THE NECESSITY OF NATURE

To understand our current world crises, it is essential to study the origins of the systems and institutions we now take for granted. This book takes a novel approach to charting intellectual, scientific and philosophical histories alongside the development of the international legal order by studying the philosophy and theology of the Scientific Revolution and its impact on European natural law, political liberalism and political economy. Starting from analysis of the work of Thomas Hobbes, Robert Boyle and John Locke on natural law, the author incorporates a holistic approach that encompasses global legal matters beyond the foundational matters of treaties and diplomacy. The monograph promotes a sustainable transformation of international law in the context of related philosophy, history and theology. Tackling issues such as nature, money, necessities, human nature, secularism and epistemology, which underlie natural lawyers' thinking, Associate Professor García-Salmones explains their enduring relevance for international legal studies today. This title is also available as Open Access on Cambridge Core.

MÓNICA GARCÍA-SALMONES ROVIRA is Global Law Fellow in the Alvaro d'Ors Global Law Chair, ICS, at the University of Navarre, and a Senior Fellow at the Erik Castrén Institute of International Law, University of Helsinki. She is the author of *The Project of Positivism in International Law* (2013) and co-editor of *Cosmopolitanisms in Enlightenment Europe and Beyond* (2013) and *International Law and Religion* (2017).

CAMBRIDGE STUDIES IN INTERNATIONAL AND COMPARATIVE LAW

Established in 1946, this series produces high quality, reflective and innovative scholarship in the field of public international law. It publishes works on international law that are of a theoretical, historical, cross-disciplinary or doctrinal nature. The series also welcomes books providing insights from private international law, comparative law and transnational studies which inform international legal thought and practice more generally.

The series seeks to publish views from diverse legal traditions and perspectives, and of any geographical origin. In this respect, it invites studies offering regional perspectives on core *problématiques* of international law, and in the same vein, it appreciates contrasts and debates between diverging approaches. Accordingly, books offering new or less orthodox perspectives are very much welcome. Works of a generalist character are greatly valued and the series is also open to studies on specific areas, institutions or problems. Translations of the most outstanding works published in other languages are also considered.

After seventy years, Cambridge Studies in International and Comparative Law sets the standard for international legal scholarship and will continue to define the discipline as it evolves in the years to come.

A list of books in the series can be found at the end of this volume.

THE NECESSITY OF NATURE

God, Science and Money in 17th Century English Law of Nature

MÓNICA GARCÍA-SALMONES ROVIRA
University of Helsinki

CAMBRIDGE
UNIVERSITY PRESS

CAMBRIDGE
UNIVERSITY PRESS

Shaftesbury Road, Cambridge CB2 8EA, United Kingdom

One Liberty Plaza, 20th Floor, New York, NY 10006, USA

477 Williamstown Road, Port Melbourne, VIC 3207, Australia

314–321, 3rd Floor, Plot 3, Splendor Forum, Jasola District Centre, New Delhi – 110025, India

103 Penang Road, #05–06/07, Visioncrest Commercial, Singapore 238467

Cambridge University Press is part of Cambridge University Press & Assessment, a department of the University of Cambridge.

We share the University's mission to contribute to society through the pursuit of education, learning and research at the highest international levels of excellence.

www.cambridge.org
Information on this title: www.cambridge.org/9781009332163

DOI: 10.1017/9781009332149

First published 2023

A catalogue record for this publication is available from the British Library

ISBN 978-1-009-33216-3 Hardback
ISBN 978-1-009-33215-6 Paperback

CONTENTS

FIGURE

PREFACE

My intuition in writing this book was that acquiring a better understanding of the history of natural law might facilitate addressing key current issues relating to the Anthropocene era and offer an insight into the development of the power of money.

The book relates how knowledge and nature were rearranged anew in the theories of natural law developed in seventeenth-century England. It locates that novelty of English natural law in its context and explains why it remains relevant today. In so doing it broadens the classical language of governance to encompass notions drawn from natural and social sciences, the theory of knowledge and natural philosophy. These notions concern health, human necessities, the light of nature, innate principles, abundance, scarcity, utility, *oeconomy*, money and, indeed, the human body, all of which have consistently been neglected in legalistic accounts of the history of international law and studies of natural law, or only with theology as a secondary element. My argument is that the Scientific Revolution was as important as the Reformation in the process that transformed natural law from a theological staple into a new philosophy for the development of Europe. I argue that the sacred idea of nature was one of the casualties of the Scientific Revolution, and the innate principles of practical reason were another. They had to give way so that natural scientists could obtain dominion over science and the humanities.

The book offers a complementary interpretation of John Locke's philosophy in relation to the important theological reading produced during the last few decades, to which, I hasten to add, I subscribe. The analysis set out also considers the naturalized aspects of seventeenth-century empirical science and medicine, which is particularly evident in Locke's work and appears in the production of his epistemology, science of money and political theory. I propose to read Locke's main theoretical writings as revolving around the core theme of (human) necessities. Furthermore, this reading is set in the context of the wider seventeenth-century scientific project of making atomism the new foundation of natural philosophy, in the corpuscular version developed in particular by Robert Boyle. I also suggest that the transformation of natural law in the seventeenth century has not been sufficiently reflected upon and that the demise of natural law never took place. The natural sciences and economics that we have inherited from that period constituted a world structured on the basis of natural law that has influenced and shaped our understanding of moral natural law anew. Far from disappearing, natural law has become embedded in the very foundations of all enlightened societies.

The thesis advanced reframes our understanding of Hobbes and Locke's political theory as a reaction to radical scepticism, Neoplatonism and the commercial spirit of England in the seventeenth century, but without ever really escaping the reach of these new ideas and worldviews. It also introduces Robert Boyle's important philosophical and economic work on nature. The book's approach relates to their naturalism and care for the public good, their medical studies, the ambiguous deconstruction of the sacred notion of nature during the Scientific Revolution and the increasingly anxious twenty-first-century debate among scientists and lawyers about how to protect nature and curb greed globally.

Without the magnanimity of the Finnish Cultural Foundation, this book would have not been possible. At the end of the process, the Olga and Kaarle Oskari Laitinen Foundation contributed to costs related to the language checking, which was undertaken by Rupert Haigh, and I was able to conclude the publishing process with a grant of the Funciva Foundation. The Osk. Huttunen Foundation awarded me a one-year research sojourn at the Faculty of Law and Clare Hall of the University of Cambridge. Thus, it was possible to carry out proper research founded on intuitions that came to me during a previous research sojourn at the Faculty of History of the same university. With characteristic generosity, Professor Annabel Brett helped me to fulfil my wish to gravitate around Cambridge. At Clare Hall, I found a wealth of brilliant people, among them historians of science, from whom I constantly learned, and a home, for which I am indebted to Professor David Ibbetson, then President of Clare Hall, and to its great fellows. The people and the vibrant academic environment in the Lauterpacht Centre provided me with the necessary motivation to continue digging despite the apparently daunting nature of the enterprise. During my stay in England, Dan Jolowicz, Matthew C. Nicholson, John Haskell and Sarah Nouwen generously invited me to present embryonic versions of this work. At home in Helsinki and in other places, my friends, colleagues and family faithfully supported my determination to understand what natural law is. They listened to primitive versions of the project; colleagues sent me their unpublished chapters, and even books, and all in all showed me that science is really the common pursuit of truth. Sometimes it is necessary to look at issues from an altogether different perspective, and in this regard, I must thank Professor Anne Orford who gave me the extraordinary opportunity of being a visiting fellow in her outstanding Laureate Program in Melbourne. Australia's design of nature is something else. Matthias Goldmann generously engineered a visiting professorship in Frankfurt through which I learned a lot, meeting many brilliant German law students. The professionalism and friendliness of Tom Randall at Cambridge University Press have been a source of confidence in the process of publishing the book. I am very grateful to the editors of this series, Jean d'Aspremont and Larissa van den Herik, who amidst their busy schedules found time for my manuscript and showed great interest in it, and also to the excellent anonymous reviewers of Cambridge University Press. At different stages, Martti Koskenniemi, Joseph Weiler, Anne Orford and Jan Klabbers have exceeded all bounds of generosity in their support. With its proverbial flexibility and openness, the University of Helsinki enabled me to continue with the task of writing the manuscript at certain key moments. I am extremely grateful to Rafa Domingo, Miguel Arrufat and Jaime García del Barrio who recently welcomed me to their new venture, the Álvaro d'Ors Chair of Global Law at the Institute for Culture and Society, University of Navarre. During these years, a great number of other colleagues and friends, too numerous to mention here, and my family have been a constant source of friendship, inspiration and love.

This book is dedicated to my sister Elsa who passed away unexpectedly last May. A geologist by training, she was a Renaissance woman, equally capable of sewing a winter coat, cooking a delicious Basque meal, talking about any current book or solving the most difficult arithmetic problems to help her engineer nieces, nephews and her students. The most precious treasure she has left to us all is her unassuming capacity to love, giving her time, her things and herself untiringly to those around her. I called her some years ago to learn how gold appeared in the world, and in this way to gain a better understanding of some of the heroes of this story, and I was surprised and enlightened by her explanation about supernovas. I hope you like the book Elsa.

Introduction

This book has three interwoven theses: The first of these concerns the Anthropocene era and contends that a more accurate understanding of the history of natural law and its impact on the development of modern Europe, which, significantly, focuses and draws on previous transformations of the concept of nature, will facilitate the addressing of key current issues in respect of that era. The second concerns the metaphysics of human nature and nature more broadly and contends that the sceptical denial of the light of moral nature and of its epistemological freedom is related to the disappearance of nature as a sacred space. The third thesis concerns the modification of natural law in England during the seventeenth century and contends that the most important seventeenth-century scientists/natural lawyers buttressed their liberal politics by means of philosophical and ethical necessitarianism. The naturalism and scientificism of necessity and needs constituted the means by which they separated moral and theological issues from governmental matters, to advocate a threshold of necessities to which each human being and each citizen is entitled and to foster the inauguration of a monetary economy. Accordingly, the first three parts of this introduction deal with the new 'Empire over nature', the context of epistemological scepticism and the new political economy of necessity. This book therefore chiefly enquires into the relations between natural law and the evidence we find of competing metaphysics of the past.[1] It asks why, despite fundamental differences, the English liberal natural lawyers agreed on so much as to the new natural law. The first three parts of the introduction are roughly divided between utopian, materialist and realist metaphysics. The fourth and fifth parts deal respectively with methodological questions and provide an overview of the chapters.

[1] On the knowledge of the past through evidence, see Aviezer Tucker: 'Historiography makes no observations of historical events, but presents descriptions or representations or constructions of such events in the presence of evidence'. Aviezer Tucker, 'Historical Truth', in Vittorio Hosle (ed.), *Forms of Truth and the Unity of Knowledge* (Notre Dame: University of Notre Dame Press, 2014), p. 238.

I Altering the Perception of Nature

Humankind's dominance of nature was articulated as a new geological epoch starting in the latter part of the eighteenth century and termed the 'Anthropocene' by chemist Paul J. Crutzen and biologist Eugene F. Stoermer more than twenty years ago. The measure they applied in assigning dates to this era was the evidence of measurable global effects of human activities, such as the concentration of 'greenhouse gases', that started during the nineteenth and twentieth centuries. Envisaging that humankind would continue to be 'a major geological force' for thousands and even millions of years to come, their proposal was to think strategically about ways in which to develop sustainable ecosystems.[2] Dominance of nature was a common trope of scholastic theology, and theologians ranging from Thomas Aquinas to Francisco de Vitoria, the leader of the Salamancan School, held that it was founded in Scripture.[3] Theologians accordingly took dominance over nature to be scriptural in origin and natural to human beings in respect of the use of nature. Further, they viewed the design of nature as being subject only to the power of God.[4] The political dream of being Lords (as Anthony Pagden described them) of all the world in the Spanish, French and British Empires had little to do with a scientific 'empire over nature', however appealing that Lordship was felt to be in relation to extracting natural resources from the new territories.[5] Instead, the ethical standpoint of reverence towards nature was dismissed among the ranks of natural scientists involved in the emerging Scientific Revolution. Consequently, the notion of nature had to be altered in such manner that its domination was permissible. Cruzen and Stoermer's chronology coincides with scholars' acknowledgment of a change in

[2] Paul J. Crutzen and Eugene F. Stoermer, 'The "Anthropocene"', 41 *Global Change Newsletter* (Stockholm: Royal Swedish Academy of Sciences) (2000), pp. 17–18.

[3] See Chapter 6.

[4] Thomas Aquinas, *Summa theologiae* q. 66 a.1. co; de Vitoria Francisco, *Comentarios a la Secunda secundae de Santo Tomás*, Vicente Beltrán de Heredia (ed.) Vol. III *De Justitia*, qq. 57/66, (Salamanca: Apartado 17, 1934), q. 66 art. 1, 73; Jaime Brufau Prats, 'La noción analógica del dominium en Santo Tomás, Francisco de Vitoria y Domingo de Soto' 4 *Salmanticensis* (1957), pp. 96–136; Annabel Brett, *Liberty, Right and Nature. Individual Rights in Early Scholastic Thought* (Cambridge: Cambridge University Press, 1997), ch. 4; Martti Koskenniemi, *To the Uttermost Parts of the Earth: Legal Imagination and International Power, 1300–1870* (Cambridge: Cambridge University Press, 2021) p. 150.

[5] Anthony Pagden, *Lords of All the World: Ideologies of Empire in Spain, Britain and France c.1500-c.1800* (New Haven: Yale University Press, 1998); Manuel Jimenez Fonseca, 'Civilizing nature. Revisiting the Imperial History of International Law 1511–1972' (PhD, Finland: University of Helsinki, 2017).

attitude towards 'nature' and the argument that that transformation was one important factor in the eighteenth-century Enlightenment and the beginning of the Industrial Revolution.[6]

This book situates that change in the perception of nature in the previous century, when scientists set out to 'range, anatomize, and ransack nature'.[7] The novelty of this way of thinking lies in the way in which the faraway and exotic 'Other' was no longer the party candidly designated as a victim in the process of plundering and pillaging.[8] Now 'nature', simply and universally, ought to be ransacked. The new trend was to demystify nature, multiply it and transmute it. For the most part, leaving behind old occult practices and alchemy, how to do that lay in new knowledge. 'Man's power over the creatures depends chiefly upon his knowledge' wrote Robert Boyle (1627–1691).[9] Boyle was the foremost natural scientist and philosopher of nature of the era, brilliant in the extreme, though also extremely pragmatic as to his goals. It is unsurprising to find that two centuries later Friedrich Nietzsche defined science in exactly that manner in his *Will to Power*: 'the transformation of nature into concepts for the purpose of mastering nature.'[10] Apparently he wrote that approvingly.[11] There is a fine line between mastering and ransacking nature that perhaps now we are starting to sense. Hence, new theories about 'Earth Stewardship'

[6] Margaret C. Jacobs points to a text of mechanics of 1744 by Newton's assistant, John Teophilus Desaguliers (1683–1744) as the first with that 'critical insight'. See Margaret C. Jacob, 'The Cultural Origins of the First Industrial Revolution', in Marcus Hellyer (ed.), *The Scientific Revolution: The Essential Readings*, (Oxford: Blackwell Publishing, 2003), p. 212; Joel Mokyr, *A Culture of Growth: The Origins of the Modern Economy* (Princeton: Princeton University Press 2016).

[7] Robert Boyle, 'Of the Usefulness of Experimental Philosophy, The First Part, Principally as It Relates to the Mind of Man' in *The Works of Robert Boyle*, vol. 3 (London Pickering and Chatto, 1999), p. 237.

[8] On some of the 'Others', see for instance, Anne Orford (ed.), *International Law and Its Others* (Cambridge: Cambridge University Press, 2009), pp. 245–386; Anthony Anghie, *Imperialism, Sovereignty and the Making of International Law* (Cambridge: Cambridge University Press, 2005).

[9] Robert Boyle, 'Of the Usefulness of Experimental Philosophy'. The Second Part. Second Section, in *The Works of Robert Boyle*, vol. 6, p. 436.

[10] 'Science – the transformation of nature into concepts for the purpose of mastering nature – belongs under the rubric "means". But the purpose and will of man must grow in the same way, the intention in regard to the whole.' Friedrich Nietzsche, *The Will to Power*, Walter Kaufmann and R. J. Hollingdale (trans.), Walter Kaufmann (ed.) (New York: Vintage, 1967 (1901, 1906)), section 610.

[11] Eli I. Lichtenstein, 'Revaluing Laws of Nature in Secularized Science', in Y. Ben-Menahem (ed.), *Rethinking the Concept of Law of Nature: Natural Order in the Light of Contemporary Science* (Cham: Springer, 2022), pp. 347–377.

turn to older traditions to revive aesthetic and moral appreciations of nature, and even to spiritual and sacred conceptions of ecological knowledge.[12] There is something about nature, scholars appear to argue, that we cannot know by simply dissecting and anatomizing it.

And yet, nature was necessary. Nature embodied the epistemic necessity of the new mechanical world. This time it was not a potential source of precious metals but of laws of motion and regularities. Laws followed principles, including the principle of causal necessity. Without nature as a container or perhaps the very articulation of all those necessary laws, what would be there to study? Moreover, knowledge about that nature was the driving force of much of the intellectual movement of the period. Transformations in the concept of 'law' in science towards 'law' either fully ruling the universe or being incapable of ruling it at all also followed from changes in the notion of 'nature'.[13]

II Nature and The Light of Nature

Utopian theology gave epistemological impetus to science. There was still so much to learn from a world created by an omnipotent God, but that was a theology without human beings. Its counterpart, the pragmatism of scientists, was the result of how they had decided to step in to replace the *designer of nature*. The idea of conceiving nature as something sacred had been in the Christian tradition that human and non-human nature alike had been created to give glory to God the Creator, each according to their specific nature. Therefore, there was a purpose to nature. By the mid-seventeenth century, on the grounds of its inviolability and the boundaries to human knowledge and dominion that it established, 'the unnecessariness of such a nature' deserving any kind of 'veneration' was declared.[14] Further, the rational human being no longer seemed to be part of nature. In the new natural law, every human being appeared a mystery.

12 See Shan Gao, 'Aesthetic and Moral Appreciation of Nature in Philosophical Traditions of China'; Fausto O. Sarmiento, 'The Antlers of a Trilemma: Rediscovering Andean Sacred Rites'; Vicenta Mamani-Bernabé, 'Spirituality and the Pachamama in the Andean Aymara Worldview', all in Ricardo Rozzi et al. *Earth Stewardship. Linking Ecology and Ethics in Theory and Practice* (Cham, Heidelberg, Dordrecht, London, New York: Springer, 2015).

13 See Lorraine Daston and Michael Stolleis (eds.) *Natural Law and Laws of Nature in Early Modern Europe. Jurisprudence, Theology, Moral and Natural Philosophy* (Surrey, Burlington: Ashgate 2008); John Dupré, *Metaphysical Foundations of the Disorder of Things* (Cambridge, Mass: Harvard University Press, 1995); Brett, *Liberty, Right and Nature.*

14 Boyle, *A Free Enquiry into the Vulgarly Receiv'd Notion of Nature*, in *The Works of Robert Boyle*, v. 10, p. 485.

If left to their own judgment, they were a threat to all humanity, and in spiritual terms they were called to respond to none but their God and conscience. What could be specifically natural about that? At the same time the human body became a central source of concern. An old Greek-Arabic tradition of household economics taking the physical needs of human nature as the foundation of politics resurged in Europe through new Latin translations. These ideas entered the philosophy of natural law quietly but firmly during the early modern period. Further, the moderation of living 'to or neere the necessity of nature', throwing off whatever threatened to interfere with a life of simplicity, was considered the model for the Reformed individual.[15] Nature, clearly articulating human necessities, represented thus the ideal of a virtuous Protestant. Around the middle of the seventeenth century the bottom line was that nature was considered to be a stream of constant needs experienced by human beings, which determined much of what followed in terms of virtue and sociability.

This physicalist idea about human nature was central to many Christian natural lawyers in seventeenth-century England working within the new science. The book explores the mixed vocation of Thomas Hobbes, Robert Boyle and John Locke, being at once natural scientists, economists, medical doctors, (al)chemists, theologians and philosophers. In the history of international law they are usually dealt with in terms of their 'philosophy of law' understood in a lego-juristic sense – except for Boyle who is usually omitted. But as a phenomenon extending now much further than 'treaties' or 'diplomatic endeavours', and encompassing all kinds of global matters and questions, both of social and of natural sciences, international law can benefit greatly from the rich approach to law that natural lawyers themselves adopted.

By emphasizing the physical aspects of the body within the pervasive dualist ideas of the period, such as Neoplatonism or Cartesianism, the great natural lawyers of the seventeenth century put aside the more intellectual view of human nature. In a period in which human beings were becoming masters and lords of empirical knowledge the light of nature was obscured. The classic notion of the light of nature illuminated the mystery of how individuals from all places and eras have searched for the good life, the virtuous life. Since Aristotle the light of nature had a

[15] In a letter from Sir Cheney Culpeper (1601–1663) to Samuel Hartlib (1600–1662), '7 November 1649', in M. J. Braddick and M. Greengrass (eds.), and Introduction, *The Letters of Sir Cheney Culpeper (1641–1657)*, (Royal Historical Society Camden Series, Vol VII, 1999), p. 360.

divine connotation. In Christian theology it was either the image of God implanted in each human being, or a certain participation in the eternal law in the divine intellect.[16] Christian natural lawyers of previous centuries had even conceived human nature, soul and body, as 'reason'. That was true of the biologist-theologian Albert the Great.[17] For his disciple, Thomas Aquinas, moral natural law was, famously, participation in eternal reason, in a great part by means of the light of nature.[18] Despite the weakening consequences of the Fall, it was thought that a human being can think, decide and view things in the world as God had created them and wished them to be. This was a spiritual or indeed a divine conception of reason, of nature and of law, unconcerned with future burgeoning struggles among philosophers of history to explain the past in terms of necessity and contingency.[19]

As recovered by the first liberals in terms of necessities, human nature again became part of a cosmology, similarly to what had been before in the natural law period of theologians. It once more encompassed political thought, natural science, religion, natural law and the incipient science of political economy. However, natural law had undergone a complete transformation, as had nature. But, after all, nature was necessary. The needs of human beings imposed themselves in the articulations formulated by social sciences, leaving very little to the

[16] See Chapters 1 and 5.

[17] Alberti Magni, *De bono*, in *Alberti Magni opera omnia*, tomus XXVIII), Henricus Kühle, Carolus Feckes, Bernhardus Geyer (Proldgomena), Wilhemus Kübel, ediderunt, (Aschendorff: Monasterii westfalorum in aedibus, 1951), pp. 259–271; Albertus Magnus, *Ethica*, ed. Borgnet, vol. VII (Paris: Louis Vivès, 1891); Georg Wieland, *Zwischen Natur und Vernunft: Alberts des Grossen Begriff vom Menschen*, Lectio Albertina 2 (Münster 1999); Jörn Müller, *Natürliche Moral und Philosophische Ethik Bei Albertus Magnus* (Münster: Beiträge zur Geschichte der Philosophie und Theologie des Mittelalters: Neue Folge 59, 2001); Stanley B., Cunningham, *Reclaiming Moral Agency: The Moral Philosophy of Albert the Great* (Washington, DC: Catholic University of America Press, 2008).

[18] Aquinas, *Summa theologiae*, I-IIae, q. 94; Riccardo Saccenti, *Debating Medieval Natural Law: A Survey* (Notre Dame: University of Notre Dame Press, 2017); Odon Lottin, *Le droit naturel chez Saint Thomas d'Aquin et ses prédécesseurs*, (Bruges: C. Beyaert, 1931); Martin Grabmann, 'Das Naturrecht der Scholastik von Gratian bis Thomas von Aquin. Nach den gedruckten und ungedruckten Quellen dargestellt', 16 *Archiv für Rechts-und Wirtschaftsphilosophie* (1922/1923), pp. 12–53; Brett, *Liberty, Right and Nature*, pp. 88–97; on Aquinas and *ius gentium* but also illuminating for natural law see, Koskenniemi, *To the Uttermost Parts of the Earth*, pp. 78–83; see also how the light of nature appeared in the legists in Rudolf Weigand, *Die Naturrechtslehre der Legisten und Dekretisten von Irnerius bis Accursius und von Gratian bis Johannes Teutonicus* (Munich: Hueber, 1967).

[19] Yemima Ben-Menahem, 'Historical Necessity and Contingency', in Aviezer Tucker (ed.), *A Companion to the Philosophy of History and Historiography* (Chichester: Wiley-Blackwell).

imagination or poetic mind. Moreover, in this new cosmology, nature could be the problem, as Hobbes had stated, or the solution, as in Boyle's theory. All the goods of nature could be multiplied and offer food and occupation for human beings' needs and their multitude of desires. In a century when all authors proclaimed the obscurity and even the extinction of the divine light of nature, the death of sacred nature as described above was being planned.[20] It is impossible to take a scientific stand about a causal necessity between these two events. Instead, I suggest that since they were unable to understand themselves and the earth as part of a unified Creation, natural scientists opted to squander recklessly what was appraised as their inheritance.

III Needs, Politics and Money

The book contends that Hobbes and Locke developed their natural law and political theory revolving around a novel doctrine of necessity and of necessities. The utopian moment in the history of Europe described above is observed from the perspective of the doctrine of necessities and comprises the promise of unlimited knowledge and unlimited economic growth – significantly through nature – in circumstances of great freedom of thought. The standpoint of the philosophers of necessity is described in the book as a response to that utopian moment, tempering that enthusiasm for the sake of the safety and well-being of human beings.[21] In making this argument, several key transformations in the conception of nature and of money are uncovered that have not thus far received attention in the histories of natural law, international law and political economy.

A neutral, scientific idea of money has been instrumental in shaping the global legal order. But it is an open question whether there are other possible explanations of what money is. Also, the debate about whether scientific money would be the best instrument for devising the public good is as old as the scientific money itself. History and theories of natural

[20] See also Carolyn Merchant, *The Death of Nature: Women, Ecology, and the Scientific Revolution* (San Francisco: Harper San Francisco, 1990).

[21] 'For seeing every man, not only by Right, but also by necessity of Nature, is supposed to endeavour all he can, to obtain that which is necessary for his conservation; He that shall oppose himself against it for things superfluous, is guilty of the warre that thereupon is to follow; and therefore doth that, which is contrary to the fundamentall Law of Nature, which commandeth to *seek Peace*. The observers of this Law, may be called Sociable'. Hobbes, *Leviathan*, Noel Malcolm (ed.), ch. 15, p. 232.

law, political economy, sociology and economics teach that money may be described in the following ways: as debt, credit, a medium of exchange, a lasting 'thing' that is not really a thing, but a measure of value, a social instrument, a political weapon, a storage facility for power, willpower, speculators' fantasy, an idol … Money is a complex reality that is particularly political and moral (a) in its relative independence from underlying reality, (b) in the way it may be distributed and (c) in the way that it is pursued within and outside the commonwealth and aligned with its principles or detached from them.

Ethical, political and economic concerns about economic inequality, the depoliticization of money and the ensuing undemocratic practices heightened after the 2008 financial crisis have prompted the resurgence of the debate about what money constitutes.[22] Despite important recent exceptions, for the most part public international law follows mainstream economics in keeping their distance from these debates.[23] Thus, international lawyers continue to reduce money to a formal medium and represent it as a 'black box' and as a function of other forces and institutions. This under-theorization veils the more theoretical and foundational thinking about what money is, undertaken within the old European tradition of theological and monetary thought, but also carried out by twentieth- and

[22] Aristotle, *Politics*, Ernest Barker trans., revised with an Introduction and Notes by R. F. Stalley (Oxford University Press, 1995); John Locke and Patrick Hyde Kelly (eds.), *Locke on Money. Vol. I and II* (Oxford: Clarendon Press, 1991); John Smithin, *Controversies in Monetary Economics* (London: Elgar Publishing, 2003); Geoffrey Ingham, *The Nature of Money* (Cambridge: Polity Press, 2004); Christine A. Desan, *Making Money: Coin, Currency and the Coming of Capitalism* (Oxford: Oxford University Press, 2014); Samuel Bowles, *The Moral Economy: Why Good Incentives Are No Substitute for Good Citizens* (London, New Haven: Yale University Press, 2016); Joseph Huber, *Sovereign Money: Beyond Reserve Banking* (London: Palgrave Macmillan, 2017); Diane Coyle, *Cogs and Monsters: What Economics Is and What It Should Be* (Princeton: Princeton University Press, 2021); Stefan Eich, *The Currency of Politics: The Political Theory of Money from Aristotle to Keynes* (Princeton: Princeton University Press, 2022).

[23] Rosa M. Lastra and others, 'Central Bank Money: Liability, Asset, or Equity of the Nation?' *Rebuilding Macroeconomics Working Paper Series, Working Paper No 20*, 25.11.2020; Rosa M. Lastra and Marcelo J. Sheppard, 'Ethical Foundations of Financial Law', in Costanza A. Russo, Rosa M. Lastra and William Blair (eds.), *Research Handbook on Law and Ethics in Banking and Finance* (London: Elgar Publishing, 2019); Isabel Feichtner, 'Law of Natural Resource Extraction and Money as Key to Understanding Global Political Economy and Potential for Its Transformation', in Poul F. Kjaer (ed.), *The Law of Political Economy: Transformation in the Function of Law* (Cambridge: Cambridge University Press, 2020); Isabel Feichtner, 'The German Constitutional Court's PSPP Judgment: Impediment and Impetus for the Democratization of Europe' 21 *German Law Journal* (2020); see also the group of researchers in justmoney.org.

twenty-first-century economists and contemporary sociologists, political economists and anthropologists.[24]

Phenomena such as that of financialization fundamentally defy the scientific and neutral explanation of money in ordering global monetary operations. Economists and political economists describe financialization as the increasing power of financial actors over the political world, society and the rest of the economy.[25] The term has 'parasitical' and negative connotations as money gradually acquires a fictitious nature, sovereign countries become heavily indebted to foreign private lenders and entrepreneurs become 'liquidified' by seeking profit for shareholders first and foremost.[26]

Today Locke's monetary ideas stand out in the context of historical monetary theory as one of the key languages that scholars employ to decode money in the contemporary global economic system.[27] One of the general concerns expressed in this literature pertains to the way in which money resists being considered a political issue in many spheres. My argument is that in his monetary writings Locke took money to be a representation of need and necessities, not of the private individual, as Aristotle had it, but of the necessities of the state, and in this manner

[24] John Maynard Keynes, *A Treatise on Money*. Vol I *The Pure Theory of Money*. Vol. II *The Applied Theory of Money* (London: Macmillan and Co., 1935; 1950 [1930]); Joseph A. Schumpeter, *History of Economic Analysis*, Elizabeth Boody Schumpeter (ed.) with an Introduction by Mark Perlman (New York: Routledge, 1987); Paul A. Samuelson, 'Some Aspects of the Pure Theory of Capital' 51 *The Quarterly Journal of Economics* (1937); Ingham, *The Nature of Money*; Bill Maurer, *How Would You Like to Pay? How Technology Is Changing the Future of Money* (Durham: Duke University Press, 2015); Stefano Sgambati, 'The Significance of Money: Beyond Ingham's Sociology of Money', 56 *European Journal of Sociology* (2014).

[25] Engelbert Stockhammer, Stefano Sgambati and Anastasia Nesvetailova, 'Financialisation: Continuity and Change – Introduction to the Special Issue' 2 *Review of Evolutionary Political Economy* (2021).

[26] Cédric Durand, *Fictitious Capital: How Finance Is Appropriating Our Future*, trans. by David Broder (Brooklyn, London: Verso, 2017); Tristan Auvray, Thomas Dallery and Sandra Rigot, *L'entreprise liquidée. La finance contre l'investissement* (Paris: Michalon, 2016); Stockhammer, Sgambati and Nesvetailova, 'Financialisation: Continuity and Change'.

[27] Joyce Oldham Appleby, 'Locke, Liberalism and the Natural Law of Money', 71 *Past and Present* (1976); Patrick Hyde Kelly, 'General Introduction: Locke on Money', in Patrick Hyde Kelly (ed.), *Locke on Money* (Oxford: Clarendon Press, 1991); Daniel Carey and Christopher J. Finlay (eds.), *The Financial Revolution in the British Atlantic World, 1688–1815* (Dublin, Portland: Irish Academic Press, 2011); Daniel Carey, 'Locke's Species: Money and Philosophy in the 1690s' 70 *Annals of Science* (2013); Daniel Carey (ed.), *Money and the Political Economy of Enlightenment*, Oxford University Studies in the Enlightenment (Oxford: Oxford Voltaire Foundation 2014); Christine A. Desan, *Making Money*; Katarina Pistor, 'From Territorial to Monetary Sovereignty' 18 *Theoretical Inquiries in Law* 2017; Stefan Eich, 'John Locke and the Politics of Monetary Depoliticization' 17 *Modern Intellectual History* (2020); Eich, *The Currency of Politics*.

began the scientification of money.[28] On the one hand, Locke was interested in promoting the monetary interests that he considered fundamental for the commonwealth to thrive. But he also foresaw the dangers posed by money, which he thought could be tempered by robust construction of the public good.[29] By integrating Locke's theory of money into the interpretative prism provided by the Scientific Revolution, the aim of *The Necessity of Nature* is also to contribute to current debate in Lockean interpretations, between Locke as the 'Evangelical political theorist'[30] and Locke as 'the inaugurator of radical capitalism'.[31] Furthermore, it analyses his ideas of the public good, which, it is argued, are also founded on the doctrine of necessities, alongside more traditional interpretations.

IV Necessity and Liberalism

Thomas Aquinas is for the most part a sort of silent discussing partner in the context of this book – providing arguments but remaining in the background. Thomas Hobbes's proposal for a political philosophy sustained by a new and robust metaphysics represented a decisive change in the seventeenth century. Aquinas's metaphysical question, 'what is good?'

[28] A contemporary account of 'the scientification of politics' in the knowledge society, in Peter Weingart, 'From "Finalization" to "Mode 2": Old Wine in New Bottles?' 36 *Social Science Information*, (1997), p. 605.

[29] John Locke, *Two Treatises of Government*, ed. with an Introduction by Peter Laslett (Cambridge University Press, 1988 [1967]). See on Aristotle, money and needs, chapter 9.2.2. below.

[30] John Dunn, *The Political Thought of John Locke: An Historical Account of the Argument of the 'Two Treatises of Government'* (Cambridge: Cambridge University Press, 1969); James Tully, *A Discourse on Property: John Locke and his Adversaries* (Cambridge: Cambridge University Press, 1980); Ian Harris, *The Mind of John Locke: A Study of Political Theory in Its Intellectual Setting* (Cambridge: Cambridge University Press, 1994); Timothy Stanton, 'John Locke and the Fable of Liberalism' 61 *Historical Journal* (2018); Paul Bou-Habib, 'Locke, Natural Law and Civil Peace: Reply to Tate' 16 *European Journal of Political Theory* (2017); Mark Goldie, in *2021, The Carlyle Lectures: John Locke and Empire*. www.history.ox.ac.uk/event/the-carlyle-lectures-2021-john-locke-and-empire

[31] C. B. MacPherson, *The Political Theory of Possessive Individualism* (Oxford: Oxford University Press, 1962); Leo Strauss, *Natural Right and History* (Chicago: University of Chicago Press, 1953); John William Tate, 'Locke, God and Civil Society: Response to Stanton' 40 *Political Theory* (2012); Neal Wood, *John Locke and Agrarian Capitalism* (Berkeley: University of California Press, 1984). See also Helga Varden commenting on Hannah Arendt's critique of the confusion between work and labour, Helga Varden, 'Locke on Property', in Jessica Gordon-Roth and Shelley Weinberg (eds.), *The Lockean Mind* (Abingdon, New York: Routledge, 2022), ch. 44.

was displaced. As discussed in Chapter 2, in the construction of his metaphysics, Hobbes no longer asks what is good, but 'what is necessary?' This shift makes Aquinas and Hobbes look like opposites. However, in reality 'necessity' was their point of contact. Annabel Brett's study as to the interpenetration of notions of nature and the city in early modern natural law is in this sense key to ascertaining how 'naturalness' in Aquinas's eternal law and in English authors from John Case to Hobbes responds to the inclinations of the human spirit.[32]

The importance of Islamic sources and their ways in contributing to the development of Christian natural law is articulated for the first time in this book.[33] Avicenna barely wrote anything on moral philosophy, except for short tracts pointing to the centrality of human needs in ethics and politics. In his important commentary on Aristotle's *De Anima* he argued against the idea of the unity of human nature, contending that the soul was not the form of the human body in the metaphysical sense. In this manner the union of soul and body, also in terms of morality and epistemology, was shattered.[34] Moreover, the fact that he was a physician and that his extensive writings were taught for centuries in all European faculties is also of relevance in seeking to understand lawyers and medical doctors' differing philosophical concerns. I analyse Locke's early training in medicine and describe the philosophical baggage that this education entailed by discussing among others some of the ideas of another great philosopher-physician, Galen (129–216).[35]

Understanding how the assumptions behind the notions of 'nature' in the 'philosophies of nature' and 'natural sciences' impacted on natural law, natural rights and political theory shows the benefits of narrowing the gap between the methods of legal reasoning and of scientific thinking. Thomas Hobbes and John Locke, whether consciously or unconsciously, tried to bridge that gap between science and law. Their new and highly sophisticated ideas on necessity produced novel ways of thinking about human freedom, government, natural law, the economy and, finally,

[32] 'The will and nature do not conflict always and in all things, for we choose many things which are by nature, such as life and health', John Case, *Sphaera civitatis*, quoted in Annabel S. Brett, *Changes of State: Nature and the Limits of the City in Early Modern Natural Law* (Princeton: Princeton University Press, 2011), on Aquinas, p. 72; and on Hobbes, ch. 5, p. 121.

[33] I have, of course, found guidance in the work of theologians and philosophers, such as Étienne Gilson, 'Avicenne et le point de depart de Duns Scot' 2 *Archives d'histoire doctrinale et littéraire du moyen age* (1927).

[34] See on Avicenna's dualism of soul and body, chapter 9.1.1. below.

[35] Dag Nikolaus Hasse, *Success and Suppression: Arabic Science and Philosophy in the Renaissance* (Cambridge, Mass.: Harvard University Press, 2016).

nature. Therefore, the book sheds new light onto the early stages in the development of what we have come to think of as liberalism. In his recent Carlyle Lectures (Spring 2022) Samuel Moyn analysed the attempts of some Cold War political thinkers to rescue the project of liberalism, with the stated purpose of ascertaining what can we salvage from these ideas of equality and universalism that were once so appealing.[36] In approaching the topic from the perspective of the Scientific Revolution and philosophical theology, *The Necessity of Nature* offers new insights into liberalism's internal contradictions: its savage inauguration of the Anthropocene as against the reordering of political institutions with a view to achieving equality; the disintegration of the sacred notion of nature and the novel quasi-naturalness of economy; the enslavement of human beings on a massive scale; and the new centrality of human needs emerging as a premise for the flourishing of any political society. Some of the themes discussed in the book bring to the fore a reminder about the theology, the economics and the politics of science. Doing that in the context of the Scientific Revolution, it is hoped, produces a much more forceful argument about the allegiances of science. Although it is very real nowadays, the presence of a methodological abyss between natural sciences reasoning and legal reasoning is unfruitful and arguably potentially dangerous both for the planet and for humanity. However, even if methodological differences are assumed and it is accepted that natural sciences and legal science are fundamentally different, it may be argued that they are similar in one respect: both have an important political aspect. I accordingly hope to underline the seriousness of the business the philosopher of law is enmeshed in and the responsibility it entails – a point scholars from other disciplines usually realize – and that it is vacuous to leave decisions on important matters of human society and human life to natural scientists alone. I hope that the book will also reveal a new Locke to a larger audience, one that is less like a liberal individualist and more like the figure presented in the theological interpretations of his work, albeit also more complex than that – a complexity that I reveal through analysis of his medical career and his medical and monetary studies. Though ambiguous in some respects, Locke was generous in devoting much effort to thinking about the public good and was tremendously committed in the way he embraced the societal responsibility of the philosophers of law.

[36] Samuel Moyn, *2022 The Carlyle Lectures: The Cold War and the Canon of Liberalism* www.history.ox.ac.uk/carlyle-lectures

V Outline of Chapters

The scepticism of the period from roughly 1645 to 1680 prompted English philosophers' attempts to rethink theology and moral and civil philosophy in their search for ideas concerning the common and the public good. This is the argument of Chapter 1. Ralph Cudworth's effort to overcome the challenges posed by fragmentation in religion and politics and to develop a philosophy helpful in uniting society, but not at the expense of liberty, demonstrate that Neoplatonism was an important force during that period. In a sceptical era, John Selden's contribution to particularism in natural law stands in parallel to the turn to universalism that was partly made possible by means of medical ideas gleaned from widespread study of Arabic medical works. A discussion of Sir Robert Filmer's life and key political ideas together with the principles of political economy he espoused follows. Given the disintegration of moral theology in that period, the commercialization of societal ties seems to have been unstoppable. Against the Macphersonian critique of possessive individualism, the chapter puts forward the opening argument that both Hobbes and Locke sought to tame the harsh society characterized by the use of credit they saw before them and that they chose to do so by means of political philosophy and natural law.

Chapter 2 analyses Hobbes's 'doctrine of necessity', which was famously so termed by Hobbes himself in his debate with Bishop Bramhall. It argues that by means of this doctrine's basis in the natural sciences Hobbes transformed natural law from an idealist to a pragmatic enterprise, from one based on natural rights to one characterized by the pragmatic employment of principles of necessity. The chapter discusses Avicenna's metaphysics of existence, through which he described 'nature', which gives precedent to what exists in the material world and depends on the necessitarian principle that 'whatever exists is necessitated by another'. Similarities between Avicenna's metaphysics and Hobbes's are analysed, and in respect of the latter the capacity of the doctrine of necessity to sustain a metaphysical framework for philosophy and politics is identified.

The implications for morality and natural law of Hobbes's skilful employment of Neoplatonist metaphysics such as Avicenna's, entailing a sharp division between the human soul and the human body, are spelled out in Chapter 3. This shows that the concept of need, rather than right is central to Hobbes's natural law and political theory. Judgments concerning needs, including the needs of others, represent a constant source of legitimacy for acting in the state of nature and in the commonwealth. A thorough analysis of the doctrine of necessity in *Leviathan*, Hobbes's masterpiece, follows. The superior and absolute sovereignty that *Leviathan* evaluates and proposes is the true and scientific concept of sovereignty in a commonwealth, by reference to the needs of human nature and also in accordance with divine command. Hobbes exploits his doctrine of metaphysics of necessity to explain that that type of absolute sovereignty is compatible with freedom; after all, each free act of every human being is necessary in the sense of a metaphysics of necessity. He also models the question of faith on the principle of necessity and famously asserts that all that was necessary to salvation was 'Faith in Christ', and 'Obedience to the law'.

Chapter 4 discusses the circle that formed around the intelligencer Samuel Hartlib (1600–1662). Its overarching argument is that utilitarian science offered guidance in finding the simplicity of the *unum necessarium* (Luke 10:42), a common theme exalted by contemporary Millenarianism of the Protestant cause. In practical terms, knowledge about necessities became the means to achieving that goal of faith. The scepticism of the period and its obvious corrupting effects on morality and devotion led to inventiveness in pursuit of substitutes for the classical moral principle of the light of reason. The Reformers worked towards a political and theological project of a utilitarian science as a means by which to reach God and reproduce Paradise on earth. Scientific knowledge about trade became central and was expressed, significantly, in the momentous Navigation Acts of 1651.

Next, I consider the theology and moral philosophy of the respected theologian and moral casuist, Robert Sanderson. The divine Sanderson despaired of the unfortunate consequences for practical morality of denying the responsibility and freedom of individuals. In its historical context his doubt amounted to finally rejecting the Calvinist doctrine of predestination. Scholars consider Sanderson's *Several Cases of Conscience Discussed in Ten Lectures in the Divinity School at Oxford* a main reference for Locke in the writing of the unpublished *Two Tracts of Government* and his foundational *Essays on the Law of Nature*. Sanderson's work sets out a moral philosophy of free will reinforced by mechanical overtones of necessary causality in reasoning. The chapter briefly analyses this type of 'mechanical conscience' and shows how Sanderson was committed to a *de facto* theory of government.

The natural philosopher Robert Boyle, mentor of John Locke, took the view that the aim of science was 'the Empire over the Creatures'. The task of Chapter 6 is to show how Robert Boyle's new political system for an economics of natural science, primarily involving the utilitarian exploitation of nature and of trade, is connected with his contribution to the development of a form of natural law and natural philosophy shorn of moral natural law. That idea drew on classical theological teachings on dominion over creatures (as set out in Genesis 1:26) together with the economic goal of making natural sciences productive – also considering the significant expansion that the British Empire was undergoing at that point in time – and a heterodox programme with alchemical roots by which anything in nature could be transmuted into another thing. Theological principles about an omnipotent and bountiful God were crucial to Boyle's plans for the achievement of broader management of nature, but as a rule he avoided consideration of anthropological theology in his scientific writings. A close reading of *Of the Usefulness of Experimentall Natural Philosophy* and of the *Aretology* helps in articulating these ideas.

Chapter 7 examines Benjamin Worsley's manifesto of natural sciences that contained utopian ideas about human capacity to overcome death, if only the right scientific approach and the right moral attitude could be achieved. Boyle was inspired by his good friend and mentor when theology and experiment became the core of his work as a natural scientist. Revelation substituted what Boyle believed was the impossibility of grasping moral natural law rationally. Therefore, the study of moral natural laws is practically irrelevant in his work. Boyle moved constantly between a self-sufficient and mechanistic idea of the physical world and recourse to an infinitely wise God as a guide to human knowledge. He wrote several ambitious works on these issues, which are nowadays considered foundational to the Scientific Revolution but remain practically unknown beyond specialist circles. The chapter looks in particular at *The Origine of Formes and Qualities according to the Corpuscular Philosophy* and *A Free Enquiry into the Vulgarly Receiv'd Notion of Nature*. These works articulate Boyle's ambition to transmute everything in nature and his momentous critique of nature, a metaphysical concept that had been part of Western culture since at least the era of the great Greek philosophers.

The transformation of the politics of government towards material necessities has deep roots in Locke's work. This is the argument of Chapter 8, which first assesses the controversy over 'matters indifferent' into which the young Locke intervened in his unpublished *Two Tracts of Government*. Public order may guide human reason, he argued, while the classic understanding of conscience, with its troublesome perplexities, appears to be demoted to the private sphere. In his *Essays on the Law of*

Nature innate principles are denied. Instead, Locke affirms the centrality of human necessities since they compel human beings to band together.

Locke's knowledge of medicine, and of the main Galenist principles, indicates the type of ideas he was familiar with at an early age. Scholars have analysed the reception in the European political tradition of the Pseudo-Aristotle's *Oeconomia* up to Robert Filmer's *Patriarcha*, where the household unites economy and politics as a kingdom. Chapter 9 evaluates in a novel manner, in the context of seventeenth century liberalism, the tradition of texts that deal with the materialist anthropology of needs, including the Pseudo-Galen's *Yconomia* and Avicenna's *Kitâb Al-siyâsa* (*Politics*) and *The Metaphysics of 'The Healing'*, in which household and humanity originate in the existence of needs. In these texts the state is the sum of individuals united through the materialist principle of human needs with an arbiter entrusted to resolve disputes about reciprocal transactions.

Chapter 10 introduces the wider context of Locke's corpuscularianism and explores what I have termed his 'doctrine of necessities. The chapter argues that his theory concerning the 'necessaries' and 'necessities', rather than 'rights', gives systematic coherence not only to his political and economic writings but to his entire philosophical theory. The chapter discusses in detail the literature dealing with moneylending that existed before Locke and demonstrates in this manner his originality.

In Locke's early writings on money discussed in Chapter 11, the key issue concerns economic phenomena that belong to an interdependent scientific system. Earlier and contemporary authors had observed the systematic aspects involved in the use of money for the nation's trade. Locke's novelty lies in the fact that he observed those systemic connections solely from the perspective of economic phenomena, and 'necessities' and the necessity of money constituted the main tool through which he described the phenomena associated with the emerging monetary economy. Instead of making the classic theological reference to usury, Locke built the theoretical foundation and normativity of money on the system of trade and its necessities, and hence on the survival of the nation. In this way he was able to gloss over the earlier theological discourse.

The goal of the final chapter is to examine the central role of necessities in the epistemological, moral and political theory of *An Essay of Human Understanding* and of the *Two Treatises of Government*. A study of the former shows Locke's preoccupation with classical moral questions such as happiness and the 'proper object of *Desire*' and how necessities helped him to strike a balance between tradition and the new science. As a rule of thumb of proper conduct, knowledge of necessities leads to the preservation of life, a human being's most important duty to God, while following desires threatens its loss if these desires are not examined with the goal of eternal life in mind. His doctrine of necessities is what made it possible for Locke to develop the theory of the public good with which, it is argued, he attempted to defeat the egoist theory of self-interest. Without a doubt, examination of his conception of property and money through the lens of human necessities shows a certain ambiguity in Locke's normative ideals. Nevertheless, my conclusion is that above other considerations underlying the capital-oriented ideals of the period, the last word of Locke's political theory is the public good represented by preservation and convenience for the commonwealth and, when possible, for the whole of humanity.

There is no study in existence that seeks to shed light on the distinctiveness of the phenomenon of modern natural law that emerged within the England of the Scientific Revolution. Rather the canonical argument is that English natural law closely followed the work done by continental authors.[37] In order to understand English originality, the book deals with fields as diverse as natural law, political theory, natural sciences, theology, moral law and monetary theory, both through the lens of primary literature and by making use of specialist works on the great natural lawyers and scientists. I have not sought to emulate, nor do I feel, that this book is in any way comparable to *The Machiavellian Moment* – Pocock's masterpiece – but that book has been an inspiration in the way in which it pinpoints core historical issues and political theory via philosophical theology. There are excellent works in existence that analyse certain notions that are key to this book from a contemporary perspective.[38] The

37 Richard Tuck, *Natural Rights Theories. Their Origin and Development* (Cambridge: Cambridge University Press, 1978); Tully, *A Discourse on Property: John Locke and His Adversaries* (1980); Knud Haakonssen, *Natural Law and Moral Philosophy: From Grotius to the Scottish Enlightenment* (Cambridge: Cambridge University Press, 1996).

38 These include the classic Leo Strauss, *Natural Right and History* (that I attempt to respond to), Thomas Piketty's *Capital* and, dealing with historically contextualized notions, Germano Maifreda, *From Oikonomia to Political Economy. Constructing Economic Knowledge from the Renaissance to the Scientific Revolution*, Loretta Valz Mannucci (trans.) (London and New York: Routledge, 2016); Keith Tribe, *The Economy of the Word, Language, History and Economics*, (Oxford: Oxford University Press, 2015); Carl Wennerlind, *Casualties of Credit. The English Financial Revolution, 1620–1720* (Cambridge: Harvard University Press, 2011) and Peter Remien, *The Concept of Nature in Early English Modern Literature* (Cambridge: Cambridge University Press, 2019). Superb studies of the ethics developed by English natural philosophers include Sorana Corneanu, *Regimens of the Mind. Boyle, Locke, and the Early Modern* Cultura Animi *Tradition* (Chicago: The University of Chicago Press, 2011) and, on the project of natural history, Daniel Carey, *Locke, Shaftesbury, and*

range of analysis of some of these works extends to larger questions that combine theology and science, although none of them deals with natural law per se.[39] *The Necessity of Nature* offers the first study of the rich phenomenon of English natural law and its enduring contribution to the rise of the British Empire and the development of Europe at the dawn of the Scientific Revolution.

Hutcheson: Contesting Diversity in the Enlightenment and Beyond (Cambridge: Cambridge University Press, 2005). The rise of the public interest is usefully explored in Vera Keller, *Knowledge and the Public Interest, 1575–1725* (Cambridge: Cambridge University Press, 2015). All these studies establish the historical context and the theoretical underpinnings of specific notions.

39 Other outstanding books that look at the history of science more thoroughly include Charles Webster, *The Great Instauration: Science, Medicine and Reform 1626–1660* (London: Duckworth, 1975) and John T. Young, *Faith, Medical Alchemy and Natural Philosophy: Johan Moriaen, Reformed Intelligencer and the Hartlib Circle* (Aldershot: Ashgate 1998) both including the aspect of science and theology; Alexander Wragge-Morley, *Aesthetic Science. Representing Nature in the Royal Society of London, 1650–1720* (Chicago: The University of Chicago Press, 2020), which combines the history of science and theology, is a rich study that opens vistas onto the Royal Society's larger project.

1

A Christian Science

Searching for the Common Good and the Public Good

1.1 Deism, Neoplatonism and the Light of Reason

Someone like Robert Boyle would emphasize that the Christian world is premised upon the action and presence of God through grace, light and, indeed, mystery in the very divine contrivance of the material world, that is, the 'argument of design'.[1] Hence, in late seventeenth-century England, orthodox Christian thought did not entail an anxious effort to relate the particular to the universal but an industrious effort to obtain a glimpse of the unknown. In a review for the publisher of J. G. A. Pocock's *The Machiavellian Moment*, Donald Weinstein remarked that the account in it of 'medieval thought was unduly Augustinian'.[2] I want to further qualify Weinstein's statement on what Pocock described as a definition of Christianity in the opening chapters of his masterpiece, which, in his view, accordingly shaped the sixteenth-century understanding of politics.[3] Pocock's narrative on the painful efforts of scholastic Christians to refer knowledge of particular and contingent historical events to categories unbounded by time and space was certainly representative of *some strands* of Christian theology. Nevertheless, Pocock's recurrent distinction between a divine eternal order and the contingent – in effect, a dual world entailing history and transcendence – was characteristic of Neoplatonic thought rather than of Christian thought more generally. Pocock went so far as to argue that the story of Florentine political thought was the history of its 'striking but partial emancipation' of that

1 Scott Mandelbrote, 'The Uses of Natural Theology in Seventeenth-Century England', 20 *Science in Context* (2007), pp. 451–480; Wragge-Morley, *Aesthetic Science*.

2 See in Richard Whatmore, 'Introduction to the New Princeton Classics Edition', in J. G. A. Pocock (ed.), *The Machiavellian Moment: Florentine Political Thought and the Atlantic Republican Tradition* (Princeton: Princeton University Press, 2016), p. xix.

3 Among a wealth of examples: 'Within the limits of that framework, the individual employed reason, which disclosed to him the eternal hierarchies of unchanging nature and enjoined him to maintain the cosmic order by maintaining his place in that social and spiritual category to which his individual nature assigned him' Pocock, *The Machiavellian Moment*, p. 49.

mould of thought.[4] He was certainly right to highlight the existence of this type of dualist thinking, for Neoplatonism had a great impact on aspects of Christian and, in particular, Arabic philosophy from at least the Middle Ages onwards.[5] The question now, of course, is: What does it matter? Why is it relevant, in a study of seventeenth-century English natural law, to distinguish between Christian theology generally and a particular Neoplatonic strand of Christian theology? This book argues that *that* distinction changes everything. First, the premise of my analysis is that the original Christian thought transcends dualities. Moreover, the struggles of several natural philosophers dealt with in the chapters that follow – in particular Robert Boyle and John Locke – to grasp the essence and unity of a Christian cosmology offer an important proof of my claim. In the words of John Dunn, Locke's voluntarism and rationalism were 'yoked by violence together' – through the force of faith more than by philosophical persuasion.[6] It is of the utmost importance, however, to witness Locke's certainty that dualism was not workable.[7]

I propose to seek an insight into the perspectives of modern natural lawyers by studying these struggles to unify thought in a philosophy of natural law – including its subsequent transformations – as framed by the influence of Neoplatonic thought, rather than in the light of Ockhamite nominalist traditions or the voluntarist traditions often employed during the twentieth century.[8] Several of the English philosophers discussed in this book sought to overcome the dualist conception of the world they

[4] Pocock, *The Machiavellian Moment*, p. 50.

[5] Pasquale Porro, 'The University of Paris in the Thirteenth Century: Proclus and The *Liber de causis*', in Stephen Gersh (ed.), *Interpreting Proclus: From Antiquity to the Renaissance* (Cambridge: Cambridge University Press, 2014), p. 264; Dragos Calma, 'Du neoplatonisme au realisme et retour, parcours latins du *Liber de causis* aux XIII–XVI siecles, 54 *Bulletin de philosophie médiévale* (2012); Dragos Calma, 'The Exegetical Tradition of Medieval Neoplatonism. Considerations on a Recently Discovered *Corpus* of Texts', in Dragos Calma (ed.), *Neoplatonism in the Middle Ages, I: New Commentaries on Liber de causis (ca. 1250–1350)* (Turnhout: Brepols, 2016).

[6] Dunn, *The Political Thought of John Locke*, p. 195.

[7] Locke's assertion that God is, in fact, everywhere, but *without being nature* (as Spinoza had it), is interesting in this regard. John Locke, *An Essay Concerning Human Understanding*, with an Introduction by Peter H. Nidditch (ed.) (Oxford: Clarendon Press, 1975), II. 17. §20. 222, and generally ch. 13–17. Arguing that unlike for Spinoza, for Locke God is not nature, but that through the latter's emphasis of God's omnipresence, God's immensity and eternity almost corresponds with infinite space and infinite duration, see generally Geoffrey Gorham, 'Locke on Space, Time and God', 7 *Ergo* (2020).

[8] Famously so by Michel Villey, 'Les origines de la notion du droit subjectif', in *Leçons d'histoire de la philosophie du droit* (Paris: Dalloz, 1962), 240–241; and generally, Michel Villey, 'La genèse du droit subjectif chez Guillaume d'Occam', 9 *Archives de Philosophie*

had inherited directly from Descartes and indirectly from Proclus and Avicenna. Deism – the establishment of religion on the basis of nature not revelation – was one of the outcomes of Neoplatonism.[9] In his examination of 'Descartes's Proof of a God from the Idea of a Necessary Existence', John Locke rejected the theological deficiency of Deism:

> The idea of the Theists' eternal Being is, that it is a knowing immaterial substance, that made and still keeps all the beings of the universe in that order in which they are preserved. The idea of Atheists' eternal Being is senseless matter. The question between them then is, which of these really is that eternal Being that has always been. Now I say, whoever will use the idea of necessary existence to prove a God, i.e. an immaterial eternal knowing spirit, will have no more to say for it from the idea of necessary existence, than an Atheist has for his eternal, all-doing, senseless matter.[10]

This passage evidences Locke's dissatisfaction with the dualist or Neoplatonic implications of the theory, since, for the devout philosopher, very little could be said about a Neoplatonic God. But after the publication of *An Essay*, according to John W. Yolton's review and M. A. Stewart's analysis of Edward Stillingfleet's critique, charges that Locke was a Deist

du Droit, Le droit subjectif en question (1964), p. 97. Despite his critique to Villey, Brian Tierney framed his discussion on rights as a response to nominalism in *The Idea of Natural Rights: Studies on Natural Rights, Natural Law, and Church Law 1150–1625* (Grand Rapids, MI and Cambridge, UK: William B. Erdmans Publishing Company, 2001); James Tully, 'Governing Conduct: Locke on the Reform of Thought and Behaviour', in James Tully (ed.), *An Approach to Political Philosophy: Locke in Contexts* (Cambridge: Cambridge University Press, 1993), p. 193; Peter R. Anstey, *The Philosophy of Robert Boyle* (London and New York: Routledge, 2000). More generally, dissociating medieval skepticism from an exclusive link with Ockham's nominalism, Martin Pickavé, 'Skeptical Arguments in the Later Middle Ages', in G. Anthony Bruno and A. C. Rutherford (eds.), *Skepticism: Historical and Contemporary Inquiries* (London and New York: Routledge, 2018).

9 M. A. Stewart notes that it 'is not always clear in seventeenth-century writers where the boundaries lie between the influences of Cartesianism, Cambridge Platonism, the views of Lord Herbert, and even traditional Scholasticism'. M. A. Stewart 'Stillingfleet and the Way of Ideas', in M. A. Stewart (ed.), *English Philosophy in the Age of Locke* (Oxford: Clarendon Press, 2000), p. 256. The use and misuse of Neoplatonism in England in the refutation of Socinianism, in Sarah Mortimer, *Reason and Religion in the English Revolution: The Challenge of Socinianism* (Cambridge: Cambridge University Press, 2010), p. 147.

10 Locke later qualifies his view: 'I answer: The idea of God, as far as the name God stands for the first eternal cause, includes necessary existence'. In John Locke, 'Deus-Descartes's Proof of a God from the Idea of a Necessary Existence, Examined', in Peter King (ed.), *The Life of John Locke with Extracts from His Correspondence, Journals, and Common-Place Books*, vol. II (London: Bentley, 1830), pp. 134–6. A similar idea than the quote in the text in John Locke, 'Remarks upon Some of Mr. Norris's Books. Wherein He Asserts P. Malebranche's Opinion of Our Seeing All Things in God' (1693) in *The Works of John Locke in Ten Volumes*, X (London: Thomas Tegg and Co., 1823), p. 255.

multiplied, albeit not altogether justly, since he believed in Revelation.[11] Deism, it is true, developed out of the changing conceptions of nature in theology and philosophy, which is one of the main themes of this book, but it was also the product of a personal choice of faith. With the adoption of Neoplatonic thought in late thirteenth-century theology and in some strands of fifteenth-century humanist philosophy, materialism crept up. In Neoplatonism, the intellectual and the material world are markedly distinguished. That very dualism would become the foundation of mechanistic philosophy. However, during the English Scientific Revolution, importantly in Boyle's case, as we will see, the suspicion began to arise that dualist philosophies were preventing knowledge.

As with any realist philosophy, the defining feature of Neoplatonism is that knowledge starts with a particular thing or individual – in it the material world is often understood in atomic terms. In turn, what differentiates materialist epistemology of Neoplatonism from other forms of realism is its scepticism, obscurity of reason or of will (a 'blind will'), the existence of an extramental giver of forms for human understanding, denial of innate principles or – however the idea is expressed – of the absence of an active unity of body and spirit, will and reason. The theological expression of that dualism is that God is not involved in the actual speculative and practical reasoning of human beings. Thus, Christian sceptics neglect the scriptural doctrine that the kingdom of God is within us.[12] The interpretation of that verse has been varied in the tradition: from Origen's Christological understanding of the *autobasileia*, by which Christ *is* himself the Kingdom, to the mystical reading that views the Kingdom as a place located in the interiority of human beings, and the ecclesiastical that more diffusedly sees the relationship of Christ and

11 As appears from John Locke, *The Reasonableness of Christianity*, with an Introduction and Notes by John C. Higgins-Biddle (ed.) (Oxford: Clarendon Press, 2000); John W. Yolton, *Locke and the Way of Ideas* (Bristol: Thomes Press, 1993), p. 169; Stewart 'Stillingfleet and the Way of Ideas'; Jeffrey R. Collins, *In the Shadow of Leviathan: John Locke and the Politics of Conscience* (Cambridge: Cambridge University Press, 2020), p. 333.

12 'Once, on being asked by the Pharisees when the kingdom of God would come, Jesus replied, 'The coming of the kingdom of God is not something that can be observed, nor will people say, "Here it is", or "There it is", because the kingdom of God is in within you' (*neque dicent ecce hic aut ecce illic ecce enim regnum Dei intra vos est*). Luke 17.20–21; 'According as his divine power hath given unto us all things that pertain unto life and godliness, through the knowledge of him that hath called us to glory and virtue: Whereby are given unto us exceeding great and precious promises: that by these ye might be partakers of the divine nature, having escaped the corruption that is in the world through lust' 2 Peter 1.3–4, *King James Version Bible Translation.*

the human beings building the Church.[13] At any rate, all of them express the real presence of the divine in the materiality of the world, even within human beings' bodies. Famously, Aristotle expressed a pre-Christian version of that scriptural doctrine in *De anima*, defining a divine element in the human mind and, since his view was convergent with Scripture, Christian theologians – particularly Albert the Great and later Thomas Aquinas – followed suit.[14] Briefly, these thinkers had described the peculiar manner in which human beings perceive and live in the world, grasping, together with God, the divine in the world and in themselves: created in the image of God as such; by means of the general principles of natural law through the divine light; or through God living within themselves and helping them to act well – that is, the Kingdom that Luke mentioned in his Gospel.[15] How scepticism shattered these epistemological and ontological principles and the evolving understanding of the light of reason in seventeenth-century England are discussed later in Chapter 5.

In the philosophical vacuum created during the long Reformation, Thomas Hobbes is usually considered the first English natural lawyer to have offered a convincing frame of thought that suited the sceptical temper of the period.[16] Hugo Grotius (1583–1645), it is true, was also constantly

[13] These three interpretations in Joseph Ratzinger, *Jesus of Nazareth: From the Baptism in the Jordan to the Transfiguration*, Adrian J. Walker trans. (New York and London: Doubleday, 2007), p. 49.

[14] Aristotle, *De Anima*, 430a10–25 in R. M. Polansky, *Aristotle's De Anima: A Critical Commentary* (Cambridge: Cambridge University Press, 2007), p. 460; about the impact of these lines, see K. V. Wilkes noting that until this passage, Aristotle was 'every physicalist's ideal role model', but after it 'he seems to put himself resoundingly in the dualists' camp', K. V. Wilkes, 'Psuchē versus the Mind', in Martha C. Nussbaum, and Amélie Oksenberg Rorty (eds.), *Essays on Aristotle's de Anima* (Oxford: Oxford University Press, 1995), p. 125; Albertus Magnus, *Ethica*, ed. Borgnet, vol. VII (Paris: Louis Vivès, 1891), Liber I, t. 7, c. 5; Paul Dominikus Hellmeier, *Anima et intellectus. Albertus Magnus und Thomas von Aquin über Seele und Intellekt des Menschen* (Münster: Aschendorff Verlag, 2011); *Aristotle's De Anima with the Commentary of St. Thomas Aquinas*; René Gauthier, 'Introduction' to Aquinas, *Sententia Libri De Anima*, vol. 45, I (Rome: Commissio Leonina, 1984).

[15] See, previous note and Timothy C. Potts, *Conscience in Medieval Philosophy* (Cambridge: Cambridge University Press, 1980), p. 45; Tobias Hoffmann, 'Conscience and Synderesis', in Brian Davies and Eleonore Stump (eds.), *The Oxford Handbook of Aquinas* (Oxford: Oxford University Press, 2012); Mónica García-Salmones Rovira, 'Natural Rights in Albert the Great: Beyond Objective and Subjective Divides', in Paolo Amorosa, Mónica García-Salmones Rovira and Martti Koskenniemi (eds.), *International Law and Religion: Historical and Contemporary Perspectives* (Oxford: Oxford University Press, 2017).

[16] Henry G. van Leeuwen, *The Problem of Certainty in English Thought: 1630–1690* (The Hague: Martinus Nijhoff, 1963); Richard H. Popkin, *The History of Scepticism: From Savonarola to Bayle* (Oxford: Oxford University Press, 2003), pp. 1–43; 174–218. Discussions on the

referred to in England, but there were other interesting native experiments. Eminent Cambridge Platonists such as Henry More (1614–1687) and Ralph Cudworth (1617–1688) attempted to establish the Neoplatonist tradition in England in the midst of the crisis in epistemology that led to British empiricism. In the context of empiricism, knowledge would be inferred from the accumulation of empirical data, and ideas about natural law and morality would be transformed through novel mechanistic and naturalist principles. By contrast, Cudworth's key principle concerned the elementary capacity to ascertain the divine order of the world and how this ability preserved responsibility and human freedom. By his own account, Cudworth wrote his main work, *The True Intellectual System of the Universe* (1678), to confute prevalent ideas of necessity and to reinstate liberty to the centre of debate concerning moral philosophy. His was a discourse about liberty, 'against the fatal necessity of all actions'.[17]

Cudworth derived the force of his ideas also from Neoplatonic sources and built on Cartesian dualism – exactly the dualism that, as we will see in this study, Boyle and Locke were trying to defeat in order to develop a new theory of knowledge. Furthermore, Cudworth's Neoplatonic defence of religion against atheism was heterodox and often received with misgivings.[18] In his recent study of Cudworth as a critic of Hobbes's radical voluntarism, Stewart Duncan shows how, in another text on morality, Cudworth – interestingly, for a Cambridge Platonist – viewed things in matter and things in morality as possessing a similar type of constituency, a sort of 'nature' that was common to such qualities as, for example,

idea of a Long Reformation in England in Jeremy Gregory 'The Making of a Protestant Nation: "Success" and "Failure" in England's Long Reformation', in Nicholas Tyache (ed.), *England's Long Reformation* (London: University College Press, 1998).

17 This is explained in the 'Preface': 'some Theists supposing God, both to decree and doe all things in us …; or that he hath nothing of morality in his nature, he being only arbitrary will omnipotent …, or by his immediate influence to determinate all actions, and so make them alike necessary to us. Again there being other Divine fatalists, who acknowledge such a Deity, as both suffers other things, besides itself, to act, and hath an essential goodness and justice in its nature, and consequently, that there are things, just and unjust to us naturally, and not by law and arbitrary constitution only; and yet nevertheless take away from men all such liberty as might make them capable of praise and dispraise, rewards and punishments, and objects of distributive justice; they conceiving necessity to be intrinsical to the nature of every thing, in the actings of it, and nothing of contingency to be found any where.' Ralph Cudworth, 'The True Intellectual System of the Universe', in Thomas Birch (ed.), *The Works of Ralph Cudworth*, vol. I (Oxford: D.A. Talboys, 1829), p. 44.

18 Sarah Hutton, 'Philosophy, Religion and Heterodoxy in the Philosophy of Henry More, Ralph Cudworth and Anne Conway', 100 *Church History and Religious Culture* (2020), pp. 158–159.

'whiteness', 'evilness' or 'goodness'.[19] Cudworth's point was to assert that things are what they are (material or moral) not by divine, arbitrary institution, but *by nature*.[20] Remarkably, Cudworth almost reified the conception of 'nature' and thus adopted a position opposite to that of Hobbes, and indeed Boyle. Against voluntarists' wild arbitrariness, both in their conception of morality and in their view of human society, Cudworth described natural order as the outcome of a just and rational God. Civil society and civil sovereignty were also expressions of that natural order. The political absolutism lurking in the sceptical and voluntarist position led him to emphasize an almost ontological public good and public conscience. With regard to Hobbes, Cudworth condemned in his main published work the atheist politics and ethics of the new natural lawyers:

> Here therefore these atheistic politicians, as they first of all slander human nature, and make a villain of it; so do they, in the next place, reproach justice and civil sovereignty also, making it to be nothing but an ignoble and bastardly brat of fear; or else a lesser evil, submitted to merely out of necessity, for the avoiding of a greater evil, that of war with every one, by reason of men's natural imbecility.[21]

It was a vain endeavour, Cudworth thought, to attempt to craft justice artificially when there was none by nature. The passage from art to force and unrestrained power would be unavoidable in that situation.[22] Artificial sovereignty of 'bodies politic' was an impossibility. Instead, there must be 'some natural bond or vinculum' that held groups of subjects together and led them to obey the lawful commands of sovereigns. In turn, sovereigns sought to secure the welfare of their subjects through their commands. Thus, the natural bond could not be other than 'natural justice'; hence, there existed 'something of a common and public, of a cementing

[19] Stewart Duncan, 'Cudworth as a Critic of Hobbes', in Marcus Adams (ed.), *A Companion to Hobbes* (Hoboken: Wiley-Blackwell, 2021). Benjamin Carter also sees Cudworth refuting Calvinist voluntarism, see Benjamin Carter, 'Ralph Cudworth and the Theological Origins of Consciousness', 23 *History of the Human Sciences* (2010), p. 31.

[20] 'It is a Thing which we shall very easily demonstrate, that *Moral Good and Evil, Just and Unjust, Honest and Dishonest* (if they be not meer Names without any Signification, or Names nor nothing else, but *Willed* and *Commanded*, but have a Reality in Respect of the Persons obliged to do and avoid them) *cannot possibly be Arbitrary things, made by Will without Nature*; because it is Universally true, That things are what they are, not by *Will* but by *Nature*.' Ralph Cudworth, *A Treatise Concerning Eternal and Immutable Morality*, with a Preface by Edward, Bishop of Durham (London: Printed for James and John Knapton, 1731), p. 13.

[21] Cudworth, *The True Intellectual System of the Universe*, vol. IV, p. 198.

[22] Cudworth, *The True Intellectual System of the Universe*, vol. IV, p. 205.

and conglutinating nature, in all rational beings'. Its origins were from 'the Deity', whose own right and authority was also founded in justice. Thus, civil sovereignty was nothing other than 'a certain participation' in that justice. Therefore, sovereignty was neither artificial, nor natural, neither regal nor popular, but 'hath a stamp of Divinity upon it'.[23] The error, Cudworth argued, was that atheists acknowledged 'nothing in nature of a public or common good, nothing of duty or obligation'. Instead, atheists made private apetite the only measure of good and transformed justice into 'utility'. Public conscience on the part of atheists was a contradiction in terms, for they argued that 'Conscience is Private Judgment of Good and Evil'. When they invoked conscience, they were only asserting rebellion, violence and fanaticism.[24] Cudworth's own view was that 'conscience also is, in itself, not of a private and partial, but of a public and common nature'. One ought to put first divine laws, justice and the common good ('the good of the whole') when they clashed with 'our own selfish good, and private utility'. This statement constitutes the core of what Cudworth saw as the only means to unite society and the body politic.[25] However, Cudworth also thought that individuals made a judgment in conscience for themselves 'a public conscience being nonsense and ridiculous'. In that sense, they could err. And yet, the rule by which such judgments in conscience were made was not 'private'. Instead, divine laws and justice and the revealed will of God – 'things more public than the civil laws' – made one responsible for one's judgment.[26] Simply put, publicness involved responsibility, also in terms of natural justice. Liberty, and not necessity, was the rule of human actions. Cudworth was adamant in his philosophical project as to the existence of the capacity to ascertain the common good among subjects, in the form of a kind of 'conglutinating nature', and the capacity to know the morality that a just God had determined.[27]

A Treatise Concerning Eternal and Immutable Morality was published posthumously in 1731.[28] His grandson Francis Cudworth Masham (1686–1731) – the son of Damaris (Cudworth) Masham (1658–1708), Cudworth's

[23] Cudworth, *The True Intellectual System of the Universe*, vol. IV, p. 206.

[24] Cudworth, *The True Intellectual System of the Universe*, vol. IV, p. 211.

[25] 'This is the only thing that can naturally consociate mankind together, lay a foundation for bodies politic, and take away that private will and judgment, according to men's appetite and utility which is inconsistent with the same.' ... 'that which is of a common and public nature, unites; but that, which is of a private, segregates and dissociates'. Cudworth, *The True Intellectual System of the Universe*, v. IV, p. 212.

[26] Cudworth, *The True Intellectual System of the Universe*, v. IV, p. 212.

[27] Cudworth, *The True Intellectual System of the Universe*, v. IV, p. 206.

[28] Cudworth, *A Treatise Concerning Eternal and Immutable Morality.*

daughter – to whom John Locke had left practically half his estate, found it among his grandfather's papers and made it available for publication.[29] The gist of its moral philosophy is that morality was *within human minds* and was not the command of the sovereign.[30] Neither the Sovereign God nor the political sovereign generated a duty to obey. Moral and political obligation arose not from a command, but from 'the Intellectual Nature of him that is commanded'. If there were no intellectual natures – presumably he meant human beings and angels – there would be no morality.[31] Cudworth envisaged metaphysics as the Neoplatonic 'scale of beings', with an archetype and different degrees of imitation in the ectype ideas – that is, 'an imprint or copy of an archetype'.[32] He rejected Descartes' argument that natures could not be eternal because (as Descartes reasoned) God would then depend on them and not the other way around. Furthermore, Cudworth asserted that the only genuine philosophy was the ancient atomistic philosophy with a Neoplatonic twist:

> Wherefore the proper and genuine Result of this old *Atomical* Philosophy, which is the Triumph of Reason over Sense, is nothing else but this, that Sense alone is not the *Criterion* or Judge of what does Really and Absolutely exist without us, but that there is a Higher and Superior intellectual Faculty in us that judges of our Sense, which discovers what is Fallacious and Fantastical in them, and pronounces what Absolutely is and is not.[33]

Cudworth considered human intellect a vital force that framed conceptions of things wherever it found something that could be understood. The

[29] 'Preface' in Cudworth, *A Treatise Concerning Eternal and Immutable Morality.* A description of Damaris by Locke to his correspondent on theology P. van Limborch in, 'Locke to P. van Limborch, on the 13th of March 1691' Letter 1375, in E. S. de Beer (ed.), *The Correspondence of John Locke* (Oxford: Clarendon Press, 1976–82), vol. IV, p. 237; on her husband see Mark Knights, 'Sir Francis Masham, 3rd Bt. (c. 1646–1723), of Otes, High Laver, Essex' in *The History of Parliament: The House of Commons 1690–1715*, ed. D. W Hayton, Eveline Cruickshanks, Stuart Handley (Cambridge: Cambridge University Press, 2002); see also John W. Yolton, *Locke. An Introduction* (Oxford: Basil Blackwell, 1985), p. 8. Peter Laslett described Francis Masham as one of the five members in the House of Commons of 'the Lockeian group in the Parliaments'. Peter Laslett, 'John Locke, the Great Recoinage, and the Origins of the Board of trade: 1695–1698', 14 *The William and Mary Quarterly* (1957), p. 381.

[30] See linking this thesis with the 'moral sense' school of English ethical theory founded by Anthony Ashley Cooper, third Earl of Shaftesbury (1671–1713), W. M. Spellman, *John Locke and the Problem of Depravity* (Oxford: Clarendon Press, 1988), p. 184.

[31] Cudworth, *A Treatise Concerning Eternal and Immutable Morality*, p. 27.

[32] Cudworth, *A Treatise Concerning Eternal and Immutable Morality*, p. 36; Cornelis de Waal, 'Locke's Criterion for the Reality of Ideas: Unambiguous but Untenable', 28 *The Locke's Newsletter* (1997), p. 35

[33] Cudworth, *A Treatise Concerning Eternal and Immutable Morality*, p. 72.

human intellect worked analogically to what he termed 'the Spermatick or Plastick Power' of Stoic and Augustinian inspiration, which generated forms in all animals 'framing an Eye here and an Ear there'.[34] He put forward two principles in relation to the question of knowledge of morality relevant here. First, that the human mind has the capacity to order the world around us, also in moral terms. Second, his adoption of an epistemology that definitively broke with the classical understanding of the light of reason. We shall see in Chapter 5 the many doubts that existed in the minds of natural lawyers and theologians of the day concerning the existence of a divine light of nature with the capacity to discriminate between good and evil. The numerous arguments they put forward as to the obscurity and weakness of this approach suffice to demonstrate the uncertainties and even despair surrounding the continuing validity of the classical natural law notion of the light of nature and sometimes even of conscience in the 17th English political context.[35] Locke was not impervious to that feeling.[36] Together with the rise of scepticism in Europe, the peculiar religious controversies of the time were certainly factors that contributed to confusion as to the idea of the world being illuminated from within by human beings' *light*. Conceptions of individual moral agency were thus entangled with notions of religious and political independence and enthusiasm. It is instructive to read that the philosopher Damaris Masham discovered in the work of John Smith, another Cambridge Platonist, the possibility of a higher principle than reason, which reason could activate. She defended that idea in her correspondence with Locke, albeit that the latter dismissed it as a species of 'enthusiasm'.[37] As late as 1701, John Edwards (1637–1716), the Cambridge divine, championed an apology for article 18 of the 39 articles of the Anglican Church, the articles dealing with the 'accursing' of those who thought that by the law of their sect and the light of nature could be saved. He criticized Locke's Deism in the same chapter, on the

[34] Cudworth, *A Treatise Concerning Eternal and Immutable Morality*, p. 135.

[35] See Margaret Sampson, 'Laxity and Liberty in Seventeenth-century English Political Thought', in Edmund Leites (ed.), *Conscience and Casuistry in Early Modern Europe'* (Cambridge: Cambridge University Press, 1988); Robert A. Greene, 'Synderesis, the Spark of Conscience, in the English Renaissance' 52 *Journal of the History of Ideas* (1991); Tymothy Stanton, 'Freedom of Conscience, Political Liberty and the Foundations of Liberalism', in Quentin Skinner and Martin van Gelderen (eds.), *Freedom and the Construction of Europe*. vol. I, *Religious Freedom and Civil Liberty* (Cambridge: Cambridge University Press, 2013).

[36] See Chapter 9 below.

[37] This story in Sarah Hutton, 'Lady Damaris Masham', *The Stanford Encyclopedia of Philosophy* (Winter 2020 Edition), Edward N. Zalta (ed.), URL = <https://plato.stanford.edu/archives/win2020/entries/lady-masham/>.

ground that Locke had – in Edwards' view – denied natural conscience.[38] Clearly, Edwards approved neither of the affirmation of the independent light of reason of the enthusiasts, which ought to be contained, nor of the denial of natural light in moral action, which obscured what was traditionally described as the voice of God in human beings. In the mostly ignored *Natural History of Superstition* (1709), by the Deist John Trenchard, 'the inward light' was equated to a hallucinatory experience.[39] The opposite attitude was displayed by the Catholic Church at the time. In 1726 it canonized the mystic John of the Cross (1542–1591) who popularized a type of rational mysticism through his works. He frequently described how God would at will communicate directly with the intellect of human beings in grace, and that was what the classic theologians had termed fruition or enjoyment: that is, to see God already in this world.[40]

Cudworth's neat adoption of Neoplatonist dualism sets itself against that classic notion of the light of reason. His Neoplatonism might be described as a type of moderate scepticism. What human intellect discovered was (ectypal) ideas modelled after the divine archetype. In other words, there was no light of nature, but human intellect *contained* the just moral and metaphysical order instituted eternally by God. Cudworth's influential work on consciousness has gained increasing attention.[41] He understood consciousness, at a higher intellectual level, as a 'return to oneself'. Udo Thiel writes that he was not employing a classical notion of conscience in

[38] 'They are to be had accursed who presume to say, Every Man shall be saved by the Law or Sect which he professes (be it what it will) so he frame his Life according to that Law and the Light of Nature 18th Article.' John Edwards, *Discourse Concerning Truth and Error. Especially in Matters of Religion* (London: Printed for Jonathan Robinson, 1701), pp. 403; 423. An extreme case was that of Quakers, see Stefano Villani, 'Conscience and Convention: The Young Furly and the Hat Controversy', in Sara Hutton (ed.), *Benjamin Furly 1646–1714: A Quaker Merchant and His Milieu* (Firenzi: Olschki, 2007).

[39] See John F. Sena, 'Melancholic Madness and the Puritans', 66 *The Harvard Theological Review* (1973), p. 304.

[40] San Juan de la Cruz, 'Cántico Espiritual. Códice A.' en *San Juan de la Cruz. Obras Completas* (*Ebook Clásicos*, 2015) Canción 13 y 14. On the notion of 'fruition' see Severin Valentinov Kitanov, *Beatific Enjoyment in Scholastic Theology and Philosophy: 1240–1335* (Doctoral Diss, Helsinki, 2006); Arthur Stephen McGrade, 'Enjoyment at Oxford after Ockham: Philosophy, Psychology, and the Love of God', in Anne Hudson, and Michael Wilks (eds.), *From Ockham to Wyclif* (Oxford: Basil Blackwell, 1987), pp. 63–88; Servais Pinckaers, 'The Place of Philosophy in Moral Theology', John Berkman and Craig Steven Titus (eds.), *The Pinckaers Reader: Renewing Thomistic Moral Theology* (Washington, DC: Catholic University of America Press, 2005).

[41] Udo Thiel, 'Cudworth and Seventeenth-Century Theories of Consciousness', in Stephan Gaukroger (ed.), *The Uses of Antiquity* (Dordrecht: Kluwer, 1991); Carter, 'Ralph Cudworth and the Theological Origins of Consciousness'.

terms of a 'perception or knowledge of something that one shares with someone else'.[42] Like other Neoplatonists before him, and, indeed, strictly following Pocock's model, described above, in which particularity is located in universality, Cudworth understood the judgment of conscience as the natural recognition of a metaphysical just order with which one ought to compare one's moral or political decisions. In Hobbes's radical sceptic epistemology, which Cudworth sought to neutralize, good and evil were moral categories that a human being could not discern naturally. Instead, whether useful or not, pleasant or painful would be the substitutes for the *morality inside* type of thinking. As triggers of knowledge, the 'pleasant' or 'painful' nature of sensations became building blocks for the new naturalist natural law. The complexity of John Locke's work, dealt with in Chapters 8 to 12, evidences that he took seriously Cudworth's critique of hedonistic morality and its corrosive consequences for the social order.

As the analysis will show, the rejection of innate ideas did not imply the absence of moral psychology, which is also one of the findings of Lisa T. Sarasohn's *Gassendi's Ethics.*[43] Gassendi's doctrine of pleasure and pain, for instance, functioned as an internally constituted moral psychology. He did not consider the classical laws of nature to be necessary in order to pursue what he thought an individual and a culture was 'instinctually' and rationally equipped for.[44] In her path-breaking study on the topic, Sorana Corneanu has described the specific solution adopted by the English *virtuosi*, the leading English figures in early modern science.[45] Cultivation of reason through science and industriousness would become, for them, one of the main tools for practising righteous moral actions. They adopted this stance on the strength of their insight that the European crisis of knowledge had massive implications for morality. Ian Harris has shown how, in relation to matters of religion, English natural lawyers of the new science opted for tolerance.[46] Their writings also evidence a process through which Cudworth's ideas connecting private reason to public conscience are refined. In a moment of generalized awe towards *Leviathan*, Cudworth stood for a return to ideas concerning the existence recognizable by

[42] Thiel, 'Cudworth and Seventeenth-Century Theories of Consciousness', pp. 81–82; 90.

[43] Lisa T. Sarasohn, *Gassendi's Ethics. Freedom in a Mechanistic Universe* (Ithaca and London: Cornell University Press, 1996). She devotes Chapter 8 to arguing about Gassendi's influence in Locke.

[44] Sarasohn, *Gassendi's Ethics*, p. 178.

[45] Corneanu, *Regimens of the Mind.*

[46] Ian Harris, *The Mind of John Locke. A Study of Political Theory in Its Intellectual Setting* (Cambridge: Cambridge University Press, 1998).

everyone of a public and common good. As mentioned above, strong echoes of this awareness may be found in the work of John Locke. The pragmatic expression that public good took in Locke's work and politics, in terms of theorizing a natural law that would make England and her economy strong and care for everyone's necessities, is the main topic of Chapters 11 and 12. At the same time, and notwithstanding an accurate perception of the dangers of individualism, the critiques of Hobbes's project levelled by Cudworth and many others were not always fair, as they represented Hobbes as being less interested in the public good than he was in reality, as I will argue in Chapters 2 and 3.

1.2 Scepticism and Moral Righteousness

Creativity in scientific and monetary matters marked the era under discussion. However, moral and religious ideas framed the directions of the new imagination. As wealth for the nation seemed nearer at hand through economic growth, the new economic and scientific activities were experienced with increasing anxiety, and philosophers looking for the right way in which to carry out economic policies came up with ingenious scientific solutions. The hope was that the new ideas would be also morally acceptable. My view on the existence of a theological framework for the new thinking reflects the perspective that this period should be regarded as the long Reformation, rather than as marking the beginning of Enlightenment.[47] This stance is justified by the fact that religious themes permeated all the issues and every text discussed here during the entire period. Moreover, the elite of Reformers that Charles Webster popularized in the 1970s, dealt with in Chapter 4, aimed to reform science, economy and faith in one stroke.[48] By contrast, the next generation of authors, dating from roughly after the beginning of the Restoration (1660), shows a certain weariness with a cultural system that guaranteed the reproduction of controversies on religious grounds. On political principle they obviously desired a united but not uniform society. However, in order to understand the gist of Robert Boyle's or John Locke's scientific and economic projects, it is not necessary to pinpoint the 'secularist' ideas in them. In fact, their scientific and societal project would be meaningless if observed as a dechristianized enterprise. The

[47] Gregory 'The Making of a Protestant Nation: "Success" and "Failure" in England's Long Reformation'; David Loewenstein and Alison Shell, 'Early Modern Literature and England's Long Reformation' in 24 *Reformation* (2019).

[48] Webster, *The Great Instauration.*

fact that Locke, at least, fought 'priestcraft' did not make him secular.[49] The naiveté of devout Whiggery was therefore not behind their commitment to producing a robust moral discourse through the sciences, that is to say, in their contribution through their scientific work to guiding the lifelong Christian effort in the choice of 'the proper object of *Desire*'.[50] It would have been a simple-minded view if they had thought, in acting out the role of scientist as priest (as they did), that real theologians and priests were redundant.[51] However, while incontrovertible evidence on that point is inaccessible to us now, there are in fact, as discussed below, ample biographical and textual indications that this was not their standpoint and that instead they were soberly attentive to what priests and theologians had to say.[52]

An alternative way to describe the history of natural law discussed in the chapters that follow would be to adopt the tradition of C. B. MacPherson, Leo Strauss and Neal Woods, by which I mean situating it in the history of Western materialism.[53] After all, Karl Marx did not borrow substantially from John Locke's ideas on money for *The Capital* on a mere whim, while also giving them an Aristotelian philosophical twist about the 'form of commodity'.[54] However, I hope to show that identifying the new thinking as the philosophers' attempt to *materialize* Christianity offers a more accurate analysis of what happened in the second half of seventeenth-century England. In other words, their efforts were directed towards embedding Christian thinking in the business of prudential government,

[49] Mark Goldie, 'Priestcraft and the Birth of Whiggism', in Nicholas Phillipson and Quentin Skinner (eds.), *Political Discourse in Early Modern Britain* (Cambridge: Cambridge University Press, 1993); Collins, *In the Shadow of Leviathan*, p. 339.

[50] On 'the proper object of *Desire*' see Locke, *An Essay Concerning Human Understanding*, II. 21.§43, p. 259. (emphasis Locke).

[51] On the scientist as a priest, see Robert Boyle, 'Of the Study of the Booke of Nature', in Michael Hunter and Edward B. Davis (eds.), *Works of Robert Boyle*, vol. 13 (London: Pickering & Chatto, 2000), p. 151; Harold Fisch, 'The Scientist as Priest: A Note on Robert Boyle's Natural Theology' in 44 *Isis* (1953); Michael Hunter, *Boyle: Between God and Science* (New Haven: Yale University Press, 2009).

[52] The obvious example is the situation of Robert Boyle's doubts of conscience, see for this Michael Hunter, 'The Conscience of Robert Boyle: Functionalism, 'Dysfunctionalism' and the Task of Historical Understanding', in Michael Hunter (ed.), *Robert Boyle (1627–1691) Scrupulosity and Science* (The Boydell Press, Woodbridge, 2000).

[53] MacPherson, *The Political Theory of Possessive Individualism*; Strauss, *Natural Right and History*; Wood, *John Locke and Agrarian Capitalism*. And see also John W. Yolton, *Thinking Matter: Materialism in Eighteenth Century Britain* (Minneapolis: University of Minnesota Press, 1983).

[54] Karl Marx, *Capital. A Critique of Political Economy*, Vol I., Samuel Moore and Edward Aveling trans. and Frederick Engels ed. (Progress Publisher, Moscow, USSR, undated [from the First English ed. 1887]) ch. 1–3.

empirical science and the capitalist economy that was well under way in Europe by that time; so confident were they in the power of Christian faith to speed economic growth and contain greed and indignity. As the diasporic Huguenot Jean Barbeyrac (1674–1744) had it in his uneven *History and Critical Account of the Science of Morality* (1728), the new philosophy sought to develop ethics and politics in a manner 'better proportion'd and adapted to the Constitution of humane Affairs'. However, in the process of achieving this, *certain* Christian moral and religious ideas had to be sifted. In that text written as an 'Introduction' to the main text on natural law by Samuel Pufendorf (1632–1694), Barbeyrac noted on at least five occasions that putting money to interest was a licit activity.[55] The single-mindedness with which the traditional moral condemnation of usury was attacked over a century evidences that making the lending of money at interest socially acceptable was considered of paramount importance for European economic and political development. The particular scientific solution to the problem of usury that Locke devised is explored in Chapter 11 in the context of the period and of his larger philosophical project.

Natural law thinking was also deeply enriched by a strand of moral theory influenced by medical notions. It is worth to consider the fact that medical notions seemed to be immune to scepticism and to lie beyond religion strife. Morality was shaped in particular during the seventeenth century by the utilitarian goals of health and the survival of the human body. The much read *The Anatomy of Melancholy* by Robert Burton (1577–1640), the librarian of Christ Church (Locke's college), exemplifies a new type of medical literature. It is largely a medical text aimed at producing a species of curative reading, combining cases and learned description of a disease that at the time appeared to be reaching epidemic proportions, especially among men.[56] Strikingly, Mary

55 Which might explain his notorious harangue against the backwardness and lack of holiness of the Fathers of the Church whose testimony went against the practice of usury, Jean Barbeyrac, 'An Historical Account of the Science of Morality, and the Progress It Has Made in the World from the Earliest Times Down to the Publication of This Work' in Samuel Pufendorf, *Of the Law of Nature and Nations*, Basil Kennett trans. (London: Printed for J. and J. Knapton et al., 1728), pp. 21; 22; 23; 26; 55. Steven Shapin discusses the high value of testimony during the earliest period of the Scientific Revolution, which might explain the efforts of Barbeyrac to invalidate the prized testimony of the Fathers, see Steven Shapin, *A Social History of truth: Civility and Science in Seventeenth Century England* (Chicago and London: The University of Chicago Press, 1994), p. 211.

56 On *The Anatomy of Melancholy*, and its combination of theological doctrines for curing I follow Mary Ann Lund, *Melancholy, Medicine and Religion in Early Modern England: Reading 'The Anatomy of Melancholy'* (Cambridge: Cambridge University Press, 2010). For an explanation of why the perception at the period of a mark increased in cases of melancholy, see Angus Gowland, 'The Problem of Early Modern Melancholy' 191 *Past & Present* (2006).

Ann Lund remarks that despite all the medical analysis, Burton identified 'want of charity' as the root of all melancholy.[57] In considering the individual's cure, in *Anatomy*, Burton prudently avoided both theological controversy and he also integrated theological doctrines. Setting aside Calvinist ideas of predestination and of the 'captivity of the human will', the text instead highlighted agency in terms of self-improvement and self-cure and hope in the mercy of God was stressed in cases of sinners' despair.[58] On the other hand, 'enthusiasm' was after the mid-seventeenth century often medically classified as madness, and thus directly disqualified from religious validity.[59]

Still, in a pre-Scientific Revolution moment, the well-known scholar John Selden (1584–1654), a savant, jurist, natural lawyer and author of rabbinical works, who held a sceptic position following Carneades, took the view that the guiding principle of the law of nature was an anti-universalist utility. Selden accordingly considered that even when lawyers, philosophers or doctors decided to take an approach based on utility their decisions were in fact very much influenced by local customs and tastes, rather than by objective (*ex natura sui*) attributes of medicines or foods. One found in the commonality of peoples not the 'simplicity' of natural law but the utility of here and now.[60] Selden's prestige in England was immense, thus his utilitarian ideas were very influential.[61] But the new science and theology both demanded universalism. Hence, Selden's theory of natural law would soon be superseded and the solution to the scepticism of reason he proposed did not take root in the crude, though erudite form in which he presented it.[62]

Still, there are at least four important matters that are shown through Selden's study on moral reason or, as he repeatedly put it, his analysis of how to tell good from evil, honourable from dishonourable, licit from illicit, and whether that was at all possible. First, it is clear how urgent the need was at the time to find a solution to this issue of moral knowledge from the immense effort Selden put into seeking to do so. Second, his work undisputedly shows that utilitarian principles were already common among

[57] Lund, *Melancholy, Medicine and Religion in Early Modern England*, p. 174.

[58] This point in Lund, *Melancholy, Medicine and Religion in Early Modern England*, p. 181.

[59] Sena, 'Melancholic Madness and the Puritans'.

[60] Joannis Seldeni, *De Jure Naturali et Gentium Juxta Disciplinam Ebraeorum*, (Bibl. Noribergensium, 1665), p. 80.

[61] Tuck, *Natural Rights Theories*, p. 162.

[62] Ofir Haivry writes that Selden's ideas and style were soon superseded 'in the new "age of reason"'. Ofir Haivry, *John Selden and the Western Political Tradition* (Cambridge: Cambridge University Press, 2017), p. 2.

English scholars at the start of the Civil War.[63] Third, his analysis shows the manner in which metaphysical conceptions of order have evolved, and that a dualist cosmology was well established. This is clear from the fact that Selden did not understand Aquinas's notion of the light of the agent intellect as the participation of human reason in God's order. Instead of a light that *is* the divine Being, the English natural lawyer explained it as a light that 'commands'.[64] Quentin Skinner has recently suggested the existence of a thread between vocabularies as to the health of the body of the state – present in particular in the work of Jean Bodin – and the abstract notion of a state that Hobbes made famous in *Leviathan*.[65] Thus medical notions were not unknown in political theory. However, Selden's approach also made it clear that medicine was not yet a theoretical tool for natural lawyers, not at least for the most knowledgeable Englishman of the time.[66]

My suggestion is also that the rise of the type of combination of Christian theology with medical morality as natural law studied in this book may be traced to the revival of Neoplatonism and the utilitarian moral philosophy that characterizes it. Moreover, as we will see in Chapter 9, it was a utilitarianism that, unlike Selden's contextual approach, could be operated as guided by universal principles. Furthermore, *moderni* theologians, Neoplatonism and Orientalism were in vogue in old Oxford, the place of study of most of the protagonists that feature in this book. In Thomas Wood's contemporary history of Oxonian scholars during the seventeenth century, we find that Thomas Lushington (1589–1661) wrote a treatise, unpublished but extensively circulated, entitled *Theology of Proclus*.[67]

63 Utilitarian ideas are common already in theologians a century early, e.g. in Francisco de Vitoria see, Mónica García-Salmones Rovira, 'The Disorder of Economy: The First *Relectio de Indis* in a Theological Perspective', in Stefan Kadelbach, Thomas Kleinlein and David Roth-Isigkeit (eds.), *System, Order and International Law: The Early History of International Legal Thought from Machiavelli to Hegel* (Oxford: Oxford University Press, 2017); Norbert Campagna, *Francisco de Vitoria: Leben und Werk. Zur Kompetenz der Theologie in politischen und juridischen Fragen* (Münster: Lit Verlag, 2010), p. 75.

64 'adeoque quae naturaliter Bona sint, quae Mala, an ejusmodi illuminatio divina Rationi ac Intellectui humano ritè disposito per Indicationem cum Imperio insinuari.' Seldeni, *De Jure Naturali et Gentium Juxta Disciplinam Ebraeorum*, p. 114.

65 Quentin Skinner, *From Humanism to Hobbes. Studies in Rhetoric and Politics* (Cambridge: Cambridge University Press, 2018), p. 345.

66 For the fame of Selden's knowledge, see Haivry, *John Selden and the Western Political Tradition.*

67 The relevance of this fact may be inferred from Dragos Calma's study of the fortunes of Neoplatonist texts and Proclus's *Elements of Theology* in particular in Europe during the previous centuries; its employment and translation is considered rather the exception than the rule. Calma, 'Du neoplatonisme au realisme et retour'.

Sometimes suspected of being a Socinian, Lushington was a contemporary of Robert Sanderson. He coincided with Sanderson at Lincoln College and later became a fellow at Pembroke College. It is apparent from his use of sources that the latter was knowledgeable about the *moderni* Parisian theologians Duns Scotus (1266–1308) and Durand de Saint Pourçain (1275–1334).[68] The metaphysics of necessity introduced in Chapters 2 and 3 flourished in Europe and also in England with the revival of Orientalism. Bishop Laud's encouragement of 'Orientalist languages' started in the 1630s by his sending John Greaves (1602–1652) to the East to bring him books; Greaves himself became an expert in the Persian language. The savant Henry Jacobs (1608–1652), who was fluent both in 'Arabick' and in Hebrew benefited also from Laud's patronage with the renewal after a hundred years being inactive of the *Socius Grammaticalis*, or Reader in Philology to the Juniors in Merton College. Both linguists were collaborators of Selden that, as Thomas Wood noted, 'Hugh Grotius' praised as 'the glory of the English Nation'.[69] Henry Stubbe (1632–1676), the radical polemicist and scholar, and good friend of both Hobbes and Locke, who wrote the *Originall and Progress of Mahometanism* (1672), fiercely defended in 1670 the contribution of ancient oriental philosophy to physics.[70] The object of his critique was a reduction of contemporary knowledge to the 'fecundity of the Cartesian Principles'. It was, Stubbe considered, first the 'Arabians' that had used chemistry in an eminent manner to help medicine, and it was they who, through their 'sectarian' use of ancient philosophy, had 'improved Chymical Pharmacy very much'. Finally, it had been 'the Aristotelian' Averroes, and 'the Galenist' Avicenna who had transmitted a divided science to Europe:

> From these two great men amongst the *Moors*, as the knowledge of Physick and Philosophy, happened to be imparted to the *barbarous Christians* of the *West*, so was there a feud propagated betwixt the *Philosophers and the Physicians*.[71]

[68] A study of the metaphysics of Scotus in light of his approval of Avicenna's metaphysics of existence in, Etienne Gilson, 'Avicenne et le point de depart de Duns Scot' 2 *Archives d'histoire doctrinale et littéraire du moyen age* (1927), p. 92.

[69] This information is all from the second volume of Thomas Wood, *Athenae Oxonienses an exact history of all the writers and bishops who have had their education in the most ancient and famous University of Oxford*, (…) (London: Printed for Tho. Bennnet at the Half-Moon in S. Pauls Churchyard, 1692). Vol. II; TCP; Early English Books Online; quote in p. 173.

[70] *Henry Stubbe and the Beginnings of Islam. The Originall and Progress of Mahometanism*, ed. Introduction by Nabil Matar (ed.) (New York: Columbia University Press, 2013).

[71] Henry Stubbe, *A specimen of some animadversions upon a book entitled, Plus ultra, or Modern Improvements of useful knowledge written by Mr. Joseph Glanvill, a member of the Royal Society* (London, 1670) TCP; Early English Books Online, pp. 53; 61; 91.

Since, for Stubbe, the 'Mahometans' were a 'sect of Christians', this praise was not necessarily understood as irreverent in relation to Christianism, however radical he himself would later become.[72] Instead, with polemical intent – perhaps as a nod to Hobbes who was fighting some battles in that direction – he declared how grave and prejudicial to knowledge was the ignorance of thinking that science in Europe had started with Descartes, Gassendi and the Royal Society.[73]

1.3 Hobbes and Locke versus Filmer on Political Economy

Heated debate arose in England over whether consent was natural or artificial in the formation of political societies – i.e. over how political obligation originates – once Aristotelianism was displaced from the centre of political discourse.[74] It is a well-known fact of intellectual history that Robert Filmer and Thomas Hobbes set the tone of the discussion, providing opposing solutions to the question, albeit with a similar preference for a strong sovereign power.[75] Filmer's notorious but original theological argument of natural obligation founded on Adam's hereditary kingdom was, of course, explosive after the end of the Civil Wars. The divine Edward Gee (1613–1660) was one of the main writers that engaged with Filmer's early series of publications during the Commonwealth period. Gee discussed Filmer's patriarchalism seriously in 1658, but ultimately

[72] Indeed, Stubbe radicalized completely this position, and inverted the terms, making of Islam the pristine Christianity, see Justin A. I. Champion, 'Legislators, Impostors and the Politic Origins of Religion: English Theories of Imposture from Stubbe to Toland', in Silvia Berti, Françoise Charles-Daubert and Richard H. Popkin (eds.), *Heterodoxy, Spinozism and Freethought* (Dordrecht: Kluwer, 1996) p. 342.

[73] Stubbe, *A Specimen of Some Animadversions*; for Hobbes and his feud with the Royal Society see, Steven Shapin and Simon Schaffer, *Leviathan and the Air-Pump. Hobbes, Boyle, and the Experimental Life*, with a translation of Thomas Hobbes *Dialogus Physicus de Natura Aeris* by Simon Schaffer (Princeton: Princeton University Press, 1985).

[74] Sophie Smith argues convincingly that Aristotelian politics were more fundamental than hitherto thought in sixteenth-century England, and that Hobbes's endeavour amounted to their transformation, Sophie Smith, 'The Language of "Political Science" in Early Modern Europe' 80 *Journal of the History of Ideas* (2019). Among the reasons for the decay of Aristotelianism in the last 30 years of the seventeenth century in Germany H. Dreizel pointed out 'the growing importance of the natural sciences', which, as we will see in Chapters 4 and 7 certainly played an important role a number of decades earlier in England, H. Dreitzel, 'Reason of State and the Crisis of Political Aristotelianism: An Essay on the Development of seventeenth century Political Philosophy' in 28 *History of European Ideas* (2002), p. 181.

[75] See Peter Laslett, 'Introduction', in Sir Robert Filmer, *Patriarcha and Other Political Works*, Peter Laslett (ed.) (New Jersey: Transaction Publishing, 2009 (1949)), p. 40.

dismissed it as ridiculous and absurd.[76] Gee had initially defended the parliamentary cause but opposed Independence, inciting to civil disobedience.[77] He later fell under suspicion of having participated in a conspiracy with Charles II and the Scots to a sufficient extent as to be imprisoned in 1651.[78] In 1658, England was for Gee a 'Nation' that was 'naturally addicted to Lawes and Liberties'.[79] In *Patriarcha* (not yet published in the 1650s), Filmer had noted that 'because the Scripture is not favourable to the liberty of the people therefore many fly to the authority of reason and to the authority of Aristotle'.[80] And so did Gee. He situated the basis of government 'upon a bottom of conscience', that is 'the light of nature' with its dual foundation of rightful law and being the expression of the will of God.[81] However, as noted above, the light of nature and the flexibility and freedom that it entails had but a dim glow in seventeenth-century English theological thinking. Following the latest Protestant line, the jurist John Selden had but cemented that general scepticism. Sceptical thought was so pervasive in the middle of the century that everyone rejected Hobbes's atheism, but the philosophical principles of necessity examined in this book were tacitly accepted as the new space for relevant discussion on politics, even by Filmer himself. Hence, decrying the *atomization* of monarchy denoted by the requirement of individual consent, Filmer considered that it was also materially impossible: 'the truth is, that amongst all them that plead the necessity of the consent of the people, none of them hath ever touched upon these so necessary doctrines'.[82]

[76] Edward Gee, *The Divine Right and Original of the Civill Magistrate from God, (as it is drawn by the Apostle S. Paul in those words, Rom 13.1). There Is No Power but of God: The Powers That Be Are Ordained by God* (London: Prin. for George Eversden, 1658) pp. 144–159. Edward Gee as the discussant of Filmer in the 1650's in Laslett, 'Introduction' in Sir Robert Filmer, *Patriarcha*; mentioning approvingly Filmer's ideas are John Hall in 1657 and Henry Stubbe in 1659 noted in Johann P. Sommerville 'Introduction', in Sir Robert Filmer, *Patriarcha and Other Writings*, Johann P. Sommerville (ed.) (Cambridge: Cambridge University Press, 1991) xiv.

[77] 'Independence' refers here to the radical group of revolutionaries of the English Interregnum who also defended the most anticlericalist position. A helpful overview in Jeffrey R Collins, *The Allegiance of Thomas Hobbes* (Oxford: Oxford University Press, 2005)

[78] S. Guscott (2004, September 23), 'Edward Gee, (bap. 1612, d. 1660), Church of England clergyman and writer.' *Oxford Dictionary of National Biography*. On Gee as an enemy of the Rump Parliament, see Quentin Skinner, *Hobbes and Republican Liberty* (Cambridge: Cambridge University Press, 2008), p. 199.

[79] Gee, *The Divine Right*, 'Preface'.

[80] Sir Robert Filmer, 'Patriarcha', in *Patriarcha and Other Writings*, p. 13.

[81] Gee, *The Divine Right and Original of the Civill Magistrate from God*, 'Preface' and p. 141.

[82] See Robert Filmer, 'Observations Upon Aristotles Politiques Touching Forms of Government with Directions for Obedience to Governours in Dangerous and Doubtfull Times' in Sir Robert Filmer, *Patriarcha and Other Political Works*, p. 174.

Evidently, there was little room for dialogue between Filmer's empirical method and Hobbes's philosophical abstraction.[83]

Peter Laslett showed years ago that Sir Robert Filmer was not the retired reactionary that critiques have made of him. Rather, together with his very large family and circle of friends, he was present in London and Westminster and involved in most of the commercial, political and intellectual undertakings of the day, notably those concerning Virginia. In the next centuries practically all the families that enjoyed political influence in colonial America would be related to the Filmers.[84] Filmer's materialist ideas on government were published in the influential 'Observations Upon Aristotles Politiques Touching Forms of Government'.[85] His few published writings established 'dominion and property' as the basis of government, insisting on the latter repeatedly, rather than on the former, and making property the grounds and main principle of government and justice.[86] Gee, who distinguished between natural and moral power – the latter being 'property or dominion' either over inanimate things or understood as authority – had noted in his preface to *The Divine Right and Original of the Civill Magistrate from God* that dissensions about civil matters could be about 'laws, property, liberty and magistratical prerogative'. However, it is illustrative of the temper of the times that he also concluded that by examining 'the nature of the thing' the most controvertible was that of 'humane interest', and only after a long discussion of issues of property did he mention the desire to rule.[87] Intriguingly, Gee commented on the 5th divine commandment (*Honour your father and mother*) in the Preface exclusively in terms of property.[88] Undoubtedly, private property was much more central to the notions of the common good at the time than had been the case during the Middle Ages.[89]

[83] On the method of Hobbes's theorizing on political representation, see Skinner, *From Humanism to Hobbes*, ch. 9.

[84] Laslett, 'Introduction' in Sir Robert Filmer, *Patriarcha and Other Political Works*, p. viii; Peter Laslett, 'Sir Robert Filmer: The Man versus the Whig Myth' 5 *William and Mary Quarterly* (1948).

[85] Filmer, 'Observations upon Aristotles Politiques Touching Forms of Government'.

[86] See generally, Sir Robert Filmer, *Patriarcha and Other Political Works*.

[87] Gee, *The Divine Right and Original of the Civill Magistrate from God*, p. 15.

[88] Gee, *The Divine Right and Original of the Civill Magistrate from God*, 'Preface'.

[89] M. S. Kempshall, *The Common Good in Late Medieval Political Thought*, (Oxford: Oxford University Press, 1999). Noting the relationship between property and common good later in Locke, see Gordon Schochet 'Guards and Fences': Property and Obligation in Locke's Political Thought' in 21 *History of Political Thought* (2000).

The imperative to expand the economy held sway. The chapters that follow argue that seventeenth-century English political philosophers and natural lawyers attempted to tame, rather than foster the materialism of the period. Thus, Hobbes and Locke's idea, it is contended, was to imbue politics with less pragmatic principles than those held by Filmer and others and to recover a basic normative sense of equality and freedom in the context of political obligation. In this regard, as suggested before, I have been persuaded by Annabel Brett's naturalist exposition of Hobbes and by John Dunn and Timothy Stanton's Neotestamentarian reading of John Locke, and not by other materialist interpretations.[90] However, there is a sense in which the MacPhersonian tradition of 'possessive individualism' captured an important element that is addressed in the work of Norman L. Jones, Craig Muldrew and Carl Wennerlind.[91] The sociopolitical context in which modern English natural lawyers started to remake philosophy was marked by scepticism and permeated by an ideology of wealth-seeking through credit that makes itself felt in their writings, and shaped their understanding of natural law.

'Observations', Filmer's last political tract, is a surprisingly rich commentary on Aristotelian political forms published in 1652, written either that or the previous year.[92] Peter Laslett considered that Locke and other critiques of Filmer made extensive use of the piece.[93] A royalist who had survived the Civil Wars, Filmer presented his ideas on the relevance of property for the success of the Commonwealth as being in fact beneficial for all sides – it is astonishing how quickly he

[90] Brett, *Liberty, Right and Nature*; Dunn, *The Political Thought of John Locke*; Timothy Stanton, 'Authority and Freedom in the Interpretation of Locke's Political Theory' 39 *Political Theory* (2011); Timothy Stanton, 'John Locke and the Fable of Liberalism' 61 *Historical Journal* (2018).

[91] Norman L. Jones, *God and the Moneylenders: Usury and Law in Early Modern England* (Oxford, UK and Cambridge, USA: Blackwell, 1989); Craig Muldrew, *The Economy of Obligation. The Culture of Credit and Social Relations in Early Modern England* (Hampshire and London: Macmillan Press, 1998); Wennerlind, *Casualties of Credit.*

[92] Since Filmer is clearly aware of Hobbes's *Leviathan*, few other possibilities remain for its date of writing. That it was probably the last political text that he wrote, apart from a tract on witches, in Peter Laslett's 'Introduction' and Brief Introduction to Robert Filmer, 'Observations Upon Aristotles Politiques', p. xxvii, and p. 133.

[93] Laslett, 'Brief Introduction' to Robert Filmer, 'Observations upon Aristotles Politiques, p. 135. See e.g. John Locke *Two Treatises of Government*, ed. with an Introduction by Peter Laslett (ed.) (Cambridge: Cambridge University Press, 1988 [1967]): 'But, that I might omit no care to inform my self in our A. full Sense, I consulted his *Observations on Aristotle, Hobs*, etc.', I. §14, p. 150.

reacted to the political sea change that had taken place.[94] Therefore, in the 1650s Filmer operated as an ideologue of materialist politics and not as the manufactured persona of Whig and Tory opposition that he would become in the 1680s. Political obligation, Filmer argued, sprang from inherited property, which was inherited first from God. This tract on Aristotelian forms of government demonstrates that Filmer knew Aristotle as well, if not better, than he knew the Scripture – which is not to say, however, that he knew either of them well, as Locke's exuberant critique in the *First Treatise* makes clear with regard to Biblical commentary.[95] The tract on Aristotle comprises first a short summary of scriptural principles that Filmer extracted from *Patriarcha*, together with its fundamental argument. He combined the theological doctrine of the dominion over the inferior creatures (Genesis 1.26–28) and enriched it with Aristotelian ideas of a house or an *oikos*, rejecting Aristotle's distinction between the household and the *polis*.[96] In *Patriarcha* published only in 1680, Francisco Suárez was the main object of criticism due to his statement that Adam had 'complete economical power', though 'only economical power, but not political'. For, affirmed the English royalist, 'economical and political societies' did not differ.[97] Filmer decided that what happened within Adam's household was in fact the first political union, a set of natural family relationships involving economic relationships between masters, servants and slaves. The first household, Adam's, was thus a kingdom, and any kingdom was an immense household. In Filmer's work, and, also in 'Observations', however, the divine rights of kings took on a notoriously possessive hue:

> Adam was the Father, King and Lord over his family: a son, a subject and a servant or a slave, were one and the same thing at first: the Father had power to dispose, or sell his children or servants; whence we find, that at the first reckoning up of goods in scripture, the manservant, and the maidservant are numbered among the possessions and substance of the owner, as other goods were.[98]

[94] See on this also Cesare Cuttica, 'Sir Robert Filmer (1588–1653) and the Condescension of Posterity: Historiographical Interpretations' in 21 *Intellectual History Review* (2011).

[95] Locke, *Two Treatises of Government*, pp. 141–263; Jeremy Waldron, *God, Locke, and Equality: Christian Foundations in Locke's Political Thought* (Cambridge: Cambridge University Press, 2002), pp. 188–194.

[96] Tully, *A Discourse on Property*, p. 56; Sommerville 'Introduction', in Sir Robert Filmer, *Patriarcha and Other Writings*, p. xxi.

[97] Filmer quotes from Suárez *De legibus*, in Filmer, 'Patriarcha', p 15; p. 17; p. 19.

[98] Filmer, 'Observations upon Aristotles Politiques', p. 136.

What Filmer described in these terms in 1652 was not merely a set of ideas concerning the fictionalized origins of government but a portrayal of the present. That was the shocking reality of Barbados and other plantations, known by everyone who cared to find out, where, in shipments to the islands, servants and slaves appeared listed as commodities.[99] Filmer revealed it to his readership in artful narrative. But to reckon with what was happening in practice in the wilderness of the commercial relations, was in a Christian commonwealth, or for that matter, in any commonwealth, very different to a philosophical, let alone theological sanctioning of it. Machiavellian notions of self-preservation were common, but Filmer's pragmatic ideas of inequality went against any minimal notion of natural law thinking.[100] However, as Peter Laslett and recently Anne Becker have argued, they realistically reflected a contemporary phenomenon, in the form of the rise of the patriarchal household experienced during the sixteenth and seventeenth centuries, which reached its climax with Jean Bodin's, *Five Books of the Republic* (1576).[101] In the extreme form proposed by Filmer, the ideology of patriarchalism justified social inequality,

99 'The Commodities these Ships bring to this Island are, Servants and Slaves, both men and women; Horses, Cattle, Assinigoes, Camells, Utensills for boyling Sugar, as, Coppers, Taches, Goudges, and Sockets; all manner of working tooles for Trades-men, as, Carpenters, Joyners, Smiths, Masons, Mill-wrights, Wheel-wrights, Tinkers, Coopers, & c. Iron, Steel, Lead, Brasse, Pewter, Cloth of all kings, both Linnen and Wollen; Sutffs, Hatts, Hose, Shoos, Gloves, Swords, knives, Locks, Keys, & C Victualls of all kinds, that will endure the Sea, in so long a voyage. Olives, Capers, Anchoves, salted Flesh and Fish, pickled Maquerells and Herrings, Wine of all sorts and the boon Beer, d'Angleterre.' Richard Ligon, *A True and Exact History of the Island of Barbados* (London: Humphrey Moseley, 1657), p. 40. More on Ligon's narrative, in the last section of chapter 6.

100 On Machiavelli at the time, Marco Barducci 'Order, Conflict and Liberty: Machiavellianism in English Political Thought, 1649–1660', in Alessandro Arienzo and Alessandra Petrina (eds.), *Machiavellian Encounters in Tudor and Stuart England: Literary and Political Influences from the Reformation to the Restoration* (London and New York: Routledge, 2013).

101 'The modern reader is only familiar with the patriarchal household in such contexts as the Court of Hamlet, King of Denmark, and it is this archaism which makes Filmer's work so anachronistic. It is worth pointing out, however, that the descendants of the Virginian planters, who became the slaveowners of the Southern States, where the heads of a classic type of patriarchal household, so that it survived until the middle of the nineteenth century even in such a rationalistic and egalitarian society as the U.S.A.' Laslett, 'Introduction', in Sir Robert Filmer, *Patriarcha* p. xxxiii. This picture, though not denied, appears to have been more complex, with a household or *oikos* that accommodated aristocratic planters and artisanal proprietorship; but it was truly more patriarchal and not less with the time, of whose increase slavery seemed to have been a causing factor. See for this, Christopher Tomlins, *Freedom Bound. Law, Labor, and Civic Identity in Colonizing English America, 1580–1865*, (Cambridge: Cambridge University Press, 2010), pp. 383–400. And on the political and intellectual changes that favoured in the seventeenth century the rise of patriarchalism in Europe,

the subjection of women in the family, the domination by a rich minority of the majority, slavery – and, above all, the elevation of property as the institution around which all other legal and political principles must revolve. Filmer placed property with notions of hierarchy and absolutism as being divinely ordered. In *Patriarcha*, apparently written in the late 1630s, Filmer warned that popular government was the cause of all sorts of vices in society. In 1652, his central argument in 'Observations upon Aristotle Politiques' was that a popular commonwealth was irreligious, poor and disrupted by dissensions and controversy – worst of all, it would not last long. Therefore, in his view, the idea then 'in fashion' – that original power lay by nature with the people – put forward by 'the modern politicians' in the early 1650s - was self-defeating.[102] The gist of Filmer's argument as to the hopelessness of popular government was again centred on property:

> Men that boast so much of natural freedom, are not willing to consider how contradictory and destructive the power of a major part is to the natural liberty of the whole people; the two grand favourites, liberty, and property (for which most men pretend to strive) are as contrary as fire to water and cannot stand together.[103]

In the context of a nation in conflict and engaged in empire-building, Filmer's standpoint concerning the impossibility of achieving wealth in a republic of free citizens was a *provocation*. The sharpness of the royalist Filmer was certainly dangerous at the dawn of a commercial empire. These frightful ideas about the disease of poverty attached to popular government and the origins of all government in the principles of property saw the light almost three decades before *Patriarcha* appeared in published in 1680. As mentioned before, they showed Filmer less a Machiavellian author than someone moved by the pragmatic spirit of the times and with vested interests in the continuation and expansion of the international economic and political system.[104] Perhaps given these motives, Filmer was effective in setting the tone of political discourse over the following decades. The

Anne Becker, *Gendering the Renaissance Commonwealth* (Cambridge: Cambridge University Press, 2020); about Bodin's text in Filmer, see Constance I. Smith, 'Filmer, and the Knolles Translation of Bodin' 13 *The Philosophical Quarterly* (1963) and Peter Laslett, note in Locke, *Two Treatises of Government*, p. 181.

102 Filmer, 'Observations upon Aristotles Politiques', p. 150.

103 Filmer, 'Observations upon Aristotles Politiques', p. 173.

104 See Tully's, almost tongue in cheek, classic conclusion that Macpherson was in effect criticizing Filmer, as ideologue of private property, rather than Locke, Tully, *A Discourse on Property*, p. 79; also hinting at the fact that Macpherson's attack on Locke missed the real culprit, that is Filmer, Dunn, *The Political Thought of John Locke*, p. 66.

political thinkers that came after Filmer had to respond to his very pragmatic approach. Moreover, his short but shrewd arguments were not easy to undo.[105] In his discussion of Hobbes's thesis that political obligation arose from consent, Filmer almost succeeded in proving that popular government as conceived by his contemporaries had an undemocratic character, on the grounds that the majority ended up oppressing the minority, and that the consent of each and every person could never be obtained. It is difficult not to agree with Peter Laslett that the second *Treatise on Government*, and not only the *First*, was Locke's response to the ideological line that held that popular government was synonymous with deprivation and dissent, as Filmer argued in 'Observations' more explicitly than in *Patriarcha*.[106] After the Civil Wars, Filmer had astutely noted Puritan beliefs as to care for the poor and horror of poverty, and accordingly pointed again to property, and not liberty, as the essence of any government.[107]

1.4 The New *Oeconomies*: Household – State – Nature

Understandings of *oeconomy* in seventeenth-century England are presented in Chapters 9 and 10, from around the time that Filmer had rudimentarily integrated the household into the political notion of a kingdom. Filmer's political principle suited English mid-seventeenth century socio-legal relations well. He was knowledgeable about the common law and the radical voluntarism evident in his conception of law and of customary law in *Patriarcha* was similar to Hobbes's.[108] However, historiography on Filmer evidences that he was an embarrassment.[109] His thin philosophical

105 See also Tully, *A Discourse on Property*, p. 55.

106 Laslett, 'Introduction', in Sir Robert Filmer, *Patriarcha and Other Political Works*, p. xlvii.

107 See, among many others, e.g. the regicide John Cooke's, *Unum necessarium: or, The poore mans case: being an expedient to make provision of all poore people in the Kingdome*, (London: pr. for Matthew Walbancke at Grayes Inne Gate. 1648).

108 'When kings were either busied with wars or distracted with public cares, so that every private man could not have access to their persons to learn their wills and pleasure, then of necessity were laws invented'; 'Customs at first became lawful only by some superior power which did either command or consent unto their beginning.' Filmer, 'Patriarcha', p. 41; p. 45.

109 A review of historiography on Filmer with that approach in Cuttica, 'Sir Robert Filmer (1588–1653) and the Condescension of Posterity'; a good example is Dunn, *The Political Thought of John Locke*, ch. 6; Peter Laslett's following remark tells everything one needs to know about his view on Filmer: 'Filmer's patriarchal mystique of kingship could almost be said to have provided for the Stuart monarchs the sort of political mythology which the doctrine of the 'Volk' provided for the Nazi dictatorship of Germany'. Laslett, 'Introduction' in Sir Robert Filmer, *Patriarcha and Other Political Works*, p. xxxvii; a more sober appraisal appears in the last edition of Filmer's work in Sommerville, 'Introduction'.

reasoning, lack of system and obscure theology and his always suspect ideas on royalist absolutism, which became unpalatable after the Civil Wars, made him unsuited for representing anything close to a viable political philosophy. One would be inclined to think, moreover, that the type of patriarchalism Sir Robert Filmer became famous for, was rather the effect of postlapsarian history and not previous to it.[110] Locke's triumph was then his ability to develop a natural law theory that both responded to Filmer's misgivings and, being founded on scientific principles, was compatible with the new *oeconomy*.[111] Fittingly, for one of the core initiators of the Scientific Revolution, the very earth would be for Robert Boyle the new *oeconomy* – a rational system in which science and empire in tandem were thought to assert the utility of knowledge. The English political philosopher *par excellence*, Thomas Hobbes, remained in spite of everything, uninterested in the new *oeconomy* and thus it is unsurprising that he was the less committed of the three philosophers to the production of theories with useful results. Philosophy was Hobbes's great love, and despite his wit and his many friends, apparently the only one, as the solitude in the anthropological theory underlining *De Cive* intimates.[112]

Many seventeenth-century English natural lawyers were natural scientists. They responded to the scepticism by having recourse to heterodox Neoplatonic sources in their search for robust philosophical foundations. However, they were also reacting to the demands imposed by economic growth in the country. The dangers posed to one's soul and virtue by greedy desire for money and other material goods could be understood via an ethical approach that conceived of the light of reason acting in each human being. In the *Summa theologiae* as a whole, Aquinas developed possibly the best theology to that point concerning the way in which material goods had been created for human beings to help them on their way to God. At the same time, following the Aristotelian and a Christian millennial tradition, the Dominican warned against the dangers of becoming too attracted to them, thus losing sight of spiritual values. In that work, Aquinas managed to maintain the almost impossible equilibrium of loving and fearing the material world, not on the grounds of its evilness, but due to the

[110] On how Jean Bodin bent Roman law in order to include a husband's conyugal power nonexistent in Roman *patria potestas* see Becker, *Gendering the Renaissance Commonwealth*, p. 195 and generally ch. 5.

[111] On Locke responding to Filmer on property, see Dunn, *The Political Thought of John Locke*, p. 66.

[112] Thomas Hobbes, *On the Citizen*, Richard Tuck and Michael Silverthorne eds. (Cambridge: Cambridge University Press, 2007); Dunn, *The Political Thought of John Locke*, p. 260.

postlapsarian weakness of human beings. Again, all the protagonists that feature in the chapters that follow worked in the shadow of Aquinas's conviction that, somehow, *some* light of reason was able to illuminate moral behaviour. My argument operates in a manner akin to a reduced version of Alasdair MacIntyre's thesis that the morality of virtues was displaced by fragmentation of concepts in the social history of modern philosophy.[113] It seems that notions such as the light of nature or the agent intellect had disappeared or become almost completely blurred by the mid-seventeenth century.[114] Moreover, the Neoplatonic dualism prevalent in metaphysics made attaining the light of reason practically impossible or, indeed, made it inaccessible. Natural lawyers were thus compelled to articulate a theory of knowledge attuned to the new natural philosophy. Chapters 4, 6 and 7 show that seventeenth-century English thinkers fascinated by the beauty and goodness of nature – in fact, its divine artistry – also naturalized economy. That is to say that they were the first to make a natural science – albeit not yet a virtuous one – of economics. This was done by employing concepts of natural sciences and medicine such as 'system' or 'necessities' and by disintegrating what they considered to be problematic aspects of moral theology in relation to economic growth.[115] The natural economy, as we will see, was understood to satisfy both the necessities of individuals and of the nation. The domain of natural law enlarged.

Opinions as to the origins of theories of capitalism must not distract from the fact that Locke was a thinker who focused on the public sphere and that he was interested in articulating a theory of the state.[116] Locke's paradoxical concern with public interest and the novelty of his theory as to individual natural rights in relation to property is analysed in detail in Chapter 12. His distrust of merchants and traders as looking out only for their own private interest, and the naturalist and complex way in which his political theory is founded in relation to private property, makes any straightforward characterization of his work as being that of

113 Alasdair MacIntyre, *After Virtue. A Study in Moral Theory* (Notre Dame: University of Notre Dame Press, 2007).

114 On the agent intellect see ch. 5.

115 On the centrality of justice for Adam Smith's project in the economy of the following century, see Istvan Hont and Michael Ignatieff, 'Needs and Justice in the Wealth of Nations: An Introductory Essay' in Istvan Hont and Michael Ignatieff eds. *Wealth and Virtue. The Shaping of Political Economy in the Scottish Enlightenment* (Cambridge: Cambridge University Press, 1983).

116 David Armitage, *Foundations of Modern International Thought* (Cambridge: Cambridge University Press, 2013), p. 125.

an early capitalist – or for that matter materialist – either unconvincing or based on the argument that our notions of capitalism have evolved in isolation from political theories dealing with the form of the modern state. Nothing could be further from the truth. Pocock's commentary (again!) on James Harrington's *Oceana* (1656) helps to ascertain the importance of Harrington's attempt – which was powerful, though ultimately unsuccessful – to reformulate the English constitution. In Pocock's view, Harrington's thinking was stuck in the feudal era. Harrington was so close to feudalism that he was unable to analyse it properly, and still described a Machiavellian state in which citizens were called upon to be soldiers. But what Harrington did in his spectacularly innovative 'Preliminaries' part in *Oceana* was to uncover the importance of the distributional aspect of land ownership to the political stability of a national constitution.[117] Interestingly, he did that by means of a scientific method that incorporated traditional medical notions concerning balance in his theory of the new English State.[118] It is not implausible to see Harrington's *Oceana* as a good lesson for Locke. In positive terms, it showed what was important for a revolutionary politician. As James Tully writes, Locke's natural right of property is designed to ground his idea that 'the world belongs to all men in the same manner'.[119] In a negative sense, the text was a warning against a conception in which – unlike that adhered to by the neighbouring Dutch – the economy of the state was thought of solely in terms of land ownership, overwhelmingly important though this was.[120] The techniques of money and commerce must become matters of state.[121] In the spirit of a good civil servant and statesman, the philosopher must make compromises. Locke argued in his *Two Treatises of Government* that material equality was normative by natural law and material inequality was by consent accepted and good. Some 12 years earlier he had written

117 See this argument and the comment on Harrington's *Oceana* in J. G. A. Pocock, *The Ancient Constitution and the Feudal Law: A Study of English Historical Thought in the Seventeenth Century. A Reissue with a Retrospect* (Cambridge: Cambridge University Press, 1987) ch. 6.

118 James Harrington, *The Oceana and Other Works of James Harrington, with an Account of His Life by John Toland* (London: Becket and Cadell, 1771) pp. 35–73.

119 Tully, *A Discourse on Property*, p. 95.

120 'But the *chief matter of Property* being now not the Fruits of the Earth, and the Beasts that subsist on it, but the *Earth it self*; as that which takes in and carries with it all the rest', Locke, *Two Treatises of Government*, §32, p. 290.

121 Istvant Hont, 'Free Trade and the Economic Limits to National Politics: Neo-Machiavellian Political Economy Reconsidered', in *The Economic Limits to Modern Politics*, John Dunn (ed.), (Cambridge: Cambridge University Press, 1990).

that abundant cash money was needed to keep the wheels of the economy moving, the land rents paid, manufacturers working and internal trade functioning. Money was thus viewed as the lifeblood of the economy, and in a country that lacked mines, the acquisition money and bullion (gold and silver in bulk) depended on the balance of trade. Locke's papers on money from the 1690s evidence continuation with these early ideas rather than change.[122] Money is therefore the most exciting and disrupting element in John Locke's philosophical project. Naturally endowed with an intrinsic value that was paradoxically consensual, money linked *raison d'état* and natural law and, as I will conclude, was the stumbling block in Locke's attempt to transform Christian morality into an empirical science.

It is essential to add that my critique to the disruption of the morality of usury in Chapter 10 is not merely a topic for antiquarians. If anything, whether to charge interest for money lending or not will be a topic for the future. In the Conclusions, I will briefly discuss two arguments put forward by John Maynard Keynes that help to substantiate this idea. In a nutshell, Keynes thought that despite the fact that the love of money had triumphed in modern Europe, it remained to be ousted by future generations.

[122] See John Locke, 'Some Considerations of the Consequences of the Lowering of Interest, and Raising the Value of Money', in Patrick Hyde Kelly (ed.), *Locke on Money* (Oxford: Clarendon Press, 1991), vol. I.

2

Hobbes's Doctrine of Necessity

2.1 Hobbes's Doctrine of Necessity and Existence

Thomas Hobbes flipped over the theory of natural law that had prevailed in Europe until the early seventeenth century by means of his 'doctrine of necessity'. Utilizing natural rights, Hobbes's novelty delivered a powerful theory whose meaning derived from his instrumental use of the principles of necessity.[1] This and the next chapters describe the main features of that doctrine and its impact on Hobbes's political philosophy, particularly in *Leviathan*.[2]

The political language of 'necessity', or in the words of its most radical exponent, 'the Doctrine of Necessity', presupposes the philosophical method of determinism. By the mid-seventeenth century, the doctrine was common among the promoters of civil religion and the new science

[1] Thomas Hobbes, *De Corpore: Elementorum philosophiae sectio prima*, Introduction by Karl Schuhmann (ed.), with the collaboration of Martine Pécharman (Paris: Vrin, 1999); Thomas Hobbes, *The Questions Concerning Liberty, Necessity, and Chance Clearly Stated and Debated between Dr. Bramhall, Bishop of Derry, and Thomas Hobbes of Malmesbury* (London: Andrew Crook, 1656) p. 14. Anne Arbor, Text Creation Partnership, 2011, http://name.umdl.umich.edu/A44010.0001.001

[2] An analysis of *De Cive*'s text shows that Hobbes held the doctrine of necessity already in that book, although he had not yet employed it with the same radical intent for absolute sovereignty that he would later display in *Leviathan*. Among dozens of examples in *De Cive*, see: 'For each man is drawn to desire that which is Good for him and to Avoid what is bad for him, and most of all the greatest of natural evils, which is death; this happens by a real necessity of nature as powerful as that by which a stone falls downward' 1.7, p. 27; 'Thus the practice of *natural law* is necessary for the preservation of peace, and *security* is necessary for the practice of natural law' 5.3, p. 70; 'Thus the security of individuals, and consequently the common peace, *necessarily* require that the *right* of using the *sword* to punish be transferred to some man or some assembly' 6.6, p. 78; 'It is necessary to the essence of a law that two things be known to the citizens: first what man or council has sovereign power, i.e. the right of making laws; second, what the law itself says' 14.11, p. 159; 'It is logically necessary consequence of what has been said that a commonwealth [*civitas*] and a church [*ecclesia*] of the same *Christian* men are exactly the same thing under two names, and that for two reasons' 17.21, p. 221. Thomas Hobbes, *De Cive. The Latin Version*, entitled in the first Edition, *Elementorum Philosophiae Sectio Tertia De Cive*, and in later editions *Elementa Philosophica de Cive*, Howard Warrender ed. (Oxford: Clarendon Press, 1983).

to explain rationally the foundation and causes of (political) things in the world. 'Necessity' was linked to faith in that the design or constitution of the world was conceived to have been decreed by God. Furthermore, the will of a human being was regarded as necessitated as opposed to free. As a moral and philosophical principle, 'necessity' emphasizes the (physical) body and downplays the spirit. Politically, what is necessary is by definition expedient. These terms are in fact synonymous to the extent that justice is implied in neither. In a system of natural law such as that of Hobbes, who attributes to each individual 'a Right to everything', natural rights are literally emptied of meaning. Instead, when one acts or appropriates things by necessity, this is always done justly.[3] In the state of nature, the importance of justice is thus confined to situations of necessity. Some years ago, Noel Malcolm termed the former description of 'a right to everything' an account of external rights, which presupposed 'a sort of moral vacuum', and the latter, about necessities of the internal standard, which is right (or just) because it is conducive to self-preservation.[4] This chapter argues that Malcolm's internal/external distinction that is a characteristic of Hobbes responds to his adoption of necessitarianism as a philosophical method. That which is necessary constitutes the internal structure of normative events and things, while Hobbes represents the contingent with an idea of what is external to the constitutions of things and thus free and unnecessary.

At the outset 'the doctrine of necessity' could be any of the following in a theological mindset: a call for duty, an abandonment of supererogatory acts or a command to leave anything that is not necessary behind (Luke

[3] Thomas Hobbes, *Leviathan* in 3 volumes, with an *Editorial Introduction* by Noel Malcolm (ed.) (Oxford: Clarendon Press, 2012), ch. 14, 198; 'Nature Has Given a Right to All Things', Thomas Hobbes, *On the Citizen*, Richard Tuck and Michael Silverthorne (eds.), with an Introduction by Richard Tuck (Cambridge: Cambridge University Press, 1998) ch. I, n. 10; see the helpful discussion in Dieter Hüning, 'Von der Tugend der Gerechtigkeit zum Begriff der Rechtsordnung: Zur rechtsphilosophischen Bedeutung des *suum cuique tribuere* bei Hobbes und Kant' in Dieter Hüning and Burkhard Tuschling (eds.) *Recht, Staat und Völkerrecht bei Immanuel Kant. Marburger Tagung zu Kants Metaphysischen Anfangsgründen der Rechtslehre* (Berlin: Duncker & Humblot, 1998). Hüning, however, does not touch on the principle of necessity, nor on 'Leviathan's disempowerment' that Locke carried out. About Hobbes's justice mostly in the commonwealth, see Tom Sorell, 'Hobbes and the Morality beyond Justice' 82 *Pacific Philosophical Quarterly* (2001).

[4] Noel Malcolm, 'Hobbes and Spinoza', in J. H. Burns and Mark Goldie (eds.), *The Cambridge History of Political Thought 1450–1700* (Cambridge: Cambridge University Press, 1991), p. 537; S. A. Lloyd terms the state of nature 'the state of universal unlimited private judgment' S. A. Lloyd, *Morality in the Philosophy of Thomas Hobbes. Cases in the Law of Nature* (Cambridge: Cambridge University Press, 2009), p. 19.

10.42). For this reason, as a philosophical method 'necessity' seems to have operated as a valuable political staple in England around the time of the Civil Wars, balancing, in the name of science, the free will of 'crypto Popish Arminianism' against that of the 'elect Brethren' of Rebellious Puritanism.[5]

'Necessity' appears as a ubiquitous key element in the contemporary theological, political, metaphysical, scientific and, with the revival of scepticism, moral discourse.[6] In extreme cases, such as in Hobbes's determinism, what seemed to be contingent was also necessary. Everything thus was necessary, voluntary actions included, since every single instance of existence was established by 'the decree of God' – that is, by necessity.[7] The problem of contingency was thus transformed into ignorance about the necessary causes, and therefore acted as a boost to scientists' endeavours.[8] Hobbes reasoned that there was always a necessary cause in any particular action. A necessary cause is at play, for example, if we are caught in a rain shower while walking outside: we had a necessary cause for going out and there was also a necessary cause for it to rain at that moment. We simply do not know the necessary causes of contingency, but they exist. 'There is no such thing as freedom from necessity', Hobbes stated. The necessary cause of a voluntary action was the will, thus voluntary actions were 'necessitated', by which he meant that they were effected by a necessary

[5] Nicholas D. Jackson does not state this explicitly. However, I have gained this insight by reading his book. Nicholas D. Jackson, *Hobbes, Bramhall and the Politics of Liberty and Necessity: A Quarrel of the Civil Wars and Interregnum* (Cambridge: Cambridge University Press, 2007).

[6] Galileo's epistemological method of drawing things out from the learner also employs it: 'but as for *the true-that is, the necessary; that which cannot be possibly otherwise* – every man of ordinary intelligence either knows it by himself, or it is impossible for him to ever know it.' Galileo quoted in J. W. N. Watkins, *Hobbes's System of Ideas. A Study in the Political Significance of Philosophical Theories* (London: Hutchinson University Library, 1965), p. 62 (emphasis by Watkins). On Galileo and Hobbes, see also, Daniel Garber, 'Natural Philosophy in Seventeenth-Century Context', in A. P. Martinich and Kinch Hoekstra (eds.), *The Oxford Handbook of Hobbes* (Oxford: Oxford University Press, 2016).

[7] Thomas Hobbes, 'Treatise on Liberty and Necessity', in *Hobbes and Bramhall on Liberty and Necessity*, ed. Vere C. Chappell (Cambridge University Press 1999), p. 36. Jean Bernhardt speaks of a 'providentialisme necessitaire de Hobbes' that captures well that idea, in Thomas Hobbes, *Court traité des premiers principes. La naissance de Thomas Hobbes à la pensée moderne*, texte, traduction et commentaire par Jean Bernhardt (Paris : PUF, 1988), p. 153.

[8] For instance referring to suppositions about the future: 'Quando autem propositio vocatur contingens, "contingens" ibi significat idem quod "ignorata", idemque est dicere, "Talis propositio est contingens", ac si quis diceret, "Utrum vera sit, an falsa, nescio"'. Thomas Hobbes, *Critique du De mundo de Thomas White*, Jean Jacquot and Harold Whitmore Jones (eds.) (Paris: Vrin, 1973), p. 391.

cause. The necessary cause 'necessitated' the voluntary action.[9] Hobbes's understanding of freedom in his dispute with Bramhall was novel within his own work and is the solution he would retain in *Leviathan* and later.[10]

Over the course of the past century or so scholars have reflected upon Hobbes's accomplishment of the mechanization of scholastic political thought for the sake of civil authoritarian peace.[11] What were his intended political and theological purposes – whether royalism and episcopacy, independency and commonwealth or merely eirenic peace and security – remains a matter of debate.[12] It is clear, however, that an emphasis on the philosophy of 'necessity' leads to the *de facto* tendencies in government. Kinch Hoekstra uses nothing short of Hobbes's entire political works as an example, arguing that when the sovereign exists *de jure* and has *de facto* power, subjects' submission to sovereignty is necessary. Moreover, the requirement of *de jure* power may appear spontaneously: it is present

[9] 'as the will itself, and each propension of a man during his deliberation, is as much necessitated and depends on a sufficient cause as anything else whatsoever'. Hobbes, 'Treatise on Liberty and Necessity', p. 21; p. 28. See also, Thomas, Hobbes, *Elements of philosophy the first section, Concerning Body* (London, Andrew Crook, 1656) Early English Books Online Text Creation Partnership, 2011, http://name.umdl.umich.edu/A43987.0001.001, p. 95. This is what Locke called 'the religion of Hobbes and Spinosa by resolving all, even the thoughts and will of men, into an irresistible fatal necessity.' Locke, 'Remarks upon Some of Mr. Norris's Books', p. 254. On Spinoza on this same question setting down to ignorance the general belief of contingent truths, see Jonathan Bennett, *A Study of Spinoza's Ethics* (Indianapolis: Hackett Publishing Company, 1984), p. 121.

[10] Noel Malcolm, 'Editorial Introduction', in Thomas Hobbes, *Leviathan*, vol. I, p. 17. See also my discussion in Chapter 3.2.5 of Quentin Skinner's work on Hobbes and rhetoric.

[11] Frithiof Brandt, *Thomas Hobbes' Mechanical Conception of Nature*, Vaughan Maxwell and Annie I. Fausboll (trans.) (Copenhagen: Levin & Munksgaard, and London: Librairie Hachette, 1928); Michael Oakeshott, 'Introduction to *Leviathan*' (Oxford: Basil-Blackwell, 1946); Jakob Hans Joseph Schneider, *Thomas Hobbes und die Spätscholastik* (Bonn: Philosophische Fakultät der Rheinischen Friedrich-Wilhelms-Universität zu Bonn, 1986); Carl Schmitt, *Der Leviathan in der Staatslehre des Thomas Hobbes. Sinn und Fehlschlag eines politischen Symbols* (Stuttgart: Klett-Cotta, 1995); Collins, *The Allegiance of Thomas Hobbes*; Skinner, *Hobbes and Republican Liberty*; Jackson, *Hobbes, Bramhall and the Politics of Liberty and Necessity*; Malcolm, *Editorial Introduction*; Jeffrey R. Collins, 'Malcolm's Leviathan: Hobbes's "Thing"' 12 *Modern Intellectual History* (2015).

[12] For the second, see Collins, *The Allegiance of Thomas Hobbes*, and Jackson, *Hobbes, Bramhall and the Politics of Liberty and Necessity*; the first by Noel Malcolm, is more an argument about the contingent moment, stating that between the late 1640s an early 1650s the situation demanded ceding some power to the Presbyterians in order to get support from the Scots. The idea would have been to revoke it as soon as it was possible, since in fact it was void to give away the powers of sovereignty, in Malcolm, *Editorial Introduction*, p. 24. On the 'eirenic' position see Skinner, *Hobbes and Republican Liberty*, p. 179. Goldsmith considered him simply ambiguous, M. M. Goldsmith 'Hobbes's Ambiguous Politics' 11 *History of Political Thought* (1990).

when the people have consented to it, or *in fact* must necessarily consent to it due to circumstances such as that the *de facto* sovereign is keeping peace and order, and covering basic necessities.[13] It seems therefore that all other political choices are rendered meaningless if the rule of necessity is taken to its logical conclusion.[14] The greater the insistence on necessity, the more intense the *de facto* theory would result and vice versa.

Hobbes has been acclaimed for his radical reconstruction of the philosophy of natural law.[15] My argument in the following chapters is that it was due to his employment of the doctrine of necessity that Hobbes was able to reinvent the tradition of natural law. Several of his key political concepts – including 'natural rights', 'Common-wealth' and the 'Christian commonwealth' – draw meaning from his multifaceted understanding and intense application of the doctrine of necessity. Furthermore, his employment of a philosophy of necessity culminated in the wholesale adoption of the metaphysics of necessity in his masterpiece of political philosophy, *Leviathan*. I suggest that Hobbes was inspired, either directly or indirectly, by the Aristotelian and Neoplatonist Arabic philosopher, jurist and physician Avicenna (Ibn-Sīnā) (circa 970–1037) and his metaphysics of existence and necessity. I also contend that Hobbes appropriated it to the extent that it was useful for his project of separation of philosophy and theology and developed it further as he dovetailed it with mechanistic philosophy. The following chapters show that through the concentration on physical body that the philosophy of existence implies, natural necessities rather than natural rights acquire the *real* central meaning and foundation of Hobbes's political philosophy.

The interest shown by both Thomas Hobbes and Robert Boyle in the work of the groundbreaking French mechanistic philosophers of necessity and contingency, René Descartes (1596–1650) and Pierre Gassendi

13 See Kinch Hoekstra, 'The de facto Turn in Hobbes's Political Philosophy', in Tom Sorell and Luc Foisneau (eds.), *Leviathan after 350 Years* (Oxford: Oxford University Press, 2004), p. 61. See also, Edwin Curley, 'Introduction' to Thomas Hobbes, *Leviathan*, with selected variants from the Latin Edition of 1668 (Indianapolis and Cambridge: Hackett Publishing Company, Inc. 1994), p. xxxiv.

14 Adopting the analysis of liberty, but reaching the same conclusion, Philip Pettit, 'Liberty and Leviathan' 4 *Politics, Philosophy and Economics* (2005), p. 148.

15 Malcolm 'Hobbes and Spinoza'; Quentin Skinner, 'Thomas Hobbes's Antiliberal Theory of Liberty', in B. Yack (ed.), *Liberalism without Illusions: Essays on Liberal Theory and the Political Vision of Judith N. Shklar* (Chicago: University of Chicago Press, 1996); Ian Hunter, 'Natural Law as Political Philosophy', in Desmond M. Clarke and Catherine Wilson (eds.), *The Oxford Handbook of Philosophy in Early Modern Europe* (Oxford: Oxford University Press, 2011), p. 480.

(1592–1655), has been extensively researched.[16] Within that scholarship of the history of science, Margaret Osler has studied the indebtedness of French philosophers of nature to the Middle Ages voluntarist discourse on the absolute power of God, in particular that of William of Ockham (1285–1347), and of the version put forward by Duns Scotus that balanced absolute power against ordained power. Osler viewed Gassendi's aim as being 'to baptize' Epicurean atomism, and that of Descartes as being to root the laws of nature in a divine source.[17]

In the fourteenth century, ideas about the absolute and thus unpredictable will of God weakened confidence in the ability to arrive at demonstrated truth in natural philosophy and theology and thus propagated general doubt, which was, however, fruitful in terms of stimulating scientific inquiry.[18] Nevertheless, the entire debate on the power of God has a complex history that started in the thirteenth century with both theologians and lawyers deeply involved in it and touching on core themes of theology, ecclesiology and moral philosophy.[19] In their search for a

[16] Jean Jacquot and Harold Whitmore Jones, 'Introduction' to Thomas Hobbes, *Critique du De mundo*; J. E. McGuire, 'Boyle's Conception of Nature' 33 *Journal of the History of Ideas* (1972); Margaret J. Osler, *Divine Will and Mechanical Philosophy: Gassendi and Descartes on Contingency and Necessity in the Created World*, (Cambridge: Cambridge University Press, 1994); Michael Hunter and Edward B. Davis, 'The Making of Robert Boyle's "Free Enquiry into the Vulgarly Receiv'd Notion of Nature" (1686), 1 *Early Science and Medicine*, (1996); Michael Ben-Chaim, *Experimental Philosophy and the Birth of Empirical Science: Boyle, Locke and Newton*, (London: Routledge, 2016).

[17] Osler, *Divine Will and Mechanical Philosophy*.

[18] Luca Bianchi, *Il vescovo e i filosofi. La condanna parigina del 1277 e l'evoluzione dell' aristotelismo scolastico* (Bergame: Pierluigi Lubrina, 1990), p. 86; Edward Grant, 'Science and Theology in the Middle Ages', in David C. Lindberg and Ronald L. Numbers (eds.), *God and Nature: Historical Essays on the Encounter between Christianity and Science* (Berkeley: University of California Press, 1986).

[19] Ludwig Buisson, *Potestas und Caritas. Die Päpstliche Gewalt im Spätmittelalter* (Köln: Böhlau Verlag, 1958); Mary Anne Pernoud, 'Innovation in William of Ockham's References to the "Potentia Dei"', XLV *Antonianum* (1970); Mary Anne Pernoud, 'The Theory of the Potentia Dei According to Aquinas, Scotus and Ockham,' XVVII *Antonianum* (1972); John Marrone, 'The Absolute and the Ordained Powers of the Pope. An Unedited Text of Henry of Ghent,' 36 *Mediaeval Studies* (1974); Eugenio Randi, *Il sovrano e l'orologiaio: due immagini di Dio nel dibattito sulla "potentia absoluta" fra XIII e XIV secolo* (Firenza: La Nuova Italia Editrice, 1987); William J Courtenay, *Capacity and Volition: A History of the Distinction of Absolute and Ordained Power* (Bergamo: Pierluigi Lubrina, 1990); Pasquale Porro, 'Henry of Ghent on Ordained and Absolute Power', in Guy Guldentops and Carlos G. Steel (eds.), *Henry of Ghent and the Transformation of Scholastic Thought. Studies in Memory of Jos Decorte* (Leuven: Leuven University Press, 2003); Theo Kobusch, 'Analogie im Reich der Freiheit? Ein Skandal der Spätscholastischen Philosophie und die kritische Antwort der Neuzeit,' in Jan A. Aertsen and Martin Pickavé (eds.), *"Herbst Des Mittelalters"? Fragen Zur Bewertung Des 14. Und 15. Jahrhunderts*, (Berlin: De Gruyter, 2004).

firm foundation for the new knowledge, the seventeenth-century natural philosophers borrowed liberally from that rich source of texts.

2.1.1 A Yearning for Necessity

The project of the 'patrons of necessity', as Bishop Bramhall mockingly labelled them, was epistemological and metaphysical and, of course, political.[20] In the spring of 1645, Thomas Hobbes and John Bramhall had a philosophical discussion on human freedom at the invitation of the Marquess of Newcastle. Since they were all in exile due to the English troubles, the debate took place at the Marquess's lodgings in Paris. A pair of excellent texts followed from it, starting with one by Bramhall (finished before the end of the summer of 1645), and a response by Hobbes, which were intended to remain private. After Bramhall's rejoinder and partly due to a misunderstanding about the publication, a further series of publications ensued that, to put it mildly, abandoned the courteous tone of the first texts and the academic style of the first encounter.[21] Nicholas D. Jackson interprets the debate, through a strongly contextualist lens, as almost a Parisian skirmish in the war taking place in England, between an Arminian royalist (Bramhall) and an almost Puritan rebel (Hobbes).[22] But if we observed the different planes and philosophical schools in which the contents of Bramhall's 'Discourse' and Hobbes's treatise *Of Liberty and Necessity* were situated, the scientific momentum of the debate cannot be denied.[23] Hobbes's discourse was about natural philosophy, epistemology and metaphysics, and in his 'antipodean way' also about theology, while Bramhall's discussion of freedom and necessity focused on humanist moral theology and philosophy.[24] Bramhall's position may

[20] 'Bramhall's discourse of liberty and necessity' in *Hobbes and Bramhall on Liberty and Necessity*, p.1.

[21] Hobbes, *The Questions Concerning Liberty, Necessity, and Chance'*, p. 59; Skinner, *Hobbes and Republican Liberty*, ch. 5.

[22] Jackson, *Hobbes, Bramhall and the Politics of Liberty and Necessity*, p. 99.

[23] On the many other aspects of disagreement, in particular political, between Bramhall and Hobbes, see Jon Perkins commentary of Bramhall's 'Castigations of Mr. Hobbes (1657)' in Jon Parkin, *Taming the Leviathan. The Reception of the Political and Religious Ideas of Thomas Hobbes in England, 1640–1700* (Cambridge: Cambridge University Press, 2007).

[24] In a letter to his friend Edmund Waller Hobbes relates his pleasant conversations in France with the third Earl of Devonshire (to whom Hobbes dedicated *De Cive*), in which the latter liked to tease him with questions about his paradoxical doctrines, in order to corner him on an absurdity. Instead of succeeding, Devonshire, 'at last finds I am of the antipodes to the schools'. Hobbes quoted in Jackson, *Hobbes, Bramhall and the Politics of Liberty and Necessity*, p. 90.

be summarized in the sentence, 'God leaves many things indifferent'.[25] In Hobbes's first response to Bishop Bramhall, the treatise *Of Liberty and Necessity*, the philosopher noted that he had drawn his doctrine of necessity 'from the nature of the things themselves', but due to its speculative and complex character, he chose not to explain what he meant by that.[26]

The moral question Bramhall and Hobbes discussed was directly linked to the problem of knowledge per se: how to reach or understand nature and what about its moral demands? Arguably, the important variations in the moral philosophy of the times, which become more radical as political strife intensified, were variations on an attempt to understand the divine plan for human beings with the scant help provided by sceptic natural reason. Was that divine plan still hidden in nature? As described by J. Sears McGee, the spiritualism of the Puritans in the early seventeenth century had threatened to make that style of religion concerned with natural law irrelevant to real life, while an excessively Calvinist emphasis on justification and predestination had brought about an alarming moral decay.[27] But, could a (wo)man be saved without having led a good life? According to Margaret Sampson, this was the question that troubled many devout citizens in England during that period.[28] Later in the century, the conclusion of an attentive and practical John Locke was clear enough:

> I cannot see of what use the Doctrine of Election and Perseverance is unlesse it be to lead men into presumption and neglect of their dutys being once perswaded that they are in a state of grace, which is a state they are told they can not fall from.[29]

Hobbes's complex programme of moral philosophy and natural law ends with the hypothesis, tested against the empirical effects of civil war, that nature, and thus God, demands the establishment of a sovereign with supreme legislative authority.[30] The fact that, in Hobbes's view, necessity

[25] 'Bramhall's Discourse of Liberty and Necessity', p. 12.

[26] 'For there is hardly any one action, how casual soever it seem, to the causing whereof concur not whatsoever is in rerum natura [in the nature of things], which because it is a great paradox and depends on many antecedent speculations I do not press in this place.' Hobbes, 'Treatise on Liberty and Necessity', p. 33.

[27] J. Sears McGee, *The Godly Man in Stuart England. Anglicans, Puritans, and the Two Tables, 1620–1670* (New Haven and London: Yale University Press, 1976).

[28] Sampson, 'Laxity and Liberty', p. 101.

[29] Locke, around May 1695, quoted from his commonplace book in John C. Higgins-Biddle, 'Introduction' to John Locke, *The Reasonableness of Christianity*, p. xviii.

[30] Hobbes's own view on the causes of the Civil Wars appears in Thomas Hobbes, *Behemoth or the Long Parliament*, Ferdinand Tönnies (ed.) with an Introduction by Stephen Holmes (Chicago: The University of Chicago Press, 1990).

was the guiding principle of Creation made this choice less repulsive. In Robert Boyle's epistemological project, 'nature' would ultimately fall apart as an epistemological category around the 1660s, weakening greatly the entire project of necessity.[31]

Debate about the influences in Hobbes's natural philosophy is far from concluded. Since Frithiof Brandt's groundbreaking *Thomas Hobbes' Mechanical Conception of Nature* (1928) recent work continues the tradition by analysing Hobbes in relation to mechanical philosophers.[32] Gianni Paganini has emphasized Gassendi's influence on Hobbes's philosophy as well as, more generally, humanist inspiration, as discussed below.[33] Daniel Garber's recent study on the context of Hobbes's natural philosophy is also worth highlighting. Together with a comparison with Galileo, which underlines various similarities between a number of philosophers of that era, Garber restates the thesis as to the striking similarity between the natural philosophy of Descartes and that of Hobbes. Significantly, Garber notes that while Descartes views God as the foundation of the first law of nature, this foundation is conspicuously absent in Hobbes. The centrality of the principle of necessity in Hobbes's philosophy of nature is implied, though not fully articulated, in Garber's subsequent analysis, which shows how closely Spinoza follows Hobbes. By way of illustration, I will quote from one of Spinoza's passages, also quoted by Garber, that revolves around law, its possible voluntarism and the 'necessity of nature' implied in the constitution of a thing, also taken to be a law:

> The word law, taken without qualification, means, that according to which each individual, or all or some members of the same species, act in one and the same certain and determinate manner. This depends either on a necessity of nature or on a decision of men. A law which depends on a necessity of nature is one which follows necessarily from the very nature or definition of a thing.[34]

The remainder of this chapter and the next chapter trace the centrality of the principle of necessity in Hobbes's work to two particular influences:

[31] See Section 2.2 and chapter 7.

[32] See Brandt, *Thomas Hobbes' Mechanical Conception of Nature*, and bibliography in note 11.

[33] Gianni Paganini, 'Early Modern Epicureanism: Gassendi and Hobbes in dialogue on Psychology, Ethics, and Politics', in Phillip Mitsis (ed.), *Oxford Handbook of Epicureanism Ancient and Modern*, (Oxford: Oxford University Press, 2020).

[34] Baruch Spinoza, *Tractatus Theologico-Politicus*, quoted by Garber, 'Natural Philosophy in Seventeenth-Century Context', p. 124. On how necessitarianism informs Spinoza's ethics see, Bennett, *A Study of Spinoza's Ethics*, pp. 111–124; Michael Lebuffe, 'Necessity and the Commands of Reason in the *Ethics*', in Matthew J. Kisner and Andrew Youpa (eds.), *Essays on Spinoza's Ethical Theory* (Oxford: Oxford University Press: 2014).

necessitarian tendencies both in French theology and Arabic philosophy. Remarkably, the language of necessity and of necessitarianism in the nature of the things that Hobbes employed in *Of Liberty and Necessity* took for granted the innovative nature of late thirteenth- and early fourteenth-century Parisian theology and philosophy. The following paragraphs briefly describe a branch of voluntarism of the thirteenth-century Parisian theologians and Avicenna's necessitarianism and highlight its similarities with Hobbes's.

2.1.2 Neoplatonist Necessary Existence of Avicenna

Ideas of necessary existence appear in the work of those Parisian theologians that sought to liberate civil and commercial life from religious rigorism and interference, while promoting a sort of theologians' rule.[35] In the past century Etienne Gilson, Jean Paulus and José Gómez Caffarena – joined in recent decades by Jos Decorte and, in particular, by Pasquale Porro and Jules Janssens – have attributed these ideas to the influence of the Arabic philosopher Avicenna.[36] Janssens writes, in his study of the very influential Gallican theologian Henry of Ghent (1217–1293), that much research is needed to ascertain how the authors of the Latin West received Avicenna's idea of necessity.[37] Aquinas, who was also inspired by Avicenna's understanding of necessity and whose writings benefit from it on occasion, is a case in point.[38] Nevertheless, Aquinas's theological

[35] Henry of Ghent acted as a leader of sorts of the secular theologians. About Henry as promoter of both secular life and of the role of the theologians, see the important works by Marialucrezia Leone, *Filosofia e teologia della* vita activa. *La sfera dell'agire pratico in Enrico di Gand*, (Bari: Edizioni di Pagina, 2014) and Anna Arezzo, *Lumen Medium. Enrico di Gand el il dibattito sullo statuto scientifico della teologia* (Bari : Edizioni di Pagina, 2014).

[36] Gilson, 'Avicenne et le point de départ de Duns Scot'; Paulus, *Henri de Gand*; Paulus, 'A propos de la théorie de la connaissance d'Henri de Gand'; José Gomez Caffarena, *Ser participado y ser subsistente en la metafísica de Enrique de Gante*, (Romae: Apud aedes Universitatis Gregorianae, 1958); Jos Decorte, 'Avicenna's Ontology of Relation: A Source of Inspiration to Henry of Ghent', in Jules Janssens and Daniel de Smet (eds.), *Avicenna and His Heritage* (Leuven: Leuven University Press, 2002); Janssens, 'Elements of Avicennian Metaphysics in the *Summa*', p. 41; Janssens, 'Some Elements of Avicennian Influence on Henry of Ghent's Psychology'; Pasquale Porro, 'Universaux et *esse essentiae*: Avicenne, Henri de Gand et le "troisiéme Reich"', 38–39 *Presses universitaires de Caen*, (2002). Fascicle titled *Le réalisme des universaux*.

[37] Janssens, 'Elements of Avicennian Metaphysics in the *Summa*'.

[38] See Stephen L. Brock, 'Causality and Necessity in Thomas Aquinas', in Constantino Esposito and Pasquale Porro (eds.), 2 *Quaestio* (2002) 217–240; Aquinas, *Summa theologiae* (2019) Textum Leoninum Romae 1888–1907, edited by Roberto Busa SJ; digitalised by Enrique Alarcón www.corpusthomisticum.org/sth0000.html

project in the *Summa theologiae* concerns the promotion of interaction between spirit and body and the integration of worldly and divine activities. His reasoning begins with the goodness (divinity) of the created world. Furthermore, much of the *Summa* revaluates positively secular activities and also points to people's dangerous tendency to become attached to them, as noted before.[39] After the appearance of evil, that attachment to the world may cause people to deviate from the first commandment: 'You shall not have other gods before me' (Exodus 20:3). Hence, in metaphysics, epistemology and practical morality Aquinas might be described as seeking to transcend the dualism of Neoplatonism. In other words, he employed Neoplatonist elements instrumentally but did not become a Neoplatonist.[40]

To Henry of Ghent's overwhelming influence as a theologian in Paris and beyond, one may add the fact that he is remembered by historians of natural law as the first author ever to devise the concept of a subjective natural right – a type of property right over one's body – similar to the way in which the concept was to be understood later in modernity, in particular by Hobbes and Locke, as is analysed in the last chapter 12.[41] Henry's very sophisticated metaphysics can be summarized in his theory as to things having three ways of being: (a) as pure essences, (b) in existence and (c) in the human mind. Henry viewed the pure essences as a sort of participation in a formal order in the divine mind and the essences in existence as the effect of God's will. In an ingenious stroke of the pen, he accordingly combined a rationalist and a voluntarist vision of God – in effect analogous to God's ordained and absolute power – that came close to sketching a dual conception of the world.[42] The doctrine of duality of essences as

39 The right use of material goods depends on a good will. *Summa theologiae*, I pars, q. 48, a. 6. co.

40 On Aquinas's Neoplatonic influences see, W. J. Hankey, *God in Himself. Aquinas' Doctrine of God as Expounded in the Summa Theologiae* (Oxford: Oxford University Press, 2004); Pasquale Porro, *Thomas Aquinas. A Historical and Philosophical Profile*, Joseph G. Trabbic and Roger W. Nutt trans. (Washington, DC: The Catholic University of America Press, 2016).

41 Tierney, *The Idea of Natural Rights*, p. 78; Virpi Mäkinen, *Property Rights in the Late Medieval Discussion on Franciscan Poverty* (Leuven: Peeters, 2001); Pasquale Porro, 'Individual Rights and Common Good: Henry of Ghent and the Scholastic Origins of Human Rights', in Andrea A. Robiglio and Hans Christian Günther, (eds.), *The European Image of God and Man: A Contribution to the Debate on Human Rights*, (Leiden, Boston: Brill 2010).

42 'Ad cuius intellectum sciendum secundum superius determinata, quod in Deo res quae ipse est, est ipsum esse eius, et non simpliciter esse, sed est quoddam necesse esse. A cuius simplicitate deficit omnis creatura, scilicet quia ipsa res quae ipsa est, non est eius esse, sed habet ab alio esse tam essentiae quam existentiae, ut supra declaratum est saepius, a quo non habet necesse esse ipsius existentiae, eo quod ex se est possibile esse, per indifferentiam

pure essences (*esse essentia*) and existing in the real world (*esse existentia*) was, as Henry also noted, originally Avicenna's.[43] The *esse essentia/esse existentia* division produced by Avicenna offered an explanation of both the universal and the particular thing.[44]

Pasquale Porro explains that Henri of Ghent is *the* Latin master that understood Avicenna in his own right in relation to the issue of the universal. First, there is the individual thing, the reality of the thing in existence. Then there is the universal, which Avicenna held to be a common definition in the mind. Lastly, there is nature, which is the essence of humanity expressed in a particular human being.[45] Thus, Avicenna writes '[t]he reality of such a thing exists either in concrete things, or in the soul, or absolutely, being common to both'.[46] In this 'being common to both' laid the secret of a novel conception of something akin to a universal. Neither Platonic exemplars nor Aristotelian universals, Avicenna's

se habens ad esse et non esse. Propter quod, sicut essentia divina dicit aliquid quod est necesse esse, sic essentia creaturae dicit aliquid cui ab alio contingit esse.' R. Macken and L. Hödl (eds.), *Henrici de Gandavo, Summa* (Leuven: Leuven University Press, 1991), art. 32, q. 5, p. 79; Porro, 'Henry of Ghent on Ordained and Absolute Power'.

43 'Et est hic distinguendum de esse, secundum quod distinguit Avicenna in fine V Metaphysicae suae, quod quoddam est esse rei quod *habet essentialiter* de se, quod appellatur *esse* essentiae, quoddam vero quod recipit ab *alio*, quod appellatur *esse* actualis existentiae. Primum esse habet essentia creaturae essentialiter, sed tamen participative, in quantum habet formale exemplar in Deo. (…) Secundum esse non habet creatura ex sua essentia sed a Deo, in quantum est effectus voluntatis divinae iuxta exemplar eius in mente divina.' R. Macken (ed.), *Henrici de Gandavo, Opera Omnia*, V, *Quodlibet* I, *quaestio* 9, p. 53. Although, according to Janssens, work needs to be done in the research of Avicennean influences in Henry, he states that '[I]t is clear that for Henry Avicenna's essence-existence distinction is of capital importance and expressed a solid metaphysical insight', Jules Janssens, 'Henry of Ghent and Avicenna', in Gordon Anthony Wilson, (ed.), *A Companion to Henry of Ghent* (Leiden Boston, Brill, 2011), p. 69; Paulus, *Henri de Gand*, p. 26; Paulus, 'A propos de la théorie de la connaissance d'Henri de Gand', p. 493. With yet another approach Bianchi also noted a double conception of God in Henry's thought, 'the God of the philosophers', with an immutable will, and 'the God of the Christians' with sovereign freedom shown in the act of creation. Bianchi, *Il vescovo e i filosofi*, p. 65.

44 Avicenna had a thorough Ḥanafi upbringing and practiced some time as a jurist according to the teachings of that school, see Dimitri Gutas, 'Avicenna's "MaḏDhab" with an Appendix on the Question of his Date of Birth' 5–6 *Quaderni di studi Arabi* (1987–1988).

45 Porro, 'Universaux et *esse essentiae*'; see the similarity in Locke, *An Essay Concerning Human Understanding*, II. 11, § 9, p. 151.

46 Avicenna, *The Metaphysics of 'The Healing'. A parallel English-Arabic text, translated, introduced, and annotated by* Michael E. Marmura, (Provo, Utah: Brigham Young University Press, 2005) Book 1, ch. 5, 24.29. A commentary of this question in Jon McGinnis, *Avicenna* (Oxford: Oxford University Press, 2010), p. 33 and Daniel D. De Haan, 'Avicenna's *Healing* and the Metaphysics of Truth' 56 *Journal of the History of Philosophy* (2018).

division between *esse essentia* and *esse existentia* gave a certain consistency like a more robust entity to the general names:

> The fact that the animal existing in the individual is a certain animal does not prevent animal inasmuch as it is animal ... from existing in it. [This is] because, if this individual is a certain animal, then a certain animal exists. Hence, animal [in as much as it is animal] which is part of a certain animal exists.[47]

Robert Wisnovsky describes thus Avicenna as a synthesizer. When he made distinct but co-implied 'thing' (essence) and 'existent', he was carrying out a compromise between different positions in the speculative theology (*kalām*) of his time (in turn also influenced by Greek philosophy), encompassing Ash'arites and Māturidītes' position that 'a thing is an existent', and Mu'tazilites and al-Fārābī's that 'a thing is a thing before it comes into being'.[48] In Avicenna's thought, the worlds of 'being' (*esse*) and 'existence' (*existentia*) are separated and distinct but connected and concomitant.[49] In the physical world what exists is everything, the real and true being.[50] In the metaphysical reality what exists is the means of understanding the essences.[51]

In the work of the voluntarist Henry of Ghent, the doctrine between the division of *esse essentia* and that of *esse existentia* seems to explain what he took to be a cosmological order composed of related essences (of natures) underlying the reality of what we see in the world – a 'necessary' order in effect that the empirical world tends to mirror.[52] Hence for sceptic natural lawyers 'necessity' determines much of the validity of natural law. *Something X ought to be X-1*, because it is in *the nature of the thing* – that is to say that it is so in the underlying order of essences, and accordingly necessary.

[47] Avicenna, *The Metaphysics of "The Healing"*, 153.29; McGinnis, *Avicenna*, p. 33; De Haan, 'Avicenna's *Healing*'; comparing Henry and Avicenna on this see, Porro, 'Universaux et *esse essentiae*'.

[48] Robert Wisnovsky, *Avicennas's Metaphysics in Context*, (Ithaca, New York: Cornell University Press, 2003) 149; 153, and generally, Chapter 7.

[49] Amos Bertolacci, 'The Distinction of Essence and Existence in Avicenna's Metaphysics: The Text and Its Context', in Felicitas Opwis and David C. Reisman (eds.), *Islamic Philosophy, Science, Culture, and Religion: Studies in Honor of Dimitri Gutas*, (Leiden: Brill, 2012), p. 271.

[50] Marmura 'Avicenna on Primary Concepts in the *Metaphysics* of his *al-Shifā'*'.

[51] Ghassan Finianos, *De l'existence à la nécessaire existence chez Avicenne*, (Bordeuax: Presses Universitaires de Bourdeaux, 2007), p. 40.

[52] 'Ordo autem iste, quia naturalis est et a natura rei, et non rationis ab opera intellectus aut voluntatis – aliterenim talis relatio rationis esset, ut patet ex iam dictis –, ideo necessario procedit ex naturali dependentia unius naturae ad alteram, qua mutuo sese exspectant ut in ipsis fundetur relatio.' R. Macken ed., *Henrici de Gandavo*, vol. XIII, *Quodlibet* IX, q.1, p. 15.

2.2 Necessitarian Metaphysics and (Human) Body in Avicenna and Hobbes

Key similarities can be seen between Avicenna and Hobbes in respect of the important method of necessity. In Hobbes's work, these culminated in *Leviathan*. The extreme deterministic stance of both philosophers thwarts further thinking on and the development of a theory of moral freedom, and indeed of a foundational political theory of freedom.[53] In Avicenna's thought, 'necessary' and 'good' appear to be linked – for Avicenna, God is no longer the 'Prime Mover' but rather the 'Necessary Existent'.[54] Jack Macintosh has recently written about the currency of this idea in seventeenth-century thinkers.[55] Furthermore, at the beginning of the fifth chapter of the first book of his *Metaphysics*, Avicenna describes 'the necessary' as primary knowledge, almost like innate ideas, that enables further knowledge: 'We say: the ideas of "the existent", "the thing" and "the necessary" are impressed in the soul in a primary way, this impression not requiring better known things to bring it about.' As to which is prior – 'the possible', 'the impossible' or 'the necessary' – Avicenna wrote:

> Nonetheless, of these three, the one with the highest claim to be first conceived is the necessary. This is because the necessary points to the assuredness of existence, existence being better known than non-existence because existence is known in itself while, non-existence is, in some manner or another, known through existence.[56]

Avicenna's argument was that 'whatever exists (other than God) was necessitated by another'.[57] As Michael E. Marmura explains, Avicenna viewed

[53] We will return to this point about Avicenna in Chapter 9.

[54] On the change from Aristotelian 'Prime Mover' to Avicennan 'Necessary Existent', see, Dimitri Gutas, *Avicenna and the Aristotelian tradition. Introduction to Reading Avicenna's Philosophical Works* (Leiden, New York, Copenhagen: Brill, 1988) p. 261; also, Miguel Cruz Hernández, 'El concepto de metafísica de Avicena', in Jules Janssens and Daniel De Smet (eds.), *Avicenna and His Heritage* (Leuven: Leuven University Press, 2002); on the object of metaphysic for Avicenna see, Ghassan Finianos, *Les Grandes Divisions de l'Être "Mawjūd" selon Ibn Sīnā* (Fribourg: Editions Univesitaires Fribourg Suisse, 1975), p. 18.

[55] Jack MacIntosh, 'Theological and Scientific Applications of the Notion of Necessity in the Mediaeval and Early Modern Periods', in Max Cresswell, Edwin Mares and Adriane Rini (eds.), *Logical Modalities from Aristotle to Carnap. The Story of Necessity* (Cambridge University Press 2016), p. 160.

[56] I am quoting here from Michael E. Marmura's translation of the chapter and also following his detailed explanation, in Marmura 'Avicenna on Primary Concepts in the *Metaphysics* of his *al-Shifā*'', p. 222; p. 234.

[57] Noted by Marmura 'Avicenna on Primary Concepts in the Metaphysics of his *al-Shifā*'', p. 234. Both for Avicenna and Henry 'necessary' and 'good' appeared to be linked.

existence as a reality, a 'brute fact' from which his reasoning commenced. 'Why is this thing here?' he asked, the answer being that it is the cause that necessitates the thing, as in a cause-effect situation that goes backwards (the cause of the apple tree is the apple), and it must be outside its own nature.[58] Daniel D. De Haan has recently referred to this as 'Avicenna's existential necessitarian metaphysics'.[59] The similarity with this and Hobbes's reasoning is evident; when in frustration about Bishop Bramhall's and his disparate discourses Hobbes writes: 'And where he saith, that it is ridiculous to say, the object of the sight is the cause of seeing, he showeth so clearly that he understandeth nothing at all of Natural Philosophy, that I am sorry I had the ill fortune to be engaged with him in a dispute of this kind.'[60]

The subject matter of metaphysics is for Avicenna 'the existent' that is necessitated.[61] Thus it produced a sort of ultrarealist ontology that gives precedence in knowledge to what exists in the real world.[62] More importantly, it produces determinism in so far as the effect necessarily follows from the efficient cause, and, as argued by Catarina Belo, arises from the fact that Avicenna is using logic to argue a metaphysical point. If something exists, it is necessitated. If it is not necessitated, then it does not exist – otherwise, the principle of non-contradiction would be violated.[63]

58 Marmura 'Avicenna on Primary Concepts in the *Metaphysics* of his *al-Shifā*'', p. 234; on possible issues of mistranslation of the word 'thingness' for 'causality' see, Wisnovsky, *Avicennas's Metaphysics in Context*, p. 161. See the opposite description in Elisabeth Anscombe's explanation of the principle of modern causality and necessity: 'The concept of necessity, as it is connected with causation, can be explained as follows: a cause C is a necessitating cause of an effect E when (I mean: on the occasions when) if C occurs it is certain to cause E unless something prevents it.' G.E.M. Anscombe, G. E. M. 'Causality and Determination' in *The Collected Philosophical Papers of G. E. M. Anscombe. Metaphysics and the Philosophy of Mind vol. 2*, (London: Basil Blackwell Publisher, 1981), p. 144.

59 'In Avicenna's *existential necessitarian* metaphysics, this entails that since every being is either necessary existence through another or necessary existence in itself, so also is every being either true through another or true in itself.' De Haan, 'Avicenna's *Healing* and the Metaphysics of Truth', p. 40. (emphasis De Haan).

60 Hobbes, *The questions concerning liberty, necessity, and chance*', p. 59; Skinner, *Hobbes and Republican Liberty*, ch. 5.

61 Amos Bertolacci, 'The Doctrine of Material and Formal Causality in the 'Ilāhiyyāt' of Avicenna's 'Kitāb al-Šifā'' 2 *Quaestio* (2002).

62 The expression of 'ultrarealism', for Avicenna in Marmura 'Avicenna on Primary Concepts in the *Metaphysics* of his *al-Shifā*'', and for Henry in Gomez Caffarena, *Ser participado y ser subsistente en la metafísica de Enrique de Gante*. With characteristic conciseness in opening up a complex matter, when Hobbes denied causality to the foreknowledge of God, he declared, in an ultrarealistic style, that 'knowledge depends on the existence of the things known, and not they on it' Hobbes, 'Treatise on Liberty and Necessity', p. 20.

63 Holding that Avicenna had a deterministic agenda, in Catarina Belo, *Chance and Determinism in Avicenna and Averroes* (Leiden, Boston: Brill 2007). In his review of Belo's

An example from Hobbes's first response to Bramhall helps highlight again the similarity with Avicenna's determinist metaphysics of existence and necessity:

> That which I say necessitates and determinates every action, that his Lordship may no longer doubt of my meaning, is the sum of all those things which, being now existent, conduce and concur to the production of that action hereafter, whereof if any one thing now were wanting, the effect could not be produced. This concourse of causes, whereof every one is determined to be such as it is by a like concourse of former causes, may well be called (in respect they were all set and ordered by the eternal cause of all things, God Almighty) the decree of God.[64]

Gianni Paganini has also described Hobbes's redesign of metaphysics as being concerned only with what exists. Paganini thinks that by rejecting a 'presumed "separate" existence of essences', Hobbes was getting rid of the matter with which 'the scholastics conjured up the existence of a "spiritual" kingdom'.[65] It is only logical that metaphysics and political philosophy would emerge very differently if the theology of 'pure essences' – its spiritual half – were to be put aside, and only a philosophy about the 'essences in existence' were considered. But Hobbes had a theological project of his own. His seventeenth-century conception of a 'decree and plan of God' that established the events that take place in the world may be as well compared with Henry of Ghent's metaphysical order of the 'nature of the thing'. In lieu of the latter's conception of a rational order of creation that the existing creation mirrors, Hobbes lays down a decree and

book Jules Janssens acknowledges that Avicenna 'defends a strict determinism regarding efficient causality, insofar as an effect necessarily results from its efficient cause'; but he also points to unresolved tensions in his thought, such as 'the identification in God between thinking and creating versus His absolute freedom' and 'the being necessary of the contingent beings by their cause versus their maintaining their possibility in themselves'. Jules Janssens, 'Book Review: Catarina Belo', *Chance and Determinism in Avicenna and Averroes*, 19 *Journal of Islamic Studies* (2008), p. 101. More recently Ozgur Koca gives a radical turn to scholarship arguing that Avicenna's necessitarianism must not be deterministic, since in Avicenna, God's creation is not mechanistic, and by distinguishing between metaphysical and physical causation. Ozgur Koca, 'Revisiting the Concepts of Necessity and Freedom in Ibn Sīnā (Avicenna) (c. 980–1037)' 59 *Sophia* (2020).

64 Hobbes, 'Treatise on *Liberty and Necessity*', p. 20.

65 Gianni Paganini, 'Hobbes's Critique of the Doctrine of Essences and Its Sources', in Patricia Springborg (ed.), *The Cambridge Companion to Hobbes's Leviathan* (Cambridge: Cambridge University Press, 2007), p. 337; Paganini is pointing to how in *Critique du de Mundo* Hobbes derided the whole project of metaphysics (what goes after physics or beyond physics) and its proponents 'as if the limits of nature could be transgressed by its doctrine.' Hobbes, *Critique du de Mundo de Thomas White*, p. 170 (my translation).

plan from which follows his deterministic confluence of necessary causes. It seems therefore that Hobbes endows thereby with religious or theological content his philosophical enterprise.[66]

In his chronology of the writing of *Leviathan*, Noel Malcolm shows that in 1642–1643 Hobbes was engaged in the refutation of Thomas White's Catholic natural philosophy and metaphysics, and in 1645 with *Of Liberty and Necessity*.[67] But the work that most occupied him, at least from 1642 onwards, was *De Corpore*, his treatise on physics, metaphysics and logic. Hobbes was grappling with its argument during the 1640s, and busy teaching mathematics to Prince Charles in France. Then he fell seriously ill in 1647, and in fact he wrote *Leviathan* between 1649 and 1651, in the middle of the production of *De Corpore*, which was finally published in 1655.[68] In a similar manner to the situation in respect of his natural philosophy and his politics, Hobbes's source of inspiration in relation to metaphysics is still the subject of scholarly debate. His contemporary and friend, the poet Abraham Cowley pointed to his inspiration in Aristotelian, Roman and Arabic philosophy. In his poem 'To Mr. Hobbes', Cowley explains that the fields ploughed by the ancients, the 'Stagirite', the 'Roman Eagle' and 'Mecha itself' no longer offered (philosophical) nourishment. What was required by the times was to 'break up tombs with sacrilegious hands' and search for 'treasures buried'.[69] A possible interpretation of Cowley's poem is that instead of a complete new beginning, what was at issue was the pillaging of tradition.[70] Paganini argues in favour of Lorenzo Valla's critical philology that ultimately rendered the word 'essence' superfluous, since

[66] According to Catarina Belo Avicenna had also defined the 'Decree' of God to explain 'the determination' of the necessary causes and reasons leading to the order of what exists: 'Determination (*qadar*) is the existence of causes (*'illa*) and reasons (*sabab*) and their harmonization in accordance with their arrangement and order, leading to the effects and caused beings. These are what is necessitated by the Decree (*qaḍā'*) and what follows from it. There is no [ultimate] reason for the action of the Creator because His action is due to His essence and not due to a motive (*dā'in*) that would incite Him to [do] something.' From Yahya Michot trans. Ibn Sīnā *Lettre au vizir ab Sa'd*, quoted in Belo, *Chance and Determinism in Avicenna and Averroes*, p. 114, and generally ch. 3.

[67] Se on Hobbes and White Tuck's rich interpretation about Hobbes's 'revolutionary utopia' Richard Tuck, 'The Civil Religion of Thomas Hobbes', in Nicholas Phillipson and Quentin Skinner (eds.), *Political Discourse in Early Modern Britain* (Cambridge: Cambridge University Press, 1993).

[68] Malcolm, 'Editorial Introduction', pp. 4–13.

[69] Abraham Cowley, 'To Mr. Hobbes', in G. Molesworth, ed., *Thomae Hobbes Malmesburiensis Opera Philosophica, quae Latine scripsit, omnia*. v. I (Londini, Joannem Bohn, 1839), iv.

[70] See also on Cowley, the Arabic philosophers and Hobbes, Nabil Matar, *Islam in Britain, 1558–1685* (Cambridge: Cambridge University Press, 1998), p. 87.

essences did not have a separate existence, and were one with existence.[71] As I have shown above, ideas about 'essences in existence' and 'essences separated from existence' appeared in medieval Parisian theology and some of them had been extracted from the work of Avicenna. Hence the novelty of Hobbes (or the humanists before him) appears to be in how they selected and combined these 'essences'. Hobbes certainly merged 'thing' and 'body' into one. In the Appendix to the *Latin Leviathan*, for instance, he wrote: 'By "body" I now understand that thing of which it can truly be said that it really exists in itself, and also has some magnitude.'[72] At any rate, the resemblance between Hobbes's metaphysics of necessity and existence and Henry of Ghent's and Avicenna's metaphysics is striking. While I am not arguing that this resemblance is complete, I contend that Hobbes's metaphysics of necessity and existence is similar to Avicenna's novel contribution in the way in which his reasoning starts with the fact of existence, and that the principle of causal necessity utilized by both is strikingly similar.

I would like to suggest that since the dualist Avicenna dealt separately and in the first place with the things existing in the material world, his philosophy of existence was useful to a committed physicalist like Hobbes- in the expression of Robert Pasnau. That is, someone for whom nothing is 'nonphysical'.[73] There is a certain development concomitant to Hobbes's choice of metaphysics of existence, his physicalism and the secularist and absolutist project. Avicenna's dualism offered the new philosophers of nature studying the physical body a strictly physicalist metaphysics.[74] On this point it is worth quoting Avicenna at length on metaphysics:

> Thus, in its own right, this science should be prior to all the [other] sciences; but from our point of view, it is posterior to all of them … As for the name of this science, it is [metaphysics,] "that which is after nature". By "nature" is not meant the power which is a principle of motion and

[71] Paganini, 'Hobbes's Critique of the Doctrine of Essences and Its Sources', p. 344; p. 351. Lorenzo Valla was an Italian humanist (1406–1457).

[72] Hobbes, *Leviathan*, vol. 3, p. 1184 (translation by Noel Malcolm); similarly Skinner writes that Hobbes's lifetime ambition was to create 'a system of philosophy grounded on the assumption that there is nothing real except bodies in motion.' Skinner, *Hobbes and Republican Liberty*, p. 208.

[73] Robert Pasnau, 'Mind and Extension (Descartes, Hobbes, More)', in Henrik Lagerlund (ed.), *Forming the Mind. Studies in the History of Philosophy of Mind*, vol. 5 (Dordrecht: Springer, 2007), p. 286.

[74] See Nicola Polloni, 'Gundissalinus and Avicenna: Some Remarks on an Intricate Philosophical Connection' 28 *Documenti e studi sulla tradizione filosofica medievale* (2017), p. 525.

> rest, but the totality of the things that come about through corporeal matter – [including the latter] power and accidents. For it has been said that "nature" is said of the natural body that has the nature, the natural body being the sensed body [along] with what belongs to it by way of properties and accidents. The meaning of "[that which] is after nature" [involves] a posteriority relative to us. For when we first observe existence and get to know its states, we observe this natural existence. As for that which this science, if considered in itself, deserves to be name, [this] is to speak of it as the science of what is "prior to nature," because the matters investigated in this science are, in [terms of] essence and generality, prior to nature.[75]

Thus, Avicenna viewed nature as all the bodies that exist and metaphysics meant 'after physics', *according to human beings' point of view*, that is starting with what exists. For Avicenna, we humans observe first the existence of body, and from that observation, we may deduce the general principles of things and nature. Despite his Aristotelianism, Avicenna's metaphysics was unrelated to the Aristotelian and scholastic idea of 'transcending' nature that Hobbes derided.[76] The latter found this point sufficiently relevant to political philosophy as to define it properly in *Leviathan* and to *distinguish* 'a certain *Philosophia prima* on which all other philosophy ought to depend', from the 'Books of supernaturall philosophy' of the scholastics. As Amos Bertolacci has noted, Avicenna's metaphysics also sought to prove, in a secondary way, 'the Necessary Existent' (the Superior Being) that 'has no cause'. But it is important to emphasize that Avicenna viewed the subject matter of metaphysics as primary 'existence', and not a divine necessary existent.[77]

Dag Nikolaus Hasse has described Avicenna's dualist epistemology, involving epistemology in two steps – rational abstraction from the physical thing that is in front of me as primary learning, followed by retrieving the understanding of the same thing as emanation from the supralunar separate intellect – as a useful antidote to scepticism. Avicenna was an optimist about the capacity of human reason to grasp things in that first step of observing existence unproblematically.[78] In fact, Avicenna regarded the first 'benefit' of his metaphysics of existence as being, in his own words,

[75] Avicenna, *The Metaphysics of "The Healing"*, 16.32–17.1.

[76] Hobbes, *Leviathan*, ch. 46, p. 1076; Paganini, 'Hobbes's Critique of the Doctrine of Essences and Its Sources', p. 344.

[77] Bertolacci, 'The Doctrine of Material and Formal Causality in the 'Ilāhiyyāt' of Avicenna's 'Kitāb al-Šifā''; Avicenna, *The Metaphysics of "The Healing"*, Book. I, ch. 6.

[78] See Dag Nikolaus Hasse, 'Avicenna's Epistemological Optimism' in Peter Adamson ed. *Interpreting Avicenna* (Cambridge: Cambridge University Press, 2013) 109–119.

'to bestow certainty on the particular sciences'.[79] To remain within the bounds of Christianity, one needed only to dispose of the second step, and hence of Neoplatonic dualism, which involved, in Avicenna's work, a separate intellect that was not God, but a supralunar giver of forms. The physicalist and the spiritualist aspects are thus set apart.

No attempt will be undertaken here of tracing the textual connections or sources from Avicenna to Hobbes. My purpose is rather to use the ideas of both philosophers to depict the capacity of 'necessity' to establish a metaphysical category that may inform religious, moral and political theory to a greater extent than has hitherto been regarded as possible in scholarly discourse. Since whatever exists is necessary in one way or another, and necessity is moreover self-evident, 'necessity' gives a sufficient metaphysical foundation to existence.

In its most pure forms, however, the paradox of the project of necessity is that philosophers *were doing* theology. Theirs was a theology marked by the non-involvement of God in the activities of the current world – a secularist theology if you will. The world that had emanated from God in Avicenna's Neoplatonism tends towards perfection with the goal of reaching the supralunar intelligent beings.[80] In its Christian version, Hobbes's 'decree of God' has also a similar metaphysical function but with more profound consequences.[81] God produces or creates the world, and continuing on a sort of autopilot, through 'necessity', things existing in the world follow God's plan. And unless there are special revelations – which are hardly to be expected – human beings remain within the limits of natural reason in control of what happens *on this side of the line*. Hobbes's project against free will might well have been concerned primarily with preventing 'ecclesiastical promotion' (i.e. intervention).[82] However, it is well buttressed by self-contained philosophical ideas about necessity that blur the spiritual aspect of free moral and political human decisions in the exposition of political philosophy, underlying, nevertheless a robust theological framework.

[79] Avicenna, *The Metaphysics of 'The Healing'*, 14.20.

[80] Robert Wisnovsky, 'Final and Efficient Causality in Avicenna's Cosmology and Theology' 2 *Quaestio* 2002; see also De Haan, 'Scientific knowledge is causal knowledge of necessary truths, and within Avicenna's metaphysics of truth, the epistemologically necessary truths of science simply conform to the metaphysically necessary truth of things, which are themselves causally dependent upon the divine First Truth that is necessary existence in itself.' De Haan, 'Avicenna's *Healing* and the Metaphysics of Truth', p. 28.

[81] A somehow similar connection is made by Alan Cromartie between Bacon's (and Hobbes's) theory of 'motion' with the theory of God 'the designer' of order, Alan Cromartie, 'The God of Thomas Hobbes', 51 *The Historical Journal* (2008), p. 863.

[82] Hobbes, *The Questions Concerning Liberty, Necessity, and Chance*, p. 2.

2.2.1 *Hobbes's Early Necessitarianism*

Hobbes's knowledge of necessitarianism was not acquired during his long sojourns in France in the 1630s and 1640s.[83] His *Short Tract of First Principles* from around 1632–1633 evidences that, as Karl Schuhmann also noted.[84] Ferdinand Tönnies described the tract as 'an intermediate stage' between Hobbes's scholasticism acquired during his early training in Oxford and his later knowledge of mechanics and mathematics.[85] The tract in question deals with the philosophy of nature and mainly with optics. Significantly, Hobbes also experimented with the devising of moral concepts on the basis of strictly physical concepts in this tract. This was done by (ambiguously) prescinding from a spiritual soul in the explanation of understanding and by pushing Aristotle's concepts in that direction. After a strictly physical explanation of the role of motion in understanding and sensing, Hobbes adds that 'Good is to every thing, that which hath active power to attract it locally'. He then notes that this definition agrees with the way in which Aristotle defined 'Good to be that, to which all things are moved'. Hobbes remarks that that 'hath been metaphorically taken, but is properly true'. Finally, he describes '*Malum* to every thing is that which hath active power to repell it' and 'Badness' as 'the power of *Malum*'.[86]

By the end of the tract, one understands that Hobbes's view is that good and evil may primarily be explained through a physical motion of attraction and repulsion – he upheld a version of that understanding of moral good and evil all the way up to *Leviathan*.[87] Hobbes's is not an altogether arbitrary explanation. It is important to make this clear, in order to reject the thesis that Hobbes was an extreme nominalist, for his explanation of good and evil is backed by a deep insight into the philosophical significance of real bodily attraction or repulsion. However, what he says about

[83] He had been already in a long trip to the continent, though. About the dates of the sojourns, see Richard Tuck, 'Principal Events in Hobbes's Life', in Thomas Hobbes, *Leviathan*, Richard Tuck ed. (Cambridge: Cambridge University Press, 1996) p. lviii.

[84] Karl Schuhmann's analysis of concordances of concepts and expressions in *The Short Tract* with Hobbes's other works, mainly the *Treatise of Liberty and Necessity*, *De Corpore* and *Elements of Law* confirms the intuition about Hobbes's authorship, despite the scholarly debate, which is discussed also by Schuhmann. Karl Schuhmann, 'Le "Short Tract", première ouvre philosophique de Hobbes', in 8 *Hobbes Studies* (1995).

[85] Ferdinand Tönnies, 'Editor's Preface', in Thomas Hobbes, *The Elements of Law*: *To Which Are Subjoined Selected Extracts from Unprinted Mss. of Thomas Hobbes*, (Cambridge: Cambridge University Press, 1927), p. xiii.

[86] Hobbes, 'Appendix I: A Short Tract on First Principles', in Hobbes, *The Elements of Law*, p. 166.

[87] Hobbes, *Leviathan*, Malcolm (ed.), ch. 6, p. 82.

good and evil is metaphysically and ontologically reductionist as to what being a human being entails. One may at least say that a human being is more than a body. Although Hobbes gave some explanation of reality, his definition of good and evil is an insufficient explanation of reality.

With regard to the doctrine of necessity, Hobbes illuminates it in *The Short Tract* as follows in principles 12 and 13 in Section I:

'12. Necessary is that which cannot be otherwise.
13. A necessary cause is that which cannot but produce the effect.'

And conclusions 11 to 14 of Section I state as follows:

'11. A Sufficient Cause is a Necessary Cause.
12. Every effect produced hath had a Necessary Cause.
13. Every effect to be produced shall be produced by a Necessary Cause.
14. Necessity hath no degrees.'[88]

In summary, Hobbes's elaboration states that any cause that is sufficient to produce an effect necessarily produces that effect. Therefore, it is contradictory to speak of a 'free agent' that has all that it needs in order to work but may or may not work.[89] Both in his *The Mechanisation of Aristotle* and in a previous article Cees Leijenhorst considers that the Jesuit Benito Pereira (1535–1610) is a plausible source for Hobbes in relation to these 'conclusions' on a necessary cause.[90] Pereira had noted that Ockham had sought to prove a statement by Avicenna while (Ockham) not mentioning Avicenna by name.[91] Leijenhorst, however, acknowledges that the reason for Hobbes's use of this unconditional necessity 'remains obscure' and that there is little evidence of its origin. More recently, Kara Richardson

[88] Hobbes, 'Appendix I: A Short Tract on First Principles', p. 152; p. 155.

[89] Hobbes, 'Appendix I: A Short Tract on First Principles', p. 167.

[90] Ceest Leijenhorst, *The Mechanisation of Aristotelianism. The Late Aristotelian Setting of Thomas Hobbes' Natural Philosophy* (Leiden, Brill, 2002); Ceest Leijenhorst, 'Hobbes's Theory of Causality and Its Aristotelian Background' in 79 *The Monist*. Causality Before Hume (1996), p. 444.

[91] Ockham argues his Quodlibet I, q. 17 from the other extreme that without free will there cannot be 'casus' or 'fortuna', since for natural agents everything that happens, happens by necessity. *Quodlibeta septem una cum tractatu De sacramento altaris venerabilis inceptoris fratris Guilhelmi de Ockam anglici sacre theologie magistri de ordine fratrum minorum* (Strasbourg : Georg Husner, 1491). On Pereira see, Constance Blackwell, 'Aristotle's Perplexity Becomes Descartes's Doubt: *Metaphysics* 3, 1 and Methodical Doubt in Benito Pereira and René Descartes', in José R. Maia Neto, Gianni Paganini and John Christian Laursen (eds.), *Skepticism in the Modern Age: Building on the Work of Richard Popkin* (Leiden, Boston: Brill, 2009).

has suggested that Avicenna might have been one of the main sources of seventeenth-century rationalism on account of his necessitarianism.[92] At any rate, Hobbes's notion of a 'necessary cause' appeared in similar terms in Avicenna's *The Metaphysics of 'The Healing'*:

> Hence with the existence of the cause, the existence of every effect is necessary; and the existence of its cause necessitates the existence of the effect.[93]

The evidence present in this text from the 1630s allows one to emphasize Hobbes's early and uncompromising position on necessitarianism. This leads to inquiry as to whether his political writings are dependent on historical events. I argue below that Hobbes gains methodological proficiency in the sequence of his political writings, until in *Leviathan* other methods are discarded in favour of this method of necessary causality. The threat of civil war – in the form of empirical proof of danger – and other political events might have influenced the sense of urgency with which he adopted the principle of necessity in his political writings.[94] A philosopher of necessity investigates how the needs of human nature relate to moral and political life. The outcome of such investigation will be a precisely defined branch of natural law founded on necessity and survival – not unlike Hobbes' project in *De Cive* and the first three sections of *Leviathan*. This looks like a more complex version of 'the older picture of Hobbes' in the words of Peter Munz.[95] The older picture indicates that Hobbes studied the natural principles of survival that lie within human beings – that is the 'strict nature' – and put them at the disposal of atheists. Nevertheless, what the evidence suggests is that he wanted mostly to reach believers by combining his philosophy of necessitarianism with the argument of divine decree.

2.2.2 Hobbes's Metaphysics of Bodies and Its Implication to Morality

The perspective of Avicennian necessity of existence described above gives new insights about Hobbes's interest in the existence of bodies

92 For instance in Kara Richardson, 'Avicenna and the Principle of Sufficient Reason' 67 *The Review of Metaphysics* (2014).

93 Avicenna, *The Metaphysics of 'The Healing'*, 127.34.

94 A more complex set of motivations transpire from Noel Malcolm's chronology, which indicates that *Leviathan* was written after the Civil War. Malcolm, 'Editorial Introduction'.

95 And Munz continued, which 'is so much more *interesting*'. Peter Munz was undermining the 'taming' of Hobbes by Howard Warrender. Munz is quoted in Watkins, *Hobbes's System of Ideas*, p. 98

and in the conception of political society that derives from it. That interest has been neglected by an important group of scholars that concentrated on his nominalism and hence individualism.[96] Of this group, I will consider in particular Yves Charles Zarka's *La decision métaphysique de Hobbes*. To be sure, Zarka's work is helpful in navigating Hobbes's attempt to unite natural philosophy and the science of politics. But the French philosopher argues that in opposition to Aristotle's metaphysics, Hobbes's foundation of politics was a 'metaphysics of separation' between knowledge and being and that he regarded truth as residing not in things but in thinking.[97]

Zarka comes to this conclusion in interpreting Hobbes's supposition as to the 'annihilation of the world'. The first line of Chapter 7 of *De Corpore* affirms that natural philosophy begins first with 'privation', by which Hobbes means, among other things, a scenario in which the universe is removed. Next, Hobbes invites us to imagine that the world is annihilated and only a thinking individual remains.[98] He would retain only a few ideas (*phantasmata*) of the bodies that had disappeared and consideration of how the things he remembered had a being without the thinking individual's mind, which would produce a conception of 'imaginary space'. That individual would obtain a conception of time by remembering how the things moved from one space to another. Zarka notes that the fundamental aspect of Hobbes's supposition of the *annihilatio mundi* is that nothing changes in our representation of the world whether it exists or not.[99] This interpretation is persuasive. However, pushing it a little bit further, it seems to me that Hobbes is eminently concerned with the physical existence of the world – i.e. with *body* and how bodies operate – both in his exposition of natural philosophy (in *De Corpore*) and in

[96] Yves Charles Zarka, *La decision métaphysique de Hobbes. Conditions de la politique*, (Paris: Vrin, 1999); interesting in this regard is David Gauthier's emphasis on individualism and his argument that the laws of nature are 'maxims for the preservation of the individual' …'The basic consideration is always the preservation of the individual'. David Gauthier, *The Logic of Leviathan: The Moral and Political Theory of Thomas Hobbes* (Oxford: Clarendon Press, 1979) p. 90.

[97] Zarka, *La decision métaphysique de Hobbes*, p. 54.

[98] 'Doctrinae naturalis exordium, optime (ut supra ostensum est) a privatione, id est, a ficta universi sublatione, capiemus. Supposita autem tali rerum annihilatione, quaeret fortasse aliquis, quid reliquum esset, de quo homo aliquis (quem ab hoc universo rerum interitu unicum excipimus) philosophari, vel omnino ratiocinari, vel cui rei nomen aliquod ratiocinandi causa imponere posset.' Thomae Hobbes, *Elementorum Philosophiae. Sectio Prima De corpore, in Opera Philosophica*, Gulielmi Molesworth (ed.) (Londini: Joannem Bohn, 1839), vol I, p. 81.

[99] Zarka, *La decision métaphysique de Hobbes*, p. 54.

political philosophy (in *Leviathan*). Hobbes's metaphysics is a *metaphysics of existence* that he exposed as a *metaphysics of body*.[100] In sum, it is a metaphysics of what is physical, in which bodies are the agent and patient of movement.[101] This is evidently a metaphysics that is important, but reduced in scope as compared to the Aristotelian metaphysics of ultimate causes. For, notes Hobbes, philosophy must not be subjected to theology, 'since when I say theology' he wrote:

> I say that the Church regulates', that is to say, establishes dogmas, whereas philosophy is about right reasoning.[102]

Hobbes viewed spiritual matters as a question of belief, not of reasoning. And one must add, he was making an interesting point in that regard. But the confusion started when he employed the framework of a Neoplatonist metaphysics, with a sharp division between the spirit and the real thing; between the human soul and the human body.[103] In that type of Neoplatonist dualism what is spiritual is outside the realm of nature. Hence in this reading, morality as a branch of spirituality is not the outcome of right reasoning; instead, not unlike Revelation, it must be taught.[104] And then, in parallel to that there are the natural laws of the human bodies. Hobbes was particularly adamant that a human being can reason about these natural laws of the human bodies.

Another famous thought experiment – Avicenna's floating man from the first book, *The Soul*, from *The Cure* – provides an unexpected

100 Supporting this argument see Noel Malcolm's discussion of the Italian Renaissance Aristotelians and their scholarship about their 'physicise metaphysics' and their similarities in this and other aspects with Hobbes. Malcolm, *Thomas Hobbes and Voluntarist Theology*, p. 69.

101 'Ego vero pro ente, et esse dicam ubique *corpus* & *actum* ? Cum ergo actus omnis, praeter ipsam corporeitatem, concipi possit generari sive produci, & rursus perire, ut quando videmus *esse album* id quod videramus antè *esse nigrum*, et sentimus *esse frigidum* quod ante senseramus *esse calidum*; concipi autem non possit quomodo talis generatio & corruptio actuum fieri possit, nisi à *corpore aliquo* & in *corpore aliquo*, solent omnes corpus illud à quo producitur vel destruitur aliquis actus, apellare *agens*, illud verò in quo producitur, *patiens*'. Hobbes, *Critique du De mundo de Thomas White*, p. 314.

102 Hobbes, *Critique du De mundo de Thomas White*, p. 433.

103 See for this also, G. Verbecke, 'Le "De Anima" d'Avicenne. Une conception spiritualiste de l'homme: Introduction sur la doctrine psychologique d'Avicenne', in *Avicenna Latinus Liber de Anima seu Sextus de Naturalibus IV-V*, Édition critique de la traduction latine médiévale par S. van Riet (Louvain, Leiden: Éditions Orientalistes, E. J. Brill, 1968).

104 Avicenna expressed this type of morality 'through teaching' most strikingly in Book V, Chapter 1 of *Avicenna Latinus Liber de Anima seu Sextus de Naturalibus IV-V*, Édition critique de la traduction latine médiévale par S. van Riet (Louvain, Leiden: Éditions Orientalistes, E. J. Brill, 1968)

background against which to interpret Hobbes's *annihilatio mundi.*[105] Avicenna invites us to imagine that one of us has been created as an adult. The sight of that individual is veiled, and she or he cannot see things in the external world. The person in question is in a state akin to floating, but without feeling the air, as in a void, and with the limbs stretched out so that they do not come into contact with each other. The world exists but for some reason it is not tangible for the floating individual, who cannot see it or feel it in any way. Avicenna's question again concerns existence: can this floating individual assert the existence of her or himself? The answer is that without a doubt she or he can do so. Avicenna's conclusion is that the reader is now aware of 'the existence of the soul as something that is not the body – not in fact *any* body'.[106] What he had asked in 'The Soul' is that we annihilate all (past and present) perception of body in order to grasp the existence of the soul. My suggestion is that once that had been done, the next step was for Hobbes, in a study entitled 'Concerning Body', to propose annihilating the present perception of the body (in terms of space, time, number etc.) in order to ascertain how we think about the body, albeit that it is not present or no longer in existence. Avicenna analyses the soul through existence by means of his thought experiment, and Hobbes followed this by analysing the body.[107]

Zarka traces the key pieces of Hobbes's metaphysics, including his focus on existence, his necessitarianism and the principle of 'necessity', but consistently refers them to Ockham's nominalism and Hobbes's own original work.[108] He thinks that the 'legal-political structure' that Hobbes designs for the human world does not correspond to a previous 'ontology' and that he describes a human being as 'separated from a world

[105] Ibn Sīnā 'Selections on Psychology from The Cure, "The Soul", in Jon McGinnis and David C. Reisman, *Classical Arabic Philosophy: An Anthology of Sources* (Indianapolis, Cambridge: Hackett Publishing House, 2007), p. 179.

[106] Ibn Sīnā, 'Selections on Psychology from The Cure, "The Soul', p. 179; see Robert Wisnovsky rejecting that Descartes's 'cogito' is related to the floating man despite a superficial similarity, Robert Wisnovsky, 'Avicenna and the Avicennian Tradition', in Peter Adamson and Richard C. Taylor eds., *The Cambridge Companion to Arabic Philosophy*, (Cambridge: Cambridge University Press, 2004) p. 103; Verbecke, 'Le "De Anima" d'Avicenne. Une conception spiritualiste de l'homme', p. 36.

[107] It is probably accurate to say that the different proposal of John Locke again shows the evolution of thinking. In *An Essay Concerning Human Understanding* he supposes a sort of floating man, who is placed by God in that state. His goal is to ascertain the idea of space, and whether it is the same with body. John Locke, *An Essay Concerning Human Understanding*, II. 13.§21, p. 175.

[108] Zarka, *La decision métaphysique de Hobbes*, p. 200; p. 211.

of things'.[109] Without claiming that there are no other valid approaches to this point of Hobbes's political philosophy, I have attempted to show that Hobbes theorized about a human being whose body is *immersed in things*, rather than separated from them. The next chapter will accordingly interpret *Leviathan* by reference to the principle of necessity. The implication of this novel approach is that Hobbes was able to found politics on a philosophy of nature, contrary to what Leo Strauss argued.[110] In response to Strauss's rich discussion of Hobbes I accept that the latter retained the public spirit of traditional political philosophy and that he was a materialist.[111] However, Hobbes was not only a materialist, as we will see below, but rather an expert on the sectionalization of social and political explanations of life. He was able to do this at the cost of reducing metaphysics to a metaphysics of existence devoted only to what is corporeal in human beings. Moreover, as a consequence of this approach, the aspect of human physical necessities assumes a central position in his political philosophy. This metaphysics of 'body' and of 'what exists' is successful thanks first to Hobbes's clever use of the principle of causal necessity, which functions as an anchor for thinking, and second by degrading all meaningful natural rights to natural necessities. The reason I have chosen *Leviathan* for particular attention is that in that text Hobbes was able to, or decided to, double down on his chosen approach by dispensing altogether with other foundational philosophies and principles in order to concentrate on necessity.

109 Zarka, *La decision métaphysique de Hobbes*, p. 366 (my translation).
110 Strauss, *Natural Right and History*, pp. 173–209.
111 Strauss, *Natural Right and History*.

3

Necessities, Natural Rights and Sovereignty in *Leviathan*

3.1 Hobbes's Necessity, Theology and Natural Laws

'Necessity is lack of power.'[1] This is the most straightforward definition that Hobbes gives about what he means by 'necessity', and one that may be taken as his most fundamental thinking on the question. This definition points to one of the deepest currents of thought on power flowing from Hobbes's theological and secular projects. Furthermore, it makes sense of his efforts to secure and seal the power of the sovereign, after all, merely a human or a group of human beings who have a 'modicum of physical power'.[2]

In many of his works, Hobbes plays with different meanings of necessity: psychological, theological, metaphysical, material and, to a lesser extent, logical in nature. These varied dimensions of necessity give a sense of unity to his political and natural philosophy and functions well together on the grounds of its theological and metaphysical underpinnings. The reasoning is about 'something', maybe a 'nature', whose necessity is (or must be) remedied by another. Hobbes's doctrine of necessity is expressed in the fact that the word 'necessity' or 'necessary' does not usually add meaning to a sentence: it can usually be avoided. But it adds a determinist philosophical aspect. Chapter 15 of *Leviathan* is paradigmatic in this regard:

> For seeing every man, not only by Right, but also by necessity of Nature, is supposed to endeavour all he can, to obtain that which is necessary for his conservation.[3]

[1] 'necessitas enim impotentia est'. Hobbes was criticizing in this passage Thomas White's use of the idea of necessity in reference to God ('*necesse esse ut Deus Seipsum diligat*'). Hobbes, *Critique du De mundo de Thomas White*, p. 372. See also in Locke, *An Essay Concerning Human Understanding*, II. 21. §13., p. 240.

[2] Counterintuitively, but in my view correctly, Warrender noted many years ago the feebleness of *Leviathan*, Howard Warrender, *The Political Philosophy of Hobbes: His Theory of Obligation* (Oxford: Clarendon Press, 1957), p. 317.

[3] Hobbes, *Leviathan*, Noel Malcolm (ed.), p. 232.

Hobbes could have written only 'by Nature' but he chooses to write 'by necessity of Nature'.[4]

3.1.1 *Within the Tradition of Power*

The doctrine of necessity also provided the basis for Hobbes's naturalism and political theory, in which he combined a description of the need for things with an exhortation to satisfy that need when it did not happen automatically.[5] Hobbes viewed God as the one who 'is everything', the 'highest best and incomprehensible' – God did not necessitate anything.[6] It is not my intention here to deliver an extended exposition of Hobbes's views on religion and God. A good idea may be obtained by combining the extremes depicted by Howard Warrender and Lodi Nauta – i.e. Warrender regarded Hobbes as holding a reasoned belief in God while Nauta attributes to him a stance of religious scepticism – with the more balanced studies on the topic by Aloysius Martinich, Richard Tuck, Jeffrey Collins and Alan Cromartie.[7] Hobbes was often quite explicit about his belief in God, utterances that, as Martinich has written, would be awkward to interpret ironically, especially in an individual as direct as Hobbes.[8] Moreover, when he wrote in *Leviathan* that there are 'subjects' and 'enemies' of God, there is little doubt that he was making the important point that authentic Christianity was about subjective belief or, in other words, about personal faith.[9] One of the most explicit statements as to God's existence in *Leviathan*, which shows that Hobbes was inspired by

[4] See also previous chapter, note 2.

[5] Perhaps similar to what Arash Abizadeh has called a hybrid interpretation of Hobbes's naturalism, Arash Abizadeh, *Hobbes and the Two Faces of Ethics* (Cambridge: Cambridge University Press, 2018), pp. 27–61.

[6] 'Ne igitur quaremus qui sit: cum sit omnia, et super omnia, et praeter omnia. Hoc ipso cognoscimus: quod a se solo perfecte cognosci potest.' Hobbes's papers, quoted in Noel Robert Malcolm, *Thomas Hobbes and Voluntarist Theology* (PhD Dissertation, Gonville and Caius College, University of Cambridge, 1982), p. 73; 'est enim Deus optimus maximus incomprehensibilis'. Hobbes, *Critique du De mundo de Thomas White*, p. 312.

[7] Warrender, *The Political Philosophy of Hobbes*; A. P. Martinich, *The Two Gods of Leviathan: Thomas Hobbes on Religion and Politics* (Cambridge: Cambridge University Press, 1992); Richard Tuck, 'Introduction' to *Leviathan;* Lodi Nauta, 'Hobbes on Religion and the Church between the Elements of Law and Leviathan: A Dramatic Change of Direction?' 63 *Journal of the History of Ideas*; Alan Cromartie, 'The God of Thomas Hobbes'; Collins, *In the Shadow of Leviathan*, p. 93.

[8] Martinich, *The Two Gods of Leviathan.*

[9] Hobbes, *Leviathan*, ch. 31, p. 554. See for this also Richard Tuck's comment on faith in Hobbes's *Critique du* De Mundo, Tuck, 'The Civil Religion of Thomas Hobbes', p. 125.

Aquinas's so-called 'five ways', can be found in the way in which he indicated his view that proof of the existence of God derived from nature and of being the cause without cause:[10]

> Curiosity, or love of the knowledge of causes, draws a man from consideration of the effect, to seek the cause of that cause; till of necessity he must come to this thought at last, that there is some cause, whereof there is no former cause, but is eternall; which is what men call God. So that it is impossible to make any profound enquiry into natural causes, without being enclined thereby to believe there is one God Eternall; though they cannot have any Idea of him in their mind, answerable to his nature.[11]

However, it was clear to everyone that this issue of religion in Hobbes's work was not as unproblematic as that. Even by today's secular standards, some of his ideas on religion come across as disrespectful and as outright heresies, and his writings contain plenty of them. Most readers, Noel Malcolm writes, found 'at least some of his theological arguments either disconcerting, or objectionable, or entirely unacceptable'.[12] Chapters 37 to 42 of *Leviathan* deliver ideas that seem to be designed to offend believers at several levels. Hobbes's satirical tone was not only employed against the classics.[13] One may even say that not only wittiness and satire but also the grotesque is one of the features that marks Hobbes's literary style. Dogmas seem to be the object of his most acerbic attacks. Certainly, he had a problem with the conflicts over dogmas, and his solution was to eliminate all of them, except one, as we will see in the next epigraph.[14] Notwithstanding all that, Hobbes's published and unpublished work contain even very pious thoughts. The remarkable third section of *De Cive*, evidence of a serious investigation of the biblical texts, is full of them. He described the natural understanding of God, at once esoteric and scriptural, as follows:

10 *Summa theologiae*, First part, q.2, art. 3: 'The existence of God can be proved in five ways … The second way (to proof the existence of God) is from the nature of the efficient cause.'

11 Hobbes, *Leviathan*, Noel Malcolm (ed.), ch. 11, p. 160.

12 Malcolm, 'Editorial Introduction', to Hobbes, *Leviathan*, p. 149.

13 See on Hobbes's satire against the classics, Quentin Skinner, '"Scientia Civilis" in Classical Rhetoric and in the Early Hobbes', in Nichola Phillipson and Quentin Skinner (eds.), *Political Discourse in Early Modern Britain* (Cambridge: Cambridge University Press, 1993), p. 85.

14 See Hobbes, *On the Citizen*, ch. 28; see also George Wright analysis of Hobbes's clarification and restatement on several of his positions on dogma and heresy in the Latin Appendix, George Wright, 'The 1668 Appendix and Hobbes's Theological Project' in *The Cambridge Companion to Hobbes's Leviathan*.

> For the reason of nature dictates only one significant name of God – *the existent* (*existens*), or simply *that which is*, and one name of relationship to us, namely God, in which are contained both *King* and *Lord* and *Father*.[15]

His discussion of infinite divisibility in the *Physical Dialogue* of 1661 is another example drawn from his writings on the philosophy of nature that shows how he viewed God's power:

> Truly, you who cannot accept infinite divisibility, tell me what appears to you to be the reason why I should think it more difficult for almighty God to create a fluid body less than any given atom whose parts might actually flow, than to create the ocean.[16]

In that period of the Restoration, misunderstandings between Hobbes and the Church were already starting to turn into open war.[17] But these problems did not interfere in Hobbes's employment of God's omnipotence as a means of defending his scientific hypothesis. His notes summarizing a book by Julius Caesar Scaliger (1484–1558), which he read before 1635, and are quoted in Noel Malcolm's dissertation entitled *Thomas Hobbes and Voluntarist Theology*, are another much earlier example of this. Hobbes's summary stated as follows:

> God's power is double: ordinary and absolute; they are both one in God, for the ordinary power is part of the absolute power. And it is altogether impious to posit anything in God which is not absolute, and which is not God himself. For all power, as it is in God and as it proceeds from him, is absolute: it is described as ordinary only with respect to us.[18]

There was, after all, something that Hobbes thought could be said about God. The idea contained in the quote above that the concept of God's power was a matter of perspective appears originally in probably the most important monograph existing on it, Aquinas's *De Potentia Dei*:

15 See Hobbes, *On the Citizen*, ch. 15, p. 179.

16 Thomas Hobbes, 'A Physical Dialogue of the Nature of the Air: A Conjecture taken up from Experiments recently made in London at Gresham College (1661)', Simon Schaffer (trans.). Appendix in Shapin and Schaffer, *Leviathan and the Air-Pump*, p. 354. Another interesting example of 'God' working as a scientific method from Hobbes's *Decameron physiologicum* in Cromartie, 'The God of Thomas Hobbes', p. 870.

17 Collins, *In the Shadow of Leviathan*.

18 The date that he read the book and the quote in Malcolm, *Thomas Hobbes and Voluntarist Theology*, p. 71 (translation by Noel Malcolm). The book was *Exotericarum exercitationum liber XV. De subtilitate, ad Hieronymum Cardanum* by J. C. Scaliger; on Scaliger see, Andreas Blank, 'Julius Caesar Scaliger', in Marco Sgarbi (ed.), *Encyclopedia of Renaissance Philosophy* (Springer, 2018).

> The absolute and the conditional (*regulatum*) are ascribed to the divine power solely from our point of view. To this power considered in itself and which we describe as God's absolute power, we ascribe something that we do not ascribe to it when we compare it with his ordered wisdom. *De potentia Dei*, Q.I, art. V.[19]

Hobbes's thinking about the ordinary and absolute power of God was in this sense heir to a tradition not limited merely to William of Ockham.[20] In that same article V, Aquinas analysed the argument that God acts 'from natural necessity'. His conclusion, like Hobbes's, was that God does not do so and that 'God can do otherwise than he has done'.[21]

3.1.2 The Tradition of Natural Laws Updated

Unsurprisingly, it is an English author, 'the judicious Hooker', who shone light on the area that was the subject of the specific divergence between Hobbes's philosophical method of necessity and previous theological doctrines. In his acclaimed *Of the Lawes of Ecclesiastical Politie*, Richard Hooker (1554–1600) asked the classical theological question on necessity: what is 'necessary unto salvation' inspired in the choice of Mary over that of Martha in Luke 10:42?[22] As a good, reformed theologian, Hooker felt the urge to clarify that 'traditions', though holy and divine, did not constitute 'supernatural necessary truth' for salvation. In a nutshell, his view was that 'scripture must contain' the description of what was necessary. He also explained that the Old Testament taught salvation through the saying 'Christ that should come' and the New Testament by showing that 'Christ is come'. He confirmed what John the Evangelist had written to be the purpose of his history: 'These things are written, that ye might believe that Jesus is the Christ, the son of God, and that in believing, ye might have life thro his name.'[23] But Hooker added a caution that urged that one should not forget the light of nature. Nature and Scripture 'both

[19] 'Can God Do What He Does Not?' Q. 1, art. V, Reply to the 5th objection. Thomas Aquinas, *Quaestiones Disputatae de Potentia Dei*, translated by the English Dominican Fathers (Westminster, Maryland: The Newman Press, 1952), Html edition by Joseph Kenny, O.P.

[20] This argument also in Malcolm, *Thomas Hobbes and Voluntarist Theology*.

[21] Aquinas, *'Can God Do What He Does Not?' Q. 1, art. V,; see* Hobbes: 'He who would demonstrate that the world was created must show that this was necessary, i.e. that it could not have been otherwise … such view denies God's omnipotence'. Hobbes critique of White quoted in Malcolm, *Thomas Hobbes and Voluntarist Theology*, p. 51. (translation by Malcolm).

[22] Richard Hooker, *Of the Lawes of Ecclesiastical Politie* (London: John Walthoe et al., 1773), p. 28.

[23] The rightly famous equivalent passage in Hobbes's *Leviathan* was thus continuing English political tradition, Hobbes, *Leviathan*, Noel Malcolm (ed.), ch. 43, p. 938.

jointly' were necessary for salvation and Hooker warned that 'the benefit of nature's light be not thought excluded as unnecessary, because the necessity of a diviner light is magnified'. The point was that with the light of nature human beings would be able to perform 'the good work' that God required of them, whatever their call in the 'church of God', or to 'whatsoever kind of society' they belonged.[24]

A thorough analysis of *Leviathan*, like the one undertaken in Section 3.2, shows the idea introduced in the beginning: Hobbes's metaphysical question is not 'is this good?' but 'is this necessary?'. In particular, the doctrine of necessity of nature guides the key question of the citizen's voluntary act of transferring his or her right and how much to transfer, and what never to transfer, as we will see below. Nevertheless, the object of that voluntary act is always 'a Good to himselfe' (the individual) (*semper Bonum est aliquod Volenti*).[25] Hobbes never specified whether that was a prudential judgment in the modern sense or an act of practical wisdom in the Aristotelian sense – a practical act illuminated by the light of reason,[26] and instance of truth. He simply asserts that only once the passions have calmed, each may know what constitutes that 'good to one self'. *How* do we know what is a good to ourselves? This is the question that Hobbes never posed.[27] Hobbes is able to avoid this key question only by having recourse to his doctrine of necessity in which he combines Christian voluntarist theology and Avicennean philosophy of existential necessity. The latter is only concerned with metaphysics and therefore eschews entirely the fundamental theme of human freedom.[28]

[24] Hooker, *Of the Lawes of Ecclesiastical Politie*, p. 136. On this question in Hooker, R. S. White writes that 'the desire to do good and shun evil, in his account, emerges not as a mysterious, God given *synderesis*, but as a rational conclusion deduced from the Law of Nature'. R. S. White, *Natural Law in English Renaissance Literature* (Cambridge University Press, 2006), p. 55. However, Hooker is quite explicit in the text above on the 'benefit of nature's light.'

[25] Hobbes, *Leviathan*, Noel Malcolm (ed.), ch. 14, p. 202.

[26] 1140b5 Aristotle *Nichomachean Ethics*: phronesis 'is a true and reasoned state of capacity to act with regard to the things that are good or bad for a human being'; '*prudentia est vera recta ratio agibilium*' Aquinas, *Summa theologiae*, IaIIae q.57 a 4co. See Rosalind Hursthouse, and Glen Pettigrove, 'Virtue Ethics', *The Stanford Encyclopedia of Philosophy* (Winter 2018 Edition), Edward N. Zalta (ed.), URL = https://plato.stanford.edu/archives/win2018/entries/ethics-virtue/. Complicating Aristotelian prudence through a study of the metaphysics of contingence, see Pierre Aubenque, *La Prudence chez Aristote*, (Paris: Presses Universitaires de France, 1963).

[27] See also Gauthier: 'Hobbes has no intelligible account of natural reason that would qualify its deliverances to be divine commands.' David Gauthier, 'Hobbes: The Laws of Nature' 82 *Pacific Philosophical Quarterly* (2001), p. 280.

[28] See more about this in chapter 9.2.

As discussed in the next section, although Hobbes was a moral philosopher, as opposed to a moralist or theologian, he did not dwell in a classical sense on epistemological questions of the light of reason or of nature in the style of many of his contemporaries, such as Robert Sanderson. Rules of natural reason are found out by reason, not dictated by reason.[29] Nevertheless, they are dictates of reason. But how are they found out? And how to apply them in the particular circumstances? Through the light of reason? Hobbes did not specify. Instead, buttressing the general argument in his necessitarianism, Hobbes glossed over the relevance of the light of reason to the political philosophy he was undertaking. Although some of Hobbes's statements imply the incapacity of human beings' reason for the supernatural, what he thought about practical wisdom is less obvious. In *Leviathan* he equated the 'Word of God' with the 'Dictates of reason'.[30] He also marvelled 'that a man endued but with a mediocrity of reason' would be able to think things 'supernaturall'. For the purposes of the commonwealth, not everyone had to 'make our own private Reason, or Conscience, but the Publique Reason' (i.e. whatever the sovereign would judge best) is 'all that is necessary for our peace and defence'.[31]

At the outset, it would appear that all that mattered in the public life of the state, 'all that is necessary', was what the sovereign declared to citizens to be best – however means the sovereign has reached that conclusion – but not what God helped the sovereign and citizens alike to choose and deliberate upon through the light of reason.[32] In turn, this raises the question of human beings' moral obligation. The laws of nature are means to achieve peace, and human beings must obey them. They originally are dictates of reason.

> These dictates of reason men use to call by the name of laws, but improperly; for they are but conclusions or theorems concerning what conduceth to

[29] See Abizadeh, *Hobbes and the Two Faces of Ethics*, p. 49. The classic article reviewing the status and evolution of understandings of 'the light of nature' in seventeenth-century England is Greene, 'Synderesis, the Spark of Conscience, in the English Renaissance'.

[30] Hobbes, *Leviathan*, Noel Malcolm (ed.), ch. 36, p. 656.

[31] Hobbes, *Leviathan*, Noel Malcolm (ed.), ch. 37, 696.

[32] A long-life student of Hobbes, the controversial Carl Schmitt would be then right when he wrote that personal piety was not accompanied in Hobbes by a devout thought. Schmitt in *Der Leviathan in der Staatslehre des Thomas Hobbes*; see the comment by Heinrich Meier, *The Lesson of Carl Schmitt: Four Chapters on the Distinction between Political Theology and Political Philosophy*, trans. by Marcus Brainard. New Essays translated by Robert Berman (Chicago and London: University of Chicago Press, 2011), p. 117.

> the conservation and defence of themselves, whereas law, properly, is the word of him that by right hath command over others. But yet if we consider the same Theoremes, as delivered in the word of God, that by right commandeth all things; then are they properly called Lawes.[33]

To assert that moral obligation (of the laws of nature) is simply natural, because it is theological, or an 'obligation to obey God in his natural kingdom',[34] approximates it to the obligation the lamb might have to run for its life, or the tiger to hunt for food. They are also acting in order to survive. The different principle that human beings may meet or not their obligations does not fundamentally change their situation in nature – and based on many statements in his texts one might legitimately conclude that Hobbes thought about moral obligations in this naturalistic sense. Thus 'augmentation of dominion over men, being necessary to a mans conservation, it ought to be allowed him.'[35] This originates 'from the natural and necessary appetite of his own conservation'.[36] Incidentally, it would be absurd to discuss the self-interest of a tiger, and equally ridiculous, as in a naturalistic view, to think of a human being as being in a state of nature occupied with her self-interest. Against the interpretation that Hobbes's political philosophy is one of absolute naturalism, it is contended here that he gradually injected into it a more metaphysical structure of thought, certainly more than he wanted to admit. To put this point in the most unambiguous way possible, 'nature' is not mere nature but 'necessity', and for him also *a metaphysical expression of God's will.* The sovereign only makes determinate that will. This argument may accommodate theories about the common good in Hobbes's moral philosophy such as that suggested by S. A. Lloyd.[37] They would certainly be coloured by modern physicalist overtones to the effect that considerations of self preservation and preservation of others enjoy preference over other moral considerations. However, the argument would still amount to one in favour of the common good. In fact, this could be the only way to explain Hobbes's strenuous efforts to get individuals out of the state of nature and keep them within the commonwealth. The way in

33 Hobbes, *Leviathan*, ch. 15. 242.

34 This is a quote from Warrender who is however not defending an absolute naturalism. The aim here is to benefit from his expression. He adds '(in his natural kingdom) based upon fear of divine power'. Warrender, *The Political Philosophy of Hobbes*, p. 10.

35 Hobbes, *Leviathan*, Noel Malcolm (ed.), ch. 13, p. 190.

36 Hobbes, *Leviathan*, Noel Malcolm (ed.), ch. 18, p. 274; Hobbes, *On the Citizen*, ch. 1, 7, p. 27.

37 S. A. Lloyd, *Morality in the Philosophy of Thomas Hobbes: Cases in the Law of Nature* (Cambridge: Cambridge University Press, 2009).

which the meaning of the laws of nature reaches across the concept of God's commands, dictates of reason and commands of the sovereign as in David Gauthier's interpretation receives also a convincing explanation with this view about an emphasis on necessitarian metaphysics expressing the will of God.[38] In all this, as I already mentioned, Hobbes leaves unexplained how we produce the reasoning on the laws of nature.

The work on Hobbes by John W. N. Watkins and Tom Sorell, who stress (metaphysical) physicalism; Annabel Brett, who provides an exposition of Hobbes's naturalism; and Quentin Skinner, who offers a close reading of Hobbes's increasingly physical notion of liberty are illuminating on these questions.[39] My contribution is to pay attention to the theological and philosophical depth and complexity of Hobbes's particular version of physicalism, arguing that it is embedded in the doctrine of necessity described thus far and also in his theological voluntarism. I remain, therefore, a step or two behind Warrender's interpretation of the theological naturalism in Hobbes's political philosophy and Noel Malcolm's early work on theological voluntarism.

3.2 The Doctrine of Necessity in *Leviathan*

The superior and absolute sovereignty that *Leviathan* analyses and proposes is the true and scientific concept of sovereignty in a commonwealth, by reference to the needs of human nature and also in accordance with divine command.[40] In terms of substance, in the first two sections of the book, entitled 'On Man' and 'On Commonwealth', Hobbes based his ideas on politics and natural law on two principles: conservation of the human body *and* of the body of the commonwealth. Furthermore, he stressed the political principle that judgment about what is necessary for that purpose belongs exclusively to the holder of each of those bodies: the individual human being and the sovereign ruler. The sovereign is also 'body', while the commonwealth is an automaton. No complex explanation of metaphysics was required for such a treatment of political philosophy, so

[38] Since my point is about Hobbes's emphasis on metaphysics of necessity, I change here David Gauthier's exposition of the sequence of the constitution of the laws of nature. Instead of Gauthier's primary theorems of reason, I would argue that they could be primary commands of God, the omnipotent creator of nature, and secondarily theorems of reason and of the civil sovereign. See Gauthier, 'Hobbes: The Laws of Nature'.

[39] Watkins, *Hobbes's System of Ideas;* Tom Sorell, 'Hobbes's Moral Philosophy' in *The Cambridge Companion to Hobbes's Leviathan*; Brett, *Liberty, Right and Nature*; Skinner, *Hobbes and Republican Liberty*; Malcolm, *Thomas Hobbes and Voluntarist Theology*.

[40] See also Curley, 'Introduction' to Thomas Hobbes, *Leviathan*, viii–xi.

Hobbes implies. He took the opportunity to criticize Francisco Suárez's rejection of a metaphysics of mechanical necessity and his overly sophisticated philosophical language.[41]

Founded on the pre-eminence of 'body' he had established in the first two sections, the English philosopher deduced his argument of political theology in the last two sections of *Leviathan*, entitled 'Christian Commonwealth' and 'On the Kingdom of Darkness', respectively. He concluded that there is no need for an exclusively spiritual commonwealth.[42] In his words, 'seeing there are no men on earth, whose bodies are Spirituall; there can be no Spirituall Commonwealth amongst men that are yet in the flesh'.[43]

Firstly 'necessities' have a pejorative connotation in Hobbes's text and are understood as 'wants': 'the common people' needed only bread and spectacle – the notorious *panem et circenses*. Understood in this sense needs denote smallness and unimportance; fear and wants, characteristically prompting individuals to employ unjust or dishonest means, and inviting 'craft' or 'crooked wisdom'. 'Needy men', never content, are inclined to continue causes of war. It is due to our need for protection that we seek another's power. Power is in itself 'a thing dependant on the need and judgment of another'.[44] However, basic necessities can also be taken to have a positive sense. Interestingly, the 'article of peace' or '[l]aws of nature' is founded on three passions: fear, desire for things that are 'necessary to commodious living' and the 'hope' that one can obtain them by means of industry. Hobbes consistently distinguished between 'basic needs' and 'conveniencies'. Thus, it is not purely 'needs', but the wish to go beyond mere basic material needs that draws human beings to

41 'What is the meaning of these words. *The first cause does not necessarily inflow any thing into the second, by force of the Essentiall subordination of the second causes, by Which it may help it to worke*? They are the Translation of the Title of the sixth chapter of *Suarez* first Booke, *Of the Concourse, Motion, and Help of God*. When men write whole volumes of such stuffe, are they not Mad, or intend to make others so?' Hobbes, *Leviathan*, Noel Malcolm (ed.), ch. 8, p. 122.

42 This idea can be approached from different angles. See Sorell: 'the distinctive purposes' of *Leviathan* are 'to show that several supposed sources of ecclesiastical authority in the commonwealth either derive from the sovereign or are spurious. There are no sources of ecclesiastical authority independent of the sovereign, still less above the sovereign, and there is no scriptural basis for his submission to a church or to a Pope, not even for the sake of Salvation.' Sorell, 'Hobbes's Moral Philosophy' p. 139.

43 Hobbes, *Leviathan*, Noel Malcolm (ed.), p. 918.

44 'To give little gifts, is to Dishonour; because it is but Almes, and signifies and opinion of the need of small helps'; 'Servitude, for need, or feare, is Dishonourable'. Hobbes, *Leviathan*, Noel Malcolm (ed.), ch. 12, p. 178; ch. 10, p. 141; 136; ch. 11, p. 152; ch. 8, 110; ch. 10, p. 134.

peaceful living.[45] Needs also constitute a principle of motion for human knowledge, since 'need' is 'the mother of all inventions'.[46]

Hobbes employed his doctrine of necessity in few but crucial moments of his masterpiece. The following five principles are the most relevant arguments about necessity and necessities that appear in *Leviathan*: (a) in the context of natural rights and the individual's capacity for reasoning in the right manner about what is necessary for self-preservation; (b) in respect of the sovereign's similar capacity to ascertain what is necessary for the body of the commonwealth; (c) in explaining how freedom and civil law are compatible; (d) in his assertion as to the *unum necessarium* for salvation; and (e) finally in his critique of the faith that seeks to understand, in Hobbes's view, unnecessarily. In the remainder of this chapter I will analyse these principles in that same order.

3.2.1 Natural Rights and Necessity

In *Leviathan* natural rights are treated as being simultaneously formidable and hollow.[47] There is no way that in the state of nature – i.e. in the absence of governmental regulation and control – each person's practical reason would limit their individual right to everything in the material world. At least, not for Hobbes. A morality based on virtues, checking and subduing greed and violence, for instance, did not work in his view. Whether he considered this approach unhelpful or unrealistic, we do not know. In an anarchical political state, the only way to secure the provision of human needs was to *reduce* those 'natural rights to everything' to the level of human necessity for survival. The birth of the commonwealth occurred when this limitation of natural rights happened. This may suggest that Hobbes was himself a materialist theorizing a society of incipient capitalism, as C. B. MacPherson argued over half a century ago.[48] However, it may also be the case that Hobbes was making a different point and that his concern lay with the inability of contemporary moral and political theories to set limits on certain people's greed. Therefore, the solution to the avarice of some and the deprivation of many was not utopia, but a political society in which necessity was the bottom line. Needs, indeed, unite human beings.[49]

[45] Hobbes, *Leviathan*, Noel Malcolm (ed.), ch. 13, p. 196.

[46] Hobbes, *Leviathan*, Noel Malcolm (ed.), ch. 4, p. 50.

[47] Malcolm, 'Hobbes and Spinoza', p. 537.

[48] MacPherson, *The Political Theory of Possessive Individualism*.

[49] I am paraphrasing from Judith Shklar, who in turn articulates a current expression of modern natural law: 'Not Morality but physical needs and laws, even the most ferocious,

Thus, the first important theoretical function of the concept of necessity in *Leviathan* appears in relation to the rights of nature. Famously 'the Right of Nature' (*Jus Naturale*) is for Hobbes, 'the Liberty each man hath, to use his own power, as he will himselfe, for the preservation of his own Nature; that is to say, of his own Life'.[50] Governed only by one's reason in this endeavour, 'every man has a Right to every thing; even to anothers body'.[51] The law of nature forbids every human being to do or to omit anything that may jeopardize the preservation of one's nature.[52] Human beings ought to use reason in accordance with the law of nature as they think appropriate for their own survival. The principle of necessity rules human judgment about the *measure of right* to be used in Hobbes's natural law. In the same paragraph in which Hobbes considers 'what is necessary' for survival as an axiom of natural law he also introduces the notion of the 'necessities of nature' as material physical goods without which the human body cannot live. The separate but complementary meanings of 'necessity' are thus laid down. Therefore, before the institution of the commonwealth each human had 'a right to every thing and to do whatsoever he thought necessary to his own preservation'.[53] But even within it, human beings cannot give away a number of rights:

> As it is necessary for all men that seek peace, to lay down certaine Rights of Nature; that is to say, not to have libertie to do all they list: so it is necessarie for mans life, to retaine some; as right to governe their owne bodies; enjoy aire, water, motion, waies to go from place to place; and all things else, without which a man cannot live or nor live well.[54]

In this approach, God has already determined that no one is entitled to give away one's right to self-preservation. Below God, each individual alone may judge what is necessary in time and space for her or his survival – that is to say, to decide both generally and in a critical instance where a real threat appears, as to survival and living well. Necessities are

keep us together.' Judith N. Shklar, 'Putting Cruelty First' in 4 *Democratiya* (2006), p. 93; see on Hobbes and the self-effacing laws of nature, Lloyd, *Morality in the Philosophy of Thomas Hobbes*.

[50] For self-defence and preservation as the core of Hobbes's natural laws, rather than peace, see Bruno Dix, *Lebensgefährdung und Verpflichtung bei Hobbes* (Würzburg: Königshausen and Neuman, 1994), pp. 1–26.

[51] Hobbes, *Leviathan*, Noel Malcolm (ed.), ch. 14, p. 198.

[52] Hobbes, *Leviathan*, Noel Malcolm (ed.), ch. 14, p. 198.

[53] Hobbes, *Leviathan*, Noel Malcolm (ed.), ch. 14, p. 198; 'quod ad conservationem sui videretur ipsi necessarium, jus erat naturale.', ch. 28, p. 483.

[54] Hobbes, *Leviathan*, Noel Malcolm (ed.), ch. 15, 234; Hobbes, *On the Citizen*, ch. 3. 14. p. 50.

therefore constant and contingent. In a condition of state of nature or of war, as noted above, 'every man has a Right to every thing; even to one another's body'.[55] In such a dark state, the first and fundamental law of nature is divided into two rules: 'to seek Peace, and follow it' and 'by all means we can, to defend our selves'. The second law of nature follows from the command to seek peace: 'to lay down this right to all things' as long as the others do the same. It is, again, each individual that judges the extent to which one may lay down one's right safely, and how much right each one regards as being conducive to the goals of peace and self-defence. In Hobbes's words, 'as farre-forth, as for Peace, and defence of himself he shall think it necessary'.[56]

In Hobbes's view, therefore, the main political question in a space ordered by the laws of nature is that after God – who has granted the rules to act to human beings – it falls to each individual to decide on the necessity of retaining or giving away (and to what extent doing so) the rights of self-preservation. Hobbes gave further specific examples of rights to activities or things that, according to the law of nature, no human being ought to consent to renounce or give away.[57] For instance, even when living in a commonwealth – despite the command of the sovereign – no one can lay aside the right to resist those that go after their life or intend to wound, enchain or imprison them. The same example was given by the theologian Henry of Ghent as to the limit of public authority, and by John Locke in the context of epistemology, as we will see in Chapter 12.[58]

On the one hand 'by necessity of nature' human beings 'choose that which appeareth best for themselves'.[59] Arguably, this is one of the unarticulated manifestations of the light of reason in Hobbes's natural law. Human beings are supposed, and assumed to be able, to deliberate properly about when a right is necessary for security or for survival – for oneself

[55] Hobbes, *Leviathan*, Noel Malcolm (ed.), ch. 14, p. 198.

[56] Hobbes, *Leviathan*, Noel Malcolm (ed.), ch. 14, p. 200.

[57] 'All men allow that any act not contrary to right reason is *right*, and therefore we have to hold that any act in conflict with right reason (i.e. in contradiction with some truth reached by correct reasoning from true principles) is *wrong* … The *Natural Law* therefore (to define it) is the Dictate of right reason about what should be done or not done for the longest possible preservation of life and limb.' Hobbes, *On the Citizen*, ch 2, p. 33; p. 40; see a comprehensive list extracted from the text of activities in the abstract that a subject cannot rationally consent to, in Curley, 'Introduction' to Thomas Hobbes, *Leviathan*, p. xxxviii.

[58] Hobbes, *Leviathan*, Noel Malcolm (ed.), ch. 14, p. 202.

[59] Hobbes, *Leviathan*, Noel Malcolm (ed.), ch. 27, p. 456.

and for others – and when it is not. On the other, human beings are often crafty, and in this regard they also ought to be presumed to seek their own benefit. Thus, the seventh law of nature states that in controversies that do not impinge on self-preservation, arbitrators are needed.[60]

3.2.2 The Needs of Others

Hobbes writes in *Leviathan* that the 'fool' is wrong. The fool questions whether injustice may not sometimes stand to reason and be the right choice and also asserts 'in his heart that there is no God'. Hobbes rejects that. The fool commits injustice and violates the natural laws in pursue of his own benefit irrationally – since, no one would sustain damage unless by error. Hence the fool is a 'harming fool' who violates the rational community of human beings. In this manner, Hobbes quietly acknowledged that 'taking away the feare of God' wreaks havoc on political theory as he saw it. Consistently with the general tone of *Leviathan*, the preservation of society also requires that the unjust and godless individual who actively seeks to damage others must be thwarted.[61]

By declaring that it was a recipe for perpetual war, Hobbes brutally unpacked the fallacy of speaking about unlimited 'rights' of human beings in relation to material things that are to be found in nature. What was meaningful, Hobbes reasoned, was to downgrade those 'rights in everything' as to reduce them to the quantity *necessary* for survival and more than that, for 'living well'.[62] Although he did not mention it, that was in accordance with all previous traditional political philosophies. This 'reduction of rights' was only possible through a combination of the law of nature, the law of the commonwealth and correct reasoning on the part of individuals.

It is only logical that quantity mattered for a phyisicalist like Hobbes, who was concerned with 'body' in all its aspects. Individuals, thus both by right and by necessity of nature, must do all in their power to obtain that which is necessary for their conservation. In times of scarcity this might be dangerous. Moreover, only antisocial people, 'by asperity of Nature', would have difficulties in ascertaining the scope of their material needs and

[60] Hobbes, *Leviathan*, Noel Malcolm (ed.), ch. 15, p. 238.

[61] Hobbes, *Leviathan*, Noel Malcolm (ed.), chapter 15, 222–224; also on this question see Kinch Hoekstra's argument that Hobbes referred to the 'explicit fool', Kinch Hoekstra, 'Hobbes and the Foole' 25 *Political Theory* (1997) 620–654; and the answer by Peter Hayes, 'Hobbes's Silent Fool: A Response to Hoekstra' 27 *Political Theory* (1999).

[62] Lloyd, *Morality in the Philosophy of Thomas Hobbes*.

try to retain things that are 'superfluous and to others necessary' (*vicino autem necessariis*).[63] Such an individual would go against nature – keeping more than he or she needs, while someone else really needs it – and would be guilty of the ensuing war, and hence deserve to be cast out of society:

> For seeing every man, not only by Right, but also by necessity of Nature, is supposed to endeavour all he can, to obtain that which is necessary for his conservation; He that shall oppose himselfe against it, for things superfluous is guilty of the warre that thereupon is to follow: and therefore doth that, which is contrary to the fundamental Law of Nature, which commandeth *to seek Peace.*[64]

MacPherson's critique was probably the most important to have been levelled against Hobbes's natural law during the previous century – one in which he characterized Hobbes's thinking as a 'political theory of possessive individualism'.[65] But MacPherson's attack against Hobbes is rendered ineffectual by means of this quote only, which denounces the antisocial behaviour of the greedy accumulator. Hobbes's notorious fear of the power of the spiritual and his defence of philosophical materialism in specific parts of *Leviathan* does not prevent him from denouncing the selfishness of the accumulator.Ostensibly, Hobbes's narrative is as much about the preservation of individuals as of human beings at large. He is clear that human beings may be evil – that many of them may be so. However, Hobbes did regard procuring one's own advantage irrationally and without limits as amounting to moral selfishness. The appetite for self-preservation is, as Hobbes saw it, an instrument of survival; and in rejecting egoism, Hobbes declared that natural law served this goal not only for one individual but for the generality of mankind.[66]

Notwithstanding this comment, it is difficult to ignore the intuition that MacPherson was onto something with his argument concerning possessive individualism. In his social history of the market, Craig Muldrew

[63] Hobbes, *Leviathan*, Noel Malcolm (ed.), ch. 15, p. 232.

[64] Hobbes, *Leviathan*, Noel Malcolm (ed.), ch. 15, p. 232.

[65] MacPherson, *The Political Theory of Possessive Individualism*; also contesting MacPherson and suggesting instead a practical science of peace for self-preservation, Otfried Höffe, 'Wissenschaft im Dienste freier Selbsterhaltung? Zum Theorie-Praxis-Verhältnis in Thomas Hobbes' Staatsphilosophie' in Udo Bermbach and Klaus-M. Kodalle (eds.), *Furcht und Freiheit. Leviathan Diskussion 300 Jahre nach Thomas Hobbes* (Opladen: Westdeutscher Verlag, 1982).

[66] As he put it in *De Cive*, 'All these natural precepts are derived from just one dictate of reason, that presses on us our own preservation and security.' Hobbes, *On the Citizen*, ch. 3. 26, p. 53.

argues that MacPherson had grasped a phenomenon that occurred in early modern England. In a period of political, religious and social disruption after the Reformation the rise of the market was felt in England with greater intensity than in other parts of Europe. The error made by MacPherson, Muldrew writes, was to think that Hobbes's political theory aimed at developing a utilitarian market model. Instead, he attributes Hobbes's emphasis on competition to the historical moment in which he was writing. With rampant growth in consumption, and neither a consistent economic policy nor a moral philosophy to guide it, in the face of increasing need for credit and monetary transactions, judicial and social culture placed great emphasis on sociability and interpersonal relations as the only means of securing them – pushing the societal system to its breaking-point. This was the *stressed* sociability that Hobbes had in mind and which gave rise to his doubts that individuals could face alone the demands of trust made by the market, as it were.[67] 'Possessiveness' was therefore taken for granted in *Leviathan* as the starting point for theorizing, in a political culture that contained a vacuum that needed to be filled. Hobbes built a cosmological order of necessity, among other reasons, as a means of replacing the exhausted sociability of trust.

3.2.3 *Naturalism*

The body and its preservation are not per se transcendental values, at least not explicitly, either in *Leviathan* or in the earlier *De Cive*, where the same doctrine is put forward.[68] However, as Tom Sorell rightly notes and I have been argued so far, there is more to Hobbes's laws of nature than 'an unmetaphysical idea of a fair or rational agreement' or 'rational self-interest alone' resonant with twentieth-century moral philosophy.[69] The doctrine of necessity asserts a metaphysical chain of necessary causes that encompasses invaluable knowledge about self-preservation, including the

[67] Craig Muldrew analyses the inability in the period of social mores of neighbourhood to cope with the increasing demands of credit, and the stress that these put into social relations in Muldrew, *The Economy of Obligation*, generally and on MacPherson – Hobbes, pp. 321–325. Studying Locke but with a much more positive account on this historical question of the promotion of interpersonal borrowing and the emphasis on trust, see recently Jon Cooper, 'Credit and the Problem of Trust in the Thought of John Locke, c. 1668–1704' 64 *Historical Journal* (2021).

[68] Hobbes, *On the Citizen*, Richard Tuck and Michael Silverthorne (eds.) ch. 3, 9, 48.

[69] Sorell, 'Hobbes's Moral Philosophy', p. 144. Sorell is responding to David Gauthier, 'Hobbes: The Laws of Nature'.

creation of the commonwealth itself. It is a scientific doctrine that provides the foundation of the new 'civil science'. It is worth noting that while in *De Cive* Hobbes still uses argumentative devices, such as 'it is self-evident' or 'it is a commonplace', in *Leviathan* he presents his ideas as a scientific truth.[70] Within Hobbes's discourse of civil science in *Leviathan* things are not 'good' or 'evil'; they are neither 'opinion' nor 'belief'. Instead, things or actions are 'necessary' or 'not necessary', without further involvement of value judgments.[71] This holds for both extreme cases and the habitual right reason. Moreover, when human beings follow correct reasoning about necessity, they are obeying the will of God.

Hobbes's naturalism makes it a stretch to declare him a mere relativist or sceptic – he saw himself as ascertaining the truth, and not as asserting that there is no objective truth.[72] After all, something that 'all men easily recognize' is that peace is good, and so are all virtues ('modesty, fairness, good faith, kindness and mercy') that rationally lead to that end.[73] The real problem, as Hobbes saw it, concerned the incapacity to make proper judgments about future goods, virtue and peace due to the irrational desire for goods now.[74] This mismatch of reason and passion was usually the case, *except* in the case of self-preservation, where reason and desire coincided. The same idea appears in the *Elements of Law* in a form that is perhaps exaggerated by the subsequent discussion on the inadequacy of transferring one's judgment to another: 'Also every man by right of nature is judge himself of the necessity of the means, and of the greatness of the danger.'[75]

[70] Hobbes, *Leviathan*, Noel Malcolm (ed.), ch. 5.

[71] To be more precise, as he stated already in *De Cive*, 'What is done of necessity, or in pursuit of peace, or for self-preservation (in the state of nature) is done rightly.' Hobbes, *On the Citizen*, ch. 3.27, p. 54. Also in the same work Hobbes notes that to the right of self-preservation that each one has is attached 'the right to use every means necessary to that end'. Hobbes defines those: 'The necessary means are those that he shall judge to be so himself.' The 'sin against the Natural Laws' may occur when someone falsifies that judgment, and pretends that something belongs to his or her self-preservation, in Latin 'ad sui conservationem pertinere', but it does not. The right and the sin arise therefore from the authentic or false judgment about the necessity of the means. Hobbes, *On the Citizen*, ch. 1. 10, p. 28; Thomas Hobbes, *De Cive*, p. 95.

[72] See Brett, *Liberty, Right and* Nature; Tuck, 'Introduction' to Thomas Hobbes, *On the Citizen*, p. xxvi; Abizadeh, *Hobbes and the Two Faces of Ethics*.

[73] It is remarkable that the very Scripture that Hobbes cited profusely to prove the laws of nature could not persuade him that the habitual state of a practicing Christian is the desire for peace ('let the peace of Christ control your hearts' Coloss. 3.15). Hobbes quoted, e.g. Coloss. 3.11 in *De Cive* to prove the tenth law of nature on fairness, Hobbes, *On the Citizen*, ch. 3.13, p. 63.

[74] Hobbes, *On the Citizen*, ch. 3. 31–32, p. 55.

[75] Hobbes, *The Elements of Law*, I, ch. 14, 8, p. 55.

3.2.4 The Needs of the Sovereign

The first two sections of *Leviathan* refrain from tying the doctrine of necessity to a theological foundation. Hobbes suggests that in the context of the new civil science it is a matter of choice as to whether one's beliefs remain secular (nature and the sovereign), thus revealing again dualistic Neoplatonism as a source of inspiration. However, the sovereign must receive all the power:

> For to every End, the Means are determined by Nature, or by God himself supernaturally: but the Power to make men use the Means, is in every nation resigned (by the Law of Nature, which forbiddeth men to violate their Faith given) to the Civill Soveraign.[76]

The very acumen about 'the necessity of retaining or giving up rights' with which nature has endowed human beings constitutes the fundamental building block of the sovereign in the second section of *Leviathan*, 'Of Common-wealth'. In other words, Hobbes also attributed to the sovereign the natural human ability to ascertain what is necessary for self-preservation, and transformed it into a *sine qua non* of the rights of sovereignty – all the rest was sedition, disobedience, rebellion and weakness. The sovereign's ability to ascertain the ultimate necessity is thus the second important theoretical employment of the doctrine of necessity. This particular use of the doctrine is a crucial aspect of the method by which Hobbes made sense of the novel meanings of authority and representation in *Leviathan* since it emphasizes the independent and almost natural life of a commonwealth:

> A *Common-wealth* is said to be *Instituted*, when a *Multitude* of men do Agree, and Covenant, *every one with every one*, that to whatsoever *Man* or *Assembly of Men*, shall be given by the major part, the *Right* to *Present* the Person of them all, (that is to say, to be their *Representative*;) every one, as well he that *Voted for it*, as he that *Voted against it*, shall *Authorise* all the Actions and Judgments, of that Man, or Assembly of men, in the same manner, as if they were his own, to the end, to live peaceably amongst themselves, and be protected against other men.[77]

Subjects are represented by the sovereign, who is authorized to act for them, and they own the sovereign's decision.[78] Representation and authority go hand in hand with a number of essential rights that show everyone

[76] Hobbes, *Leviathan*, Noel Malcolm (ed.), ch. 42, p. 916.

[77] Hobbes, *Leviathan*, Noel Malcolm (ed.), p. 264, and generally ch. 18.

[78] Noel Malcolm, 'Editorial Introduction' in Thomas Hobbes, *Leviathan*, vol. I, p. 16; Quentin Skinner, 'Hobbes on Representation' 13 *European Journal of Philosophy* (2005); Hanna Fenichel Pitkin, *The Concept of Representation*, 14–37.

where the sovereign power 'is placed, and resideth'. In sum, these include all the rights that ensure that no corruption and disintegration of the body of the sovereign occurs, that it can act with a unified voice in the legislative, executive and judicature, and defend the body of the commonwealth (i.e. its own body).[79] As he had done with the individual human being and the citizen, Hobbes also combines the principle of necessity with illustrations of its material needs in relation to the commonwealth.

The source of the sovereign's rights was partly natural and partly artificial – in the Latin text Hobbes refers to rights *ex rei natura deducta*. 'Soveraign rights' are deduced 'from the nature, need and designes of men, in erecting of Common-wealths, and putting themselves under Monarchs, or Assemblies, entrusted with power enough for their protection'.[80] While the covenant of the commonwealth is artificial, its ends are not: securing the capacity of nourishment of citizens, protection from within and without and, in consequence, peace:

> The only way to erect such a Common Power, as may be able to defend them from the invasion of Forraigners, and the injuries of one another, and thereby to secure them in such sort, as that by their owne industrie, and by the fruites of the earth, they may nourish themselves and live contentedly; is, to conferre all their power and strength upon one Man, or upon one Assembly of me, that may reduce all their Wills, by plurality of voices, unto one Will … and therein to submit their Wills, everyone to his Will, and their Judgments, to his Judgment.[81]

The big theme of the economy of the commonwealth pressed almost entirely into the important matter of levying taxes became thus one of the irrenounceable rights of sovereignty. Traders and labourers were kept busy by 'necessity or covetousness'. The commonwealth ought to provide for the poor, 'as far-forth as the necessities of Nature require', but only for those that 'by accident unevitable, become unable to maintain themselves by their labour'.[82] More generally, the commonwealth had 'necessities', and

[79] Hobbes, *Leviathan*, Noel Malcolm (ed.), ch. 18, p. 278.

[80] Hobbes, *Leviathan*, Noel Malcolm (ed.), ch. 20, p. 314.

[81] Hobbes, *Leviathan*, Noel Malcolm (ed.), ch. 17, p. 260.

[82] Hobbes, *Leviathan*, Noel Malcolm (ed.), ch. 30, p. 532; p. 538. In the Latin version Hobbes notes the canonical and theological principle that in extreme necessity by natural right everything is common, and in order to avoid trouble for the rest of the citizens, he recommends intervention of the sovereign: 'Cum enim in Summa necessitate existentibus, aliena surripere, aut etiam rapere, jure naturae permissum sit, ne Civitati alias molesti sint, à Civitati alendi sunt, neque singularium Civium incertae charitati relinquendi.' Hobbes, *Leviathan*, Noel Malcolm (ed.), ch. 30, p. 539. On this principle see, Tierney, *The Idea of Natural Rights*, pp. 69–77.

arising from the 'Office of the Sovereign Representative', the sovereign had the power 'of Judging of the Necessities of the Common-wealth'.[83] To illustrate this idea Hobbes related the passage in the Gospel in which Jesus asked the disciples to go into a village and take a donkey to carry him into Jerusalem (Matthew 21:2, 3). No one, neither the owner of the donkey nor the disciples, questioned whether the title of that 'necessity' was sufficient or doubted whether the Lord ought to be 'judge of that necessity' (*neque utrum Dominus necessitates illius Iudex sit*). In England, this principle was certainly one of the central constitutional questions of the century and one apt to make feelings run high, as the unfortunate Charles I found to his cost. Hobbes's lesson was uncompromising: the content of subjects' 'obedience' in a commonwealth was that 'the Kings word, is sufficient to take anything from any Subject, when there is need; and that the King is Judge of that need'.[84]

Hobbes's method of exposition is original, but hardly any topic was more debated in the years before the Civil War than the sovereign's judgment about the 'important question of necessity'. In *Rex v Hampden* (1637), John Hampden was tried for refusing to pay the Crown ship money (a form of tax hitherto confined to coastal regions), the levying of which had been extended to inland areas. The Crown alleged that the preservation of the kingdom 'is only intrusted to our care'. Apparently, the strongest blow against the royal prerogative was made by Hampden's counsel, Oliver St. John, who argued that the Crown had not been able to prove the existence of imminent danger, in relation to which the tax was apparently being levied, since there had been a delay of seven months in receiving supplies. However, disagreement as to the question of necessity as a matter of fact, of law and of constitutional principle existed among the 12 judges adjudicating on the matter in the special Court of Exchequer Chamber. Over half of them thought the King was sole judge of that necessity; some considered that he was sole judge, but that he had to levy money through parliament. Others considered that the King's judgment about necessity could be checked.[85]

83 Hobbes, *Leviathan*, Noel Malcolm (ed.), ch. 30, p. 520.

84 Hobbes, *Leviathan*, Noel Malcolm (ed.), ch. 20, p. 318.

85 Richard L. Noble, 'Lions or Jackals? The Independence of the Judges in Rex v. Hampden, 14 *Stanford Law Review* (1962); *Complete Collection of State Trials, and Proceedings for High Treason, and Other Crimes and Misdemeanours*, v. I, (Dublin: Graisberry and Campbell, 1793), p. 570. See also the detailed reasoning by Henry Parker in *The Case of Shipmony briefly discoursed*. Notoriously, Parker dismissed in the pamphlet the argument of the King's counsellors that dominion of the seas was necessary for the survival of England,

In *Leviathan*, Hobbes held it as madness for the power to levy taxes for the benefit of the commonwealth – 'the Nutritive faculty' – to be taken away from the sovereign and bestowed on a general assembly. It amounted, in Hobbes's view, to one of the dangerous divisions of power within a commonwealth, which will paralyze it, 'most often for want of such Nourishment, as is necessary to Life, and Motion'.[86] More generally, the commonwealth would be endangered if citizens were able to place obstacles in the path of the sovereign's attempts to raise money 'for the necessary uses of the Common-wealth' (*Pecuniarum necessarium ad salutem Civitatis*), on the grounds that they had a 'propriety' on goods and lands that was exempted from the 'Soveraigns Right to the use of the same'. In a similar manner to the situation of the sole judgment of the individual about his or her necessity and security, it was only the head of the commonwealth that 'foreseeth the necessities and dangers' that lay ahead. In order to avoid the contraction of the whole system – as in a human body when a disease prevented the blood from passing from the heart through the veins – the sovereign would be forced to discipline the people, 'or else the Common-wealth must perish'.[87]

3.2.5 *The Necessary Freedom*

The third key employment of the principle of necessity in *Leviathan* works to ease the tension between individual freedom and absolute sovereignty and to introduce Hobbes's idea of the compatibility of freedom with civil laws. 'Feare, and Liberty are consistent', Hobbes noted. For example, in a sinking boat, one would throw one's goods into the sea *willingly* in order to save one's life. '*Liberty*, and *Necessity* are consistent', he continued, since necessity is simultaneously natural and necessary, like water flowing freely through a channel.

> *Liberty*, and *Necessity* are consistent ... so likewise in the actions which men voluntarily doe: which, because they proceed from their will, proceed from *liberty*; and yet, because every act of mans will, and every desire, and inclination proceedeth from some cause, and that from another cause, in a continuall chaine, (whose first link is in the hand of God the first of all

Henry Parker, *The Case of Shipmony briefly discoursed, according to the Grounds of Law, Policy, and Conscience. And most humbly presented to the Censure and Correction of the High Court of Parliament, Nov. 3. 1640*. Printed Anno Dom. 1640. Thomason Tracts Catalog information TT1, p. 2.

86 Hobbes, *Leviathan*, Noel Malcolm (ed.), ch. 29, p. 512.

87 Hobbes, *Leviathan*, Noel Malcolm (ed.), ch. 29, pp. 514–515.

> causes,) they proceed from *necessity*. So that to him that could see the connexion of those causes, the *necessity* of all mens voluntary actions, would appeare manifest.[88]

With the paradox of the necessity of 'voluntary actions' Hobbes reaches the pinnacle of his theological philosophy. Every free action of an individual was at once free and necessary, which, as the quote above shows signified for Hobbes that it also proceeded necessarily from a cause. Significantly, Noel Malcolm writes that none of Hobbes's earlier writings appear to have been important in relation to the composition of *Leviathan*, except a number of points set out in *Of Libertie and Necessitie*, the outcome of his debate with Bramhall mentioned previously, and specifically, the example of the behaviour of water given above. The differences in this same passage in the manner in which it appears in *De Cive*, where Hobbes distinguished between 'liberty' and 'servitude', strike me as important in showing the novel metaphysics of intensified necessity at work in the construction of *Leviathan*. The author of *De Cive*, it is true, defined liberty in a mechanical style as the absence of obstacles to motion. But he granted liberty to the son or slave of the family to the extent that he would not be prevented from 'doing all he can and trying every move that is necessary to protect his life and health'. Hence, he relativized the opposition of liberty and slavery: both a free man and a slave *served*, but the scope of that service differed: the former served only a commonwealth and the latter also his or her fellow citizen. Quentin Skinner argues that in his earlier presentation of civil science in *Elements of Law* (1641) and *De Cive* (1642) Hobbes drew on the work of the classical theorists of eloquence, Cicero and Quintilian, and reacted to them. Indeed, it is possible to recognize that attitude in Hobbes, who reacted tactlessly (probably intentionally) to that type of classicism.[89] The very frontispiece of *De Cive* shows 'Sapientia' quoting from the Bible: 'Pro. 8:15. *Per me Reges regnant et legum conditores iusta decernunt*' ('By me kings reign, and rulers decree what is just').[90] However, notwithstanding his stated pursuit of wisdom and his critique of rhetoric, Hobbes's own method remained largely rhetorical in this and other passages.[91] Skinner notes Hobbes's change of heart in *Leviathan*, in which he praises rhetoric. He also suggests that the reason for this change of

88 Hobbes, *Leviathan*, Noel Malcolm (ed.), ch. 21, p. 326.

89 That lack of tact is termed by Skinner 'satirical deflation'. Skinner, '"Scientia Civilis" in Classical Rhetoric and in the Early Hobbes', p. 85.

90 The original frontispiece is reproduced in Thomas Hobbes, *De Cive, The Latin Version*.

91 'True Wisdom is simply the knowledge [scientia] of truth in every subject' Hobbes, 'Epistle Dedicatory', in *On the Citizen*, p. 4.

heart can be inferred from Hobbes's comment in *Behemoth* that the Civil War was a triumph of rhetoric over rationality, the inference being that the former (rhetoric) 'cannot after all be safely ignored'.[92] I wish to add that Hobbes's confidence in the power of his scientific method of necessity in his masterpiece may also have played an important part. In *Leviathan*, Hobbes is no longer interested in a response to humanism, and neither does he need to do so, for affirmation of his own mature philosophical method occupied him. At this point, he confides to his readers his view that all human liberty is in the last instance necessary and determined by an omnipotent God. Human actions always proceeded from an individual's will and thus from liberty; 'and yet' every inclination and appetite in human beings responded to a chain of uninterrupted causes – that is 'they proceed from *necessity*'.[93] Hobbes no longer relied on persuasion, but on his own metaphysics of necessity to convince the reader. Though it may appear slightly paradoxical, I am arguing that as Hobbes thought that he had encountered the true *scientia civilis*, and he felt confident about it, eloquence was no longer a threat, but a useful tool.[94] The story of Hobbes's progressive detachment of his critique to rhetoric is therefore arguably a narrative about his final ability to incorporate the doctrine of necessity into his political philosophy.

In his study on the evolution of Hobbes's notion of liberty, Quentin Skinner has also shown how it changed up to its final articulation in the Latin version of *Leviathan*. This notion of liberty is substantially the same as the English version, but more concise and clearer:

> When someone, due to fear of shipwreck, throws his goods into the sea, he does it willingly, and if he had wished he could have avoided doing it. Therefore he did it *freely*. So too, a man who pays a debt out of fear of imprisonment pays it *freely*.[95]

92 Skinner, 'Scientia Civilis', p. 93; Hobbes, *Behemoth or the Long Parliament*.

93 Hobbes, *Leviathan*, Noel Malcolm (ed.), ch. 21, p. 326. (emphasis by Hobbes).

94 Tom Sorell argues that '*Leviathan* does not break the mould of the civil science that is found in *De Cive* and *The Elements of Law*' which I would agree with; but I would add that the scientific method of necessity is better and more intensely applied, Sorell, 'Hobbes and the Morality Beyond Justice', p. 234; on Hobbes's science of politics but without envisaging a concrete evolution of method, see the classic, M. M. Goldsmith, *Hobbes's Science of Politics* (New York: Columbia University Press, 1966). Strikingly, Goldsmith did no see Hobbes operating within a system of metaphysical necessity, which Goldsmith attributed only to Kant ('Hobbes does not anticipate Kant's attempt to formulate a necessary system of categories'), p. 43.

95 The point Hobbes's conciseness in translation by Skinner; Hobbes quoted by Skinner, and his translation, Skinner, *Hobbes and Republican Liberty*, p. 137.

Skinner also points out the crucial distinction Hobbes added to his previous discussions of liberty following his debate with Bramhall. The impediment to freedom becomes now an 'external impediment', and liberty 'the absence of external impediments' that Hobbes contrasts with the 'intrinsical limitations' of the nature of things.[96] I want to benefit from Skinner's point in my argument about Hobbes's doctrine of necessity. According to Hobbes, there was no scope for freedom in the constitution of the things – that is, internally – since things or human beings were only responding to how they were:

> But when the impediment of motion, is in the constitution of the thing it selfe, we use not to say, it wants the Liberty; but the Power to move; as when a stone lyeth still, or a man is fastened to his bed by sickeness.[97]

Due to its intrinsic limitations, Hobbes finds no relevant difference between the constitution of the thing (the stone) and the constitution of the commonwealth. The issue is not lack of freedom but intrinsic limitation by the given nature. The configuration of the commonwealth determines citizens' actions:

> When therefore our refusal to obey, frustrates the End for which the Sovereignty was ordained; then there is no Liberty to refuse: otherwise there is.[98]

Beyond what he termed the 'internal' way of being of things, Hobbes's progressive mastery of the doctrine of necessity enables him to identify the metaphysical existence of people, things and events weaved together by a series of necessary causes. Obedience to the civil laws that in fact impose external impediments, Hobbes explains, represents an internal limitation to which the citizen has consented freely. To accept the terms of the covenant and submit to them (despite fear) means to act freely, even in the case of the individual who has been conquered.[99] Although citizens find themselves compelled to obey and submit to external, physical limitations, that

[96] Hobbes quoted by Skinner, *Hobbes and Republican Liberty*, p. 130; 'The water is said to descend *freely*, or to have *liberty* to descend by the channel of the river, because there is no impediment in that way, but not across, because the banks are impediments. And though the water cannot ascend, yet men never say it wants the *liberty* to ascend, but the *faculty* or *power*, because the impediment is in the nature of the water, and intrinsical.' Hobbes letter to Newcatle responding to Bramhall, quoted in Skinner, *Hobbes and Republican Liberty*, p. 132.

[97] Hobbes, *Leviathan*, Noel Malcolm (ed.), ch. 21, p. 324.

[98] Hobbes, *Leviathan*, Noel Malcolm (ed.), ch. 21, p. 338.

[99] Skinner notes Hobbes's assumption 'that the idea of acting willingly and the idea of acting freely are simply two names for the same thing', Skinner, *Hobbes and Republican Liberty*, p. 138.

necessity is the consequence of their free previous acceptance. However, Hobbes added further depth in terms of metaphysical determinism to the reasoning with his idea that 'liberty and necessity are consistent'. An individual that, e.g., submits to a conqueror does so freely. But the chain of necessary causes, involving will, desires and inclinations by which he or she ends up in that position have in fact been necessary. 'So that to him that could see the connexion of those causes, the *necessity* of all mens voluntary actions, would appeare manifest.'[100] And all this reasoning seems to originate in Hobbes's faith that behind that necessity was the very will of God – that is, its providence, understood in the peculiar physicalist way he increasingly conceived it:[101]

> And therefore God, that seeth, and disposeth all things, seeth also that the *liberty* of man in doing what he will, is accompanied with the *necessity* of doing that which God will, & no more, nor lesse.[102]

Hobbes's theology and philosophy of necessity enables him to employ this thick sense of 'liberty as necessity' by which he avoids conflicts between an individual's free will and God's superior will, and thus attempts to dispel the mystery of human freedom. These two wills, he suggests, will always identify, no matter how unaware we human beings are of that fact. Hobbes seems sincerely content with his (re)discovery of the doctrine of necessity, which effectively allowed him to make political obligations a great deal more stringent, and this within a Christian cosmology. But to him only appears to have escaped the deterministic overtones of the theory, incompatible with a commitment to Christian freedom and that that, in fact, appears to be non-Christian in flavour, as attested to by the general appraisal of his theory as materialistic or atheistic.

In other places of *Leviathan,* his understanding of freedom is less deterministic. In a commonwealth, the liberty of each subject consisted in the absence of regulation by the law, which could not regulate all actions. Thus, 'it followeth neessarily, that in all kinds of actions by the laws praetermitted, men have the Liberty of doing what their own reasons shall suggest for the most profitable to themselves'.[103] Crucially, liberty was not to be found

[100] Hobbes, *Leviathan*, Noel Malcolm (ed.), ch. 21, 326. (emphasis Hobbes).

[101] Malcolm, 'Editorial Introduction', to Thomas Hobbes, *Leviathan*, p. 180; see on this question also, Agostino Lupoli, 'Hobbes and Religion without Theology' in A. P. Martinich and Kinch Hoekstra (eds.), *The Oxford Handbook of Hobbes* (Oxford University Press, 2016).

[102] Hobbes, *Leviathan*, Noel Malcolm (ed.), ch. 21, p. 326.

[103] Hobbes, *Leviathan*, Noel Malcolm (ed.), ch. 21, p. 328.

in the total absence of laws or in exemption from the law. This would be 'absurd': laws and the sword were essential to the commonwealth.[104]

As noted in the first section of this chapter, Hobbes's definition of 'the right of nature' as 'the Liberty each man hath to use his power, as he will himselfe, for the preservation of his own Nature' possesses a strong connotation of justice as necessity in keeping with traditional natural law. To preserve oneself is a normative principle of human nature, and human beings are not free to disdain it: self-preservation is, as it were, in the constitution of human nature. To use one's power to preserve oneself is right and just because it is necessary, and vice versa. Hobbes notes that he considered 'Liberty' in this context as an 'absence of externall Impediments', which, he adds, might exist ('which Impediments, may oft take away part of a mans power to do what hee would do') but 'cannot hinder him from using the power left him, according as his judgment and reason, shall dictate him'.[105] Hobbes seems to suggest that the right of nature to require preservation prevails, no matter what external impediments exist. The liberty to act to give effect to the power of self-preservation accordingly takes precedence over any form of obedience to the law. Civil laws that prevent preservation appear to be the only case in which natural liberty prevails in the commonwealth.

3.2.6 *Faith and Necessity*

In the third part of *Leviathan*, 'Of a Christian Common-wealth', Hobbes set out to deduce from Biblical texts 'all rules and precepts necessary to the knowledge of our duty both to God and man', the rights of the sovereign and the duties of the citizen. His interpretation was undertaken on the basis of natural reason alone, 'without Enthusiasm, or supernaturall Inspiration'.[106] This was followed by an agonistic critique of divines, martyrs, saints and clerics from almost all ages, the doctors of the Church included, for coveting the power that, as Hobbes argued in the *Leviathan*, belonged, by the will of God, to the Christian sovereign alone.[107] The

104 Hobbes, *Leviathan*, Noel Malcolm (ed.), ch. 21, p. 328. See about this, also Skinner 'Thomas Hobbes's Antiliberal Theory of Liberty'.

105 Hobbes, *Leviathan*, Noel Malcolm (ed.), ch. 14, p. 198.

106 Hobbes, *Leviathan*, Noel Malcolm (ed.), ch. 12, p. 186; ch. 32, p. 584.

107 Still, Hobbes's critique to the Fathers of the Church is mild compared to Jean Barbeyrac's acrid comments, mentioned before, Barbeyrac, 'An Historical Account of the Science of Morality'. An interpretation of Hobbes's purge of doctrine as a project to eliminate fears of the afterdeath and traces of the religion of the gentiles in Tuck, 'The Civil Religion of Thomas Hobbes'.

civil law or secular law is thus made divine law, and a commonwealth's sovereign is the representative of God on Earth.

The fourth key usage of the principle of necessity is in this third part of the book the analysis of Luke 10:42, *unum est necessarium*, in particular in the last chapter entitled 'Of What Is *Necessary* for a Mans Reception into the Kingdome of Heaven'.[108] Hobbes walked well-trodden paths in this part, rehearsing historical arguments made by secularist authors against the mendicants in the famous thirteenth century controversy that occurred after the foundation of the Dominican and Franciscan orders.[109] In a word, Hobbes's disparaging comments amounted to the assertion that a believer 'needs no Witnesse', hence martyrdom and other testimonies of faith were meaningless unless one were engaged in the conversion of 'infidels'.[110] The works of William of Saint Amour, the main secular controversialist in the mendicants' affair, were ostensibly obscure and yet apparently well known in the period, as Hugo Grotius's correspondence also proves.[111] Notwithstanding Hobbes's familiarity with the secularist textual tradition, his central argument as to the transformation of the civil commonwealth into a church entailed the reduction of faith to two articles by means of his doctrine of necessity.[112] 'All that is Necessary *to*

108 'And she had a sister called Mary, which also sat at Jesus' feet, and heard his word. But Martha was cumbered about much serving, and came to him, and said, Lord, dost thou not care that my sister hath left me to serve alone? Bid her therefore that she help me. And Jesus answered and said unto her, Martha, Martha, thou art careful and troubled about many things: but one thing is necessary: and Mary hath chosen that good part, which shall not be taken away from her.' *The Holy Bible, King James Version*; see also Lupoli, 'Hobbes and Religion Without Theology'

109 Thomas of York, 'Traktat Eines Franziskans zur Verteidigung der Mendikanten Gegen Wilhelm von St. Amour vom Jahre 1256/1257 "Manus, Qui Contra Omnipotentem Tenditur,"' in *Bettelorden und Weltgeistlichkeit*, Max Bierbaum (ed.) (Münster und Westfalen: Aschendorffschen Buchhandlung, 1920); Georges de Lagarde, *La Naissance de l'esprit Laïque. Au déclin du Moyen Age*, Third edition, vol. I (Louvain, Paris: Nauweelaerts, 1956); Andrew Traver, *The Opuscula of William of Saint-Amour. The Minor Works of 1255–1256*, Beiträge zur Geschichte der Philosophie und Theologie des Mittelalters. Neue Folge 63 (Münster: Aschendorff Verlag, 2003); William of Saint-Amour 'De Periculis Novissimorum Temporum', with a Translation and Introduction by G. Geltner, Dallas Medieval Texts and Translations (Paris, Leuven, Dudley: Peeters, 2008).

110 Hobbes, *Leviathan*, Noel Malcolm (ed.), ch. 42, p. 788.

111 Hugo Grotius answered to his friend Jean de Cortes in 1633 that he was right to state that the works of William of St Amour belonged to obscure matters and come to light by public custom (Opera Gulielmi de Sancto Amore, et quae ad res illius temporis, ut recte dicis, obscuras pertinent, in lucem protrahi ex usu est publico.) Hugo de Groot, *Briefwisseling van Hugo Grotius*, vol. 5 ed. B.L. Meulenbroeck (The Hague, Martinus Nujhoff), p. 133.

112 See on this Noel Malcolm.

Salvation, is contained in two Vertues, *Faith in Christ*, and *Obedience to Laws*.' There was no law more divine than the law of nature, which could be narrowed down to obedience to 'our Civill Soveraigns'.[113] Hobbes's famous conclusion was that all the faith required to achieve salvation was encapsulated in the statement that 'Jesus is the Christ'. Nothing more, but nothing less. 'Therefore, this Article alone is faith sufficient to life eternall; and', he added, crucially, 'more than sufficient is not Necessary'.[114]

To conclude this review of the main uses made by Hobbes of the doctrine of necessity in *Leviathan*, I will mention one significant principle from the last section of the book about the politics of knowledge, in which Hobbes problematized the term *hypostasis*. This was his own critique of the Fathers of the Church as they tried to reason about the faith, ironically enough given his own invitation to do the same.[115] It appears only in the Latin version of *Leviathan* in '*De regno tenebrarum*', translated by Noel Malcolm as follows:

> It is indeed true that there is no word in the Greek language corresponding to the word "persona". Yet there was no need (*Necesse tamen non erant*) for them to use the word "hypostasis", since there was no need to explain the mystery (*cum necesse non esset ut mysterium explicaretur*).[116]

Since the theory developed in *Leviathan* with regard to Nature, God, or the Civil Sovereign, was determined in a frame of thought establishing a chain of causes, Hobbes, as noted above, did not assess whether things were good or evil, but whether they were or not necessary.[117] In this sense, necessity was both a value judgment, about 'scientific' truth, and about how things were or ought to be in a commonwealth of human beings.

Chapter 2 has set forth an argument as to the likely inspiration of Hobbes's doctrine of necessity in the work of Avicenna and other Parisian theologians that borrowed from him, and has noted its characteristic of

113 Hobbes, *Leviathan*, Noel Malcolm (ed.), ch. 43, pp. 930–932 (emphasis Hobbes).

114 Hobbes, *Leviathan*, Noel Malcolm (ed.), ch. 43, p. 938; p. 942.

115 That after the 1690s a natural history of religion evolved as a Hobbesian genre among heterodox writers, sceptical of doctrines asserted on Church councils and defending heresy as 'free opinion' in Collins, *In the Shadow of Leviathan*, p. 321.

116 Hobbes, *Leviathan*, Noel Malcolm (ed.), ch. 46, pp. 1068–1069. He despaired: 'But I am afraid that it is impossible to bring the Universities to such a compliance with the actions of state, as is necessary for the business.' Also a diatribe against the same tendency at the university to exceed the boundaries of what was 'necessary' for one to know and instead start disputations 'against the necessary power of the sovereign' in Hobbes, *Behemoth or the Long Parliament*, p. 55.

117 Hobbes, *Leviathan*, Noel Malcolm (ed.), ch. 42, p. 916.

placing the body and its needs at the heart of natural, moral and political philosophy. Chapter 3 has described core aspects of the doctrine of necessity in Hobbes's philosophical work and has explored the doctrine as applied in *Leviathan.* Hobbes seems to rely on a metaphysical principle of necessity that shapes existing things and causal processes, such as human beings' free will, and endows them with normativity, such as the liberty to preserve oneself, as an individual or a commonwealth. Moreover, with the complete adoption of the doctrine of necessity in *Leviathan* Hobbes also endorses a deterministic view of human freedom. The chapter has shown that the doctrine of necessity reverberates at all levels of Hobbes's work and culminates in consideration of how it fulfils the decree of God in *Leviathan.*

4

Reformers on the Necessary Knowledge

4.1 Useful Knowledge as the Only Necessary Knowledge: Benjamin Worsley in Context

G. E. Aylmer, later Charles Webster and, more recently, Thomas Leng have all made efforts to rescue Benjamin Worsley (1618–1677) from undeserved obscurity.[1] Worsley was a surgeon, a speculator, a scientist and a civil servant. In the 1640s he became a prominent member of the circle around Samuel Hartlib, who was an intelligencer and ideologue for the Protestant universal cause of knowledge and Independency. In August 1650 the Rump Parliament appointed Worsley as secretary to the new Council of Trade. This organ functioned until the end of 1651, during which time the first Navigation Act was enacted. In 1668 Worsley became a member 'of the select committee on trade, assistant to the Secretary of the Trade Council in 1670, and finally himself Secretary and Treasurer to the Council for Trade and Foreign Plantations of 1672'.[2] As a nonconformist, he resigned from his post the following year, when the Test Act of 1673 excluded Independents, Catholics and other nonconformists from civil service. He was replaced by no other than John Locke. The pith of Worsley's and Locke's fellowship may easily be described by references to the themes of nature, duty to the public, and the scientific study of economy through plantations and the laws of trade. These issues were also of intense concern to English Reformers in the mid-seventeenth century, as this chapter explores.

In several ways, Benjamin Worsley epitomized the new ethos of the Reformers – that informal group of post-Puritan and Protestant ideologues

[1] G. E. Aylmer, *The State's Servants: The Civil Service of the English Republic, 1649–1660* (Boston: Routledge & Kegan Paul, 1973), p. 270; Webster, *The Great Instauration*; Thomas Leng, *Benjamin Worsley (1618–1677). Trade, Interest and the Spirit in Revolutionary England* (Suffolk: The Royal Historical Society, The Boydell Press, 2008).

[2] Aylmer, *The State's Servants*, p. 271.

that managed to control English cultural and political life during the two decades between the Civil Wars and the Restoration and, in some respects, even beyond that point. Worsley had no personal wealth. His innumerable projects and the industrious life he led did not help him increase his fortune; he proved unable to make one and was possibly uninterested in doing so. In a eulogy of sorts, Lady Ranelagh (1615–1691), the famous sister of Robert Boyle, sent his brother a letter of condolence when Worsley, his devoted friend, and Henry Oldenburg (1618–1677), the German first Secretary of the Royal Society, died around the same time in September 1677: '[t]hey have left noe blot upon their memorys (unless their not having dyed rich may goe for one)'.[3] Worsley also lacked prominent social status and, although he claimed he had a degree from Trinity College Dublin, it appears that he completed no formal education beyond that of a seven-year apprenticeship to a barber surgeon. But Worsley was a man of many parts. Moreover, his hands-on approach was significant within the Reformer milieu, which was characterized by an 'Adamic epistemology', in Joanna Picciotto's expression, meaning that they regarded productive labour as the means of achieving the perfect combination of experience or experiment and innocence in life.[4] John T. Young relates how experiments occupied much of Worsley's time at periods, such as during his alchemical mission to the Netherlands.[5] Moreover, experiments were the door to productive knowledge. Useful knowledge thus became the only knowledge necessary[6] and represented precisely the theological content that the expression evokes.

Through the lens of his correspondence, one may often observe Worsley engaged in an activity of extracting secrets and experimental demonstrations from others for the greater good of the Reformers' cause – the service of the Lord and spiritual service – that was to be realized through

[3] 'Lady Ranelagh to Boyle 11 September 1677', in Michael Hunter, Antonio Clericuzio and Lawrence M Principe (eds.), *The Correspondence of Robert Boyle vol. 4, 1668–1677* (London: Pickering & Chatto, 2001), p. 454.

[4] Joanna Picciotto, *Labors of Innocence in Early Modern England* (Cambridge: Harvard University Press, 2010), p. 4.

[5] Young, *Faith, Medical Alchemy and Natural Philosophy*, generally Chapter 7.

[6] In a letter to his tutor, Robert Boyle stated as much: 'The other human studies I apply myself to, are natural philosophy, the mechanics and husbandry, according to the principles of our new philosophical college, that values no knowledge, but as it hath a tendency to use.' According to the editors of Boyle's correspondence this is the first mention of the Invisible College. Boyle to Isaac Marcombes, 22 October 1646, in *The Correspondence of Robert Boyle vol 1, 1636–61*, p. 42.

very concrete projects.[7] In his charmingly millenarian way, in expectation of the transformation of society, Worsley was something of a genius of creativity, industriousness and innocence. Intelligent and powerful people around him, such as Hartlib, John Dury (1596–1680), Robert Boyle, Sir Henry Vane (1613–1662) and the first Earl of Shaftesbury (1621–1683), obviously respected him.[8]

The scientific and commercial community of the Hartlib circle developed ideas for educational reformation and economic revival during the 1640s. They were first inspired by French Huguenots proposals, importantly by Pierre le Pruvost, that contemplated both the resources of the colonies, such as fishing and husbandry, and the poverty and unemployment at home. When the proposals proved to give too much control over natural resources and land to the state and to foreigners, the Reformers themselves wary of the old system of royal patents, put on their thinking hats.[9] Worsley assumed a leadership role on the question of colonial trade. The Reformers' writings show fear of the state – a feeling that private owners had to be free. However, as Kevin Dunn writes, at the same time they suffered from 'a fear of the private' that the private Corporation embodied.[10] This dichotomy led the Reformers to explore groundbreaking avenues by which to forge a relationship between private and public interest. Their approaches embody the ideal of mutual support among the communion of saints within millenarian visions of prosperity of the nations and mankind – 'mens salvation and peoples good' – without losing sight of

7 Worsley's sojourn in the Netherlands had the aim of obtaining from the chemist Johan Glauber a process to extract gold from tin scoria that, according to the mediator in the negotiations, would serve well 'the Commonwealth of England', see Young, *Faith, Medical Alchemy and Natural Philosophy*, p. 226; Worsley's letters, e.g. to William Potter, the inventor and real money expert of the period are an attempt to learn from his ideas and thus 'making good the rich promises of God to his people', and at once to improve Potter's spirit. 'Then give me also leave to say I care not much for your demonstrations, nor doe indeed weigh them so much as I do your spirit.' Copy Extract in Scribal Hand A, Benjamin Worsley to Potter, 17 November 1658, Ref. 26/33/6A-B; Copy letter In Scribal Hand A, Benjamin Worley to Potter, 7 April 1658, 39/2/62A-63B in M. Greengrass, M. Leslie, M. Hannon (eds.), *The Hartlib Papers*, Published by The Digital Humanities Institute, University of Sheffield [available at: www.dhi.ac.uk/hartlib]

8 This appears, among other places in Hartlib's correspondence.

9 Webster, *The Great Instauration*, p. 227; p. 370–372; M. J. Braddick and M. Greengrass (eds.), and Introduction, *The Letters of Sir Cheney Culpeper (1641–1657)*, (Royal Historical Society Camden Series, vol. VII, 1999), p. 133; p. 227; p. 243.

10 Kevin Dunn, 'Milton among the Monopolists: *Areopagitica*, Intellectual Property and the Hartlib Circle', in Mark Greengrass, Michael Leslie and Timothy Raylor (eds.), *Samuel Hartlib and Universal Reformation: Studies in Intellectual Communication* (Cambridge: Cambridge University Press, 1994), p. 182.

the practical aim of achieving a thriving English economy, following the example of success offered by the Dutch. The different paths to God, and 'the *unum necessarium*' – that is 'Jesus Christ' – thus emerged within a unified religious framework of natural science, technology and material wealth that justified 'the great Necessity of a generall Reformation of Common Learning'.[11] The stress among the most important writings by the Reformers lay in distribution of knowledge in the case of Hartlib, national success through international trade in that of Worsley and 'Englands prosperity' in William Potter's writings on money, to name only three of the abundant strands of thought on the issue of government current during this intellectually fertile period.[12]

The most characteristic feature of the Reformers' writings is how they viewed the path to achieving greatness, wealth, honour and truth as being no longer rooted in humanist-inspired worldviews, let alone in humanist virtue. Rather, they look at once to science and to the dramatic increase in material exchanges and wealth that trade, bureaucracy and even chemistry could bring about. They constitute a sort of hiatus in the history of natural law, but quite a fascinating one. The aim of their endeavours was still theological, the philosophy in some cases Neoplatonist, but despite the recurrence of the mantra of 'light' in their writings, their working method was authentically empirical. It revolved around the study of the material aspects of life for practical purposes. There is no longer interest in normative ideals that entitle the individual to a natural right to food from their neighbours' overly abundant harvest. The concern now lay in how to produce scientifically better and more abundant food, more professional shipping for trade, and crucially, more credit money for coping with debt and increasing trade amidst a money shortage problem in England that

[11] *The Letters of Sir Cheney Culpeper*, p. 244. 'Reformation of Schooles Designed in Two Excellent Treatises. The First whereof summarily sheweth the great Necessity of a generall Reformation of Common Learning' is the title of one of Jan Comenius's texts translated into English in 1642, Ref. 14/1/2A-B, 1642 in *The Hartlib Papers*. See also, John Amos Comenius, *Unum Necessarium*, Vernon H. Nelson (trans.) (Winston-Salem: Moravian Archives, 2008) p. 25.

[12] Samuel Hartlib, *Considerations tending to the happy accomplishment of Englands reformation in church and state: humbly presented to the piety and wisdome of the high and honourable court of parliament* (London, s.n., 1647); Benjamin Worsley, *The Advocate* (London, printed by William Du-Gard, printer to the Council of State, 1651). Early English Books Online Text Creation Partnership, 2011 http://name.umdl.umich.edu/A96937.0001.001; William Potter, *Humble Proposals to the Honorable the Councell for Trade: And all merchants and others who desire to improve their Estates* (London: pr. for Edward Husband, 1651). Early English Books Online Text Creation Partnership, 2011 http://name.umdl.umich.edu/A55526.0001.001

had been going on for more than half a century. Carl Wennerlind writes that the alchemists, with their experiments all over Europe to transmute base metals into gold, were only sent packing once an efficient credit system became operational in late seventeenth-century London.[13] What we regard today as nonsense (the endeavour to produce gold through alchemy) can also be viewed as a symptom of the urgency of the need for economic growth and of the intellectual and philosophical climate in which credit money was invented.

Together with Jan Amos Comenius (1592–1670), Hartlib was 'chief architect of parliamentary policy' during the Long Parliament and beyond until the Restoration.[14] In the 1960s Hugh Trevor-Roper argued, spectacularly, that three foreigners had been the philosophers of the Puritan Revolution: Comenius, Hartlib and Dury.[15] The first was a Bohemian and the other two were exiles from Catholic Prussia – but not fully foreign. Hartlib probably had an English mother and Dury was of Scottish origin.[16] Trevor-Roper took the view that it was Comenius, Hartlib and Dury's Baconianism combined with the expectation of the Millenium – or in methodological terms, their belief in 'useful knowledge', messianism and metaphysics – that proved to be, in the late 1630s, a source of inspiration for the English country party that was at once Puritan and Baconian.[17]

[13] Carl Wennerlind, 'Credit-Money as the Philosopher's Stone: Alchemy and the Coinage Problem in Seventeenth-Century England' 35 *History of Political Economy* (2003).

[14] Michael Hunter, Antonio Clericuzio and Lawrence M. Principe. 'Samuel Hartlib (born c. 1600–died 1662), German Educationalist, Social Reformer, Author.' *Electronic Enlightenment Biographical Dictionary*. Robert McNamee et al. (ed.) Vers. 3.0. University of Oxford. 2018. Web. 2 Dec. 2019.

[15] Hugh Trevor-Roper, 'Three Foreigners: The Philosophers of the Puritan Revolution' in *The Crisis of the Seventeenth Century* (Indianapolis: Liberty Fund). Hartlib apparently did not recognize Hobbes's peculiar talent. He described him as 'a witty brain' and seemed to have trusted others on the basis of derisive comments of his skills on mathematics. Notes by Hartlib Ref. 30/4/53A-60B; 29/5/29A-42B; 30/4/81A-85A: 81B, 83B in *The Hartlib Papers*.

[16] Dury was author of tracts dealing with subjects as suggestive as 'How to travel profitably in the law' and in '*Digitus dei* a proof that the lost Jewish nation had been found among the natives in American and of the cruelty of the Spaniards towards them' and was more generally an Irenist and architect of Protestant reunion. Peter Damian-Grint, 'Reverend John Dury (born 1596–died 1680), Scottish Churchman, Theologian.' *Electronic Enlightenment Biographical Dictionary*. Ed. Robert McNamee et al. Vers. 3.0. University of Oxford. 2018. Web. 2 Dec. 2019. The tracts are named in Hartlib's correspondence in the collection *Electronic Enlightenment Scholarly Edition of Correspondence*, ed. Robert McNamee et al. Vers. 3.0. University of Oxford. 2018. Web. 1 Dec. 2019.

[17] Trevor-Roper, 'Three Foreigners'; G. H. Turnbull, *Hartlib, Dury and Comenius: Gleanings from Hartlib's Papers* (Liverpool: University Press of Liverpool, 1947).

John T. Young, Carl Wennerlind and Lawrence Principe have studied the intellectual underpinnings of the Hartlib circle's alchemical project, thus contributing to our understanding of its broader spiritual and social endeavours. On the one hand, the Hartlib circle pursued scientific understanding of the world in all its complexity through the lenses of devout Protestant Reformers. In other words, they saw the world as the unified work of God the Creator and were, generally, wary of relativism and fearful of the sheer amount of information that the world provided. On the other, the experiments they undertook for decades, in all seriousness, to transform base metals into gold and silver aimed at generating the bullion that – shrewd economic thinkers and experienced merchants as they were – they knew England was in desperate need of.[18]

4.1.1 *Jan Comenius and Sir Cheney Culpeper on Nature*

The recovery of the dominion over nature would accomplish the Reformers' ideal about man's return to a state of grace. That was the true end and reward of the scientific study of nature, as famously expressed by Francis Bacon (1561–1626) and echoed by John Milton (1608–1674) in *Paradise Lost*.[19] This way of linking knowledge and dominion over nature had been, of course, the endeavour of theologians and philosophers since at least the thirteenth century. Thomas Aquinas, whose theology both Reformers and John Locke knew well, wrote about this question four centuries earlier in his *Summa theologiae*. In the Garden of Eden, Aquinas remarked, human beings did not need animals for survival, clothing or vehicle. They got their food from the tree of Paradise, they were naked without suffering of lust and other sins and the strength of their bodies made vehicles unnecessary. However, human beings needed animals 'for acquiring an experimental knowledge of their nature, signified by the fact that God put animals in their charge to give them names, which designated their nature'.[20] Dagmar Capková has noted that the new perspective with regard to theological

[18] Young, *Faith, Medical Alchemy and Natural Philosophy*; Wennerlind, 'Credit-Money as the Philosopher's Stone'; among other books by Principe, see Lawrence M. Principe, *The Secrets of Alchemy* (Chicago, London: University of Chicago Press, 2013).

[19] This is the argument of the groundbreaking study by Webster, *The Great Instauration*, 16; 59; Francis Bacon, *The Great Instauration* (New York: Start Publishing, 2012); John Milton, *Paradise Lost*, David Scott Kastan (ed.) (Indianapolis: Hackett Publishing Co., Inc, 2005) Book IV.

[20] 'Indigebant tamen eis ad experimentalem cognitionem sumendam de naturis eorum. Quod significatum est per hoc, quod Deus ad eum animalia adduxit, ut eis nomina imponeret, quae eorum naturas designant.' Aquinas, *Summa theologiae*, I, q. 96 a.1. ad 3.

tradition that the Reformers contributed was that philosophy must abandon its position of '*ancilla theologiae*' and, together with 'politics', become 'its true natural sister'.[21]

The savant Jan Comenius stayed in England between 1641 and 1642 on the invitation of some prominent members of the English Parliament. His *Naturall Philosophie* comprised an amalgam of old and current ideas. As he acknowledged, the aim of the book was to harmonize 'whatsoever truth either Aristotle hath; or Galen, the Chymicks, Campanella and Verulamis (Bacon)'.[22] The observation that 'as there is nothing in the understanding which was not first in the senses, there is nothing in the belief, which was not first in the understanding' is an important empirical and rationalist message contained in the book.[23] Comenius also described in *Naturall Philosophie* the method of learning that might be followed by future Protestant Reformers. Starting with the senses and continuing with reason and the Bible, matter was apprehended through the senses, the spirit (nature) by reason and the light by the Bible. Inspired by Luis Vives and Campanella, this was considered the right order to follow. It intended to throw away the 'Gentiles' that Aristotle embodied in different ways. On the strength of this, Comenius crafted a working definition of 'Nature' for the Reformers:

> But that all these things (created) might continue in their essence, as they were disposed by the wisdom of God, he put into everything a virtue, which they call Nature, to conserve themselves, in their essence, yea, and to multiply, whence the continuation of the creatures into this very day, and this *Moses* intimated.[24]

In *Naturall Philosophie*, the 'spirit' was not something spiritual, but rather it appeared to be that virtue called 'nature'. Nature 'spreading forth her virtue through all things' made it possible for those things to endure over time. Significantly, the aim of scientific study was to discover the divine order *entrusted* to Nature. With this understanding of nature, Comenius, who

21 Dagmar Capková 'Comenius and His Ideals: Escape from the Labyrinth' in Mark Greengrass, Michael Leslie and Timothy Raylor (eds.), *Samuel Hartlib and Universal Reformation. Studies in Intellectual Communication* (Cambridge: Cambridge University Press, 1994), p. 90.

22 Jan A. Comenius, 'Preface' of *Naturall philosophie reformed by divine light, or, A synopsis of physicks by J. A. Comenius* (London: Printed by Robert and William Leybourn for Thomas Pierrepont, 1651). Early English Books Online Text Creation Partnership, 2011, http://name.umdl.umich.edu/A34110.0001.001. I am using the translation of his work produced later to help its popularization as noted by Webster, *The Great Instauration*, p. 113.

23 Comenius, 'Preface', *Naturall philosophie reformed by divine light.*

24 Comenius, *Naturall philosophie reformed by divine light*, p. 16.

was a synthesizer rather than an original, took two important steps: First, the traditional importance of God's providential care of nature receded:

> God's omnipotencie concurring no longer immediately unto particular things, (as before) but nature it self, always spreading forth her virtue through all things, which thing derogates nothing from the Providence of God ... for it comes ... from his power, that such an immutable durability can be put into the universe, through such a changeable mutability of particulars, so that the World is as it were aeternall.[25]

Nature united thus the divine knowledge and matter. In common with the Reformers, Comenius understood 'Nature' as an expression of divine order in the material world, to which God had confided the future of matter – God was not involved in the particulars. In this way, theology lost its pre-eminent place in the circle of knowledge. By means of his second move, Comenius personalized and feminized 'Nature'. That was also important, since he was proposing the revival and approval of a newly conceived atomism, which required a substitute for the Aristotelian category of 'substance'.[26] The 'spirit of nature' would meet that need:

> From the same spirit is the custody of the bounds of nature; for example, that a horse grows not to the bigness of a mountain, nor stays at the smalnesse of a cat.[27]

For Sir Cheney Culpeper (1601–1663), another core member of the Hartlib circle, the true aim, end and center of nature was gold.[28] Hence to 'move the

[25] Comenius, *Naturall philosophie reformed by divine light*, p. 17. Compare with Aquinas, *Summa theologiae*, III, q. 6, art. 1, 'Reply to Objection 1. 'We may consider a twofold order between creatures and God: the first is by reason of creatures being caused by God and depending on Him as on the principle of their being; and thus on account of the infinitude of His power God touches each thing immediately, by causing and preserving it, and so it is that God is in all things by essence, presence and power.'

[26] 'Democritus erred not altogether, in making Atomes the matter of the World: but hee erred in that hee believed, that they were aeternall ... by reason that he was ignorant of that which the Wisdom of God hath revealed unto us, that the Atomes were conglutinated into a mass, by the infusion of the Spirit of life, and began to be distinguished into forms, by the coming in of the light.'; 'For example, the spirit of a dog being included in its seed, when it begins to form the young, doth not form it wings or fins, or hands, &c. because it needeth not those members: but four feet, and other members, in such sort, as they are fit for that use to which they are intended.' Comenius, *Naturall philosophie reformed by divine light*, p. 30; p. 35.

[27] Comenius, *Naturall philosophie reformed by divine light*, p. 35.

[28] 'Nature hauinge (in golde) arriued at her ayme, ende, or center, of simple puritye shee there doethe, nay muste set downe, For the wisdome of God in nature is suche as that Natura nihil facit frustra; yf shee haue once attained her ende, shee there keeps an euerlastinge sabbothe; except (by an ingenuous artiste) shee bee (as it were) drawne backe from her center of reste; Now the better to discouer howe nature is put into a newe motion, it were well

spirit' of nature constituted the goal of natural philosophy (*for motus generat calorem*) in order to arouse it from its slumber and make it produce more, be more fruitful, become more open to scientific study. Culpeper was a lawyer, a private scientist and a civil servant who worked on agrarian and economic reform, natural law and chemistry and who participated in the Parliamentarians' cause to his own economic detriment. He was promoter of the cause of the Palatine, acted as advisor and donor on many of Hartlib's scientific and educational projects and was one of the fifteen members of the Commission that the Rump Parliament established to regulate and promote trade.[29] Culpeper was, with the other members of Hartlib's circle, an enemy of monopolies, of private Corporations and the King, which at once attempted to monopolize trade and conscience.[30] As a consequence of what M. J. Braddick and M. Greengrass have called his 'animist chemical universe', Culpeper deliberated at length on the need to observe the workings of nature.[31] Intriguingly, in relation to these ideas Culpeper referred mostly to the experiments carried out in the Hartlib circle at the time to produce the 'phylosophers stone' or the 'elixir' by which to convert base metals into gold. In its utmost state of purity, nature produced gold; the task of the chemist was thus not to dissolve but to observe how from the impurity 'in her dominions' nature continued 'in motions & action' until it reached the perfection of gold.

> And truly it is vpon these & the like consideration, (touched very sparingly in the bookes) that I haue insisted, nowe these many yeeres, beinge as confidently assured that these distractions & pullinge of nature to peeces,

woorthe our consideration, what are natures endes in all her motions, & (by an vniversall consente of writers) wee shall finde them to be, selfe preseruation, & selfe increase, & this, as by a continuall increase of her owne vigour, soe allsoe by castinge forthe whatsoeuer hathe the nature of enmity againste her.' *The Letters of Sir Cheney Culpeper*, p. 354.

29 M Greengrass (2008, January 03). Culpeper, Sir Cheney (bap. 1601, d. 1663), advocate of political reform and technological innovation. *Oxford Dictionary of National Biography*. Retrieved 11 May 2020. Culpeper's estate suffered greatly from his father's opposition to his support to the Commonwealth.

30 'they (merchants) and all other monopolizinge Corporations of Merchantes, may perhaps finde (ere longe) imploymente inought to defende theire paste incroachements vpon the liberty of the subjectes & truly the monopoly of trade will proue as greate a greeuance (when rightly vnderstoode) as any in this kingdome whatsoeuer, nexte vnto that monopoly of Power which the [K-ing] claimes; & beleue it, nowe wee are pullinge downe of suche monopolies wee shall starte a greate many which yet ly hid in the bushes but the greate monopoly muste firste downe; & then the monopoly of trade, the monopoly of Equity, (a thinge which nowe begins to be lookt into), & the monopoly of matters of conscience & scripture (a very notable monopoly), all these & many more wee shall haue in chace & what one hownde misses another will happen in the sente of & thus will Babilon tumble, tumble, tumble tumble.' Culpeper to Hartlib, 4 March 1645/6, in *The Letters of Sir Cheney Culpeper*, pp. 269–270.

31 M. J. Braddick and M. Greengrass, 'Introduction' in *The Letters of Sir Cheney Culpeper*, p. 144.

> may perhappes be a meanes of our gettinge those rights which natures containes, in that simple perfection wherein wee finde her in all things; but that to exalte nature to the exurebancy which is attributed to the phylosophers stone; there needes onely suche a reincrudation as the seedes of the earthe receiue after theire autumnall ripenes; And yf (insteade of these subtile mannuall operations), wee wowld more obserue the intentions, wayes & actions of nature, wee might (without cumbringe our selues about many thinges) more easily attaine that vnum necessarium, that beste parte, which is soe muche & soe vniversally desired.[32]

In its natural state of repose, nature possessed 'rights', in the sense of benefits, valuable information about natural resources and how to imitate nature in its production of them. The Reformer-scientists desired those rights of nature, and specifically gold.

But as we saw with Comenius, nature took 'nothing from the Providence of God'.[33] Hence in *Natural Philosophy*, the Czech Comenius applied his method of deciphering the Bible through scientific investigation, crucially starting with matter. In this effort 'Nature' as a virtue or spirit connected both ends – empiricism and the Bible. If this did not happen, then true knowledge and wisdom was not acquired. John T. Young quotes also a letter by Worsley to Hartlib from 1657, in which he acknowledged that true analytical and comprehensive knowledge was not acquired if 'the lawes, course & motions, of nature itself' did not produce the harmony of 'the lawes, mysteryes, Revelations & discoveryes spirituall' that always offered 'Constancy, Simplicity, Identity, Homogeneity, Unity'.[34]

4.1.2 *A 'Professor of Necessities'*

In 1668 an elderly Comenius dedicated a booklet entitled *Unum necessarium*, a testament of sorts published in Amsterdam, to the Prince Palatine. In this short work, Comenius wrapped the Neotestamentarian principle in a reformed philosophical doctrine of necessities.[35] He described the life of human beings as a 'perpetual frustration' of 'deep-rooted desires',

[32] Culpeper concluded the paragraph as follows: 'I doe be fore I am aware too much beate upon this subjecte, as beinge that I knowe mr. Woorslyes ingenuity will finde finally woorthe its observation' In this particular quote Culpeper appears to play with the meaning of 'the unum necessarium' suggesting ambiguously also material wealth. Culpeper to Hartlib, 14 August 1649. *The Letters of Sir Cheney Culpeper*, p. 352; pp. 354–355.

[33] Comenius, *Naturall philosophie reformed by divine light*, p. 16.

[34] Young, *Faith, Medical Alchemy and Natural Philosophy*, p. 239.

[35] Comenius, *Unum Necessarium*; Luke 10.42.

and the natural sciences – philosophy and religion – as 'huge labyrinths' from which the wise attempted to escape. Both the sacred and profane history of humankind appeared as a collection of failures on the part of individuals and societies to distinguish between the necessary and the unnecessary in the pursuit of human desires:

> but there always is this one unfortunate root underneath, that men omit NECESSITIES and think, speak and act in regard to NON-NECESSITIES. In reference to this it has been said, "We are ignorant about necessities, because we learn about non-necessities." And in imitation of this: we lack necessities because we work at collecting non-necessities. We do not concern ourselves about necessities, because we occupy ourselves with non-necessities. We do not attain necessary ends, because not sticking to the necessary means, we degenerate to what is impertinent. And so we fall short of our best vows (even if they are kept in the mind), because we are hindered from the *best* by slipping because of inferior things that are only *good*.[36]

The foolishness of Solomon came from tasting both the necessary good and the unnecessary evil, or Nimrod's extension (as the 'hunter of men') of the dominion granted by God to human beings over the fishes, the birds and the animals of the earth, to other men – which could be a veiled criticism of slavery by Comenius.[37] He detailed the practices that he considered unnecessary, such as trampling over human beings' liberty, rule by violence, and the 'Greedy' who 'ignorant of the limit of riches, heap up the goods of this life beyond necessity, and by unnecessary bother about them multiply the labors and troubles of life'.[38]

But what is it that is necessary in everything, and how can it be distinguished from the unnecessary? Or, as Comenius put it, 'how can that one necessary thing be found in such a turmoil of non-necessities?' That was the theory that the Czech wanted to articulate. The modern author of the brief 'Introduction' of *Unum Necessarium* noted that the most valuable part of the text, even comparable to Milton's *Paradise Lost*, is the last chapter.[39] With the perspective offered by the Reformers and Independents' unique philosophical project, the entire endeavour might be taken to epitomize a world that was lost with the Restoration but was yet strangely present in the work of future scientists – among them Locke's. Through

36 Comenius, *Unum Necessarium*, p. 28. The translator notes that it was not clear whether the author was quoting and to what extent.

37 Comenius, *Unum Necessarium*, p. 24.

38 Comenius, *Unum Necessarium*, p. 28.

39 C. Daniel Crews, 'Introduction' in Comenius, *Unum Necessarium*, p. 2.

this wonderfully simple text, Comenius explained the supernatural function of utilitarian science. The point was to find the 'use' of each thing for human beings – i.e. the *unum necessarium* in everything – according to 'the nature of the thing':

> The true definition of each thing must be attended to, also the end of the thing, or the purpose, and how the thing may most suitably be used for its own purpose. For if this is found, it will be that very thing which is most necessary to it.[40]

For example, the use of water, was to 'moisten us'. Hence, 'the one thing necessary for it' was to be humid, liquid and fluid. These utilitarian views were combined with astonishing simplicity with Christ's teachings as they appear in the New Testament: excessive concern with earthly things, excessive desire for power and excessive riches are hindrances. Desires ought to be limited to what is necessary. Comenius also prescribed rules for each individual, university, nation and church and for the whole world, tailored to different spheres of life, in respect of the Neotestamentarian rule of the *unum necessarium*. Interestingly, he started by pointing to the *property* of each one over her own 'body, the mind and the immortal spirit' that each individual ought to value highly 'persuaded that they are your property (your field, so to speak, garden, and paradise)'. One ought to learn to know oneself, and 'use and enjoy' (*uti-frui*) oneself.[41] However, all this should be done while keeping the desires that all normal human beings have under check, without extending 'desires beyond necessity' and being content 'with the necessities that come from the hand of God'.[42] What Comenius was after, perhaps more acutely at the end of his life, was Christian poverty of spirit or detachment of material things endowed with the peculiar features of a utilitarian Protestantism. 'Therefore', wrote Comenius in his Christian Pansophy, 'the art of growing rich in God truly consists in praying and working, in economy and frugality'. He continued:

> I wish nothing else to be understood by this than the perpetual tabulation of necessary things, so that when anyone has an honest desire (for things relating to this or the future life) it may be clear what means he needs, and how these means are to be used, so as to go directly to his goal and always to arrive at it.[43]

[40] Comenius, *Unum Necessarium*, p. 33. Thus, one must 'learn to know the order of the world.' Kerstin Jergus, 'Comenius Jan Amos, 1592–1670' in M.A. Peters eds. *Encyclopedia of Educational Philosophy and Theory*, (Singapore: Springer, 2016) p. 200.

[41] Comenius, *Unum Necessarium*, p. 38.

[42] Comenius, *Unum Necessarium*, p. 41.

[43] Comenius, *Unum Necessarium*, p. 57; on the 'Pansophy' or 'overall wisdom', see Jergus, 'Comenius Jan Amos, 1592–1670'.

That was a written guide, a table, in respect of desires, not only as to which were honest, but also, as to how to satisfy them. Comenius thus transformed the deliberation about necessities into a science. He recommended that in the academies a 'professor of NECESSITIES or of FRUGALITY' would work together with the professors of medicine and theology.[44] Furthermore, in his view the cause of excesses in the government of human society lay in rulers' excesses and in the machinations of pettifogging lawyers that generated 'the labyrinths of law', leading to conflict and absence of peace. He also recalled the words of the German jurist Nicolaus Vigelius (1529–1600) with respect to 'how much damage jurisprudence' was doing to the glory of God and public welfare.[45] The problem was that people sought in the law and in legal process that which was beyond what was necessary – which was, compliance with God's tribunal in individuals' conscience.

Comenius finished the book with a pious prayer in the last chapter (chapter 10), in which he confessed to having found the *unum necessarium*, and again warned against luxuries, which he scorned.[46] His last petition to God in that chapter is as follows: 'Grant me to warn other men properly about these things, and to tell them how foolishly they act when they neglect necessities and give themselves entirely to non-necessities.'[47]

This last book by Comenius, written in simple language, evidence how rich and complex the language of necessities could be for a pious and enlightened seventeenth-century Protestant. Economic, scientific and theological themes belonged together, and the 'professor of necessities' was to communicate them in connection with each other, becoming a moral philosopher in the process. That professor was, in a word, a moral teacher of desires, or of what not to desire if it went beyond necessity, teaching that through the empirical method. Economic prosperity was not about luxury, but about industriousness, frugality and scientific knowledge about what was really necessary.

[44] As well, as a 'professor of laconic eloquence', Comenius, *Unum Necessarium*, p. 57.

[45] About the method of the German lawyer Nicolaus Vigelius see, Harold J. Berman, *Law and Revolution. II: The Impact of the Protestant Reformations on the Western Legal Tradition* (Cambridge: Harvard University Press, 2003), p. 124.

[46] He warned the Moravians, his own people, with the Bohemians, Silesians, Poles and Hungarians: "Luxury ruined the Bohemians," said a wise northern king, who hated luxury. But in a short time the same will have to be said about you, Poland, unless you swiftly come to the one thing necessary, frugality. For the beginning of sins is the haughtiness of Sodom, and an excess of bread and abundance of leisure (Ezek. 16:49)' Comenius, *Unum Necessarium*, p. 85.

[47] Comenius, *Unum Necessarium*, p. 86.

4.1.3 *Robert Boyle: Between Nature and Utilitarian Science*

Faced with the prospect of working alone in the laboratory, a young and precocious Robert Boyle wrote to Worsley in the following terms: 'I intend to court Nature as eagerly as <such a> disaccomodated Solitude will permit me.'[48] Worsley was not only Boyle's friend but also his mentor in chemistry.[49] The young Anglo-Irish Boyle contributed decisively to the making of modern chemistry by developing it as an 'independent, fundamental and philosophical' discipline. He would also become one of the artificers of the Scientific Revolution. What distinguishes Boyle from the outset from the other members of the Hartlib circle was his independence of means. The benefit of his immense wealth – he was the youngest and beloved son of the First Earl of Cork – both facilitated extraordinarily his works as a scientist and as promoter of science, and contributed to a strain of unreality in his character.[50] Young Boyle's conception of a 'Nature' of which he was enamoured in 1647 – according to his correspondence, almost literally – changed rapidly in the years that followed, with new philosophical influences of a more empiricist, quasi-Epicurian and utilitarian bent. Thus, in the unpublished *Of the Study of the Book of Nature* (probably written around 1650), which could be considered his transitional text on the path from being a moralist to becoming a natural philosopher, he summarized what might well be considered one of the core working principles of his philosophy of nature:[51]

> God has furnish't Man with such a Multiplicity of Desires; & whereas other Creatures are content with those few obvious & easily attainable Necessarys that Nature has almost every where provided for them; In Man alone every sense has numerous greedy Appetites, for the most part for Superfluitys & Daintys; that for the Satisfaction of all these various Desires, he might be olblig'd with an inquisitive Industry to range, anatomize & ransacke Nature, & by that concern'd survey come to a more exquisite knowledge of the Workes of it; & consequently to a profounder admiration of the Omniscient Author.[52]

[48] 'Boyle to (Worsley?), late February 1647', in *The Correspondence of Robert Boyle vol I 1636–1661*, p. 49.

[49] Hunter, *Boyle: Between God and Science*, p. 70.

[50] The 1st Earl of Cork was 'the richest man in Britain', Lawrence Principe, 'In Retrospect: the Sceptical Chymist', 469 *Nature* (2011) p. 30; Hunter, *Boyle: Between God and Science.*

[51] The date in Michael Hunter and Edward B. Davis 'Introductory Notes', in *Works of Robert Boyle*, vol. 13 (London: Pickering & Chatto, 2000), p. xxxvii.

[52] Boyle, 'Of the Study of the Booke of Nature', in *The Works of Robert Boyle*, v. 13, p. 156.

Boyle attributed the motive for the manipulation and exploitation of nature to the urge to satisfy the multiplicity of human desires for 'Superfluities' that, crucially opposing Comenius, went beyond 'Necessities'. Knowledge about nature and devotion to the Creator would ensue from this working with nature. In this early text, Boyle declared that only human beings' desires, many superfluous and a source of greed, forced them to plunder nature. In this sense, Boyle was announcing, a century in advance, the theory that would make Adam Smith famous. Chapter 6 analyses this important aspect of Boyle's thinking in detail. 'Since the world is a Temple, Man surely must be the Priest', wrote Boyle some pages before.[53] How can one explain this desire to ransack the very temple in which God was to be adored, given that Boyle was later justly remembered as one of the most pious and good men in England?[54] Arguably, it was the fragmentation of matter and spirit, characteristic of mid-seventeenth century empiricism that explains the 23-year-old Boyle's breathtakingly savage homily. His odd tripartite division of the main assets in a 'man's library', 'the Booke of nature, the book call'd Scripture and the booke of Conscience' makes one suspicious of the separate handling of the different 'books'.[55] For Boyle, the laws of nature, essentially the laws of motion, had nothing to do with conscience, as discussed in detail in Chapter 7 in relation to his more mature texts on nature.

One important way in which the Reformers carved out a space for 'man' and his workmanship in God's creation was through their economic plans and dreams of wealth. But in practice, the issues surrounding riches were not so easy to deal with, as evidenced by the pious Boyle's scruples. He was particularly troubled by his conscience in later life in relation to his financial transactions, about which he was extremely skilled, and his love for a 'morality of cases' was unable to sooth him in his predicament.[56] However,

[53] Boyle, 'Of the Study of the Booke of Nature', in *The Works of Robert Boyle*, v. 13, p. 151.

[54] Hunter, *Boyle: Between God and Science.*

[55] Boyle, 'Of the Study of the Booke of Nature', in *The Works of Robert Boyle*, v. 13, p. 147.

[56] Hunter, 'The Conscience of Robert Boyle'. About Boyle's financial skills, for instance, it is telling that those receiving salaries in the New England Company, mainly missionaries and teachers preaching the Gospel according to its 1662 Charter, asked to be paid in 'necessaries' and not money, since they had difficulties 'how to come by commodities at their needs'. Boyle, representing the Company, wrote ordering a different course of action. A rise of salary was decided that 'will put them to find out a means to accommodate themselves with conveniencys since they shall find soe much more commodities for their mony'. The reason was that 'the way of remitting mony' sent overseas to pay their salary would be put at 25 pounds in advance and thus 'augment the Revenew more considerably than now is'. The plan for improvement of the stock for the Company was undertaken, rather than

it appears that he was entirely untroubled in relation to his scientific work, which he described – and would restate – as plundering the work of creation in pursue of economic gain and satisfaction of 'greedy Appetites'. Moreover, this activity was necessarily preceded by an incredible amount of theoretical work towards the deconstruction of what tradition had considered a sacred understanding of nature. Boyle did, however, suffer from what appear to have been terrible crises of faith. In one of Boyle's interviews with pious men, in order to help him, the Bishop of Salisbury charitably advised him in the summer of 1691 to reject and slight them as 'mere effects of Distempers of the Body or the Brain' declaring that they 'were Mechanical Effects', arising from 'Distempers of the Animal Spirit'.[57] It is not uncommon to find these types of crises of faith occurring at some point in the lives of individuals who lead admirably charitable lives. Hence, they may cast light either on Boyle's saintly life or on the fragmentation of his reason.

4.2 All-Encompassing Human Necessities

4.2.1 Hartlib's 'Office of Publick Address'

Serving God's 'Glory and the Public' was a fundamental aim of the Reformers that found expression in many different projects.[58] Comenius proposed the foundation of a Baconian Universal College in London in *Via Lucis*, a text written during his stay in that city. Their members, dedicated to knowledge and public service, would communicate with colleagues throughout the world, thus forming an 'Invisible College'.[59] Furthermore, in 1635 Hartlib had started a membership list for a Society

the minimalist scheme of working for necessities proposed by the missionaries. 'Boyle to the Commissioners of the United Colonies in New England. 28 April 1669', in Michael Hunter and Edward B. Davis eds. *The Correspondence of Robert Boyle, vol. 4*, p. 133.

57 See Robert Boyle, 'Appendix: The Text of the Interviews' *Robert Boyle (1627–91)* in *Scrupulosity and Science*, p. 90.

58 From the salutation of a letter dated 30.8.1658 to Samuel Hartlib from Peter Figulus (1617–1670), a reformed priest from Bohemia and son in law of Comenius, 'Deare Sir, You refresh my bowells as many times as I see a letter written with your owne hands: I having this for a token of Gods speciall loue to the mankind & especially to the Common Cause of Protestants, if he pleases longe to continue yours & Mr Dury's life: no lesse then Mr Comen*ius* his. Hee being nowe in this his old age very variable & unstable in his resolutions. God helpe us all to serve his Glory & the Public as much as wee can!' Ref. 9/17/20A-22B, in *The Hartlib Papers*.

59 Webster, *The Great Instauration*, p. 49; note the similarity with the Invisible College of international lawyers, Oscar Schachter, 'The Invisible College of International Lawyers' 72 *Northwestern University School of Law* (1977–78).

of Reformation and Correspondence.[60] More broadly, Comenius is largely remembered for developing the Christian philosophy he called 'Pansophy', as mentioned, which had humanist and Neoplatonists roots and sought to achieve universal harmony and provide education to solve the world's conflicts and overcome that 'labyrinth' that a human being was, promoting the universal school as a workshop of humanity, an *officina humanitatis*[61] – thus giving the *officia humanitatis* of the classics a technical and administrative expression.

Charles Webster read in the early exchange of letters (1646–1647) between Boyle and Worsley the beginning of what Boyle also termed the 'Invisible College', an actual scientific association that occurred when Bacon's writings and empirical method were incorporated into Protestant piety, or in other words the *reunion of utilitarianism and utopia*. Although Hunter debates the extent to which Boyle's 'Invisible College' amounted to anything substantial,[62] there is evidence to support the thesis, discussed further in this chapter, that distinctive ideas about commerce and exploitation of the material world as a way to God resulted from the fellowship of Worsley, Boyle and a few others. Far from belittling its importance, Joanna Piccioto suggests that the 'Invisible College' was in a way *everything*: an idea of a sacred corporate persona identified with the intellectual commons that decisively contributed to the formation of a new public sphere in seventeenth-century England.[63] Concern with the public realm was certainly one of main Hartlib's preoccupations. One may add that the 'Invisible College' represents what most visionaries of the new Protestant experimentalists had in common: industriousness, love of science and of humanity, a desire for glory for their country and sincere piety. However, as is the case of any social enterprise, at the end of the day only a handful of individuals were able to share the kind of intense communication that would enable them to be part of such a *sui generis* fellowship as the 'Invisible College'. Their own texts and pamphlets offer glimpses of the complex and rich English public sphere – military, merchants, politicians, the Church and the various social classes – that make this group of intellectual Puritans look, in context, decisively minuscule.

60 Stephen Clucas, 'In Search of "The True Logick": Methodological Eclecticism among the "Baconian Reformers"', in Mark Greengrass, Michael Leslie and Timothy Raylor (eds.), *Samuel Hartlib and Universal Reformation: Studies in Intellectual Communication* (Cambridge: Cambridge University Press, 1994), p. 72.

61 Capková 'Comenius and His Ideals, p. 79; Jergus, 'Comenius Jan Amos, 1592–1670'.

62 Hunter, *Boyle: Between God and Science*, p. 67.

63 Picciotto, *Labors of Innocence*, p. 126.

It is fascinating to observe how this method of experimenting with matter was put at the service of the actual cultural Reformation of England. Samuel Hartlib addressed a discourse to the Court of Parliament, published in 1647 as *Considerations tending to the happy accomplishment of Englands reformation in Church and State.* The gist of the address is the proposal contained in his acclaimed 'Office of Publick Address in Spirituall and Temporall Matters'.[64] However, the tract is also a masterful account of what a reformed commonwealth amounts to and how it should be applied in England, leading one to understand, indeed to explain why, despite the impracticalities involved in the whole scheme of the proposed Office, the Anglo-German Hartlib rose to inspire the men of the Long Parliament.

Hartlib was both scientifically minded and personally unambitious, an expert in trade and in the reformed religion. Despite not being personally wealthy, he acted as a disinterested and generous patron of many artists and scientists. The tract *Considerations* amounts to the strangest combination of piety, Protestantism, and trust in scientific research, putting each individuals' gifts at the service of 'the publick': the commonwealth embracing the particular situation of each citizen through bureaucracy, promotion of industriousness and prosperity. Hartlib depicted one of the goals of the commonwealth as being to establish 'superstructures of Gold, Silver, and Precious Stones' on a spiritual foundation. This idea was couched in a very pedagogical style, in which the arts of 'Trade' (embodied in the marketplace) were to be directed towards the practical organization of the commonwealth. *Considerations* reveals Hartlib to be a genius of Protestant Reformation and a very original thinker – a forerunner in intriguing ways of our present internet society with its systems of communication and exchange and, significantly, an expert in finances in terms of the specific legal-economic instruments he proposed with which to finance the Office, alongside, obviously, his proposal to deprive the official Church of its vast wealth. At the same time, Hartlib's proposals in *Considerations* make it clear why he sometimes trod a fine line between utopianism and being fair game for ridicule and satire and, as Mark Jenner has argued, in need of being able to prove that at least some of his ambitious plans were remotely feasible.[65] However, I wish to highlight here only three of

[64] Webster, *The Great Instauration*; Greengrass, Leslie and Raylor (eds.) *Samuel Hartlib and Universal Reformation.*

[65] Mark Jenner, '"Another *Epocha*"?: Hartlib, John Lanyon and the Improvement of London in the 1650s', in Mark Greengrass, Michael Leslie and Timothy Raylor (eds.), *Samuel Hartlib and Universal Reformation. Studies in Intellectual Communication* (Cambridge University Press, 1994), 343–356; see also Michael Hunter's Review of this book commenting that

the many intriguing points he made – points that, I would contend, also appear in different guises in the work of Locke. First, there is the fact that the reformed commonwealth nurtured the original micro-macrocosm analogies that Young and others mention as being typical of Hartlib's circle and the pansophic method, or in his words:[66]

> The Nationall Covenant doth bind Us for the redresse of our Evils, to settle our Church, our Civill State, and our particular Persons in a Reformed condition.[67]

Second, there is the manner in which Hartlib benefited from Comenius's principle of starting with matter, in order to establish the Erastian principle that the secular magistrate ought to be first in rank, guiding 'men' in their natural condition:

> The Advancement of this Kingdome (the Universall Kingdome of God) is the proper sphere of a Christian reformed Magistrate: First, as he is Gods Vicegerent [sic] over men, as they are in the condition of nature, and inhabitants of the world. Secondly, as hee is a Nursing Father to the Church within his dominion.[68]

Next in order after the magistrate was the communion of saints or 'Administration of Grace' that acted through love and care for the 'mutuall good in Spirituall and Temporall things' of everyone.[69]

Finally, the third principle is his description of the 'Office of Spirituall and Temporall Adresses' that Hartlib introduced as a 'Common Center of Repose', in which everyone may expect 'satisfaction for all their Lawfull desires'.[70] The 'Center' was in essence a place where all members of the commonwealth would 'come to give information of the Commodities which they have to be imparted unto others'.[71] People might need servants, have jobs to offer or seek employment. All these things were 'Usefull and profitable', convenient in 'Spirituall and Bodily Concernments'; the exchange

the projects of Hartlib's preferment 'were in fact speculative and of questionable validity, comparable to the schemes which were to evoke the satire of Swift and others in the late seventeenth and early eighteenth centuries' Michael Hunter, 28 *The British Journal for the History of Science* (1995), p. 469.

66 Young, *Faith, Medical Alchemy and Natural Philosophy*, p. 240.

67 Hartlib, *Considerations*, p. 6.

68 Hartlib, *Considerations*, p. 17.

69 That was expressed in sharing of gifts, knowledge and burdens, the entertainment of which was work of the 'faithfull Ministers of the Gospel' Hartlib, *Considerations*, p. 18.

70 Hartlib, *Considerations*, p. 36.

71 Hartlib, *Considerations*, p. 37.

of scientific research was also contemplated.[72] The process worked by registering and then sharing through the Office information about goods and other things. Hartlib proposed wildly impossible deadlines and times for registration – perhaps influenced here by his Prussian upbringing, albeit that, according to Charles Webster, Hartlib was inspired on this issue by a Frenchman, Théophraste Reanudot (1586–1653) and his *Bureau d'Adresse*.[73] The fact that his grandfather on his mother's side had been an agent of the English Baltic Company and his own father a merchant for the King of Poland, and later owner of a house of credit in Elbing, may have influenced the manner in which he employed the analogy between the Office and a great market:[74]

> If say, we consider this, we shall find what Conveniency the Use of Exchange-meetings doth bring to a Particular sort of Men who are called Merchants; the same, and farre greater will this Office bring to the whole Society of all Men, for all their Mutuall Occassions and Accommodations wherein they have need to incounter with one another so that this Office will be a Center of all mens satisfactions to gaine their Interest in each other for mutuall help.[75]

In a key sentence summarizing his project, Hartlib stated 'that this Office should bee erected properly for the Relief of Humane Necessities'.[76] Hartlib thus exploded the boundaries of a sober theological concept of supply of the needs of human nature for subsistence, with the extremely wide enumeration of services of the Office for relieving 'Humane necessities'. Certainly, human necessities were a matter of public service and it fell to 'none but to a supreme Magistrate to establish such an Office, and to Order it for the Proper Ends and Uses whereunto it should serve'.[77] Hartlib's Office emphasized ideas of love, care and citizenship of the communion of saints and of exchange of human beings' gifts and goods in the reformed commonwealth and even beyond, without necessarily transforming the notion into a question of capital, or materialism in itself, although Webster notes that its function was entirely economic.[78] Perhaps Hartlib was also thinking of something akin to a utopian society of mutual service, closer to modern ideas of social welfare than merely to

[72] Hartlib, *Considerations*, p. 40.
[73] Webster, *The Great Instauration*, p. 67.
[74] G. H. Turnbull, *Samuel Hartlib. A Sketch of His Life and His Relations to J. A. Comenius* (Oxford: Oxford University Press, 1920).
[75] Hartlib, *Considerations*, p. 40.
[76] Hartlib, *Considerations*, p. 37.
[77] However, Hartlib was of course himself applying for funding. Hartlib, *Considerations*, p. 42.
[78] Webster, *The Great Instauration*, p. 375.

charitable activities for the relief of the poor – the latter's welfare, however, was also taken into account in that they would be exempted from payment for registration. The institution was divided into an 'Office of Bodily Addresses', dealing with 'worldly Concernments', an 'Addresse of Accommodations' and an 'Addresse of *Communications*' both dealing with all 'Inward things' relating to 'the Soules of Men', by which Hartlib meant scientific rather than spiritual matters.

Webster described Hartlib's 14-year struggle, aided by his circle, to establish the Office, entailing a constant stream of new schemes, petitions to Parliament and the unsuccessful submission of proposals for funding, and how any hope of establishing the Office died with the Restoration. However, it is also clear that through his correspondence and his circle in effect Hartlib *embodied* the Office of Communication during his almost 40 years in England, from the date he arrived in Cambridge in 1625.[79] The list compiled by Webster from Hartlib's papers, of distribution of labour for a possible installation of the Office in the form of a new college at Oxford University illustrates the importance of Worsley's and Boyle's role in this project. This may have represented the point at which Boyle's 'Invisible College' project melded with the plans for the Office.[80] Here is the list:

Office of Divinity – Dury
Office of Mechanics – Boyle
Office of Agriculture and Traffick – Worsley and Culpeper
Office of Experimental Philosophy – Worsley, Coxe and Boyle
Chamber of Rarities – Caspar Godeman
Medicine – Gerard Boate, Worsley and Justin van Ascher

Worsley's role at the Oxford branch of the Office comprised the department of experimental philosophy, trade and agriculture and medicine and it shows both the esteem in which Hartlib held him, visible often in his correspondence and that of other members of the circle, and the areas in which he was thought to be an asset. Again, nothing would come of these designs. Instead, more realistic ways to serve science and the public were found. Boyle moved to Oxford at the age of 27 and later returned to London as

[79] This was done in the context of adoption of Bacon's writings and assuming as the task of his life the fostering of *Verulamian designes* in his adopted nation. Robert G. Franck, 'John Aubrey, F. R. S., John Lydall, and Science at Commonwealth Oxford', 27 *Notes and Record of the Royal Society of London*, (1973), p. 205; the network of correspondence that he directed during the Commonwealth was known also as 'the Office of Addresses' see, Sarah Hutton, *British Philosophy in the seventeenth Century* (Oxford: Oxford University Press, 2015), p. 56.

[80] Webster, *The Great Instauration*, p. 72.

an established scientist and pursued an academic career as a professional scientist in the company of other natural philosophers of the new science. John Wilkins (1614–1672), Christopher Wren (1632–1723), John Wallis (1616–1703) and William Petty (1623–1687) – who, as a professional civil servant, did not last long at the university – joined forces as members of Oxford's *eruditi* and founded the Oxford Experimental Philosophy Club around 1650 or even before, which seems to have been one of the outcomes and means for the advancement of experimental scientific activity in which the Reformers together with others participated.[81] The young John Locke's name appears in a list of the members of that exclusive Oxford club aimed at bringing about innovation in learning.[82] Locke had been elected to a Junior Studentship at Christ Church Oxford in the summer of 1652, and his membership explains the remarkable empirical research skills demonstrated in his studies of money. After all this empirical approach was the method for the study of things rather than of words.[83]

4.2.2 'A Well-Regulated Plantation'

The other obvious means by which Hartlib's aspirations in respect of his Office could be fulfilled was by pursuing a career as a civil servant. In view of the trajectory of Worsley's earlier career, Aylmer, writing in 1975, marvelled at his 'surprising appointment' to the 1650 Council of Trade, which, I think, can only be explained by reference to Worsley's connections with Hartlib's circle.[84] Aylmer also took a sceptical view of the idea that the obscure Worsley could have been 'an originator of such major legislation' as the Navigation Acts of 1651, the Enumerated Commodities Act of 1663 and the Plantations Duty Act of 1670.[85] His association with the promoter of the 'Office' and his circle, however, provides a quite realistic framework for that type of administrative legislation. Also, a clearer picture of Worsley's role in the passage of the Navigation Acts emerges from the major studies by Charles Webster on the Reformers' project, which shed light on the wider scientific, religious and political purview of the Hartlib circle, and Thomas Leng's in-depth study of Worsley's economic thinking

81 Franck, 'John Aubrey, F. R. S.'
82 Webster, *The Great Instauration*, p. 167; Karen Iversen Vaughn, *John Locke. Economist and Social Scientist* (Chicago: The University of Chicago Press, 1980), p. 6.
83 Capková 'Comenius and His Ideals', p. 83.
84 Aylmer, *The State's Servants*, p. 270.
85 Aylmer, *The State's Servants*, p. 272.

and political career.[86] Among other projects, Worsley was involved, in the mid-1640s, in schemes for developing the productivity of the plantations, particularly those in Virginia, with the goal of resuscitating England's economy. However, as an Independent it was the appearance of the Rump Parliament that afforded him the political opportunity, to secure appointment on 1 August 1650 as secretary to the commissioners in the Council of Trade, the new body for the advancement of trade established by it.[87] He did not delay in taking action in this post. In his words, he had been 'the first sollicitour for the act for the incouragement of navigation, and put the firs fyle to it, and after writ *The Advocate* in defence of it'.[88]

Also one of the members of the above-mentioned Council of Trade from 1650 onwards, in autumn 1645 Culpeper wrote to Hartlib giving his opinion on a memorandum, probably written by Worsley, entitled 'Proffits humbly presented to this Kingdome' – a document he termed the 'Woorsteley-s-Propositions'.[89] A discussion of Culpeper and Dury's comments on them evidences the Reformers' ambiguous attitude towards wealth. While they were literally obsessed with material riches, their proposals were for the most part intended to lead to general prosperity. Their writings on trade constantly discuss material equality among the brethren, social justice, moderation and restraint in terms of 'the necessities of nature' and the state's role in meeting them. Thus, when Culpeper discussed levying new taxes he advised that they ought not to be laid 'upon nothing that serves for sobriety & necessity' and instead on 'all things that have the nature of superfluity' – in other words, 'upon all the merchandise of Babylon'. Merchants and buyers of luxurious products would accordingly carry the burden of taxation, while 'eyther poore, or (yf riche yet) soe sober as to live to, or neere the necessity of nature' would be free.[90] The question of the promotion of the Plantations became, significantly, another of those instances in which promoting the fortunes of private

[86] Thomas Leng, 'Commercial Conflict and Regulation in the Discourse of Trade in Seventeenth-Century England' 48 *The Historical Journal* (2005); the same *Benjamin Worsley (1618–1677)*; the same '"A Potent Plantation Well Armed and Policeed": Huguenots, the Hartlib Circle, and British Colonization in the 1640s', 66 *The William and Mary Quarterly*, Third Series, (2009); the same 'Shaftesbury's Aristocratic Empire' in John Spurr (ed.) *Anthony Ashley Cooper, First Earl of Shaftesbury 1621–1683* (Surrey, Burlington: Ashgate, 2011).

[87] Leng, *Benjamin Worsley (1618–1677)*, p. 13.

[88] Worsley quoted in Webster, *The Great instauration*, p. 464; pp. 462–465; Kelly, 'General Introduction: Locke on Money', p. 7.

[89] Culpeper to Hartlib, n.d. Autumn, 1645, *The Letters of Sir Cheney Culpeper*, p. 243.

[90] Culpeper to Hartlib, 7 November 1649, *The Letters of Sir Cheney Culpeper*, p. 360.

citizens should have worked hand in hand with augmenting the grandeur of England. Culpeper concurred with John Dury, the divine, that the 'Woorsteley-s-Propositions' could not be advanced 'excepte the intereste as well as the authority of a State be ingaged with it' and took the view that what Worsley proposed – a regulated plantation – was in essence what the Hugenot Pierre le Pruvost had proposed years earlier.[91]

In a letter sent that same autumn, Dury explained to Culpeper why it was not a good idea to convince Pruvost to ask for a personal patent for the Plantation project. Two years later, however, Culpeper was still asking Hartlib whether he and Dury had written effectually to 'mons. Pruvoste' about 'whether he will quitte that resolution of taking mens states & disposing of them without theire consente'.[92] Culpeper meant by this the system of land tenure involving taking leases directly from the state set out in the proposal for a state-sponsored American colony developed by Pruvost and his colleague Hugh l'Amy.[93] Webster relates that this aspect of state land leases encountered opposition among the liberal Reformers and was one of the reasons for preventing the realization of the French project. He also discloses that Pruvost and l'Amy had in fact been working on projects for settling French Protestants in Virginia to work with manufacturers of salt and silk and with olive farmers and vineyard owners since 1629. Back then, the creation of a colony named 'Carolina', in which l'Amy would had been 'Receiver general of Rents', was their sole concrete proposal. However, it came to nothing.[94]

Dury explained to Culpeper that while it was a bad idea for the state to grant land leases, the system of patents was, on both personal and practical grounds, not much of an improvement. First, it would look like 'a Monopolie in Trade', and Pruvost was adverse to it. Second, he and his friends were 'strangers' (foreigners) and 'there would bee so much oppositon of Envie & jeallousie against him' that the project would never get off the ground. Finally, no one would want to invest in a private venture like that. Instead, Dury concurred with Pruvost in arguing that the 'Authority of the state' must intervene since only in this way could the 'maintaining of that order by which all the work is to be effectuall' be achieved. Thus, Dury concluded, 'his patent would be an ordinance which the State should make for the Regulating of its owne proffit'. What would, in Dury's view, be the state's interest in the plantation? In what seem like

91 Culpeper to Hartlib, n.d. Autumn, 1645, *The Letters of Sir Cheney Culpeper*, p. 243.
92 Culpeper to Hartlib, 13 October 1647, *The Letters of Sir Cheney Culpeper*, p. 307.
93 Culpeper to Hartlib, 13 October 1647, *The Letters of Sir Cheney Culpeper*, p. 308; Webster, *The Great Instauration*, pp. 371–372.
94 Webster, *The Great Instauration*, pp. 371–372.

notions originating in Pruvost's plan, Dury pointed to the 'advantage of Employing the poore and idle people, who bring many distempers to the body of a State, because they cannot walke Reglarly and profitable'. Jobs, skills, virtue and personal reform would ensue for the mass of the people that 'bee sette a work by Land and Sea'. Further, added Dury, showing thereby that he was also well versed in trade discourse, it would give people the opportunity to

> improove their states and employ their stockes to better advantage for themselves and the public then hitherto they have done: (by which meanes the subjects become as it were the Factors, and the State by a prudentiall addresse is the Princepall tradere, and doth manage all their meanes with equalitie for their good) but the stoles and Estates of Forrainers will be drawen in, to increase the trade and make it beneficiall to the Public. The greater a stocke is, the more profit it doth yeeld.[95]

The colonies ought to be managed, in fact, like great companies. Eventually Pruvost returned to France. This led to the cosmopolitan-Protestant colour of the enterprise draining away, and it is accordingly unsurprising that the plantation ideas soon gained a nationalist hue. Although the memorandum entitled 'Proffits humbly presented to this Kingdome' is not signed, and Culpeper does not refer to it by its title, Webster, who published the text from amongst Hartlib's papers, thinks that the tract is connected to Benjamin Worsley, while also Braddick and Greengrass, who edited Culpeper's letters, note that the 'Woorsteley-s-propositions' is probably the text of 'Proffits humbly presented to this Kingdome'.[96]

Worsley's 'Proffits humbly presented to this Kingdome' anticipated some of the elements of both the Navigation Acts and *The Advocate*. However, it sketched a project that was simultaneously less detailed and much more ambitious.[97] The economic reform started with better husbandry, the use of fertilizer (the much discussed and advertised 'salt-petter' in the Hartlib circle), the improvement of the fishing industries and of production of national commodities such as wool and other clothes, and above all, rationalization of production from the rich soil of the plantations to boost the economy of the Kingdom as a whole. With a view to the future British Empire Worsley's skill in seeing the bigger economic picture is breathtaking. If England no longer needed to import her commodities from Spain, Italy, etc., but could establish

[95] Dury to Culpeper n.d. Autumn 1645, *The Letters of Sir Cheney Culpeper*, p. 235.

[96] Note by the editors in *The Letters of Sir Cheney Culpeper*, p. 243; 'Proffits' is published in Webster, *The Great Instauration*, pp. 539–546.

[97] *The Advocate* is a tract by Worsley in which he defended and explained the value of the Navigation Acts, see below.

> a well regulated plantation as wee shall cleerly and orderly describe with such lawes and constituons (*sic*) in it That the most yea all of those commodities wee now fetch from other partes, may bee had within our owne dominions and that at very inferiour rates especially those countries we will plant being also ordered and improoved according to the former manner, and government of our praescribed Husbandrie.[98]

The English nation would be thus able 'to receiving the wholl benefit both of the Commodities it selfe and monopolysing also the trading for them into their owne hands', which would afford her a strategic position that came from the perception that the nations that now produced these commodities, wines, fruits, sugar, drugs and so on 'were ours by Conquest and possession'.[99] The ensuing material benefits were indeed immense: cheap products for domestic households, better quality of commodities, increase in trade and shipping, outdoing the Hollanders, enlargement of the dominions, increased revenues and profits arising from taxes paid in the Plantations, bullion and money 'Banckt and Hoorded', leading to more discoveries, the attraction of ambassadors and artists to the country, and the deprivation of 'neighbour Kingdoms of their rich manufacturers'. In sum, as England rose the nations about her 'must necessarily as much decay and weaken'.

> For as wee sending our owne commodities every where abroad and that at gainfull rates, not standing in need of returning others for them, dayly take in without laying out, and soe stil add and improve the wealth and stock of the Kingdome.[100]

England would be feared, respected, and able to 'dictate the laws', preserve peace among the countries and 'sit as judge an Umpire of al Christian differences'. To 'wealth and honour' would be 'annexed a Reformation of lawes, and an establishment of rightousness amongst us', a 'Propagation of the Gospel', 'Reformation of Education', 'Advancement of Learning by men appointed and maintained to keeping an Universall Correspondency by erecting of Threasure Houses for the Collection of the History of Nature, for experiments both Chymicall and Mechanicall and by increasing of choice and public Libraries', 'conversion of the Jewes' was 'shortly to be expected and without a doubt at hand', and finally 'Union of reconciliation throughout all the christian at least all the Protestant Churches'.[101]

98 Benjamin Worsley 'Proffits humbly presented to this Kingdome', in *The Great Instauration*, p. 540.

99 Worsley 'Proffits humbly presented to this Kingdome', p. 542.

100 Worsley 'Proffits humbly presented to this Kingdome', p. 545.

101 Worsley 'Proffits humbly presented to this Kingdome', p. 545.

In a word, Worsley envisaged England as a combination of Messianism and the Great Instaurator.[102] And all this, one should not forget, was to be started with *one well regulated plantation.*

Leng notes Worsley's 'cynical' or 'amoral stance' in preferring 'commerce' to 'virtue' in this and other texts leading to the Navigation Acts.[103] Furthermore, Culpeper's pointed recommendation, in 1645, to 'Mr Woorstleys finall aime' that '(not this family, Cownty, Nation, but) whole mankinde' ought to benefit from the scientific study of trade, hinted at the reservations that aggressive nationalism in trade and otherwise provoked among the Protestant Reformers.[104] And yet, as transpires from his letter to Hartlib, Culpeper was impressed by this scientific promotion of the laws of trade – and how could he not be?

But rather than merely being the result of Worsley's nationalistic inclinations, or just another example of mercantilist thinking, 'Proffits humbly presented to this Kingdome' may also be read as the perfect example in early economic science of the narrow application of the empirical method to the study of wealth conscripted to a certain nation. One nation would indeed flourish, the others decay or even perish. Pure empiricism signified leaving aside the analysis – and, in effect, isolating its proposals – from moral and religious considerations about the common good, and this despite the Puritans' deeply religious and universalist aims. That the principle of 'starting with matter', if applied specifically to the production and most efficient trade of certain commodities would lead to this type of outcome, speaks, indeed of the amorality of the scientific method itself, and also of Worsley's clever way of applying it.

4.2.3 *The Knowledge of Trade*

Worsley's authorship of *The Advocate* was among his accomplishments as a civil servant. A brief but remarkably pedagogical tract on the 'Canon and Laws of Trade', *The Advocate* was a defence of the Navigation Acts that was presented in August 1651 to the Council of State and published the following year. While critics of the Acts were asking why they did not present full-throated promotion of free trade, Worsley generally defended 'the enclosed market' facilitated by them.[105] In the context of discussion as to

102 Webster, *The Great Instauration.*

103 Leng, *Benjamin Worsley (1618–1677)*, p. 192.

104 Culpeper to Hartlib, n.d. Autumn 1645, *The Letters of Sir Cheney Culpeper*, p. 243; Leng, *Benjamin Worsley (1618–1677)*, p. 192.

105 Leng, 'Commercial Conflict and Regulation in the Discourse of Trade in Seventeenth-Century England', p. 950.

how the commonwealth ought to foster trade, Worsley explained in *The Advocate* that as a private individual observes the rules of trade in order to gain prosperity, so must a nation observe the same care of *a shopkeeper*: to buy at first hand where commodities were cheaper, to fetch commodities from the immediate places of their production or growth, to send commodities to places where they were most needed, and to send all commodities to their farthest or utmost market where they would naturally tend to yield the highest price.[106] The advancement of shipping that the Navigation Acts promoted would be ideal for these activities and a means 'in som measure, to recover us'.[107] Other points made in *The Advocate*, such as noting how the Dutch were benefitting in their trade from having a bank, would have to wait four decades to be implemented. However, that was ultimately undertaken in the 1690s with the foundation of the Bank of England. As noted earlier, in 1672 Locke acted as Worsley's secretary at the Council for Trade and Foreign Plantations for one year, and then replaced him in that position.[108] The influence of Worsley's ideas as expressed in *The Advocate* and probably in a number of other texts diligently copied into Locke's notebook is evident in the latter's writings on money: the need for research and information, the analogy of how the private man (shopkeeper or farmer) and the nation should act if both wished to become richer, the centrality of foreign trade for the nation, the importance of money as the lifeblood of the economy.[109] But while Worsley advocated a low-interest rate for money, considering that 'the Easiness or Lowness of interest' in Holland benefited trade, Locke's central point when writing on money was to prove that the interest rate ought to be left at its 'natural value', as we will see in Chapter 11.[110]

Worsley devoted the bulk of *The Advocate* to explaining scientifically to the Council of State why the Dutch, whose design had been 'to laie a foundation to themselvs for ingrossing the Universal Trade, not onely of Christendom, but indeed of the greater part of the known world', had beaten out the English nation in all economic areas.[111] Their 'Care' in

[106] Worsley, *The Advocate*, p. 13.
[107] Worsley, *The Advocate*, p. 13.
[108] See about this institution in William Letwin, *The Origins of Scientific Economics. English Economic Thought 1660–1776* (London and New York: Routledge, 2003), p. 162.
[109] Worsley, *The Advocate;* Kelly, 'General Introduction: Locke on Money', p. 7; Leng, 'Commercial Conflict and Regulation in the Discourse of Trade in Seventeenth-Century England'.
[110] Worsley, *The Advocate*, p. 10.
[111] Worsley, *The Advocate*, p. 1.

big and small issues of trade policy had helped them achieve this. Thus, Worsley set out to show the 'clear waie of Governing it (trade)'.[112] A detailed account of the markets that the Dutch had conquered was presented: 'East-land', the 'Baltick Sea', Greenland, Rusia, 'East-India', the fishing coast of England, 'Spain, Canaries and the Straighs', as well as the markets for specific products, such as cloth manufacturing and – in 'East-land' and the 'Baltick Sea' – 'most necessarie Commodities' such as 'Masts, Timber, Hemp, Pitch, Tar, Copper, Iron, Salt-peter, all sorts of Grain, Pot-ashes' and the like. Moreover, he gave figures illustrating the dramatic reduction in English shipping over a short period, from 200 to 16 in the trade to East-land, whereas 'the Hollanders' employed 'no less than 600 Sail'.[113] In short, Dutch shipping was cheap, since they had become masters of the commodities employed in shipbuilding while the English had been forced to employ their services. And that was the way in which the money of the nation had gone to Holland. Moreover, the Dutch were able 'to under-sell' the English in practically all commodities that were common to the English and the Dutch. Whereas the latter were extremely careful to keep up 'the Repute' of their manufactured products, they also overbid the English in foreign commodities. The situation run 'thus in a Circle, each part of it (as wee said) strengthening another part' with the result that the nation's stock was diminishing day by day.[114] Worsley considered that the wisest path to break that vicious circle was to imitate the Dutch and carefully apply the laws of trade, described as the 'Canon or rules Belonging to Manufacturers', and whose core message was the need for focusing on the quality and increase of manufactures, at home, and in the colonies:

1. 'That although Divine Providence, in the greatness of his Wisdom, hath place natural commodities, som here, som there; yet no Manufacture or artificial commoditie, but may possibly bee had or transplanted into anie Countrie.
2. That all Manufactures (especially such as are of Necessitie) if they are of a certain goodness, They are (like Coin) of a certain value and price also; so on the contrarie. If of an uncertain goodness, They, & c.
3. That two persons selling or making commodities of a like goodness, hee shall have the preference of the Market, that will sell them the cheapest. *And so two Nations likewise.*

112 Preface, Worsley, *The Advocate.*
113 Worsley, *The Advocate*, p. 6.
114 Worsley, *The Advocate*, p. 5.

4. That the cheapness of Manufactures, and artificial commodities, doth altogether depend upon the plenty and cheapness of the matter, and upon the like cheapness of price, for Handie-labor.'[115]

Worsley seemed to state by rule number 1 that while natural resources were naturally located in different areas of the globe, both the production of artificial commodities and manufacturers had no limits and could be set anywhere. Moreover, there was no impediment to the English complying with these 'few' but 'unalterable Laws in all Manufactures' in the case of wool, and the fact that they had not done it only attested to their 'want of the like Care, as our Neighbours'.[116] Manufacturers were apt to be transplanted; moreover, they were like money – they had a certain value within the wider economic picture, and well-produced commodities were more valuable than others.

Civil servants entrusted with the responsibility to administer state affairs naturally thought in terms of social welfare. The introduction to Worsley's text states as much in his narrowing down to two reasons the need for careful consideration of 'Matters of Trade'. These amounted first to the '*Safetie*, *Unanimitie*, or *Defence* of this Nation', and next

> to preserv and maintein this Countrie: calling also to minde, how many times I have heard it urged, That here is no other means to quiet or keep up the spirits of the poorer sort of people: No other to give them Imploiment, or to finde a vent and Incouragement for their Labors (when they have wrought) and consequently no other to provide against the wants and distempers of them, and of the Generalitie, but solely by Trade, and by a due Order and Regulation of it.[117]

Nevertheless, Worsley's *The Advocate* also constituted modern economic thinking in terms of the benefit of the means of production locally through very flexible establishment of manufacturers and subsequent global trade. As he had noted in 'Proffits humbly presented to this Kingdome', 'Manufacturs being halfe if not the major part of the riches of all Kingdomes', whereas history had provided abundant examples, 'raysing themselves from Nothing to a greatness solely by them.'[118]

In different terms than 'value chains' – which was developed later, following fragmentation of the unity between capital, manufacturing and labour – together with the multiplication of manufactures, this was

[115] Worsley, *The Advocate*, p. 8.
[116] Worsley, *The Advocate*, p. 8.
[117] Worsley, *The Advocate*, p. 4.
[118] Worsley 'Proffits humbly presented to this Kingdome', p. 544.

exactly what Worsley was proposing.[119] Thomas Leng has argued that political discourse in the second half of the seventeenth century was neither mercantilists in the almost caricatured way in which that concept tends to be understood, nor a government defending itself from the rest of the countries. In the context of the ideas circulating in political debate, foreign trade was not depicted as a cake of finite size in relation to which one ought to defend one's portion. Instead, Worsley, and others were also very aware of both the conflictual and enterprising nature of trade, sometimes arguing about its unlimited possibilities when managed as a matter of state.[120] The aspect of competition is visible in Worsley's invitation to outdo the Dutch – in the same way that the Dutch had outdone the English, in a polished but firm manner – and in his belief in the (quasi-natural) existence of a series of trade laws that, if applied carefully, would help England to recover and take advantage of unlimited possibilities. The regulation of trade promised both wealth and social order.

As we have seen Worsley's lasting contribution was to study trade scientifically, developing laws of trade and of manufactures. It's clear that for the English Reformers trade had become the issue on which the other political and social questions hinged. Security and preservation of the nation and employment and thus provision for the wants of the people would certainly materialize through scientific trade and scientific production, and this perspective was also accompanied by the hope that it would realize an elusive utopian goal of a new kingdom of wealth, science and faith. With their versatile skills and their determination to apply modern empirical methods the Reformers certainly contributed to the reform of knowledge in England in many respects and to the scientific and regulated development of the Empire, particularly concerning the new legislation of trade and novel thinking about it. These were regarded as being independent from classic natural law and therefore functioned outside the usual sphere of moral laws. Nevertheless, behind the Reformers' schemes, principles of distributive justice within the commonwealth were also usually at stake.

[119] Joost Pauwelyn, 'Is Globalization Finally Re-balancing? Novel Ways of Leveling the Playing Field for Labour', in George P. Politakis, Tomi Kohiyama and Thomas Lieby eds. *Law for Social Justice* (International Labor Office, 2019).

[120] Leng, 'Commercial Conflict and Regulation in the Discourse of Trade in Seventeenth-Century England'.

5

Necessity, Free Will and Conscience

Robert Sanderson

5.1 Logician and Theologian

5.1.1 An English Casuist

Dealing at this point with a real theologian enables us to imagine the greater picture that any pious and well-read English natural lawyer – and there were many in existence in the period under discussion – would have in mind when referring to primary knowledge as 'necessary'. Furthermore, this chapter explores the formidable efforts that Christian theologians made to maintain a unified sense of the world's view, with coherent science, politics, and faith, in the face of rampant scepticism, mechanistic philosophy and fragmentation of faith and political representation.

This chapter explores how the divine Robert Sanderson (1587–1663) sought to develop a theological doctrine of free will that made sense of the moral life of a free individual. Sanderson simultaneously posited a metaphysics of necessity and a doctrine of free will, while developing a notion of conscience founded on mechanical laws. By many accounts, his work was an inspiration to John Locke.[1] Scholars have written about its influence on conscience and natural law in John Locke's early writings and have shown, in particular, that Sanderson's *Several Cases of Conscience Discussed in Ten Lectures in the Divinity School at Oxford* was a main reference for Locke in the writing of the unpublished *Two Tracts of Government* and his foundational *Essays on the Law of Nature*. However,

[1] Wolfgang von Leyden, 'Introduction', John Locke, *Essays on the Law of Nature*, The Latin text with a Translation, Introduction and Notes, together with Transcripts of Locke's Shorthand in his Journal of 1676, W. von Leyden (ed.) (Oxford: Clarendon Press, 1954); Philip Abrams, 'Introduction' in John Locke, *Two Tracts of Government* (Cambridge: Cambridge University Press, 1967); Robert Horwitz, 'Introduction' in John Locke, *Questions Concerning the Law of Nature*, with an Introduction, Text and Translation by Robert Horwitz, Jenny Strauss Clay, and Diskin Clay (Ithaca and London: Cornell University Press, 1990); Harris, *The Mind of John Locke*; Stanton, 'Authority and Freedom'; Stanton, 'Freedom of Conscience, Political Liberty and the Foundations of Liberalism'.

none of them has engaged with Sanderson's ideas in their own right. This is the aim of the present chapter.

In the dangerous decades from prior to the death of Charles I to the Restoration of Charles II (1640–1660) Sanderson developed a complex understanding of conscience and *the laws* by which it worked that stood somewhere between classical and reformed theology, civil religion and natural philosophy. Influenced through several channels by a metaphysics of necessity, that inspiration was nowhere more conspicuous than when he grounded the definition of legislative power as a right and as public jurisdiction on the fact that '[t]he Law hath a necessitating power' – that is, law carries the sword.[2] Sanderson's metaphysics of a dual structure of the world composed of necessary truths and contingent or indifferent things has complex roots. What might seem its most obvious source – fashionable seventeenth-century French mechanistic philosophers – does not, in view of his biographical writings, appear to tell the whole story about the origin of his ideas.

Peter Lake once highlighted Sanderson's Calvinist, 'dourly pessimistic view of human nature', evidenced by his zealous preaching against sin, which often bordered on Puritanism.[3] Sanderson's life, however, shows that by temperament he could hardly share the Puritan radicalism displayed during 'the English troubles'. His biographer Izaak Walton described him as a virtuous man who led an innocent life and found just one fault in his character, which was that he was 'too timorous and bashful'.[4] Certainly, moderation and humility were his constant message, and despite his theological and philosophical tendencies, he abhorred social radicalism. Lake argues that Sanderson remained within Calvinist orthodoxy, alarmed

[2] 'Seventh lecture: Concerning the Obligation of Humane Laws, in relation to the Efficient Cause thereof,' Robert Sanderson, *Several Cases of Conscience Discussed in Ten Lectures in the Divinity School at Oxford* (London: Printed by Tho. Leach, and are to be sold by John Martin [etc.], 1660). Hathi Trust, p. 236; p. 240. Sanderson substituted 'compulsive' by 'necessitating power' in his quote of Aristotle, *Nichomachean Ethics*, Book X, 1180a18–22: 'the paternal command has not the required force or compulsive power (not in general has the command of one man, unless he be a king or something similar), but the law *has* compulsive power, while it is at the same time a rule proceeding from a sort of practical wisdom and reason.' Aristotle, *Nichomachean Ethics* David Ross trans., Revised with an Introduction and Notes by Lesley Brown (Oxford: Oxford University Press, 2009).

[3] Peter G. Lake, 'Serving God and the Times: The Calvinist Conformity of Robert Sanderson' 27 *Journal of British Studies* (1988), p. 82; p. 89; 'Sanderson, Robert (1587–1663)' J. Sears McGee, 23 September 2004 https://doi-org.libproxy.helsinki.fi/10.1093/ref:odnb/24627

[4] Izaak Walton, *The Life of Dr. Sanderson, Late Bishop of Lincoln; to which is added, some short tracts or cases of conscience written by the said Bishop* (London: Printed for Richard Marriott, 1678), Early English Books Online Text Creation Partnership, 2011, http://name.umdl.umich.edu/A67467.0001.001 p. 16.

by the pride and social disruption he witnessed in communities of radical Puritans. Lake also explains that in the face of the high level of anxiety caused by the fact of sin, the Puritans developed a sort of comforting strategy in the experimental predestinarian tradition, which they reinforced in the practice of peers' assurance by the godly Puritan community.[5] As discussed in the following text, Sanderson's Calvinism was certainly not uncompromising, and Lake's point is, in short, that to describe Sanderson as an *Anglican* divine obscures more than it tells. However, Sanderson's Anglicanism can be seen in his respect for the law and preference for order and public peace.[6] In fact, it may be argued that from the ample palette of Reformation England, Sanderson used what he thought could be helpful to his own soul, to his pastoral care, to his Church, and to his country.[7]

Sanderson's very widely read ten lectures, *De obligatione conscientiae*, were delivered at Oxford in 1647, but only published in 1660 after thorough revision.[8] The editor of an 1851 reprint of the Latin text and translator of a summary of the lectures was no other than the professor of Moral Philosophy and Master of Trinity College at the University of Cambridge, William Whewell (1794–1866), well known among international lawyers for having endowed the first ever chair of international law. Whewell praised Sanderson's adequate use of Aristotle and, but for Sanderson's approach to the issue of the divine rights of kings, described the lectures as probably the best example of the Ethical School that 'preceded the influence of Hobbes and Descartes'.[9] The prestigious Latin translator Robert Condrington produced the English text of 1660. Both the Latin and the English editions are dedicated to Robert Boyle who paid a pension to Sanderson to enable him to prepare them for publication.[10] The first half of the lectures cover moral philosophy while the second half cover legal and

5 Lake, 'Serving God and the Times', p. 100; McGee, *The Godly Man in Stuart England*, p. 173.

6 McGee, *The Godly Man in Stuart England*, pp. 114–170.

7 In the preface to his Sermons of 1657 'in zeal for the safety and honour of my dear Mother, the Church of England, which hath nourished me up to become a Christian and a Protestant, that is to say, a pure Christian without any other addition or epithet'. Robert Sanderson, 'Preface', in William Jacobson (ed.), *Robert Sanderson Works*, (Oxford: Oxford University Press, 1854) vol. 2, p. liv.

8 Sanderson, *Several Cases of Conscience*; Robert Sanderson, *De obligatione conscientiae. Praelectiones decem*, with Notes and abridged Translation by William Whewell (Cambridge: Cambridge University Press and London: John W. Parker, 1851).

9 Whewell, 'Editor's Preface', in Robert Sanderson, *De obligatione conscientiae*, p. iii.

10 Michael Hunter notes the express request of Boyle who, as noted before, suffered from an scrupulous conscience and personally welcomed the relief provided by Sanderson's advise, Hunter, 'The Conscience of Robert Boyle', p. 74; Hunter, *Boyle: Between God and Science*, p. 100.

political teaching, but, due to their casuistic character, involving focus on boiling political cases, they rather belong to the genre of political treatise.

Ahead of the content, Sanderson wrote in the Preface to the reader that a 'Necessity did inforce' him to close himself into his study and review the text. He had been practically forced to publish the lectures since they were about to be published both in England and on the Continent without his permission. A candid request from a publisher convinced him that it was best to take the process into his own hands, despite his doubts and evident modesty. Sanderson was a Royalist.[11] He was appointed Regius Professor of Divinity by Charles I in 1642 and later ejected from his Professorship by the Parliamentary Commissioners. Harassed by members of the new regime, the affronts and violence he suffered only convinced him further of the value of religious moderation. Charles II reinstated him in 1660 and soon afterwards made him Bishop of Lincoln. Sanderson had assisted the King's father, Charles I, in diverse tasks in the 1630s and, in captivity along with other divines during 1647 and 1648, on points on conscience.[12]

From 1606 to 1619 Sanderson was a fellow at Lincoln College, coinciding in Oxford with Thomas Hobbes, who lived at Magdalen Hall, at least from 1603 to 1608. He became a Reader of Logic in 1608 and his lectures were first printed in 1615. They reached eleven editions by 1741 and became a sort of textbook in 'both Universities' (Oxford and Cambridge).[13] Sanderson's *Logicae Artis Compendium* follows the Neoplatonist Porphyry's reading of Aristotle, a practice common among scholars in the history of philosophy.[14] However, the characteristics of his later deployment of the causal principle of necessity were not yet apparent in that text on logic.[15] As a

[11] Together with the 'counsel of his Peers', 'the will of the Prince, from whose Arbitration and Command alone, all Rogations of Lawes are either established, or made void, is the only adequate, and efficient Cause of Publick Laws'. However, as he noted, in England kings never 'exercise their Legislative power as to impose any Laws on their subjects without their own consent', Sanderson *Several Cases of Conscience*, p. 246; p. 264.

[12] Whewell, 'Editor's Preface', in Robert Sanderson, *De obligatione conscientiae*; Walton, *The Life of Dr. Sanderson, Late Bishop of Lincoln.*

[13] William Jacobson, 'Introduction', in William Jacobson (ed.), *The Works of Robert Sanderson in Six Volumes* (Oxford: Oxford University Press, 1854), vol. I, p. 24; Walton, *The Life of Dr. Sanderson, Late Bishop of Lincoln*, 19.

[14] Robert Sanderson, *Logicae Artis Compendium* (Oxon: Iosephus Barnesius, 1615); A. C. Lloyd, 'Neoplatonic Logic and Aristotelian Logic I, 1 *Phronesis* (1955), p. 58.

[15] In Chapter 19, *De Locis à Causa et Effectus* in the explanation of the five principles Sanderson did not employ the method of 'necessity'; his epistemology back then made it superfluous: 'I. Posita causa, ponitur effectus'; II. Posito effectu ponitur causa; III Qualis causa, talis effectus; IV. Propter quod unumquodque est tale illud est magis tale; V. Causa Natura prior est effectu' (Sanderson, *Logicae*, p. 183).

logician, it was only natural that he would follow the common contemporary method of syllogism to resolve cases of conscience. However, the mark of Erastian modernity in his series of lectures on cases of conscience, which were soon to become a theme only bothered about by antiquarians, was remarkable. English moral casuistic would not survive to the eighteenth century, making the reedition by Whewell the more interesting.

Sanderson deployed modern mechanistic philosophy to overcome scepticism, and insisted on obedience to positive law, in which he recognized the will of God. Moreover, he attributed the right to make ecclesiastical laws to the bishops, but he concluded that the complete exercise of that right and power, even the organization of the initial meeting of bishops, depended on the supreme magistrate.[16] Without knowing the extent of the revisions he undertook in 1659 it is impossible to decide whether the lectures of the future Bishop of Lincoln were a case of Hobbism predating Hobbes– another expression 'of the genius' that governed the unhappy and fascinating age, according to Skinner's description of the context of Hobbes's political thought. Instead, Sanderson might simply have been a political proselyte of the philosopher of Malmesbury.[17] Notwithstanding the allegiances involved, Sanderson's thought (vis-à-vis that of Hobbes) shows clear originality in terms of the method by which he rooted the moral duty to obey the law in a complex theory of a mechanical conscience and moral uprightness.

5.1.2 *Predestination, Necessity and Free Will*

The particular context of Sanderson's early interest in the category of 'necessity' was worthy of the 'laberynthine religious history of the period' and quite to be expected from a politically engaged young English

[16] Sanderson, *Several Cases of Conscience*, p. 272.

[17] The seventh chapter dealing with obligation of human laws starts with Prov. 8.15 'Per me reges regnant, et Legum conditores justa decernunt', Sanderson, *Several Cases of Conscience*, p. 67. The same quote that already Hobbes had used in *De Cive*, as early as 1641, Howard Warrender, 'The Early Latin Versions of Thomas Hobbes's *De Cive*', s6-II *The Library* (1980). Hobbism of Anglican divines and Dissenters appeared more developed during the second decade of the Restoration, notoriously in the case of Samuel Parker's, *Discourse of Ecclesiastical Polity* see for this Richard Ashcraft, *Revolutionary Politics & Locke's Two Treatises of Government* (Princeton: Princeton University Press, 1986); Quentin Skinner, 'The Ideological Context of Hobbes's Political Thought' 9 *The Historical Journal*, (1966) p. 296.

theologian.[18] By the 1620s, the epicentre of English theological debate had a clear doctrinal focus. After the rise of Arminianism, King James's attack on it prompted by a Calvinist impulse of his – and also for political reasons – and the international Synod of Dordt (1618–1619) organized by the Dutch Reformed Church, the tone was set for further discussion.[19] 'The Quinquarticular controversy' between the Calvinists and the Armenians related to the doctrines of predestination and grace, that ramified into five different points concerning the following: (1) original sin; (2) 'irrespective' election and reprobation ('irrespective' indicating whether someone had listened to the good news of the Gospel or not); (3) particular redemption; (4) irresistible grace; and (5) final perseverance.[20] Sanderson's theological positions on these questions appear in a letter-testimony he wrote to the Dean of Salisbury, Thomas Pierce, before the Restoration. His theological stand in turn offers valuable insight into the origins of the unique metaphysics of the English casuist. The reputed Royalist divine Henry Hammond (1605–1660) published part of that letter in a collection together with the thoughts and letters of friends.[21] The other part was obtained directly through another letter, dated 15 March 1678, this time from Pierce, due to the efforts of Sanderson's biographer. Reportedly, Sanderson resisted Pierce's entreaties to publish that information for a long time.[22] After all, he had been sharpening his ploughshare in the forges of the Philistines. But eventually he yielded to his friend's petition.

In the part of the letter in Hammond's possession, Sanderson described his theological path and his radical change of views from 1625 onwards.[23] As a young divine, he had read the 'learned Hooker', followed by Calvin's *Institutions*, which had greatly guided him in relation to his belief in predestination. Sanderson had accordingly become a 'sublapsarian', which

[18] Nicholas Tyacke, *Anti-Calvinists: The Rise of English Arminianism, C. 1590–1640*, (Oxford: Clarendon Press, 1990), p. xiv.

[19] Tyacke, *Anti-Calvinists*, p. 41; Hillel Schwartz, 'Arminianism and the English Parliament, 1624–1629, 12 *Journal of British Studies* (1973).

[20] J. B. S Carwithen, *The History of the Church of England* (London: Baldwin and Cradock, 1829) vol. II, p. 245.

[21] Henry Hammond, *Charis kai eirene, or, A pacifick discourse of Gods grace and decrees in a letter of full accordance / written to the reverend and most learned Dr. Robert Sanderson by Henry Hammond* (London, for R. Royston, 1660) Early English Books Online Text Creation Partnership, 2011 http://name.umdl.umich.edu/A45400.0001.001

[22] Walton, *The Life of Dr. Sanderson, Late Bishop of Lincoln*; The letter in *The Works of Robert Sanderson in Six Volumes*, vol. VI, p. 351.

[23] Jacobson, 'Introduction' in *The Works of Robert Sanderson in Six Volumes*, vol. I, p. v.

is to say that he held the belief that God had foreknowledge about the Fall when He decreed who was predestined to achieve salvation.[24] In 1625, Parliament was convened and he was chosen as one of the clerks of the convocation for the diocese of Lincoln. His participation there gave him occasion to study the doctrine of salvation for himself, rather than simply continuing to rely on Calvin. As a result, he entirely abandoned Calvinist predestination views, although, as we will see in the following text, he retained other aspects of Calvin's theology.

During the parliamentary session, he discussed these issues with an unidentified man who recommended to him a work entitled *Variarum difficiliumque speculativae* (1623) that had recently been published in Paris by a Spanish bishop, Francisco de Arriba.[25] The Spaniard claimed in an introductory letter to the Pope Gregory XXV that the argument proposed a solution of a different, but related controversy, that of *de auxiliis. De auxiliis* had stirred up Catholic theologians after the Council of Trent ended in 1563, on the topic of the proper balance between divine sovereignty and free human will, between determinism and Pelagianism. The controversy *de auxiliis* started with a debate in Salamanca in 1582 between the Dominican Domingo Bañez and the Jesuit Prudencio de Montemayor, and the polemic arrived in Leuven with the Jesuit Leonard Lessius (1554–1623), when he contested the determinism of Michael Baius. It took definite international flight with the publication of *The Reconciliation of Free Choice with Gifts of Grace, Divine Foreknowledge, Providence, Predestination and Reprobation* (1588) *for several Articles of the* Prima Pars *of St. Thomas Aquinas* by the Jesuit Luis de Molina. A papal commission was established. In a pastoral move to avoid further dissension, it concluded in 1607 with a universal prohibition by the Pope Paul V to publish any more on the question. Robert J. Matava has written on the controversy *de auxiliis* recently, contrasting the theocentrism of the Dominicans with the

[24] In contrast to supralapsarians: 'a person who believes that God decreed the election or non-election of individuals to salvation even before the Fall', *Collins Online English Dictionary.* In the Introduction to Sanderson's letter, Dr Pierce wrote to Mr Walton that 'Sanderson discerned a necessity of quitting the Sublapsarian way, of which he had before a better liking, as well as the Supralapsarian, which he could never fancy.' *The Works of Robert Sanderson in Six Volumes*, vol. VI, p. 352. For the history of the controversy of Arminianism, Calvinism, the Quinquarticular controversy and James I in England Carwithen, *The History of the Church of England*, generally ch. 22. According to Sanderson, John Calvin was a supralapsarian.

[25] Francisco de Arriba, *Variarum difficiliumque speculativae theologiae quaestionum libri quatuor* (Parisiis: apud Laurentium Sonnium, 1623).

anthropocentric position of the Jesuits.[26] It might be that the death of the Pope in 1621 cleared the way for new publications on the question, and de Arriba's was one of them.[27] De Arriba's *Variarum* seemed to have been a popular work in England in the seventeenth century, since bequests of at least three copies are registered as having been made before 1648 to the libraries of three Oxford colleges.[28]

Initially, Sanderson was baffled, feeling that he was reading the work of a charlatan. However, he persevered until he finished the work. Although inspired by Scotus, de Arriba's *Variarum* has neither the depth nor the density of style of Scotus. Nonetheless, it amounts to around 3000 pages of metaphysical reasoning about time and God. Moreover, de Arriba was no nebbish. First bishop of Segovia, then elected bishop of Ciudad Rodrigo – he died in 1623 before he could accept the bishopric – he was a doctor in theology and, as a biographical note in the book asserts, confessor to the French queen, the Spanish Anne of Austria, future mother of Louis XIV. Sanderson's letter highlights the content of books III and IV, the former arguing in support of 'the coexistence of all things past, present and future, *in mente Divina realiter ab aeterno*' and 'not simply *praesentialitatem objectivam*'. The fourth book contains an argument as to the

> twofold manner of God's working ad extra; the one, *sub ordine Preadestinationis*, of which Eternity is the proper measure; the other, *sub ordine Gratiae*, whereof Time is the measure. And that God worketh *fortiter* in the one, though *not irresistibiliter*, as well as *suaviter* in the other, wherein the Free Will hath his proper working also.[29]

In other words, predestination was not irresistible and human beings possessed free will to respond to grace – a statement by which in effect Sanderson stopped being a Calvinist. Apparently, the issue was not momentous enough for Sanderson to take a strong political position in

[26] Matava actually calls for a recovery on the unresolved question R. J. Matava, 'A Sketch of the Controversy *de auxiliis*', 7 *Journal of the Jesuits Studies* (2020) p. 422; p. 446; Jackson, *Hobbes, Bramhall and the Politics of Liberty and Necessity.*

[27] Another book was, for instance, by Diego Álvarez, O.P., *De avxiliis divinae gratiae et humani arbitrii viribus, et libertate, ac legitima eivs cvm efficacia eorvndem avxiliorvm concordia liberi duodecim* (Cologne: Antonius Boetzerus, 1622).

[28] Among others from different religious inclinations, bequested to Jesus College on his death by the 1st Baron Herbert of Cherbury (1583–1648) the Deist philosopher and diplomat regarded highly by Descartes, Grotius, Gassendi, and Marsenne; by William Paddy, the royal physician, in 1634 to St John's College, and another of Ralph Kettel, the third president of Trinity College bequested to that college in 1643. From the database of the libraries at Oxford University.

[29] *The Works of Robert Sanderson in Six Volumes*, vol. VI, p. 353.

relation to it since he remained private on the question his entire life. Instead, the reading of *Variarum* probably helped the good bishop to appease his conscience. Sanderson concluded that the acts of the Synod of Dordt remained in his study afterwards 'only to fill up a room to this day' and that

> from the result of his whole performance I was confirmed in this opinion, that we must acknowledge the work of both Grace and Free Will in the conversion of a sinner. And so likewise in all other events, the consistency of the infallibility of God's fore-knowledge at least, though not with any absolute, but conditional Predestination with the liberty of man's Will, and the contingency of inferior causes and effects.[30]

Sanderson's doubts concerning the extreme Calvinist views of a divine decree of predestination and the way in which he resolved them show that in the early decades of the seventeenth century, Catholic, Anglican and Reformed theologians might possess sturdy arguments that helped their consciences and their pastoral work and endowed their understanding of moral life with a common sense approach.[31] Beyond that metaphysical discourse carried on by theologians, the office of the magistrate as a legislator was supposed to determine and fixed 'in time and place' much of that contingency.

5.2 The Mechanical Conscience

5.2.1 The Age of Conscience

In his *Several Cases of Conscience* Sanderson set out the method by which right moral behaviour may be ascertained. He articulated, in a remarkable manner, the way in which contingent moral action became necessary in a framework of thinking in which God's will is necessary, and moral reasoning is guided by necessary syllogisms.

Margaret Sampson argued some years ago that in the seventeenth century Hugo Grotius and other eminent natural lawyers transformed casuistry into modern political thought.[32] Kant poured scorn on the political moralism of this group in his *Perpetual Peace*, describing them as 'miserable

[30] *The Works of Robert Sanderson in Six Volumes*, vol. VI, p. 353.

[31] See also David S. Sytsma, 'Aquinas in Service of Dordt: John Davenant on Predestination, Grace and Free Choice', in Jordan J. Ballor, Matthews T. Gaetano and David S. Sytsma (eds.), *Beyond Dort and De Auxiliis. The Dynamics of Protestant and Catholic Soteriology in the Sixteenth and Seventeenth Centuries* (Leiden, Boston: Brill, 2019).

[32] Sampson, 'Laxity and Liberty in Seventeenth-Century English Political Thought'.

comforters'.[33] I argue in this chapter that in mid-seventeenth-century England, Robert Sanderson devised a method of assuring the tranquility of conscience that drew on natural philosophy and a command of positive law. Along with many of his contemporaries, Sanderson suffered many doubts about the simple 'postlapsarian recognition of the natural law through right reason' – that is to say, that after the weakness following original sin it was possible to know how to practice moral good.[34] On the one hand, the illumination of the light of reason was commonly considered to be no more than a faint spark in Reformation England. On the other hand, in a politically divided nation, the rationalist method of submitting people's consciences to the practice of reasoning through complex causal syllogisms, deprived of life, was not only an exhausting practice, but one that could lead to ominous political results. Sanderson's final proposal was then to complement the syllogistic method with a way of guiding one's conscience through human ordinances and, in this manner, end the tortuous process of inquiry to find the right action.

Izaak Walton mentioned the books that Sanderson always had to hand and knew almost by heart: Aristotle's *Rhetoric*, Aquinas's *Secunda Secundae*, Cicero's *De officiis* and the *Elementa Jurisprudientiae* by the Oxford civilian Richard Zouche, his contemporary.[35] In his lectures on conscience, however, Sanderson preferred Scotus and Durandus 'and some other of the most subtile School-men' over Aquinas. Further, he simplified many of the traditional notions, importantly *synderesis*, meaning conscience or the light of nature.[36] Nevertheless, Sanderson's lectures on cases of conscience are an ambitious and multifaceted work in which he proposed an original philosophical method to explain what he calls 'the Rule of Conscience', where he was mainly concerned with the *how* of the moral reasoning. I emphasize next the ways in which Sanderson employed the principle of logical

33 Martti Koskenniemi, 'Miserable Comforters: International Relations as New Natural Law' in 15 *European Journal of International Relations* (2009).

34 Greene, 'Synderesis, the Spark of Conscience, in the English Renaissance', p. 196.

35 Walton, *The Life of Dr. Sanderson, Late Bishop of Lincoln.* Zouche's *Elementa* is a quite well-arranged systematic study of the civil law, with little theory, containing private and public law, ecclesiastical law and a good section on maritime commercial law. Richardi Zouchei, J. C., *Elementa Jurisprudentiae, definitionibus, Regulis & Sententiis selectioribus Juris Civilis, Illustrata* (Lugd. Batavorum, Johannes & Daniel Elsevirii, 1652). Richard Zouche was a Royalist civil lawyer, described as 'clearly the most distinguished civilian [lawyer] that Oxford produced in the seventeenth century' quote in P. Stein, 'Richard Zouche (1590–1661)', *Oxford Dictionary of National Biography* (2004, September 23). On Zouche's patriarchalism and on his *jus inter gentes* see Martin Clark, *The 'International' and 'Domestic' in British Legal Thought from Gentili to Lauterpacht* (PhD London School of Economics, London, January 2020), p. 66.

36 Sanderson *Several Cases of Conscience*, p. 19.

and causal necessity as a method by which to attain security of conscience. This standpoint went far beyond the theological doctrine under which certain truths and morals were necessary for salvation. The core message of Sanderson's lectures on conscience was ethical in nature.[37]

The will of God is the rule of conscience, and the way to fulfil that law in the practice of morality is to do it mechanically – that is, by following necessary reasoning according to a hierarchy of laws. This, in a nutshell, was Sanderson's message. He devoted many pages to a theory of conscience based on the rule of the Supreme Legislator – God – and to the method of ascertaining it. In the very substantial second part of the lectures, Sanderson made a sort of de facto case, stating that not only were human laws the surest guide for conscience, but that it was necessary, even in politically disrupted times, to obey human laws as the embodiment of the will of God.

According to Camille Slights, Sanderson's *De obligatione conscientiae*, together with Jeremy Taylor's *Ductor dubitantium* (1660), constituted the main reference work of seventeenth century Anglican casuistic moral philosophy.[38] This gives a sense of his position among contemporary moral philosophers, in a century that has been referred to as 'the age of conscience' – and casuistry has been argued to be the context of the main changes in political thought during that period, while even Hobbes is discussed seriously as being a casuist.[39] Anglican casuists' position about how to produce evidence in doubtful moral cases was termed *probabiliorism*, and its focus was on reason. Probabiliorists insisted that in case of doubt, it was safer to consider themselves bound in the face of an obligation, while they decried the laxity of (Jesuit) probabilism.[40] Sanderson explained it as follows: 'it is safer to obey the conscience doubting, than the Conscience doubting not to obey.'[41] The inviolability of individual conscience was

[37] Sanderson's biographer felt incapable to describe the immense value of the work stating only 'That they continue to this day, and will do for ever, as a compleat standard for the resolution of the most material doubts in Casuistical Divinity.' Walton, *The Life of Dr. Sanderson, Late Bishop of Lincoln*, p. 45.

[38] Camille Slights, 'Ingenious Piety: Anglican Casuistry of the Seventeenth Century' 63 *The Harvard Theological Review* (1970).

[39] Keith Thomas, 'Cases of Conscience in Seventeenth Century England', in John Morrill, Paul Slack and Daniel Woolf (eds.), *Public Duty and Private Conscience in Seventeenth Century England. Essays Presented to G. E. Aylmer* (Oxford: Clarendon Press, 1993), p. 29; p. 44; Margaret Sampson, '"Will You Hear What a Casuist He Is" Thomas Hobbes as Director of Conscience' 11 *History of Political Thought* (1990).

[40] George L. Mosse, 'Puritan Political Thought and the "Cases of Conscience"' 23 *Church History* (1954) 109–118; Slights, 'Ingenious Piety'.

[41] Sanderson, *Several Cases of Conscience*, p. 216.

paramount for them and they also acknowledged the inability to grasp the innumerable circumstances of human affairs. Hence no categorical decision for or against sin was usually asserted.[42]

Certainly, not every casuist was a political thinker. Furthermore, only those authors that were ready or had the skills to produce theoretical novelties to justify a case of conscience developed national and international political thought in any significant way.[43] In view of Sanderson's lectures on the obligations of conscience, there is a strong case to be made that he aimed at doing precisely that to develop a moral philosophy compatible to *Leviathan*'s Erastian politics from within the ranks of the English Church. However, in the very ambiguous role that Sanderson attributed to the light of nature ('the *light* proceeding from this *law* is extremely obscured by that grievous ruine which followed the fall of Adam'), his own obscure use of the notion of synderesis and his employment of the Gersonian-Calvinist concept of 'instinct of Nature', Sanderson's lectures on conscience also embodied a rationalist epilogue in the decline, during the English Renaissance, of the idea of synderesis as a spark of conscience.[44]

5.2.2 Albert the Great, Aquinas and Ralph Cudworth on the Agent Intellect

Sanderson's light of nature is distinct from the light of the agent intellect of Aristotle, Albert the Great and Aquinas.[45] It is clear from his reworking of the light of nature and of the notion of conscience that he was knowledgeable

42 Slights, 'Ingenious Piety'. Probabiliorism is one of several commonalities between Sanderson and earlier Puritan casuists such as William Perkins (1558–1602), see Mosse, 'Puritan Political Thought and the "Cases of Conscience"'.

43 García-Salmones, "The Disorder of Economy? The First Relectio de Indis in a Theological Perspective'; Mónica García-Salmones Rovira', 'The Impasse of Human Rights' 21 *Journal of the History of International Law* (2019); Sampson, 'Laxity and Liberty'.

44 'The *light* proceeding from this *law* is extremely obscured by that grievous ruine which followed the fall of Adam, and from hence arise those thick clouds of *Ignorance* and *Error* in which all his posterity whilst we live in this World, are invelopped. But the providence of God hath so most wisely ordered it, that in the common wrack it hath some off more unhurt that many other of the Faculties: for it hat pleased God that certain propositions, and practical principles ... a spark of the Divine Fire which in the great conflagration was preserved in the ashes of it, should still remain, that so in our breasts and most inward parts, he might have the Preachers of his will.' Sanderson, *Several Cases of Conscience*, p. 132; Greene, 'Synderesis, the Spark of Conscience, in the English Renaissance'.

45 Albertus, *Ethica*; *Aristotle's De Anima with the Commentary of St. Thomas Aquinas*; Jonathan Lear, *Aristotle. The Desire to Understand* (Chicago: University of Chicago Press, 1988); Hellmeier, *Anima et intellectus*, p. 217.

about the tradition but wanted to reshape it according to the new ideas and the political situation. Conscience worked under the 'rule of the Law' and 'ordained' previous actions.[46] Thus, conscience could be explained as like 'the science of the heart' and 'no more than the heart's consciousness'. In both cases, it referred either to the fact that many individuals have the same knowledge, or that an individual knows many things. Furthermore, conscience applied 'the universal knowledge, or knowledge of the law' to the particular knowledge or 'the knowledge of the fact'.[47] Adopting Luther's position, Sanderson rejected the Biblical reference to the illuminative act of the light of reason – 'Thy light of Lord is signed over us' – and with it, the classical integration of philosophy and the Bible.[48] Hence Sanderson would propose a 'syllogisticall' conscience as we will see in detail.[49]

Therefore, Sanderson's description of the light in the mind seemed at the outset like a rule of law, to be applied to the particular case at hand. The light of intellect of the Christian theological tradition relates to knowledge, virtue and human nature in more complex and richer ways than being a rule of law. Albert the Great was, significantly, one of the first authors to take Aristotle up on that and Aquinas followed suit. Aristotle's description as a light of the potential intellect and the agent intellect in *De anima* III is one the most commented upon chapters in the history of philosophy:[50]

> Since just as in every nature there is something that is the matter in each class (this is what is all those things in potentiality), but another is the cause and agent (by causing all things, e.g. art with respect to the matter that has undergone it), it is necessary also that in the soul these differences belong. And there is one such mind by becoming all things, another by making all, as some sort of hexis, e.g. light; for in some way also light makes potential colours actual colours.[51]

46 'The Law which is written in our Hearts, and is as it were a rule of well living may be called Conscience'.

47 Sanderson, *Several Cases of Conscience*, p. 5; p. 7.

48 'I here shall willingly take no notice of that Text in the fourth *Psalm* and sixth verse, which is commonly produced by the Latin Fathers especially of the latter *times*, and by the Schoolmen, for a proof of this Conclusion, the words are *Signatum est super nos lumen vultus tui domine, Thy light oh Lord is signed over us*, because that interpretation of the words are grounded on a bad translation, & seemeth not to appertain to the mind and scope of the Prophet.' Sanderson, *Several Cases of Conscience*, p. 117; that this was from Luther's inspiration, in Greene, 'Synderesis, the Spark of Conscience, in the English Renaissance', p. 203.

49 Still he sometimes appears to remain within tradition: 'The proper act of Conscience, to wit, the *application* of the light which is in the mind by the discourse of *reason* to particular Acts.' Sanderson, *Several Cases of Conscience*, p. 13; p. 29.

50 Lear, *Aristotle. The Desire to Understand.*

51 Aristotle, *De Anima*, 430a10–17. Polansky, *Aristotle's De Anima: A Critical Commentary*, p. 460; Wilkes, 'Psuchē versus the Mind', p. 125

For Albert and Aquinas this sort of light – the agent intellect and its counterpart the potential intellect – was (a) participating in God and, at the same time, (b) a new living being in the sense that the intelligent being in question was a particular woman or man. The light of the agent intellect depends on God. It is alive and is akin to a light that illuminates the truth of the particular thing. Their position broke the link with the idea defended by the Andalusian philosopher Averroes (1126–1198) about an intellect connected with human beings but 'separated from the body, as a substance that exists on its own'. In his commentary on Aristotle's *De anima*, written between 1267 and 1268, Aquinas summarized his intense polemic against the Averroist separated intellect, noting, that 'the theory in question (of Averroes) is an implicit denial of the existence of thinking in the human individual'.[52] In this context thinking, also thinking about the moral act, is a core notion as between God, the human spirit and the human body.

Albert also followed Aristotle in respect of the idea that we need to accept 'the virtues as innate in us, and that according to the act of thus accepted virtues, we are not changed, but perfected'. The reasoning behind this was that as 'in every nature each thing was perfected and not altered, when it acquired the virtue of its natural power, then the virtues cannot be a gift that reaches man from the outside'.[53] Albert wanted to explain in this context the connection between the virtuous act and the light of the agent intellect, with the tenets of his theory of creation as a hierarchy of forms (influenced by Neoplatonism) that participate in the divine light in gradual descent.[54] The closer the individual was to the first source (*fontem primi*) of the light, the more simple, spiritual, more authentic and pure would be the manner in which she would be illuminated in order to be virtuous in his or her actions. On the other hand, at a greater distance from the prime source, the individual's intellectual light would be perceived as no more than a faint image, and ultimately only something similar to an obscure reflection. 'The agent intellect' Albert explained, 'is a divine particle' but not one that had divine substance and nature, rather, according to a participation

52 *Aristotle's De Anima with the Commentary of St. Thomas Aquinas;* Gauthier, 'Introduction' to Aquinas, *Sententia Libri De Anima*, §689–690; §694–695; the same Neoplatonist explanation in Avicenna : 'Même l'acte de pensée n'est pas exclusivement une initiative humaine, il s'explique toujours par l'intervention d'un principe transcendant à l'homme', Verbecke, 'Le "De Anima" d'Avicenne. Une conception spiritualiste de l'homme', p. 73.

53 'sed nos sumus virtutes innati suscipere, et suscepta virtute secundum esse actu non alterati, sed perfecti sumus: sicut in tota natura omnis res non alterata sed perfecta est, quando suae naturalis potestatis virtutem attingit: igitur virtutes non possunt esse donum quod extrinsecus hominibus adveniat.' Albertus, *Ethica*, Liber I, t. 7, c. 5.

54 Hellmeier, *Anima et intellectus*, p. 216; p. 221.

in God of quality and power. Albert noted the fact that human beings' agent intellect was separated from the first source of light and pinpointing this as the origin of our freedom: 'This divine particle is free due to its separateness and it makes us to be lords (*dominos*) of our acts.[55]

In the dense, barely one and a half pages constituting Chapter 5 of his *Ethica*, Albert raised at least four relevant points. First, the dependency of a virtuous human's action on a light in the individual's intellect participating in God. Second, the manner in which this dependency occurs within human nature, i.e. through the participation of human understanding in divine understanding. Third, the freedom of the acting individual. Fourth, the way in which a human being may understand everything in the world by means of the light of the agent intellect, since the world is potentially in our intellect. Moreover, as the intellect individuates human beings that is, constitutes each human nature, enables knowledge and moral perfection – being the source of happiness, prudence and wisdom – the idea of the agent intellect connects in Albert natural philosophy, metaphysics and epistemology.[56] It seems to be the case that Albert was asserting that human beings are created to think, decide and act as God had done when creating the world.

Arguably, Albert's and Aquinas's emphasis on the light in the intellect did not result in an intellectualized conception of human beings, for the 'thinking' referred to by the theologians was for both speculative and practical purposes. Aquinas's conclusion that the cause and root of goodness in human beings is reason must be placed in the context of the light-truth-goodness chain.[57] Physical body appears relevant when Aquinas buttresses goodness in the will of acting human beings. The human virtues perfect the human desires in using (the world) in a manner that allows the human being to perform good acts. Prudence, as the virtue of acting on the basis of the right reason, requires that the human being possesses good principles guiding action, which is to say that they have good aims when acting – and in a virtuous individual, desires follow these goals. The virtuous individual has therefore good

[55] 'Hoc quidem modo dicendo divinam particulam, intellectus agentis divina particula est non quidem per substantiam et naturam divinam, sed secundum participationem proprietatis et virtutis, et analogiam typicae imagines ad prototypum, quod omnium est causa efficiens et formalis per aliquem modum. Haec divina particula ex separatione libera est, et facit nos esse dominos nostrorum actuum. Et ex quod divina est, formalis est ad esse et bene esse. Divinum et certissimum est hoc quod omnis causa est in nobis.' Albertus Magnus, *Ethica*, Liber I, t. 7, c. 5; Hellmeier, *Anima et intellectus*; Lee, 'St. Thomas and Avicenna on the Agent Intellect'.

[56] Henryk Anzulewicz, 'De Intellectu et intelligibili des Albertus Magnus: eine Relektüre der Schrift im Licht ihrer peripatetischen Quellen' XXV *Przegląd Tomistyczny* (2019).

[57] *Summa theologiae*, I, q. 79, a.11; I–II, q. 66. a.1. co.

desires. It is the good or right will of a human being that possesses these good aims, which also depend on knowledge.[58] In this wider picture *conscience is an act*: the application of knowledge (not of a rule). It is also an acknowledgement or judgment of what we did or should not have done.[59]

The way in which 'body' comes into the picture is more original in Albert's thinking. Although he repeatedly expressed the idea that the pinnacle of perfection in human being is a vital process in which the intellect is perfected to the point at which one no longer needs the resources of knowledge acquired by the senses, he was not a spiritualist. As Wieland has argued, to avoid the impression that Albert's work expresses a 'denaturalizing' theory of the human being, one should also consider Albert's extensive works on nature and animals, which adduce the idea that human beings' senses are completely penetrated by the rational.[60] This, Wieland continues, amounts to a statement on Albert's part that it is through the sense of touch that the human being is the most intelligent of living beings. To put it in more precise terms, the issue concerns a 'theory of penetration of reason' in the entire human being, body and soul, whereas reason is understood in this ample sense of intellect, speculative and practical reason.[61] As Albert wrote concisely in *De bono*, 'human nature is reason'.[62]

The Cambridge Neoplatonist Ralph Cudworth accepted the existence within the human mind of a universal 'innate cognoscitive Power', a view he acknowledged as having been inspired by the famous passage about mind as light in Aristotle's *De anima*.[63] However, he explicitly rejected

58 *Summa theologiae*, I-II, q. 56, a.3.6.

59 *Summa theologiae*, I, q. 79, a.13.

60 For instance, when Albert states that the intellect penetrates and impregnates all soul and body: 'Et similiter intellectus qui in homine excellentissum est, omnes animae particulas et corporis ad se format'. Albertus Magnus, *Ethica*, Liber X, t. 2, c. 3; Wieland, *Zwischen Natur und Vernunft*.

61 Wieland, *Zwischen Natur und Vernunft*.

62 'Natural right is thus nothing else than the right of reason as it is its due (*sive debitum*), in as much as nature is reason' Alberti Magni, *De bono*, in *Alberti Magni opera omnia*, tomus XXVIII), Henricus Kühle, Carolus Feckes, Bernhardus Geyer (Prolegomena), Wilhemus Kübel, ediderunt (Aschendorff: Monasterii westfalorum in aedibus, 1951), n. 270.22.

63 'For the Soul having an Innate Cognoscitive Power Universally (which is nothing else but a Power of raising Objective Ideas within it self, and Intelligible Reasons of any thing) it must needs be granted that it hath a Potential Omniformity in it. Which is not only asserted by the Platonists, that the Soul is *all things Intellectually*, but also by *Aristotle* himself *That the Souls is in a manner All Things*'; 'they (Created Intellects) have them all (the Actual Ideas of all things) Virtually and Potentially comprehended in that one Cognoscitive Power of the Soul, which is a Potential Omniformity' Cudworth, A *Treatise Concerning Eternal and Immutable Morality*, p. 134.

the idea that that power could be active or alive, and that, thereby, it was divine. Indeed, accepting the testimony of the Neoplatonist interpreters of Aristotle, he rejected the notion of the agent intellect:

> As for that Opinion, that the *Conceptions of the Mind* and intelligible Ideas or *Reasons* of the Minds should be raised out of the Phantasms by the strange Chymistry of an Agent Intelligence; This is founded on a Mistake of *Aristotle's* Meaning, who never dreamed of any such a Chimerical Agent Intelligence, as appears from the Greek Interpreters that best understood him.[64]

Despite the pioneering Neoplatonic project that Ralph Cudworth carried out, his scepticism prevented him from following Albert's ambitious project of 'nature as reason'. Thus, Cudworth lowered the bar in the endeavour of ever ascertaining what really happens in the collaborative work between brain, mind and soul and how does it happen – in other words, with what tradition has called natural law. The disenchantment with what is best in a human being, the divine element in us, would bring thinkers to search for rationality through other means.

5.2.3 *Necessary Discursive Reasoning*

Sanderson's philosophical efforts and minutely logical description of how to achieve purity of conscience may be explained, from a theological perspective, as promoting an alternative safest moral way, in the face of scepticism, both for the individual and the community. In Biblical terms, Sanderson linked evidence of a truth with its necessity for the achievement of salvation.[65] In turn, his study of morality integrated the causal principle of necessity into syllogistic reasoning to create a secure guide on how to act. The way a philosopher such as Buridan explained the rationality of ethics through its inscription in a causal order was, though similar, less ambitious than Sanderson's, since the former recognized our imperfect access to the knowledge of that order, and the multitude of circumstances

[64] Cudworth, A *Treatise Concerning Eternal and Immutable Morality*, p. 146.

[65] 'The most necessary truths and such as sufficed to bring our forefathers (in the primitive and succeeding times) to heaven are so clearly revealed in scripture and have been so universally and constantly consented unto by the Christian church in a continued succession of times as that to doubt of them must needs argue a spirit of pride and singularity at least ... But in things less evident (and therefore also less necessary) no man ought to be either too stiff in his own private opinion or too peremptory in judging those that are otherwise minded' from the Sermon preached by Sanderson before the King at Berwick in 1639, quoted in Lake 'Serving God and the Times', p. 105

that would remain beyond our grasp.[66] Sanderson's employment of causal necessity in moral philosophy and metaphysics gave his work a particular mechanical bent, which must surely have appealed to pious students of the new science such as Robert Boyle and John Locke.

Sanderson delimited the sphere of conscience as dealing with things 'spiritual' or 'supernatural', but also with things *moral* which he defined as entailing 'whether they be *good* or *evil, lawfull* or *unlawfull, free* or *necessary*', and essentially depending on whether they led to or avoided sin.[67] His moral categories of good, lawful and necessary are categories drawn from voluntarist theology – the same categories he also transferred to the human legislator as wholly contingent on God's will. Crucially, these are not moral categories operating in the sphere of practical reason and allowing one to discern right from wrong. Sanderson's scepticism, visible in his description of the obscured light of reason, forced him to develop every moral category from elaborations deduced from the supreme law, i.e. the will of God. His clarification of how the liberty of conscience pertained to the judgment and not to will is a good example of this. He considered that only a positive law requiring that *one thinks in a certain manner* about the world – absent a necessary truth backing it – would force or violate the operation of conscience. Sanderson drew a sharp distinction between the situation in which the magistrate commanded something because it was thought to be 'necessary', or prohibited something because it was considered 'unlawful', which was contrary to the freedom of conscience; and the situation in which the thing begun to be classified as 'necessary and lawful' only after the command of the magistrate, but not before:

> The first Necessity which anteceded the Law, and is supposed by it to be some cause of it, is contrary to the liberty of the Conscience; but the other, which followeth the Law and proceedeth from it as an effect thereof is not repugnant to it; The reason of this difference is, because the antecedent necessity which the Law supposeth, doth necessarily require some assent of the *practical judgment*; but to the following necessity which proceedeth from the Law, the consent of the will is sufficient to the performance of that outward work which by the Law is commanded.[68]

66 About Buridan on this point see Christophe Grellard, 'Probabilisme et approximation du vrai au xive siècle' in Jean-Philippe Genet ed., *La vérité. Vérité et crédibilité: construire la vérité dans le système de communication de l'Occident (XIIIe-XVIIe siècle)* (Paris: Éditions de la Sorbonne, École française de Rome, 2017), p. 70.

67 'I call that *lawful* which may be done without Sin, and that *free*, which without Sin may be omitted; now the same thing (any one circumstance being added or taken away, or anyways changed) may be made *unlawful* of that which was *Lawful*, and *necessary* of that which before was free', Sanderson, *Several Cases of Conscience*, p. 82; p. 121.

68 Sanderson, *Several Cases of Conscience*, p. 202.

An act *indifferent* in its own nature, when it was commanded by the law, became 'honest and necessary'; when forbidden, 'evil and unlawful.' The action did not change in itself or in its own nature, physically or morally. But the obligation that the law brought into existence changed an act from one freely carried out into a necessary act.[69]

Therefore, only the will of God was the measure of good and of what was necessary, and anything that was God's will was necessarily good.[70] Human will was absolutely free, 'blind' and undetermined, but was in 'potential to another', and this meant that 'it is necessary that there should be some Law or Rule, which may direct it in the acting'. Thus the 'office' of the conscience: of examining, judging, and informing must be guided by a certain rule. In all cases, one must follow 'the rule of law which is certain', and not the example of other men, which was uncertain.[71] In the account of Sanderson's *Lectures*, the 'proper Rule of Conscience' was obviously solely the will of God, the 'supreme law-giver', in whatever way God had revealed his will to human beings. Furthermore, the will of God was disclosed in two ways: through 'authority' and 'the discourse of reason'. Next to the will of God ('the immediate rule of conscience') was 'the light of reason'.[72] But the bottom line was how an individual's conscience could discover, through a clouded and obscured light of reason, what was good, lawful or necessary – or the opposite – in any given case. Initially, Sanderson framed the knowledge of the moral act as a dual syllogism of demonstrative knowledge.

> Every thing that is unjust is to be eschewed.
> Every theft is unjust, therefore
> Every theft is to be eschewed.

The first is provided by the law of nature, the second by reason and the third is the conclusion that conscience brings. The second syllogism is the application of the previous conclusion to a particular fact.

> All Theft is to be eschewed
> This which is now propounded to me to be done is
> a Theft, therefore it is to be eschewed[73]

[69] Sanderson, *Several Cases of Conscience*, p. 225.

[70] Quoting Damascenus approvingly, he wrote 'Quod vult Deus id bonum esse necesse est; cujus scilicet Voluntas boni mensura est'. Sanderson, *De obligatione conscientiae*, p. 112.

[71] Sanderson, *Several Cases of Conscience*, p. 81.

[72] Sanderson, *Several Cases of Conscience*, p. 116; p. 126; p. 143.

[73] Sanderson, *Several Cases of Conscience*, p. 14. (emphasis Sanderson)

Sanderson viewed the most proper definition of conscience as being when 'the last conclusion in the course of both syllogisms' was established.[74] The light of nature had a crucial role in this dual syllogism. As noted, Sanderson was inconsistent with regard to the 'light innate' – a sort of sparkling or fire that made human beings the image of God – claiming at times that it was practically obscured, while affirming at others that some principles may be 'known by the light of Nature, or Revelation'. Thus, the light of nature made it possible for individual human beings to grasp the principle that 'no unjust thing is to be done'.[75] At any rate, he placed greater emphasis on what he termed 'the light acquired' through the discourse of reason. In summary, Sanderson employed four main types of notions of the light of nature in his lectures on conscience: the 'light of nature' per se, which sometimes referred specifically to the obscured image of God in human beings, while at other times described any type of light in human reason; the 'light innate', which was the spark of the divine image in human beings; 'the light inferred', which established what was necessary for every Christian to believe; and 'the light acquired', which determined what was necessary for any human being according to natural law and discursive reasoning.

The first sentence of the first syllogism – '[e]very thing that is unjust is to be eschewed' – was as a matter of fact the main, and apparently sole principle of the law of nature that human beings captured almost intuitively or innately – it was nevertheless quite a powerful one.[76] The 'upright conscience was the conscience capable of reaching the conclusion of the second syllogism with true and certain knowledge of the passions involved and could 'demonstrate it by the next cause'. If the upright conscience could conform itself to the next rule in the syllogism it was upright respectively. If it could also do so in relation to the superior rule – i.e. the first syllogism – it was absolutely so.[77] Sanderson applied here his mechanical idea that rules like 'causes' worked with 'a kind of subordination':

> From the *Law of Nature* many particular Propositions of things to be done, like so many *Conclusions* from their *Principles,* are deduced by the *discourse of Reason* to the use of the Conscience; In which, unless we orderly

[74] Still three other relative ways to understand conscience were: the knowledge of the first universal principle about avoiding evil, the very process of reasoning contained in the two syllogisms and, a final definition, adequate to the era of empiricism, 'the aggregate knowledge of many particular acts of which the whole account of our life and conversation doth consist', Sanderson, *Several Cases of Conscience*, pp. 13–16.

[75] Sanderson, *Several Cases of Conscience*, p. 15; p. 132.

[76] Sanderson, *Several Cases of Conscience*, p. 15.

[77] Sanderson, *Several Cases of Conscience*, p. 108.

> proceed from the first unto the last, we shall be apt to erre, as already I have expressed; we must therefore be very carefull, that in every part of the *Discourse* the proceeding be legitimate, that those things that follow, may aptly depend upon those which go before, *and that the consequence be necessary*; lest the Conscience being mis-led, do not dictate *this* or *that* or otherwise to the *will* than what it ought to do.[78]

If the conscience had to proceed mechanically following a sort of necessary chain of propositions in order to be upright, when the 'discourse of reason' did not operate properly, remorse would automatically ensue:

> Those things, which being violated, do leave a Remorse upon the Conscience, do oblige the Conscience for so it must necessarily be, that all remorse, or reproof of Conscience must proceed from the sense of some obligation, as all other effects do follow their causes.[79]

With the classics, Sanderson saw that the process of reasoning was key to acting well. He departed from their view that we already possess all the knowledge but fall short of truth through passions and imagination. Sanderson's theory was constructed by diminishing analysis of desires and imagination, and by laying stress on faulty reasoning – failure to follow the necessary steps – as causing the frustration of God's will in human beings and deviation from our obligations.[80]

5.2.4 *The Necessity of Obedience*

Notwithstanding the value attributed to the principle of freedom of conscience, it is startling how Sanderson made freedom of conscience

[78] Sanderson, *Several Cases of Conscience*, p. 144 (emphasis mine); 'E Lege naturæ deducuntur per discursum Rationis ad usum Conscientiæ, multæ particulares de rebus agendis Propositiones; velut Conclusiones ex suis Principiis. Qua in re, nisi a primo ad ultimum rite procedatur, proclive est errare; ut ante dictum est. Quare diligenter videndum, ut in singulis partibus *discursus* legitimus fiat *processus*; utque posteriora quæque a prioribus apte pendeant, et ex eis necessario consequantur: ne Conscientia in errorem prolapsa voluntati aliud aliterve, quam oportuit, dictet.' Sanderson, *De obligatione conscientiae*, p. 125.

[79] Sanderson, *Several Cases of Conscience*, p. 179.

[80] 'Next at "All intellect then" he [Aristotle] applies what has been said to a particular accidental factor in movement or action, explaining why we go amiss in our actions. "All intellect" he says, "is right", by which he means that we never err about the first principles of action, about such truths as "it is wrong to do harm to anyone" or "injustice is never right", and so on. Those principles correspond to the equally infallible first principle of the speculative reason. But as for the consequences of these first principles, if we apprehend them aright it is because our thought is consistent with our grasp of the principles, whereas if we deviate from the truth the fault lies in our reasoning. Appetition and imagination (motive-principles likewise) may be, on the other hand, either right or wrong. Hence if we

compatible with an absolute insistence on external obedience to the law, as the 'safer' way in all doubtful cases he presented. As soon as the method of functioning of the mechanical conscience in necessary matters was established, he moved on to explain why human laws had binding force. Positive laws that determined particulars and dealt with 'things indifferent' – such as tariff levels, what merchandise may or may not be lawfully exported or imported in such and such a country, what garments were suitable for what university degree, what statutes were dispensable – had no binding force per se, because 'God alone is that Law-maker.'[81] Only things that were binding as a consequence of the nature of the matter – as an internal cause – were obligatory in themselves. Things indifferent were binding by virtue of God's commandment to obey the lawgiver.[82] As a matter of fact, Sanderson wondered whether 'these things indifferent' were not 'the most proper and the only most fit matter of Humane Laws', a large field in which 'the power of man might exercise it self'.[83]

Firstly, there was Sanderson, the natural lawyer, condemning the presumption of a human lawgiver who, on a matter that was in itself 'morally indifferent', would dare to impose an obligation founded 'on the truth of the thing'. Morally indifferent things could only become obligations 'that induce a necessity' on the basis of the possession of legitimate authority, and not on truth – i.e. 'formally' but not 'materially'. Although the subject must obey outwardly, in cases of this type his or her conscience remained free. Secondly, Sanderson decried that 'wild Reformation', the 'Innovators' that would rather 'against all common sense' take 'away from the world all indifferency' rather than 'grant unto the Magistrate any power of determining of Rites & Laws altogether'. In Sanderson's view, to deny the magistrate that power amounted to 'fight[ing] against the Laws and Constitutions of both Kinds' ecclesiastical and political'.[84]

Instead, he argued that human law must always be binding, at least formally, due to 'the inbred depravity of the human heart' and 'the craft of the old serpent' – the innate depravity of the human heart also made

act amiss it is, in the last analysis, because we fall short of what we intellectually know; and our previous conclusion stands, that the final motive-impulse comes from the object of desire.' *Aristotle's De Anima. In the version of William Moerbecke and the Commentary of St Thomas Aquinas* (1951, Book III, Lectio 15, § 826).

81 Sanderson, *Several Cases of Conscience*, p. 176.

82 Sanderson, *Several Cases of Conscience*, p. 177.

83 Sanderson, *Several Cases of Conscience*, p. 222.

84 Sanderson, *Several Cases of Conscience*, p. 223; p. 227.

punishment necessary.[85] Sanderson's insistence on obedience was characteristically Anglican.[86] However, Sanderson's peculiarity lies in his transferal of that Anglican ideal to a civil commonwealth. In his lectures on conscience, he applied the religious requirements of obedience to church laws, sincere participation in rituals and avoidance of theological controversy to the moral demand to submit to and obey civil laws and to the obligation to avoid conflict. John William Packer once distinguished the 'spirit of martyrdom' of the Laudian cleric Henry Hammond in 1649, when dealing with the same issue of obedience to the Conqueror, from Sanderson's 'spirit of accommodation'.[87] The correspondence between the two men is also indicative of the consistency of Sanderson's doctrine rather than only of Sanderson's accommodation. The violation of any just obligation 'only in the Case of Necessity, not otherwise to be avoided' was framed within an imaginary conversation

[85] 'Furthermore, seeing both are certain, that the Consciences of Men are free, and ought to be so, which Liberty no Humane Power can, or may infringe; And that an *Obligation* is a kind of a Bond, and doth induce a necessity, which seemeth to be opposite, and to fight with *just Liberty* (for neither is the any ways free who is bound, neither can he be free to both, who by some necessity is bound to either) that it plainly may appear that this Obligation of Conscience, of which we now do treat, may consist with the just Liberty of Conscience, we must necessarily in this place give you another distinction, which is, that the *Precepts* of Humane Law may be taken two ways, either *formally* for the *Act* it self of giving the precepts, or *materially* for the thing precepted; If the Law giver therefore should intend an Obligation, or impose on the Subject a necessity of obeying, from giving the Precept of this Law taken *materially*, that is, from the necessity of the thing it self which is precepted, which notwithstanding in the truth of the thing, was not necessary before that Law was made, he in that very fact should lay a force upon the Conscience of the Subject, which should be repugnant to the Liberty of it; But it he should derive his Obligation from giving the precept of his Law taken *formally*, that is from the legitimate Authority with which he himself is invested that gives it (a moral indifferency of the thing precepted in the mean time remaining, and in the same state in which it was before the Law was made) although the obligation followeth which imposeth on the Conscience a necessity of obeying, yet the inward Liberty of the Conscience remaineth uninjuried and intire'. Sanderson, *Several Cases of Conscience*, p. 200; p. 217; p. 286.

[86] McGee, *The Godly Man in Stuart England*, pp. 94–100.

[87] John William Packer, *The Transformation of Anglicanism. 1643–1660, with Special Reference to Henry Hammond* (Manchester: Manchester University Press, 1969), p. 180. On Sanderson's counsel for 'accommodation' see: 'so it is more likely, and it is to be presumed that the lawful Heir hath a greater care of the safety of his people (…) than he who having newly usurped the supreme Magistracy will be more careful, it is likely, to establish his newly acquired Greatness, than to procure the safety of the publick, and therefore the lawful Heir had rather that as modestly as they could they should accommodate themselves to the present affairs for their own safety, than to run into a certain destruction, by making an unreasonable, and an unsuccessful opposition against one that overpowers them.' Sanderson, *Several Cases of Conscience*, p. 175.

between one's conscience and 'the oppressed power, to whom my Obed. is justly due', who observing the 'Necessity of the present case, & of all the Circumstances thereof' would consent to one's manner of external compliance.[88] This position about political obedience was not far from Hobbes's *de facto* theory.

> As far therefore as the peace and safety of that society of which that Citizen is a Member doth require, so far he is bound to obey the commands of that person, who *de facto* is the chief Magistrate in that society.[89]

Secondly, human law must be binding, since in Sanderson's architecture the lawgiver was the supreme power:

> The Law-giver out of the plenitude of his power doth prescribe and constitute the Law, which the inferior Judge is no lesse bound for the future to observe than the people themselves.[90]

To all appearances, by the time the Royalist Sanderson gave his lectures he had already accepted the defeat of Charles I, who was still alive at that point.[91] Hence he pleaded with his audience to adopt a position of passive civil obedience to the usurper for the sake of the survival of the nation, but without giving him anything belonging to the rightful heir or to the Church.[92] In fact, as a casuist, he argued extensively that people were bound to obey the usurper's law. Subjects were not bound on the grounds of the tyrant's law, which, lacking right, was unlawful, but only to law 'equivocally'. However, 'according to the condition of humane affairs, there may be such an exigency of necessity', which meant that subjects were failing in their dual 'duty' to themselves and England, if they did not obey – any citizen in this situation was 'not bound to the law but to himself and to his Country'. The reasons he adduced were to avoid provoking the wrath of the holder of the sword that at his pleasure could take lives and fortunes away, 'from hence is the first necessity of obedience'. The obligation of any 'prudent' and 'honest man' was to consider the

88 Packer, *The Transformation of Anglicanism*, p. 181.

89 Sanderson, *Several Cases of Conscience*, p. 172; see on Hobbes de facto theory, Hoekstra, 'The de facto Turn in Hobbes's Political Philosophy'.

90 Sanderson, *Several Cases of Conscience*, p. 250.

91 Charles execution occurred on the 30th January 1649. His references to the suffering Christ killed for reasons of expediency, implying the impersonation by the captive King, a common theme of the Restoration, may have been added later when he revised the text. Sanderson, *Several Cases of Conscience* p. 66; see on this Collins, *In the Shadow of Leviathan*, p. 33.

92 Sanderson, *Several Cases of Conscience*, p. 173.

real 'present situation' and endeavour 'to live safely, and in peace' and also to safeguard 'Fields, Houses and possessions': in a word, the issue at hand was 'the advantage of himself and of his fellow-Citizens'.[93] Other reasons were gratitude for government and the much worse situation in which everyone would end up otherwise, and Sanderson went on to describe the dreaded state of nature without giving it that name.[94] He ultimately adopted the same reasoning in his resolution of 'the Case of the Engagement', when Parliament, frightened by the growing Royalism of Scottish Presbyterians, imposed a new oath of allegiance in 1650. Camille Slights termed Sanderson's appeasing attitude in the Engagement controversy 'ingenious piety'.[95] It may equally be described as a divine's common sense, sowing unity and peace of conscience after a civil war, instead of promoting a war of all against all.

The last reason from which arose 'the third necessity of obeying the *present power*' was that 'no man is born only for himself, but for public profit'.[96] In this way, Sanderson described the extent to which 'the duty of Conscience' bound Charles's subjects to the dictator who sat 'in the throne of supremacy'. Interestingly, in Sanderson's theoretical explanation de facto rule was an imperative not limited to the state of exception of 1647 but a general feature of government: '[w]hatsoever is to be done in a peculiar reference to its end, ought to be done, as shall appear most necessary and profitable' for achieving that end, he wrote in a clearly Hobbesian turn.[97] Since the 'tranquility and safety of Humane society' were both the purpose of civil government and of obedience to it, Sanderson distinguished 'three things very necessary' for their preservation: the 'defence of our Country', 'the administration of right' and 'the care of Commerce and Merchandize, concerning buying, selling, exchanging, and all manner of contracts', respectively 'Distributive' and 'Commutative Justice'. Without these three elements, human society would again be in a terrible state of nature:

93 Sanderson, *Several Cases of Conscience,* p. 169; in the almost absence of latitude for resistance to authority, to those whom God has given the power to make laws, Sanderson resembles also William Perkins although Sanderson has more of a pragmatic approach, Mosse, 'Puritan Political Thought and the "Cases of Conscience"', p. 114.

94 See in next page, quote of note 98.

95 Slights, 'Ingenious Piety'.

96 Sanderson, *Several Cases of Conscience,* p. 171.

97 'When therefore our refusal to obey, frustrates the End for which the Sovereignty was ordained; then there is no Liberty to refuse: otherwise there is.' Hobbes, *Leviathan*, Noel Malcolm (ed.), ch. 21, p. 338.

> all things presently will run to ruine, all things and all places will be filled with Plunder, Slaughter, Deceit and Injuries, the lives of the most innocent Citizens, their Wives and Fortunes will become prey, and a sport unto the lusts of our armed Superiors.[98]

The solution to this particular moral case, no doubt weighing heavily on the consciences on many of the King's subjects in 1647, offers another perspective on Sanderson's method of describing the necessity of certain aspects of the functioning of the world that bound conscience. He articulated, in the contemporary idiom of necessity, what was perceived by many to be the contemporary 'common good' in stressing the need to obey the government and human laws and in the reasons he gave for doing so. This perspective was expressed when he gave his lectures in 1648 at which point obedience to the Commonwealth was stressed, and again at the beginning of the Restoration in terms of obedience to the returning King.[99]

According to Sanderson, also, certain rules applied in respect of doubts of conscience over compliance with the law – essentially concerning the necessity of the law in question. Laws that were possible to the majority but impossible to a minority could be lawfully made when 'some extraordinary great cause, and a manifest necessity' required it. However, those who could not comply – for instance, in relation to the payment of a large tax 'for the necessary use of the Commonwealth' – were exempted from the application of the law, though obliged to disclose with simplicity 'the slendernesse of their Estate' and pay what amount they could. In respect of 'a very grievous law', an honest citizen ought to see all the qualifications and clauses of the law to avoid being snared, but 'if any evident or necessary cause for the good of the Commonwealth' so required one had to obey the law, even 'with the ruin of his whole Estate.' Sanderson gave many appropriate examples, but his conclusion was clear: 'every good man is to prefer the publick above all private interests.' On the face of an extremely burdensome law, the bottom line for a private individual to decide between economic survival and compliance was the presence of 'some remarkable necessity or fear of publick danger.'[100]

Several Cases of Conscience evidenced a very learned scholar, a devout and moderate divine, and an eirenic politician. But Sanderson could be also uncompromising about certain things. First, that preserving rightfulness

[98] Sanderson, *Several Cases of Conscience*, p. 172.

[99] Sanderson, *Several Cases of Conscience*, p. 240; Kempshall, *The Common Good in Late Medieval Political Thought*.

[100] Sanderson, *Several Cases of Conscience*, p. 204.

of a pure conscience in business and in politics according to the 'Purity of the Gospel of our Saviour Christ' was in all respects fundamental. Second, that the pursue of the ends of the Civil power, the preservation of the people, ought to be done in peace, tranquility and with honesty and godliness, and not by 'the enlargement of Empire' as 'the Politicians of this world do affirm'.[101] Evidently, Robert Boyle and, to a great extent, John Locke did not share the latter point. But they fully agreed on the first of these points, which constitute an English type of model for a good Christian and peace-loving politician, characterized by rigour, honesty and piety.[102]

A Hobbesian politician of sorts as well, Sanderson felt that his world had fallen apart but not his God, and found in piety, reason and country what he valued most: moral uprightness. Moreover, the Anglican divine and the Reformers dealt with in the two previous chapters shared a foundation of a metaphysics of necessity embodied by the pursuit of necessary knowledge, obedience to the magistrate and the necessary mechanical reasoning for human conscience. Thereby they compensated for the fall of tradition and scepticism of reason while enlarging the possibilities of action in their troubled and stimulating world.

101 Sanderson, *Several Cases of Conscience*, p. 208; p. 209.

102 In the *2021 Carlyle Lectures* by Mark Goldie Locke's ambiguity about the Empire was apparent, but also how in a certain way that model of politician shaped Locke's actions. The impact of that model in the development of the British Empire would deserve further study.

6

The Grand Business of Nature

6.1 The *Oeconomy* of Nature

Robert Boyle's status as a scientific pioneer, and the many emotional insecurities that this entailed may have fuelled his notorious feud with the formidable author of *Leviathan*.[1] But whatever the reasons for their enmity and whoever prevailed in their feud, it is certain that Boyle's philosophical work on natural law is mostly known nowadays only within specialist circles, while Hobbes, on account of his theory of natural law, is recognized today as the author of probably the most important theory of the state in modernity. The scope of Boyle's influence in the context of natural law is, however, another matter entirely. This chapter is concerned with just one aspect of Boyle's proposal regarding knowledge: the way in which he connected nature, theology and economy through science as a multiplier of sorts. The task of this chapter is thus to show how Boyle's new political system for an economics of natural science, primarily involving the utilitarian exploitation of nature and of trade, connected with his contribution to the development of natural law and natural philosophy, stripped of moral natural law. Natural law was thus rendered non-human. The theoretical problem that Boyle set himself to address was to ascertain the way in which the activity of matter (as opposed to spirit) related to God.[2] Descartes's denial of the activity of powers in

[1] 'Those Fellows of Gresham who are most believed, and are as masters of the rest, dispute with me about physics. They display new machines, to show their vacuum and trifling wonders, in the way that they behave who deal in exotic animals which are not to be seen without payment. All of them are my enemies.' Thomas Hobbes, 'Dedicatory Epistle to Samuel Sorbière', Hobbes's *Physical Dialogue* (1661). Boyle's and Hobbes's feud is described in Shapin and Schaffer, *Leviathan and the Air-Pump: Hobbes, Boyle, and the Experimental Life*, quote at p. 347.

[2] This appears so in different levels of theoretical abstraction in his works of natural philosophy, and is also clearly expressed: 'So that to me, who desire to have it explained how an immaterial Substance can move matter, and consequently, how God can do it, it will be no satisfaction to say, that the Rational Soul can move the Body 'tis joined to, since that Power

nature, against Aristotle and Aquinas's ideas, and his attribution of all the work in matter to God through his laws of nature may have acted as a spur to Boyle's work in the realm of natural philosophy.[3] Boyle, however, thought that human reason could carry out this theological exercise only by investigating matter. Remaining within the Baconian tradition, his goals were at once devotional and utilitarian: he sought to expand human beings' dominion over 'matter'. He did this as a transitional figure who operated within the broader intellectual context of early modern or Renaissance Europe characterized by the appearance of anti-Aristotelian perceptions of nature that increasingly enlarged the scope of human beings' dominion over it.[4] Theological principles about an omnipotent and bountiful God were crucial to Boyle's plans for the achievement of broader management of nature, but as a rule, he avoided consideration of anthropological theology in his scientific writings.[5] Boyle's idea of recovering the bountiful God might well be compared with the provident ruler that the Arminians had recovered half a century earlier. They rejected the punitive God of Calvin and asserted that by attributing reason, will and affection to human beings, which were only diminished not destroyed by the sin of our first parents, Adam and Eve, God provided human beings

is referred merely to God's appointment: and the question is, how God himself can be conceived to move matter.' Robert Boyle, 'Advices about Judging of Things Said to Transcend Reason. third advise.' in Michael Hunter and Edward B. Davis eds. *The Works of Robert Boyle vol 9. Publications of 1678–1683*, p. 404.

3 The context of Cartesian occasionalism is presented usefully in Benjamin Hill, Henrik Lagerlund and Stathis Psillos 'Introduction' in the same eds. *Reconsidering Causal Powers: Historical and Conceptual Perspectives* (Oxford: Oxford University Press, 2021).

4 Since the Second World War this argument has been explored with increasing degree of concern. In recent years it has accelerated with the intensification of the environmental crisis, R. G. Collingwood, *The Idea of Nature* (Oxford: Oxford University Press, 1978 [1945]) p. 93, partly intellectual history of science, partly an ecofeminist project in Carolyn Merchant, *The Death of Nature. Women Ecology and the Scientific Revolution* (San Francisco: Harper & Row, 1990). For Merchant, Newton's scientific work is the culmination of the death of nature through the conceptual world of corpuscularianism, domination and manipulation of nature and progressive economic development, while Boyle appears as a quite marginal figure; Bruno Latour, *We Have Never Been Modern*, Catherine Porter (trans.), (Cambridge: Harvard University Press, 1993); see also from a theological perspective, recently Jacob Holsinger Sherman 'Reading the Book of Nature after Nature' 11 *Religions* (2020). Boyle as a transitional figure between the Aristotelian system and experimental diversification of science in Anstey, *The Philosophy of Robert Boyle*, p. 4.

5 This dualism is illuminated by Peter Harrison and John Henry's debate. See Peter Harrison, 'Voluntarism and Early Modern Science' 40 *History of Science* (2002); John Henry, 'Voluntarist Theology at the Origins of Modern Science: A Response to Peter Harrison' 47 *History of Science* (2009), p. 104; Peter Harrison, 'Voluntarism and the Origins of Modern Science: A Reply to John Henry' 47 *History of Science* (2009) 223–231.

with natural sociability.[6] Only Boyle, instead of focusing on the moral aspects, he worked with the material aspects of human beings' divine government. The disappearance of moral natural law from the concerns of seventeenth century natural philosophers, I argue, placed human beings outside nature and subjected nature to a new lord and master: the human being. The sophistication of Boyle's philosophical investigation of the concept of nature was instrumental to this endeavour.

The first important natural philosopher of the seventeenth century to describe nature as an *oeconomy* was Sir Kenelm Digby (1603–1665).[7] Peter Remien has recently reinstated Digby as the thinker of the *oeconomy* of nature, which, in Remien's view, was predicated on an ontology that

[6] James Moore, 'Calvinians, Arminians, Socinians: Popular Sovereignty and Natural Rights in Early Modern Political Thought', in Ian Hunter and Richard Whatmore (eds.), *Philosophy, Rights and Natural Law. Essays in Honour of Knud Haakonssen*, (Edinburgh University Press, 2019), p. 23.

[7] Kenelm Digby, *Two Treatises: In the One of Which The Nature of Bodies; in the other, The Nature of Mans Soule, is Looked Into* (London: Print. for John Williams, 1645). Digby combined mechanic philosophy, a species of atomism and Aristotelianism. According to Antonio Clericuzio he was one of the most influential natural philosophers of mid-seventeenth century, see, Antonio Clericuzio, *Elements, Principles and Corpuscles. A Study of Atomism and Chemistry in the Seventeenth Century* (Springer, 2000), p. 81. A political interpretation of why despite his brilliance as a thinker Digby remained in his time and in historiography an outsider, in a word, because as a Catholic he had his own agenda for the new science, John Henry, 'Sir Kenelm Digby, Recusant Philosopher' in G. A. J. Rogers, Tom Sorrell and Jill Kraye (eds.) *Insiders and Outsiders in the Seventeenth Century* (London and New York: Routledge 2009); a helpful overview of his natural philosophy by Betty Jo Dobbs, 'Studies in the Natural Philosophy of Sir Kenelm Digby', 18 *Ambix* (1971) 1–25; see also about Digby's project of illuminating the historical corruption of Aristotle's philosophy and thus of blocking Pomponazzi's materialist Aristotelianism, and about Digby in England and his displacement by the new Epicureanism, Dmitri Levitin, *Ancient Wisdom in the Age of the New Science. Histories of Philosophy in England, c. 1640–1700* (Cambridge: Cambridge University Press, 2015), pp. 468–474; pp. 688–692; Digby's discussion on gravity and the sun is remarkable, while he broke new ground, in particular, as a biologist on embryology, see M. Foster (2009, January 08). Digby, Sir Kenelm (1603–1665), natural philosopher and courtier. *Oxford Dictionary of National Biography*. https://doi-org.libproxy.helsinki.fi/10.1093/ref:odnb/7629. The ambivalence of Hartlib towards Digby is notable. Evidently charmed by the Catholic natural philosopher, not the least reason for that being that Digby was 'in very good favour with the lord protector' and that Digby had hired Hartlib's 'chemical son' Clodius in his laboratory, it is plain that it was not appropriate to talk about Digby as one of their own, for instance in his correspondence with Boyle 'Letter Hartlib to Robert Boyle, 8 May 1654' in *The Correspondence of Robert Boyle*, vol. 1 1636–1661, pp. 169–179; Digby is allotted with the 'Cartesians', 'Armians' and 'Calvians' and their failed philosophical and theological discourses, in 'Letter Hartlib to John Worthington 22 February 1659'. See Hartlib Papers, www.dhi.ac.uk/hartlib/context. See more on the political context of Digby and his endorsing of Blackloism, in Jeffrey R. Collins, 'Thomas Hobbes and the Blackloist Conspiracy of 1649' in 45 *The Historical Journal* (2002), 305–331.

separated humanity from nature.[8] Remien goes on to describe how Boyle employed Digby's *oeconomy* for a different purpose – that of expressing God's governance of the system that the natural world constituted.[9] My reading of Digby differs from Remien's, as I emphasize his project of defending the compatibility of the new science with faith. From within the ranks of mechanical and atomist philosophies, Digby, a prominent biologist in the history of science, wrote in protest against their impending turn to materialism, and hoped to show that the whole *oeconomy* of nature could not be merely a concatenation of material and causal effects, but the work of a designer.[10]

6.1.1 The Last Atom

The following interpretation offers a fresh context for Boyle's work. I suggest that Boyle's novelty lay not in showing God's sovereignty over the *oeconomy* (something Digby had already done), but in seeking to perfect on an intellectual level Digby's naturalist project by distancing through his use of chemistry the philosophical natural explanations of nature from moral or religious accounts.[11] Furthermore, Boyle did this by using utopian theology as a foundation that would also serve his utilitarian ideas. His atomism required the deconstruction of past knowledge, displacing moral or religious epistemologies about nature – for the goal was to enlarge knowledge – while a theology of abundance sanctioned the extraction of material benefits from the pursue of natural sciences. In more personal

[8] Remien, *The Concept of Nature in Early English Modern Literature*.

[9] Remien explains that Digby had been obscured and dismissed from histories of ecology since he did not fit the main narrative of how ecology developed, summarily, unrelated to mechanical philosophy. Remien, *The Concept of Nature in Early English Modern Literature*, p. 33 and generally ch. 1.

[10] Digby concludes accordingly his first massive treatise on the nature of bodies: 'And when you have once gained thus much of your selfe, to gree unto an orderly course and generation of any single effect; by the power of a material cause working it, raise but your discourse a straine higher, and looke with reverence and duty upon the immensity of that provident Architect, out of whose hands these masterpieces issue, and unto whom it is as easie to make one linke alone: and then you will no longer sticke at allowing the whole *oeconomy* of those actions; to be nothing else, but a production of material effects, by a due ranging and ordering of materiall causes.' See also his nuanced account of the 'vis formatrix', Digby, *Two Treatises*, p. 289; p. 400.

[11] In his unpublished papers, when praising atomism Boyle placed together 'Gassendus, Magnenus (1590–1679, author of Democritus revived or On Atoms, 1646) and Des Cartes' with 'our deservedly famous Countryman Sir Kenelme Digby' see Richard S. Westfall, 'Unpublished Boyle Papers Relating to Scientific Method. II' in 12 *Annals of Science* (1957), p. 111.

terms, as a scientist, Boyle appeared fascinated with matter and motion. Moreover, the fact that we know God and discover the composition of the world through matter and motion explains Boyle's adoption of the method of isolating matter through mechanical theory, both philosophically and experimentally.[12]

Thomas Hobbes had noted in *The Elements of Law* that 'every man by natural necessity desireth his own good', and then he went on in *Leviathan* to attribute to each human being in the state of nature a natural right to everything, referring mostly to material goods in nature for which one may need to fight in times of scarcity.[13] Thus arose the struggle characteristic of his state of nature. Boyle's rejoinder to this sociological theory was that the desire for one's good was not merely a 'human thing' or a 'necessity' – that it was God who desired the good(s) and knowledge for human beings, and took care that those who were industrious received them:

> For, not content to have provided him all that was requisite either to Support or Accommodate him here, he hath been pleas'd to contrive the World so, that (if Man be not wanting himself) it may afford not onely Necessaries and Delights, but Instructions too.[14]

Nature was thus the solution for humanity, not, as Hobbes had claimed, the problem. In Boyle's normative theory of nature, God the Creator and 'munificent Benefactor', who had endowed the earth richly, was the premise for producing a philosophy of nature. In turn, human beings disappeared from the ambit of the philosophical questions posed by the leading exponent of the new experimental philosophy.[15] Human nature got lost in a theory describing two opposites – the intangible God and a system

[12] 'And, if an Angel himself should work a real change in the nature of a Body, 'tis scarce conceivable to us Men, how he could do it without the assistance of Local Motion; since, if nothing were displac'd or otherwise mov'd than before, (the like hapning also to all external Bodies to which it related,) 'tis hardly conceivable, how it should be in it self other, than just what it was before.' Robert Boyle 'Of the Excellency of Grounds of the Corpuscular or Mechanical Philosophy' in *The Excellency of Theology Compar'ed with natural Philosophy* (as both are objects of men's study) (London: Printed. for Henrry Herringman, 1674; Early English Books Online Text Creation Partnership, 2011, p. 22, http://name.umdl.umich.edu/A28966.0001.001

[13] Hobbes, *The Elements of Law*, n. 14.12 and chapter 3 of this book.

[14] Robert Boyle, 'Of the Usefulness of Experimentall Philosophy, The First Part, Principally as it Relates to the Mind of Man' in *The Works of Robert Boyle*, vol. 3 (London Pickering and Chatto, 1999), p. 232.

[15] Robert Boyle, 'The Christian Virtuoso: Showing That by Being Addicted to Experimental Philosophy a Man Is Rather Assisted, Than Indisposed to Be a Good Christian', in *The Works of Robert Boyle*, vol. 11, p. 303.

or *oeconomy* of physical nature. We saw in Chapter 2 that the individual remembering the now-disappeared corporeal world in Hobbes's thought experiment of the *annihilatio mundi* was still able to remember its conception of body with some accuracy. Some centuries earlier Avicenna had carried out a similar experiment – about a floating man who does not feel or see the corporeal world but knows that he exists – to affirm the existence of the human soul. In Boyle's experiment of the *annihilatio mundi* only an atom survives:

> If we should conceive, that all the rest of the Universe were annihilated, except any of these entire and undivided Corpuscles (…) it is hard to say what could attributed to it, besides Matter, Motion (or Rest,) Bulk, and Shape.[16]

Hobbes had devised a political philosophy for the masses with the tools of his own version of mechanistic natural philosophy. Boyle would in turn produce a popular philosophy of nature with natural laws from which rational human beings were exempt.[17] By means of that philosophy of nature, Boyle, who was at once a forceful and chaotic publicist, also developed economic science or, in other words, principles for making science economically productive for the state, an empire in the making.[18] Michael Hunter noted years ago the danger of taking a narrow approach to the Royal Society's appeal to utility by 'assuming that it referred exclusively to practical, everyday needs'.[19] The breadth and depth of Boyle's thinking helps to overcome this danger, and to ascertain that – strikingly in his case – he was able to be attentive to both grand theory and, to a lesser extent, to daily needs. His economic science is rich, with a background in alchemy, and intriguingly, was destined to establish chemistry as real natural philosophy. At the same time, he articulated his ideas in simple terms destined to reach everyone.

[16] Robert Boyle, *The Origine of Formes and Qualities. According to the Corpuscular Philosophy* in *The Works of Robert Boyle*, vol. 5, p. 315; p. 317.

[17] That this separation contained the seeds of deism transpires in James E. Force, 'The Newtonians and Deism' in James E. Force and Richard H. Popkin (eds.) *Essays on the Context, Nature and Influence of Isaac Newton's Theology* (Dordrecht, Boston, London: Kluwer Academic Publishing, 1990).

[18] Boyle reflected the difficulties he encountered sometimes with his method of writing composition in sections that with his innovative and all-encompassing inquisitive mind might lead to chaos especially when long periods had elapsed in subsequent revisions, see more about this in Hunter and Davis, 'The Making of Robert Boyle's "Free Enquiry into the Vulgarly Recevi'd Notion of Nature" (1686).

[19] Michael Hunter, *Science and Society in Restoration England* (Cambridge: Cambridge University Press, 1981) p. 89.

Boyle devoted many hundreds of pages to showing the interdependence between the new practical science, the products arriving from the empire and the welfare of the country.[20] Between utopia, represented by theology, and scepticism, presented as natural philosophy, human beings re-emerged in his economic science at once as passive subjects of needs and delights, and as lords of nature, and hence industrious agents of change and transmutation.[21] Knowledge and the exploitation of physical nature thus formed a unity:

> And 'tis chiefly by the Knowledge, such as it is, that Experience, (not Art) hath taught Us, of these differing Qualities of Bodies, that we are enabled, by a due application of Agents to Patients, to exercise the little Empire, that we have either Acquired or Regained over the Creatures.[22]

At the same time, consideration of how to multiply the goods of nature and rendering them profitable became a ubiquitous trope in Boyle's studies, published writings and lists of enquiries to fellow scientists and fellow travellers.[23]

6.1.2 *The Multiplier*

Multiplication through investment in science was in the air in the seventeenth century, as we saw in Chapter 4. Boyle's closest friends would also use the argument of multiplication to interest him in rather far-fetched economic schemes. When, for instance, his sister, Lady Ranelagh mediated between him and Benjamin Worsley in 1666 to prompt her brother's investment of 500 pounds in a new project, she argued in those terms. This time the business involved the cultivation of senna, herb with medicinal powers that Worsley had received from Barbados and for whose cultivation he wanted to obtain a patent from the King:

[20] Emphasizing the importance of practice for the great thinkers of the Scientific Revolution see, including Boyle, John Henry, *The Scientific Revolution and the Origins of Modern Science*. Third edition (Hampshire, New York: Palgrave, Macmillan, 2008); also noting the experience with products gained through the new great voyages, see R. Hooykaas, 'The Rise of Modern Science: When and Why?' 20 *British Journal for the History of Science* (1987).

[21] That Bacon was also interested in transmutation, in Catherine Wilson, *Epicureanism at the Origins of Modernity* (Oxford: Clarendon Press, 2008), p. 22.

[22] Boyle, *The Origine of Formes and Qualities according to the Corpuscular Philosophy*, p. 298.

[23] Michael Hunter writes that Boyle was in no way ambivalent about the benefits of trade, personally investing large sums in the East India Company, 'enjoying the benefits of trade while professing that his real interest was in scientific inquiry', Hunter, *Boyle: Between God and Science*, p. 169.

> I may sudainely be able to give you a particular accoumpt of the course Mr. W. (Worsley) thinks of taking to make his senna presently a Commodety & to Multiplye it to great quantities which appears to me neither disingenuous not unpoliticke.[24]

Boyle's theorization of his ideas on economic science occurred through a series of lengthy writings entitled *Of the Usefulness of Experimentall Natural Philosophy* published over a period of eight years (1663–1671).[25] It was nevertheless a theme that would appear in his writings more generally. *Usefulness* advocated the multiplication of commodified natural goods through two channels: naturalists' activity, experiments, alchemy, the study of mines and so on; and managing trades and labour, the introduction or alteration of crafts, businesses or professions, their change of locality and the introduction of engines in manufacturing processes.[26]

In the second half of the seventeenth century, Boyle and his collaborators raised the status to those practicing experimental science almost to become a social class of its own, as Steven Shapin and Simon Schaffer demonstrated some years ago.[27] Experience of scientific knowledge about nature was to be channelled towards utility for economic and theological purposes. Michael Ben Chaim has shown the ways in which Boyle considered experimental philosophy the paradigm of science at the service of a theology of divine workmanship. Boyle perfected the purification of the Christian religion from the supposedly vulgar metaphysics of the Schools that opened the way both to acknowledgment of God, Creator and Designer and to

[24] 'Lady Ranelagh to Boyle 18. September 1666'; in a previous letter she had explained at length the details, both in *The Correspondence of Robert Boyle*, vol. 3, 1666–1667, p. 239; p. 235. Despite Worsley's and Lady Ranelagh's insistence in their correspondence, the clever Boyle did not seem too convinced of that particular prospect, or at least that it should be carried out of his own pocket.

[25] The series on 'The Usefulness of Experimentall Philosophy' amount to more than 500 pages in total in the modern edition of Boyle's works. The Usefulness of Natural Philosophy I and II Sect. 1, in *The Works of Robert Boyle* vol. 3, pp. 189–561; The Usefulness of Natural Philosophy II, Sect. 2 (1671) *The Works of Robert Boyle* vol. 6, pp. 389–541.

[26] Among his letters there is also an intense correspondence about mines with several persons, which show again how Boyle unites erudite science with economic production. For instance, Samuel Colepresse, a virtuoso who died in 1669, answered a list of eighty-nine queries about mines that he was studying. Judging by his answers, Boyle's queries were, though extremely detailed, mainly about the characteristics of areas where mines with diverse minerals may be found, and about the quantities and processes to yield the minerals, in particular tin and silver. The letter also answers a query about 'fiery meteors', suggesting that Boyle was suspecting the possible relation of the origin of heavy elements such as gold with supernova explosions. 'Colepresse to Boyle. 1 February 1667', in *The Correspondence of Robert* Boyle, v. 3, p. 290.

[27] Shapin and Schaffer, *Leviathan and the Air-Pump: Hobbes, Boyle, and the Experimental Life.*

vast knowledge about His Design.[28] Moreover, Boyle was probably propelled into new realms of knowledge by the undeniable nationalism and Independency, both in political and scientific terms, of his millenarian mentors – particularly Benjamin Worsley – who operated outside the strictures of a formal education or school. The development of science, economy and religion were uniquely connected in mid-seventeenth-century, England through Boyle's uncompromising boldness.[29] Certainly, the Reformers of the previous generation were no dilettanti. However, Boyle far outshone them in sophistication – Comenius's basic ideas about a 'professor of necessities' that we saw in Chapter 4 and *Of the Usefulness of Experimentall Natural Philosophy* are worlds apart, in particular due to Boyle's intimate knowledge of the imperial trade – though Comenius is more profound in anthropological terms. As a matter of fact, Boyle became a professional politician of experimental science and sought to advance science and to make it profitable. This trait is visible even in his earliest works and was possibly inherited from his father, the luxury-loving Earl of Cork. It is also to be found in the work of the alchemical authors that inspired him and in that of the Baconian Reformers. In fact, knowledge and profit were the Royal Society's two stated goals and were not merely declared defensively in response to criticism levelled in the 1660s that the Royal Society was made up of gentlemen who killed time by playing with experiments, but as congruent principles within the pragmatist ideas of the period.[30]

Behind Boyle's drive to deconstruct nature, as analysed in Chapter 7, was a thirst for knowledge and scientific curiosity for managing the system or *oeconomy* of nature to the utmost limits, which also ultimately aimed

28 Ben-Chaim, *Experimental Philosophy and the Birth of Empirical Science.*

29 John Henry, 'The Scientific Revolution in England', in Roy Porter and Mikuláš Teich (eds.), *The Scientific Revolution in National Context* (Cambridge: Cambridge University Press, 1992), p. 182.

30 Thus, the Society's historian, Thomas Sprat, wrote that its aims were to produce 'faithful *Records* of all the Works of Nature or Art' and to 'accomplish this, they have indeavor'd, to separate the knowledge of *Nature*, from the colours of *Rhetorick*, the devices of *Fancy*, or the delightful deceit of *Fables*. They have labor'd to inlarge it, from being confin'd to the custody of a few; or from servitude to private interests. They have striven to preserve it from being over-press'd by a confus'd heap of vain, and useless particulars; or from being straitned and bounded too much up by General Doctrines. They have try'd, to put it into a condition of perpetual increasing; by settling an inviolable correspondence between the hand, and the brain. They have studi'd, to make it, not onely an Enterprise of one season, or of some lucky opportunity; but a business of time; a steddy, a lasting, a popular, an uninterrupted Work. They have attempted, to free it from the Artifice, and Humors, and Passions of Sects; to render it an Instrument, whereby Mankind may obtain a Dominion over *Things*, and not onely over one anothers *Iudgements*. And lastly, they have begun to establish these Reformations in Philosophy, not so much, by

at imitating God the Creator. Boyle's philosophical effort expressed in his own way the zeal for economic prosperity of the Reformers, who would, as a matter of course, transform that zeal into theology. In the last few decades, important studies have considered Boyle's significance as a natural philosopher. Rose-Mary Sargent and Philip Anstey have rightly recovered from undeserved obscurity the systematic character of a philosophy that appears from the outset wonderfully asystematic. Later thinkers, such as John Locke and Isaac Newton (1643–1727), evidently found inspiration for their own theories in it.[31] As a rule, however, Boyle's ideas on the economics of science are glossed over, which is surprising as they appear to constitute a powerful engine in his theoretical effort. J. R. Jacob famously interpreted Boyle's political programme for atomism as being solely a religious attack against the scholasticism of Jesuits and papists.[32] Boyle's programme does not, however, really justify that characterization when one takes account of the context in which he worked. Catholics, including the French Pierre Gassendi and the English Sir Kenelm Digby, among others, were the most prominent atomists of the period.[33] Moreover, as discussed in Chapter 4, the economic problem was also a *religious* problem.[34]

Recently studies of Boyle have started to highlight the utilitarian aspects of his work not dealt with by previous scholars. For example, Matthew Day

any solemnity of Laws, or ostentation of Ceremonies, as by solid Practice, and examples: not, by a glorious pomp of Words; but by the silent, effectual, and unanswerable Arguments of real Productions.' Thomas Sprat, *The History of the Royal Society for the Improving of Natural Knowledge* (London: Printed for J. Martyn and J. Allestry, 1667), Early English Books Online Text Creation Partnership, 2011, http://name.umdl.umich.edu/A61158.0001.001 p. 61. Shapin and Schaffer, *Leviathan and the Air-Pump;* Latour, *We Have Never Been Modern*, p. 15. On the critiques, see for instance Margaret Cavendish gendered critique on their 'useless experiments' Lisa T. Sarasohn, 'A Science Turned Upside Down: Feminism and the Natural Philosophy of Margaret Cavendish' 47 *Huntington Library Quarterly* (1984); the satire in plays such as Thomas Shadwell's *The Virtuoso* performed first in 1676, and with success in the next thirty years, where the main role, Sir Nicholas Gimcrack, apparently Boyle, weighed the air for the sake of knowing how much it weighed. Steven Shapin, 'Pump and Circumstance: Robert Boyle's Literary Technology 14 *Social Studies of Science* (1984), p. 498; p. 517.

31 Boyle's intense experimental attitude and reticent attitude to draw conclusions had a complex epistemic goal of showing the multiplicity of sources of truth, see about this Rose-Mary Sargent, *The Diffident Naturalist: Robert Boyle and the Philosophy of Experiment* (Chicago: The University of Chicago Press, 1995); Anstey, *The Philosophy of Robert Boyle.*

32 J. R. Jacob, 'Boyle's Atomism and the Restoration Assault on Pagan Naturalism', 8 *Social Studies on Science* (1978).

33 Sarasohn, *Gassendi's Ethics;* Digby, *Two Treatises.*

34 This point was made for instance by Charles Webster in an article suggesting a broad Reformation and Puritan socioeconomic framework of the Scientific Revolution, Charles Webster, 'Puritanism, Separatism and Science', in David C. Lindberg, and Ronald L. Numbers (eds.), *God and Nature. Historical Essays on the Encounter between Christianity and Science*

has noted that the extant textual evidence makes it impossible to argue that Boyle's interest in political economy was comparable with his interest in nature. However, he argues that Boyle was involved in a project of framing economy as technology. Thus, his invention of an instrument to discriminate between real, degraded and counterfeit money amounted to an attempt to eliminate the human dimensions of money.[35] Also Michael Hunter argued not long ago that probably no one wrote more or better than Boyle in his time about the application of science.[36] But on the whole Boyle's huge significance as a philosopher of nature has remained within the confines of what we would call today natural sciences, and not always without controversy.[37] His name is either absent from histories of the birth of seventeenth-century natural law and political economy or used to denote a peripheral figure who conceived corpuscularianism as a sort of conduit between atomism and Aristotelian and Cartesian natural philosophy and inspired others with his tour de force in experimental philosophy. Significantly, he is often linked to William Petty – whose genius was apparent, for instance, in *Political Arithmetic* (1676) – and to John Locke, possibly the natural lawyer of the seventeenth century whose influence remains strongest today.[38] Petty and Boyle's mutual inspiration and

(Berkeley: University of California Press, 1986); it is more generally the argument of his masterpiece, Webster, *The Great Instauration.* With the specific approach of the Calvinist work ethics it was the argument of the classic Max Weber, *The Protestant Ethic and the Spirit of Capitalism.*

35 Matthew Day 'Restoration Commerce and the Instruments of Trust: Robert Boyle and the Science of Money' 29 *History of the Human Science* (2016), pp. 3–26.

36 Michael Hunter, 'Boyle on the Application of Science', in Jan-Erik Jones (ed.), *The Bloomsbury Companion to Robert Boyle* (London, New York, Oxford, New Delhi, Sydney: Bloomsbury Academic, 2020).

37 For instance, as I understood it, the debate between Alan Chalmers and William Newman is partly about the role Boyle played in the Scientific Revolution as a philosopher, where Newman considered that it was crucial, and I tend to agree with him. See for instance, Alan F. Chalmers, 'Boyle and the Origins of Modern Chemistry: Newman Tried in the Fire' 41 *Studies in History and Philosophy of Science* (2010); and the response, William R. Newman, 'How Not to Integrate the History and Philosophy of Science: A Reply to Chalmers' 41 *Studies in History and Philosophy of Science* (2010).

38 Andrea Finkelstein, *Harmony and the Balance: An Intellectual History of Seventeenth-Century English Economic Thought* (Anne Arbor: University of Michigan Press, 2000); Maifreda, *From Oikonomia to Political Economy;* Akos Silvado, 'The Ontology of Sir William Petty's Political Arithmetic' 26 *The European Journal of the History of Economic Thought* (2019). On the complex question of the Boyle-Locke relationship see Peter R. Anstey, 'Boyle's Influence on Locke', in Jan-Erik Jones (ed.), *The Bloomsbury Companion to Robert Boyle*, p. 48; Ben-Chaim, *Experimental Philosophy and the Birth of Empirical Science;* and adopting a critical standpoint about 'the great influence theory' through a study of Locke's early writings, see Jonathan Craig Walmsley, *John Locke's Natural Philosophy (1632–1671)* (PhD, King's College London, 1998; Reformatted, 2008).

friendship is well known, as is the fact that Locke started work as a theorist around the same time he began to work with Boyle.[39]

'Philosophers', Boyle wrote, 'may have Acquisition of wealth more in their power than in their aim.'[40] However, Boyle's programmatic goal of uniting theology and philosophical knowledge with the goal of making that union useful and profitable is ubiquitous in his work.[41] If his studies had any purpose beyond giving glory to God, generating knowledge and satisfying his prodigious curiosity, it was to achieve 'substantiall Productions to answer the Necessities and Furnish the Accommodations of Humane Life' and to facilitate that the 'artificer learn to make the utmost profit' in order to serve the 'Oeconomical prudence'.[42] In this manner, Boyle's project of knowledge emerges as supported on three pillars: theology, natural science and economy. It is no coincidence that he rectified Bacon's distinction between 'Luciferous' experiments, providing knowledge or light, and 'Fructiferous' experiments, which were to the advantage of one's interests, by coining the term 'Lucriferous' – given that, to the attentive scientist, each implied the other.[43] His statement that the difference between a 'trade' and an 'experiment' lay 'not so much in the Nature of the thing', but in the fact that the former 'had the Luck to be applied to Human Uses, or by a Company of Artificers made their Businesse, in order to their Profit' offers a clue to his way of thinking.[44] Shorn of economic considerations, Boyle's theology and science remain enigmatic and lacking in the extraordinary relevance they appear to have had in the broader social and political context of his time.[45]

6.1.3 *Natural Philosophy without Moral Natural Law*

Boyle primarily promoted the study of chemistry, an eminently practical science emerging from alchemy and involved with elements, compounds

[39] In Dublin, Boyle learned from Petty the newest anatomical techniques, for instance, Hunter, *Boyle: Between God and Science*, p. 88.

[40] Robert Boyle, 'Of the Usefulness of Experimentall Philosophy. The Second Part. Of its Usefulness to promote the Empire of Man over things Corporeal, 1663. The First Section of it's Usefulness to physick', in *The Works of Robert Boyle*, vol. 3, p. 296.

[41] 'Man's power over the creatures depends chiefly upon his knowledge' Robert Boyle, 'Of the Usefulness of Experimentall Philosophy. The Second Part. Second Section, in *The Works of Robert Boyle*, vol. 6, p. 436.

[42] Boyle, 'Of the Usefulness of Experimentall Philosophy. The Second Part', p. 394; p. 398.

[43] Boyle, 'Of the Usefulness of Experimentall Philosophy'. The Second Part. Second Section, p. 434.

[44] Boyle, 'Of the Usefulness of Experimentall Philosophy'. The Second Part. Fifth Section, p. 422.

[45] Incidentally, a study assessing how much Adam Smith borrowed from Boyle remains to be done.

and atoms – or corpuscles, as he called them – and this fact is of the utmost importance in this story.[46] A theory of matter is present in his work that entails interconnected – mechanical – elements that comprise a system and possess an intelligence – implying (mechanical) affections. According to Boyle, these attributes undoubtedly come from God and do not call for a theory about human beings or about analogies related to them.[47] William Newman has underlined that the fundamental characteristic of Boyle's atomism is that it was studied from the perspective of a chemist – not from a physicalist – who observes the impossibility of further physical division and evoked images of autonomy and ultimately individualism.[48] More recently, it has been noted by Alexander Wragge-Morley that Boyle imagined God as 'a transcendentally skilled chemist'.[49] That was certainly his own model to imitate.

Boyle's investigations are rich and complex, combining Aristotelian ideas of atoms as substances that he borrowed from the German physician Daniel Sennert (1572–1637), only to reject the notion of substance in favour of that of the identity of atoms or corpuscles.[50] Those corpuscles, Boyle emphasized, gained particularity or identity in their interaction with their environment – that is, within the *oeconomy* of nature.[51] This theory is both beautiful and far-reaching but strictly not concerned with human beings, whereas his economics of science employs the same method of ignoring the moral aspect of human agency while focusing on utility. This specific Boylean call would generate dramatic changes in future conceptions of natural philosophy and would emphasize his utilitarian goals. I have little doubt that he was one of the key artificers of the seventeenth-century transformation of natural law. Furthermore, his social importance, the relevance of his philosophical and theological work and his commitment to the discipline of chemistry far removed from human spirit justify the focus on his work in this chapter. Ethics and moral philosophy were of

[46] Lawrence Principe enumerates the central goals of alchemy in the early modern period, that he terms 'its golden age': 'achieving metallic transmutation, producing better medicines, improving and utilizing natural substances, understanding material change', Principe, *The Secrets of Alchemy*, p. 121.

[47] Boyle, *The Origine of Formes and Qualities*, p. 302.

[48] William R. Newman, *Atoms and Alchemy. Chymistry and the Experimental Origins of the Scientific Revolution* (Chicago: The University of Chicago Press, 2006), p. 164.

[49] Wragge-Morley, *Aesthetic Science*, p. 69.

[50] Newman, *Atoms and Alchemy*, pp. 164–189. We will see more about Sennert below; see also Peter R. Anstey, 'Robert Boyle and the Heuristic Value of Mechanism' in 33 *Studies in History and Philosophy of Science* (2002).

[51] Boyle, *The Origine of Formes and Qualities*.

little relevance in the approach he took, which was based on chemical analysis, and in how he thought anew a theology about divine Creation and human beings' dominion over nature (Genesis 1:26–31). Boyle's laws of nature are laws of motion, not moral laws, and the dominion of human beings over nature is about deconstructing and reconstructing nature, traditionally reserved to the omnipotence of God – the Lord of the nature of things – and about extracting economic profit from it.[52]

That was a blend of creationism, science and economy that constituted a fresh start for natural law in lieu of the great ethical contemporary traditions that may be summarized as falling into these four categories: (1) Aristotelian-Thomistic virtue ethics, or a morality of virtues (2) the ethics of the nature of the thing of the modern and late scholastics, expressed either as a morality of precepts or a morality of rights (3) the ethics of needs of the Greek-Arabic medical traditions, or a morality of needs and (4) the Puritan ethics, of a morality of industriousness and utility.[53] Robert Sanderson's seventeenth century casuistic and mechanistic moral philosophy cannot be considered to be in competition with Boyle's ideas, but rather to supplement them. Moral cases concocted with sceptical epistemologies backed by the institutional authority of the Anglican Church completed what experiments could not provide: guidance in respect of individuals' moral behaviour. Thus, the traditional grand moral natural

[52] Transmutation is even denied to Jesus Christ in Aquinas, *Summa theologiae* III, q. 13. a. 2 'But the transmutation of creatures, inasmuch as they may be brought to nothing, corresponds to their creation, whereby they were brought from nothing. And hence even as God alone can create, so, too, He alone can bring creatures to nothing, and He alone upholds them in being, lest they fall back to nothing. And thus it must be said that the soul of Christ had not omnipotence with regard to the transmutation of creatures.'

[53] The following seminal texts can be considered representative of these traditions: Aristotle, *The Nicomachean Ethics*; Aquinas, Thomas, *Summa theologiae*; *Quodlibet* IX, *Henrici de Gandavo, Opera Omnia*, XIII, R. Macken (ed.) (Leuven: Leuven University Press, 1983); *Durandi de Sancto Porciano. Scriptum super IV Libros Sententiarum. Prologus et Distinctiones 1–3 Libri Primi*. Guy Gildentops (ed.) (Leuven: Peeters, 2019); Francisco de Vitoria, *Comentarios a la Secunda secundae de Santo Tomás*, Vicente Beltrán de Heredia (ed.) Vol. III *De Justitia*, qq. 57/66, (Salamanca: Apartado 17, 1934); Hugo Grotius, *The Rights of War and Peace*, with and Introduction by Richard Tuck (ed.) from the Edition by Jeand Barbeyrac (Indianapolis: Liberty Fund, 2005) in 3 vols.; Simon Swain, *Economy, Family, and Society from Rome to Islam: A Critical Edition, English Translation, and Study of Bryson's Management of the Estate* (Cambridge: Cambridge University Press, 2013); *Avicenna Latinus Liber de Anima seu Sextus de Naturalibus IV–V*; Max Weber, *The Protestant Ethic and the Spirit of Capitalism*, Talcott Parsons trans. with an Introduction by Anthony Giddens (London and New York: Routledge Classics, 2001). See also, Terence Irwin, *The Development of Ethics. A Historical and Critical Study. II: From Suárez to Rousseau* (Oxford: Oxford University Press, 2008).

law theories experienced a substantial decline in the face of the underlying normative project of experimental science and of industriously exploiting, enjoying, and investigating nature as the way to God carried out by Boyle and others.

Sorana Corneanu's groundbreaking description of a species of morality that evolved in Europe during the seventeenth century – which she calls 'Regimes of the Mind' – also positions Boyle as legitimizing the experimental line of enquiry against speculative and metaphysical modes of thinking. The method of ascertaining truth through experimental philosophy had both scientific and therapeutic import, and therefore moral value for the mind.[54] However, as Boyle depicted it, the experience of training the mind is remarkably self-centred. It connected, as in a solipsism, the search for supernatural truths with the humility of the industrious scientist. In the absence of a study of human beings, core social and communitarian aspects and rules of morality also disappear.

Therefore, Boyle's emphasis on multiplication, I argue, results from a lack of a solid doctrine of morality in his theoretical work. In the absence of a theory of virtues concerning social life, justice or other invocations of social morality founded on principles of natural law, multiplication and growth become the means of addressing human needs and of satisfying desires. Moreover, an ethics of multiplication placed no limit on the expectations concerning profiting from or exploiting nature by those involved in natural science and trades. Multiplication was at once a scientific method and a source of theological truths about the bountiful Creator by which the contemporary problem of poverty and that of overcoming Hobbes' anthropology of struggle, with its atheist tendencies, could be approached.[55] Boyle employs 'multiplication' as the worldly and social counterpart to the solitary and therapeutic introspection of the individual. Experimental philosophy offered both. He regularly insisted that the love of God manifested itself in the bountiful material goods of nature, the suitability of human bodies to relish them, and the duty of human beings to multiply nature's goods. This theology of abundance was fundamentally alien to the asceticism of the Puritans that Max Weber famously described at the beginning

[54] Corneanu, *Regimens of the Mind*, especially ch. 4.

[55] The poor were not only the vagrant sort of individuals. In the study of political arithmetic (1695) by Gregory King, 'the poorest sort' meant the third class that comprised 51 per cent of the population that had an average income of between six and twenty pounds a year, 'labouring people and outservants', 'cottagers and paupers', 'household of common sea men and soldiers', and around 30.000 vagrants, see for this, Keith Wrightson, *Earthly Necessities, Economic Lives in Early Modern Britain, 1470–1750*, (London: Penguin Books, 2002), p. 449; p. 452.

of the twentieth century.[56] It appears therefore that Boyle's work opened a new avenue for thinking about morality among them. In Boyle's written works only a very narrow set of virtues and desires appear to be relevant for human beings as creatures of God. Boyle has been described as a lay theologian, a description that is also supported statistically since almost half of his numerous texts are religious in nature.[57] When he wrote about natural philosophy and natural sciences, he candidly acknowledged that his aim was not to do theology, and yet his theological arguments often led to one all-encompassing and underlying theme: God has given human beings dominion over bountiful nature and creatures and it is good and right to know, relish, multiply and make them productive.

Boyle was an erudite author, gifted natural philosopher and a man of intense faith with a strong grounding in the Bible and deep scholastic knowledge. While his convoluted prose sometimes makes him appear slightly priggish, he was above all an extremely bold scientist.[58] He would approve of and employ any tools available for the acquisition of knowledge: theology, philosophy, experiments, alchemy, even perhaps private revelation.[59] Ironically, despite being guided in several respects by the supernatural and esoteric, his contribution to natural law represented a novel and intensively desacralized understanding of nature. The ethical significance of *A Free Enquiry into the Vulgarly Receiv'd Notion of Nature* and his devastating critique of the traditional personification of nature that even Reformers such as Jan Comenius rather reaffirmed than destroyed, entailed the disintegration of 'human moral nature' as a concept.[60]

[56] Weber, *The Protestant Ethic and the Spirit of Capitalism*, pp. 102–125; cfr. on Boyle 'Puritanical' attitudes, Henry, 'The Scientific Revolution in England', p. 201.

[57] Edward B. Davis, 'Boyle's Philosophy of Religion' in *The Bloomsbury Companion to Robert Boyle.* A similar *Physico-Theology* by the divine William Derham (1657–1735) in Merchant, *The Death of Nature*, p. 248.

[58] A certain impatience with Boyle's self-righteousness, and perhaps also with the tradition protecting the hero, transpires in the classic Shapin and Schaffer, *Leviathan and the Air-Pump.*

[59] Boyle noted that he did not dare to affirm with the Paracelsians and Helmotians that science may be revealed by angels, but he encouraged to have recourse to the 'Father of lights' (in the plural number) in 'The Usefulness of Natural Philosophy.' in *The Works of Robert Boyle*, vol. 3, p. 276. See for instance, Michael Hunter ed. *Robert Boyle Reconsidered* (Cambridge: Cambridge University Press, 1994); Jan W. Wojcik, *Robert Boyle and the Limits of Reason* (Cambridge: Cambridge University Press, 1997); Lotte Mulligan, 'Robert Boyle, 'The Christian Virtuoso' and the Rhetoric of 'Reason' in Robert Crocker (ed.) *Religion, Reason and Nature in Early Modern Europe* (Dodrecht, Boston, London, Kluwer Academic Publishers, 2001) and Jan-Erik Jones ed. *The Bloomsbury Companion to Robert Boyle.*

[60] Boyle, *A Free Enquiry into the Vulgarly Receiv'd Notion of Nature*, in *Works of Robert Boyle*, vol. 10.

'Nature' was substituted by a new complex system of mechanical forces – an *oeconomy* susceptible to and, in a sense, awaiting the intervention of the chemist. That was the highest expression of the dominion of human beings over natural goods. The *oeconomy* or system of nature constituted Boyle's minimalist metaphysics, which was nevertheless remarkably more rational (and mechanistic) than the millenarian relativism of his friend Benjamin Worsley.[61] Some sort of minimal system beyond the chaos of the Epicureans was necessary in order to make sense of the world.[62] But ideas such as Hobbes's metaphysics of necessity, let alone those of the scholastics, were only barriers to knowledge.

Germano Maifreda's archaeology and Keith Tribe's philological study of the concept of 'economy' in modern Europe help to ascertain how avant garde Boyle's approach was.[63] He abandoned the traditional but narrow understanding of economy as management of the household, even if expanded to the state as advocated by Bodin.[64] The management of nature as a whole ensued. As noted above, Boyle probably borrowed the term *oeconomy*, attributed to nature, from Digby's natural philosophy. However, it was Boyle who first combined three elements: (1) the new epistemological and metaphysical transformation of natural categories (that is, the grouping of the natural world into species etc.), thus diluting Aristotelian substances in his theory of atomism; (2) the socioeconomic purpose of pursuing 'the Empire of Man' in a systematic manner over 'inferior' creatures; and (3) lifting of 'the boundaries of nature', of how natural beings and things are found naturally, in order to multiply its 'productions'.[65] A visionary of the British Empire and beyond, Boyle would identify nature with the physicality of the entire globe. Boyle's economy did address the organization of the management of the world to meet human needs, but it did so with

[61] On the relativism of Worsley see next chapter, and Leng, *Benjamin Worsley (1618–1677) Trade, Interest and the Spirit in Revolutionary England*, p. 190.

[62] A way he had to put this theme was to deny that every matter may be dissolved by fire: 'Why may not Nature associate in divers Bodies the more minute Elementary Corpuscles she has at hand too firmly to let them be separated by the fire?' Robert Boyle, *The Sceptical Chymist*, in *The Works of Robert Boyle*, vol. 2, p. 238.

[63] Maifreda, *From Oikonomia to Political Economy*; Tribe, *The Economy of the Word, Language, History and Economics*, especially ch. 2.

[64] We will see more about this question in Chapter 9. On Bodin and Pseudo-Aristotle *Oeconomia*, see Becker, *Gendering the Renaissance Commonwealth*.

[65] Boyle's philosophical effort is especially novel in Boyle, *The Origine of Formes and Qualities* and Boyle, *A Free Enquiry into the Vulgarly Receiv'd Notion of Nature*.

a breathtakingly global perspective. It had the goal of extracting from, imitating and multiplying productively a system called nature.[66]

My analysis is simple. Boyle's own project of *exaggerating* the economy and resources of nature was not Scriptural. Instead, it grew out of his scientific genius and the economy of the world in which he lived. This included the enjoyment of his immense inherited fortune, a trading and colonial empire in the making, and the urge felt by entrepreneurs or 'projectors', in the parlance of the time, planters and merchants, among others, to make the acquisition of wealth appear respectable. Whether he was personally candid or disingenuous has been much discussed in the literature, for he adopted a low profile and had a modest public persona.[67] However, the authenticity of his deep religious faith cannot be doubted.

His outlook, in common with that of the Reformers, was utopian in combining care for the poor and contemplation of industrious labour, as the path to heaven, with the alluring promise of private richness, evolving autonomously from moral philosophy. The theology of abundance resulted from an independent interpretation of the Bible in accordance with the millenarian tradition of seventeenth-century English Puritans' world view. Their belief in the promise of return to a bountiful Paradise on earth is portrayed in Charles Webster's *The Great Instauration*.[68] Moreover, Boyle displayed a penchant for highlighting the value of pleasure that did not form part of a wider theory of moral philosophy but probably stemmed from his Epicureanism. Boyle was a critical scholar and a stoical experimental scientist, and his alchemical interests only rarely betrayed him; hence, he hardly raised the suspicion of being a charlatan. Moreover, he became a natural scientist due to the knowledge he acquired at an early age as to the increasing possibilities for public wealth offered by the dominions of the British Empire – if they were well managed. His intrepid scientific spirit worked hand in hand with an impatience in relation to finding means of obtaining wealth, which was typical of the alchemists but not unrealistic in his case, except for the fact that he tended to omit the vexing aspects of moral human nature in his theoretical works.[69] After all, human beings had been expelled

66 On 'imitation' and 'multiplication' of nature, Robert Boyle, 'Of the Usefulness of Experimentall Philosophy. The First Part', p. 212. The notion of system appeared in works on husbandry a bit later, and among the French physiocrats in the next century. Adam Smith flattered himself a century later about his new principles founded on a system of natural liberty, and 'systems of political oeconomy', see Tribe, *The Economy of the Word*, p. 55.

67 Shapin and Simon Schaffer, *Leviathan and the Air-Pump*.

68 Webster, *The Great Instauration*.

69 See on alchemists and money, Wennerlind, 'Credit-Money as the Philosopher's Stone'.

from Paradise for some reason, a Christian belief that he tended to gloss over in his writings. Thus his position was marked by utopian optimism neglecting the dangerous aspects of human beings' nature. Despite his massive theological discourse, the question that Boyle never asks is: will this activity, etc. result in a better, or more righteous individual or a more just society?

6.2 The Fact of Man

6.2.1 *Voluntarist Law*

In the longer perspective of Boyle's many theological writings, it is perplexing that he eschewed any effort to rationalize the relationship between God and human beings. *The Christian Virtuoso* (1690), his last major work, defined law in moral terms as the positive law that God had explicated to human beings through supernatural Revelation, according to which intelligent and free agents ought to regulate their actions. Differently, inanimate bodies could not restrain, or incite their actions, and they were moved by 'real Power'.[70]

Thus, God's noblest creatures – human beings – had been guaranteed 'an explicit and positive law' that showed them what kind of obedience and worship God expected. Notwithstanding the requirement of obedience to God's law, a human being 'can by reason, without it (Revelation) either not at all, or but rovingly, guess at' the contents of that law. Motivation to comply with divine law thus stemmed less from human conscience than the threat of terrible penalties and the promise of eternal bliss.[71] Boyle denied the Deist view that everything after the formation of the universe was directed by 'the settled laws of nature':

> For, beside the insuperable difficulty there is to give an Account of the first formation of things, which many (especially Aristotelian) Deists will not ascribe to God, and besides that the Laws of Motion, without which the present State and Course of things could not be maintain'd, did not necessarily spring from the nature of Matter, but depended upon the Will of the Divine Author of things.[72]

Deists thus disregarded providence, while Boyle considered or did not deny that the laws of motion may originate in the will of God and not

[70] Robert Boyle, 'The Christian Virtuoso', in *The Works of Robert Boyle*, vol. 11, p. 301.
[71] Boyle, 'The Christian Virtuoso', p. 303.
[72] Boyle, 'The Christian Virtuoso', p. 301.

'necessarily' in any feature of matter. Non-rational bodies in nature were incapable of understanding or knowing the 'Will of the Legislator' and thus of *obeying* any law because, in Boyle's voluntarist conception of law, such obedience always required a rational and free agent. As he plainly wrote in 'Free Enquiry into the Vulgarly Receiv'd Notion of Nature':

> But to speak strictly, (as becomes Philosophers in so weighty a matter) to say that the *Nature* of this or that Body, is but *the Law of God prescrib'd to it*, is but an improper and figurative Expression. For, *besides* that this gives us but a very defective *Idea* of *Nature*, since it omits the general Fabrick of the World, and the Contrivances of particular Bodies, which yet are as well necessary as Local Motion itself, to the production of particular *Effects* and *Phaenomena's*; *besides* this, I say, and other imperfections of this *Notion of Nature*, that I shall not here insist on, I must freely observe, that, to speak properly, a *Law* being but a *Notional Rule of Acting according to the declar'd Will of a Superior*, 'tis plain, that nothing but an Intellectual Being can be properly capable of receiving and acting by *a Law*.[73]

Logically, therefore, non-rational bodies were ruled out from having any position in a system of (voluntarist) natural laws. Hence the laws of motion were *not properly* laws either, but the result of God's providential acts of power, and also of divine endowments of power upon His creatures. This was the way in which Boyle combined God's active involvement (or 'general concourse') in the laws of motion with the causal powers of matter in motion to give impulse to further movement in matter.[74] Boyle's providential and voluntarist theology of power, defending, in relation to moral law, a voluntarist law and an anti-intellectualist position, represented the crowning moment of one of the most successful scientific careers in modern science. Margaret Osler famously attributed Boyle's ideas to Gassendi's influence and the latter's 'baptism of Epicure'.[75] I hope, however, to show that Boyle's natural philosophy had

[73] Robert Boyle, 'Free Enquiry into the Vulgarly Receiv'd Notion of Nature, in *The Works of Robert Boyle*, vol. 10, p. 457 (emphasis Boyle).

[74] More about Boyle's concept of the laws of nature is discussed below in 7.2.4. Francis Oakley has recently linked this statement of Boyle with Francisco de Suarez's statement that the term 'natural law (lex naturae)' was in relation to physical nature 'metaphorical since things which lack reason are not capable of obedience', in *De legibus ac Deo legislatore*, in Francis Oakley, 'The Rise of the Concept of Laws of Nature Revisited' in 24 *Early Science and Medicine* (2019), p. 23 (Suarez quoted from Oakley's text). My argument is that Boyle's complexity reaches beyond the use of metaphors.

[75] Margaret J. Osler, 'The Intellectual Sources of Robert Boyle's Philosophy of Nature: Gassendi's Voluntarism and Boyle's Physico-Theological Project', in Richard Kroll, Richard Ashcraft and Peter Zagorin (eds.), *Philosophy, Science, and Religion in England 1640–1700* (Cambridge: Cambridge University Press 1992).

important original aspects based on his own theology and political economy. Sincere and pious thoughts of devotion to God and of the importance of virtue, such as his youthful statement that 'the Souuerain and greatest Necessity of all (for a man) is to be Vertuus' abound in Boyle's writings.[76] These were often coupled with an insistence on the centrality of desires and pleasure, which gives his ideas an aspect of realism that balances his more spiritual utterances. This approach also offers insight not devoid of value against intellectualist positions that seemed to belong to another world.[77] However, since Boyle's ethical ideas are not unified by an overarching theory of morality and his approach to virtues is not systematic (only some of the virtues are addressed), they often appear unbalanced, reflective of the cultivation of individuality and generally confusing in terms of moral theory. Humility, gratitude, love and trust, delight in abstract truth, docility and openness to veiled truths, modesty of mind, government of reason and, crucially, industriousness are the virtues he mentions repeatedly. However, justice and other social virtues are conspicuously absent from his writings.[78]

But the novelty of Boyle's work as a natural philosopher lies in the remarkable inattention to human beings evinced by his system of nature. In *The Origine of Formes and Qualities*, probably his most important philosophical piece, Boyle introduced and explained the species of atomism he defended: corpuscularianism.[79] He developed in that text an understanding of nature and nature's possibilities that was to be put at the service of chemistry and its profitable management. Certainly, human beings were the scientific and economic managers of the new system.[80] In this regard, Peter Remien notes in his ecological study on the concept of nature in early modern literature that Boyle's 'anthropocentric teleology' of the 'utility of man' in tension with the welfare of other species would reappear forcefully later in Darwin's understanding of species as 'a diffuse set of interconnecting

76 Robert Boyle 'The Aretology', in John T. Harwood (ed.), *The Early Essays and Ethics of Robert Boyle* (Carbondale: Southern Illinois University Press, 1991), p. 39.

77 On this 'humane' aspect of Epicureanism see Wilson, *Epicureanism at the Origins of Modernity*, p. 11.

78 See the recent overview by Sorana Corneanu, 'Boyle's Moral Philosophy' in *The Bloomsbury Companion to Robert Boyle.*

79 About how his ideas developed after *The Origine of Formes and Qualities*, see John Henry, 'Boyle on Cosmical Qualities', in Michael Hunter (ed.), *Robert Boyle Reconsidered* (Cambridge: Cambridge University Press, 1994).

80 That Boyle opened the door to a conception of nature by which we 'directly manipulate the microstructures of things' with independence of how human beings conceive those bodies is noted in Laura S. Keating, 'Boyle on Qualities', in Jan Erik Jones (ed.), *The Bloomsbury Companion to Robert Boyle*, 169–197, p. 192.

centres of interest'.[81] My point here concerns the fact that human epistemology and human nature were not integrated in Boyle's scientific project. Humans stand, as it were, outside nature. Human beings were '*de facto* in the world', rational and sensible human beings that perceived the entities in the world in a manner that, in Boyle's view, did not suit the way matter was ordered in reality, i.e. as a combination of atoms.[82] Human beings also had spiritual souls, which also placed them beyond the range of the radar of atomism and consequently of the nature Boyle was studying.

Arguably, a more intense desacralization of non-human nature occurred when the human being was considered separately from nature, and taken to be merely as a *user* of the natural world. The next two sections discuss Boyle's scattered ideas on morality, and Boyle's paradoxical and alternative enchantment/disenchantment with nature.[83]

6.2.2 Aretology: *Embracing Human Body*

Boyle chose not to publish his early work *Ethics* or *Aretology* for good reason. This piece, which rather amounts to a compilation of different texts, represents a youthful attempt to write a weighty piece, but falls a little short of succeeding. A mixture of interesting thoughts, borrowings from similar works by other authors, sanctimonious discourse and advice on education (when he started to write it, he was 18 years old!) are united in the 1991 edition of the work. The piece pales in comparison with his more mature works. However, John Harwood is right in noting that Boyle was already a naturalist when he composed the texts.[84] Although he perhaps had not yet

81 Remien, *Concept of Nature*, pp. 42–46.

82 'But now we are to consider, that there are *de facto* in the world certain sensible and rational Beings, that we call Men, and the body of Man having several of its external parts, as the Eye, the Ear, &c. each of a distinct and peculiar Texture, whereby it is capable to receive Impressions from the Bodies about it, and upon that account it is call'd an Organ of Sense, we must consider, I say, that these Sensories may be wrought upon by the Figure, Shape, Motion, and Texture of Bodies without them … Whence Men have been induc'd to frame a long Catalogue of such Things as, for their relating to our Senses, we call Sensible Qualities; and because we have been conversant with them, before we had the use of Reason, and the Mind of Man is prone to conceive almost every Thing (nay even Privations, as Blindness, Death, &c.) under the notion of a true Entitie or Substance as it self is, we have been from our Infancy apt to imagine, that these Sensible Qualities are Real Beings, in the Objects they denominate.' Boyle, *The Origine of Formes and Qualities* in *The Works of Robert Boyle*, vol. 5, p. 316.

83 I am borrowing the term from Han van Ruler, 'Minds, Forms, and Spirits: The Nature of Cartesian Disenchantment' 61 *Journal of the History of Ideas*, (2000).

84 John T. Harwood, 'Introduction' in Harwood ed. *The Early Essays and Ethics of Robert Boyle*.

discovered the delights of experiment, *The Aretology* is valuable in showing how Boyle's thinking on ethics functions in relation to the body, and in particular the *animal* body, and in illuminating his method, which lays the foundations for his later work. The most remarkable aspect of the text is how Boyle combined exalted theological ideas about the happiness in contemplation with a close description of morality as a pathology, or doctrine of affections, and an emphasis on the pleasures of the body.[85] This duality of spirit and body in his exploration of morality and virtue, which is present throughout his works, seems to originate in his scepticism as to the capacity of reason to ascertain truth in practical terms and to recognize natural law, that, as we saw before, he explicitly articulated in *The Christian Virtuoso* near the end of his life. Among many other instances in that text, he referred to notions and principles 'that God hath planted' in the 'Mind of Man' that were 'fit to make him *sensible* that he ought to Adore God'. His was a natural religion lived through 'sentiments' towards 'the transcendent Goodness of God', the 'continual and munificent Benefactor' that would allow human beings to pass 'from Natural to Reveal'd Religion'. The radical spiritual and the sensuous are two extreme and recurrent positions in his works. After all, 'experience', one of his main working concepts, has its origins principally in the senses.[86]

On the other hand, as early as in the *Aretology* Boyle declined to share the spiritualism of radical Puritans who, against all common sense, disregarded the need for, and possibility of, good works on the grounds of justification of believers by faith only. The workings of businesses, life experience, law and punishment, as well as the very nature of free will, attested to the fact that an individual was free and would thus be accordingly virtuous or vicious:

> we wil onely heere set down the most Christian and Rationall Opinion: which is that tho in Spirituall and Supernaturall Matters, the Will be not indifferent to Good and Evill, but (not withstanding its Liberty) cannot but

[85] Without mentioning him, Boyle adopted the theological tradition of Thomas Aquinas in locating happiness in the individual's 'Vision and Fruition' of God. 'Cum ergo ultimus finis quasi exterior humanae voluntatis sit Deus, non potest esse quod aliquis actus voluntatis sit interior finis; sed ille actus erit ultimus finis interior quo primo hoc modo se habebit ad Deum, ut voluntas quietetur in ipso. Haec autem est visio Dei secundum intellectum, quia per hanc fit quasi quidam contactus Dei ad intellectum; cum omne cognitum sit in cognoscente secundum quod cognoscitur; sicut etiam corporalis tactus ad delectabile corporeum inducit quietationem affectus.' Aquinas, IV *Sent.* d. 49, q.1.a.1; Mary Beth Ingham, *La vie de la sagesse: Le Stoïcisme au Moyen Âge* (Fribourg: Academic Press Fribourg, 2007), p. 80; see on 'fruition' also ch. 1, footnote 42.

[86] Boyle, 'The Christian Virtuoso', p. 301; p. 303.

> Sin yet in the Exercise of Civill Vertus (and Aeconomicall Arts) a man out of his owne Free-will may give himself either to Vertu or Vice, and approve or disapproveth thing proposed, as himself pleases: and by consequent that it is naturally in his Power to be Virtuus or Vitius as himself will.[87]

The dualism is apparent: in spiritual matters the human will 'cannot but sin'. But in real, practical life, Boyle argued in his unpublished work on ethics, the divine determinism typical of radical Puritans was useless. John Henry has argued that the link between the way in which the religious situation evolved in England and the spectacular development of science in the late seventeenth century, often termed the Scientific Revolution, was a theological method translated into natural science. Anglicans, Reformers and Puritans alike, constantly adapting to a middle way between Geneva and Rome, were wary of rationalist reason in theology, had a preference for commonsense reasoning and a commitment to minimalist doctrine. This method, Henry notes, was also employed in natural sciences to ascertain the truth about nature, as facts, without an ideological bias.[88] This picture fits some aspects of Boyle, who, exactly as Henry describes, took distance from both Puritan and Hobbesian ideas of corrupted human nature when discoursing about 'civil life' and opted, with English common sense, for a middle way of personal virtue. He thus rejected both 'Aristoteliticians' who, in not allowing 'the Cherishing of passions so far as to enable them to discompose the mind' lead people away from virtue, and 'Stoicks' who would have the 'wise man' settled 'in that Immoveable Constancy, that no impulsions of the Sensitive Appetite should be able to make wander from the dictates of Reason'. Passions were good for many reasons that Boyle listed in *Aretology*, and renouncing them stemmed from and evidenced the 'Blockish stupidity of the Stoicks'.[89]

However, Boyle went further than this and was novel in certain respects. Probably influenced by French moralists, he celebrated a human nature created by God for delights, even though he lacked, as stated above, a serious theological anthropology. His fearlessness about the consequences of that deficiency may be perhaps attributed to satisfaction with his own

87 Boyle, 'The Aretology', p. 43.

88 Henry, 'The Scientific Revolution in England'; and Henry, 'Sir Kenelm Digby, Recusant Philosopher'.

89 Where Aristotle would argue in favour of tempering the passions and the Stoics in favour of a life 'Without Passions', Boyle wrote that 'the Wise man' was 'Above them'. Boyle 'The Aretology', p. 18.

version of right reason. In the context of the evolution of English views of right reason – as described in Chapter 5, and for instance expressed by John Spurr and Robert A. Greene – which faintly preserved some sort of illumination of principles of natural law in the capacity of reasoning, Boyle's understanding of right reason is perplexing, distinctive and novel.[90] Sorana Corneanu has contributed greatly to illuminating Boyle's approach. As she explains, Boyle's right reason belongs neither to a tradition of illumination nor to principles of natural law. However, it is a moral conception, for it concerns the mastering of the passions and ordering of intellect and governing the mind through virtuous inquiry (of empirical, Baconian influence), possessing the interesting goal of 'growing' in (natural) knowledge.[91] This idea is discussed further in the last two sections, but it is worth noting at this juncture that Boyle regarded also quantity as crucial in this area.[92]

Also, religious axioms guided Boyle's work, which places him outside the seventeenth-century trends of waning of the religion's role in relation to doing science. It is more accurate to describe it as a straightforward example of the relatively recent separation between the realms of science and religion – in this case, moral laws being removed from the realm of natural philosophy – discussed by Peter Harrison.[93] Some contemporary authors had sought to integrate with creativity the array of main philosophical and theological foundations in the idea of moral reason, which also connects with the political principles of absolutism. Thus the light of nature had an extraordinary burden of tasks to perform in *The Darknes of Atheism Dispelled by the Light of Nature: A Physico-Theologicall Treatise* by the physician Walter Charleton (1619–1707), a friend of Hobbes and Lady Margaret Cavendish and translator of Epicure. He described the light of nature as a 'Domestick oracle' and 'the Magna charta of all temporal knowledge', and in fact understood it as offering instruction

[90] John Spurr, '"Rational Religion" in Restoration England' 49 *Journal of the History of Ideas* 563–585 (1988); Greene, 'Synderesis, the Spark of Conscience, in the English Renaissance'.

[91] Corneanu, *Regimens of the Mind*, generally ch. 4 and p. 128.

[92] See further on Boyle's description of the 'abstracted reason' that reach few of the 'Multitude of things knowable' opposed to the experience and revelation, Corneanu, *Regimens of the Mind*, p. 133.

[93] Peter Harrison, *The Territories of Science and Religion* (Chicago: The University of Chicago Press, 2015); also a critique to a once hegemonic distinction between religion and science in the historiography of the Scientific Revolution, in Alexander Wragge-Morley, *Aesthetic Science: Representing Nature in the Royal Society of London, 1650–1720* (Chicago: The University of Chicago Press, 2020).

about truth.[94] However, in respect of practical deliberation concerning moral action, Charleton referred also to an *indifference* both of will and of intellect (towards good or evil) on the basis of the experience of how inconstant and changing was an individual's judgment about things. He illustrated his explanation of probabilities in respect of moral judgment by reference to scales. 'Below uncontrollable Necessity', rational judgment would not be absolutely indifferent, but experience or reasons would usually tip the scale in one direction or another, thus recognizing the good to be chosen.[95] Similarly to Hobbes's determinism, Charleton argued as follows:

> That every man, in whom the *Light of Nature* is not damp't by *Fatuity*, either native and temperamental, or casually supervenient, hath this or *impress* of an *especial Providence*, decreeing and disposing all events, that have, do, or shall befall him.[96]

The light of nature became thus an 'intestine Dictator'.[97] Robert Sanderson's efforts to construct a mechanical conscience, as discussed in Chapter 5, are indicative of the daunting challenge involved in producing a working concept of practical reason and conscience during that period. Ultimately, Boyle's decision not to make moral philosophy part of his project of knowledge is captured in his statement in the *Aretology* that 'knowledge of Ethicks, though helpful, was not absolutely necessary'.[98] Bypassing the middle ground of theories about the truth of practical reason or of moral natural law, he devoted his energies to the experimental sciences and his scientific interest remained constraint to physical body. Nevertheless, he took the view that his investigations into matter offered enough material for those searching for divine things. What he called 'Inferior sort of truths' might lead directly to 'Divine truth' and at the same time dispose the mind towards the habit of searching for truth.[99]

[94] Walter Charleton, *The Darknes of Atheism Dispelled by the Light of Nature: A Physico-Theologicall Treatise* (London: Printed for William Lee, 1652), Early English Books Online Text Creation Partnership, 2011, http://name.umdl.umich.edu/A69728.0001.001, p. 15; p. 41.

[95] Charleton, *The Darknes of Atheism Dispelled by the Light of Nature*, p. 271.

[96] Charleton, *The Darknes of Atheism Dispelled by the Light of Nature*, p. 170. Charleton's praises Hobbes for having proved the natural immortality of human soul in *Leviathan*, p. 90. Lisa Walters 'Epicurus and Gender in the British Newcastle Circle: Charleton, Hobbes and Margaret Cavendish' in Lisa Hopkins and Tom Rutter (eds.) *A Companion to the Cavendishes* (York: Arc-Humanities Press, 2020).

[97] Charleton, *The Darknes of Atheism Dispelled by the Light of Nature*, 170; Eric Lewis, 'Walter Charleton and Early Modern Eclecticism' 62 *Journal of the History of Ideas* (2001).

[98] Boyle 'The Aretology', p. 54.

[99] Boyle, 'The Christian Virtuoso', p. 304.

In conclusion Boyle's *Aretology* is indicative of the fact that from an early age he was too much of a student of the human body, and a naturalist – and one probably under the influence of Gassendi and perhaps Aquinas too – to neglect pleasure or desire. Gassendi's doctrine of a moral psychology, structured by seeking pleasure and avoiding pain may have inspired him more than anything else: hence his apology for Epicure at the beginning of the text, which is similar to the one he inserted in *The Usefulness*.[100] Examples of and comparisons between human beings and how wolves, sheep and dogs act figured prominently in Boyle's rather biological ethics in some parts of *Aretology*.[101] Affections, he wrote, were so natural to 'man' that 'he can as soone devest himself of being an animal, as exempt himself of the Commotions of his Appetites'. Beyond that and, not without some shade of unreality, he also noted that animals were usually content 'to Satisfy nature', whereas human beings' passions were literally inexhaustible: 'once overflown the Bankes of Reason' they 'ar like a Fire blowne up by the Feuel of their Enjoyments into a greater Flame'. However, Boyle was not a wholehearted Gassendist. Dmitri Levitin has also recently interpreted Boyle as increasingly rejecting the dogmatic reductionism of Epicurean atomism.[102] Although observance of the fact of 'unlimited desires' of human beings keeps cropping up in his economic writings, in terms of theory, he seems to have approached the issue of morality from the other end: the animal body. But when dealing with the theme of the usefulness of science, Boyle milked the question of human beings' unlimited desires for utilitarian purposes.

The question arises as to how he reconciled the economic promotion of the satisfaction of manifold and inexhaustible desires with his earnest entreaties to engage in contemplation and to have faith? How can godly piety triumph over hedonism if, as we will see below, science ought to serve economy through the promotion of unlimited pleasures? Boyle's written works do not acknowledge any conflict between these two positions, and his repeated and ambiguous utterances with regard to Epicureanism, together with the fact that he set aside moral

100 Osler, 'The Intellectual Sources of Robert Boyle's Philosophy of Nature'; on Gassendi's ethics, see Sarasohn, *Gassendi's Ethics: Freedom in a Mechanistic Universe*; Boyle, 'Of the Usefulness of Experimentall Philosophy', p. 237. In the past century Robert Kargon denied originality to Boyle who would have been simply introducing Gassendi's Epicureanism in England, Robert Kargon, 'Robert Boyle, and the Acceptance of Epicurean Atomism in England' 55 *Isis* (1964).

101 Boyle 'The Aretology', p. 13; 16; p. 17; p. 51; p 76.

102 Levitin, *Ancient History in the Age of the New Science*, pp. 707–711.

philosophy for good, make his work difficult to critique from this angle.[103] Boyle's focus on hedonism largely resulted from his reluctance to delve into the complexities of human nature and his refusal to become a moral philosopher – as Gassendi was and John Locke would become – while amplifying human desires in his project for the utility of science.

6.3 The Grand Business of Nature

Utilitarian ideas as to the use of nature had appeared in different ways, sometimes in a subtle manner, often quite explicitly in the work of renowned Catholic theologians of the sixteenth century, such as Francisco de Vitoria.[104] In analysing the question of dominion as 'use', Vitoria elaborated on a common theme for Parisian theologians, at least after the early fourteenth century – the enjoyment of 'the tree of life' for the benefit of human beings.[105] Vitoria commented that God's prohibition on eating from another tree, 'the Tree of Paradise' could be interpreted as a negation of the idea that human beings were true lords of the Earth. Instead, he argued, human dominion over goods was complete, despite the limitations that God had set in respect of that tree. In view of the specific definition of 'dominion as a right to use' – i.e. dominion divided into a bundle of rights – the prohibition concerning 'the Tree of Paradise' posed no difficulties. The Bible made it clear that God had prohibited human beings from *eating* from the tree. However, eating was only one of the possible uses that it offered. Human beings 'could benefit from that tree through other uses, thus, to give the brutes of its fruits or to cut branches

[103] The ambiguity about one's position towards Epicureanism seemed common, for instance, Samuel Parker (1640–1688) hid his own influences of Gassendi-Epicurean materialism by pointing to the arrogance of Epicure and Descartes alike in claiming to know what the soul was, Levitin, *Ancient Wisdom in the Age of the New Science*, p. 666. On Parker see, Jon Parkin, "Parker, Samuel (1640–1688), bishop of Oxford." Oxford Dictionary of National Biography. September 23, 2004. See also, Wilson, *Epicureanism at the Origins of Modernity.*

[104] On the utilitarianism of Vitoria see Mónica García-Salmones Rovira, 'Francisco de Vitoria on the Theology of Dominion and Secular Natural Rights', in José Maria Beneyto (ed.), *Empire, Humanism and Rights* (Cham: Springer, 2022); Campagna, *Francisco de Vitoria: Leben und Werk*, p. 75.

[105] Providing e.g. in Durandus de Saint Pourçain, pure and strengthening food that facilitated inmortality, *Durandi a Sancto Porciano, Ord. Praed. et Meldensis Episcopi, In Petri Lombardi Sententias Theologicas Commentariorum libri IIII, Venetiis, MDLXXI. Ex Typographia Guerræa.* (Republished: Ridgewood, New Jersey, The Gregg Press Incorporated, 1964), lib. 2 d. 19 q. 1.

off it for his or her uses or for other uses'.[106] In short, the tree had multiple uses, some of which were allowed to human beings while others were not. Vitoria's conclusion was that God gave human beings dominion over all things, notwithstanding the fact that he excluded some uses from that dominion. Because *dominium* signified a right to use, the prohibition of some uses did not hamper humanity's dominion over all the goods of the earth.[107] The entitlement to use also entailed the important conclusion that human beings could employ the goods of creation 'not for all, but only for the licit uses'.[108]

6.3.1 Aquinas's Theology of Use

There is little doubt that Thomas Aquinas's theology was a *theology of use*, by which I mean a method of thinking about problems relating to the science of God in which a free agent, a human being, is thought to be acting, rightly or wrongly upon a reality that has been given or presented to her. At the deepest anthropological level, the 'good' of human beings is described in the *Summa theologiae* as the use with a good will of anything in the world – a world in which God also participates.[109] Hence, 'the good of human beings, absolutely considered, is a good operation viz. the good use of things that are possessed'; the ultimate good to be possessed being, of course, God. In opposition to that, 'sin' amounts to the bad use

[106] 'Dubium aliud est de ligno paradisi: quomodo homo est dominus illius postquam vetitum est ei? Ergo aliquid Deus servavit sibi cujus non dedit homini dominium. Concedo. Parum est hoc quod aliquid sit cujus non dederit Deus homini dominium, postquam dedit multorum aliorum dominium. Vel dico quod etiam dedit ei dominium illius ligni, quia solum ei prohibuit ne comederet de illo. Poterat tamen uti eo ligno ad alios usus, scilicet ut daret brutis poma illius, vel excindere ramam illius ad usus suos, vel ad aliud; et hoc non prohibuit Deus. Sed solum ne comederet de illo. Ita quod homo non erat dominius omnium rerum ad omnes usus utamur illo, sicut ne dominus est dominus servi ad omnes usus, quia non ad occidendum. Et sic Deus communicavit homini dominium rerum, licet aliqui usus illarum sint excepti. Et sic propositio nostra generaliter sumpta est vera, quia homo habet dominium omnium rerum.' de Vitoria, *Comentarios a la Secunda secundae de Santo Tomás*, q. LXII, art. 1, p. 73.

[107] See on the notion of dominion in Francisco de Vitoria, Brett, *Liberty, Right and Nature*, ch. 4 and generally.

[108] de Vitoria, *Comentarios a la Secunda secundae de Santo Tomás*, q. LXII, art. 1, p. 69; p. 73.

[109] A good will is the will acting in accordance with reason, since 'reason is the cause and root of the good of human beings.' *Summa theologiae*, I. II, q.66 a.1.co; I.II, q. 18, a. 5 and I.II, q. 61, a. 2. I am mainly employing Alfred J. Freddoso's translation, in combination with the Latin original at the Corpus Thomisticum project, and also making small changes in it myself. New English Translation of St. Thomas Aquina's *Summa Theologiae* by Alfred J. Freddoso, www3.nd.edu/~afreddos/summa-translation/TOC.htm.

of things.[110] In response to the question of whether happiness may lie in riches, Aquinas answered that happiness lies neither in natural nor in artificial riches. The reasoning behind this conclusion is that natural riches simply sustain the lives of human beings, and surely happiness should be based on something more than that which achieves physical survival. On the other hand, Aquinas held that artificial riches were 'for the sake of natural riches, since they would not be sought except that things necessary for the sustenance of life (*necessariae ad usum vitae*) are bought with them'.[111]

Therefore, artificial riches had even less the character of an ultimate end, since their meaning merely reinforced that of natural riches in making possible human beings' use of the gift of life.

Aquinas defined virtue as good use of free will (*bonus usus libero arbitrio*).[112] Furthermore, in the *Prima Secundae*, he described how the virtuous act of choosing was done either with regard to human acts or to doing or using things (*facere re or uti re*).[113] In respect of doing things, Aquinas gave the example of the physician whose aim is to promote health; while in respect of using things, he gave the example of a greedy human being whose aim is to acquire money. He also defined pleasure as either 'knowing' only or 'knowing that one possesses certain things' such as honour or fame. The pleasure that accompanies the possession of things arises from the fact of 'making use of them or being able to make use of them'.[114]

Coming closer to the topic of nature Aquinas also argued that in Paradise animals were inferior to human beings in terms of use, government and characteristics. In the order of nature superior beings use and govern inferior beings. The reason for human beings' superiority was that only they possessed universally the virtue of prudence, while certain other

110 Aquinas was explaining why sin has more the character of evil than punishment. *Summa theologia*, I pars, 48.a 6. co.

111 *Summa theologiae* I.II, q.2.a.1.co.

112 *Summa theologiae*, I.II, q.55.a.1 ad.2.

113 *Summa theologiae*, I.II, q. 13. a. 4. co.

114 'Reply to objection 1: The objects of the operations are themselves pleasurable only insofar as they are joined to us either (a) through cognition alone, as when we take pleasure in thinking about or looking at certain things, or (b) in some other way along with cognition, as when one takes pleasure in knowing that he possesses some good, such as riches or honor, etc., that is pleasurable only if it is apprehended as possessed. For as the Philosopher says in Politics 2, "To think of something as one's own is a great pleasure that proceeds from the natural love one has for himself." For having things of this sort is nothing other than making use of them or being able to make use of them, and this occurs through an operation. Hence, it is clear that every pleasure is traced back to an operation that is a cause of it.' *Summa theologiae* I.II, q.32.a1.ad.1

animals have it to a limited extent.[115] Finally, in the well-known passage on the use of natural goods in the section devoted to the sins against justice, *Summa theologia* q. 66 a.1. co, in response to the question of whether the use of goods was natural to human beings Aquinas famously answered:

> I respond: There are two possible ways to think about an exterior thing:
> (a) with respect to the nature of the thing, which is not subject to human power, but only to the power of God, whom all things obey at will;
> (b) with respect to the use of the very thing – and in this sense a human being has natural dominion over exterior things, since by his reason and will he can make use of exterior things for his own utility as almost things made for his sake.

Human dominion over nature was therefore limited to the use of goods for their utility while human beings lacked the power over the configuration of 'the nature of the thing' that only God possessed. However, since human beings are endowed with reason, their dominion was not merely physical, like that of lower animals, but also involved a type of dominion over certain creatures:

> For as was established above [q. 64, a. 1], things that are less perfect or less complete exist for the sake of things that are more perfect or more complete. And this is the line of reasoning by which the Philosopher proves in *Politics* I that the possession of exterior things is natural to human being. Now this natural dominion over other creatures that belongs to human being in accord with his reason, in which the image of God consists, is made manifest in the very creation of man in Genesis 1, where it says, "Let us make man to our likeness and image and set him above the fish of the sea, etc.

God the Creator was therefore, according to Aquinas, the sovereign with absolute power over the design of the Creation – a power which human beings did not enjoy. In his answer to the first objection, Aquinas made a distinction in relation to the concept of 'dominion'. 'God' had 'the principal dominion (*principale dominium*) over all things'. It was a result of God's providence that certain things were ordered towards the bodily sustenance of human beings. This meant that human beings had 'a natural dominion over things as regards the power to use them (*ad potestam utendi ipsis*)'. Aquinas therefore viewed human beings' 'natural d*ominium*' as 'a power to use'. Their 'natural dominion' amounted to 'use'.[116]

115 *Summa theologia*, I. q. 96. a.1.co; *Summa theologiae*, I-II. q.1 a1.co 'Differt autem homo ab aliis irrationalibus creaturis in hoc, quod est suorum actuum dominus.'

116 *Summa theologiae*, II-IIae q. 66, a. 1. ad 1. 'Ad primum ergo dicendum quod Deus habet principale dominium omnium rerum. Et ipse secundum suam providentiam ordinavit

In response to the second objection, as to justice – the statement in the New Testament (Luke 12:18) that 'the rich man is reprimanded' and that accordingly material, exterior goods are unnatural for human beings – Aquinas explained that the rich man's error was to think that the exterior goods were principally his own, in the sense that he had not received them from another (i.e. from God).[117] In response to the third objection – Ambrosius's statement that human beings 'cannot transform nature' – Aquinas replied that this argument was only about a dominion over things as regards 'their natures', which, as he had noted, belonged to God alone.

The fact that 'use' had such an important role in Aquinas's theology about human beings in relation to nature derives from the supposition that human beings are free moral agents in a created world who act upon spirit and matter. Moreover, in order to have power, which may be Aquinas's fundamental category in respect of human beings, there has to be something towards which the exercise of that power or dominion aims, apart from oneself.[118] As Stathis Psillos has put it, in Aquinas's work powers are both innate qualities and exist in relation to something else, there is a purpose to them.[119] Human beings use their 'will' and 'reason' in the same way that they use 'money' or 'food'. The use of the material world, 'reason' or 'will' could be good and then they led to God or, in the opposite case, to evil.

6.3.2 *Knowing the Bountiful Nature*

Boyle's utopian theology furnishes what I have referred to above as the 'multiplier', i.e. his project of turning science into a real agent of the economy. This comprised, first, an anthropology of unlimited desires that resulted in a perhaps not eternal but definitively exponential increase in consumption of divinely designed, inexhaustible and, to that point, mostly unknown natural resources that were hidden in the bowels of the earth,

res quasdam ad corporalem hominis sustentationem. Et propter hoc homo habet naturale rerum dominium quantum ad potestatem utendi ipsis.'

117 However, it is noticeable that following the mendicant tradition, in the *Summa tertia pars* when he discussed the perfections of Jesus as an individual man, Aquinas noted that 'condemning all riches' Jesus showed the highest degree of liberality and magnificence, while he exercised liberality giving 'to the poor what was given to Himself.' Aquinas, *Summa theologiae*, III, q.7, a. 2, 3co.

118 This is visible in the *Summa*, but specially in Aquinas, *Quaestiones Disputatae de Potentia Dei*; Riccardo Saccenti, *Debating Medieval Natural Law: A Survey* (Notre Dame: University of Notre Dame Press, 2017), p. 77.

119 Stathis Psillos, 'The Inherence and Directedness of Power' in *Reconsidering Causal Powers: Historical and Conceptual Perspectives*, p. 58.

situated in faraway and exotic territories or within potential or invisible (atomic) mixtures. Second, the multiplier emerges in the improvement of production through the multiplication of trades, by which Boyle appears to have meant the specialization and refinement of works, crafts and techniques that he saw taking place around him and that would greatly increase production. Scientists were crucial in improving knowledge of the products of nature, developing new working techniques and acting as mediators of knowledge between economic actors. Scientists like Boyle began the study of political economy in the modern sense of concentrating on the usefulness of (natural) objects for economic production.[120] This, I argue, is Boyle's paradigm shift.

His most characteristic stance appeared in the seminal *Of the Study of the Booke of Nature* of around 1650 in which he wrote that 'God created the World for a Double End', being 'the manifestation of his owne Glory' and 'the Good of Men, principally of the Elect'.[121] But he was also specific in repeatedly stating his position in respect of a qualified utilitarianism of creation as universal knowledge:

> tho' I judge it erroneous to say in the strictest sense, that every thing in the Visible World was made for the Use of Man; yet I think'tis more erroneous to deny, that any thing was made for ends Investigable by Man.[122]

Utopian theology also comprised the complex vocation of 'priest', 'natural scientist' and citizen of the British Empire that Boyle himself seemed to embody. With regard to the rest of inanimate and irrational creatures unable to acknowledge how much they owe their Creator, 'Man' he wrote in the *Of the Usefulness of Experimentall Natural Philosophy* was 'born the Priest of Nature'; by investigating nature, God received glory. To praise God was human beings' 'natural right'.[123] Not only did pleasures abound in the world, but also knowledge, which implied industriousness,

120 Karl Marx mocked in a footnote to the first chapter of *The Capital* the 'fictio juris' in 'bourgeois societies' that 'everyone as a buyer possesses an encyclopedic knowledge of commodities.' Instead, Marx argued in the bulk of the text: 'The use values of commodities furnish the material for a special study, that of the commercial knowledge of commodities.', which is exactly what Boyle proposed, Marx, *The Capital*, p. 27; p. 53.

121 Robert Boyle, 'Of the Study of the Booke of Nature' in *The Works of Robert Boyle*, vol. 13, pp. 147–172, p. 149. The idea is repeated in Boyle, 'Of the Usefulness of Experimentall Philosophy, The First Part', in *The Works of Robert Boyle*, vol. 3, p. 217.

122 Boyle, 'A Disquisition about the Final Causes of Natural Things, in *The Works of Robert Boyle*, vol. 11, p. 87; p. 95.

123 Boyle, 'Of the Usefulness of Experimentall Philosophy, The First Part', in *The Works of Robert Boyle*, vol. 3, p. 238.

even perhaps martyrdom. Similarly to the ancient right to priesthood among the Jews, so 'Reason' was 'a Natural Dignity' and 'Knowledge a Prerogative' that could 'confer a Priesthood without Unction or Imposition of Hands'.[124] The world was a 'sacrament' (*Verbum visibile*) – a visible sign of God.[125] Boyle's beautiful and groundbreaking stance is clear here. That was a very concrete means of praising God that went beyond specialized circles of *virtuosi* and was being proposed, in fact, to anyone who cared about natural sciences and the Empire. However, he was also breaking with theological tradition in two ways. As it classically considered that inanimate and irrational creatures praised God just by the fact of *being*; secondly, without a theory of morality, the danger of utopian pragmatism in Boyle's proposal loomed large. Around the years he wrote *The Usefulness* Boyle became a member of the Council for Foreign Plantations (1660–1664) and was appointed to the committees of Jamaica and New England, and it is not unreasonable to think that his new situation as a civil servant put Boyle's rare imagination to work.[126]

Few other modern English writers were more sophisticated than Boyle in combining natural philosophy, faith and economy. Intimations about the expansion of the empire underlined his image of the 'World' as a 'Ship'.[127] Such metaphors, of which he used plenty, adapted the traditional theological metaphors on the economy of salvation to the exigencies of the British Empire.[128] The world, he argued, was not merely an 'Inne', as the divines noted, with the idea that life is a journey and Christians found in the world every refreshment in the manner of a traveller who finds a place

124 He gave the example of 'the Elder Pliny' for his curiosity in watching how the Vesuvius erupted as 'a martyr of Physiologie. For we daily see Alchymists hazard their Lives on Minerall Experiments in Furnaces'. Boyle, 'Of the Usefulness of Experimentall Philosophy' in *The Works of Robert Boyle*, vol. 3, p. 201; quote in p. 203.

125 Boyle, 'Of the Usefulness of Experimentall Philosophy, The First Part', in *The Works of Robert Boyle*, vol. 3 p. 232; p. 238.

126 See also how important was for Boyle his careful use of rhetoric and other means of communication: 'metaphors were to the mind what microscopes were to the eye', in John T. Harwood, 'Science Writing and Writing Science: Boyle and Rhetorical Theory', in Michael Hunter (ed.), *Robert Boyle Reconsidered* (Cambridge: Cambridge University Press, 1994), p. 51; and John T. Harwood, 'Introduction', in John T. Harwood (ed.), *The Early Essays and Ethics of Robert Boyle* (Southern Illinois University Press, 1991), i-lxix. See also Hunter, *Boyle: Between God and Science*, p. 110.

127 Boyle, 'Of the Usefulness of Experimentall Philosophy, The First Part', in *The Works of Robert Boyle*, vol. 3, p. 218.

128 For the economic metaphors more generally in the Christian theological tradition see, Giacomo Todeschini, "Quantum Valet? Alle origini di un'economia della povertà," 98 *Bulletino Dell'istituto Storico Italiano per Il Medio Evo e Archivio Muratoriano* (1992).

to stop. The world indeed offered everything 'to feed Man and delight him'. However, references to the 'Inne' suggested interruption of one's journey, whereas the image of 'the Ship' gave the impression of the traveller being helped 'to convey him towards his Journey's end'. Moreover, the image of the ship illuminated the fact that God had created nature, not only for Christians' satisfaction, but also for their instruction. On this point, Boyle employed another metaphor – that of God as a benevolent donor, who would not withdraw from human beings' knowledge concerning his endowment. It would be irreverent to assume that God 'sends them to Sea disprovided of *Sea-Charts* and Mariners Compass, and other requisite helps to steer their Course by, to the desired Harbour'.[129] An elaboration of the older and remarkable paragraph of *Of the Study of the Book of Nature* that was mentioned in Chapter 4 appears in *The Usefulnesse of (Experimentall) Naturall Philosophy.*[130] It summarizes Boyle's ideas with regard to theological principles about the design of God in the creation of nature and of human beings and about a realist emphasis on body. As mentioned, the work contains no reflection on possible moral tensions arising in relation to the fulfilment of unlimited desires, but merely enthusiasm for their multiplying effect in terms of consumption, industriousness and knowledge. The passage merits being quoted at length:

> And 'twas perhaps, *Pyrophilus*, to ingage us to an industrious indagation of the Creatures, that God made Man so indigent, and furnish'd him with such a multiplicity of Desires; so that whereas other Creatures are content with those few obvious and easily attainable necessaries, that Nature has every where provided for them; In Man alone, every sense has a store of greedy Appetites, for the most part of Superfluities and Dainties, that to relieve his numerous Wants, or satisfie his more numerous Desires, He might be oblig'd with and inquisitive Industry to Range, Anatomize, and Ransack Nature, and by that concern'd survey come to a more exquisite Admiration of the Omniscient Author. To illustrate this subject yet a little further, *Pyrophilus*, give me leave to observe to you, That Philosophers of almost all Religion have been, by the contemplation of the World, mov'd to consider it under the notion of a Temple.[131]

[129] 'A wise Merchant, that sends Persons, he loves, to a farre Country, to think that he would furnish their Cabinets with Plenty of Provision, soft Beds, fine Pictures, and all other accommodations for their Voyage', Boyle, 'Of the Usefulness of Experimentall Philosophy, The First Part', in *The Works of Robert Boyle*, vol. 3, p. 218.

[130] See the chronological table of writings in The Robert Boyle Project, Birkbeck, University of London: *www.bbk.ac.uk/boyle/media/pdf/Boyles-writings-chronological.pdf*

[131] Boyle, 'The Usefulness of Natural Philosophy', in *The Works of Robert Boyle*, vol. 3, p. 237. Despite his utilitarian views Boyle wrote an early unpublished text (1647–1648) in which he condemns purposeless cruelty with creatures, and states that God created 'them for other

The Epicurean tone of praising desires is habitual in Boyle's work – he never appears austere or abstemious, and certainly not Puritan, rather touching on the merry aspect of Creation. Particularly in *The Usefulness*, in which this paragraph appears, Boyle observed the 'indigence' of human beings and their inclination to satisfy not only necessities but multifold and unlimited desires. In the context of the project of applying science, unlimited human desires become a manifestation, even an *opportunity*, to relish the bounty of the Creator, and not a negative tendency. Moreover, many of Boyle's theological, philosophical and metaphysical convictions are disclosed gradually in that important text of *The Usefulnesse*. Boyle explained his apologetic style by stating that he was addressing it to some religious people, afraid that the scientific knowledge of nature would shake belief. On the contrary, he argued, explaining that observation of God's 'Workmanship' in nature was one of the main methods for strengthening faith. Accepting his own explanation, and as mentioned before, Boyle's insistence on the usefulness of science has been in the literature partly attributed to critiques concerning irreligiosity and impractical activities carried out by the Royal Society.[132] However, the text is much more than a pious exercise of apology. At once a normative programme and a manifesto for scientists, Boyle brings out the big guns within the text in the form of the economic possibilities hidden in nature and in natural science. On the other hand, in the second part, which deals with 'Physick' (medicine) and the amelioration of medicinal remedies, the discourse is about 'necessity' and the economic aspect recedes from view almost completely, save that the importance of providing cheaper remedies for the poor is mentioned.[133] The economic discourse returns in the lengthy second part of Section II, which is devoted to proving the usefulness of natural philosophy in contributing to the profitability of trades.

Ends, besides Man's Seruice & Aduantages.' Malcolm Osler comments the text in the context of animal experiments increasingly practiced by the members of the Royal Society, including Boyle. Malcolm R. Oster, 'The "Beame of Divinity": Animal Suffering in the Early Thought of Robert Boyle' 22 *The British Journal for the History of Science*, (1989), p. 175.

132 Hunter, *Boyle: Between God and Science*; Sprat, *The History of the Royal Society for the Improving of Natural Knowledge*, p. 61. Shapin and Schaffer, *Leviathan and the Air-Pump;* Latour, *We Have Never Been Modern*, 15–18; Sarasohn, 'A Science Turned Upside Down'; Shapin, 'Pump and Circumstance: Robert Boyle's Literary Technology', p. 498; p. 517.

133 Noting that it was important to investigate cheap remedies; some 'cannot imagine that what doth not cost much Money in the Shops, can do much good in the Body; as if God had made Provision onely for the Rich, or those People that have Commerce with China or the India's.' Boyle, 'Of the Usefulness of Experimentall Philosophy. The Second Part' in *The Works of Robert Boyle*, vol. 3, p. 382.

With their capacity for pleasure and for praising the Almighty in the creatures human beings were singled out from the rest. Moreover, since human beings were the only ones capable of 'enjoy, use and relish' the rest of the beings, living and inanimate, the latter had been made for the former, not for God, not for themselves:

> For it is no great presumption to conceive, that the rest of the Creatures were made for Man, since He alone of the Visible World is able to enjoy, use, and relish many of the other Creatures, and to discerne the Omniscience, Almightinesse and Goodnesse of their Author in them, and returne Him praises for them.[134]

The 'necessaries of life' were abundantly provided in nature for every creature. However, the other animals were *limited* to 'necessaries', whereas all the material goods in the entire Creation were at the disposal of human beings:

> The Earth produces him an innumerable multitude of Beasts to feed, cloath, and carrie him; of Flowers and Jewels to delight and adorne him; of Fruits to sustaine and refresh him; of Stones and Timber, to lodg him; of Simples, to cure him; and in Summe, the whole sublunary World is but his Magazine. And it seems the grand businesse of restlesse Nature so to constitute and manage his Productions, as to furnish him with Necessaries, Accommodations and Pleasures.[135]

More than anything desires were the means decreed by God to prevent human beings' passivity towards nature and promote their (intellectual) industriousness. In the first three essays contained in *Of the Usefulness of Experimentall Natural Philosophy*, Boyle urges the argument that the industrious study of nature was a source of power, riches and faith – industriousness and its variants is probably the most repeated word in the text. Natural philosophy 'is not only Delightful, as it teaches us to Know Nature, but also as it teaches us in many Cases to Master and Command her'.[136] The possibilities that studying nature gave to the naturalist to imitate, multiply and improve its wonderful phenomena was in a sense the 'Empire of Man, as a Naturalist over the Creatures'. It consisted in 'a much more satisfactory kind of Power or Sovereignty' than the most common

[134] Boyle, 'Of the Usefulness of Experimentall Philosophy' in *The Works of Robert Boyle*, vol. 3, p. 216.

[135] Boyle, 'Of the Usefulness of Experimentall Philosophy' in *The Works of Robert Boyle*, vol. 3, p. 229.

[136] Boyle, 'Of the Usefulness of Experimentall Philosophy' in *The Works of Robert Boyle*, vol. 3, p. 211.

forms of political sovereignty. The latter was often the consequence of ambition, bloody struggles, crime or even simply chance. The former, Boyle argued, was innocent.[137]

6.3.3 *Technology from the Plantations*

Boyle's most remarkable employment of economic ideas appeared in the third part of *Of the Usefulness of Experimentall Natural Philosophy*, in which he was already thinking in terms of industrial manufacture. His distinction between bare necessities and what may now be termed luxuries was again introduced. 'It is not only to the Trades that minister to the necessities of Mankind' he noted 'but to those also that serve for man's accommodation and delight, that Experimentall philosophie may bring Improvements', including, 'perfums', 'making seweetmeats', embelleshing 'the Face with cosmeticks, and divers others of the like voluptuous nature'.[138] Boyle's innovation here lay not so much in his proposal for the improvement of crafts but in his ability to mediate between all economic positions involved as a spokesman for science.[139] In this process it was essential that artisans trusted the natural scientists. If 'tradesmen' were to disclose some of their experiments to 'practicall Naturalists', Boyle argued, 'the difussed knowledge and sagacity of Philosophers' would be able to improve them markedly.[140]

Furthermore, his narration of how a combination of *transplanting* commodities[141] to which improved techniques were applied, with the result of multiplying the employment of workers ('mechanical hands') reveals him as something akin to a seer in respect of the future Industrial Revolution. Firstly, importing and exporting commodities would also bring about the idea of the multiplying effect. For foreign natural goods were sometimes more productive, such as the wonderful exuberance of the Indian corn or

137 Boyle, 'Of the Usefulness of Experimentall Philosophy' in *The Works of Robert Boyle*, vol. 3, p. 212.

138 Boyle, 'Of the Usefulness of Experimentall Philosophy' in *The Works of Robert Boyle*, vol. 3, p. 417.

139 That Boyle was not especially original in this particular idea of improving the crafts for economic benefit may be seen from Vera Keller, 'Scarlet Letters: Sir Theodore de Mayerne and the Early Stuart Color World in the Royal Society', in Vera Keller, Anna Marie Roos, and Elizabeth Yale (eds.), *Archival Afterlives. Life, Death, and Knowledge-Making in Early Modern British Scientific and Medical Archives*, (Leiden, Boston: Brill 2018).

140 Boyle, 'Of the Usefulness of Experimentall Philosophy' in *The Works of Robert Boyle*, vol. 3, p. 399.

141 Boyle, 'Of the Usefulness of Experimentall Philosophy. Second Part. Second Section', 412.

the Chinese rice. Moreover, exploiting new ideas had a direct impact in augmenting production, and thus profit:

> For these Inventions of ingenious heads doe, when once grown into request, set many Mechanical hands a worke, and supply Tradesmen with new meanes of setting a livelihood or even enriching themselves.[142]

It is important to emphasize Boyle's originality here in noting the possibilities of profit for the entrepreneur in allegiance with 'science'. In studies of the cultural roots of the Industrial Revolution, reducing labour costs through mechanization in order to gain profit for the entrepreneur is considered to be the vital insight, in contradistinction to the public policy mantra of putting the poor to work. However, this principle is situated much later in time, around the mid-eighteenth century.[143] But Boyle's advice for combining new technologies with an increase in 'mechanical hands' to the trader or owner of a manufactory in the widely read *Of the Usefulness of Experimentall Natural Philosophy*, as 'more advantagious to him' was given a century earlier. Sometimes Boyle urged the employment of more chemical processes, where mechanic devices were common. In cases where no technology was applied, he noted again with his futuristic emphasis in multiplication that things 'that ought to be done mechanically' still undertaken 'by the labour of the Hand, may with far more ease and Expedition (the quantity considered) be performed by Engines'.[144]

Boyle's own notorious report of 'a recent Instance of the transplanting of Arts and Manifactures' may conclude this section. He recalls how a foreigner travelling from Brazil to Europe with some sugar canes happened to stop in Barbados, and there 'an English Planter that was curious' obtained not only some sugar canes from him but also 'some Hints of the way of cultivating and using them'.[145] The importance of the story was for him that 'the Introduction of one Physico-Mechanical Art' may put many hands to work. Without offering further detail, he added that

[142] Boyle, 'Of the Usefulness of Experimentall Philosophy' in *The Works of Robert Boyle*, vol. 3, p. 399.

[143] Margaret C. Jacobs points to a text of mechanics of 1744 by Newton's assistant, John Teophilus Desaguliers (1683–1744) as the first with that 'critical insight' in Margaret C. Jacob, 'The Cultural Origins of the First Industrial Revolution' in Marcus Hellyer (ed.), *The Scientific Revolution: The Essential Readings* (Oxford: Blackwell Publishing, 2003), p. 212.

[144] Boyle, 'Of the Usefulness of Experimentall Philosophy' in *The Works of Robert Boyle*, vol. 3, p. 478.

[145] Boyle, 'Of the Usefulness of Experimentall Philosophy' in *The Works of Robert Boyle*, vol. 3, p. 424.

'I had the particular opportunity to learn by Enquiry, that … the Blacks, living as Slaves upon that spot of the Ground, and imploy'd almost to tally about the planting of Sugar, amount at least to between five and twenty, and twenty thousand persons'. He also gave some figures to show 'how Lucriferous in that place this so recent Art of making Sugar is, not onely to private man, but to the publick'.[146] Boyle's conclusion was, in his own words, '*That the Experimentall philosopher may not only Improve Trades, but multiply them*' (emphasis by Boyle).[147]

Two things are noticeable in this narration. Boyle was thinking in this case of a lucrative endeavour for private individuals and the public – in sum, for the economy of the empire as a whole. Moreover, his exposition of the conditions of labour of the slaves in Barbados seems to suggest that he not only approved of them but wanted to see them adopted in his own country. Workers in England ought to be employed as the slaves were employed already in the Plantations – this is what his suggestions as to importing the labour techniques used in Barbados appears to suggest. The 'mechanical art' applied to slaves' work in the plantations would equally make trades and manufacturers in England more profitable, which, with hindsight, would appear to make the slaves on the plantations the unwilling initiators of the English Industrial Revolution.

Boyle's mention of the mechanical arts used in Barbados refers to a manufacturing process used in sugar mills involving advanced chemical and mechanical technologies that raised sugar production and consumption in England to much higher levels than had previously been the case.[148] Eric Otremba describes how the English scientific community attributed the success of sugar-making in Barbados to the *ingenios*, a type of furnace

[146] Though 'scarcely credible', he had obtained the following numbers from one of the ancient Magistrates of the Island of Barbados. This amounted to shipping off to England 'ten thousand Tun', each tone 'two thousand Pund weight of sugar' which amounted to 'twenty millions of Pounds of that Commodity'. Boyle, 'Of the Usefulness of Experimentall Philosophy' in *The Works of Robert Boyle*, vol. 3, p. 425.

[147] Boyle, 'Of the Usefulness of Experimentall Philosophy' in *The Works of Robert Boyle*, vol. 3, p. 425. As noted before, Robert Boyle used this word to emphasize the union between light or knowledge and profit, that had been distinguished by Bacon as 'luciferous' versus 'fructiferous' experiments, Peter R. Anstey, 'Philosophy of Experiment in Early Modern England: The Case of Bacon, Boyle and Hooke' in 19 *Early Science and Medicine* (2014), p. 111.

[148] 'In turning the pith of the sugar cane plant into white crystalline sucrose, the ingenios of the Atlantic basin relied upon a series of mechanical and chemical processes which were highly sophisticated for their day' Eric Otremba, 'Inventing Ingenios: Experimental Philosophy and the Secret Sugar-makers of the Seventeenth-Century Atlantic' 28 *History and Technology* (2012), p. 122.

or mill for processing sugar cane, and to the clever plantation owners who ran them. However, this view neglected the contribution of the sugar-making know-how possessed by slaves and servants, which, as Otremba argues, was ultimately the critical factor in the entire enterprise.[149] Richard Ligon's well-known *A True and Exact History of the Island of Barbados* (1657) both describes and sketches the *ingenio* in detail and gives a very melancholy account of the conditions of life and work of the European servants and slaves involved in operating it. He thereby informed the English and European public of both the incredible possibilities offered by the island and of the conditions under which these possibilities were being exploited. Both African slaves and Christian servants, who were of Irish extraction or European captives of war, were 'commodities': the former were owned by the plant owners for life, the latter for five years. Ligon emphasized the terrible heat common in the island for eight months of the year, under which the thousands of servile workers laboured for ten hours a day in the field. Then there was the *ingenios* furnace to contend with. Some masters were good, some not. Ligon's narration makes clear that under these conditions slaves often committed suicide or ran away.[150] Boyle had read Ligon's history of Barbados thoroughly and made numerous annotations.[151] To see him engrossed in the technological and horticultural detail of the natural history of the 'ingenious Lingon' but apparently unengaged by the sociological aspects of the narrative casts his remarks on the virtues of Barbados's 'mechanical hands' in a sombre light.

I contend that his declaration of the usefulness of the scheme while remaining silent on the conditions of labour results directly from Boyle's glossing over human nature in the context of his studies of nature. That would evolve into the tragic side of the Scientific Revolution. The European practice of slavery was almost two centuries old by that point,

[149] Otremba, 'Inventing Ingenios'. More generally, that 'the practick part' contained much knowledge not easily transferable was however soon realized by the fellows of the Royal Society, despite their early confidence on the force of intellect and deriding comments of ignorant and 'rude mechanics' Michael Hunter, *Science and Society in Restoration England* (Cambridge: Cambridge University Press, 1981), p. 104.

[150] This information in Richard Ligon, *A True an Exact History of the Island of Barbados* (London: Humphrey Moseley, London, 1657) Early English Books Online Text Creation Partnership, 2011 http://name.umdl.umich.edu/A48447.0001.001

[151] Describing Boyle's method of annotations his notes on Ligon's *A True and Exact History of the Island of Barbados* are mentioned in Iordan Avramov and Michael Hunter, 'Reading by Proxy: The Case of Robert Boyle (1627–1691) 25 *Intellectual History Review* (2014), p. 42. Boyle also mentions the 'Ingenious Mr. Lygon' about a fruit in the Caribbean in *The Origine of Formes and Qualities.*

with the Spanish Empire's requirements for workers promoting the horrific business, but without offering any justification for it. This only happened when utilitarian ideology gained ground among European philosophers. In her study on the justifications of slavery through political economy Anne Charlotte Martineau explains how around sixty years later the physiocrat François Melon (1675–1738) pointed out in an *Essai politique sur le commerce* (1734) that the significance of slavery lay in its 'utility' rather than whether it was contrary to morality or religion.[152]

Therefore, the salient issue is not how far Boyle was prepared to go in order to defend his project of useful experimental science, but rather to observe how soon a utility-oriented science that made no attempt to incorporate the moral nature of human beings within its epistemic realm would render compromises with matters contrary to fundamental morality and prejudicial to human beings unavoidable – even in the hands of its best practitioners. As a consequence of the utilitarianism human beings become the exploitators of nature, instead of their guardians, as well as utilitarianism's victims. The utilitarian lack of moral anthropology in science, which place human beings outside nature, leaves nature and human nature unprotected on the face of future utilitarian schemes.

152 See about this, Anne-Charlotte Martineau, 'Comment et pourquoi écrire l'histoire du droit international? Le cas de l'abolition de l'esclavage' 18 *Clio@Themis* (2020), pp. 1–15, p. 14.

7

Robert Boyle, the Empire over Nature

7.1 Nothing Is Necessary: Benjamin Worsley Revisited

Robert Boyle's immersion in the life of an experimental chemist seems to have been preceded by his encounter as a teenager with the virtuoso Benjamin Worsley and strengthened by the enthusiastic support of Samuel Hartlib. Boyle's early correspondence shows that his personality partook of much of Hartlib's capacity for inquiry and for sharing scientific matters with others, and therefore that he had the potential to be a key player in the realm of science himself. An important number of writings showing his inclination to theory from an early age indicate, as we have seen, that Boyle was already a (moral) philosopher. However, according to Michael Hunter, Worsley was 'his evident mentor' in such matters as chemistry and experiments.[1] It may have been the case that Boyle's social status and wealth prevented a more common student/mentor relationship. Nonetheless, Worsley's intellectual ascendancy over Boyle is visible in their early correspondence. And then there is, of course, the Irish connection. Worsley was working in Ireland by 1640 and Boyle himself was born at the iconic Lismore Castle. Boyle's father, the First Earl of Cork, was one of the main seventeenth-century English planters in Ireland, and Boyle was his youngest son; Cork and his second wife Catherine Fenton (1588–1630) had 15 children. Cork's legacy in the history of Ireland was impressive though controversial, mainly due to his activities as a land grabber. Nicholas Canny has argued that Boyle's bent towards practical science as a divine command, advancement of social discipline and broad Protestantism, neither sectarian nor marked by absolute conformity, were characteristics inherited from his father. Boyle would pursue the trajectory indicated by these tendencies with growing confidence and erudition throughout his career. Canny's suggestion was that the encounter with the Hartlib circle was a propitious

[1] Hunter, *Boyle: Between God and Science*, p. 70; see also, Harwood, 'Introduction' in *The Early Essays and Ethics of Robert Boyle*, p. lxiii.

circumstance in Boyle's scientific career, but not much more, for the seed was planted in Ireland.[2] This seems accurate also in view of the pains his father took to provide him with an exquisite social and intellectual education, in England (Eton) and, in particular, in Florence, Rome and Geneva.[3] Thanks to his wealth Boyle was very soon acknowledged as a 'mecenas' by other important scientists, and only after that as a scientist. It was in terms of patronage that a young William Petty (1623–1687) wrote to an even younger Boyle. The physician and economist Petty (to whom we will return later) was four years Boyle's senior and engaged in a rivalry with Worsley in the management of certain Irish affairs that would signify a permanent disadvantage for the latter. Boyle's admission, at a precocious age, to the Hartlib circle probably stems from his extraordinary position in society.[4] Interestingly, Canny also mentions the possibilities of experimentation and creativity offered by Ireland. Every new administrator thought himself to be destined to improve on what others had done before, and Boyle's father seems to have been only one of the most entrepreneurial of them. Meanwhile, the natives looked on in resignation or rebelled in their misery.[5]

Thomas Leng points out that Worsley's part-time practitioner scientist approach would be overridden by the impending Scientific Revolution, which involved the ever more sophisticated standards of method, experiment and exposition that Boyle represents.[6] Although Worsley was only nine years older than Boyle, they belonged to different generations of scientists, and even different worlds, in this respect. Another difference – and a feature of Boyle I want to highlight in this chapter – is how well-read in the most modern philosophy of the time he was. Partly as a consequence of his aristocratic and opulent upbringing and partly of his own erudition, criticism of and active struggle against the 'vulgar' – understood as that which has not been subjected to proper critical reflection – is a key thread that runs through his writings.[7] *A Free Enquiry into the Vulgarly Receiv'd Notion of Nature*, analysed in the following text, represents the culmination of this

[2] Nicholas Canny, *The Upstart Earl. A Study of the Social and Mental World of Richard Boyle, First Earl of Cork, 1566–1643* (Cambridge: Cambridge University Press, 1982), pp. 139–150.

[3] His family connections propitiously allied themselves with the Parliamentarians after the War. This biographical information in Hunter, *Boyle: Between God and Science*.

[4] Hunter, *Boyle: Between God and Science*, p. 51; Harwood, 'Introduction', p. xxii.

[5] Canny, *The Upstart Earl*.

[6] Leng, *Benjamin Worsley (1618–1677) Trade, Interest and the Spirit in Revolutionary England*.

[7] Michael Hunter notes several times the lavishing expenses for his children by the First Earl of Cork that must have left a character trace in Boyle, Hunter, *Boyle: Between God and Science*, p. 27. The social station of Boyle may be illustrated by the correspondence cited by Michael Hunter between the first Earl of Cork and the tutor in Geneva of Francis and

critical endeavour and shows its fruitfulness as well as the risks involved in the wielding of Boyle's elitist razor.[8] Certainly, he was an experimental philosopher, with equal stress on each of those words. Moreover, he belonged to an intellectual network that allowed him to meet personally many philosophers, scientists and virtuosi, and, strikingly, also to know well and admire the work of the Epicurean Pierre Gassendi when he was barely 20 years old.[9] For instance, on 9 May 1648 Hartlib copied for Boyle an extract from a letter from Sir Charles Cavendish to William Petty, in which Cavendish – in addition to noting how much Hobbes had liked a letter from Petty and describing an important experiment as to whether vacuums exist – wrote as follows about Gassendi's forthcoming book on the life of Epicurus:

> your worthy friend and mine Mr. Gassendi is reasonable (*sic!*) well, and hath printed a book of the life and manners of Epicurus since your going from hence. He hath now in the press at *Lyons* the philosophy of Epicurus, in which I believe we shall have much of his own philosophy, which doubtless will be an excellent work.[10]

Robert Boyle, Isaac Marcombes. Marcombes urged Cork not to allow that the boys got a too clear grasp of their "greatness" and wrote to him that "every one thinks that because I belong to my Lord of Corke I must have the Philosophical stone" Hunter, *Boyle: Between God and Science*, p. 45; John Harwood highlights the years of financial strain during the civil wars, in which the Earl died and his landed property and inheritance to his children remained in an uncertain position. Harwood, 'Introduction' in *The Early Essays and Ethics of Robert Boyle*. By 1645, when he returned to England, Boyle could have access to his immense inheritance, considering in particular that (although a favourite) he was just the youngest of many children. Michael Hunter reports that Boyle, a teenager, inherited rentals of about 3.000 pounds a year, which made him the equivalent to a millionaire of the twenty first century. His fortune required a great deal of administration, and trouble. Not the least of it caused by the fact that extensive parts of Boyle's land had been confiscated from the Church by his father. Since the money of those rentals could have been employed to help spreading the Gospel and in the cure of souls, this would prove to be later a source of anxiety for the conscience of the pious Boyle. Hunter, *Boyle: Between God and Science*, p. 40 and generally Chapter 2, and Hunter, 'The Conscience of Robert Boyle'.

8 Already for instance in the unpublished *Aretology* that he wrote as a teenager: 'And by Seeming Vertus I heere understand, Certin splendid and less observed Vices, opposed to other Vices more generally taken Notice of and Condemn'd, which therefore the Ignorant Vulgar mistake for reall Vertus.' Boyle, 'The Aretology', p. 135.

9 Boyle writes that the counsels Hartlib gave to the tutor John Pawson for applications 'to make to those three mathematicians, can promise a great deal of probability for their success: specially *Gassendus*, a great favourite of mine, I take to be a very profound mathematican, as well as an excellent astronomer, and one, that has collected a very ample treasury of numerous and accurate observations of all, that belongs to the abstruse science of those sublime bodies.' 'Robert Boyle to Samuel Hartlib, 8 May 1647', *The Correspondence of Robert Boyle*, vol. 1, 1636–1661, p. 59.

10 Samuel Hartlib to Robert Boyle to 9 May 1648, *The Correspondence of Robert Boyle*, vol. 1, p. 66.

This was the sort of information that interested Boyle. If Boyle was from the beginning a philosopher, Worsley and Boyle's interests in common – in terms of nature and in relation to esoteric principles and economic ideas – may be summarized in few words: trade and plantations, alchemy, medicine and astrology. Lawrence Principe has shown that Boyle never abandoned his pursuit of the philosopher's stone, and has enumerated his changing motives in relation to that activity 'as a tool for dissecting nature', for the production of medicines and for enabling his philosophy of nature to ascertain the truths of theology.[11] These motives indicate that Boyle followed in Worsley's footsteps and also frame the recurring topics that prompted the Scientific Revolution. They comprise the achievement of a flourishing public economy, care of the human body, veneration of the spirit and an avidness in the pursuit of knowledge about nature.

7.1.1 Mentoring Boyle

Three of Worsley's letters, which take the form of essays imparting knowledge, particularly show the heritage that the administrator, scientist and millenarian shared with Boyle, the wealthy aristocrat, enlightened scientist and governor of the New England Company. None of them have an identified recipient and only the first two identify Worsley as the author.[12] The editors of Boyle's correspondence considered that the author of the third and longest letter written in late 1658 or early 1659 was also Worsley and the recipient Boyle. John T. Young remarks that Hartlib was circulating these two letters as there are several copies of it among his papers, and he describes them as 'something of a manifesto of natural philosophy', as indeed they are.[13] The tone of the second letter is rather casual, as if written to a close friend; the overall content points with some probability to Boyle also being the recipient. Common themes such as microscopes, names – such as Ahasuerus Fromanteel (1607–1693) the glass and watchmaker – the key themes of 'air' and the purpose of natural philosophy, at once high and useful, recur throughout the three letters.[14] Worsley also thanked the

[11] Lawrence M. Principe, *The Aspiring Adept. Robert Boyle and His Alchemica Quest* (Princeton: Princeton University Press, 1998), p. 7.

[12] The first two letters of June and July 1648, that is, of more than a decade earlier are found also among Hartlib's papers copied in a single document with Worsley indicated as his author and with no recipient.

[13] Young, *Faith, Medical Alchemy and Natural Philosophy*, p. 222, n. 54.

[14] Antonio Clericuzio's study on some papers contained in Boyle's *History of Air*, that were in reality authored by Worsley proved that the latter's role on the development of Boyle's

recipient for the copy of a letter from 'Dr. Goddard' – probably the physician Jonathan Goddard (1617–1675) whom Quentin Skinner paired with Boyle as 'the religious forces' among the Founding Fellows of the Royal Society.[15] It was in Goddard's lodgings, moreover, that the first embryonic group of what was to become the early Royal Society was to meet after 1645, because he had a machine for grinding glasses for telescopes and microscopes.[16] Boyle was associated with this group at least since 1646.[17]

In the first letter, Worsley described a certain glass for the microscope that Fromanteel had given to him that after special rubbing and grinding magnified the vision of things to a measure hitherto unknown to him. Worsley commented that the microscope was as good as some made in France, of whom 'Mr. Petty' (William Petty) had assured him that he possessed one, 'Mr Hobbes of Paris giving it to him'. Worsley then begged his addressee to bring up the topic of optics when he met with Petty and to try to see the latter's microscope, so that they could later compare it with Fromanteel's. In the second letter, written in Amsterdam, Worsley explained at length why Fromanteel's glasses were of such importance – in a nutshell, they buttressed the design argument of nature.[18] In an environment of convinced atomists, by showing the beauty of creation to its most minuscule aspect, they proved that God was its designer, and that nature was not the outcome of mere chance. The first philosophical and theological reason for this was that they helped to prove the maxim by which, above any other method, the wisdom of God might be ascertained.

natural philosophy was more important than thought previously. Antonio Clericuzio, 'New Light on Benjamin Worsley's Natural Philosophy' in *Samuel Hartlib and Universal Reformation. Studies in Intellectual Communication* (Cambridge: Cambridge University Press, 1994).

15 Quentin Skinner, 'Thomas Hobbes and the Nature of the Early Royal Society' in 12 *The Historical Journal* (1969), p. 225.

16 This was the account of the mathematician John Wallis (1716–1703) describing the members of the meetings and the places where they met, quoted in Thomas Birch, 'The Life of the Honourable Robert Boyle', in *Works of the Honourable Robert Boyle* (London: Pr. For J and F. Rivington et al. 1772), v. I, p. xlii.

17 In his biography of Boyle Thomas Birch made the link between the cryptic 'Invisible' or 'philosophical college' which Boyle mentioned sometimes in this period between 1646 and 1649, and this first group of scientists. The Invisible College could not be the Hartlib circle, as also noted by Michael Hunter, for the very reason that Boyle reported to him about it in a letter to satisfy his curiosity, Hunter, *Boyle: Between God and Science*, p. 66. On the Invisible College see also section 4.2.1.

18 Thomas Leng thinks that the addressee was Hartlib; but the editors of Hartlib's papers still keep it open. As I wrote above, I think that it might be Boyle. Copy Letters, Benjamin Worsley to?, 22 June 1648, 27 July 1648, Ref. 42/1/1A-2B: 2B Blank, in *The Hartlib Papers*.

Looking at the singular individuals of any species through the glasses, one might observe that they had 'not only a numericall forme as the schooles say, but an outward visible externall character or difference to distinguish them one from another'. Not only every man, but every animal, and in Worsley's example 'every sand is knowne by its name'. The glasses had helped him see that every grain of sand was different in colour, form and shape, although they all seemed round in the hand. The second motive was that in the bigger project of classifying plants, the microscope greatly facilitated investigation into 'seeds and flowers'. Worsley considered that 'this [little] Atlantis', and 'Unknown part of the Creation', unexplored at the time could fill many scientific volumes in the future.[19] With regard to his scientific manifesto, also touching on the rejection of the vulgar, Worsley was straightforward:

> For I now having abdicated much reading of Bookes, vulgare received Traditions & common or Schoole opinion, have divided knowledge into Divine & humane. For divine I acknowledge none to be the necessary Rule of faith but what the spiritt of god hath sett doune plainely, in simple & univocall tearmes & easy to the understanding of any, looking upon all poynts contreoverted, as the opinions but at best, if not the Inventions & pryde of men … For humane knowledge I honour only that which is immediately deduced from or built upon Reall, & certayne Experiments; & those so many as to make an infallible universall; seeing according to the Schooles, science is not of particulars.[20]

Worsley's manifesto on natural sciences was a petition for theological independence, with no 'necessary rule of faith' or philosophical principle beyond faith in experimentation on a vast scale. His argument was that among 'good men' there ought not to be 'difference of opinion', since the Spirit of God was 'one' – a statement that seems rather terse and even eccentric in his ideological and political context.[21] However, it is possible that Worsley's charm lay precisely in that capacity to urge a mental state oblivious of the surrounding reality, an attitude that probably imparted much creative freedom to Boyle. The aim was practical: a 'natural history' or observations and description of the geography and

[19] Benjamin Worsley to?, 22 June 1648, 27 July 1648, in *The Hartlib Papers*. The grain of sand as an explanans was apparently a common trope of seventeenth-century atomists, see e.g. in Thomas M. Lennon, *The Battle of the Gods and Giants: Legacies of Descartes and Gassendi. 1655–1715* (Princeton: Princeton University Press, 2014 (1993)), p. 142.

[20] Benjamin Boyle to?, 22 June 1648, 27 July 1648, in *The Hartlib Papers*.

[21] Copy Letters, Benjamin Worsley to?, 22 June 1648, 27 July 1648' in *The Hartlib Papers*.

peoples of the world, in the style of the geographical editor and compiler Samuel Purchas (1575–1626), but infused with the new scientific spirit.[22] Great knowledge would be thus produced on (among many other things that he listed) the fruits and products of nature, plants, fish and minerals, 'convenient or pleasurable for mans use or in things hurtfull & inconvenient' and, on whether '[i]ts use medicinall, oeconomicall & mechanicall either by Inhabitants or by other Countries' could be advanced.[23] No better example of what Vera Keller has called 'the wish list' may be found: a dramatized enumeration of knowledge, reconceptualized as shared desires, projected as an alluring future and thus transformed into public interest.[24]

Moreover, for the industrious Worsley, these were not theoretical or utopian proposals. He would ascend on several occasions to the highest echelons of the only institutions that could make something of them during his lifetime. We saw in Chapter 4 that he was closely involved, during the Interregnum, in the Council of Trade and Commonwealth in promoting trade scientifically through the Navigation Acts. Thomas Leng has traced, by reference to Worsley's expert reports, copied by John Locke in his *Notebook*, the way in which Worsley planned – in the Council of Trade of 1668 and, later in the Council for Trade and Foreign Plantations (1670–73) – the regulation of trade from the late 1660s onwards. He achieved his aims by promoting single commodities, and in particular sugar. Thus, he wrote a substantial report to the Duke of Buckingham (1628–1687) in the summer of 1668, in which he noted that through the reduction of taxes, encouragement of cultivation and careful management it was feasible for the plantations of the West Indies 'to make us the sole Masters of Sugar to all the world'. He opined, according to Leng somewhat over-optimistically, that the sugar trade could soon amount to 1 million pounds.[25] Worsley's was indeed a good example of how to undertake applied science.

[22] Worsley specifically praises the possibilities that Purchas' works offered. Copy Letters, Benjamin Worsley to?, 22 June 1648, 27 July 1648' in *The Hartlib Papers*; see also David Armitage, 'Samuel Purchas (bap. 1577, d.1626), geographical editor and compiler and Church of England clergyman', *Oxford Dictionary of National Biography*, https://doi.org/10.1093/ref:odnb/22898.

[23] Copy Letters, Benjamin Worsley to?, 22 June 1648, 27 July 1648, *The Hartlib Papers.*

[24] Keller, *Knowledge and the Public Interest, 1575–1725.*

[25] Thomas Leng notes that two centuries later sugar's trade produced still half that figure, Leng, *Benjamin Worsley (1618–1677) Trade, Interest and the Spirit in Revolutionary England*, p. 150.

7.1.2 *Worsley the Prophet*

The style of Worsley's third letter is much more prophetic, perhaps cabalistic.[26] In it he disclosed to Boyle the 'Great Instauration and Reformation' of medicine, his reasoning swiftly jumping, without philosophical elaboration, from 'physicks' to 'Scripture'. As a rule, Worsley promised results impatiently, even results of the most extraordinary kind, and despite his erudition, his writing style was that of the memorandum writer.[27] This letter is no exception. The theme of the letter was about the 'nature & essence of Health', inquiring about 'what may dissolve this natural & well constituted Oeconomy of nature', by which he referred to a healthy human body. The key question was whether death was 'laid upon us by a fatality or necessity or no' and his remarkable answer was that *it was not*.[28]

After a brief introduction, he recommended robust knowledge of aetiology, the doctrine of causes of distempers, and the production of 'hystoryes' of the best 'methods used in Medicine in all ages and nations'.[29] In sum, his substantial argument amounted to attributing the cause and power of human beings' death to the Devil and to human worldly desire:

> Death as it had no entrance at the beginning into Adam, soe noe power fatality or necessity over the Posterity of Adam since. by or from any Law or Decree of God originally or Inevitably occasioning of it He (not soe far as we read in his word) either appointing of Death, or requiring any thing of his Creature, tending or leading in the least to Death.[30]

If death was unnecessary, God, the 'great buylder of nature', was not responsible for human deaths and could not be charged with having

[26] Worsley puts in parallel 'the science of a Schooleman, of a Caballist of an Universall Scholar with that of an Ideot or a common Clowne', 'Worsley to Boyle, (late 1658-early 1659)', in *The Correspondence of Robert Boyle*, v. 1, p. 309; for Christian Kabbalah though not dealing with seventeenth-century England, see Peter J. Forshaw, 'Christian Kabbalah' in Glenn Alexander Magee (ed.), *The Cambridge Handbook of Western Mysticism and Esotericism*, (Cambridge: Cambridge University Press, 2016).

[27] The size of his library also speaks about his erudition. It counted 1857 books, sold after his death, Leng, *Benjamin Worsley*, p. 174.

[28] Worsley pointed here to some sort of secret society: 'Liberation from the common state of mortality & corruption: which state there are some perhaps in the earth (though not knowne save unto some few) who presume & that not without ground they shall see.' 'Worsley to Boyle, (late 1658-early 1659)', *The Correspondence of Robert Boyle*, v. 1, p. 308; p. 310.

[29] 'Worsley to Boyle, (late 1658-early 1659)', *The Correspondence of Robert Boyle*, v. 1, p. 307.

[30] 'Worsley to Boyle, (late 1658-early 1659)' *The Correspondence of Robert Boyle*, v. 1, p. 312.

produced a 'system' that was disproportionate or allowed 'Deorganization into the body'.[31] On the contrary God had promised human beings the spirit of life. The 'Rarefaction & Coagulation' that occurred in the human body was attributable to the devil, who was a lier, and 'Lye' himself.[32] 'Satan' had the power to 'alter the whole frame and Oeconomy of this our outward & humourall substance'. Death followed the 'rule & Dominion permitted to him in the Aire'. Boyle's lifelong interest in the study of air is perhaps illuminated by Worsley's following claim:

> Now if man have a power in his spirit greater then that of the Divell who is no more than a spirit, nor so much indeed as one of our spirits. If man also through the wisedome of his spirit knoweth how to temper the aire how so to correct it or medicate it as to avoid the evill influences of it ... All which wee must plainely say we beleeve Possible, then Death for this Reason as well as for the former is not fatall.[33]

The argument made was that the 'causes of death' were 'partly Physical partly mysticall or Theosophicall'.[34] In that vein, Worsley proceeded to enumerate a strict 'Traine' of causation the result of which was the death of human beings at the end of the chain. First, 'the pretious spirit' in a human being consented to be subjected to the flesh, the light of sense and the light of his imagination – i.e. the 'light created by the spiritus mundi' – and thus was 'throwne downe from it owne true station and seate'. In a second stage a *desire* for the world appeared. This subjection of the spirit to flesh 'introducing & kindling a lust in the spirit of man to a union with the spirit of the world'. In Worsley's account it was human desire for the world that ultimately caused natural death:

> And for as much as the desire giveth Increment to the soul every soul or spirit growing both in bulke as its desire is more or lesse powerful & strong & growing in nature according to the nature of that with which & Into which its desire is fixed & placed Through this desire or lust therefore of the pretious mind or spirit of man after an union with the outward light glory or goodly appearance of the spirit of the world (which desire or lust the scripture calls sin as being the roote of all sin) the spirit or mind itselfe doth insensably & by degrees transforme it selfe & is become transformed into the very Nature of the spirit of the world soe loosing & by degree insensably puting of its own nature which is a spirit of light.[35]

[31] 'Worsley to Boyle, (late 1658-early 1659)', *The Correspondence of Robert Boyle*, v. 1, p. 314; p. 315.
[32] 'Worsley to Boyle, (late 1658-early 1659)', *The Correspondence of Robert Boyle*, v. 1, p. 313.
[33] 'Worsley to Boyle, (late 1658-early 1659)', *The Correspondence of Robert Boyle*, v. 1, p. 311; p. 312.
[34] 'Worsley to Boyle, (late 1658-early 1659)', *The Correspondence of Robert Boyle*, v. 1, p. 317.
[35] 'Worsley to Boyle, (late 1658-early 1659)', *The Correspondence of Robert Boyle*, v. 1, p. 315.

Finally, by this transformation of their spirit, human beings became subject to any inconvenient motion that produce bodily corruption and distempers. Therefore, 'Death' had no 'power of soveraignity of absolute necessity from it selfe' or from 'some unknowne Accident or Fate'. The wisdom needed to overcome death must therefore come from above.[36]

Was the pious Boyle allured or scandalized by the declaration about the possibility of eternal life on earth? While it would be idle to attempt to guess Boyle's state of mind after reading this remarkable letter, strikingly, Alexander Wragge-Morley has recently argued that Boyle's experiments concerning the transmutation of camphor included an ambitious theological programme to explain the process undergone by the corpuscles in a human body when dying and also when resurrecting: the potential presented by experimental science lay, for him, in knowing *how* God had resurrected human beings.[37] It may also be noted that during the years of correspondence with Worsley on earthly desire as the cause of human death, Boyle, as we have seen, was developing the topic of the usefulness of experimental philosophy to supply and satisfy the multifold and unlimited human desires that he sanctioned. Furthermore, according to Worsley, there was nothing to detain the march of humanity towards making a paradise on earth. Worsley himself was a riddle when one attempts to reconcile his lifelong and vigorous pursuit of trade, prosperity for his country and mastery of the knowledge about the particulars of nature and its material benefits (admittedly involving much personal inconvenience to him) with his principled rejection of the *desire for the things of the world* and his definition, presented earlier, of the materialist spirit as the true cause of human death. Was this a fragmentation of the Reformers' personality, the inevitable outcome of their Neoplatonist division between the earthly and spiritual life? Or perhaps mid-seventeenth-century Puritan consciousness was still too strong, and an edict to refrain from the satisfaction of desire was the price Reformers had to pay for pursuing the politics of science that promised to satisfy all desires?

7.2 The Transmutator of Nature

Boyle did not share Worsley's millenarian radicalism, nor was he such an extreme relativist. Paradoxically, one of the greatest experimentalists

[36] 'Worsley to Boyle, (late 1658-early 1659)', *The Correspondence of Robert Boyle*, v. 1, p. 317.

[37] Wragge-Morley, *Aesthetic Science. Representing Nature in the Royal Society of London, 1650–1720*, pp. 40–60.

in history did not have complete confidence in the sufficiency of experiment alone, and rather considered that the pursuit of theoretical natural philosophy was fundamental, as his extensive theoretical work shows. In that sense, Hobbes's critique of experimentalists, and especially of Boyle, was overstated.[38] For the undeniable fact was, in Boyle's view, that natural reality was not merely an atomist compound that had resulted from chaos. In the important *The Origine of Formes and Qualities according to the Corpuscular Philosophy* (published in 1665 but, according to the publisher, written much earlier), Boyle located his corpuscularist philosophy between materialist atomism and Aristotelianism and its particular ways of acknowledging purpose in the physical world.[39]

7.2.1 God's Concurrence

Atomism accurately represented the underlying structure of matter, according to Boyle, but its premise that the natural world was the result of only repeated and occasional chance in the motion of atoms was flawed. Aristotelianism explained intelligence in matter by introducing substantial forms that were able to keep nature as it was; for instance, heated water would always return to coldness, and to reproduce the same nature. Similarly, it was a matter of observation that species had the capacity to reproduce themselves maintaining the same nature. But while in Boyle's view atomism could not convincingly explain the reality and beauty of nature, he found that there was also 'no necessity of admitting substantial forms' of the Aristotelian type, since accidents and matter alone could explain the phenomena of nature.[40] This statement is better understood by turning to his own theory. The only thing of which

[38] See about Hobbes's critique, Shaffer and Shapin, *Leviathan and the Air Pump*, p. 151. On Boyle as a theoretician, see Anstey, *Robert Boyle Natural Philosophy*; Peter Alexander, *Ideas, Qualities and Corpuscles. Locke and Boyle on the External World* (Cambridge University Press, 1985); and generally Jan-Erik Jones, ed. *The Bloomsbury Companion to Robert Boyle* (London, New York, Oxford, New Delhi, Sydney: Bloomsbury Academic, 2020).

[39] Boyle, *The Origine of Formes and Qualities* in *The Works of Robert Boyle*, vol. 5; on Boyle and final causes see, Boyle, 'A Disquisition about the Final Causes of Natural Things, in *The Works of Robert Boyle*, v. 11, p. 87, note 95. And Antonio Clericuzio 'God and the Physical World in Boyle's Thought' in Humbertus Busche (ed.) with collaboration by Stefan Heßbrüggen-Walter, *Departure for Modern Europe / Aufbruch in das moderne Europa. A Handbook of Early Modern Philosophy (1400–1700)* (Hamburg: Felix Meiner Verlag, 2011), p. 1041.

[40] Robert Boyle, *The Origine of Formes and Qualities* in *The Works of Robert Boyle*, vol. 5; A. C. Crombie, *Science, Art and Nature in Medieval and Modern Thought* (London and Rio Grande: The Hambledon Press, 1996) p. 69.

Boyle seemed to be completely certain was of the *necessity* that God had once created the world as now it is:

> So that according to my apprehension, it was *at the beginning* necessary, that an Intelligent and Wise Agent should contrive the Universal Matter into the World, (and especially some Portions of it into Seminal Organs and Principles,) and settle the Laws, according to which the Motions and Actions of its parts upon one another should be regulated.[41]

Unlike the 'Cartesian Laws of Motion' Boyle's use of 'laws' here seems to refer to a law that operated only within *the jurisdiction of a microcosm*, as to form the innumerable structures and bodies in nature through mechanical affections. Unlike Epicurus, who conceived the world as 'brute and unguided matter', for him there existed a *regulation* of order, and even more, a certain *governance*.[42] God had put the world in motion, but not only that. Boyle accepted, with only a few reservations, that the Creator had established a certain order or system of nature that was guaranteed continuity by imbuing some species, mainly plants and animals, with the information (the seminal principles) that would enable them to reproduce themselves and continue in nature. Timothy Shanahan, Peter R. Anstey and Antonio Clericuzio have discussed Boyle's theory on God's 'general concourse' for 'the conservation and efficacy of every particular physical agent' at length.[43] This theory can be summarized as

[41] Boyle, *The Origine of Formes and Qualities* in *The Works of Robert Boyle*, vol. 5, p. 354.

[42] 'I do not at all believe, that either these *Cartesian Laws of Motion*, or the *Epicurean casual Concourse* of Atoms, could bring meer Matter into so orderly and well contriv'd a Fabrick as This World; and therefore I think, that the wise Author of Nature did not onely *put Matter into Motion*, but when he resolv'd to make the World, did so regulate and *guide the Motions* of the small parts of the Universal Matter, as to reduce the greater Systems of them into the Order they were to continue in; and did more particularly contrive some portions of that Matter into Seminal Rudiments or Principles, lodg'd in convenient Receptacles, (and as it were Wombs,) and others into the Bodies of Plants and Animals', Boyle, *The Origine of Formes and Qualities* in *The Works of Robert Boyle*, vol. 5, p. 353. For the more general late seventeenth and eighteenth century 'nomological image of nature' as 'a collection of laws and law-governed entities', or as a system, see also specially, Catherine Wilson, 'From Limits to Laws: the Construction of the Nomological Image of Nature in Early Modern Philosophy' in Lorraine Daston and Michael Stolleis (eds.) *Natural Law and Laws of Nature in Early Modern Europe. Jurisprudence, Theology, Moral and Natural Philosophy* (Surrey, Burlington: Ashgate 2008), p. 13; also Oakley 'The Rise of the Concept of Laws of Nature Revisited'.

[43] Timothy Shanahan, 'God and Nature in the Thought of Robert Boyle' in 26 *Journal of the History of Philosophy* (1988); Anstey, *The Philosophy of Robert Boyle*, ch. 7; Clericuzio, 'God and the Physical World in Boyle's Thought', p. 1042.

meaning that it is God's active involvement in the world that guarantees the efficacy of the laws of motion.[44] The idea is consonant with Boyle's voluntarist conception of laws as an act of will, as discussed in chapter 6. I agree with Peter Anstey that Boyle's natural philosophy is an elaborated and cautious *via media* between occasionalists, who viewed God as acting constantly in each event in a world devoid of causal agents, and deists, who regarded the world as working after the Creation only through natural laws.[45]

Multiple sources have been suggested as the originators of these ideas of Boyle.[46] However, whatever the specific sources involved, it is plain that Boyle's active God in nature and his God-fearing tone when he was writing as a theologian is much toned down in his two most important works on natural philosophy, *The Origine of Formes and Qualities according to the Corpuscular Philosophy* and *A Free Enquiry into the Vulgarly Receiv'd Notion of Nature*, which described interdependent systems of motion. These works conveyed the message that the scientist ought to have lordship and dominion over the natural world and traditional Aristotelian theories were preventing that conquest. There is hardly any other way of reading Boyle's oscillation between the position of a pious theologian of nature and that of an ambitious natural scientist than to read him as struggling with internal conflict. For it is the work of God, as Boyle acknowledged, that he aimed at once to know and praise – and to undo. Human beings were, in his thinking, potential managers of the physical world and in order to understand how the system of nature was constituted, the only things necessary were experiments and God. Experiments were needed as the only way to his constant double aim: 'discover the cause of her (nature's) Phenomena, or to imploy her productions', that is acquiring

[44] Anstey, *The Philosophy of Robert Boyle*, p. 168, and generally Chapter 7.

[45] Anstey, *The Philosophy of Robert Boyle*, ch. 7; Shanahan, 'God and Nature in the Thought of Robert Boyle, 26 *Journal of the History of Philosophy* (1988); also in Finnish, Jouni Huhtanen, 'Robert Boyle, luonto ja luonnonlaki' 31 *Tieteessä tapahtuu* (2013).

[46] Recently Edward B. Davis has traced Boyle's sources for natural theology and the main principle that 'the voice of nature is the voice of truth' to the Huguenot jurist, statesman and apologist Philippe de Mornay (1549–1623), and through him to Thomas Aquinas, whom de Mournay, however never mentioned. Davis writes that we cannot fully understand Boyle's philosophy of religion apart from this central fact [of the 'formative' and 'formidable' influence of de Mornay].' Davis, 'Boyle's Philosophy of Religion', pp. 259. The Earl of Cork, the three Reformers, Hartlib, Dury and Comenius, his Eton education and Gassendi are mentioned as sources of Boyle's voluntarism in Wojcik, *Robert Boyle and the Limits of Reason*, p. 201; Peter R. Anstey suggests William of Ockham, Anstey, *The Philosophy of Robert Boyle*, p. 174; p. 179.

knowledge and multiplying production.[47] To develop science, metaphysical questions that simply sought to cover up ignorance must be avoided.

7.2.2 *The Uncertain Boundaries of Natures*

Continuity in nature is probably the issue that most fascinated Boyle and was, significantly, what offered the Anglo-Irish chemist the most potential for manipulation. The 'natural state' of bodies he considered to be a 'most usual state', not an absolutely fixed one. Therefore, by the law of nature, the accidents of a body would remain, unless a competent destructive cause operated. If that cause operated – for instance, if fire was applied to wood – no supposedly (Aristotelian) substantial form would be able to prevent it from happening and preserve all those accidents in a body.[48] Hence the central meaning of chemistry emerged in *The Origine of Formes and Qualities* as that of a science of transmutation of natures.

Boyle confessed to being agnostic about whether there were 'sufficient and necessary' boundaries limiting the species of natural bodies.[49] The only

47 'I recon it among the felicities of the present Age, that in Philosophical Inquiries, Experience is not now, as in the Schools it formerly was, either wholly neglected or for the most part rested (?) to comport with Theoryes, that were framed without regard had to it. But I am sorry I see cause to add to what I have been saying that as much as we magnify the necessity of Experiments in our conceits with the Peripateticks about nature, we seem not yet to be sensible of this acknowledged necessity, when we contest with the particular difficulties that frequently occur, when we our selves are to discover the cause of her Phenomena, or to imploy her productions.' *Royal Society*, 'Boyle Papers', vol. 9, fol 1r. Boyle Manuscripts online, in the *Robert Boyle Project*, www.bbk.ac.uk/boyle.

48 'And as, when there is no competent destructive Cause, the Accidents of a Body will by the Law of Nature remain such as they were, so if there be, it cannot with reason be pretended, that the substantial Form is able to preserve all those Accidents of a Body, that are said to flow from it, and to be as it were under its care and tuition; for if, for instance, you expose a Sphaere or Bullet of Lead to a strong fire, it will quickly loose (not to mention its Figure) both its Coldness, its Consistence, its Malleableness, its Colour, (for 'twill appear of the colour of fire,) its Flexibility, and some other Qualities, and all this in spight of the imaginary substantial Form, which, according to the Peripatetical Principles, in this case must still remain in it without being able to help it.' Boyle, *The Origine of Formes and Qualities* in *The Works of Robert Boyle*, vol. 5, p. 347.

49 'For I confesse, that I have not yet, either in *Aristotle*, or any other Writer, met with any genuine and sufficient Diagnostick and Boundary, for the Discriminating and limiting the *Species* of Things, or to speak more plainly, I have not found, that any Naturalist has laid down a determinate Number and sort of Qualities, or other Attributes, which is *sufficient* and *necessary* to constitute all portions of Matter, endow'd with them, distinct Kinds of Natural Bodies.' Boyle, *The Origine of Formes and Qualities* in *The Works of Robert Boyle*, vol. 5, p. 356; see also Jan-Erik Jones, 'Boyle's Natural Kind Realism' in Jan-Erik Jones (ed.), *The Bloomsbury Companion to Robert Boyle*, p. 211.

requirement he ascertained in nature was that of the system or *oeconomy* of the universe with (some) matter possessing the seminal information and its motion being regulated by mechanical affections (powers affecting and sustaining the nature or structure of things) that constituted the laws of motion. The chief goal of chemistry became 'the mechanical production' of natures. Chemistry was understood to be a practical science, a useful science but, in Boyle's conception, also a philosophical science. Sometimes experiments might be made that were not profitable, but only instructive, and only a *mere alchemist* would resist that form of unprofitable activity.[50] Nevertheless, the purpose of chemistry was mainly to be useful in relation to the multiplication of nature. Manipulating the particular natures of anything in the world for transmutation, reproducing natures through matter and increasing the number of active bodies artificially would in Boyle's words result in an increase of 'the Inventory of Mankind's Goods'.[51]

The volatility of nature that Boyle described overlapped with other disciplines, and also impacted on culture and society, thus destabilizing long-established truths. As he explained, if a base metal were to be transmuted into one that displayed all the accidents of gold, in terms of its content or 'Stamp', people would 'take it for true Gold without scruple', use it in economic transactions without further ado, and let academics dispute among themselves whether it was real gold.[52] In an important sense, morality and social sciences were thus made plausibly dependent on chemistry and its potential of transmutation. The world was a 'self-moving engine' composed of small particles of diverse sizes, and the various combinations, figures or stamps that could appear in it were 'almost innumerable' – as were, accordingly, the possible transmutations. Boyle asserted that *anything* could eventually be transformed into *anything*. Following the Reformers of the previous generation, his programme for the science of chemistry was precisely that: to try to put the components of the world into motion and thereby into new orders.

> So that though I would not say, that Any thing can immediately be made of Every thing, as a Gold Ring of a *Wedge* of Gold, or Oyl, or Fire of Water; yet since Bodies, having but one common Matter, can be differenc'd but by Accidents, which seem all of them to be the Effects and Consequents

[50] 'But a Transmutation is neverthelesse more or lesse real, for being or not being Lucriferous, and since That may inrich a Brain, that may impoverish a Purse, I must look upon your humour as that of an Alchymist, rather then of a Philosopher, if I durst not expect that the Instructiveness in such an Experiment will suffice to recommend it to You.' Boyle, *The Origine of Formes and Qualities* in *The Works of Robert Boyle*, vol. 5, p. 423.

[51] Boyle, *The Origine of Formes and Qualities* in *The Works of Robert Boyle*, vol. 5, p. 373.

[52] Boyle, *The Origine of Formes and Qualities* in *The Works of Robert Boyle*, vol. 5, p. 323.

> of Local Motion, I see not, why it should be absurd to think, that (at least among Inanimate Bodies) by the Intervention of some very small *Addition* or *Substraction* of Matter, (which yet in most cases will scarce be needed,) and of an orderly *Series of Alterations*, disposing by degrees the Matter to be transmuted, almost of any thing, may at length be made Any thing.[53]

The empiricist-chemist accordingly became the re-maker of nature. For nature must be useful. In this sense, it is clear that nowadays 'futurist' writers with transhumanist leanings display the same 'science-fictional emphasis' about (human) nature.[54] In particular, the ends of the science of chemistry were eminently pragmatic. Knowledge had also the aim of acquiring (economic) power to 'exercise the little Empire, that we have either acquir'd or regain'd over the creatures', and to carry out practical business.[55] But the business was different from the science. In this sense, the transmutation, by some mechanical means, of a base metal into gold, differed from the plan or projection for turning some hundred or thousand parts of baser metal into gold or silver, with the help of one part of powder of gold. Hence, 'though Projection includes Transmutation, yet Transmutation is not all one with Projection'.[56]

Boyle's corpuscularisn did not mean that he renounced the principle of necessity altogether. For 'the secret correspondencies and Alliances' between bodies that Boyle could not fail to observe constituted, in his view, the *oeconomy* or system of nature. In this regard, despite the complex combinations discussed in the previous chapter by which he excepted human beings from participation in natural laws, these natural laws appeared in Boyle's case immanent in nature and not imposed by the will of God – ultimately inspired more by Aquinas, as Davis has suggested, than by Ockham.[57] Boyle's

53 Boyle, *The Origine of Formes and Qualities* in *The Works of Robert Boyle*, vol. 5, p. 332.

54 See William T. Lynch's review of Steve Fuller, *Knowledge: The Philosophical Quest in History*, in William T. Lynch, 'Social Epistemology Transformed: Steve Fuller's Account of Knowledge as a Divine Spark for Human Domination' in 3 *Symposion* (2016), pp. 191–205.

55 Boyle, *The Origine of Formes and Qualities* in *The Works of Robert Boyle*, vol. 5, p. 298

56 Boyle, *The Origine of Formes and Qualities* in *The Works of Robert Boyle*, vol. 5, p. 365.

57 This is not to tell that Davis draws a link between Aquinas and Boyle's mechanical laws. Instead, he suggests a rather loosely and indeed visible inspiration in the physical world as a source of truth, Davis, 'Boyle's Philosophy of Religion'. A classic view that saw a more radical break after the Scientific Revolution appears e.g. in Francis Oakley, 'Christian Theology and the Newtonian Science: The Rise of the Concept of the Laws of Nature' in 30 *Church History* (1961). Aquinas balanced his position also responding to the necessitarianism of Averroes, Maimonides and Avicenna in the *Questiones disputatae de potentia Dei*, q. 1, a. 5: 'And this is where they erred, for they thought that the created order was commensurate with divine goodness, as if apart from that order divine order could not have been

mechanical laws of nature and his notion of nature seemed so original partly due to the absence of human beings. But while Boyle was adamant that the physical world is a source of truth, the core of his project of knowledge is to put forward the dominion of human beings to manipulate and to remake that truth. In his writings on natural philosophy, what human beings utilize and transmute became an impersonal system or economy of nature that possessed an occult harmony of secret alliances and mechanical affections between clusters of corpuscles that had been established by the design of the Creator.

7.2.3 *God's Arbitrary Will and Humans' Right Reasoning*

Boyle's proposal for a working notion of nature was that of a minimal metaphysical *constitution*, a system or *oeconomy*. The idea of the *oeconomy* of nature originated, as we saw, in Kenelm Digby's *Two Treatises on The Nature of Body and on the Nature of Mans Soul*.[58] The notion had a manifold meaning of interconnectedness and unity for Digby.[59] It was a certain order and settled course that existed in nature, as well as a sort of agency that 'hath set on foot due and plain causes to produce known effects'.[60] Moreover, it amounted to a sufficiently strong basis on which the 'searcher of nature' could understand natural causes without jumping to supernatural explanations. It would be irreverent to engage 'the Almighty Architect' any time a particular effect in nature was to be explained. For with the first foundation of nature's design, figures of plants and animals had been already produced. That was the *oeconomy* of nature: a 'complex assemblement, or chain of all the causes that concur to produce this effect', a language by which to decipher the 'wise Author of nature in the masterpiece of the creature'.[61] Moreover, the *oeconomy* of nature was distributive,

expressed. It is clear then that God absolutely can do otherwise than he has done.' See, Pernoud, 'The Theory of Potentia de Dei According to Aquinas, Scotus and Ockham', p. 73. I discuss in section 7.2.4 the debate between Peter Harrison and John Henry on voluntarism in the scientific context of Boyle.

58 Digby, *Two Treatises*; Remien, *The Concept of Nature in Early English Modern Literature*.

59 To which might be related his faith in the powder of sympathy that cured wounds at a distance. The following quote is an example of the ideas of forces operating at a distance: 'For nature hath so ordered the matter, that when dense parts stick close together, and make the length composed of them to be very stiff; one cannot be moved but that all the rest (which are in that line) must likewise be thereby moved: so that if all the world were composed of atoms close sticking together, the least motion imaginable must drive on all that were in a straight line, to the very end of the world'; see also his discussion of the principle 'No corporeall nature can operari in distans' Digby, *Two Treatises*, p. 104; pp. 172–174.

60 Digby, *Two Treatises*, p. 43; p. 104.

61 Digby, *Two Treatises*, p. 124; p. 179; p. 214; p. 283; p. 289.

and entailed specific material causes that produced a conjuncture of the required effects for the propagation of species. Therefore, 'no such supplements' – by which Digby meant anthropomorphic signifiers – were needed in explanations of natural philosophy. The 'distribution of nature' was enough and notions such as the *compassion* of the elements, when the Halcyon laid her eggs at sea, were superfluous and non-philosophical.[62]

All these elements of Digby's *Two Treatises* – the *oeconomy* of nature, the intellectualist understanding of the Creation, the rejection of anthropomorphic intrusions and an unspecified concourse of a divine agent in the effects occurring within the natural system – also appeared in Boyle's thought, albeit in a perfected and developed form. The single most important difference between Digby and Boyle was that the latter did not include moral natural law in that rational oeconomy of nature, and instead held a radical voluntarist understanding of the moral law given through Revelation.

That is not to say that Boyle's right reason was not rationalist or moral. Some years ago, John Spurr described the definitive transformation of the notion of 'right reason' in late seventeenth-century England from 'the faculty which fused man's knowledge of what is good with his desire to be good' that 'so raised him towards knowledge of and participation in the nature of God', to the 'sterile, morally-neutral notion of "discursive reason"'.[63] As mentioned before Sorana Corneanu has broadened and enriched this view and described Boyle's specific redescription of the classic notion. The right reason as an instrument of the intellectual soul to discover, through the light of nature and practical virtue, the moral principles of moral natural law, became in the work of Boyle and others a complex combination of attitudes. But it is true that in Boyle's work right reason mainly signifies *correct* reasoning assisted by Revelation.[64] As explained by Corneanu, in knowing the richness of the physical world

62 Digby, *Two Treatises*, p. 398.

63 Spurr, '"Rational Religion" in Restoration England', p. 570.

64 Boyle's peculiar understanding of right reason, e.g. in the 'Appendix to The Christian Virtuoso': 'Right reason may be looked upon as a catholick principle, of which philosophy is but an application, and the dictates of particular philosophies, such as the Peripatetik, the Platonick, the Epicurean, etc, are but particular corollaries, which are not always truly drawn, and on that account may always be questioned or examined, and may, I fear, oftentimes be justly rejected; and this holds, especially, when in the examen, he that makes it is assisted by the discoveries made by revelation from whose heavenly light, in reference to divers subjects, the intellect may receive such a benefit, as the air does in a clear day from the beams of the sun, by which it is both enlightened and expanded.' Boyle, 'The Christian Virtuoso I. Appendix' in *The Works of Robert Boyle*, v. 12, p. 423.

through experimental work, discursive reason displayed moral connotations when aided by self-mastery in view of passions, difficulties and pains during the repeated exercise of experiment, and by modesty and docility in order to cultivate a continuous attitude of openness to new information. In sum, its moral goals comprise education of the mind in the path to truth and growth in virtue.[65] Therefore, Boyle's right reasoning has a moral dimension, albeit one that was relatively novel and idiosyncratic at the time. The ambiguous premises of *virtuosity*, despite not being in principle aimed solely at elite thinkers, appeared in this light and charges of elitism abounded.[66] This understanding of right reasoning was reinforced by Boyle's weak standpoint on innate ideas.[67] The 'light' of Revelation was then to provide benefit to right reason 'as the air does in a clear day from the beams of the sun, by which it is both enlightened and expanded'.[68]

This section and the next show that the Anglo-Irish natural philosopher produced a revolution in thinking about natural law when he theorized, as both a lay theologian and as a natural philosopher, an intelligible physical world that runs in parallel to his voluntarist conception of moral natural laws. In the movement of their natures, the natural elements of the world had a purpose, whereas the moral purpose of human beings' actions was not accessible from within our nature – we rather obey the law of the commander. The insight that there was a disconnect between the right reason of God and that of human beings had been characteristic of Protestant thought since Luther, and the ensuing Protestant rejection of the production of rational accounts of human morality by reference to divine eternal

[65] Corneanu, *Regimens of the Mind*, p. 127–129, and generally ch. 4; Thomas Holden, 'Robert Boyle on Things Above Reason' in 15 *British Journal for the History of Philosophy* (2007), p. 290.

[66] Corneanu pairs Boyle and Locke in their inspiration in Bacon's and the Royal Society virtuosi' experimental program and the early modern *cultura animi* tradition, drawing from classical Skeptic, Stoic, Galenist and Augustinian sources. Corneanu, *Regimens of the Mind*. The elitism of the experimentalists of Gresham College was an issue at the period, importantly for Hobbes who criticized the fact that they set a limit of members, 50 men plus Barons and above and so on, see Schapin and Shaffer, *Leviathan and the Air Pump*, ch. 4; and for Margaret Cavendish, see Sarasohn, 'A Science Turned Upside Down'.

[67] Boyle admits 'innate, or at least primitive *Ideas* and Rules of true and false' in the context of the rules that enable the operation of the intellectual reason, but his position is not so clear on practical reason. Boyle, *A Discourse of Things above Reason*, p. 73. Holden notes that 'Boyle systematically resists committing himself in the debate over the existence of innate ideas but concedes that the mind has innate dispositions to assent to certain propositions and to reject others' … 'such as the law of noncontradiction and other fundamental principles governing logical and mathematical (and perhaps ethical) thought'. See Holden, 'Robert Boyle on Things Above Reason', p. 288.

[68] Boyle, 'The Christian Virtuoso I. Appendix' in *The Works of Robert Boyle*, v. 12, p. 423.

law.[69] Boyle added to it the undoing or deconstruction of the more general notion of the *nature* that human beings and the rest of physical nature were previously understood to have in common, also in Anglican theology. From the perspective of inanimate and irrational nature, J. R. Milton notes that that 'kind of intimate blend of the moral with the physical would have seemed entirely natural' to the readers of Richard Hooker's *Laws of Ecclesiastical Polity*, whose definition of natural law includes irrational creatures, as did Aquinas's and the Roman tradition.[70] As late as 1672 the aim of the influential *An Inquiry into the Laws of Nature* by the Anglican divine Richard Cumberland was to use natural philosophy as a means of showing that moral natural law was obligatory – albeit he employed already a modern notion of 'laws' and of 'nature', as we will see.[71] Boyle's deconstruction of the notion of physical nature not only reached a climax in the fading tradition of right reason, but also served his ambitious utilitarian project concerning economy and knowledge, for human beings were presented as free agents in dominion of nature and of the laws of nature.

7.2.4 The Viewpoint in Boyle's Laws of Nature

In view of Boyle's dualism in considering human and physical nature to be apart, it is possible to argue that Boyle was a voluntarist moral theologian and an intellectualist natural theologian. Descartes' thought has been

[69] Luther articulated this discontinuity in *The Bondage of the Will*, see for this Quentin Skinner, *The Foundations of Modern Political Thought* (Cambridge: Cambridge University Press, 1978), vol. II, p. 5 and generally ch. 1; on the Protestant position more generally see Knud Haakonssen, 'Divine/Natural Law Theories in Ethics' in Daniel Garber and Michael Ayers (eds.) *The Cambridge History of Seventeenth Century Philosophy* (1998) vol II, 1317–1357; p. 1325.

[70] See J. R. Milton, 'Laws of Nature' in Daniel Garber and Michael Ayers (eds.) *The Cambridge History of Seventeenth Century Philosophy* (Cambridge: Cambridge University Press, 1998) vol. I, p. 681; Francis Oakley, *Natural law, Laws of Nature, Natural Rights. Continuities and Discontinuities in the History of Ideas* (New York, London: Continuum, 2005) p. 70; Brett, *Liberty, Right and Nature*, p. 95; Jan Schröder, 'The Concept of (Natural) Law in the Doctrine of Law and Natural Law of the Early Modern Era', in *Natural Law and Laws of Nature in Early Modern Europe*; also pointing out Boyle's novelty, Anstey, *The Philosophy of Robert Boyle*, p. 158; Oakley, 'The Rise of the Concept of Laws of Nature Revisited', p. 25. On natural law as the participation of the eternal law: all laws participate in the right reason of God, and hence all laws derived from eternal law, in Aquinas, *Summa theologiae*, I-IIae, q. 91, a.2.col; q. 93, a. 3.

[71] Richard Cumberland, *A Treatise of the Laws of Nature*, translated, with Introduction and Appendix, by John Maxwell (1727), with a Foreword by Jon Parkin (ed.) (Indianapolis: Liberty Fund, 2005); Jon Parkin, *Science, Religion, and Politics in Restoration England: Richard Cumberland's De Legibus Naturae* (Rochester, New York: The Boydell Press, 1999), ch. 6 and p. 7.

described by Edward B. Davis and Margaret Osler as displaying analogous complexities.[72] The fecundity of the debate between John Henry and Peter Harrison as to whether voluntarist theology was an important aspect of the origins of modern empirical science is useful, among other reasons, for the deeper insight into Boyle's project of 'undoing nature' that it provides, and is worth summarizing briefly here.

Henry and Harrison have both highlighted that the core issue for the experimentalists was a pragmatic approach by which to find a workable method for human reason, which everyone acknowledged to be very weak. Henry takes the view that the pre-eminence accorded by experimentalists to God's omnipotence meant that their ideas were defined as being the result of voluntarist theology.[73] Harrison, on the other hand, has analysed the emphasis placed during the seventeenth century on the damage caused to human beings' cognitive capacities by the Fall. He takes the view that focus on a postlapsarian reason (a reason darkened by original sin) illuminates phenomena that others have attributed to the explanatory force of the thesis of voluntarist theology.[74] However, Harrison has noted that Boyle was exceptional for his era in attributing a minor role to the Fall of Adam and Eve in the state of weakness of human reason: it appears that Boyle simply thought that God had created reason that way.[75] One may also add Corneanu's argument that Boyle's moral doctrine revolves around growth in knowledge: a sort of enlightenment obtained from observation and studies of the physical world, which presupposes rather than denies the role of reason.[76]

72 Edward B. Davis, *Creation, Contingency, and Early Modern Science: The Impact of Voluntarist Theology on Seventeenth-Century Natural Philosophy* (PhD Dissertation, 1984, Indiana University), pp. 67–121; Osler, *Divine Will and the Mechanical Philosophy*, pp. 118–152.

73 Whether for the seventeenth century scientists developing a novel idea of 'the laws of nature', voluntarist theology had explanatory power or only justificatory power is debated between John Henry and Francis Oakley, the latter emphasizing the explanatory nature and the continuation with the medieval theological tradition of God's absolute and ordained power. See generally Oakley, 'The Rise of the Concept of Laws of Nature Revisited'; Henry, 'Metaphysics and the Origins of Modern Science, p. 91, and recently, Lichtenstein, 'Revaluing Laws of Nature in Secularized Science'.

74 Henry also makes the point that Harrison is studying more the abilities and powers of human beings' intellect and will within the context of theological anthropology and he was concerned with God's abilities and omnipotence. John Henry, 'Voluntarist Theology at the Origins of Modern Science', p. 104.

75 Harrison notes that Boyle's Adam did not possess the wisdom of Heaven, but through Christian religion we may reach the perfect knowledge of natural philosophy, Peter Harrison, *The Fall of man and the Foundations of Science* (Cambridge: Cambridge University Press, 2007), p. 219; see also, Wojcik, *Boyle and the Limits of Reason*, p. 104

76 Corneanu, *Regimens of the Mind*, p. 116.

The three positions taken by Henry, Harrison and Corneanu are helpful to my argument that Boyle urged a conception of a non-human physical world, instead of the holistic conception of nature common to both before and during his era. Boyle viewed the physical world as being at once sustained by the concurrence of God and perfectly rational. As Harrison noted in an early article, the 'arbitrary will of God' did not signify randomness for most authors writing during the seventeenth century. Certainly, for Boyle it implied rational design.[77] Moreover, it also precluded the necessitarianism of the Avicennan type we have seen employed by Hobbes.[78] What was crucial in Boyle's case, was whose point of view was adopted. Thus, 'the laws of nature as they were at first arbitrarily instituted by God, so, *in reference to him*, they are but arbitrary still'.[79]

[77] 'Indeed, the whole enterprise of physico-theology is premised upon that very possibility of discerning rational design in the cosmos which was called into question by earlier voluntarists.' Harrison, 'Voluntarism and Early Modern Science', p. 74; p. 78.

[78] Although Boyle seems to have benefitted from Avicenna sometimes, he skipped the references to him and other Islamic authors, as was apparently general custom in the period, and retained only Galen throughout. Another reason for his neglect of Avicenna, beyond the customary, might have been that the latter had declared categorically the impossibility of transmuting metals from a scientific and philosophical point of view. Moreover, the Arabic philosopher believed that human beings were not created by God, but by a separate principle, the giver of forms, and that there could be spontaneous generation of human beings without procreation, for instance after a natural disaster. Some Aristotelians from Northern Italy such as the Renaissance philosopher Pietro Pomponazzi and his students had valued these aspects of Avicenna. But despite his usual boldness, that particular idea did not go well with Boyle. In a letter to Henry Stubbe distancing himself from Stubbe's mockery of miracles, Boyle rejected the principles put forward by 'those Enemys to Christianity' (apparently referring to Pomponazzi), that declared that the planets by themselves may produce such influences as generation of human beings without the intervention of God. See on Avicenna and alchemy, Bruce T. Moran, 'Paracelsianism' in Glenn Alexander Magee (ed.) *The Cambridge Handbook of Western Mysticism and Esotericism*, (Cambridge: Cambridge University Press, 2016); Georges C. Anawati, 'Arabic Alchemy' in Roshdi Rashed (ed.) *Encyclopedia of the History of Arabic Science. Technology, Alchemy and Life Sciences*, vol. 3. In collaboration with Régis Morelon, (London, New York: Routledge, 1996), p. 877; I follow here on Avicenna and Pomponazzi, Dag Nikolaus Hasse, 'Arabic Philosophy and Averroism' in James Hankins (ed.) *The Cambridge Companion to Renaissance Philosophy* (Cambridge: Cambridge University Press, 2007); Stubbe was criticizing Valentine Greatrakes who claimed to have powers to cure; also the Anglican Church castigated him. See 'Boyle to Henry Stubbe. 9 March 1966', in *The Correspondence of Robert Boyle*, v. 3, p. 99. See on this question and miracles, Clericuzio, 'God and the Physical World in Boyle's Thought', p. 1045.

[79] Boyle, 'The Christian Virtuoso I. Appendix' in *The Works of Robert Boyle*, v. 12, p. 423. (emphasis mine) Osler noted with reference to this statement how 'Boyle was a thorough-going voluntarist'. Margaret J Osler 'Robert Boyle on Knowledge of Nature in the Afterlife' in James E. Force and Richard H. Popkin (eds.). *Millenarianism and Messianism in Early Modern Culture. Vol. III The Millenarian Turn: Millenarian Contexts of Science, Politics, and Everyday Anglo-American life in the Seventeenth and Eighteenth Centuries* (Springer, 2001), p. 46.

The physical world was neither necessary nor the best possible world. But that was irrelevant, since Boyle was concerned with understanding, as a path to the Designer and the acquisition of knowledge, the evident intelligence and harmony that it possessed.[80] From a human perspective, the physical world was rational, and perhaps necessary. Furthermore, it was Boyle's firm preference for a more scholastic understanding of God the Creator and sustainer of the world that gave his theory of a harmonious natural world a metaphysical foundation. It did not seem to Boyle to be inconsistent with a rational world endowed with a settled course or order that God concurred in what happened within it – a view bordering on occasionalism. On the contrary, only the limitless immensity of the wisdom of God could have endowed the world with what seemed from a human perspective to be a rational design. For instance, in a favourite example of his, a description of the composition of the fluids contained in an egg was very rational, but it tells us nothing about how the chick's muscles, feathers and body develop. The same could be said about outer space or how the minerals are produced in the 'Bowels of the Earth'.[81] Boyle's theology thus appears incompatible with an emphasis on a strong concept of the physical laws of motion, such as Descartes's.[82] Boyle's laws of motion are plainly God's work.[83]

[80] 'We may, indeed, know by the consideration of his works, and particularly those parts of them that we ourselves are, both *That he is*, and in a great measure *What he is not*; but to understand thoroughly *What he is*, is a task too great for any but his own infinite Intellect'. Robert Boyle, 'A Discourse of Things Above Reason. Inquiring Whether A Philosopher Should Admit There Are Any Such,' in *The Works of Robert Boyle*, v. 9, p. 367.

[81] Boyle, '*The Sceptical Chymist*' in *The Works of Robert Boyle*, v. 2, p. 296. How Locke followed Boyle in this Scriptural tradition of Solomonic scepticism, in Harrison, *The Fall of Man and the Foundations of Science*, p. 221.

[82] Thus, unlike Boyle's case, John Henry argues that the real stimulus to a development of secular theology by philosophers of nature during the Scientific Revolution 'was the need to justify the concept of laws of nature, with its awkward inherent implication that inanimate bodies are somehow capable of "obeying" such laws.' John Henry, 'Metaphysics and the Origins of Modern Science: Descartes and the Importance of Laws of Nature' in 9 *Early Science and Medicine* (2004), p. 96. In this question of the natural law common to human beings and persons Selden produces a thorough review of authors referring to animals' behaviour with natural law obligations, importantly against 'adultery'. He concludes, however, that animals do not have rights or obligations in the sense human beings have them in natural law terms, and – interestingly being himself a consciencious lawyer – that often the authors' words referring to 'laws' or other such notions with regard to animals are 'homonyms', e.g. in the case of Ulpian's *Institutiones*. Moreover, he notes that to state that natural law applies to animals – that cannot be just and cannot be unjust – in the same sense than to human beings would deny the existence of the honest and the vile, the good and the evil, Seldeni, *De Jure Naturali et Gentium Juxta Disciplinam Ebraeorum*, Book I, ch. 5, p. 73.

[83] John R. Milton, 'The Origin and Development of the Concept of the "Laws of Nature"' 22 *European Journal of Sociology* (1981); John Henry, 'The Theological Origins of the Concept of Laws of Nature and Its Subsequent Secularisation', in Neil Spurway (ed.), *Laws*

Here Harrison's thesis about theological debate occurring in politics and science being directed by diverse understandings of the consequences of the Fall is also helpful.[84] We have noted already that Boyle was remarkable among his English peers in ascribing but small importance to the Fall in relation to our reasoning capabilities, arguing instead that human reason was weak by Creation. In this regard, my suggestion is that Boyle represents a turning point in thinking about reason. His theory appears as a strategy to shift thinking about right reason away from theological controversy and darkness or obscurity of the light of reason towards the study of physical nature and Revelation, where one ought to find guidance for reasoning. Obviously, this standpoint also served the Royal Society's political programme of experiment and free enquiry for laymen more generally during the Restoration.[85]

7.2.5 Selden, Milton, Cumberland and Boyle on Weakness of Reason

In 1640 the great John Selden first propounded his theory of natural law and the law of nations based on the weakness of reason. Nevertheless, through his immense scholarship – which was, significantly, both scholastic and Jewish in character – Selden was able to complicate his understanding of right or natural reason as God's command deriving from voluntarist theology. Thereby he alternated between offering proof of the lack of consensus among peoples on the principles of natural law and acknowledging that the light of the 'active intellect' of a righteous person may ascertain evident truths. Selden was adamant that right reason, the reasoning of 'a non-depraved mind', deduced natural principles from nature about living well by reference to the honest and the good. He seemed to suggest that a non-corrupted mind received better the communications of God and angelic creatures, very much in the manner that Albert the Great had highlighted that for a person closer to God is easier to ascertain natural law.[86] And he showed that right reason was present in all historical sources, whether

of Nature, Laws of God? Proceedings of the Science and Religion Forum Conference 2014 (Newcastle upon Tyne: Cambridge Scholars Press, 2015).

[84] Harrison, *The Fall of Man and the Foundations of Science.*

[85] See on 'freedom of inquiry' as a common Restoration theme among laymen, Spurr, '"Rational Religion" in Restoration England', p. 566.

[86] See J.P. Sommerville, 'John Selden, the Law of Nature, and the Origins of Government', 27 *The Historical Journal* (1984), p. 440.

theological, philosophical or legal in nature – a right reason that he was careful to distinguish from 'utility'. However, right reason was uncertain and one ought always to be cautious about it, as evidenced by the fact that people around the world often appeared to follow evil customs and laws, apparently out of ignorance. Moreover, it was impossible to extract a legitimate cause of obligation simply from 'the nakedness of free reason'.[87] If, as the ancient philosophers had done, a state of nature in which human beings both lived in 'the love of freedom' and 'the use of reason' were to be simulated, how would one establish what distinguished the licit from the illicit or how to enforce compliance with obligation? One may always back out of any contract without consequences. Hence, Selden thought that right reason must be supported with authority.[88]

Robert Sommerville White has described the evolution of right reason in John Milton's thinking in the years of the Interregnum. White argues that Milton initially adhered to a more benign type of reason that took inspiration from Aquinas and entailed a natural impulse to comply with natural law as the work of justice and moral good. Following more negative events in the political life of the Commonwealth, Milton became increasingly pessimistic about the capability of right reason to ascertain natural law obligations. What also transpires from White's analysis is that the perception that after the Fall, with only a dim light of conscience, 'we are on our own, without God's direct guidance' is a constant principle in Milton's work.[89]

The case of the divine Richard Cumberland (1631–1718) is interesting. Already writing within the context of the New Science, he attempted to reinsert human beings into the framework of created nature alongside animals and physical nature. Cumberland's response to Hobbes's natural law of self-preservation appears as an original utilitarian understanding of the common good, as preservation of all, and the notion of a common system composed of a rational God, nature and rational human beings. If our first

[87] '*ex nudo rationis liberae*'. Seldeni, *De Jure Naturali et Gentium Juxta Disciplinam Ebraeorum*, pp. 81; 89–91 and generally Book I and ch. 6 and 7.

[88] Seldeni, *De Jure Naturali et Gentium Juxta Disciplinam Ebraeorum*, p. 91. On Selden and right reason see also Haivry, *John Selden and the Western Political Traditions*, p. 225. Selden's integration of nature, law and history in Harold J. Berman and John Witte, Jr. 'The Integrative Christian Jurisprudence of John Selden', in R. H. Helmholz and Mark Hill (eds.), *Great Christian Jurists in English History* (Cambridge: Cambridge University Press, 2017); Sommerville, 'John Selden, the Law of Nature, and the Origins of Government'.

[89] White, *Natural Law in English Renaissance Literature*, p. 228 and generally ch. 9.

parents would have 'deliberated', they could have understood from 'the Nature of Man' that we experience 'the greatest Advantages' from 'mutual Assistance in a Social State.' Piety to God and their parents and benevolence should have been the way to promote 'true happines' to their children, which could not be achieved 'by initiating' human beings in the Mysteries of Atheism, and exhorting each to claim everything to himself and so immediately "to commence Robbers and Murderers of one another."[90]

Jon Parkin describes *A Treatise of the Laws of Nature* 'as one of the founding and possibly most enduring texts of Anglican rationalism'.[91] Cumberland was conversant with Pufendorf, who found inspiration in the former's idea of God's punishment and rewards having effects during the lives of human beings on earth.[92]

> But the good and bad Consequences (thus naturally known from the Nature of Things) of such human Actions, because they are fore shewn by God, to Men deliberating concerning their Actions, in order to incline them to, or deter them from, Action, are intirely in the Nature of Rewards and Punishments, by which a Law receives its Sanction.[93]

The structure of natural laws coincided then with the earthly rewards and punishments. According to Cumberland, happiness founded on utilitarian principles is the reward of the Author of nature when an individual acts with benevolence, which is one of his key concepts. 'Advantages and Disadvantages, which God himself pronounces annex'd to human Actions, and by which we are admonish'd to pursue those, and avoid these, are really and truly Rewards and Punishments.'[94] The evidence of these rewards and punishments when an individual acts or does not according to his or her nature prove the existence of the natural laws.[95] The nature of the thing 'represents' to reason what is best to do, and from the idea of God, one understands that this was a divine command. Thus was the voluntarism of divine

[90] Cumberland, *A Treatise of the Laws of Nature*, p. 181; Parkin, *Science, Religion, and Politics in Restoration England: Richard Cumberland's De Legibus Naturae;* Jon Parkin, 'Richard Cumberland', Oxford Dictionary of National Biography, https://doi-org.libproxy.helsinki.fi/10.1093/ref:odnb/6887; Knud Haakonssen, 'The Character and Obligation of Natural Law According to Richard Cumberland' in M. A. Stewart (ed.), *English Philosophy in the Age of Locke*, v. 3 (Oxford: Clarendon Press, 2000), pp. 29–48; Roger Crisp, *Sacrifice Regained. Morality and Self-interest in British Moral Philosophy from Hobbes to Bentham* (Oxford: Clarendon Press, 2019), p. 33; *Linda Kirk, Richard Cumberland and Natural Law. Secularisation of Thought in 17th Century England* (Cambridge: James Clark & Co, 2022) 29–45.

[91] Parkin, *Science, Religion, and Politics in Restoration England*, p. 173.

[92] Parkin, *Science, Religion, and Politics in Restoration England*, pp. 205–211.

[93] Cumberland, *A Treatise of the Laws of Nature*, p. 181

[94] Cumberland, *A Treatise of the Laws of Nature*, p. 183.

[95] Crisp, *Sacrifice Regained*, p. 39.

law tempered. With his insistence on recovering the notion of the common good shared by human beings and physical nature, Cumberland was primarily reacting to Hobbes's natural right to everything in the state of nature.[96] His target was Hobbes's comparison of the benefit and concord existing among animals, where, unlike in the case of human beings (so Hobbes) no strife about honour, or acknowledgement of precedence or wisdom existed.[97] Cumberland's language of natural philosophy is at points remarkably close to Digby's and, especially, to Boyle's.[98] His main thesis deals with the existence of a system in which everybody and every agent influences others.

Cumberland concluded 'from this Order among the Laws of Nature' – meaning the laws of motion – that this principle operated both among human beings and in physical nature. Therefore, he placed the 'intellectual system' of rational creatures alongside the laws of mechanics of the 'material system'.[99] Its location within this map of ideas provides Cumberland's right reason with a basis on which to judge the 'nature of the thing', according to which the laws of motion also worked. Hence, 'the Command' or 'the Permission, of the Law of Nature', amounted to 'right Reason, pronouncing concerning those things which are necessary to the common Good, according to the Nature of Things'.[100]

Boyle did not absolutely reject the metaphysical notion of the nature of things. However, he did not consider that the right reason had immediate capacity to judge, according to the nature of things, either in relation to morality or matters of natural philosophy. Moreover, as articulated in Jan Wojcik's *Robert Boyle and the Limits of Reason*, Boyle was steadfast in contending that the obscurity of reason is creational and that therefore theologians and sects could contribute little to the matter. In fact, as I have noted earlier in view of his challenging goal of knowing the deep structure of the material world, his main contribution was to incorporate the theological point as to the darkness of reason into natural philosophy and to find alternative ways to overcome it – famously, through the experimental method.

[96] Cumberland, *A Treatise of the Laws of Nature*, p. 211; Haakonssen, 'The Character and Obligation of Natural Law According to Richard Cumberland', p. 34. About the common good tradition, see Kempshall, *The Common Good in Late Medieval Political Thought*.

[97] Patricia Springborg, 'Hobbes's Materialism and Epicurean Mechanism, 24 *British Journal for the History of Philosophy* (2016), p. 828.

[98] Cumberland, *A Treatise of the Laws of Nature*, p. 185. Haakonssen considered that his main influence were the Cambridge Platonists, but also mentions Boyle in passim, see Haakonssen, 'The Character and Obligation of Natural Law According to Richard Cumberland', p. 32.

[99] Cumberland, *A Treatise of the Laws of Nature*, p. 185.

[100] Cumberland, *A Treatise of the Laws of Nature*, p. 214.

I would contend that when he employed theological language Boyle's interest mostly lay in highlighting our ignorance in order to urge the continued search for more truth or more knowledge about the physical world, and to eradicate many of the dogmas that existed at the time. This nescient attitude triggered boldness in building hypotheses and industriousness in experiment. Further, it also helped to attain moral perfection through growth in knowledge.[101] Specifically, the assumption that God the Maker concurred in the activity of the laws of motion went a long way to showing the extent to which the harmony of the physical world remained unknown. Thus, as Boyle argued, no valid proof had been presented against occasionalism thus far. In this regard, no one could prove that it was unwarranted 'to have recourse, without necessity to the first Cause'.[102]

It is possible to argue that Boyle's aim in *The Origine of Formes and Qualities* was to establish the proof he regarded as being missing: that qualities such as bulk, figure, rest, situation and texture were second causes of motion, which could eventually replace recourse to occasionalism.[103] Boyle's novelty was to stress that the rationality of the world was not accessible to us immediately and neither was it available solely through abstract reasoning of the Aristotelian sort, nor indeed that of Hobbes, but mainly through experiments.[104] As discussed earlier, Boyle made explicit his voluntarism in morality in *The Christian Virtuoso*. Although his pursuit of knowledge had a moral aspect, moral law was accessible to human beings almost exclusively through Revelation. Darkness

[101] Corneanu, *Regimens of the Mind*, p. 129. Hobbes could not stand this attitude: 'If the profession of causal nescience was acceptable to, even celebrated by, experimentalists, to Hobbes it constituted a damning admission that the experimental programme was not philosophical.' Schaffer and Shapin, *Leviathan and the Air Pump*, p. 141.

[102] Boyle does not mention Digby, but seems a fair opponent here. Digby adopted a position against presuming occasionalism.

[103] 'If these (bodies) have no inherent motion and power to communicate it, they have really and properly no power to act, but only are Instruments acted and mov'd by the first cause. I will not now examine, whiter tho motion be granted to be the chief of second Causes, some other things, such as Bulk, figure, rest, Situation and Contexture, may not entitle Natural bodys to the name of Phisical Agents, especially according to Cartesius, who will have rest to be, not a privation, but a positive thing in Nature, as well as Motion. But whatever become of this question, in Answer to the Objection, I say, that we ought to be far more carefull that our Notions be agreeable to the nature of things, than to the Opinions of Men, or Termes of Art. (…) And I thinke it may be considered, whiter it be not more safe, as well as pious, in a doubtful case, to Attribute a power that <must> be lodg'd some where, rather to an omnipotent Spirit, than to senseless Matter, it being a less dangerous error to derogate from bodys, than from God.' *Boyle Papers* volume 10, folios 38–40 edited in Peter Anstey, 'Boyle on Occasionalism: An Unexamined Source' 60 *Journal of the History of Ideas* (1999).

[104] That Hobbes was disqualified as dogmatic by Boyle and other members of the Royal Society, in Shapin and Schaffer, *Leviathan and the Air Pump*, pp. 129–139.

therefore reigned not outside, in the corpuscular world that would eventually be revealed to us through experiment, but inside us.

In his study addressing why the natural philosophers became secular theologians, John Henry demonstrates how crucial it was for seventeenth-century natural philosophers to discover the laws governing the natural world. Descartes, who was the forerunner in respect of this approach, made it clear that the laws of nature were innate to human beings: 'They [the laws of nature] are all inborn in our minds just as a king would imprint his laws on the hearts of all his subjects if he had enough power to do so.'[105] Boyle was evasive about that type of imprint or participation, or of any participation of natural laws in human nature. The change of perspective was crucial in his natural philosophy and psychology. The relevant attitude was to search for the pristine rationality of the physical world through external enquiry.[106] Due to their free will, human beings were exceptional creatures within the physical world and, as it were, stayed in the new science outside nature. Robert Boyle was the natural philosopher who possibly most effectively and with the most far-reaching influence developed a description of how physical nature worked – nature being the outcome of a divine design – without employing a robust notion of natural law or of the laws of nature.

7.3 Undoing Nature

Boyle wrote in 1666, but only published in 1685, his famous critique and deconstruction of classic substantiations and personifications of Nature, *A Free Enquiry into the Vulgarly Receiv'd Notion of Nature*, which Michael Hunter and Edward Davis have described as 'one of the key texts of the Scientific Revolution'.[107] As he often did, Boyle drew on several traditions. At the same time his approach is original and impressive, reflects his adoption of the perspective of the natural scientist who studies matter over the perspective of a theologian, and entails rejection of animistic

[105] Descartes quoted in Henry and see generally, Henry, 'Metaphysics and the Origins of Modern Science', p. 102; Steinle, 'From Principles to Regularities: Tracing 'Laws of Nature' in Early Modern France and England' in *Natural Law and Laws of Nature in Early Modern Europe*, p. 226.

[106] Richard Rorty, *Philosophy and the Mirror of Nature* (Princeton: Princeton University Press, 1979), p. 137.

[107] The date is given by Boyle in the Preface, see Boyle, *A Free Enquiry into the Vulgarly Receiv'd Notion of Nature*. Hunter and Davis, 'The Making of Robert Boyle's "Free Enquiry into the Vulgarly Recevi'd Notion of Nature" (1686), p. 204. J. E. McGuire, 'Boyle's Conception of Nature' 33 *Journal of the History of Ideas* (1972) 523–542; Osler, 'The Intellectual Sources of Robert Boyle's Philosophy of Nature; Anstey, *Robert Boyle Natural Philosophy*.

explanations of the activity of matter.[108] I argue next that Boyle moved constantly between a self-sufficient and mechanistic idea of the physical world and recourse to an infinitely wise God as a guide to human knowledge. He disintegrated in the process a metaphysical concept – nature – that had been part of Western culture at least since the time of the great Greek philosophers.

7.3.1 *The Unlimited Reason*

The crucial epistemological point for Boyle was that only God knew perfectly all the possible contingency 'conjunctures of Circumstances, into which *Matter*' could be put, divided and moved, in accordance with divine laws. The world was an 'Automaton' and attributing the cause of a particular operation or quality 'to the nature of things' was to avoid recognizing our ignorance, while attributing the glitches in the system – the 'Anomalities' – to chaos was equally unhelpful in the search for knowledge, and detrimental to religion.[109] As Jan Wojcik put it '*God's infinite* understanding', the intelligence of the Creator is thus probably the fundamental axiom of Boyle's natural philosophy:[110]

> For the Characters and Impressions of Wisdom, that are Conspicuous in the curious Fabrick and orderly Train of Things, can, with no probability, be referr'd to blind Chance, but must be to a most Intelligent and Designing Agent.[111]

God was 'Supream and Absolute Lord, and if I may so speak, proprietor of the Whole Creation' who had a 'Sovereign Right' to dispose of what exists in the world. He was 'Independent, Free and Wise', a 'Just Agent' that may 'by the Irregularities and Exhorbitance in the world' punish the wicked. We know some of God's ends in making the world, while others are 'hid in the Abyss of the divine Wisdom and Counsels'.[112] In

108 See on this, depicting perhaps a slightly too naïve Boyle, Jane E. Jenkins, 'Arguing about Nothing: Henry More and Robert Boyle on the Theological Implications of the Void' in Margaret J. Osler ed. *Rethinking the Scientific Revolution* (Cambridge: Cambridge University Press, 2000), pp. 153–179.

109 Boyle, *A Free Enquiry into the Vulgarly Receiv'd Notion of Nature*, in *The Works of Robert Boyle*, v. 10, p. 493.

110 Wojcik, *Robert Boyle and the Limits of Reason*, p. 213 (emphasis Wojcik).

111 Boyle, *A Free Enquiry into the Vulgarly Receiv'd Notion of Nature*, in *The Works of Robert Boyle*, v. 10, p. 519.

112 Boyle, *A Free Enquiry into the Vulgarly Receiv'd Notion of Nature*, in *The Works of Robert Boyle*, v. 10, pp. 493–494.

Boyle's view, for all we know about theology, God could be chastening human beings through physical nature – not arbitrarily, but wisely. He suggested that exceptional events, though often beyond human understanding, did not strictly deprive the world of its rationality *from the perspective of God*: the Creator may well have a reason that we do not know about. Granted that he worked on the basis of the sceptical reason of the experimentalists, it is nevertheless illuminating to regard Boyle's practical project of knowledge and utility of nature as being rooted more in God's infinite wisdom, as a firm springboard for launching research above apparently rational but limited possibilities, than in human beings' limited reason. Providence was a surer way to knowledge and reality than nature.[113] In this sense, I am inclined to adopt the opposite pair of the equation set out in Jan Wojcik's, *Robert Boyle and the Limits of Reason*. Instead of focusing solely on humanity's limited reason, Boyle's thought is interpreted here by reference to his belief in the unlimited richness of the world God had created, of which so much remained still to be discovered.[114] Even the fact that 'some objects are disproportionate to her (reason)' serves Boyle in his urge and curiosity to understand the world and how it works:[115]

> As when we attentively consider the dimensions of space, or … those of the Universe, we may by tryal perceive that we cannot conceive them so great, but that they may be yet greater, or if you please may exceed the bounds, how remote soever, which our former conception presum'd to assign them.[116]

[113] 'I shall, at present, only observe to you, that the Case is very differing between Providence and Nature, and therefore there is no necessity, that the Objections, I have made against the Later, should hold against the Former.' Boyle, *A Free Enquiry into the Vulgarly Receiv'd Notion of Nature*, in *The Works of Robert Boyle*, v. 10, p. 493.

[114] 'And besides the inscrutable Perfections of God, some of his Works are such, that, notwithstanding the compleat Knowledge of them surpasses our Forces; yet there remains so many things, as well worthy to be known, as possible to be attained by us, that they will allow Exercise enough to the Wits of all the Philosophers in the World.' See also on the principle of non-contradiction, Boyle refers e.g. to true propositions that 'we may think to be contradictory that really are not so' emphasising not only the limits of reason but sometimes the mismanagement and mis application of reason, and generally the immense possibilities of knowledge. On accepting apparent, not real contradiction see, Holden, 'Robert Boyle on Things Above Reason' pp. 302–308; also Corneanu, *Regimens of the Mind*, p. 216.

[115] On 'emotional excitement' as one important factor behind the Scientific Revolution, Margaret J. Osler, 'The Canonical Imperative: Rethinking the Scientific Revolution' in the same (ed.) *Rethinking the Scientific Revolution* (Cambridge: Cambridge University Press, 2000), pp. 3–22.

[116] Boyle, 'A Discourse of Things above Reason' in *The Works of Robert Boyle*, v. 9, p. 386.

Due to his conviction that human beings have limited reason, Boyle can certainly not be regarded as a scientist of 'extreme modesty', but as a bold thinker, imitating the 'boldness' of 'Verulam' (Bacon), eager to learn from the unlimited wisdom of God:[117]

> For in the Divine Nature, Power, Wisdom, and other Attributes, there is a Faecundity that has produc'd a World of Contrivances, Laws and other things, that exceedingly surpass both the Number and Variety, that the dim and limited Intellect of Man could reach to, by framing and compounding *Ideas*, without the assistance of the Patterns afforded by the Works and Declarations of God.[118]

His faith in an infinitely wise designer led Boyle to be open as a matter of principle to the possibility of something similar to what Kyle Stanford has termed 'unconceived alternatives' by which to understand the physical world – alternative lines of thought to a scientist's line of investigation, that are for him or her as a rule, quite hard to accept, despite their seriousness and even their confirmation through evidence.[119] I take Boyle's standpoint to be one of the situations in the history of science in which, in the words of Peter Harrison, invocation of the supernatural has been a 'key presupposition for scientific investigation' of '"successful" scientific theories'.[120] Boyle's ambitious project of knowledge involved the view that the consistent observation of everything – including both normal and anomalous events – offered opportunities to gather information about the physical world. It is instructive to read his correspondence with Locke on this point: the latter reported from France in 1677 and 1678 meticulously in respect of on one key argument of *A Free Enquiry* that concerned denial of the Aristotelian teleology of nature: the existence of 'anomalies' and 'monsters', in other words, irregularities – this is a topic recurrent in Boyle's correspondence also with other students. Locke, for instance, had studied a case in which a French youth had grown claws instead of nails after a bout of smallpox, and had even met the youth in question.[121] This

117 Wojcik, *Robert Boyle and the Limits of Reason*, p. 219. About Bacon's boldness see Boyle, 'A Discourse of Things above Reason' in *The Works of Robert Boyle*, v. 9, p. 382.

118 Boyle, 'The Christian Virtuoso', v. 12, 325; see also Corneanu, *Regimens of the Mind*, p. 136.

119 See for instance in P. Kyle Stanford, 'Darwin's Pangenesis and the Problem of Unconceived Alternatives' 57 *British Journal for the Philosophy of Science* (2006), 121–144, and at book length in P. Kyle Stanford, *Exceeding Our Grasp: Science, History, and the Problem of Unconceived Alternatives* (Oxford: Oxford University Press, 2006). See also, Shapin and Schaffer, *Leviathan and the Air Pump*, pp. 147–148.

120 Peter Harrison, 'Naturalism and the Success of Science' 56 *Religious Studies* (2020), p. 276.

121 'Locke to Robert Boyle, 6 August 1678' in *The Correspondence of John Locke in 8 volumes*, E. S. de Beer (ed.) (Oxford: Clarendon Press, 1976), v. I, p. 599.

absence of regularity made clear to scientists their ignorance about the phenomena. This in turn motivated them towards greater study, thereby coming closer to the Creator and, significantly, acquiring greater mastery of the physical world.

Moving constantly, between God and Science, as Michael Hunter has argued, Boyle retreated again towards a stronger form of natural law with respect to 'powers', and by the end of the *A Free Enquiry into the Vulgarly Receiv'd Notion of Nature*, he boldly concluded that the world possessed a certain constitution endowed upon it by God.[122] For it 'became the Divine Author of the Universe to give it such a Structure, and such Powers, and to establish among its Parts such general and constant Laws' that were best suited 'with his Purposes in creating the world'.[123] And in what appears to be a proposed theory of God's government of the world founded on empirical observation, Boyle observed that ensuring the welfare of human beings and other creatures was God's aim in making the world:

> First, though Men, and other animals be furnish'd with Faculties or Powers, and other Requisites, to enable them to preserve themselves, and procure what is necessary for their own welfare, yet this Provision … is made with reference to what regularly, or most usually happens to Beings of that Species or Sort that they belong to.[124]

The provision or welfare was again an incentive to think the unthinkable: the supernatural and the preternatural. Very often, when pointing to preternatural events, people only described a particular situation without grasping the wider laws of motion involved. Hence, cold air was a natural agent agreeable to the 'Catholick laws of motion' both when it turned rain into snow and when it caused disease – both cases displayed the infinite wisdom of God.[125] Moreover, by maintaining a tension between the freedom of God and the constitution of the physical world, Boyle's argument become objective. Only God knew everything: he was the Absolute Lord and proprietor and

[122] Hunter, Boyle: *Between God and Science.*

[123] Boyle, *A Free Enquiry into the Vulgarly Receiv'd Notion of Nature*, in *The Works of Robert Boyle*, v. 10, 399.

[124] Boyle, *A Free Enquiry into the Vulgarly Receiv'd Notion of Nature*, in *The Works of Robert Boyle*, v. 10, p. 496.

[125] 'The two foregoing Observations may be farther illustrated, by considering, in what sense Men speak of things which they call *Praeter-natural*, or else *Contrary to Nature*. For divers, if not most, of their Expressions of this kind, argue, that *Nature* is in Them taken for the Particular and Subordinate, or, as it were, the Municipal Laws establish'd among Bodies.' Boyle, *A Free Enquiry into the Vulgarly Receiv'd Notion of Nature*, in *The Works of Robert Boyle*, v. 10, p. 524.

had sovereign rights over his Creation.[126] Nevertheless, the laws of motion seemed to be above God's will in Boyle's view. The laws of motion seemed immutable and when it appeared that they did not work, that was only an illusion generated merely by our ignorance of divine wisdom.[127] Boyle addressed this issue in quite a convoluted manner, as was common among mechanic philosophers who took a strong stand in rejecting the suggestion of spiritual activity in nature. For Boyle, God's governance of the world was thus constitutional - as in political theory - with powers and laws distributed both to inanimate and animate beings. The thrust of his argument was to cast doubt on the possibility that the course of nature could be altered by means of miracles and angels rather than by human beings. However, he admitted supernatural interventions when human beings were concerned.[128]

7.3.2 The 'Unnecessariness' of Nature[129]

The discussion set out above helps to assess the broad scope of Boyle's project of natural law, which had moral, theological and epistemological foundations. I will conclude the chapter by briefly noting the utilitarian

[126] 'I shall only tell you in general, that I see no necessity, that Intelligibility to a *humane Understanding* should be necessary to the Truth or Existence of a thing; any more then that Visibility to a *Humane* Eye, should be necessary to the existence of an Atome, or of a Corpuscle of Air.' Boyle, 'Some Advices about Judging of Things Said to Transcend Reason' in *The Works of Robert Boyle*, v. 9, p. 398.

[127] Boyle, *A Free Enquiry into the Vulgarly Receiv'd Notion of Nature*, in *The Works of Robert Boyle*, v. 10, p. 567.

[128] 'And *tho'* I think it probable, that in the Conduct of that far greatest Part of the Universe, which is merely Corporeal, the Wise Author of it does seldom *manifestly* procure a Recession from the settled Course of the Universe, and especially from the most Catholick Laws of Motion: *Yet*, where Men, who are Creatures, that He is pleas'd to indow with Free Wills, (at least in reference to things not Spiritual,) are nearly and highly concern'd; I think he has, not only sometimes by those *signal* and *manifest* Interpositions we call *Miracles*, acted by a Supernatural way, but, as the Sovereign Lord and Governor of the World, doth divers times, (and perhaps oftner than mere Philosophers imagine) give by the Intervention of Rational Minds, as well united, as not united, to human Bodies, divers such determinations to the Motion of Parts in those Bodies, and of Others, which may be affected by Them, as by Laws merely Mechanical, those Parts of Matter would not have had: By which Motions, so determin'd, either Salutary or Fatal *Crises's*, and many other Things, conducive to the Welfare or Detriment of Men, are produc'd.' Boyle, *A Free Enquiry into the Vulgarly Receiv'd Notion of Nature*, in *The Works of Robert Boyle*, v. 10, p. 517.

[129] Boyle's second reason to oppose the notion of a nature that deserves any kind of 'veneration' is 'the unnecessariness of such a nature'. The hypothesis supporting his argument in this case is that the common matter of all bodies having been divided into innumerable minute parts by 'the wise author of nature' and disposed in the order that now is constituted, which could be done by 'mere local motion of matter (not left to itself, but skilfully guided at the

and economic implications of turning the physical world into a philosophical system in which human beings are assigned the role of external managers – which amounts to an attempt to replace God. Boyle's romantic language of 1647, when he intended 'to court nature', changed drastically over the next two decades into a possessive passion that literally and figuratively led him to the desire to 'Range, Anatomize, and Ransack' nature.[130] The differences between his understanding of 'nature' in the early 1650s and that which he expressed in this later text are important. In the 1650s he saw nature as an 'agent' of God, 'his greate Substitute' that could be compared for its prudence to a 'Wise man'.[131] However, 15 years later he sought to pull apart this idea of nature as a mediator of God in his *A Free Enquiry*. Contemporaries understood the text also in this way.[132] To return to Digby's important *Two Treatises*, despite his expressed aim, they still contained plenty of expressions that seemed to give prominence to 'Nature', thus masking a lack of knowledge as to the causes of certain phenomena, as Boyle pointedly noted. Expressions exhibiting that personification are abundant: 'nature worked by the like instruments as art useth'; 'nature teacheth us that gravity is no quality'; 'the way most practiced by nature'; 'nature doth the same'; 'the oeconomy of the wise nature'.[133]

However, Boyle did not only undertake terminological purifications. In *A Free Enquiry into the Vulgarly Receiv'd Notion of Nature* his stance reflected a double paradox: (a) a natural scientist seeking to deny the existence of 'nature' and (b) employing dozens of experiments – not abstract thinking – in order to establish theological principles, such as his theory of the existence of a universal system, or of the universe as a 'Fabrick' created

beginning of the world) – if (I say) we suppose these things together with God's ordinary and general concourse, which we very reasonably may, I see not why the same phenomena that we now observe in the world should not be produced, without taking in any such powerful and intelligent being, distinct from God, as nature is represented to be.' Boyle, *A Free Enquiry into the Vulgarly Receiv'd Notion of Nature*, in *The Works of Robert Boyle*, v. 10, p. 485.

130 Carolyn Merchant's study on Bacon and the ransacking of nature indicates that here Boyle was borrowing from him, Carolyn Merchant, 'The Scientific Revolution and *The Death of Nature*' 96 *Isis* (2006).

131 'God's 'greate Substitute Nature (which is nothing but The Active Power & Law by him plac't in the World, & all the Ingredients of it) moves to hir Ends with the compleatest prudence imaginable: (being upon that account justly compar'd y Aristotle, to a Wise man)' Robert Boyle, *Study of the Book of Nature*, in *The Works of Robert Boyle*, vol. 13, p. 170.

132 'I therefore look upon this work as the new system of a new philosophy which fundamentally overthrows the foundation – namely, Nature, – of all views hitherto held in philosophical matters.' The summary is by David Abercromby, physician and Boyle's protegé, quoted in Hunter and Davis, 'The Making of Robert Boyle's "Free Enquiry into the Vulgarly Recevi'd Notion of Nature" (1686), p. 204.

133 Digby, *Two Treatises*, p. 123; p. 167; p. 187.

initially by God. In short, his message was that the 'Atomical Hypothesis' meant that one could do away with the concept of nature.[134] The alternative he proposed was the idea of a mechanical system of bodies affected by 'the power of Contiguous bodies', composed of atoms of matter lacking any intelligent principle of their own.[135] In the strictest Epicurean style Boyle encouraged disbelief in the existence of 'nature', since there was 'no proof' of it. It was a matter of 'Philosophy, where we ought not to take up any thing upon Trust, or believe it without Proof'.[136] In common with other mechanical philosophers and theologians, his aim was to expose the ambiguities of the vulgar notion of nature, and in particular, all the metaphysics embedded in an abstract notion which obscured the real knowledge of natural phenomena.[137] The vulgar notion of nature took, according to Boyle, a so-called 'nature' as cause, an agent, a mediator, and in the worst case a semi-deity. The 'commodious forms of speech' on 'nature' supposed the 'truth of it' rather than proving anything. Axioms such as 'nature does not make anything in vain' or 'nature abhors a vacuum' functioned like a blanket covering the fact that the scientist did not know the truth of the matter.[138] 'For to vouch Nature for a Cause, is an Expedient, that scarce be wanting to any Man, upon any occasion, to seem to know what he can indeed render no good reason for'.[139] To attribute either to nature or to chaos the design of the world was an empty signifier in both cases – it was in a sense more scientifically honest, in Boyle's view, to avoid answering metaphysical questions when so little knowledge was at the disposal of the scientist. The experimental scientist ought to be more cautious in the activity of hypothesizing than had hitherto been the case.[140] Boyle took the view that a divinized notion of 'nature'

[134] Boyle, *A Free Enquiry into the Vulgarly Receiv'd Notion of Nature*, in *The Works of Robert Boyle*, v. 10, p. 535.

[135] Boyle, *A Free Enquiry into the Vulgarly Receiv'd Notion of Nature*, in *The Works of Robert Boyle*, v. 10, 505.

[136] Boyle, *A Free Enquiry into the Vulgarly Receiv'd Notion of Nature*, in *The Works of Robert Boyle*, v. 10, p. 484. To put it in Epicurus's own words, in the translation by David Sedley, Boyle carried out a 'reasoning based on empirical data' David Sedley, 'Epicurus *On Nature Book XXVIII*' 3 *Chronache Ercolanesi*, pp. 5–83, p. 27.

[137] The study of similar endeavours by the Belgian Arnold Geulinck (1624–1669) and Balthasar Bekker (1634–1698) in van Ruler, 'The Nature of Cartesian Disenchantment'.

[138] Boyle, *A Free Enquiry into the Vulgarly Receiv'd Notion of Nature*, in *The Works of Robert Boyle*, v. 10, p. 462; p. 464.

[139] Boyle, *A Free Enquiry into the Vulgarly Receiv'd Notion of Nature*, in *The Works of Robert Boyle*, v. 10, p. 451.

[140] Boyle, *A Free Enquiry into the Vulgarly Receiv'd Notion of Nature*, in *The Works of Robert Boyle*, v. 10, p. 465. See on how Boyle view his own standpoint employing the experimental

was unnecessary metaphysics, and even prejudicial to the glory of God. Moreover, as noted above, attempts to imitate or dissect nature created 'scruples of conscience' in the activity of transmutation:

> For many have not only looked upon it, as an *impossible* thing to compass, but as something of *impious* to attempt, the removing of those Boundaries which *Nature* seems to have put and setled among her Productions. And whilst they look upon her as such a venerable thing, some make a kind of scruple of Conscience, to endevour so to emulate any of her Works, as to excel them.[141]

Joel Mokyr has written that 'Irreverence is a key to progress'.[142] And it might be the irreverence of the most devout that brings about a more radical change.

The conclusion of *Of the Usefulness of Experimentall Natural Philosophy* shows the broad vision that the author had about the utilitarian possibilities offered by a disaggregated nature.[143] Boyle's activity moved between the natural and the artificial unproblematically, since anything and everything in nature, states and processes included, could be used as resources to be exploited. Nevertheless, as far as the history of international law is concerned, the most striking insight to be drawn from Boyle's *A Free Enquiry into the Vulgarly Receiv'd Notion of Nature* is that Boyle both undid nature and did not shatter the boundaries of natural law. Natural law remained a key concept, which, through his critique and deconstruction of nature, became entrenched as a way of scientific thinking. Apart from defining nature as a 'Cosmical mechanism' and the particular

method in a manner promoting that the scientist did not rush into hypothesis, Shapin and Schaffer, *Leviathan and the Air-Pump. Hobbes, Boyle, and the Experimental Life*, pp. 22–79.

141 Boyle, *A Free Enquiry into the Vulgarly Receiv'd Notion of Nature*, in *The Works of Robert Boyle*, v. 10, p. 430

142 Joel Mokyr, *A Culture of Growth: The Origins of the Modern Economy* (Princeton: Princeton University Press 2016), p. 17.

143 'Though what I have hitherto discours'd, hath almost solely related to the neglected uses of Particular Bodies: yet I would not have You thence take occasion to imagine, that there are not other Natural things whereof divers Uses may be made, that men have hitherto either ignored, or overseen. By *other Natural things* I mean *the* different *states* of Matter, or of Bodies, (such as Rarity and Density, Fluidity and Firmness, Putrefaction and Fermentation, may seem to be,) as also *the* more operative qualities, such as Heat, Cold, Gravity, & c. *the* Laws of Local Motion among the parts of Matter; and *the* present Fabrick of the Universe, and specially that of our Terrestrial Globe and its Effluviums; to which might be added other things in Nature, that are not properly *Bodies* in the usual sense of that word, but may be called *Things Corporeal* as they belong to Bodies, and entirely depend on them.' Boyle, 'The Usefulness of Natural Philosophy II, sect. 2 (1671)', in *The Works of Robert Boyle*, vol. 6, p. 540.

nature as 'the individual mechanism', the laws of nature *as laws of motion* remained key to his main definition of nature.[144]

Bodies were 'determined to act' not by any 'inherent Appetite or Inbred Knowledge' but 'by virtue of the Original Frame of Things and established Laws of Motion'.[145] In this definition, the *laws of motion* were the *laws of nature* and what was natural now was identified with strict matter in such a way that 'the natural' became severed from any realist notion of rightful or just order that had been among the assets of Western philosophical thought since the early Greek era.[146] Hence there was no 'nature', but a macrocosm and a microcosm. The great system of the universe was universal and particular. This automaton – the earth – whose laws were mechanical was a 'fabrick' in which nothing acted in isolation, but upon the influence of the power of contiguous bodies, especially of air.[147] Boyle's way of depersonalizing nature and the same time generating objectivity was, as we saw, to describe nature as a system or *oeconomy*.[148] What had previously been 'nature' was now identified with the original sense of the Greek word *oikonomia*, the idea of an environment that comprised a complex system capable of being administered successfully.[149]

[144] 'If I were to propose a Notion, as less unfit than any I have met with, to pass for the *principal Notion of Nature*, with regard to which, many Axioms and Expressions, relating to that Word, may be not inconveniently understood, I should distinguish between the *universal*, and the *particular* Nature of things ... *Nature*, in general, is The *Result* of the *Universal* Matter, or *Corporeal Substance of the Universe, considered as it is contrived into the present Structure and Constitution of the World, whereby all the Bodies, that compose it, are inabled to act upon, and fitted to suffer from, one another, according to the settled Laws of Motion ... the particular Nature*, of an *Individual Body*, consists in the *general* Nature, *apply'd to a distinct portion of the Universe*. Or rather, supposing it to be plac'd, as it is, in a World, fram'd by God, like Ours, it consists in a *Convention of the Mechanical affections* (such as Bigness, Figure, Order, Situations, Contexture, and Local Motion) *of its parts*, (whether sensible or insensible) *convenient and sufficient to constitute in*, or *to entitle* to, *its particular Species or Denominations, the particular Body they make up, as the Concourse of all these is considered as the Principle of Motion, Rest and Change in that Body*.' Boyle, *A Free Enquiry into the Vulgarly Receiv'd Notion of Nature*, in *The Works of Robert Boyle*, v. 10, pp. 466–467.

[145] Boyle, *A Free Enquiry into the Vulgarly Receiv'd Notion of Nature*, in *The Works of Robert Boyle*, v. 10, p. 528.

[146] For a review see Crombie, *Science, Art and Nature in Medieval and Modern Thought*, pp. 67–87.

[147] Boyle, *A Free Enquiry into the Vulgarly Receiv'd Notion of Nature*, in *The Works of Robert Boyle*, v. 10, p. 521.

[148] Boyle, *A Free Enquiry into the Vulgarly Receiv'd Notion of Nature*, in *The Works of Robert Boyle*, v. 10, p. 469.

[149] Carlo Natali, 'Oikonomia in Hellenistic Political Thought', in André Laks and Malcolm Schofield (eds.), *Justice and Generosity* (Cambridge: Cambridge University Press, 1995), p. 95; p. 98; Tribe, *The Economy of the Word*; Maifreda, *From Oikonomia to Political Economy*.

Chapters 6 and 7 have described two interrelated aspects of Robert Boyle's scientific programme: its goal of serving the economy of nation and empire through science and its transformation of the metaphysical foundations and principles of the traditional notion of nature. My suggestion is that Boyle was inspired in these endeavours by the previous generation of Reformers, and in particular by his former mentor and friend Benjamin Worsley. Robert Boyle was probably the most important thinker in England in displacing Aristotelian principles and replacing them with atomist ones. Apart from Creation by God, metaphysical principles were rendered unnecessary in the constitution of the physical world which was, in Boyle's account, of the atomist-corpuscular type. Moreover, only the epistemological method of experiment remained necessary. The horizon of knowledge could be always broader, deeper, and more thorough than at present – an attitude that was maintained by the profession of permanent doubt and an attitude marked by the desire for deconstruction. In Boyle's conception of the world, human beings are a fact, and he judged human beings' peculiar way of knowing the material world – evidently not directly through its atomic structure – markedly irrelevant in relation to the revolution in knowledge that was underway.

Nature became an impersonal system or an *oeconomy* for human beings to know, to administer and to exploit. In this approach humanity is the manager of that *oeconomy*. The natural system is considered a means to worship God and to human beings' growth in knowledge and material goods.[150] All in all, Boyle emerges as both an extraordinary scientist and an analytical philosopher. Nevertheless, he employed a utopian theology that lacked a critical anthropological perspective and he held conflicting positions that moved from expressions of awe towards God, towards possessiveness and recklessness, in respect of divine Creation. While Boyle seemed uncompromising in undoing notions of nature and in putting the system of nature at the service of economic profit, the natural lawyer John Locke, with a more realistic view about the effects of human greed, would distance himself from some of Boyle's most radical positions.

[150] 'And I further conceive, that he settled such Laws or Rules, of Local Motion, among the parts of the Universal Matter, that by his ordinary and preserving Concourse, the several parts of the Universe, thus once completed, should be able to maintain the great construction, or System and Oeconomy, of the Mundane Bodies, and propagate the Species of Living Creatures'. The woman's body and human beings' body more generally are also an *oeconomy*. 'the Oeconomy of the human body is so constituted by the Divine Author of it, that it is usually fitted to last many Years, if the more General Laws, settled by the same author of the Universe, will permit it.' Boyle refers to the 'Oeconomy of the Womans Body' in relation to the plentiful resort of milk to the breasts after giving birth that might produce fever. Boyle, *A Free Enquiry into the Vulgarly Receiv'd Notion of Nature*, in *The Works of Robert Boyle*, v. 10, p. 469; p. 542; p. 545.

8

Locke's Early Writings

8.1 Independent Judgment of Conscience, Public Order and Public Interest

John Locke's early writings show his concerns divided between the reality of a multiplicity of political, moral and religious standpoints articulated often as individuals' consciences, and the public good and interest. He valued both viewpoints – diversity and unity – and wanted to retain them in his developing political theory.[1] Initially, he also ascertained the immense political and social tension that characterized the times. In the *Two Tracts on Government* (1660) and the *Essays on the Law of Nature* (1662–4) (or *Questions Concerning Natural Law*) he neither expressed clearly what he meant by the notion of conscience, nor seemed to have yet decided whether he had to dispense with it altogether. But what is plain is that for the sake of public order and public interest, in these texts the individual's judgment of conscience tends to be internalized and receives little independent space for operation with regard to both natural law and the secular law of civil society.

8.1.1 The Governance of 'Matters Indifferent'

In the *Two Tracts on Government*, comprising one English and one Latin text among Locke's unpublished papers, civil society is a public space in which matters become necessary by the power of the magistrate and his or her ensuing legislation. Many things *indifferent* – i.e. the magistrate's usual area of activity – thus become necessary. The context of Locke's interest in these ideas is a debate spanning decades on the topic of 'matters indifferent' or *adiaphora* that in the years immediately preceding his

[1] For the study of Locke's interest in diversity as a project of a natural history of 'man', see Carey, *Locke, Shaftesbury, and Hutcheson: Contesting Diversity in the Enlightenment and Beyond*.

writing of the text had become particularized in details of worship and ceremonies, such as the use of surplice by the ministers, and the writings produced in its context.[2] At its heart was the question of whether matters of religious ceremony, considered to be morally indifferent, could be left to be decided according to one's conscience. The pamphlets that were written were divided between representatives of the Anglican Church that considered the issue of ceremonies to be confirmed, not decreed, by English law, and an amorphous group of Puritans, Independents and other Reformers that doubted their legality and even the appropriateness of positive law as a medium of intervention in such matters of conscience.[3] When in Oxford, Locke wrote a very close response to Edward Bagshaw's *The Great Question Concerning Things Indifferent in Religious Worship*, derisively referring to the 'patrons of liberty' and 'patrons of freedom' when addressing Bagshaw and his adherents.[4]

The lack, at the time, of an accepted unified authority in religious matters is evidenced in the fact that the contest of pamphlets turned into an effort to convince the adversaries of what was really necessary and what was not. Bagshaw employed a ubiquitous notion of 'necessity', meaning that the circumstances demanded a solution to the problem of jurisdiction about indifferent things. Some reform ought to be carried out, since many religious doctrines and their public status seemed doubtful at that point in time. The other camp considered instead the matter legally settled. Occasionally the pamphlets described 'necessity' as having theological content, referring to the idea that the

[2] Philip Abrams, 'Introduction' in John Locke, *Two Tracts on Government*, (Cambridge: Cambridge University Press, 1967), 1–111; Johann P. Sommerville, 'Conscience, Law, and Things Indifferent: Arguments on Toleration from the Vestiarian Controversy to Hobbes and Locke,' in Harald Braun and Edward Vallance (eds.), *Contexts of Conscience in Early Modern Europe, 1500–1700* (Houndmills: Palgrave Macmillan, 2004), pp. 166–179; Jaqueline Rose, 'John Locke, 'Matters Indifferent', and the Restoration of the Church of England' 48 *The Historical Journal* (2005). The debate had started almost a century ago with 'The Vestiarian controversy', or dispute over clerical dress, in the context of Puritans' attempts for reform and the response of the Anglican Church, see B. Usher, 'Participants in the vestiarian controversy (act. c. 1563–c. 1570).' *Oxford Dictionary of National Biography*. Retrieved 21 May. 2019, from www.oxforddnb.com/view/10.1093/ref:odnb/9780198614128.001.0001/odnb-9780198614128-e-92778

[3] A chronological list of the main pamphlets intervening in the dispute, by Philip Abrams, in John Locke, *Two Tracts on Government*, Appendix II, p. 252.

[4] Edward, Bagshaw, *The Great Question Concerning Things Indifferent in Religious Worship briefly States and tendred to the Consideration of All Sober and Impartial men*, third ed. (London, 1660), Early English Books Online Text Creation Partnership, 2011, http://name.umdl.umich.edu/A29126.0001.001; Locke, *Two Tracts of Government*, p. 122; p. 128.

doctrine of faith to be believed 'for necessity of salvation' ought not to be established by a public legislative authority.

Some, like the exposition to Parliament of 'divers ministers of sundry counties in England' but published under the name of Cornelius Burgess and entitled *Reasons Shewing the Necessity of Reformation of the Publick 1. doctrine, 2. worship, 3. rites and ceremonies, 4. Church-government and discipline,* denounced the abuse of authority when 'indifference' became 'necessary' by command of just authority.[5] Since the spiritual law gave liberty in such things, the text highlighted, among many other issues, the danger for consciences in determining 'things of this nature for Publick use in the Administration of Publick Ordinances'.[6] In *No Necessity of Reformation of the Publick Doctrine of the Church of England,* John Pearson responded that the public law was only confirming, not establishing the truth of the doctrines of religion and other matters. Anticipating an argument repeated later, in the Restoration years, Pearson stressed the original separation of Church and State:

> that the Articles made in K. *Edward* 6. time were *not ratified by Parliament,* it no way opposeth them who thinke our Articles established by Law: because no man imagines that our Articles were under the Consideration of any Parliament in the days of *Edward* 6.[7]

The newly named chaplain to Charles II in Ordinary, Henry Savage, wrote in *Reasons Shewing that there is no need of such a Reformation of the Publique Doctrine* that things indifferent had been made necessary by 'the intervention of human authority'. Aware of the turmoil this entailed, he pointed out that if the key questions to be answered in respect of the Church, doctrine, liturgy, rites, ordination, episcopacy and discipline were to be 'set aside till men be agreed, we must never expect any whilst the world stands'.[8] In *Some Necessity of Reforming the Publick Doctrine of the*

[5] Cornelius Burgess, *Reasons shewing the necessity of reformation of the publick 1 doctrine, 2. worship, 3. rites and ceremonies 4. Church-government and discipline, reputed to be (but indeed, not) established by law. Humbly offered to the serious consideration of this present Parliament. By divers of sundry counties in England* (London: Printed by Ja. Cottrel., 1660), Early English Books Online Text Creation Partnership, 2011, http://name.umdl.umich.edu/A77860.0001.001

[6] Burgess, *Reasons shewing the necessity of reformation of the publick*, p. 38.

[7] John Pearson, *No necessity of reformation of the publick doctrine of the Church of England,* (London: Printed by J.G. for Nathaniel Brooke, 1660) Early English Books Online Text Creation Partnership, 2011, http://name.umdl.umich.edu/A53894.0001.001, p. 26. The point that this would become a common argument in the period of the Restoration in Collins, *In the Shadow of Leviathan,* p. 38.

[8] Henry Savage, *Reasons shewing that there is no need of such a reformation of the publique 1. Doctrine. 2. Worship. 3. Rites & Ceremonies. 4. Church-Government. 5. Discipline. As it is pretended by reasons offered to the serious consideration of this present Parliament, by divers*

Church of England, William Hamilton responded shrewdly that Pearson had responded to the 'ministers of sundry counties' as a theologian, while they were writing to the Parliament on the point of 'publiqueness, and authority'.[9] Finally, Bagshaw contributed to the debate, also from a theological perspective, this time on the Puritan side.

Locke, or perhaps one of his patrons, rightly ascertained the danger of *The Great Question* with regard to political stability, for Bagshaw's text is a well-balanced and pious defence of freedom of conscience in matters indifferent and could well have tilted the balance in the opposite direction. The issue would finally be decided two years later through the intervention of the Lord Chancellor, the Earl of Clarendon (1609–1674), and of Parliament, which enacted new legislation.[10] A Whiggish perspective would tend to portray the moment in the early Restoration period in which Locke wrote his *Tracts* as being like a romance between Charles II and his people that ended in 1662 with the monarch's 'succumbing' to the Anglican Church in the Act of Uniformity.[11] Within this contextualist interpretation, Locke was still enchanted when he wrote about his conviction that supremacy in government is necessary and that chaos would result from freedom in respect of indifferent things.

ministers of sundry counties in England (London: Printed for Humphrey Robinson,1660). Early English Books Online Text Creation Partnership, 2011, http://name.umdl.umich.edu/A94222.0001.001, p. 17.

9 'To all which you answer nothing, but that the Doctrines of that Article, *as considered in themselves*, are *undoubted truths:* Which is true enough, but nothing to Rhombus, as we have often said. For the Ministers speak of the *doubtfullness* as proceeding from their *too great generality*, and *unfitness* to exclude errors by; and of their *doubtfullness* of *publiqueness, and authority*'. William Hamilton, *Some necessity of reformation of the publick doctrine of the Church of England. Or a modest and brief reply to Dr Pearson's modest and learned, No necessity of reformation of the publick doctrine of the Church of England. Directed to Dr Pearson himself* (London: Printed for John Sherley1660), Early English Books Online Text Creation Partnership, 2011, http://name.umdl.umich.edu/A45377.0001.001, p. 13.

10 Clarendon said in Parliament that there was the need for 'some law, that may be a rule to that indulgence, that under pretence of liberty of conscience men may not be absolved from all the obligations of law and conscience'. Quoted in Abrams, 'Introduction' in John Locke, *Two Tracts of Government*, p. 36. Despite Clarendon's attempt that a moderate standpoint prevailed, according to Ian Harris more than nine hundred clergymen not using the *Book of Common Prayer* were ejected from their positions as a consequence of the Act of Uniformity. Harris, *The Mind of John Locke*, p. 70. About the moderate position of Clarendon see Paul Seaward, 'Edward Hyde, first earl of Clarendon (1609–1674), Politician and Historian' (2008, October 04). *Oxford Dictionary of National Biography*. https://doi-org.libproxy.helsinki.fi/10.1093/ref:odnb/14328

11 Goldie, 'Priestcraft and the Birth of Whiggism', p. 224.

8.1.2 *Locke's* Tracts on Government *and Judgment about Necessary Things*

Regardless of passing political sentiment, *The Tracts* show the very first stages of Locke's lifelong investigation of public order, articulated as an early study of how secular law contributed to it. Order and peace were grounded in law, in what God in his infinite wisdom 'hath made necessary', which in Locke's *Tracts on Government* had little reference to defending the position of the Church of England. That necessity referred to magistracy according to the natural constitution of the world as God had established it. The focus of Locke's discussion therefore turned to describing the scope of magistracy. Once matters such as customs or education were decided by the magistrate, individuals could not invoke independent judgment of conscience, despite the fact that those matters had been indifferent before the law or ordinance was enacted. If this were not the case, the reach of the magistrate's power would be minimal.[12] The space for intervention of the magistrate could touch every indifferent aspect of civil society and, once encroached upon, any issue could become necessary. In effect, it was unavoidable that the magistrate governing civil society through law will touch upon issues of conscience. 'Tis is true', noted Locke quoting Bagshaw, '[*who would have his conscience imposed upon*] and

> tis as true, who would pay taxes, who would be poor, who almost not be a prince? And yet these (as some think them) burdens, this inequality, is owing all to human laws and those just enough, the law of God or nature neither distinguishing their degrees not bounding their possessions.[13]

The problem with individual conscience was that there were as many consciences as there were citizens. If the magistrate must please every individual, he or she must simply have 'not a power to make laws but worlds'.[14] Someone, thought Locke, had to produce the 'circumstantial determinations' about a matter that has become necessary and the law-maker was 'judge alone of that necessity', not the conscience of each individual.[15] Therefore the possibility of making an independent judgment

[12] Locke, *Two Tracts on Government*, p. 129.
[13] Locke, *Two Tracts on Government*, p. 138.
[14] Locke, *Two Tracts on Government*, p. 137.
[15] Locke, *Two Tracts on Government*, p. 147; 149. In the question of 'matters indifferent' Jaqueline Rose argues that Locke deliberately failed to distinguish between ecclesiastical and secular authority, thus 'refraining from distinguishing a particular role for the clergy', Rose, 'John Locke, 'Matters Indifferent', and the Restoration of the Church of England', p. 617; p. 621.

of conscience about outward things opposing the magistrate must be excluded in public matters that have become necessary by the latter's activity. For the young, virtuous and conforming Locke, the public activities in which the magistrate engaged were good, since they corresponded to the rational magistrate acting within order, established by God for the public good.

> Whereas the magistrate commands the obedience of the outward man by authority settled on him by God and the people, wherein he is not to expect immediate inspirations but is to follow the dictates of his own understanding, and establish or alter all indifferent things as he shall judge them conducing to the good of the public.[16]

Public activities of the magistrate were also broadly conceived:

> all indifferent actions, of whatsoever sort they may be, lie under the power of him to whose discretion are delivered the liberty, fortunes and the life itself of every subject.[17]

Locke's early authoritarianism seemed far from his later political principles of limiting government to the preservation of a set of material or outward tenets that he subsumed under the title of 'Property': 'Life, Liberties and Estates'.[18] However, close inspection reveals that even his mature political works make it clear that the first thing individuals do upon entering into civil society is to place their possessions under 'the Jurisdiction of the Government'.[19]

Perhaps the *Tracts* betray an early conservative standpoint, or possibly simply a lack of technique.[20] Locke could not see *yet* how individuals' obedience to their conscience was compatible with securing peace, order and the necessities of the nation – all of which were matters of the utmost concern to him in this period of his life and which he considered to be envisaged in the divine design.[21] From the beginning of his political works and,

[16] Locke, *Two Tracts on Government*, p. 150.

[17] Locke, *Two Tracts on Government*, p. 230.

[18] Locke, *Two Treatises of Government*, II § p. 123.

[19] Locke, *Two Treatises of Government*, II § p. 120.

[20] I tend to agree with Ian Harris that Locke had early on the vision, but initially he lacked the technique, Harris, *The Mind of John Locke*, p. 14. About conservativism, see Abrams, who writes that the *Two Tracts* are 'in every sense profoundly conservative works.' Philip Abrams, 'Introduction' in John Locke, *Two Tracts of Government*, p. 4.

[21] All historical evidence points to the sincerity of Locke's statement in the Preface of the *English Tract*: 'As for myself, there is no one can have a greater respect and veneration for authority than I. I no sooner perceived myself in the *world* but I found myself in a storm, which hath lasted almost hitherto, and therefore cannot but entertain the approaches of a calm with the greatest joy and satisfaction'. Locke, *Two Tracts on Government*, p. 119.

as we will see in the next chapters, until the end of it, Locke was equally concerned with (a) individual interest and public good, (b) with the difficulty that individuals experienced in being fair towards others, and thus (c) with the ensuing impossibility of order without the objective application of authority and power. In his realistic portray of Locke, John Dunn approached this idea in more controversial terms, writing that despite the fact that he understood some of Hobbes's claims, Locke's lifelong nightmare was to be taken as a Hobbist. In turn, Jeffrey Collins describes the charges of Hobbism, in particular in natural law, and his slow detachment of Hobbes's ideas on sovereignty.[22] In the early *Two Tracts* he proposed to achieve a balance between individual and public interest through the activity of the prudent magistrate(s):

> And hence rises one of those necessities of government – that since men were not like (being favourable judges in their own cause) to be well satisfied with the equity of others, and would be ready to judge that others made use of their liberty, to their prejudice with neglect of this rule of equity, it was requisite to settle a peace and society amongst men that they should mutually agree to give up the exercise of their native liberty to the disposure and prudence of some select person or number of men who should make laws for them which should be the rule of their actions one towards another and the measure of their enjoyments, but this by the by.[23]

Famously Locke based the need for magistracy on God, as he tended to do in respect of almost everything that he found good or important in politics, society and philosophy – except, interestingly, money.[24] However, his was not the late medieval idea of the divine right of kings, but the (Aquinean, and also Boylean) conception of what individuals understood rationally to be necessary on the basis of how God had constituted the world.[25] Magistracy, like other human affairs 'squared the economy of the world' designed by God.[26] The early writings expressed the view that no explicitly divine command

[22] Locke's 'Hobbist nightmare' in Dunn, *The Political Thought of John Locke*, p. 81; Collins, *In the Shadow of Leviathan*, pp. 315–359.

[23] Locke, *Two Tracts on Government*, p. 138.

[24] More about this in ch. 11 and see Locke, *Two Treatises of Government, II* §46, §46, §50.

[25] The argument of design is dealt with extensively from its theological perspective in James Tully, *A Discourse on Property. John Locke and His Adversaries* (Cambridge: Cambridge University Press, 1980), p. 38.

[26] Some 'presumptuously' complained that God had not put human affairs in the right posture, Locke, *Two Tracts on Government*, p. 136. The centrality of God in Locke's politics was proposed first by Dunn, *The Political Thought of John Locke*, and also later by Harris, *The Mind of John Locke*; by Timothy Stanton, for instance in Timothy Stanton, 'Authority and Freedom in the Interpretation of Locke's Political Theory' 39 *Political Theory* (2011), 6–30

based on the Bible should be expected since 'the light of nature' instructed human beings 'in the necessity of laws and government and magistrate with power over them'.[27] That was in Locke's view the will of God, and if at some point God's will changed so that the result was 'either [to] abolish magistracy or restrain its power from things of the sanctuary', magistracy would become also 'needless'.[28] In the meantime, obedience to the magistrate and, quite literally, respect for the rule of law, was due when legislating about indifferent things so that one was 'therefore not left free':[29]

> God wished there to be order, society and government among men. And this we call the commonwealth. In every commonwealth there must be some supreme power without which it cannot truly be a commonwealth; and that supreme power is exactly the same in all government, namely legislative.[30]

The single issue excepted from the power of the magistrate was religion, which was in Locke's view not a matter of indifference. Since individuals were not masters of religion, it was *not* among the things that they surrendered to the jurisdiction of the magistrate. And since the activity of the legislator constituted only '[o]rdinances of men and the products of their authority', they did not impose on conscience.[31]

However, in the English Tract conscience was '*opinion* of the truth of any practical position, which may concern any action as well moral as religious, civil as ecclesiastical regarding truth';[32] whereas magistracy 'with no commission to examine the hearts' meant governance of outwardly

and by Paul Bou-Habib, for instance in Paul Bou-Habib, 'Locke, Natural Law and Civil Peace: Reply to Tate' 16 *European Journal of Political Theory* (2017). A response to Stanton with regard to this reading, by John William Tate, 'Locke, God and Civil Society: Response to Stanton' 40 *Political Theory* (2012), pp. 222–228, and the reply by Stanton, 'On (Mis) interpreting Locke: a Reply to Tate', 40 *Political Theory* (2012), pp. 229–236. Famously, on the face of some of Locke's materialist principles, Leo Strauss argued that Locke was being deceitful when insisting about God as the foundation of morality, society and politics, Leo Strauss, *Natural Right and History* (The University of Chicago Press, 1953). Seemingly following Strauss in this point is Horwitz, 'Introduction' in John Locke, *Questions Concerning the Law of Nature*. My reading aims to make sense of God's foundational position in Locke's thinking, together with some of his materialist tenets. A comprehensive appraisal of Locke's writings and life, makes the argument of conceit untenable.

27 Locke, *Two Tracts on Government*, p. 170.
28 Locke, *Two Tracts on Government*, p. 136.
29 Locke, *Two Tracts on Government*, p. 122.
30 Locke, *Two Tracts on Government*, p. 232.
31 Locke, *Two Tracts on Government*, p. 139.
32 Locke, *Two Tracts on Government*, p. 138 (emphasis mine). Here Philip Abrams notes the similarity with Hobbes' notion of conscience in the *De Corpore*, p. 138.

indifferent things. Matters such as 'theft and chastity' were 'necessary and oblige conscience' even when the magistrate remain silent: the magistrate did not need to invent new laws in those natural law matters, but only declare and enforce the old.[33] While spiritual matters were not within the proper realm of the magistrate, human legislation could not, nonetheless, avoid touching on their substance.[34] Hence, Locke challenged Bagshaw to show 'where civil things end and spiritual begin'.[35]

A slightly more sophisticated definition of conscience appeared in the Latin Tract, in which Locke distinguished four categories of law: (1) Divine, including natural and positive law: whatever that law reaches is 'always and everywhere necessarily good or evil'; (2) human law, whose proper matter constituted things indifferent that became necessary when legislated upon; (3) the law of charity, that made necessary things left indifferent by God and magistrate; and (4) the category encapsulated in the following words:

> Besides the above-named laws there remains the other called monastic or private, which a man imposes on himself and by a new, superinduced obligation renders necessary things hitherto indifferent and not bound by previous laws. And this law is twofold, either of conscience or of contract. The law of conscience we call that fundamental judgment of practical intellect concerning any possible truth of a moral proposition about things to be done in life. For it is not enough that a thing may be indifferent in its own nature unless we are convinced that it is so.[36]

It is worth noting how, unlike Ralph Cudworth, Locke pointed to 'conscience' as early as the *Tracts* only with regard to his definition of a private law. As it was dependent on our convictions anyone could extend the law of his or her conscience beyond the human law and natural law and impose further obligations on oneself – obligations that the thing 'in its own nature' may not demand from conscience. However, in this context, the areas or subject matters of the different laws appear well delimited, at least in his theoretical definition.[37]

[33] Locke, *Two Tracts on Government*, p. 223.
[34] Locke, *Two Tracts on Government*, p. 145.
[35] Locke, *Two Tracts on Government*, p. 138.
[36] Locke, *Two Tracts on Government*, p. 224.
[37] In this regard, I see things different than Timothy Stanton who writes that in the *Two Tracts* Locke was still simply following Robert Sanderson – although, as exposed in this chapter, he was also following Sanderson. As this and other passages show Locke presented in his first political tracts already original ideas, precisely about his reworking of the notion of conscience. See Timothy Stanton, 'Freedom of Conscience, Political Liberty and the Foundations of Liberalism', p. 148.

In his study of Locke's thought, Ian Harris writes that the philosopher devised a notion of civil order in which it was possible to 'distinguish two distinct spheres' and 'conscientious attacks on the civil order in the name of worship were spurious'. Harris also notes that reason had an intellectual authority for Locke, which he stressed in his *Essays on Natural Law* through the possibility of it attaining certainty. In a civil society in which 'conscience could expect to be informed by reason' or 'Scripture interpreted in reasonable terms', Locke's solution, as outlined in his *Essay on Toleration*, was that conscience and civil order could be reconciled.[38] I follow a different line of argument from Harris and would stress that Locke reconceptualized conscience from the beginning. However, I believe that Harris and I are in agreement as regards the basic premise that Locke's delimitation of the spheres of action demanded the sacrifice of fundamental epistemological, moral and ecclesiastical principles.[39] Locke could work out that reconciliation of the claims of civil order and conscience only at the expense of delivering a new understanding of conscience, as we will see in this chapter. A conscience informed by reason – and in a sense subjected to reason – was no longer the watchdog and guardian of reason cherished by Christian tradition.[40]

In sum when thinking of public society, conscience and reason, Locke argued that questions concerning necessity of salvation were a matter of private conscience on which the magistrate could not impose any obligation. On any matter of outwardly indifferent things (moral, religious, civil and ecclesiastical) on which magistrates judged it necessary to act, they simply acted within their jurisdiction. Conscience was to be dealt with

[38] Harris, *The Mind of John Locke*, p. 76.

[39] Since 'to turn this argument into a resolution of the problem implied ignoring questions about truth and the nature of the church.' Harris, *The Mind of John Locke*, pp. 60–77; p. 123.

[40] M. V. Dougherty summarizes Aquinas doctrine, which may serve as representative of that tradition and be conveniently noted here: The formation of conscience depends directly from God and from the knowledge of God's law which also avoided malformation of conscience. Individuals operated the innate principle of practical reasoning that 'good is to be done' when the concrete situation arose; and they did so, helped by the illumination of the synderesis or light of nature. M. V. Dougherty, *Moral Dilemmas in Medieval Thought. From Gratian to Aquinas*, (Cambridge: Cambridge University Press, 2011), pp. 13–40; p. 33, and on Aquinas, pp. 124–159. In his *Mirror of Conscience* St. John Capistran (1385–1456) who studied law with Pietro degli Ubaldi and theology with Bernardine of Siena, stressed that one needed to act always according to one's conscience, and when every other external source seems to contradict one's conscience, hence indicating an erroneous conscience, the ultimate and supreme guide for conscience was to pray to God with faith for the necessary wisdom, Ioannes Capistranus, *Speculum Conscientiae. Tractatu universi Iuris* (Venice: F. Ziletti, 1584), p. 328.

sensitively, particularly where scrupulous consciences were concerned, but the magistrate ought not to listen to scrupulous people.[41] Everyone had to obey when the legislator rationally ascertained that a certain regulation was necessary – that very regulation transformed an indifferent matter into a *necessary* one.[42] At any rate, the area of public reason that the magistrate deemed necessary did not overlap with the area of conscientious salvation that the individual understood to be necessary. In turn, individual conscience had no 'authority' in the public realm. Conscience was rather the shrine in the depths of the soul where the individual met with her God.[43]

Throughout the *Two Tracts* the main philosophical technique employed by Locke is a rather simple classification of a matter as necessary or not in a determined space: the outward space of the public or the inner space of the individual's conscience. He defined what he meant by 'necessary' in the English Tract:

> I answer: That things may be necessary, (i) in their own nature and so are all comprehended within the law of God; (ii) *ex suppositione*, as being the means to some requisite end, so meat is necessary to him that would live etc, such were the things here – and so things indifferent may become necessary before they are enjoined and oblige the prince before they are commanded the people, and such a necessity (which I say still the magistrate is judge of) is sufficient for their imposition.[44]

Put briefly, something that was necessary followed the design of God, nature and causal reasoning – and it is noteworthy that Locke employs the example of meat, which constitutes a natural necessity that the sovereign himself must respect. As we saw in Chapter 3, the main arguments of Hobbes's *Leviathan* is that beyond matters of survival the sovereign was the only judge of 'the necessity' of anything. Locke still argued that the magistrate was the ultimate judge, albeit that he differed from Hobbes in identifying the necessity of the nature of things as an expression of the will of God, and teleological necessity *ex suppositione* as in principle above the reasoning of the magistrate, who nevertheless remains the judge of it.

Locke's theoretical project on government and his first publication on political theory ambitiously resulted in a threefold plan: to delimit the proper activity of the magistrate to indifferent things, that were

41 Locke, *Two Tracts on Government*, p. 138.

42 Locke, *Two Tracts on Government*, p. 221.

43 'And this is why God so frequently and so particularly claims the heart and spirit for himself, and calls the mind and the inner depths of the soul shrines dedicated to his worship, and requires a spirit obedient to himself as if it were the only worshipper that he prizes.' Locke, *Two Tracts on Government*, p. 211; p. 213.

44 Locke, *Two Tracts on Government*, pp. 150–151 (notes omitted).

nevertheless often rational matters, while in moral matters the magistrate was only declaring the old (natural) law; to further and encourage the disappearance of private spiritual conscience from debates on civil society; and to suggest the idea of a space for civil society, a public reason, between the workings of both government and individual conscience. Before turning to this last aspect as it appeared in his subsequent writings on natural law, I will comment briefly on the manner in which Locke dealt with the moral dilemmas that emerged in the period.

8.1.3 Moral Perplexity Erased

Another method by which to explain how Locke faced the controversy over indifferent matters and proposed a solution to it entails investigating the issue in terms of the problem of moral perplexity being erased from political theory.[45] Through recourse to a civil magistracy whose laws were described as exclusively dealing with outward matters, and by declaring an internalized private law of conscience, Locke discarded the understanding of the controversy as a moral dilemma, which was at the core of Bagshaw's argument.[46]

In his edition of the *Two Tracts on Government*, Philip Abrams remarks that Locke's argumentation passed over the more theologically oriented definitions of conscience available in his time.[47] He would have aimed at avoiding that type of specific theological debate in order to focus instead on questions of political authority. However, his discussion of passive and active obedience makes it obvious that morality was at the heart of his outlook, no matter how hard he tried to circumvent theology and moral

[45] It is not unfair to suggest that Luther's fundamental challenge to authority in the name of conscience provided a useful background for Locke and many others to understand the type of revolts that might occur against the sovereign of the commonwealth if given sufficient space. See on Luther's challenge to the 'fundamental criterion' of the authority of the Church. Popkin, *The History of Scepticism*, pp. 3–16.

[46] One could find 'many' who were 'utterly unsatisfied with the Lawfulness' and convinced of 'the uselesseness' of many or most 'Ceremonies', 'Whose consciences, how erroneous soever, yet are to be tenderly and gently dealt with; lest by our Rigid commanding what they can by no means comply with, we bring them, unto that dangerous Dilemma, either of breaking their Inward Peace and Comfort, by doing outwardly, what they do not inwardly approve of: or else of running themselves upon the Rock of Poverty and Prejudice, by disobeying what is commanded.' Edward, Bagshaw, *The Great Question Concerning Things Indifferent in Religious Worship*, p. 12.

[47] Abrams in Locke, *Two Tracts on Government*, note 138. For the complex position of Hobbes see Stanton, 'Freedom of Conscience, Political Liberty and the Foundations of Liberalism', pp. 141–147.

philosophy. It also shows Locke's early strategy of pointing to the authority of the magistrate as willed by God. Locke defined the power of the magistrate as regulatory and coercive. An active obedience corresponded to the former, and a passive obedience to the latter. The subject was bound by the law 'whether just or unjust' and must passively endure it because a private citizen could never 'oppose the magistrate's decree by force of arms'.[48] The distinction was taken directly from Robert Sanderson – who evidently flirted with Hobbesian principles – without acknowledgement.[49] Sanderson summarized a very long explanation with the following axiom: 'It is alwayes necessary therefore to be subject, but not alwayes necessary to obey'.[50] If the matter was 'unlawful' the magistrate sinned 'in commanding', but neither the magistrate's sin nor his or her bad faith freed the individual from the obligation to passively obey the positive law. For, Locke wrote, the measure of obedience lay not in the magistrate's intention, but in 'his expressed will, which establishes obligation'.[51] Only if the substance of the law was unlawful – that is to say, contrary to the law of God – was the subject discharged from the obligation of active obedience.

Notwithstanding his avoidance of a direct discussion on conscience, Locke dealt substantively with a case of perplexity that affected many individuals throughout the Restoration period in England – we have seen, for instance, that Benjamin Worsley's nonconformism led to the collapse of his very successful political career in 1673. As the Puritans and Independents described their case, in opposing conformity with Anglican religious ceremonies they were protecting the liberty of their consciences – which dictated that they must disobey. Therefore, to avoid the moral conflict between disobeying their consciences or disobeying the human law (ecclesiastical and secular), they proposed further reform of the laws. If, in line with the position of the official Church, there was no need for the law to be reformed, the Puritans were in a situation of perplexity, having to choose between two evils: either to violate their conscience or to violate the law.[52]

48 Locke, *Two Tracts on Government,* p. 221.

49 In his writings of the late 1640s Sanderson seems to be aware of Thomas Hobbes *De cive*; that Locke borrowed from Sanderson was already noted by von Leyden, 'Introduction' in John Locke, *Essays on the Law of Nature*, and Stanton, 'Freedom of Conscience, Political Liberty and the Foundations of Liberalism'. Jaqueline Rose even writes that on certain points of the *Two Tracts* 'Sanderson could justly have sued for plagiarism', Rose, 'John Locke, "Matters Indifferent" and the Restoration of the Church of England', p. 614.

50 Sanderson, *Several Cases of Conscience Discussed in Ten Lectures,* p. 198–199. See also ch. 5.

51 Locke, *Two Tracts on Government,* p. 221; Sanderson, *Several Cases of Conscience Discussed in Ten Lectures,* p. 157.

52 As Edward Bagshaw wrote, see note 46.

The diffusion and ultimately erasure of moral dilemmas from political theory and theology had already, at this point, a very long history. As explained by M.V. Dougherty a rationalist shift had occurred in canon law and theology from Gratian to the Glossators of the *Glossa ordinaria*. The issue of perplexity is portrayed in distinction 13 of the *Decretum*, where Gratian declares that no dispensation is permitted from natural law, 'except perhaps when one is compelled to choose between two evils'. The rationalist *Glossators* instead viewed moral dilemmas as merely epistemological problems and not as moral entanglements: they constituted *a failure to understand* that characterized situations in which individuals regarded themselves as being in a dilemma, and perplexed by it, when in reality they were not.[53] Perplexity was more the result of negligence and lack of reasoning than a situation of future moral growth in which the individual faces a new moral challenge. Rationalist canon lawyers thus produced a type of reasoning that aimed at blocking situations of perplexity, transforming them into epistemological conundrums in need of external guidance. However, the opinions in play multiplied along with the development and production of moral guiding works. In the effort to overcome the numerous subtleties of the moral casuists, this rejection of perplexity would continue in Jean Barbeyrac's early eighteenth century account of the 'Science of Morality' and its demand for moral certainty.[54] It would do so, of course, within the ideology provided by the metaphysics of necessity of mechanistic philosophy described in Chapters 2 and 3:

> it may sometimes fall out, that for want of Care or Attention, we may, in some uncommon Cases, not know how to apply them (the Rules of Conduct); or cannot methodically demonstrate the necessary Connexion of some remote Consequences, with the first Principles of Morality.[55]

In opposition to the rationalist tendency to distrust bemusement in respect of (moral) knowledge, Vasilis Politis and Constance Blackwell

[53] The *perplexitas* of Gregory's 'moral entanglement' was subsumed, via the Glossator's apparent *perplexitas* of lack of understanding into 'moral confusion', and thus into situations in which an agent faced with 'moral uncertainty' needed the assistance of a (probable) authority. For the content of this paragraph see, Dougherty, *Moral Dilemmas in Medieval Thought. From Gratian to Aquinas*, pp. 13–40; p. 33; pp. 198–203.

[54] 'A Man before he can arrive at this State of Doubt and Perplexity, so as to be at a loss which side of the Question to take, in Points relating to this own Conduct; must first have negligently over-look'd Maxims, so clear, as to be self-evident; and so easy, as to be obvious in every Case of Practical Duty.' Barbeyrac, 'An Historical and Critical Account of the Science of Morality', p. 8.

[55] Barbeyrac, 'An Historical and Critical Account of the Science of Morality', p. 10.

view the *aporie* or perplexity as an important element since Aristotle in helping to achieve knowledge of reality by means of a voyage of personal discovery.[56] Blackwell writes that in translations of metaphysics employed in the fifteenth and sixteenth centuries *aporia* was given a meaning that more properly reflects that of *dubito*, and thereby the meaning of Aristotle's project of discovery of knowledge through puzzlement was also modified.[57]

In legal works, the notion of perplexity during the Renaissance had become independent of the thinking of theological and canon lawyers and of moral discussion, which included factors such as the deceiving devil and the malformed conscience.[58] Legal discourse nevertheless suffered from the same multiplication and diversity of opinions among lawyers that made sceptics like Montaigne despair of the prospects of there being any certainty about justice.[59] This tradition transformed perplexity into a methodological theme of legal reasoning that, in effect, involved an attempt to avoid *non liquet* in the application of the law. Gottfried Wilhelm Leibniz's anti-humanist text *Casibus Perplexis in Jure*, published in 1666 crystallized the

[56] Following Vasilis Politis, Constance Blackwell reads chapter III of Aristotle's *Metaphysics* defining the *aporie* or puzzlements as a means to reach the knowledge of being in metaphysics. Aristotle wanted in that chapter 'to orient the reader of the *Metaphysics* through the *aporeo* towards a voyage of personal metaphysical discovery.' In a truly complex manner, it is the *aporie* itself, what gives orientation to the knowledge seeker. "Those who search without first engaging with *aporiai* are like people who don't know where they need to be going; moreover, they do not even know whether or not they have found what they are searching for. For the end [of a search] is not clear to such a person, but it is clear to the person who has first raised *aporiai*." (995a 34–b 2)' Aristotle quoted in Vasilis Politis, *Routledge Philosophy Guide to Aristotle and the Metaphysics*, (London and New York, 2004), p. 65; Blackwell, 'Aristotle's Perplexity becomes Descartes's Doubt'.

[57] Blackwell, 'Aristotle's Perplexity becomes Descartes's Doubt', p. 232.

[58] In between Gratian and the Glossators, Aquinas asserted that giving a certain supposition, one may be perplexed. For instance, a previous bad deed, a theft, might put an individual in a situation of perplexity, in which he or she might be unable to restore the goods without causing a bigger harm (perplexity *secundum quid*). But God never permitted individuals to be in a situation of pure perplexity (perplexity *simpliciter*). This did not mean that an individual could not suffer from dilemmas due the activity of the devil or to a malformed conscience. As noted above, individuals operated the innate principle of practical reasoning that 'good is to be done' when the concrete situation arose; and they did so, helped by the illumination of the synderesis or light of nature. However, if one did not know the law of God, the synderesis was not enough. And an apparent moral dilemma might ensue from a malformed moral conscience. Dougherty, *Moral Dilemmas in Medieval Thought*, pp. 124–159.

[59] On the narrowing notion of perplexity among lawyers in the Renaissance, on Montaigne and Leibniz, see Stéphan Geonget, *La notion de perplexité a la Renaissance* (Genève: Roz, 2006), p. 57, and generally ch. 1.

issues in play during the period and offered solutions as to the method by which the judge could apply the law in cases of apparent impossibility due to the conflicts of laws in relation to contingent facts. One can always decide in doubts about the law by having recourse to the mind of the legislator, wrote Leibniz.[60] The tendency in the seventeenth century seems to have been to throw into the lap of the sovereign whatever puzzlements of (moral) knowledge, and trust that he or she would have greater insight into the matter. In this regard, Hobbes's *Leviathan* captures the mood of the times.

Timothy Stanton discusses how Robert Sanderson had preached against the obstinacy of one who voluntarily remains, due to 'his own error', in a situation of 'fearful perplexity'.[61] The context of that discussion of perplexity is a critique of political subjection in a situation of doubtful conscience, and it appears in the fourth sermon, preached to clerics in 1634, of a large collection of his homilies.[62] The issue under discussion was whether one should participate in what one considers to be an unjust war. Sanderson advised obedience to the Prince 'for conscience sake'. If an individual had already passed judgment in his or her own conscience against it, Sanderson wrote that that matter had become unlawful for the individual. 'Yet let him know thus much withal', added Sanderson dramatically 'that he sinneth too in disobeying the Magistrate'.[63] In agreeing that, for the sake of the Commonwealth, the prince's command took priority over individual conscience, Sanderson's conclusion supported a prevailing contemporary trend in the theory of the state and in moral theology.[64] However, for a casuist and a preacher responsible for guiding consciences, his position was remarkably emphatic.

60 Gottfredus Guilielmus Leibnüzius *Disputatio inauguralis de casibus perplexis in jure*, (Lipsiensis, JU Bacc, Georgi Hagen, Universitatis Typogr., 1666) p. 5; p. 31. That this text is the end of the evolution of perplexity in law, in Geonget, *La notion de perplexité à la Renaissance*.

61 See Stanton's discussion that takes another path in Stanton, 'Freedom of Conscience, Political Liberty and the Foundations of Liberalism', p. 140.

62 Robert Sanderson, 'The Fourth Sermon' in *XXXVI Sermons*, Isaac Walton (ed.) (London: Printed for B Tooke and others, 1689), Early English Books Online Text Creation Partnership, 2011 http://name.umdl.umich.edu/A62128.0001.001 pp. 59–78.

63 Sanderson, 'The Fourth Sermon', p. 74.

64 The matter was not original since Pope Hadrian VI, Domingo de Soto and Hugo Grotius had contributed to the discussion on doubtful conscience when going to war. One of the main concerns in Grotius's *De Iure Praedae* appears to be that of how to reduce this type of lingering doubt about the justice of the war in the subjects' conscience, that is to say, in the minds of those actually involved in fighting in a war: 'those persons who are bound by the law of a state'. On this issue, Grotius followed the lead of the Spanish scholastics, especially the Salamancan theologians Vitoria and Domingo de Soto who had refuted

For the sceptical Locke, on the other hand, moral perplexities about the practice of moral good in political action reflected ignorance about how politics work. In contradistinction to Hobbes, who stated that the will of the prince contained the will of the subjects, Locke did not deny diversity.[65] He borrowed much from Sanderson's analysis of the formation of conscience for his future project of reason, and in particular the latter's advice to an individual to the effect that conscientious action should involve '[examining] well the Principles and Grounds of his opinion'.[66] However, he evidently disagreed with Sanderson's resolute guidance of other people's consciences. In the *Two Tracts*, Locke's proposal was instead to leave conscience aside from political discourse. He blocked the appearance of moral dilemmas and boldly confronted the issue of perplexity in relation to nonconformism as a problem to be solved through a new political theory. As described earlier, he established a clear distinction of three realms in the *Two Tracts on Government*: matters indifferent that, when legislated by the magistrate became necessary; moral natural law dictated by God and nature that the magistrate only confirmed; and individual conscience about one's spiritual concerns. If these three realms were distinct, neither moral dilemma nor perplexity existed for non-Anglican Protestants. If they discovered that their individual consciences dictated something opposite to the law, as clearly happened in respect of religious ceremonies, Locke argued that they did not need to put away conscience for the sake of authority. That was not what conscience was about: conscience was a private law, and what the magistrate legislated were outward actions of the public realm, either confirming matters of natural law or indifferent ones.

the opinion of the Dutchman Adrian Florisz (tutor and regent of the Emperor Charles V), later Pope Hadrian VI. In cases where subjects suffered from moral doubt about the legitimacy of a command, Florisz had defended that the decision of the individual subject prevailed, regardless of the consequences. Narrowing down the question to soldiers, Soto rejected this ample leeway for disobedience on the ground of the danger of dissolution of the commonwealth. Hugo Grotius, *Commentary on the Law of Prize and Booty* ed. with and Introduction by Martine Julia van Ittersum (Indianapolis: Liberty Fund, 2006), p. 67; On Florisz and Soto, see Rudolf Schüssler, *Moral im Zweifel. Die scholastische Theorie des Entscheidens unter moralischer Unsicherheit* v. I (Paderborn: Mentis, 2003), pp. 132–143, especially, p. 141; on Florisz and Grotius, see also Merio Scattola, 'Law, War and Method in the Commentary on the Law of Prize by Hugo Grotius', in *Property, Piracy and Punishment: Hugo Grotius on War and Booty in De Iure Praedae – Concepts and Contexts*, Hans W. Blom (ed.) (Leiden, Boston: Brill, 2009). This information is taken almost verbatim from Garcia-Salmones, 'The Impasse of Human Rights', p. 543.

65 Skinner, 'Hobbes on Representation'; Carey, *Locke, Shaftesbury, and Hutcheson: Contesting Diversity in the Enlightenment and Beyond.*

66 Sanderson, 'The Fourth Sermon', p. 72.

This crude solution involving the delimitation of different realms did not relieve Puritans' feelings. Moreover, it proved to be historically unsatisfactory since it did not match the reality of conflict between conscience and conformism and the numerous objections made following the enactment of the Act of Uniformity. The name of the Act is in itself telling. External activity and conscientious decisions on spiritual matters touched one another as a matter of course and were sometimes in violent opposition to one another. To assert that the magistrate embodied the public reason was thus not a solution that Locke entertained for long, since uniformity or conformity of action was against one of the two principles of enhancing public order and cherishing individual conscience that seem to have founded his political ideas from the beginning. It is therefore extremely paradoxical that 'conscience', as a notion of political theory, would be the casualty of his own political writings. But the *Tracts* provided Locke with a good start in terms of thinking about perplexity in politics and looking for ways to search for a new notion of the public in a divided Commonwealth.

The discovery of the Chapel Hill manuscript in 2016 has been interpreted along the lines of Locke's commitment, earlier than it was thought, around 1667 to more toleration.[67] However, Locke's goal, as also interpreted by J. C. Walmsley and Felix Waldmann remained unchanged: 'to ensure the moral conduct of a political subject'.[68] After the *Two Tracts* the time had come to explore the next candidate to embody the public reason: natural laws.

8.2 Undoing Conscience

8.2.1 No Innate Principles

In a series of disputations on the law of nature written probably between 1662 and 1664 Locke next divided an individual's moral faculties between reason, which operated on the basis of external sensorial data; and conscience, understood in an even more restricted sense than in the *Tracts*. His clear rejection of the existence of innate principles in human nature can be seen as early as in the *Essays on the Law of Nature*. Timothy Stanton takes the view that Locke's design in denying innateness in respect of conscience was to

[67] 'Locke asks whether "religion" as legislated by the magistrate should extend "any farther then a beleife of god in general. but not of this particular worship."' Context and analysis of the manuscript and Locke's quote, in J. C. Walmsley and Felix Waldmann, 'John Locke, Toleration, and Samuel Parker's *A Discourse of Ecclesiastical Politie* (1669): A New Manuscript', *Modern Intellectual History*, (2021) 1–36, p. 16.

[68] Walmsley and Waldmann, 'John Locke, Toleration, and Samuel Parker's *A Discourse of Ecclesiastical Politie* (1669)', p. 16.

avoid, in those early works, any notion of the idea of law being based on conscience.[69] The *Essays* contain a series of disputations on natural law, which probably originate from Locke's teaching and are written in the old scholastic style. Wolfgang von Leyden discovered them among the papers contained in the Lovelace collection in the early 1940s.[70] Locke did not consider that innateness works well in reality and therefore he devised a naturalist epistemic certainty for the law of nature, which was still rudimentary, though also original. It was important for his political theory that in the *Essays on the Law of Nature* he also denied that practical moral judgment about one's interest, when the occasion arises, could be a source for the law of nature.

The novel solutions adopted in the *Essays* reflect, again, both worry and his commitment in relation to the multiplicity of consciences. That was articulated as the absence of innateness, meaning crudely that your conscience is your opinion, and his view that it is impossible to judge what is in the self-interest of someone else, or in other words, that your opinion ought to be respected after all. His theory in the *Essays on the Law of Nature* therefore extended well beyond the mere separation between civil and religious or ecclesiastical matters in politics. For in declaring that practical judgment about one's interest was illegitimate to found a public sphere Locke was identifying and disarming the very core of conscience in natural law. Natural law, he thought, must be somewhere else, not in conscience.[71] A conception of 'conscience' that, as he saw happening, leads to systematic preference for private interest was no longer politically useful.[72] Locke's

[69] 'The effect of this suggestion was to expunge from the idea of conscience any notion of law. In Locke's subsequent writings conscience featured as a mental capacity which pronounced judgment upon actions by acquitting or condemning them, but which did not itself legislate.' Stanton, 'Freedom of Conscience, Political Liberty and the Foundations of Liberalism', p. 149.

[70] There have been so far two editions of these disputations, and the title given to them has been a matter of some debate. Wolfgang von Leyden termed them *Essays*, while Robert Horwitz, Jenny Strauss Clay and Diskin Clay classified them rather in the genre of *quaestiones disputatae*. The name of *Essays* is, however, the most used by scholars. I have quoted generally from the Horwitz, Clay and Clay edition that adopt a more literal approach in the translation, which is helpful for my purposes of identifying key notions, as will become clear in this section. von Leyden, 'Introduction', John Locke, *Essays on the Law of Nature*; Horwitz, Strauss Clay, and Clay in John Locke, *Questions Concerning the Law of Nature*.

[71] In this sense, see Paul Bou-Habib on the argument that Locke was searching for a common public reason already in the *Essays on the Law of Nature*, Bou-Habib, 'Locke, Natural Law and Civil Peace: Reply to Tate'.

[72] Cfr. James Tully that sees Locke's and other contemporaries' rejection of the notion of conscience on the grounds that it was too radical or too submissive to authority, James Tully, *An Approach to Political Philosophy: Locke in Contexts* (Cambridge: Cambridge University Press, 1993), p. 180.

misgivings about moral and political theories founded on self-interest revealed his early novel focus on public interest and human necessities. In view of what he described in his early writings on the law of nature as the scarcity of goods in nature and the covetous nature of human beings, he did not regard self-interest as a viable political principle.[73]

In respect of the period between the *Essays on the Law of Nature* and the *Two Treatises of Government* Peter Laslett and John Dunn emphasized the important biographical factor of Locke moving away from Oxford and its academic life, to Exeter House and the Shaftesbury circle of politics and public life.[74] My argument in this section is that the key biographical factor that marked Locke's intellectual life in Oxford was his encounter, as early as 1658, with the fascinating influence of Robert Boyle and his constellation of scientific and theological ideas, especially the method of reasoning from nature's design, more visible in the *Essays* than in the *Two Tracts*.[75]

Against all tradition, Locke declared that the witness of conscience was no rational proof of the existence of a divine power that presided over the

73 James Tully, *A Discourse on Property: John Locke and his Adversaries* (Cambridge: Cambridge University Press 1980), p. 102.

74 Dunn, *The Political Thought of John Locke*, p. 27.

75 Peter R. Anstey gives this earlier date of Boyle and Locke meeting on the basis of entries of that year in Locke's medical notebook. Anstey, 'Boyle's Influence on Locke', p. 40; von Leyden, mentions the meeting, however, he did not mention Boyle as an influence in his learned introduction to the *Essays*. von Leyden, 'Introduction', John Locke, *Essays on the Law of Nature*, p. 11. Noting the important influence of Robert Boyle see in particular, Carey, *Locke, Shaftesbury, and Hutcheson: Contesting Diversity in the Enlightenment and Beyond* and Ben-Chaim, *Experimental Philosophy and the Birth of Empirical Science*. Samuel Pufendorf's *Elementa Jurisprudentia* (1660) whose copy Locke had in his possession, and was considered by von Leyden a clear inspiration to the disputations, appears to be a text very different in principle, tone and form. The *Elementa* is composed by juridical definitions, seemingly written for consultation of statemen, a text, indeed of civil and international law. Pufendorf acknowledged his debt to Grotius and Hobbes. Despite very broad general themes common to natural lawyers of seventeenth century, such as the discussion of the place of self-interest or the question of sociability in natural law, it suffices to note that the law of nature is for Pufendorf 'the dictate of reason', which Locke explicitly rejected: 'Less accurately, it seems to me some say it is a dictate of reason; for reason does not so much lay down and decree this law of nature as it discovers and investigates a law which is ordained by a higher power'. Locke, *Questions Concerning the Law of Nature*, p. 101. Pufendorf, however, like Locke noted that 'the state of need of human life' prompts the union with other human beings. But that is something that Hooker, had also pointed out. See Samuel von Pufendorf, *Two Books of the Elements of Universal Jurisprudence* (1660) William Abbott Oldfather trans. 1931; revised by Thomas Behme. With an Introduction by Thomas Behme (ed.) (Indianapolis: Liberty Fund, 2009), p. 206; p. 213; for the point on Hooker, see Horwitz, 'Introduction', p. 15. Hanna Dawson has studied in detail Pufendorf's and Locke's naturalism in later works in, Hanna Dawson 'The Normativity of Nature in Pufendorf and Locke', 63 *The Historical Journal* (2020), pp. 528–558.

world.[76] That was unconventional, but quite logical in the context of his overall argument. In the first disputation, 'Is there a Rule of Morals, or Law of Nature Given to Us? Yes', Locke announces what would be the very Boylean foundation of his doctrine of natural law. We cannot doubt the existence of God – the fact that 'someone presides over the world' – on the grounds of the marvellous design and 'constant course of nature'.[77] No matter how uncertain, there was 'nothing in this world' that did not acknowledge 'fixed laws which are suited to its own nature'.[78] Therefore, through reason working on physical things through the senses, human beings arrived at the knowledge of God and his works.[79] The question Locke asked next was whether human beings could be the only creature without a law and jurisdiction, something he denied:

> This law of nature can, therefore, be so described [as a law] because it is the command of the divine will, knowable by the light of nature, indicating what is and what is not consonant with a rational nature.[80]

While in the *Two Tracts* an individual's conscience tends to be regarded as a spiritual sphere and a private form of law specific to the individual, in the *Essays on the Law of Nature* the very notion of conscience is contested. The denial of innate principles of speculative thinking and practical morality constituted Locke's decisive theoretical move in the English context to undo the conception of conscience as being what naturally leads human beings towards good and against evil.[81] Differently, Locke's

[76] Locke, *Questions Concerning the Law of Nature*, p. 163.

[77] 'For he has commanded the heavens to turn in their perpetual revolution, the earth to abide in its place, the stars to shine, has fixed limits to the unruly sea itself, has prescribed for every kind of plant the manner and season of its germination and growth; and all creatures in their obedience to his will have their own proper laws governing their birth and life'. Locke, *Questions Concerning the Law of Nature*, p. 95. See John Dunn that in Locke's design of an ethic, 'the touchstone which he set up was always the relation between Creator and created', Dunn, *The Political Thought of John Locke*, p. 26, and generally.

[78] Locke, *Questions Concerning the Law of Nature*, p. 96.

[79] Colman terms this natural law, perceived through the senses, empiricist natural law, John Colman, 'Locke's Empiricist Theory of the Law of Nature' in Peter R. Anstey (ed.) *The Philosophy of John Locke: New Perspectives*, (London and New York: Routledge, 2003), pp. 106–126.

[80] Locke, *Questions Concerning the Law of Nature*, 101; The grounds of our obligation 'because He wills', and the extent of our obligation was delimited by 'the declaration of his will'.

[81] John W. Yolton noted in his classic *Locke and the Way of Ideas* that Locke was not altogether original since the seventeenth century had witnessed some critique to naïve forms of innatism, as Yolton's review of the state of the matter shows. However, when his denial of innatism appeared developed in the *Essay of Human Understanding* Locke was breaking new ground as an epistemologist and moralist. Yolton, *Locke and the Way of Ideas*, pp. 26–71.

proposal is then to study the design of God as expressed in the rational nature of a human being. Hence Locke obscured the role of conscience in grounding the morality of human nature, the traditional role of conscience as the discoverer of the law of nature, witness of God's voice and so on.

Both Aquinas and Locke regarded virtue as being the aim of moral life, and in both cases the law of nature responded to the nature of human beings, making them happy if they complied with it and miserable if they did not. However, in Aquinas's work, the theological obligation of natural law arises from the participation of human beings' reason in the eternal reason of God. In respect of this idea, Aquinas was, after all, developing Aristotle's theory of light in mind – that 'non-human element in us: mind, which is divine', as we saw in Chapter 5.[82] In Locke's *Essays*, the obligation to obey natural law arises from a debt from 'the right of creation'.[83] Unlike Aquinas, Locke argued human beings' independency from God as a metaphysical question; God and human beings occupied separated and disconnected worlds. The result of Locke's erasure of conscience, both as guidance for life and morality and as a divine element in human beings, resulted in his law of nature being startlingly naturalist and also in his remarkably naturalist epistemology. The naturalism arises since Locke's light of nature is acquired only by the force of nature (*naturae vi*) and humanity's 'sagacity' through the senses.[84] Furthermore, Locke's concern was to deal with human beings as also within the jurisdiction of the law of nature, together with the rest of the creatures. The new naturalist moral natural law is thus the core difference between Locke and Boyle, and how the former tempered the latter's utopianism.

Naturalism is therefore Locke's answer to the much quoted query from his friend Gabriel Towerson of All Souls in a letter of 1661 addressed to Locke: 'I would willingly know of you whether you think the law of nature can be evinced from the force of conscience in those men who have no other (divine) rule to square their actions by'.[85] In the disputations on the

82 Aristotle, *The Nichomachean Ethics*, Book VI; Lear, Aristotle. *The Desire to Understand*, p. 146.

83 Aquinas, *Summa theologiae* I, q. 12.2; Cornelio Fabro, *La nozione metafisica di partecipazione secondo S. Tommaso d'Aquino*, (Roma: Edivi 2005). How Aquinas's idea of participation in the divine reason was understood by English seventeenth century moralists in Horwitz discussion, Horwitz, 'Introduction' in Locke, *Questions Concerning the Law of Nature*, p. 13.

84 Locke, *Questions Concerning the Law of Nature*, p. 120. To Richard Tuck's argument that Locke's theory of obligation is very loose may be noted that rather than about a theory of obligation Locke writes about a moral theory of body. Tuck, *Natural Rights Theories*, p. 169. See also similiarities with Albert the Great in the section 5.2.2. on the importance of body.

85 Abrams, 'Introduction' in John Locke, *Two Tracts of Government*, pp. 11–15.

law of nature, Locke answers Towerson's question partially in the negative, since the light of nature derived 'from the force of nature', and not from 'the force of conscience', whereas in principle it was accessible to everyone who put in the necessary effort to do so. In Locke's teaching role at Oxford, it would have been odd to ignore the notion of conscience altogether in lectures on the law of nature. However, the few clues Locke provided indicate that in his understanding conscience had little relation to the law of nature. He added that 'we would not want this (the light of nature) to be understood as some kind of light internal to human being, implanted by nature' (*non ... a natura insita*).[86] Instead, he meant 'the kind of truth whose knowledge man can, by the right use of those faculties with which he is provided by nature, attain by himself and without the help of another'.[87]

Inscription, therefore, was not the origin of the knowledge of the law of nature, as he also forcefully, almost aggressively, argues in the third *quaestio* entitled 'Is the Law of Nature inscribed in the minds of men? It is not'. In that text, Locke concluded 'that no principles, either practical or speculative, are inscribed in the souls of men by nature'.[88] Famously this idea is the linchpin of Book I of *An Essay Concerning Human Understanding* and it is remarkable that Locke deduced much of the reasoning of this third disputation from the brutish quality of the 'barbarous and rude peoples', as well as from children.[89] Already, therefore, in the *Essays on the Law of Nature* Locke employed cultural variation to undermine innate principles by means of his biased reading of the fashionable natural history of human beings as expounded in travel literature.[90]

8.2.2 *Common Necessities and Not Interest*

In the *Essays*, the knowledge produced through the law of nature was *necessary* knowledge. The law of nature was perpetual and universal, binding

[86] Locke, *Questions Concerning the Law of Nature*, pp. 118–119.

[87] Locke, *Questions Concerning the Law of Nature*, p. 119. Later he defined 'the light of nature' as the mutual aid of 'reason and sense', p. 153.

[88] Locke, *Questions Concerning the Law of Nature*, p. 139; p. 151.

[89] Locke, *Questions Concerning the Law of Nature*, p. 144; p. 145; p. 147.

[90] The peoples in Brazil and Saldanha Bay did not acknowledge a God, as Locke noted in Locke, *Essays on the Law of Nature*, pp. 173–175. But according to the same travellers, they, the Caribbeans, the much cited Tupinamba in Brazil, and other groups that Locke incorporated to his list with the years, showed other signs of recognition of divinity, such as fear of supernatural powers or desire for a place in after life. Locke's reading was thus biased, consistently neglecting the parts in which the travellers described aspects of the customs that affirmed a Stoic understanding of human nature, see these ideas in Carey, *Locke, Shaftesbury, and Hutcheson: Contesting Diversity in the Enlightenment and Beyond*, especially ch. 3.

'throughout all ages and over the entire globe'. It 'would be necessary for human nature to change before this law could either change or be abrogated'. It 'necessarily' followed 'from the nature of a man', as it followed from 'the nature of a triangle that its three angles are equal to two right angles'. These ideas about the epistemic certainty obtained through the law of nature did not amount to moral determinism. A large element of Locke's argument resides in the contention that knowledge of natural law requires each *individual* to look for it and then choose freely whether to obey it. Locke regarded the argument as to the disadvantage that would ensue in the absence of the law of nature. There would be 'no religion, no society among men, no faith'. All human beings had the duty to investigate the law of nature, since to 'surrender' to the morals of others or be 'driven athwart [from reason] by their passions' was like closing one's eyes while crossing a road – one would not be better off if one were blind.[91]

By the law of nature, all human beings are friends among themselves and are united by common necessity.[92] Adopting a modern idiom, Wolfgang von Leyden translated *communi hominum necessitate* as 'common interests', and thereby situated Locke in the natural law tradition of interests that without a doubt the philosopher was attacking in the *Essays*.[93] The more literal 'common human necessity' rendered in the latest translation makes it easier to follow the argument.[94] Since Locke regarded the principle of 'common necessity' as grounding both positive agreements (together with interests) and the bond established by the law of nature, the accuracy of the translation is vital. As he wrote in the *Essays* the consensus of mankind could first be divided into 'positive consensus and a natural consensus'. The first happened 'when some common necessity or advantage draws men to it (*communi hominum necessitate, et commodo*)'. However, unless the argument made by some (Hobbes) prevailed that 'in the state of nature war is common', Locke took the view that 'by the law of nature all men should be friend of one another and joined together by a common necessity (*communi necessitudine conjunti*)'.[95] In this paragraph,

91 Locke, *Questions Concerning the Law of Nature*, p. 227; p. 229; p. 231; p. 233.

92 'ex lege naturae omnes homines inter se amici sint, et communi necessitudine conjunti'. Locke, *Questions Concerning the Law of Nature*, p. 174.

93 The first translator of the *Essays* noted that he had preferred to adopt modern idioms, except when the argument required otherwise, von Leyden, *Essays on the Law of Nature*, p. 91; p. 161.

94 On his choice for a literal translation see, Diskin Clay, 'Translator's Introduction' in Locke, *Questions Concerning the Law of Nature*, p. 88.

95 Locke, *Questions Concerning the Law of Nature*, p. 174.

we see Locke hesitating between the accuracy of Hobbes's description of the state of nature at war and his own proposal of a more peaceful one.

The remarkable last essay is entitled 'Does the private interest of each individual constitute the foundation of the law of nature? It does not'. Instead, the *Essays* propose the naturalist bent towards necessity in human beings that the law of nature followed. In his preference for the notion of common 'necessities' over each individual's interest as the foundation of natural law, Locke reinforced both the naturalism of his law of nature and the activity of reason as the means of discovering natural law – nothing was left to the unpredictable and uncertain interests of individuals. He accordingly declared that necessities were the main principle that united society, together with a certain natural social inclination. He did not find it important to dwell on necessities but took them as a given:

> Then, [he perceives that he is] impelled to form and preserve a union of his life with other men, not only by the needs and necessities of life (*vitae usu et necessitate*), but [he perceived also that] he is driven by a certain natural propensity to enter society and is fitted to preserve it by the gift of speech and the commerce of language.[96]

Necessities and a certain sociability were the origins of society. It was, however, not lacking in importance that in Locke's view 'necessities' had an exclusively *unifying* effect among human beings, while interests had a divisive effect – exactly the contrary may be equally plausible.[97] This can be explained by observing how 'necessities' could be predicated on each individual and on all individuals in a continuum. Instead, individuals seeking their own interest would consistently oppose the common interest and common good. At any rate, this is the way in which Locke employed the terms. On that ground, the concept of necessities offered a much better basis for theorizing on the notion of the public.

Moreover, individuals' judgments on their particular interest did not amount to a necessary judgment in naturalist terms. He reformulated the utilitarians' claim that 'each individual is free to judge by himself what would be of advantage to himself (*utile ipse*) [simply] as

[96] Locke, *Questions Concerning the Law of Nature*, p. 169. As scholars have noted already, Locke's duty of human beings to the Creator is also formidable. Human beings were subjected to Him, by 'supreme right and supreme necessity' (*summa necessitate*).

[97] See about this type of thinking of 'uniting interests', Pierre Force, *Self-Interest before Adam Smith: A Genealogy of Economic Science* (Cambridge University Press, 2007); and how it would evolve see Albert O. Hirschmann, *The Passions and the Interests. Political Arguments for Capitalism before its Triumph*, with a Foreword by Amartya Sen and an Afterword by Jeremy Adelman (Princeton University Press 2007).

the occasion arises (*pro re nata*)', inquiring whether the search for self-interest was 'not only lawful (*licitum*) for him but even necessary (*necessarium*)'. His answer to this was as follows: 'This we deny.'[98] Locke's response to Carneades and his followers is possibly his most accurate moral portrait.[99] A realistic champion of duty living in a society obsessed with private wealth, who, more generally, viewed human nature as being infected with the vice of covetousness.[100] Instead, human life was 'full of duties', and many virtues amounted simply to helping others 'at one's expense'. Heroes gained their place in the stars not by virtue of 'monies piled up and acquired from all sources', but 'by toil, dangers, by generosity'. They had not pursued 'their own private gain, but the public interest (*utilitate publicae*) and that of 'the entire humankind' (*totius humani generis*)'.[101] Locating the basis of one's duty in avarice meant making an appeal to vice, while it was impossible that the law of nature would be concerned with the interest of each and every individual *at the same time*. He insisted that 'we deny that each individual is free to judge by himself what be of advantage to himself [simply] as the occasion arises'.[102] Self-love would later be described in an *Essay Concerning Human Understanding* as having often 'a great hand' in 'unreasonableness'.[103] Interest was not the measure of the rightness of an action, but its consequence. And that was good for the economy as well, since 'as virtue increases, so does wealth (*pecunia*) itself'.[104]

More pragmatically, 'nature' produced 'a fixed abundance of things for the benefit and use of men'. The products of nature were 'deliberately distributed' in a fixed manner, and not when peoples' avarice or needs increased. Empirically one ascertained that material things are limited: desires or needs might increase, but things would not increase:

[98] Locke, *Questions Concerning the Law of Nature*, p. 239.

[99] Locke is criticizing in the last question Carneades's argument that the law of nature is founded in self-interest. Locke, *Questions Concerning the Law of Nature*, 239.

[100] English society in the seventeenth century is depicted with greed as one of the most widespread vices by C. B. MacPherson, *The Political Theory of Possessive Individualism*; also in Istvant Hont and Michael Ignatieff, 'Needs and Justice in the *Wealth of Nations*: an Introductory Essay', p. 41; as a chaotic economy were sudden and widespread demand of credit lacked clear legal rules and moral check in Muldrew, *The Economy of Obligation.*

[101] Locke, *Questions Concerning the Law of Nature*, p. 240; p. 241.

[102] 'Verum negamus id cuique licere quod ipse pro re nata judicet sibi commodum fore' (Locke/ von Leyden 1954, p. 206); Locke, *Questions Concerning the Law of Nature*, 239. See Tully, *A Discourse on Property*, p. 46–48.

[103] Locke, *An Essay Concerning Human Understanding*, II, 23, §2., p. 394.

[104] Locke, *Questions Concerning the Law of Nature*, p. 243; p. 251.

> Whenever either the desire or necessity (*aut cupido, aut necessitas*) for possessions increases among men, the limits of the world are not automatically extended. Food, clothing, adornment riches, and all other such goods of this life are placed in common. And whenever one man seizes for himself as much as he can, he takes away from another as much as he piles up for himself. Nor is it possible for anyone to grow wealthy except through someone else's loss.[105]

Years, later, in the *Two Treatises* Locke historicized the scarcity of goods as a consequence of the introduction of money. Before money was introduced, in early societies, there was plenty for all, who only took from nature what they needed. In his unpublished *Essays* concerning the law of nature, the presumption was not only that goods were restricted, but that a state of scarcity existed due to increasing needs and individuals' greed, which, importantly, ought not to be encouraged. A perpetual 'state of war' would necessarily follow from a law of nature based on self-interest.[106] It is perhaps no coincidence that where the immensely rich Boyle discovered abundance and plenty in nature, Locke the modest landowner saw measured quantities of goods proportionate to the needs of the people.[107] Given limited quantities, unlimited covetousness – which was assumed in theories concerning the basis of the law of nature in self-interest – was certain to generate extreme inequalities and shortage of necessities for many. That doctrine was in Locke's view incompatible with a 'sense of humanity' and 'concern for society':

> On this supposition, it follows, first that men are bound to something which cannot come about. For (in such a case) each individual is bound to secure and to possess the greatest possible supply of things useful to him. And so long as this is the case, it is necessary that as little as possible is left for another, since it is certain that no gain accrues to you which is not taken from another.[108]

This made it clear that if the law of nature were based on the judgment of each individual's interest it ought to be constantly violated: '[t]hat law whose violation is necessary cannot be the primary law of nature'.

Observed closely, Locke's denial that 'the standard of rightness is private interest (*utilitatem propriam*) and all duties of life are founded on it', did

105 Locke, *Questions Concerning the Law of Nature*, p. 245.

106 Locke, *Questions Concerning the Law of Nature*, p. 250.

107 Locke, *Two Treatises of Government*, II § 32–33. On Robert Boyle and the principle of abundance in nature see ch. 6; and noting that in Locke's view 'Nature' was 'not a bountiful mother' since it required much effort to sustain the human life, Harris, *The Mind of John Locke*, p. 10.

108 Locke, *Questions Concerning the Law of Nature*, p. 247.

not signify a denial of the relevance of private interest. He rejected the claim that 'the common right [jus] of men and the private interest of each individual (*utilitas cujusque privata*) are things opposed to one another'. On the contrary, 'the law of nature is the greatest defence of the private property of the individual'.[109] He also stressed on several occasions that 'nothing was so conducive to the common advantage of the individual' and nothing 'so protective of the safety and security of men's possessions, as the observance of the law of nature'.[110] Locke denied, however, that each individual had the capacity to judge what was good for another individual. If the matter were left to individual assessment, other individuals would not obtain justice and fair treatment.[111] Thus was the question of how to channel self-interest into public interest broached in the *Essays on the Law of Nature.*

In the *Two Tracts*, Locke discarded private conscience as the foundation of public order. He concluded his *Essays on the Law of Nature* by denying that private judgment about one's advantage could be the foundation of public interest. Reason was considered to be a faculty of argumentation aided by the senses, and, in principle, not bound to individual conscience. Through reason, one could discover God's design for the world and for him or her as a rational being, which was what natural law amounted to.

Writing in the 1960s, Marie-Dominique Chenu pointed to the sceptical position held by Abelard (1079–1142) and to his proposal of a morality of intentions to signal the awakening of subjective conscience: 'The human being discovers herself as a subject.' ('L'homme se découvre como sujet'),[112] Imagining human beings as a 'great microcosmos', to be 'cleared from the morality of nature' became a revolutionary tool by which to move subjective creation of moral value to the forefront, at the expense of the objective order of things.[113] Locke seemed to be willing to undo this centenary

109 Locke, *Questions Concerning the Law of Nature*, p. 237; p. 238–239.

110 Locke, *Questions Concerning the Law of Nature*, p. 238.

111 'For no one can be a fair and just assessor of what is good for another, and under the guise of self-interest, you simply deceive the person to whom you claim the freedom to do what is useful.' *Questions Concerning the Law of Nature*, p. 239.

112 M.-D. Chenu, *L'éveil de la conscience dans la civilisation médiévale*, Conférence Albert-Le-Grand, 1968, (Paris : Libraire J. Vrin, 1969), p. 15 (my translation). See also Jean Olivet, 'Abelardo', in Inos Biffi and Constante Marabelli (eds.) *Figure del pensiero medievale. La fioritura della diallettica X-XII secolo* (Milano: Jaca Book, 2005), p. 373.

113 'L'adaptation de l'examen de conscience, non seulement à la personnalité de chacun, mais aux divers états de vie et professions, représente un remarquable effort d'intériorisation, y compris dans la manière de juger les fonctions de la vie sociale, dans l'objectivité des relations humaines transformées par la société marchande nouvelle.' Chenu, *L'éveil de la conscience*, p. 45.

process of subjectivization through conscience and return to objective nature, albeit that in the process he passed through the separation of conscience and reason.

The main theoretical question ahead was that of how to outline the workings of individuals' reason in a manner capable of serving public conscience and achieving public advantage. My argument is that Locke's key notion in that process was that of 'necessities'. Chapter 10 analyses Locke's doctrine of necessities and Chapter 11 examines his ideas on money. Locke's early writings on money show that he continued to observe the issue of common necessities as crucial to achieving a sound understanding of how the state operates and that he astutely began to bridge the gap between theoretical notions of private advantage and public interest with the help of monetary scientific thinking. But before that I will expose in the next chapter the impact of Locke's studies of medicine in his biography and also the type of philosophy of necessities and needs and of utilitarian economics centred around the household characteristic of philosophers-physicians.

9

Medicine, *Oeconomy* and Needs

9.1 The *Oeconomy* of Needs

9.1.1 *Resituating Locke's Natural Law in a Philosophy of Necessities and Needs*

It is essential to observe the empiricism and necessitarianism of philosopher-physicians, however broadly, to grasp what 'needs' meant for John Locke, and this is done in the two sections that follow. When investigated in the context of the study of the human body, human needs resulted in physicalist theories, close to materialist determinism. Philosophical thinking that situated the origin of human society, and subsequently of the household or of the state, in the deficiency exemplified by human needs, arose within an existential metaphysics of necessity.[1] This is how Avicenna explained what a human being is in his commentary to Aristotle's *De anima*:

> Arising from the characteristics of human beings it is necessity itself that induces them to talk and to teach, then another necessity induces them to give and receive according to the measure of justice, and finally other necessities to arrange meetings or assemblies and discover the arts.[2]

Human needs were both empirically and conceptually grounded in that type of metaphysics. But this was before Locke. The effort to integrate this type of materialist thinking into a Christian cosmology resulted in the doctrine of necessities.

1 Whatever exists necessarily through another (that is, everything in the world) is contingent on that relation that has caused it. Only the Necessary Existent (God) is necessary in itself. See Wisnowsky, *Avicenna's Metaphysics in Context*, pp. 245–263 and Wisnowsky, 'Final and Efficient Causality in Avicenna's Cosmology and Theology'.

2 'Ex proprietatibus ergo hominis est ipsa necessitas quae eum induxit ad discendum et docendum et alia necessitas quae eum induxit ad dandum et recipiendum secundum mensuram iustitiae et deinde aliae necessitates, veluti facere conventus et adinvenire artes.' Avicenna, *Avicenna Latinus Liber de Anima seu Sextus de Naturalibus IV-V*, Liber V, c. 1, p. 73.

Ian Harris notes that in *An Essay on Toleration* the functions of government were already explicitly about 'terrestrial interests' and that the content of the magistracy was viewed to uphold natural law understood as 'self-preservation'. In the context of this strategy, Locke's aims would largely have involved placing religious and ecclesiastical defiance *outside* the authority of the magistrate – in the troubles that arose from religious dissidence in the years after the end of the Commonwealth, as partly described in the previous chapter.[3] This separation could obviously be maintained only as long as there existed a homogeneous moral culture in which indifferent matters were minimal, and indeed indifferent to truth and moral good. Otherwise, it was government that ought to become minimal. Locke argued in *An Essay on Toleration* that religion should be separated from government in respect of the interests of civil society.[4] As is well known, that text urges limitation of the role of government to 'the necessity of the state and the welfare of the people', which seems to indicate that by 1667 Locke had made up his mind with regard to governmental ambitions in the public sphere.[5] Harris argues that in order to establish a distinction between religion and magistracy, Locke had envisaged at least as early as 1667– and, as the previous chapter shows, probably earlier – a government whose exclusive business was 'the present life'.[6] Given that Locke grounds the business of public government on the concept of human necessities and the necessities of the nation, a complementary examination of Locke's employment of the material aspects and necessities of the state is called for.

I will argue next that the impetus to transform the politics of government towards the satisfaction of material necessities is deeply embedded in Locke's work. That enterprise of detaching government from classical conceptions of the good life and Machiavellian politics dovetailed with his medical studies. It is possible to observe how a wider scientific project for transforming the humanities was carried on, in which religious toleration, though instrumental, merely constituted a part of the whole. The entire project benefits from Neoplatonists interpretations of human beings to promote social sciences and direct their inquiries towards what is material in human life. My plan is therefore to remain faithful to Locke's vocabulary of 'necessity' and 'needs' across his works and distinguish that vocabulary

[3] Harris, *The Mind of John Locke*, p. 111; p. 115 and generally Chapter 4.

[4] John Locke, 'An Essay on Toleration', in Mark Goldie (ed.), *Locke Political Essays* (Cambridge: Cambridge University Press, 1997).

[5] Locke, 'An Essay on Toleration', p. 142.

[6] Harris, *The Mind of John Locke*, p. 113.

from less specific notions such as 'common interests'. As we saw in the previous chapter, he wrote in his early *Essays on the Law of Nature* that, through the law of nature, human beings were friends joined together by 'common necessity', and that positive compacts were made as well by 'common necessity and advantage'.[7] From *An Essay on Toleration* onwards, Locke began to address the issues of 'needs' and 'necessity' with a firmer hand.

The change of focus from issues of ecclesiastical politics, as discussed earlier, towards philosophical aspects of medicine, as discussed in the present chapter, also illuminates the new understandings of natural law Locke worked with in the *Two Treatises of Government* (which are examined in the last section of Chapter 12). The concept of 'needs' and 'necessities' opens up a different avenue of interpretation than Harris's in respect of several of the philosopher's standpoints on government, economics and natural law. The surprising degree to which, for the greater part of his life, Locke was involved with medicine and medical studies explains his expert knowledge about the main philosophical traditions and intellectual debates among physicians. For our purposes, an overview of some of the main principles of Galenism will show what physicalism meant for philosopher-physicians. The unique writings of (mainly) philosopher-physicians on *Oeconomy* or household management illustrate the importance of physicalist theories of 'needs' employed outside the context of Aristotelian politics or ethics in premodern economic thinking. I argue that Locke employs them instrumentally in his political and scientific project of focusing on necessities of the human being and the state. In particular, Avicenna – who was (after Aristotle) one of the greatest polymaths in vogue in the European Middle Ages and the Renaissance – wrote two texts on ethics of the household, of which only one has been published so far, in Arabic, in which he placed 'needs' at the centre of a cosmological vision of human beings. Further, in his commentary to Aristotle's *De anima,* he displayed the explicit Neoplatonism of his dualist conception of human being, with a soul whose activities were independent of the physical body. In turn, Avicenna explains human beings in society through the needs of their physical body. The fundamental distinction with Aristotle is that for Avicenna soul and body are two coexisting principles, whereas for Aristotle the soul informs the human body.[8] Therefore when Gérard

[7] Locke, *Questions Concerning the Law of Nature*, p. 174.

[8] 'oportet autem ante omnia declarare quod haec anima quae est apta recipere intelligibilia ex intellectu materiali, non est corpus nec forma existens in corpore.' Avicenna, *Avicenna Latinus Liber de Anima seu Sextus de Naturalibus IV-V*, Liber V, c. 1, p. 81.

Verbecke wrote that Avicenna had a spiritualist conception of human being, he was referring only to one part of the dualism.[9] For as we will see he also proposed a materialist or physicalist view of human beings founded in their needs. And both spiritualist and physicalist conceptions were inserted in the necessitarian metaphysics that characterizes the Arabic philosopher.[10]

9.1.2 *Studying and Practicing Medicine*

We know that after studying classic languages, logic and rhetoric, the Bible and natural philosophy couched in an Aristotelian curriculum, Locke pursued medical studies in all seriousness. This was in the late 1650s.[11] Perhaps one reason for that was that in order to remain in Oxford after obtaining his Master of Arts in June 1658, he had two choices: take orders with a view to receiving tenure or change course in his career. He chose the latter, obtaining a faculty studentship in medicine to continue his studies. Later, when he entered high politics he would write that he 'pitched upon the study of physic' due to its distance from 'public affairs'.[12] Perhaps his dislike of scholastic disputation was another reason for choosing medicine. Locke studied within the classic Galenic system that formed part of the syllabus.[13] It is worth noting that the fact that Galen was outdated in

[9] Verbecke also notes that there is in Avicenna no exposition about free will or freedom, and that the aspect of determinism prevails in that spiritualism: 'Avicenne semble avoir pris conscience beaucoup plus nettement de la dépendance de l'homme, de son insertion dans une sorte de déterminisme universel, que de son autonomie et de sa consistance personnelle. L'homme est grand par son moi spirituel, mais ce "moi" ne lui appartient pas vraiment.' Verbecke, 'Le "De Anima" d'Avicenne. Une conception spiritualiste de l'homme', p. 73.

[10] See the literature mentioned in Chapter 2.

[11] On the question of John Locke, medicine and philosophy see Kenneth Dewhurst, *John Locke (1632–1704) Physician and Philosopher. A Medical Biography. With and Edition of the Medical Notes in his Journals* (London: The Wellcome Historical Medical Library, 1963); Patrick Romanell, *John Locke and Medicine: A New Key to Locke* (New York: Prometheus Books, 1984); J. R. Milton, 'Locke, Medicine and the Mechanical Philosophy', 9 *British Journal for the History of Philosophy* (2001); Walmsley, *John Locke's Natural Philosophy (1632–1671)*; and from a different more spiritual perspective, Corneanu, *Regimens of the Mind.* Connecting medicine and economics in Locke see William Coleman, 'The Significance of John Locke's Medical Studies for His Economic Thought' 32 *History of Political Economy* (2000), pp. 711–732; and Locke and other authors, such as William Petty, Maifreda, *From Oikonomia to Political Economy.*

[12] According to Peter Laslett 'Oxford frustrated him, but he was not yet master of himself enough to make his way in the world there or outside'. Peter Laslett, 'Introduction', John Locke, *Two Treatises of Government*, p. 23.

[13] Dewhurst, *John Locke (1632–1704) Physician and Philosopher.*

important respects did not mean that he had become irrelevant in Oxford. After all, it is telling that many years later, in *An Essay Concerning Human Understanding*, Locke used Galenic language rather than that of the *moderni* Paracelsus (1493–1541) or of Jan Baptist van Helmont (1580–1644).[14] However, Locke read widely in the field and, following the renewed interest in medicine that took place at Oxford University, kept up with modern trends and new ideas.[15] The physician of his father sent to Locke a book from Santorio Santori (1561–1636), the Venetian physicist and pupil of Galileo as early as 1661. Santori seems to have been one of the first serious medical proponents of empirical trials and corpuscularianism.[16] As discussed in the previous chapters, that theory described matter as the disposition and number of corpuscles within space, with the aim of describing everything purely through recourse solely to matter and its mechanical affections. In the version favoured by Boyle, however, no bones were made about the insufficiency of matter to explain the forces and powers of corpuscles.[17] Also, *De statica medicina* was one of Santori's books that featured in Locke's library.[18] It is quite amusing, though also apparently revolutionary text of medical aphorisms proved by Santori through the use of a 'weighing chair'. As he described the instrument in his *Commentaria in Primam Fen Primi Libri Canonis Avicennae* (1625), a dining room chair was suspended from the ceiling in a hidden manner and rested above a finger's height from the floor. It amounted to a system of scales whereby one could

[14] This point is made by J. R. Milton who analyses the absence in the *Essay* of references to Helmontian ideas – from van Helmont, Dutch physician, chemist and mystic, Milton, 'Locke, Medicine and the Mechanical Philosophy', p. 240.

[15] About the foundational Galenic system established by sixteenth century medical humanism and the new ideas and currents in Oxford after the 1650s in Robert G. Franck, Jr. 'Medicine', in Nicholas Tyacke (ed.), *The History of the University of Oxford. Seventeenth-Century Oxford*, vol. IV (Oxford: Clarendon Press, 1997), p. 516; p. 535. The wider interest beyond academic context is proved by the several translations into middle English since the late fourteenth century in Faye Marie Getz, 'The *Method of Healing* in Middle English', in Kudlien Fridolf and Richard J. Durling (eds.) *Galen's Method of Healing: Proceedings of the 1982 Galen Symposium* (Leiden: Brill, 1991).

[16] See on Santori and his importance for corpuscularianism in England, Fabrizio Bigotti, 'A Previously Unknown Path to Corpuscularism in the Seventeenth Century: Santorio's Marginalia to the Commentaria in Primam Fen Primi Libri Canonis Avicennae (1625)' 64 *Ambix* (2017). That the (unsuccessful) physician of his father sent Locke a text by Santori appears in a letter to Locke of 1661, Dewhurst, *John Locke (1632–1704) Physician and Philosopher*, p. 9.

[17] On Boyle and his corpuscularianism see Clericuzio 'God and the Physical World in Boyle's Thought'.

[18] John Harrison and Peter Laslett, *The Library of John Locke* (Oxford: Oxford University Press, 1965), n. 2546.

ascertain the moment at which the amount of food ingested exceeded the counterweight, as the chair would sink at that point. In Santori's words:

> which quantity or weight of salutary food is advisable for somebody, and how high the insensible transpiration in the individual bodies should be, one weighs comfortably with the chair.[19]

Santori documented scientifically, in *De statica medicina*, the importance of the balance of ingestion and bodily discharges, in particular through insensible perspiration, which came to be known as basal metabolism: that is, the energy the body needs to perform life-sustaining activities. The ideal balance between the quantity of food that an individual ingested and the waste through perspiration resulted in a healthy individual.[20] Suggestive parallels with Locke's discussion of the balance of trade that are found in his writings on money can be detected in *De statica medicina's* main message concerning balance in the human body.[21] Balance, as we will see, was a fundamental principle among the philosopher-doctors, albeit not, arguably, in Locke's case. Moreover, the fact that his library contains over four hundred books on medicine and science puts Santori's exceptional work in perspective.[22]

Locke's interest in the work of the Vratislavian philosopher and physician Daniel Sennert (1572–1637) is clearer: Locke possessed several of his works, read them very closely[23] and made numerous entries in

[19] See for this, Santori's quote, the drawings and a picture of a replica of the chair Teresa Hollerbach 'The Weighing Chair of Sanctorius Sanctorius: A Replica' 26 *NTM Zeitschrift für Geschichte der Wissenschaften, Technik und Medizin* (2018), p. 125.

[20] Section I, Aphorism VI: 'If eight pounds of meat and drink are taken in one day, the quantity that usually goes off by insensible perspiration in that time, is five pounds.' Section III, Aphorism XIV: 'Robust persons discharge their food for the most part by perspiration. Those not so strong by urine, and the weak chiefly by an indigested chyle.' For the idea of the balance and Sanctori's quote, Garabed Eknoyan, 'Santorio Sanctorius (1551–1636) – Founding Father of Metabolic Balance Studies', 19 *American Journal of Nephrological Studies* (1999), p. 231.

[21] In his impressive history of balance Joel Kaye has recently shown the interactions of Galenism with medieval economic and political thought that took place in the thirteenth and fourteenth centuries. He tells a story of promotion of the idea of balance and self-ordering in politics, economy and nature that collapsed after the disastrous plague in Europe in mid-fourteenth century. Joel Kaye, *A History of Balance, 1250–1375: The Emergence of a New Model of Equilibrium and Its Impact on Thought* (Cambridge: Cambridge University Press, 2014).

[22] William Coleman discusses some other connections between Locke's medical studies and his economic thinking, Coleman, 'The Significance of John Locke's Medical Studies for His Economic Thought'; Harrison and Laslett, *The Library of John Locke.*

[23] Sennert studied philosophy in Wittemberg from 1593 to 1597, and medicine in Leipzig, Jena, Frankfurt am Oder and Berlin, and received his medical degree from Wittemberg in 1601, John Ruhräh, 'Daniel Sennert' 46 *American Journal of Diseases of Children* (1933).

his notebooks on Sennert's *Opera*.[24] Sennert's work combines Galenic and Paracelsian medicine, which were competing schools at the time. The former was the classic Greek tradition inherited through the Arab authors, and the latter a sixteenth-century school of chemical medicine related to Paracelsus.[25] The reason Sennert gave for the prestige that the physician-philosophers Galen (129–200 CE) and his codifier Avicenna (980–1037) possessed among seventeenth-century theoreticians of medicine was that despite their 'paganism' (*Ethnicismum*), they had, like Christians, always been occupied with 'the dignity of life'.[26] This statement sheds light on Locke's own recourse to medical writers and principles and concepts, in particular that of 'necessities'. The concept of necessities is peculiar in creating a link between the Judeo-Christian tradition as expressed in both the Old and the New Testaments – which views food and other necessities as part of God's plan and care for human beings and sees their provision to the poor as the ultimate expression of charity – and the Greek and Arabic authors discussed here.

Sennert's interests in medicine and philosophy, as well as in alchemy and chemistry – as mentioned in the first volume of *Opera* – made these

[24] In Harrison and Laslett, *The Library of John Locke*, n. 2617, the books are Danielis Sennerti, *Opera*, 2 vol. (Lugduni: 1656) and *Aphorismi ex Institutionibus medicis Sennerti*, Francofurti, 1653. The medical books that appeared more in Locke's notebooks are Sennertus *Opera*; Velschius, *Sylloge Curationum et observationum med.* (1667) and Helmont, *Ortus medicinae* (1652) in that order, Sennert being the first, with much difference. See for this, G. G. Meynell, 'John Locke's Medical Notebooks and Medical Reading' 41 *Medical History* (1997), pp. 473–486. The facts of Locke's early medical studies in Jonathan Walmsley, '"Morbus"- Locke's Early Essay on Disease', 5 *Early Science and Medicine* (2000), pp. 366–393. Doubts expressed in Walmsley's article about Locke's early allegiance to Boyle in his thinking about medicine are responded in Peter R. Anstey, 'Robert Boyle and Locke's "Morbus" Entry: A Reply to J.C. Walmsley' 7 *Early Science and Medicine* (2002), pp. 358–377. See also the helpful analysis of the influence of Sennert in Boyle in Newman, *Atoms and Alchemy*.

[25] About the battle in France between Galenic rationalism and neo-Paracelsians see Laurence Brockliss, 'Seeing and Believing: Contrasting Attitudes towards observational autonomy among French Galenists in the First Half of the Seventeenth Century', in W. F. Bynum and Roy Potter (eds.), *Medicine and the Five Senses* (Cambridge: Cambridge University Press, 1993).

[26] 'Ipse toties Galeno & Avicennae Ethinicismum obiecit: an verò ipse Christiano vitam dignam semper egerit, aut Christiano digna docuerit & scripserit, viri docti & candidi iudicent.' In his view chemists were neither philosophers nor doctors, though extremely useful. Sennerti, *Opera omnia*, tomus primus, p. 192.

two physicians, especially the Arab, inexhaustible sources of knowledge.[27] An Aristotelian, Sennert nevertheless parted ways with the Greek philosopher on the question of atomism. Antonio Clericuzio has suggested that Sennert was instrumental in propounding the new version of Christian atomism developed in the seventeenth century.[28] Sennert explained that with regard to atomism he followed the pre-Aristotelians, importantly through the writings by Julius Caesar Scaliger, and 'among the doctors, Avicenna, Fernelius and many others', in respect of the theory that 'in the compounded bodies minimal corpuscles retained their form in its integrity after mixing'.[29] In other words, in material bodies that were compounded or mixed – practically the majority of bodies – one may find the original elements, 'the atoms which are minimal corpuscles', maintaining always its integrity. Mixing entailed the rearrangement of elements rather than completely new substantial forms. The learned Sennert could barely contain his enthusiasm:

> That doctrine of the ancient that is, that the elements and simple bodies maintained their nature in its integrity after composition, is the key to nearly the entirety of natural science, and specially of its part of medicine and chemistry.[30]

[27] Sennerti, *Opera omnia*, tomus primus, p. 182. Avicenna's pharmacological work was one of the strengths of his own version of Galenism. Nancy G. Siraisi, 'Avicenna and the Teaching of Practical Medicine', in *Medicine and the Italian Universities* (Leiden, Boston, Köln: Brill, 2001) 63–78; Dewhurst, *John Locke (1632–1704) Physician and Philosopher*, p. 184; p. 205.

[28] Clericuzio mentions previous scholarship dealing with the question, but it exceeds my purposes to present it here. See Antonio Clericuzio 'Minima to Atoms: Sennert', which is ch. 1 in Clericuzio, *Elements, Principles and Corpuscles*, pp. 9–34. Avicenna seems to have still missed the question of motion, size and arrangement of the particles, in the same, p. 12.

[29] 'Et praecipuè Avicenna … statuítque, elementa in misto formas suas perfectas & integras retinere, dissecta tamen & minutim concise, ita ut eroum particulae ordine quodam compositae & connexae mutuò aliae aliis cohaerescant. Avicenna, Fernelius sequitur'. Sennerti, *Opera omnia*, tomus primus, p. 120. On Jean Fernel (1448–1558) and the question of divine powers of 'seeds', see Hiro Hirai, *Medical Humanism and Natural Philosophy: Renaissance Debates on Matter, Life and the Soul* (Leiden, Boston: Brill 2011). According to McGinnis, Avicenna's atomism has been obscured in the history of philosophy partly by some parts of his works not being translated, although Sennert evidently knew about it. Jon McGinnis, 'A Small Discovery: Avicenna's Theory of Minima Naturalia' in 53 *Journal of the History of Philosophy* (2015). Sennert also mentions Philoponus, Albertus, Aureolus and Zimara among those who accept the theory.

[30] 'Et ista antiquorum doctrina, quòd scilicet elementa & simplicia corpora suam naturam integram in compositis servent, clavis est ad totam ferè naturalem scientiam, & maximam Medicine & Chymiae partem.' Sennerti, *Opera omnia*, tomus primus, p. 120. Scaliger was the father of the philologist and historian Justus Scaliger.

The occult qualities in nature – all those elements not visible to eye or microscope – were a matter of wonder and fascination to scientists of the era. They were testimony both to how much could still be learned and, crucially, to how little was still known about nature.[31] It was 'the highest imprudence to deduce everything from what was manifest' wrote Sennert quoting the 'very penetrating Scaliger'.[32]

During the 1660s, Locke was devoted with growing intensity to medical studies at the highest level, and also to medical practice. From at least the summer of 1667 onwards he worked closely together with the London physician, Thomas Sydenham (1624–1689), who was, incidentally, an expert on epidemics. Locke accompanied him on his many visits to patients, in keeping with both the Hippocratic and Galenic traditions, in which both clinical observation and experience were of fundamental importance for physicians. Locke assisted Sydenham in the production of what would become the standard textbook of medicine over the next two centuries: *Observationes medicae* (1676).[33] Sydenham's description of an 'epidemic' constituting a 'diversity of diseases' despite the fact that symptoms and external characters 'appear to the careless observer to coincide' illuminates his and Locke's shared interest in the important theme of diversity in respect of empirical studies.[34] Among the critiques made by Renaissance lawyers in their disputes with physicians as to which was the superior science, law or

[31] In the late thirteenth century in Montpellier the physician Arnau de Vilanova expressed that ignorance in the following manner: 'disagreement among scholars has *still* not come to an end, the specific cause of this or that symptom is *still* not known; we don't know exactly what *lepra* is, or exactly what all the prognostic signs signify, and so on.' Quoted in Michael McVaugh, 'The "Experience-based Medicine" of the Thirteenth Century', in *Evidence and Interpretation: Studies on Early Science and Medicine in Honor of John E. Murdoch*, 14 *Early Science and Medicine* (2009), p. 127.

[32] Sennerti, *Opera omnia*, tomus primus, 109. For Jean Fernel the occult qualities that caused the plague were 'transnatural', see Brockliss, 'Seeing and Believing', p. 71.

[33] His collaboration with Sydenham during the period 1667–1674 was so close that apparently it cannot be firmly established to whom of them, Sydenham or Locke to attribute two essays on Locke's hand *Anatomia* (1668) and *De Arte Medica* (1669). On the relationship of Sydenham and Locke, see Peter Anstey, 'The Creation of the English Hippocrates' in 55 *Medical History* (2011). Also, Kenneth Dewhurst, 'Locke and Sydenham on the teaching of Anatomy', 2 *Medical History* (1958). It is telling that John Ruhräh, historian of medicine and pediatrics considered in the past century that Sydenham had been influenced by Bacon, Boyle and *Locke*. John Ruhräh, *Pediatrics of the Past: An Anthology* (New York: Paul B. Hoeber, 1925), pp. 321–333.

[34] Thomas Sydenham 'Medical Observations Concerning the History and the Cure of Acute Diseases' in *The Works of Thomas Sydenham* trans. from the Latin edition of Dr. Greenhill by R. G. Latham (ed.) (London : New Sydenham Society, 1868), p. 32.

medicine, they argued that medicine was an experience-based art (not a science) and empirical, and they also pointed to the (impossible) diversity of its subject matter.[35] In the seventeenth century, Sydenham embraced those facts with intelligence and made clinical medicine attractive again. Lockean scholars have argued convincingly that the experienced Sydenham liberated Locke from unrealistic and self-imposed demands to know everything about diseases, of which little could be learned with certainty without more advanced technology, or even with it.[36] Leaning more towards observation, clinical experience and common sense, without neglecting science, Sydenham was evidently a model scientist for Locke.[37]

Locke's studies and work with Boyle, with other Oxford physicians and with Sydenham show plainly that during his early formative years he kept up with the latest theoretical and practical advances in medicine.[38] Whether Locke followed Boyle, at least for some time, in his effort to make medicine more scientific, or more chemical, which is not unlikely, does not influence the fact that he was deeply knowledgeable in respect of both the classic and chemical systems.[39] Nevertheless, Locke was as usual, ambiguous and cautious on which theory to adopt, while at the same time he engaged in the practice of medicine.

[35] 'Quod fuisse principium multarum rerum experientiam colligendi, quae fuit materia medicinae, quam vocatis empericam, idem Galienus autor est.'c. xix, 1; 'Scientiam autem medicinae si negaverim esse nobis, cum hypocras ipsam, artem appellet expresse teneat Galienus et probet Averroys, nec vester denegat Avicenna, num mihi iure poteris succensere? c.X, 14; 'Procedit medicus, sed coniectura magis quam Ratione'. C. xi, 17; 'Quin etiam non ne sunt infiniti numeri, et inifinitae proportiones in rebus, quae vobis notae non sunt: quem ve si non fuerint uniformiter appropinquate, principium habeant irrestaurabilis nocumenti?' c. xvi, Coluccio Salutati, *de Nobilitate Legum, et Medicinae* (Venetiis: Pederzani, 1542).

[36] Jonathan Craig Walmsley makes an appealing case in this regard in his doctoral dissertation, Walmsley, *John Locke's Natural Philosophy (1632–1671)*; Dewhurst, *John Locke (1632–1704) Physician and Philosopher*; Romanell thought that at a certain point Locke surpassed Sydenham's scepticism, Romanell, *John Locke and Medicine*, p. 140. On Locke's view of 'the weakness of our senses' as 'the cause of our ignorance' see Milton, 'Locke, Medicine and the Mechanical Philosophy', p. 234.

[37] Famously he sided Sydenham with Boyle, Huygenius and Newton, as the 'Master-Builders' in 'advancing sciences' in 'The Epistle to the Reader' of *An Essay Concerning Human Understanding*, p. 9; and in his letter to William Molyneux of 1693, after Sydenham had passed away, quoted in Dewhurst, *John Locke (1632–1704) Physician and Philosopher*, p. 309.

[38] Arguing that Locke's medical research was original and cutting edge though he never published it, Jonathan Walmsley, 'John Locke on Respiration' 51 *Medical History* (2007).

[39] The study about how Boyle's urged to make the work of the Galenists more sophisticated in Michael Hunter, 'A Suppressed Critique of Seventeenth-Century medical Practice and Its Significance', 41 *Medical History* (1997), pp. 322–361.

However, he remained non-committal during this period, probably due to his responsibilities as a civil servant and perhaps also due to the desire to be able to devote time to gathering knowledge and writing the philosophical work he was contemplating.[40] In turn, the preparation he undertook for his main written works, in the form of the writings and drafts he produced between 1665 and 1675, strengthens the argument that his studies – which included medicine as well as political issues about governance of religious toleration – were instrumental in shaping and renewing his thinking on political and philosophical matters.[41] He continued to study medicine in France (1675–1679) and Holland (1683–1689), a country to which he fled in moments of political trouble.[42] Whether he had more secretive goals while abroad is a matter of speculation.[43] It is known, however, that while in France and Holland, Locke prayed a great deal in the churches of those countries – mostly Catholic churches in France – and undertook a consistent study of their cultures, natural resources, local businesses and money in the style displayed by the physicians and economic geographers Gerald (1604–1650) and Arnold Boate (1606–1653) in their *Irish Naturall History*.[44] He stayed in Montpellier, then the hub of Neo-Paracelsism, from January 1676 to February 1677.[45] Locke's notes in his French diary show that while in that city he spent a great deal of time in the 'Physick Garden', studying plants and herbs and producing mixtures. The following quote appears in his diary: 'Disputation at the Physick Schoole. *Much* French, *hard* Latin, *little* Logic *and little* Reason'. This would appear to indicate that he missed a more rationalist standpoint among physicians while in Montpellier.[46] The question of how Locke valued reason and logic in medicine seems not unimportant, for in 1684 while in Holland, he wrote a similar remark in

[40] His lifelong practice as a physician, sometimes with spectacular results, such as helping to prevent a natural abortion of the fourteen-year-old Lady Dorothy Ashley (1656–1698), who gave birth some months later to Anthony Ashley Cooper, the third Earl of Shaftesbury (1671–1713), or being pressed by friends and neighbours to treat them as a medical doctor, in Dewhurst, *John Locke (1632–1704) Physician and Philosopher*.

[41] See also Romanell, *John Locke and Medicine*, p. 15.

[42] This biographical facts in J. R. Milton, 'Locke's Life and Times', in Vere Chapell (ed.), *Cambridge Companion to Locke* (Cambridge: Cambridge University Press, 1994).

[43] Maurice Cranston, *John Locke. A Biography* (New York: The Macmillan Company, 1957), pp. 246–253; Philip Milton, 'John Locke and the Rye House Plot' 43 *The Historical Journal* (2000).

[44] As described by Webster, *The Great Instauration*, p. 428.

[45] Brockliss, 'Seeing and Believing'; Milton, 'Locke's Life and Times'.

[46] *Locke's Travels in France 1675–1679, as Related in his Journals, Correspondence and Other Papers*, with an Introduction by John Lough (ed.), (Cambridge: Cambridge University Press, 1953), p. 50.

his journal following from another discussion, this time at the University of Leiden: 'I suppose their studys tend most to practice for in disputeing noe one that I heard urged any argument beyond one or 2 syllogisms.'[47]

9.1.3 Galenism

The sources from which Sennert, Sydenham, William Harvey (1578–1657), Locke and many others learned were so rich that objections about the division of disciplines appear meaningless. In the case of Sennert, as noted earlier, he rejoiced at the rediscovery of ancient atomism. Roger K. French describes the discoverer of the forceful systole and pulse, Harvey, proposing 'a heart-centered Aristotelian microcosm', even though he also appreciated Galenic investigations of brain and nerves, in which the role of the brain as the controller of the body was highlighted. Harvey's Aristotelianism is also present in his philosophical description of how animals satisfy physical needs: all things in nature 'desire the Good, and the Good for the animal is to seek food and drink, cooling respiration, generations of its kind, and so on'.[48]

However, Galen (129–215 AD) – a Greek physician who tended to gladiators as well as the imperial family of Marcus Aurelius – is probably the overarching reference for physicians due to the number of his works that were at the disposal of seventeenth-century scholars and the ambition of his *œuvre*. As noted earlier, Galen was very much read in the context of medical studies during that period, not perhaps as the guiding star of the moment but as someone to criticize and overcome, who was nonetheless indispensable in the process of moving forward in the philosophy of science.

In the Renaissance, the revival of sciences had been thought to demand a return to classical antiquity, still on its way during the sixteenth and

[47] 'Journal Entry, 31.10. 1684', Dewhurst, *John Locke (1632–1704) Physician and Philosopher*, p. 261.

[48] In this passage, quoted from French, he notes that Harvey believed he was 'following Aristotle' Roger K. French, 'The Languages of William Harvey's Natural Philosophy' 49 *Journal of the History of Medicine and Allied Sciences* (1994), pp. 24–51, p. 28. On Harvey, as Aristotelian and modern, see Dagmar Provijn, 'Bloody Analogical Reasoning', in Erik Weber, Dietlinde Wouters and Joke Meheus (eds.), *Logic, Reasoning and Rationality* (Dordrecht, Heidelberg, New York, London: Springer, 2014). Galen adapted Plato's principle that the soul is divided into three powers, the rational, the spirited and the desiderative. He disagreed with Aristotle that the heart was the centre of the soul. Instead, the heart was for him the place of the spirited part, that is the one that desires victory and dominion and the liver the location of the desiderative, while reason was located in the brain and was superior to the others. See for this Galen, *On the Doctrines of Hippocrates and Plato*, trans. and commentary by Phillip de Lacy (ed.) (Berlin: Akademie Verlag, 1981) vol. 1.

seventeenth centuries.[49] Galen was both a philosopher and logician and, together with his impressive experience with the workings of the human body, it is his philosophical argumentation (and his wit) that gave his writings their enduring appeal.[50] Strictly logical in his reasoning and, as Robert J. Hankinson notes, empiricist but not an Empiricist, Galen frequently observed in his writings that knowledge is tested and starts through the experience of the senses, and that imparts certain knowledge.[51] In *Natural Faculties*, which is devoted to showing the natural sympathy and powers of the organs of the human body, he dealt in philosophical vein with the production of blood through the nutritive faculty.[52] His theory evolves in the text through the startling image of bread becoming blood. A good deal of the book is devoted to distinguishing philosophically between 'the two sects in medicine and philosophy', which might be termed vitalism or Aristotelianism and atomism, and arguing against the

49 Susan P. Mattern refers to this phenomenon. It started in the sixteenth century with the anatomist Vesalius who convinced that science would be resuscitated only by returning to its roots in Antiquity paid homage to Galen and criticize him in his work *Fabrica*. Susan P. Mattern, *Galen and the Rhetoric of Healing* (Baltimore: John Hopkins University Press, 2008), p. 13.

50 For biographical facts and about the transmission of his works, that despite several disappearances and recovery in translations from Arabic appears to have retained his main theses, see Mattern, *Galen and the Rhetoric of Healing*, pp. 1–27. On Galen as a philosopher see Jonathan Barnes, 'Galen on Logic and Therapy' in Richard Durling and Fridolf Kudlien (eds.) *Galen's Method of Healing* (Leiden: Brill, 1991); P. N. Singer, 'Galen and the Philosophers: Philosophical Engagements, Shadowy Contemporaries, Aristotelian Transformations', in P. Adamson, R. Hansberger and J. Wilberding (eds.), *Philosophical Themes in Galen* 114 *Bulletin of the Institute of Classical Studies Supplement* (2014), pp. 7–38; R. J. Hankinson, 'Galen and the Sceptics (and the Epicureans) on the Unavoidability of Distress', in Caroline Petit (ed.) *Galen's Treatise Περὶ Ἀλυπίας (De indolentia) in Context* (Leiden, Boston: Brill, 2019), pp. 155–179; P. N. Singer, 'A New Distress: Galen's Ethics in Περὶ Ἀλυπίας and Beyond', in the same; Antoine Pietrobelli, 'Arabic Περὶ Ἀλυπίας: Did al-Kindî and Râzî Read Galen?', in the same. Key works in which Galen combined medicine and philosophy are for instance, Galen, *On the Natural Faculties*. Translated by A. J. Brock. Loeb Classical Library 71 (Cambridge: Harvard University Press, 1916); Galen, *On the Doctrines of Hippocrates and Plato*; *The Diagnosis and Treatment of the Affections and Errors Peculiar to Each Person's Soul*, P. N. Singer trans, in Peter N. Singer (ed.) *Galen Psychological Writings* (Cambridge: Cambridge University Press, 2013).

51 R. J. Hankinson, 'Galen on the Limitations of Knowledge', in John Wilkins, Tim Whitmarsh and Christopher Gill (eds.), *Galen and the World of Knowledge* (Cambridge: Cambridge University Press, 2009), p. 214; Galen, *On the Natural Faculties*, Book 1, xiv, p. 87; Gassendi has been pointed as the main influence in Locke and subsequent empiricism, see David Fate Norton, 'The Myth of "British Empiricism"' 1 *History of European Ideas* (1981), pp. 331–344. But in this weak sense of empiricism Galen deserves some credit, probably via Boyle and Sydenham.

52 I have used A. J. Brock that refers to them as 'faculties' and sometimes as 'powers', Galen, *On the Natural Faculties*; Philip J. van der Eijk and P. N. Singer term them 'capacities', Philip J. van der Eijk and P. N. Singer 'Introduction' in *Galen Works on Human Nature* (Cambridge: Cambridge University Press, 2018).

latter.[53] The attribution of such a large role to 'these absurd little particles' would, in his view, annul the perspective necessary to the scientist and make distrust the method of observation adopted by those engaged in the study of the human body.[54] Instead, he argued that from the beginning nature had given an inborn faculty to each of the organs of the body – the kidneys, the liver etc. – which ensured that human beings and animals could continue living. Atomists, on the other hand, argued that there was no substance or faculty peculiar to nature or to the soul, but that they resulted from the way in which corpuscles, which suffered no change from their original form, arranged themselves. In *Natural Faculties* Galen laid out the logical consequences of atomism and applied it to other levels of the study of the human being up to the denial of innate principles:

> According to the other school [the atomists], none of these things exist in the natures [of living things], nor is there in the soul any original innate idea, whether of agreement or difference, of separation or synthesis, of justice or injustice, of the beautiful or ugly; all such things, they say, arise in us from sensation and through sensation, and animals are steered by certain images and memories.[55]

Galen is not a materialist in that work. Nature is provident in that she endows natural animal organs with capabilities. In the opinion of that great observer of the human body, this personification of nature – her artistry in crafting bodies rather than anonymous forces – was the only way to understand life.[56] After corpuscularism took hold of

[53] 'What, then, are these sects, and what are the logical consequences of their hypotheses? The one class supposes that all substance which is subject to genesis and destruction is at once continuous and susceptible of alteration. The other school assumes substance to be unchangeable, unalterable, and subdivided into fine particles, which are separated from one another by empty spaces.' Galen, *On the Natural Faculties*, Book I, xii, p. 45.

[54] 'It was, of course, a grand and impressive thing to do, to mistrust the obvious, and to pin one's faith in things which could not be seen!'. Galen, *On the Natural Faculties*, Book I, xiii, p. 63.

[55] Galen, *On the Natural Faculties*, Book I, xii, p. 47.

[56] 'For, if there were not an inborn faculty given by Nature to each one of the organs at the very beginning, then animals could not continue to live even for a few days, far less for the number of years which they actually do. For let us suppose they were under no guardianship, lacking in creative ingenuity and forethought; let us suppose they were steered only by material forces, and not by any special faculties (the one attracting what is proper to it, another rejecting what is foreign, and yet another causing alteration and adhesion of the matter destined to nourish it); if we suppose this, I am sure it would be ridiculous for us to discuss natural, or, still more, psychical, activities – or, in fact, life as a whole.' Galen, *On the Natural Faculties*, Book II, iii, p. 127. Christopher Gill notes that underlying the idea in Galen's 'high naturalism', that is of nature with a design, common also to Plato's *Timaeus*

English scientists' imagination, it was certainly a question of timing that, as we saw, Boyle would attack precisely that personifying principle of nature for preventing knowledge;[57] similarly Locke would deny in his early *Essays on the Law of Nature* the innate principles in the human soul.

The complexity of Galen's understanding of the soul is testimony to the many avenues and multiple works through which he sought to understand the interactions between the soul and the body.[58] Sorana Corneanu describes the ways in which early English empiricists benefited from an assortment of spiritual and psychological traditions as to the cultivation of the mind and its healing – a culture of 'Regimens of the Mind', as she calls it. Certain of Galen's work were among these traditions, together with the Bible, the Stoics and St. Augustine.[59] Nevertheless, Galen seems to have held a physicalist notion of soul, distinct from other more spiritual writings, in certain works of disputed chronology.[60] French moralists, the Epicurean Gassendi included, had despaired in this regard of Galen's determinism, as summarized by the remarkable title, 'The capacities of the soul depend on the mixtures of the body', which is to say that the soul's capacities depend on the balance of its humours as between hot, cold, dry and wet elements.[61] In that text, Galen's argument came down to the contention that, since sick and healthy bodily factors greatly influence the soul, food and education may shape the moral character of the child – and that the

and to Aristotle, lies the existence of a Creator, a craftman or demiurge, see Christopher Gill, *Naturalistic Psychology in Galen and Stoicism* (Oxford: Oxford University Press, 2010), pp. 64–84.

57 In his remarkable *A Free Enquiry into the Vulgarly Receiv'd Notion of Nature*, see Chapter 7.

58 Summarized as ethical, nutritional, pathological, philosophical and embryological or biological discussions, by Peter N. Singer, 'General Introduction', in *Galen Psychological Writings* (Cambridge: Cambridge University Press, 2014), pp. 1–41. See generally on this question, Gill, *Naturalistic Psychology in Galen and Stoicism.*

59 Corneanu, *Regimens of the Mind: Boyle, Locke, and the Early Modern Cultura Animi Tradition*; Corneanu refers to such texts as, Galen, *The Diagnosis and Treatment of the Affections and Errors Peculiar to Each Person's Soul.*

60 Galen, *The Capacities of the Soul Depend on the Mixtures of the Body*, in *Galen Psychological Writings.* That *The Capacities* could have been written in an early stage, rather than being a culmination of his career is argued by Peter N. Singer, 'Introduction' to *The Capacities of the Soul*; described as a late work in Gill, *Naturalistic Psychology in Galen and Stoicism*, p. 142.

61 A good balance in a body means to be in the best state with regard to its own nature, which is assessed with regard to its activities, see Galen, *Mixtures*, in P. N. Singer and Phillip J. van der Eijk (eds.), Piero Tassinari collaborator, *Galen Works on Human Nature* (Cambridge: Cambridge University Press, 2018), p. 78. It has been argued that Jansenists agreed with a

nutrition adults choose makes their souls better or worse.[62] Just as 'practices and studies' were destructive of vice and productive of virtue, so too was 'nurture', i.e. food and drink.[63] Taking the view that 'self-styled Platonists' had not understand Plato, he stated as follows:

> So, then, let those who are unhappy with the notion that nourishment has the power to make some more self-controlled, some more undisciplined, some more restrained, some more unrestrained, as well as brave, timid, kind quarrelsome and argumentative – let them now have some self-control, and come to me to learn what they should eat and drink. They will derive the greatest benefit with regard to the philosophy related to their characters; and in addition to this they will make progress in the capacities of their rational souls, too, becoming more intelligent, with regard to virtue, and having better memories. In addition to nourishment and drink, I shall also teach them about winds, mixtures of the ambient air, and even about which countries are to be chosen and which avoided.[64]

For the medical doctor with a particular interest in nutrition, the ingestion of necessities, food and drink, constituted a source of moral virtue in quite literal terms.[65] Hence the physician of the soul and the physician of the body become more than analogical terms.[66] Locke was not in complete disagreement with this approach in a long note on 'Memory' and

physicalist transmission of sin through generations, see Anthony Levi *French Moralists: The Theory of the Passions 1585–1649* (Oxford: Clarendon Press, 1964), p. 239.

[62] Galen, *The Capacities of the Soul Depend on the Mixtures of the Body*, p. 401.20.

[63] 'We at least, however, know that every foodstuff is brought down first to the stomach, where it undergoes a preliminary "working" and after this, is taken via the veins leading to that organ from the liver, and produces the humours in the body, from which are nourished all the other parts, and along with them the brain, heart and liver; and in the process of being nourished they become hotter than themselves, or colder, or wetter, being assimilated to the capacity of the dominant humours.' Galen, *The Capacities of the Soul Depend on the Mixtures of the Body*, p. 401.17; p. 404.4.

[64] Galen, *The Capacities of the Soul Depend on the Mixtures of the Body*, p. 401.3. For a comment, see Peter Singer, that terms Galen's position in this text 'informed materialism', as different to 'pure materialism' Peter N. Singer, 'Introduction' in 'The Capacities of the Soul Depend on the Mixtures of the Body', p. 340. See especially the discussion by Jaques Jouanna, 'Does Galen have a Medical Programme for Intellectuals and the Faculties of Intellect? in *Galen and the World of Knowledge*. On this type of 'technically atheist materialism' in Galenism, see Gowland, 'The Problem of Early Modern Melancholy', p. 110.

[65] See the discussion of this idea on a much abstract level in Plato, Aristotle and Plotinus, in Peter Adamson, 'Making a Virtue of Necessity: *Anangkê* in Plato and Plotinus' 8 *Ètudes platoniciennes* (2011), pp. 8–30.

[66] See his view in Galen, *On the Doctrines of Hippocrates and Plato*, p. 299.

'Madness', in which he described the moment when the ideas of memory have faded and for some unknown reason imagination takes hold of the other faculties:

> If that were once known it would be no small advance towards the easier cureing of this maladie and perhaps to that purpose it may not be amisse to observe, what diet, temper, or other circumstances they are that set the imagination agog and makes it very active and imperious.[67]

Furthermore, one of Galen's main concerns in *Capacities of the Soul* was how to explain diversity, and Galen thought that nutrition went a long way towards offering insights into it:

> But those who hold that the soul is not benefitted and harmed by the mixture of the body have no account to give of the differences among children, and have no cause to provide of any of the benefits which we derive from daily regime, nor indeed, of the distinction of character traits.[68]

Thus Galen thought that by listening to those able to 'cleanse' us – both physicians of the body and honest mentors – we would be able to diminish the principle of evil that, in disagreement with the Stoics, the Greek physician identified as residing in every human being. However, he regarded matter as not per se a principle of evil. Galen declared himself agnostic about the immortality of the soul as propounded by Plato, while expressing doubts that something which was not material could be affected by the body, as happened in respect of drugs, wine and so on. However, as he noted, his argument was 'not destructive of the fine things arising from philosophy' but rather 'for guidance and for teaching of a point within those things of which the philosophers are ignorant'.[69] All in all, it seems that in *The Capacities* Galen sought to press on a sceptic audience his idea that nutrition was crucial for both bodily and psychological health, and that he was convinced that his arguments were superior to those of the philosophers.[70]

Notwithstanding his rhetorical goal, the importance Galen attributed to the study of food and nutrition ought not to be underestimated. Galen

[67] Locke quoted in Dewhurst, *John Locke (1632–1704) Physician and Philosopher*, p. 101. It is informative to know that in this period Locke was reading *Don Quixote*, John Lough, 'Locke's Reading During his Stay in France' in s5-VIII *The Library* (1953), p. 256; don *Quixote* was also a favourite of Sydenham who once remarked that the best book to start the study of Medicine was Cervantes's master piece, see Ruhräh, *Pediatrics of the Past: an Anthology*, p. 327.

[68] Galen, *The Capacities of the Soul Depend on the Mixtures of the Body*, p. 409.

[69] Galen, *The Capacities of the Soul Depend on the Mixtures of the Body*, p. 405.4.

[70] Singer, 'Introduction' to *The Capacities of the Soul Depend on the Mixtures of the Body*, p. 342.

had a philosophical bent and an inquisitive mind, and the manner in which that framework of thought articulated his interest in human needs was through the systemic exposition of human subsistence. The organs of the human body administered the nutrients, so to say, as experts or specialized agents that acted within an association whose members were naturally disposed to act together:

> For I believe that I shall prove that the organs which have to do with the *oeconomia* (*οἰκονομίαν*) of the nutriment, as also their faculties, exist for the sake of this nutritive faculty. For since the action of this faculty is assimilation, and it is impossible for anything to be assimilated by, and to change into anything else unless they already possess a certain community and affinity in their qualities, therefore, in the first place, any animal cannot naturally derive nourishment from any kind of food, and secondly, even in the case of those from which it can do so, it cannot do this at once.[71]

As this quote shows, Galen's view was that an *economy of nutrition* exists within the human body and the food and drink needed to sustain life in the external world. An important tradition of texts called *Regimens of Health* (*Regimina sanitatis*) that would be ubiquitous in Europe from the thirteenth to the sixteenth century arose, via the Arabs, from Galen's works. It constituted studies of the things that belonged to the environment external to the human body and were necessary for its subsistence.[72] In another text devoted specifically to food, *On the Properties of Foodstuffs*, Galen refers to food as being what in all respects maintains the body of the animal being nourished in an unchanged state, that is, just as the body was when it received it. Hence, the 'precise definition of a food' is 'when there is no qualitative alteration of the body of the consumer', as distinct from medicines or drugs.[73] According to John Wilkins, Galen's decision as to which foods to include in *On the Properties of Foodstuffs* was based on 'Value' – i.e. foods that were useful (*khrêsimos*) to the human body were listed while others were excluded.[74] This

[71] Galen, *On the Natural Faculties*, Book I, ch. X, p. 33.

[72] The six things that were in them food and drink, air, motion and rest, sleeping and being awake, hunger and satisfaction, and the accidents of the souls, Wolfram Schmitt, *Medizinische Lebenskunst, Gesundheitslehre und Gesundtregimen im Mittelalter* (Berlin: Lit Verlag, 2013), pp. 1–10; p. 45.

[73] Galen, *On the Properties of Foodstuffs*, with a foreword by John Wilkins, translation by Owen Powell (ed.) (Cambridge: Cambridge University Press, 2003), Book I, p. 34.

[74] John Wilkins, 'Foreword' in Galen, *On the Properties of Foodstuffs*, ix–xxv, p. ix. This is the same sense and notion in which it was described the social utility of a citizen for the Athenian citizen body in the times of Plato and Aristotle. A citizen that payed his taxes, behaved himself, served in expeditions, obeyed orders, was useful (*khrêsimos*) to the city. A citizen that was good or useful (*khrêstos*) to Athens more generally cares for the body of the

was not a utilitarian ideological conception, but rather a notion concerning what makes a fitting contribution to the healthy maintenance of the body. As the thirteenth-century Montpellier physician Cardinalis puts it, the physician 'is more concerned with utility than with truth' (*medicus plus attendit utilitatem quam veritatem*).[75] The study of this system or economy of nutrition was therefore of the essence in medical texts and manuals and also allowed one to focus on what was useful to the human body while dealing as a matter of course with material stuff. After all, physicians discussed what was most embedded in matter for human beings – their bodies. Besides, Galen argued, by starting from the body one could reach the soul.

9.2 Physicians and *Oeconomia*

9.2.1 Towards a Politics of Household

From the late thirteenth century onwards, a number of authors who were physicians by training wrote on economic matters, extricated from the normative constraints that the Bible and the Aristotelian *Ethics* and *Politics* imposed on European theologians. *On the Man's Management of his Estate* by Bryson, an obscure Greek Neopythagorean living probably in the first century and the Pseudo-Aristotle's *Oeconomia* are usually their sources.[76]

city, its interests and harmony, above his own advantage. Kenneth James Dover discovers an almost general convergence between *khrêstos and khrêsimos* (useful) in texts depicting the good or useful citizen. Describing the difficulty of giving an hypothetical authentic meaning of *khrêstos*, he provides the following quote: 'In Hyp. iv 37 (Hypereides, *Defence of Euxenippos*) a good (*khrêstos*) citizen is described as a man who cares (*phrontizein*) for the city's interests and for the *homonoia*, "harmony," "like-midedness," of the citizens, to such an extent that he is in all circumstances prepared to subordinate his own advantage *vis-à-vis* other citizens to the advantage of the city *vis-à-vis* other cities.' Kenneth James Dover, *Greek Popular Morality in the Time of Plato and Aristotle* (Berkeley: University of California Press, 1974), p. 296. On Galen expert employment of words, see Françoise Skoda, 'Galien lexicologue', in Michel Woronoff, Simone Follet and Jacques Jouanna (eds.), *Dieux, héros et médecins grecs. Hommage à Fernand Robert* (Besançon: Institute des Sciences et Techniques de l'Antiquité, 2001).

75 Quoted in Luis Garcia Ballester, 'Arnau de Vilanova (c. 1240–1311) y la reforma de los estudios médicos en Montpellier (1309): El Hipócrates latino y la introducción del nuevo Galeno.' 2 *Acta Hispanica ad Medicinae Scientiarumque Historiam Illustrandam*, (1982), p. 104; on Cardinalis see Danielle Jacquart, *Dictionnaire biographique des médecins en France au moyen âge*, Nouvelle edition sous la direction de Guy Beaujouan (Genève: Librarire Droz, 1979).

76 *The Book of Bryson, On the Man's Management of his Estate* in Simon Swain, *Economy, Family and Society from Rome to Islam: A Critical Edition, English Translation, and Study of Bryson's Management of the Estate* (Cambridge: Cambridge University, 2013).

The former was evidently inspired by Book I of Aristotle's *Politics*, albeit that he produced a fairly independent text of it. The latter was much better known and famous scholars such as Nicholas of Oresme and Leonardo Bruni are among its translators.[77] Galen was impersonated as the author of the *Yconomia*, an epitome of Bryson's *Management*, which was translated into Latin from the Arab in 1300 by Armengaud Blaise (1264–1312). Blaise, a minor physician in Montpellier, is also remembered as the nephew of the Valencian Arnau de Vilanova (1240–1311), the renowned master of the medical faculty of Montpellier in the end of the thirteenth century. Physician, alchemist and theologian, Arnau was instrumental in the complete incorporation in universities in the West of the Galenian corpus.[78]

Texts derived from Bryson can be found in Arabic, Latin and Hebrew, and now in several other languages, published at different dates over a span of more than a thousand years. The research carried out by Martin Plessner, Giuseppe Baldassarre, Mauro Zonda and Simon Swain have illuminated the main aspects of the history and historiography of the texts.[79] The chapters on property, slaves, wives and the education of sons are the four that recur in the diverse translations. Carlo Natali describes the first

[77] See Christos P. Baloglou, 'The Tradition of Economic Thought in the Mediterranean World from the Ancient Classical times Through the Hellenistic Times Until the Byzantine Times and Arab-Islamic World', in Jürgen Georg Backhaus (ed.) *Handbook of the History of Economic Thought: Insights on the Founders of Modern Economics* (New York, Dordrecht: Springer, 2012), pp. 7–91; pp. 26–30.

[78] Arab and Hebrew were languages common in his birthplace, Valencia (Spain) in the mid-thirteenth century, as his biographers note, while he did not understand Greek. Vilanova employs already around fifty works by Galen in his writings; the new curriculum of 1309 in Montpellier benefitted from the new mass of translations. Ballester, 'Arnau de Vilanova (c. 1240–1311) y la reforma de los estudios médicos en Montpellier (1309)', p. 123; p. 128; Michael R. McVaugh, 'Armegaud Blaise as a Translator of Galen', in Edith Sylla and Michael R. McVaugh (eds.), *Texts and Contexts in Ancient and Medieval Science* (Leiden: Brill, 1997), pp. 115–133; Manfred Gerwing, 'Arnaldus de Villanova', in Henrik Lagerlund (ed.) *Encyclopedia of Medieval Philosophy* (Springer, Dordrecht, 2011) https://doi.org/10.1007/978-1-4020-9729-4_55

[79] Martin Plessner, *Der Oikonomikoc des Neupythagoreers 'Bryson' und sein Einfluss auf die islamische Wissenschaft* (Heidelberg: Carl Winters's Universitätsbuchhandlung, 1928); the Latin manuscript with the title *Yconomica Galieni*, pp. 205–214; see translation in German of Bryson's text by Plessner, *Der Oikonomikoc des Neupythagoreers 'Bryson'*, pp. 214–259. On the German-Jewish Orientalist Plessner see Amit Levy, 'A Man of Contention: Martin Plessner (1900–1973) and his Encounters with the Orient' 10 *Naharaim*, pp. 79–100; Giuseppe Baldassarre, 'Musonio Rufo e l'Economico di Brisone', in *Studi in onore di Anthos Ardizzoni*, a cura di Enrico Livrea e G. Aurelio Privitera, (Roma: Edizioni dell'Ateneo & Bizarri, 1978); Maurizio Zonta, 'Fonti Greche e Orientali dell' Economia di Bar-Hebraeus nell'opera La Crema della Scienza' 52 *Annali* (1992) Supplemento; the translation of Bryson into English by Swain, *Economy, Family and Society from Rome to Islam*. On the earlier

chapter of Bryson's *On the Man's Management of his Estate* as putting forward 'an anthropological theory of trade and money based on medical considerations'.[80] Swain has also more recently highlighted its 'commercial anthropology' in stark contrast to Aristotle's.[81] Baldassarre and Swain have shown that the issues of wives and education are not devoid of interest in themselves.[82] Baldasarre took the view that the stoic philosopher Musonio Rufo (25–95 CE) was inspired by Bryson's emphasis on the equality of husband and wife and of the importance of fostering harmony in marriage. Musonio went beyond Bryson's stress on economic partnership and dealt with the spiritual partnership of the married couple.[83]

In his in-depth study of the reception of Bryson's *On the Man's Management of his Estate*, Swain argues that it was the socio-economic background of Islamic countries that made them receptive to Bryson's ideas, at least until the decline in agricultural production that took place in the eleventh century.[84] He quotes, for instance, the ninth-century intellectual Qusṭā ibn Lūqā who affirmed that intelligent people would put their money in 'landed estates and high value properties, which produce money day after day' if one was careful to 'develop and improve' them.[85] Yassine Essid has also studied the way in which this genre evolved in Islamic countries in his *Critique of the Origins of Islamic Economic Thought*, which focuses on *Tadbīr al-Manzil* (*The Science of Household Administration*). Bryson's impact in Islamic countries represents in Essid's words 'an important moment in economic thought for Islam'.[86] In that evolution, Avicenna's *Kitâb Al-siyâsa*

translations from Greek to Arab see Uwe Vagelpohl, 'The User-Friendly Galen. Ḥunayn ibn Isḥāq and the adaptation of Greek medicine for a new audience' in Petros Bouras-Vallianatos and Sophia Xenophontos (eds.), *Greek Medical Literature and Its Readers: From Hippocrates to Islam and Byzantium* (London and New York: Routledge, 2018).

80 Natali, 'Oikonomia in Hellenistic Political Thought', p. 105.

81 Swain, *Economy, Family and Society from Rome to Islam*, p. 37.

82 Baldassarre, 'Musonio Rufo e l'Economico di Brisone'; Swain, *Economy, Family and Society from Rome to Islam*, pp. 42–44.

83 Baldassarre, 'Musonio Rufo e l'Economico di Brisone', pp. 42–45.

84 Swain, *Economy, Family and Society from Rome to Islam*, pp. 87–108; Yassine Essid, *A Critique of the Origins of Islamic Economic Thought* (Leiden, New York, Köln: Brill, 1995), p. 182. See also Islahi, who is more skeptic about the influence of Bryson but also recognizes its impact, Abdul Azim Islahi, 'The Myth of Bryson and Economic Thought in Islam' 21 *Journal of King Abdulaziz University – Islamic Economics* (2008); for more historical context see Benedikt Koehler, *Early Islam and the Birth of Capitalism* (Lanham, London: Lexington Book, 2014) and Angeliki E. Laiou 'Exchange and Trade, Seventh-Twelfth Centuries' in *The Economic History of Byzantium: From the Seventh through the Fifteenth Century* (Washington, DC: Dumbarton Oaks Studies, Trustees for Harvard University, 2002) vol. 2.

85 Swain, *Economy, Family and Society from Rome to Islam*, p. 80.

86 Essid, *A Critique of the Origins of Islamic Economic Thought*, p. 182.

('The Book of Politics') is considered to have been the first translation of Bryson's ideas into Arabic.[87] Essid notes that Islam 'both as a religion and as a political reform' emphasized 'the economic aspects of life', in particular 'trade', and did not encourage an ascetic lifestyle or advise against the acquisition of property. A moral approach to money was nevertheless required, exemplified by the obligation to help the poor and disincentivization of taking money as an end in itself.[88] These are all traits shared by the original Bryson that has come to us from its modified Arabic translation.

Some years ago, Nancy G. Siraisi highlighted that the topic of household and family appears to have been of interest to academic physicians since at least the early fourteenth century. She pointed to Blasius of Montpellier, who translated the Pseudo-Galenic *Yconomia*; to Bartolomeo da Varignana (died 1321) in Bologna, who commented on the Pseudo-Aristotle *Oeconomia*; and to Bartholomaeus de Brugis (died 1356), who wrote about *Oeconomia* in Paris.[89] Only from the early fifteenth century onwards were the *libri morales*, *Ethics*, *Politics* and the *Oeconomia* officially part of the curriculum of the University of Bologna. However, Siraisi discovered a commentary of the Pseudo-Aristotle *Economics* by the physician and master of the Faculty of Arts and Medicine in Bologna, da Varignana.

Da Varignana argued that nature provided food for all animals, but 'the natural foods' for human beings were bread, meat and wine which demanded agriculture. On the basis of the need of agriculture, he argued that private property (*possessio*) was natural for human beings.[90] Related to that was his view that Aristotle's natural *servus*, included also those working for a daily pay. Siriasi also highlights da Varignana's bold standpoint on usury, perhaps influenced by the Bolognese jurists, taking it to be self-evident that

87 Ibn Sīnā, *Kitâb Al siyâsa* (*The Book of Politics*), published with an Introduction in three parts by Louis Cheikho, 21 *Al-Mashriq* (1906), pp. 966–973; 22 *Al-Mashriq* (1906), pp. 1037–1043; 23 *Al-Mashriq* (1906), pp. 1073–1078. I am grateful to Mehdi Ghaedsharaf for his translation of the text into French and I have translated it into English.

88 Essid, *A Critique of the Origins of Islamic Economic Thought*, p. 5; p.196; and generally, pp. 179–228. Ibn Sīnā, *Kitâb Al siyâsa*.

89 The author writes that in the fifteenth century physicians would be paid extra if willing to teach the *Politics* (20 Bolognese lire) and *Economics* (5 Bolognese lire), Nancy G. Siraisi, 'The Libri morales in the Faculty of Arts and Medicine at Bologna: Bartolomeo da Varignana and the Pseudo-Aristotelian Economics', in 20 *Manuscripta* (1976), p. 110.

90 'si natura providet animalibus de nutrimento multo magis et perfectis ... sed alimentum hominis sunt [sic] panis, caro et vinum et tallia et homo naturaliter fruitur illis ad suum nutrimentum ... sic ergo possessio secundum naturam naturaliter inest homini ... agricultura immediate est homini naturalis possessio.' Bartolomeo da Varignana, Pseudo-Aristotelian *Economics*, quoted in Siraisi, 'The *Libri morales* in the Faculty of Arts and Medicine at Bologna', p. 113.

without moneylending the needy would die and cities and kingdoms would fall and, since it was accepted freely, as the borrower needed money, usurious charges were just.[91] Siraisi's short summary of da Varignana's text reveals an early combination of economic and medical ideas and evidences how by limiting the exposition to those disciplines, a physician might downplay the Aristotelian economic tradition condemning usury.[92]

The form of monetarism advanced in texts about the household by early fourteenth-century physicians such as da Varignana, is at odds with the hands-on approach of the commentary of the same Pseudo-Aristotelian *Oeconomia* by the humanist Giorgio Valla, published in Venice in 1501. In the encyclopedic *De rebus expetendis et fugiendis*, an embryonic specimen of the future genre of *natural histories*, Valla devoted around 50 pages of packed text to analysing the household through a comment on the three books of the Pseudo-Aristotelian *Oeconomia.*[93] The first book is a detailed discussion of the best foods for human beings, based on Galen's *On the Properties of Foodstuffs*. The second book describes the norms of the family and the function (*officio*) of the *pater familias*, which was, in a word, to educate his sons in virtue. In common with Avicenna's own text on management of the household, discussed in the next section, the ideal for the man was to practise a liberal profession, enter the military or undertake a public office. The wife administered the house within the walls of the building and the husband went to the market.[94] Valla repeated Cato's view as to the most important aspects of family life – to feed the family, then to feed the family well, and thirdly to dress them well. He explicitly rejected as dishonourable the idea that the *pater familias* might practise moneylending:

91 'videtur woud uxura sit iusta et licita. quia quod voluntarie fit etiam ipso patente. hoc videtur esse iustum ... maior patet ex hoc, quia violentum secundum philosophum primo politice est inustum. Ergo per oppositum violentum est iustum.' Bartolomeo da Varignana, Pseudo-Aristotelian *Economics*, quoted in Siraisi, 'The *Libri morales* in the Faculty of Arts and Medicine at Bologna', p. 115.

92 See also with a comparison with Giles of Rome, Roberto Lambertini, 'L'arte del governo della casa. Note sul commento di Bartolomeo da Varignana, agli "Oeconomica"' 17 *Medioevo* (1991).

93 Georgii Vallae Placentini, *De expetendis et fugiendis rebus opus* (Venetiis, Ac Studio Ionannis Petri Vallae, 1501). On this text and natural history, see Brian W. Ogilvie, 'Natural History, Ethics, and Physico-Theology', in Gianna Pomata and Nancy G. Siraisi (eds.), *Historia: Empiricism and Erudition in Early Modern Europe* (Cambridge: MIT Press, 2005).

94 Vallae, *De expetendis et fugiendis rebus opus*, Book II, c. cliii. Notable exceptions to this view were Musonius Rufus, and Bryson, as seen before. See on the former in Ilaria Ramelli, 'Transformations of the Household Theory Between Roman Stoicism, Middle-Platonism, and Early Christianity', 2–3 *Rivista di Filosofia Neo-Scolastica* (2008); and on the latter in Swain, *Economy, Family and Society from Rome to Islam*, p. 43; p. 85.

> In the laws the thief is condemned for double, the money-lender for cuadruple, how worse does the city regard a money-lender than a thief may be inferred in this way. Be the practice of usury far from the *pater familias*.[95]

In the third book, Valla deals with husbandry, animals and implements, even creating an annual calendar of activities to carry out on the farm. Together with Galen, his sources are classic Roman authors, such as Virgil, Cato and Varro.

Valla's classic naturalism, however, was not a typical example of Italian humanists commenting on *Oeconomy*. Anna Becker has recently shown that Leonardo Bruni (1370–1444) and many other fifteenth-and sixteenth-century Italian humanists employed the Pseudo-Aristotelian *Oeconomia*, via Aquinas's general commentary on Aristotle, to define a city whose fundamental 'essence' lay in its households. The term *oikonomia*, which had been retained by medieval translators, became in Bruni's translation of Aristotle's *Politics* 'disciplina rei familiaris'.[96] In a circular manner, since both household and city were natural to human beings, households were connected to the purpose of the city: the common good. A household was a space for providing the necessities of life, and humanists viewed the city as the household's context.[97] In turn, service to the city or the state represented the means by which to achieve ethical perfection in the Renaissance.[98] Bruni also displayed the ambivalence of the Quattrocento humanists. He dedicated the book to Cosimo de Medici (1389–1463) and included the prince in the picture of the *Oeconomia*, since wealth was one of the requisites for him to achieve greatness.[99] *Oeconomia* diverges from what Aristotle had stated in the *Politics* and *Ethics* about the distinction between natural and unnatural wealth, of which only the former was virtuous. Despite this fact, it was still generally believed at the time that Aristotle was its author.

[95] Vallae, *De expetendis et fugiendis rebus opus*, Book II, c. p. cliiii (my translation).

[96] Because 'Bruni takes the principle of avoiding transliterations generally quite seriously'. Eckart Schütrumpf, *The Earliest Translations of Aristotle's Politics and the Creation of Political Terminology* (Paderborn: Wilhelm Fink, 2014), p. 40; the importance of Bruni's translation of *Economics* is apparent, e.g., in Anthony R. D. Padgen, 'The Diffusion of Aristotle's Moral Philosophy in Spain ca. 1400–ca. 1600', 31 *Traditio* (1975).

[97] Becker, *Gendering the Renaissance Commonwealth*, pp. 13–48.

[98] Benjamin G. Kohl and Ronald G. Witt, 'Introduction' in Benjamin G. Kohl and Ronald G. Witt (eds.) with Elizabeth B. Welles, *The Earthly Republic: Italian Humanists on Government and Society* (Philadelphia: University of Pennsylvania Press, 1978), pp. 3–24.

[99] Baloglou, 'The Tradition of Economic Thought in the Mediterranean World', p. 29; James Hankins, 'The "Baron Thesis" after Forty Years and Some Recent Studies of Leonardo Bruni', 56 *Journal of the History of Ideas* (1995).

Something akin to the Pseudo-Aristotelianism of *Oeconomia* had also arrived in the England of the Reformation. Together with the authentic works of Aristotle, the Aristotelian John Case (died 1600) was teaching the *Oeconomica* in the last quarter of the sixteenth century in Oxford.[100] But in the following century, William Ames (1576–1633), the renowned Puritan theologian, discouraged lawyers from undertaking such studies of practical ethics: 'although there may be some usefulness and necessity of household economy and politics for jurisprudence, the principal usefulness and necessity is nevertheless theology's'.[101] Anna Becker has studied how this type of household economics became foundational in the European theory of the state when Jean Bodin employed it to underline that, unlike the polity as such, the household was strictly necessary for human happiness.[102] We need not follow in more detail the complex narrative that reaches its zenith in the total politicization of the household carried out by Sir Robert Filmer analysed in Chapter 1. Filmer's political patriarchalism identified the household with the *polis* and equated the economical and political societies with one another.[103]

9.2.2 *Politicization and Depoliticization of Needs*

Unlike the Pseudo-Aristotle, the other tradition of *Oeconomia*, that of Bryson, followed, among others, by Pseudo-Galen and Avicenna, was founded on the opposite principle of the depoliticization of material needs, disconnecting from the polis both the household and the means by which to satisfy such needs. The pragmatism and materialism of

[100] Charles B. Schmitt, *John Case and Aristotelianism in Renaissance England* (Kingston and Montreal: McGill-Queen's University Press, 1983), pp. 20–22; pp. 175–178; on Aristotelian thinking in England, Smith, 'The Language of "Political Science" in Early Modern Europe'. In mid-seventeenth century the scholastic curriculum of Cambridge also included '*Oeconomica*, or principles of domestic government', William T. Costello, *The Scholastic Curriculum at Early Seventeenth-Century Cambridge*, (Cambridge: Harvard University Press, 1958), pp. 38–40; the Catholic natural philosopher and diplomat Sir Kenelm Digby donated to the Bodleian Library at Oxford University in 1634 the manuscript of Bruni's Pseudo-Aristotelian *Economica*. https://medieval.bodleian.ox.ac.uk/catalog/manuscript_4248

[101] Ames quoted in Mordechai Feingold, 'The Humanities', in Nicholas Tyacke (ed.), *The History of the University of Oxford: Vol. IV Seventeenth Century Oxford* (1997), p. 308.

[102] Becker, *Gendering the Renaissance Commonwealth*, pp. 114–115.

[103] Filmer, *Patriarcha and Other Political Works*, p. 15; p. 17; p. 19. Viewing the *Oeconomia* as a sort of constitutional science in Italy during the sixteenth and seventeenth centuries that developed and sustained the political and cultural idea of the patriciate, see Daniela Frigo, *Il padre di famiglia. Governo della casa e governo civille nella traditizione dell' "economica" tra Cinque e Seicento* (Roma: Bulzoni, 1985).

philosopher-physicians thus found expression in the metaphysics of existence that the concept of 'needs' seemed to embody. It is the here and now of what the human body requires that orders the first communities of human beings, while Avicenna devised an entire cosmology on the basis of needs in a chapter of his *Metaphysics of Healing*. Bryson, Pseudo-Galen and Avicenna's treatises on household management did not acknowledge a hierarchy of soul and body or between the very existence of a human being and the matters connected with that – crucially, property. Together with the clear aim of acquisition of wealth specified in Bryson's economic anthropology, the primary focus is food. It is remarkable that he did not concentrate on the household manager's food-producing activities, but rather on food as the element that gave meaning and foundation to the enterprise of a household. The matter of food and needs as the fundamental issue uniting human beings may seem a trivial note in a minor tradition, but it appears to lead towards bigger questions. The competition for necessities, the naturalization of money, the morally unqualified aim of wealth seeking, and, ultimately, the detachment of moral philosophy from discussions of economic themes all converge in subsequent texts.

The Bryson-Avicenna tradition differed from Plato and Aristotle's discussion on needs in that in the former the householder and his household's needs and wealth are the key focus. Plato's *Republic* also begins with needs, because 'none of us is self-sufficient, but we all need many things'. Accordingly, people started 'to live together as partners and helpers'.[104] However, the tension between needs and luxury immediately follows in the text. On the one hand, Glaucon, one of the speakers in the dialogue, decried the fact that the city is concerned only with providing necessities that maintain the good health of citizens. This referred to the notorious 'city for pigs'.[105] On the other hand, Socrates singles out the luxurious city as the exclusive motive for war.[106] This tension, which is present in every

[104] Plato, 'Republic', G. M. A. Grube and C. D. C. Reeve (eds.) in *Plato: Complete Works*, with and Introduction and Notes by John M. Cooper (ed.); Associate Editor, D. S. Hutchinson (Indianapolis, Cambridge: Hackett Publishing Company, 1997), n. 369c.

[105] Plato, 'Republic', n. 372d. This connection is made in Swain, *Economy, Family, and Society from Rome to Islam*, pp. 27–108.

[106] 'Then we'll have to seize some of our neighbors' land if we're to have enough pasture and ploughland. And won't our neighbors want to seize part of ours as well, if they too have surrendered themselves to the endless acquisition of money and have overstepped the limit of their necessities? That's completely inevitable, Socrates. Then our next step will be war, Glaucon, won't it? It will. We won't say yet whether the effects of war are good or bad but only that we've now found the origins of war. It comes from those same desires that are most of all responsible for the bad things that happen to cities and the individuals in them.' Plato, 'Republic', n. 373 d.

political community, between need and wealth is omitted in the works of the authors of this medical tradition of the *Oeconomica*, which do not discuss needs in the context of the political common good. In its place, a description of the economic circle that results from the interrelation of needs is offered, together with emphasis of the need for a depoliticized arbitrator in quarrels concerning property.

Furthermore, in the first book of Aristotle's *Politics*, the fundamental association – the family – was naturally instituted 'for the satisfaction of daily recurrent need'. The marked naturalistic aspect was tempered by his statement in the very first sentence of Book I that '[o]bservation shows us, first that every city [polis] is a species of associations, and, secondly, that all associations come into being for the sake of some good'.[107] Aristotle connected the necessaries of life with his classic ideal of ethical life, the good life and the common good of the city. On the one hand, the art of acquiring property belonged to the management of the household, 'for without the necessaries, even life, as well as the good life is impossible'. On the other, also in the household, the amount of property that sufficed 'for the good life' was 'not unlimited'.[108] The state of mind of those who pursued 'mere accumulation' as the main purpose of the household was that of those concerned 'about living, rather than about living well'. There was moreover 'an unnecessary form of the art of acquisition', which was, in a word, 'exchange' – in particular commerce. On the other hand, 'the necessary form' of acquisition was concerned with 'the provision of subsistence'. Aristotle's critique of greed, tyranny and unnatural wealth, all in that packed Book I, must be framed within the ideal of a temperate life championed in *Politics*.[109]

Aristotle did not write the *Oeconomia*, but it is generally recognized that he made a far-reaching contribution to economic thinking through his theory on needs. In the impressive and complex commentary on

[107] Aristotle, *Politics*, translated by Ernest Barker; revised with and Introduction and Notes by R. F. Stalley (Oxford: Oxford University Press, 1995), 1252al; 1252b2.

[108] The difficulties into which Aristotle run with his statement that the citizens ought to have leisure for politics and not provide for their daily wants (inimical to excellence) are analysed by Soran Reader 'Aristotle on Necessities and Needs' in Soran Reader (ed.), *The Philosophy of Need* (Cambridge: Cambridge University Press, 2006); see also Christopher Rowe, 'Needs and Ethics in Ancient Philosophy', 57 *Royal Institute of Philosophy Supplement* (2005).

[109] 'What they seek appears to depend on the activity of acquisition, they are thus led to occupy themselves wholly in the making of money.' Aristotle, *Politics*, 1257b35. That discussion of public finances, monopoly and money was sophisticated and justifies its enduring impact.

justice set out in Chapters 3–5 of Book V of *The Nichomachean Ethics*, Aristotle wrote that 'needs' are the measure of the exchange of goods and are what holds the process of exchange together.[110] He also noted that 'money has become by convention a sort of representative of need'.[111] 'Exchange' was clearly used as an economic term in this context, although a few paragraphs earlier the word was used more broadly to mean communication – a more fundamental social interaction in the context of a polis.[112] Arguably, Aristotle's economic thinking on this point may be situated between the important interpretations made by Moses Finley and Joel Kaye. *Koinonia* (exchange) Finley noted, was a pregnant term in Aristotle's work, the meaning of which oscillated between 'association', in its less dense conception, and 'community' as its highest level.[113] Finley's point was that Aristotle was not carrying out an economic analysis, since in his discussion on money as an equalizer in the market, the philosopher had never lost sight of the polis as a whole. He was, so Finley thought, discussing politics. Kaye, on the other hand, has undertaken a monetarist reading of Aristotle's discussion on money and uniformly interprets Aristotle's employment of the concept of exchange in Book V

[110] 'That need holds things together as a single unit is shown by the fact that when men do not need one another, i.e. when neither needs the other or one does not need the other, they do not exchange, as we do when someone wants what one has oneself, e.g. when people permit the exportation of corn in exchange for wine.' Aristotle, *The Nichomachean Ethics*, 1133b7–9. For the importance of this reasoning on needs, see for instance Ricardo F. Crespo, *Philosophy of the Economy: An Aristotelian Approach* (Cham: Springer, 2013), pp. 17–29.

[111] 'All goods must therefore be measured by some one thing, as we said before. Now this unit is in truth need, which holds all things together (for if men did not need one another's goods at all, or did not need them equally, there would be either no exchange or not the same exchange); but money has become by convention a sort of representative of need; and this is why it has the name "money" (nomisma)—because it exists not by nature but by law (nomos).' Aristotle, *The Nichomachean Ethics*, 1333a26–29.

[112] 'But in associations for exchange this sort of justice does hold men together – reciprocity in accordance with a proportion and not on the basis of precisely equal return. For it is by proportionate requital that the city holds together. Men seek to return either evil for evil – and if they cannot do so, think their position mere slavery – or good for good – and if they cannot do so there is no exchange, but it is by exchange that they hold together. This is why they give a prominent place to the temple of the Graces – to promote the requital of services; for this is characteristic of grace – we should serve in return one who has shown grace to us, and should another time take the initiative in showing it.' Aristotle, *The Nichomachean Ethics*, 1132b30–1133a5.

[113] 'The point to my digression is to underscore the overtones of the section in the *Ethics* on exchange: *koinonia* is as integral to the analysis as the act of exchanging.' Moses I. Finley, 'Aristotle and Economic Analysis' 47 *Past and Present* (1970), p. 8.

of *Ethics* as referring to the exchange of goods and services.[114] As I understand it, Aristotle neither utilizes exchange purely as a political term nor purely as an economic term in this short text, but combines both meanings.

Differently, the redirection of the household, or of the estate, solely towards agriculture and property and away from politics and the city is a common theme in Bryson's text. The principles put forward there and in Avicenna's *Kitâb Al-siyâsa* cannot be described as individualistic, but they fundamentally deal only with private economic matters. They advise the wealthy man how to become wealthier in a dignified manner and take for granted the legitimacy of using slaves or servants for the benefit of their owners.[115] The central theoretical category in Bryson's work is to be found in the first book, which deals with 'Property', while Avicenna offered a more metaphysical explanation in that first section of *Kitâb Al-siyâ*, as we will see in the following section. However, in both cases, everything starts with the human body's need for food.

Those premises resulted in a theory of the *Oeconomia*, established on the foundation of human needs. With the intervention of a first-class philosopher and physician like Avicenna in the genre of the 'Arabic *Oeconomia*', human needs became the element that united 'the family of humans'. Avicenna had synthetized a Neoplatonism of necessary existence, as we saw in Chapter 2. In his view, human thinking starts with the empirically present, the existent. Next, reasoning in reverse, he proceeded to search for the cause for which that existent thing was necessary. Thus, almost against common sense, the fruit is necessary

[114] 'And if equality of exchange is required to ensure social communication, and equalization requires commensuration, then money, the line-instrument of commensuration, is the essential connecting element in the geometry of exchange. By binding exchangers and goods through its role as a medium or connection line, money holds the community together'. Joel Kaye, *Economy and Nature in the Fourteenth Century. Money, Market exchange, and the Emergence of Scientific Thought* (Cambridge: Cambridge University Press, 1998), p. 52.

[115] This sort of landed enterprise was not uncommon in the Mediterranean economy. 'The fact, also, that great aristocrats made their money primarily from land and from imperial donations reduced their interest in investment in trade, and thus to some (unknown) extent kept an important source of capital only partially available to merchants. This aspect must not be exaggerated, for, as we have seen, the production of large estates was commercialized. But it was an inhibiting factor to greater expansion. In sum, the volume of transactions increased, the role of the Byzantine merchant increased, the exchange economy was active, but there were also barriers and negative factors.' Angeliki E. Laiou 'Exchange and Trade, Seventh-Twelfth Centuries', p. 759.

to the tree, and not the other way around.[116] 'Human needs' also appeared in Avicenna's *Kitâb Al-siyâsa* and later in *The Metaphysics of "The Healing"* as the links in an existential chain of necessity. A common critique levelled by scholars working in this sphere is that Avicenna's intellectualism lacks a theory of moral practical reasoning.[117] This is visible in particular since there is no moral law that makes sense of human needs, beyond their empirical existence. As a consequence of the all-important role attributed to human needs in the absence of an ethical or political context, a minimalist version of a natural law of necessity results from Avicenna's philosophical elaboration. His *Metaphysics of the Healing* argues that human needs were the reason to found the society of humans and the household, and from that he extrapolates the foundation of the state. In these materialist terms, the only ruler that the state required was a prophet or sage who as an arbitrator would adjudicate in respect of conflicts about property and other transactions.

In the texts discussed in this and the next section, the reasoning on *Oeconomy* starts with an individual-based theory of needs, which develops into a domestic and naturalistic outlook on food and other necessaries of life, and also notes the competition assumed to occur with other human beings who are 'partners in necessity'. *The Nasirean Ethics*, written in Persia around 1235 by Avicenna's commentator Naṣīr al Dīn al Ṭūsī, explodes the limits of the genre with two new and independent books on ethics and politics. However, it also establishes the second discourse on 'Economics' on the basis of similar ideas about the needs of human

[116] Robert Wisnovsky writes that 'Avicenna applied the distinction between essence and existence to the relationship between final and efficient causes as a way to pre-empt the circularity that loomed behind the Neoplatonists' scheme of procession and reversion … [and] was led to invent a new metaphysical basis for his philosophy' in the process. Wisnowsky, 'Final and Efficient Causality in Avicenna's Cosmology and Theology', p. 101.

[117] Critiquing that Avicenna wrote so little on ethics, Majid Fakhry, *Ethical Theories in Islam* (Leiden: Brill, 1994), pp. 85–88; among authors of the Middle Ages, Abd al-Latif equally criticized him on that point, Cecilia Martini Bonadeo, *Abd al-Latif al-Baghdadi's Philosophical Journey: From Aristotle's Metaphysics to the 'Metaphysical Science'* (Leiden: Brill, 2014), p. 180. Avicenna received a Neoplatonised Aristotle which as explained by Robert Adamson produced in some of the authors an intellectualism to the effect that 'it would seem that the "practical" part of philosophy involves only the actions themselves, and not grasping the ethical principles which are put into practice.' Peter Adamson, 'The Arabic Tradition' in John Skorupski (ed.), *The Routledge Companion to Ethics* (London and New York: Routledge, 2010), pp. 63–75; p. 65.

nature.[118] The first two paragraphs summarizing Avicenna's ideas on the issue are worth quoting:

> Whereas mankind needs food for the preservation of the individual; and the food of the human species cannot be procured without the organization of techniques, such as sowing, harvesting, cleaning, pounding, kneading and cooking; and the arrangement of such processes cannot conceivably be effected save by the collaboration of helpers, and the application of tools and utensils, and the consumption therein of long periods of time; (this being contrary to the case of the food of other animals, which is prepared naturally, so that their urge is limited to the search for fodder and water, in accordance with the demand of nature; and when they have stilled the access of hunger and thirst, they refrain from further motion), and since the restriction of mankind to the amount of their day-by-day need would inevitably bring about the exhaustion of supplies and a dislocation of their mode of life, it being impossible to contrive in one day the quantity of food which forms the daily ration:
>
> This being so, the need has befallen to store the necessaries of life and to keep them safe from the rest of one's fellows, who are partners in necessity; but safeguarding cannot be effected without location, in which food and sustenance will not spoil, and which – at the times of sleep and waking, by day and night – will restrain therefrom the hand both of the unjust and the predator.[119]

The survival of mankind and the individual, and thus needs are the theoretical framework for the organization of life. The severance of the discipline of economics from politics and ethics is thus made through focusing on human needs.

Bryson's *On the Man's Management of his Estate* has a convoluted history. The Greek original is only preserved in a few fragments, while the earliest complete text is in Arabic. The translation into Arabic is thought to be from around 900 AD.[120] Interpolations of Galen's *Natural Faculties* or a closely related work appear to explain the medical tone of its introduction. Its chapter on 'Property' starts by noting how God placed in man the faculties he needs for the sustenance of his body and his well-being.[121] There

[118] Naṣīr al-Dīn al Ṭūsī, *The Nasirean Ethics*, translated by G. M.Wickens, (London: George Allen & Unwin Ltd., 1964); according to Yoyo Hambali *The Nasirean Ethics* 'set the pattern for subsequent works on practical philosophy in the Islamic tradition.' Yoyo Hambali, 5 *Turats* (2009), pp. 53–66, p. 53.

[119] al Ṭūsī, *The Nasirean Ethics*, 153.

[120] About the fragments in Greek sources Friedrich Wilhelm, 'Die Oeconomica der Neupythagoreer Bryson, Kallikratidas, Periktione, Phintys' 70 *Rheinisches Museum für Philologie* (1915); Swain, *Economy, Family and Society from Rome to Islam*, p. 38.

[121] 'At the same time He made him wanting, mutable, and ceasing; and because of this man stood in need of replacing and restoring what was dissolved from him. (3) I mean by the term "faculties" (i) the faculty which each one of his body parts uses to derive from food what is similar to it, in the quantity in which it needs it; (ii) the faculty which changes and

'is a need of many other different crafts' to procure all that human beings and animals require for subsistence. Thus plants 'need' cultivation, animals 'need' feeding' and other activities. However, despite their potential to know the crafts, human life is so short that it is impossible for a single individual to have mastery of all crafts. However, 'for the management of his life a man needs all the crafts.' Moreover, a similar connection exists between the crafts: 'each one of the crafts ... needs another'. The text continues:

> and (since) it was impossible for one man to be expert in all of them, all people needed one another for managing their lives, and for this reason people needed to form cities and live together in them to help each other with the crafts.[122]

Although everyone needed one another, their particular needs were not exactly the same, and the value of the things they needed also differed.[123] Disagreements would arise for this reason and barter would not be enough to solve the problems caused by disparities in need. The market would not work properly if a certain product's availability varied 'owing to greater or lesser availability on the market, the level of people's need of it, or their lack of need of it, or of excessive amounts of it at different periods, and people's use of each product at any time'. Accordingly, it was suggested that barter was not enough for the proper functioning of the market. What was said about products also held true for the crafts themselves. It was at this point that money appeared, in the form of coins made from gold, silver and copper that were instrumental in allowing prices to be set for all items:

> Whoever has possession of these substances (gold, silver and copper) we have named becomes, as it were, one who has possession of all the products he needs.[124]

converts the foodstuff so that it becomes similar to the body part that is to be nourished by it: thus if what is to be nourished by it is flesh, it becomes flesh, if it is bone, it becomes bone, and if it is nerve, it becomes nerve; (4) (iii) the faculty which retains in the body part what has been attracted to (the body part) while it remains fluid and until it becomes solid and is joined to (the body part); '... of this he needs to replace what is dissolved from him by movement, and the replacement is the foodstuff which nourishes him.' 'The Book of Bryson, On the Man's Management of his Estate' in Swain, *Economy, Family, and Society from Rome to Islam: A Critical Edition*, p. 5.

122 'The Book of Bryson, On the Man's Management of his Estate' in Swain, *Economy, Family, and Society from Rome to Islam: A Critical Edition*, p. 6

123 See also Aristotle on this point about exchange on occasion of needs and money as a representation of need above.

124 Bryson, 'On the Man's Management of his Estate' in Swain, *Economy, Family, and Society from Rome to Islam: A Critical Edition*, p. 7.

Life was made 'good' through the possession of wealth, and thus Bryson set out 'to explain the best way to manage it, through (the acquisition and preservation of) property, and its expenditure'. He briefly noted that it was not worthwhile being unfair in business because trade was mostly about reputation, and recommended as the best rule that everyone stay in the craft of his or her ancestors, since all crafts were needed and it would produce chaos if everyone tried to change their place in society. With reference to the preservation of property, he counselled balancing expenditure and acquisition and seeking to procure a surplus of possessions for accidents that suddenly diminish property could happen at any time. The optimal would be of course the condition of the manager of an estate who acquires more than is expended. Bryson also advised against uncertain capital investments and, in general, any sort of difficult undertaking, since profit and even capital might be lost in the venture. He likens one who buys land despite lacking time to develop it to 'a greedy man who eats something he cannot digest' and characterizes such a person as a bad manager.

Bryson continues: '[t]he fourth consideration required for the preservation of wealth is that the man should not invest his money in anything that is slow to leave his hands'. Gems and that sort of thing would be most inconvenient in this regard. The fifth consideration was to be quick in parting with merchandise but slow to sell real estate. In this case, although the promise of higher profit would be tempting, wealth would be better secured in a long run through real estate.[125] With regard to the expenditure of wealth Bryson names a number of vices that one ought to avoid, which, in summary, amount to not being able to judge, understand and attend *what are the real needs* at a given time and in a given place – an economic science of needs is what this seems to suggest. Bryson also declared that 'the sordid man' was odious and that a good manager was not mercenary, since he spent little on himself but gave surplus money generously to family, friends and the poor, while keeping something aside as a safeguard against the vicissitudes of fate.

In sum, Bryson's is a useful treatise for entrepreneurs who own real estate. It combines strict economic reasoning with a sense of the virtues expected of a good landowner and of the knowledge about practical needs. Its most striking feature is that it is conceived only for private citizens and their fortunes, with neither political context, city or state, nor a higher political ruler that governs the state.

[125] See Swain 'Introduction' in *Economy, Family, and Society from Rome to Islam: A Critical Edition.*

9.2.3 *Avicenna's* Kitâb Al-siyâsa (Politics), *the* Metaphysics of "The Healing" *and the Pragmatic Politicization of Needs*

Interest in Avicenna's philosophical works was less intense in the Renaissance than in the two previous centuries, which, in the judgment of Dag Nikolaus Hasse, is evidenced by the small number of new printings that occurred. However, the situation was different with his medical works. His *Canon Medicinae* was the most translated Arabic book during the Renaissance, and the standard textbook in the universities of many countries well into the eighteenth century.[126] Avicenna was an extraordinary systematizer of Galen's work and also included original theories of his own. While he was a very prolific philosopher, as mentioned earlier, he wrote virtually nothing on ethics in his encyclopaedic works and only very short and focused treatises on sin and the science of ethics. Albert the Great notes in *De Bono* how Avicenna in his commentary in *De anima* considers that all moral customs are about opinion and non-necessary, and therefore that the Arabic philosopher did not put forward a natural law theory.[127] In fact, Avicenna briefly presents a utilitarian way of understanding morality in his *De anima*:

> It is for the utility of society that of all actions that a human being usually does, there are some of them that are not licit.[128]

These that are not licit one should teach to children to avoid them, in a different way for a boy and a girl, and they would 'quasi naturally' understand when this is taught to them.[129]

[126] Also a list of the printed Latin editions of Arabic physicians and other scientists before 1700, in Dag Nikolaus, Hasse, *Success and Suppression. Arabic Sciences and Philosophy in the Renaissance* (Cambridge Massachusetts, London: Harvard University Press, 2016), p. 8; p. 19; p. 357. Averroës (1126–1198) was not only expositor of the works of Aristotle but also chief *Qāḍī* or judge in Córdoba and court physician to the Spanish Caliph. Among many others, McGinnis also mentions Abū Bakr Muḥammad ar-Rāzī (born 864) who wrote, *Doubts about Galen*, Jon McGinnis 'Natural Knowledge in the Arabic Middle Ages' in Peter Harrison, Ronald L. Numbers and Michael H. Shank (eds.), *Wrestling with Nature: From Omens to Science* (Chicago: University of Chicago Press, 2011); see also McGinnis on some philosophical attempts to combining Galen and Islam, while always maintaining a certain theological perspective, visible, if nowhere else, in key concepts employed in the translation of Aristotle, p. 63.

[127] Alberti Magni, *De bono*, n. 499.

[128] 'Et propter utilitatem societatis est ei proprium ut, ex omnibus actionibus quas solet agere, sint quaedam actiones quas no licet agere', Avicenna, *Avicenna Latinus Liber de Anima seu Sextus de Naturalibus IV-V*, Liber V, c.1, p. 74.

[129] 'quod docetur dum est puer et coalescit in eo, et a pueritia consuescit audire quod has actiones non licet agere, ita quod conception horum fit ei quasi naturalis.' Avicenna, *Avicenna Latinus Liber de Anima seu Sextus de Naturalibus IV-V*, Liber V, c.1, p. 74.

Louis Cheikho, the editor of *Kitâb Al-siyâsa* at the beginning of the twentieth century, thought that *Al-siyâsa* was one of these treatises on moral custom, despite its name (*The Book on Politics*), and that it was the book mentioned in passing by the historian of medicine Ibn Abī Uṣaybiʿa.[130] *Kitâb Al-siyâsa* is regarded by other scholars as Avicenna's *Politics*, since it starts with an introduction explaining why politics are needed, which, as we will see, boils down to the fact that 'any human from king to vasal needs to eat, for this is the way that their life is sustained'.[131] But Avicenna seemed to understand politics also as 'moral management', which is made clear in one passage dealing with the 'politics of the soul': one carries out politics starting with management of oneself.[132]

Kitâb Al-siyâsa starts in the style of a theological text praising Allah for the graces and benefits given to all creation and especially to human beings. Avicenna then seeks to undergird theoretically the argument put forward by Bryson and others as to a net of needs that put humanity in motion.[133] God, Avicenna wrote, had created human beings as the best, most complete and balanced creatures, endowing them with the possibility to tell the difference between just and unjust. God had also differentiated between Creator and creature, landlord and tenant, government and the governed. Through these differences, human reason had a means by which to acknowledge the existence of God. 'Difference' therefore amounted to a method of reasoning that he continued to employ in the section entitled 'The Difference Among People in Terms of Characters and Level', in which he explained that God had given his graces differentiating

[130] Quoted narrating the following story: 'Another of my neighbors was a man named Abū Bakr al-Barqī, who was born in Khwārizm. He was a renowned jurist, devoting himself entirely to jurisprudence, Qur'anic exegesis and ascetic practices. But he felt an inclination for the sciences and asked me to write commentaries on certain books for him. I wrote for him "al-Hāsil wal-Mahsūl," comprising nearly twenty volumes, and also – in the field of ethics – a book entitled "Virtue and Sin." These two books are to be found only with him for he never lent them to anyone for copying.' Ibn Abi Usaibia, *History of Physicians* (1971) www.tertullian.org/fathers/ibn_abi_usaibia_01.htm.

[131] Ibn Sīnā, *Kitâb Al-siyâsa.* A later version of this edition is listed among Avicenna's minor works in Jules L. Janssens, *An Annotated Bibliography on Ibn Sīnā, (1970–1989): Including Arabic and Persian Publications and Russian Refences* (Leuven: Leuven University Press, 1991), p. 72

[132] 'when a man's politics towards his souls is at its best, there is no need for someone else to impose his policy on him and to follow and implement another's policy.' Ibn Sīnā, *Kitâb Al-siyâsa*, p. 972. He uses politics in another sense when recommending the debates among children in the education of the son. 'Then they sometimes are friends and sometimes they argue. And by forgiving themselves, they will improve themselves. This is the best preparation for politics.' Ibn Sīnā, *Kitâb Al-siyâsa*, p. 1076.

[133] Ibn Sīnā, *Kitâb Al-siyâsa.*

individuals in terms of reason and opinion, possessions, household and so on. If everyone were equal and at the same level, he argued, corruption and annihilation would ensue, and 'this is why there is competition and jealousy and what appears to be cruelty and wickedness'.[134] However, the sages knew that if everyone were king, humanity would be annihilated. If everyone were rich, no one would be willing to help others with kindness, and in the opposite situation, if everyone were poor, all would starve:

> and there is differentiation in their substances, and the existence of this differentiation in their situations considers the reason for their continuation and the cause of their satisfactions.[135]

Difference also meant satisfaction of different needs. By 'difference' Avicenna referred literally to diversity. In the *Metaphysics of the Healing* it is evident that utilization of 'difference' is one of Avicenna's favoured means of logical reasoning – a means of mapping physical reality in his mental world.[136] In *Kitâb Al-siyâsa* difference was the reason for continued survival of creatures, also within human society.

There was also *need*, which functioned as a reversal of the process of differentiation and connected what had been differentiated. In *Kitâb Al-siyâsa* needs made everyone equal. Both the king and the vassal equally needed to eat in order to survive and preserve their personality.[137] Avicenna describes how a human being differs from the other animals, who were passive when satiated. A human being prepares food in order to eat it and save what is left after the meal, and thus 'needs' a place to preserve that stored food and helpers to guard it. And the only one who would help him collaboratively in that enterprise would be a wife. That was the origin of the family. With the coming of children, 'there would be many more in need of a meal', and he would 'need' companions and servants to help with these tasks. They would look up to him from the standpoint of vassals or members of a crowd:

> In this case, be either king or vassal, or owner or crowd, or ruler or ruled, or master or servant, all they are equal in that each one in the universe needs the meal that keep his spirit and cause his body to survive. And he needs a

[134] Ibn Sīnā, *Kitâb Al-siyâsa.*

[135] Ibn Sīnā, *Kitâb Al-siyâsa.*

[136] Avicenna, *The Metaphysics of 'The Healing'*, p. 21; p. 25; p. 29; p. 34; p. 81; Finianos, *De l'existence à la Nécessarie Existence chez Avicenne*; Jon McGinnis, 'Logic and Science: The Role of Genus and Difference in Avicenna's Logic, Science and Natural Philosophy, 18 *Documenti e studi sulla tradizione filosofica medievale* (2007).

[137] Ibn Sīnā, *Kitâb Al-siyâsa*, p. 970.

> guardian to safeguard himself and where he lives, where he rests from his efforts and he needs a wife in order to take care of his house for him and she guards his property and he needs the child that does the work when he is old and gives him a helping hand when he is old, and continues his generation, and enlivens his reputation when he is old; and he needs servants that carry the heavy weights and when they meet there is an owner and possessor, and a vasal and possessed.[138]

Situating this interconnected necessity of the human family in the context of the management of the estate by the male owner entails everyone on the estate working together to meet the needs of everyone, albeit that the proprietor is responsible for the subsistence of all whom he is charged with protecting. This requires that the owner be an honest and just man. Avicenna provides an ethical discussion of the means for healing of the soul of the estate owner, in the style of Galen's counselling by a good honest friend: self-examination and self-punishment for breaking bad habits or indulging in vices and corruption.[139]

Unlike Bryson, Avicenna's section on how to obtain one's wealth turns to Aristotle. There were two groups of people, he explained. The first group constituted those that could subsist due to inherited wealth or thanks to the people around them. God inspired the second group that needed nourishment to get it through commerce and industry. Avicenna commended industry as more durable than commerce, since property was perishable and inconstant. He divided industry into men of state, scholars and men of war or soldiers. Moreover, in the section on servants (not slaves), Avicenna noted that although they might occasionally be punished, and the authority of the owner of the estate must be clear, there was a need for optimal conditions of labour. He argued, for instance, against constant change in tasks that does not allow the person to work well, and ultimately to be human. 'Therefore, this work is considered a moral virtue for the servant, which cannot be forsaken, and it is like the essence and nature of a person who is not separate from man'. The servant ought not to be afraid that he or she will be dismissed. Hence, the master ought to give the servants to understand that their position in the estate is secure and stable. 'This is a great sense of humanity, of grandeur and dignity.'[140]

Avicenna develops further the political aspect of the issue of human needs in Book Ten, Chapter 2 of *The Metaphysics of 'The Healing'*,

[138] Ibn Sīnā, *Kitâb Al-siyâsa*, p. 970.
[139] Ibn Sīnā, *Kitâb Al-siyâsa*.
[140] Ibn Sīnā, *Kitâb Al-siyâsa*.

following the tradition of texts centred on needs described so far, but now delineated as a building block of society.[141] In short, Avicenna argued that the difficulties existing in a society that was united through the materialist principles of human needs must be supervised by a type of prophet-legislator – an arbitrator of sorts. Despite his divine calling the prophet-legislator would not attempt to interfere in civil society beyond resolving disputes over 'yours and mine'. Neoplatonic dualism – the strict demarcation between the materialist origins and functioning of society and its spiritual aspect – is the most conspicuous principle in the chapter:

> We now say: It is known that the human differs from the rest of the other animals in that he does not lead a proper life if isolated as a single individual, undertaking the management of his affairs with no associate to help him satisfy his basic needs.[142]

Avicenna held that the needs of each human being must be complemented by the undertakings of another of his or her own species. He described this by reference to the same traditional chain of diverse crafts connecting supply and needs. One would sew, another would make the sewing needle, yet another would provide vegetables, while a further person would 'bake for him'. Neither the benevolence nor the interest of the baker, as stated famously by Adam Smith, but their mutual 'needs' would motivate him to bake for his fellow human being according to Avicenna. It seems that Smith would add to the materialist 'needs' of Avicenna generating society, the marginal profit produced through entrepreneurship.[143] It was evident then, Avicenna concluded, that 'man's existence and survival' required partnership:[144] 'Partnership is only achieved through reciprocal transactions just as this is inescapably needed in the various trade practices that belong to [man].'[145] Reciprocal transaction involved law and justice, which must have 'a lawgiver and a dispenser of justice'. The lawgiver must be someone who would not 'leave people to their private opinions' with regard to what was lawful. The survival of humanity depends on the

141 Avicenna, *The Metaphysics of 'The Healing'*.

142 Avicenna, *The Metaphysics of 'The Healing'*, Book 10, ch. 2, 1; also Avicenna, *Avicenna Latinus Liber de Anima seu Sextus de Naturalibus IV-V, Liber V, c.1*, p. 73.

143 'it is not from the benevolence of the butcher, the brewer, or the baker, that we expect our dinner, but from their regard to their own interest.' Adam Smith, *An Inquiry into the Nature and Cause of the Wealth of Nations*, Edwin Cannan (ed.) (London: Essex Street, 1904), p. 16.

144 Avicenna, *The Metaphysics of 'The Healing'*, Book 10, ch. 2, 1–2.

145 Avicenna, *The Metaphysics of 'The Healing'*, Book 10, ch. 2, 2.

lawgiver, without whom people would not otherwise recognize justice, 'each considering as just what others owe them, unjust what they owe others'.[146]

Avicenna connected the material and spiritual realms, *The Metaphysics of "The Healing"* by noting that it was impossible that providence, which had supplied human needs in respect of tiny things such as 'the growing of hair on the eyebrows' would not have envisaged a righteous legislator. If 'the First Principle and the angels after Him' exist, one who was necessary 'to introduce the order of the good' must also exist. 'A prophet, therefore, must exist, and he must be a human'.[147] When this man comes to life, the main principle governing the prophet's legislation was to let the people 'know that they have a Maker, One and Omnipotent'.[148] However, the legislator ought not to involve people in anything relative to doctrine. Politics and religion ought to be separated. This would only confuse people, and their religion. Moreover, people understood such elevated matters only with great difficulty – only a few would achieve understanding of them. A danger was also latent in trying to instil doctrinal matters in people. It 'might even lead them to adopt views contrary to the city's welfare, opposed to the imperatives of truth'.[149]

This chapter has discussed literature that has been available in the West since the thirteenth century, derived from Greek and Arabic sources, in which the concept of needs and necessities is related both to physicalist guides to explaining the origins of human society through needs and to managing a man's estate, himself and the State. This literature employs the notion of needs and imbues it with a strong physical meaning that concerns nourishment, shelter and diverse crafts required for the economy. Furthermore, Avicenna's texts, in particular, bestow a strong metaphysical meaning on the notion of needs that relates to connecting people and making them equal on grounds of their common precariousness, the existence of diverse classes due to human differences, and to the diverse crafts needed in the economy. There exists therefore a combination of diverse historical understandings of *oeconomy* as a home or an estate, even as a state, some stressing its potential political elements, and other undermining them. All appear to be influenced by physicians' literature and a Neoplatonic metaphysics of necessity. Especially the Brysonean and Avicennean Arabic strand narrowed down ethics, politics

[146] Avicenna, *The Metaphysics of 'The Healing'*, Book 10, ch. 2, 2. An idea to be found in Locke's *Essays on the Law of Nature*, as we saw earlier.

[147] Avicenna, *The Metaphysics of 'The Healing'*, Book 10, ch. 2, 3.

[148] Avicenna, *The Metaphysics of 'The Healing'*, Book 10, ch. 2, 4.

[149] Avicenna, *The Metaphysics of 'The Healing'*, Book 10, ch. 2, 5.

and even theology to a physicalist focus on material needs, chiming well with modern sceptical tendencies in natural law as to the capacity of an individual's human mind to ascertain what was right and just. The background to subsequent writings on political economy was thus prepared.

Locke's emphasis on human necessities already in his early philosophical works possibly originated from his reading of the philosopher-physicians and his experience as a physician. To my knowledge, this emphasis has not come under scrutiny, except perhaps by Karl Marx, who in view of his foundational use of it for his materialist enterprise and his evident knowledge of Locke's work in *The Capital* seemed quite enthusiastic about the notion of necessities.[150] In Chapters 10, 11 and 12 I analyse what use Locke made of his doctrine of necessities in his monetary, epistemological and political writings. With the background of the *oeconomy* of needs described in this chapter, his ideas on the necessity of money appeared tied to larger (Arabic and European) medical and materialist traditions of needs:

> for money being a Universall commodity, and as necessary to trade as food is to life, every body must have it at what rate they can get it, and unavoidably pair deare when it is Scarce.[151]

150 Karl Marx, *Capital. A Critique of Political Economy*, Vol I., Samuel Moore and Edward Aveling trans. and Frederick Engels ed. (Progress Publisher, Moscow, USSR, undated [from the First English ed. 1887]).

151 John Locke, 'Some of the Consequence that Are Like to Follow Upon Lessening of Interest to 4 per Cent' (1668) in Patrick Hyde Kelly (ed.), *Locke on Money*, v. I (Oxford: Clarendon Press, 1991), p. 172.

10

Money and the Doctrine of Necessities

10.1 Locke's Doctrine of Necessities

Thinking in terms of necessities of the nation in the context of the monetary system allowed Locke to introduce the public element that private money owners lacked.[1] The entire question of money moves thereby from a moral-theological system to a system of moral-natural philosophy. In all this philosophical and theoretical work, the notion of necessities becomes central. The celebrated argument by Joyce Appleby about Locke's conviction of the existence of a natural economic order on which mercantilism was advanced does not chime with Locke's corpuscularianism. Among other reasons, to a committed empiricist, a minimal articulation of any natural order would require lots of experiments. Nature had certainly an order, but there was very little about that order we could say in the present state of science. Instead, in his economic thinking, Locke endorsed the argument of human necessities: necessities of the (economy of the) state and concern for the public and the shaping role of public legislation.[2] But it was also Locke's theoretical premise of the disintegrative principle of corpuscularist atomism that demanded the certainty of the notion of necessities.

10.1.1 A Changing Perspective: Corpuscularianism

Human beings are back in the world in the philosophy of John Locke. We encounter them as beings *in nature*, in their dual capacity as rational

[1] Public debt in form of tallies and 'Exchequer orders' circulated extensively from one person to another between 1667 and 1672, until the King stopped payment in January 1672, the notorious 'Stop of the Exchequer', to start borrowing afresh.J. Keith Horsefield, *British Monetary Experiments 1650–1710* (London: G. Bell and Sons, 1960), pp. 1–10; C. D. Chandaman, *The English Public Revenue 1660–1688* (Oxford: Clarendon Press, 1975).

[2] Joyce Oldham Appleby, *Economic Thought and Ideology in Seventeenth Century England* (Princeton: Princeton University Press, 1978), pp. 242–279; Daniel Carey responded to this argument on Locke's naturalism with a sophisticated analysis on the recoinage controversy in Daniel Carey, 'Locke's Species: Money and Philosophy in the 1690s' 70 *Annals of Science* (2013). More about this later in the chapter.

explorers of elusive knowledge and as created natural beings endowed with powers and necessities. The following three chapters describe Locke's response, as an economist, a moral philosopher, an epistemologist and as a political philosopher, to the magnificent challenge that corpuscular philosophy posed in the English context. Following Boyle, Locke accepted atomism in natural sciences.[3] The goal of making real science – that is empirical knowledge – of social endeavours appeared clear. But atomism was hardly helpful for making theory with social content that would confront Hobbes's individualist and atheist political science. I suggest that Locke's doctrine of necessities allowed corpuscularianism to be launched in natural sciences at full speed without discomposing all social institutions and ensure that social sciences could partake of the new science. Moral natural law was in that sense modernized. This chapter explores how Locke benefited from a generalized language of necessities in the context of a theory of money, government, natural law and knowledge. Furthermore, he imbued the political meaning of the concept of necessities with a specific theoretical content inspired partly by theology, economy and medicine.

English corpuscular philosophy held that the physical world could be explained without Aristotelian forms or substances. In this manner, teleological thinking in natural philosophy and ethics lost much of its meaning.[4] Locke's rejection of Aristotelian reasoning on virtues, despite his own proposal of rational morality, may be put in the context of its incompatibility with corpuscular anti-teleological principles.[5] As we saw in Chapter 7,

[3] The study of the influence of Boyle in Locke's philosophy is still in an early stage. Matthew Priselac, Jan-Erik Jones and Hilarie Kochira have made a strong case with regard to the importance of corpuscularianism for Locke's discussions in *An Essay of Human Understanding*. Matthew Priselac, *Locke's Science of Knowledge* (New York and London: Routledge, 2017); Jan Erik-Jones refers in particular to *The Origin of Forms and Qualities* by Robert Boyle, for instance to the seventeenth-century philosophical debates on natural kinds – such as in biology, 'the species'. Jan Erik-Jones, 'Boyle's Natural Kind Realism' in Jan Erik Jones (ed.), *The Bloomsbury Companion to Robert Boyle* (2020). Locke knew that work so well that, according to Jan-Erik Jones, he was even able to detect and criticize its gaps of reasoning. Jan-Erik Jones, 'Locke vs. Boyle: The Real Essence of Corpuscular Species', 15 *British Journal for the History of Philosophy* (2007), pp. 659–684; Hylarie Kochiras, 'Locke's Philosophy of Science', *The Stanford Encyclopedia of Philosophy* (Spring 2020 Edition), Edward N. Zalta (ed.), https://plato.stanford.edu/archives/spr2020/entries/locke-philosophy-science/.

[4] I am considering here English corpuscularianism in its own right. The dependencies and continuities in mechanic Cartesianism to theological and teleological thinking have been discussed, for example, by Osler, *Divine Will and the Mechanical Philosophy*.

[5] 'And, however Aristotle or Anacharsis, Confucius, or any one amongst us, shall name this or that action a virtue or a vice, their authorities are all of them alike, and they exercise but what power every one has, which is to show what complex ideas their words shall stand for:

corpuscularist authors considered it productive for science to narrow the scope of the philosophical approach to the physical world to a conception of a natural system held together through powers, qualities and forces. That is to say, the frame and course into which matter and motion were set in the beginning by God was the start of reasoning for the naturalist. Corpuscularianism is explained, for instance, masterfully in Robert Boyle's *The Origins of Forms and Qualities* in terms that the only thing in nature that possessed something distinct from matter was the human being, with an 'immaterial Form and a humane Body'.[6] Next, in explaining particular natural phenomena of this 'great Automaton, the World', it was argued that the naturalist must pay attention only to the 'doctrine of qualities', meaning the qualities of matter: size, texture, shape and motion, or lack of motion. In Boyle's view, this understanding of material bodies as an aggregate of qualities gave an element of convention, of agreement, even of arbitrariness to other conceptions such as naturalists' classification of aspects of physical nature into species, or indeed into 'natures'.[7] In effect, he was hinting at the fact that in view of the emerging corpuscularianism and its infinite possibilities in relation to knowledge, contemporary science still offered a poor and positivist conception of the natural world.[8] Did scientists know

for without showing a law that commands or forbids them, moral goodness will be but an empty sound'. John Locke, 'On Ethics in General' in Peter King (ed.), *The Life of John Locke with extracts from his Correspondence, Journals, and Common-Place Books*, vol. II (London: Bentley, 1830), pp. 129–130.

6 Robert Boyle, *The Origin of Forms and Qualities (according to the Corpuscular Philosophy)* (Oxford: Pr. By H. Hall, Printer to the University, Davis, 1666), p. 157–158.

7 'For the World being once constituted by the great Author of Things, as it now is, I look upon the *Phaenomena* of Nature to be caused by the Local Motion of one part of Matter hitting against another, and am not so fully convinced, that there is such a thing, as Natures designing to keep such a parcel of Matter in such a state, that is clothed with just such Accidents, rather then with any other. But I look upon many Bodies, especially fluid ones, as frequently changing their state, according as they happen to be more or lesse agitated, or otherwise wrought upon by the Sun, and other considerable Agents in Nature'; 'there is scarce any Natural Body, wherein the Form makes so strict, durable, and indissoluble an Union of the parts it consists of'. Boyle, *The Origin of Forms and Qualities*, p. 167; p. 183; p. 194. Locke uses this theory for instance in explaining 'substance', Locke, *An Essay Concerning Human Understanding*, II.23. §4–5, pp. 297–298.

8 'Whatever Men talk in Theory of Substantial Forms, yet That, upon whose account they really distinguish any one Body from others, and refer it to this or that *Species* of Bodies, is nothing but a Aggregate or Convention of such Accidents, as most men do by a kind of Agreement, (for the Thing is more Arbitrary then we are aware of) think necessary or sufficient to make a Portion of the Universal Matter belong to this or that Determinate *Genus* or *Species* of Natural Bodies'. Boyle, *The Origin of Forms and Qualities*, pp. 61–62. See Richard H. Popkin, 'Preface' in Henry G. van Leeuwen, *The Problem of Certainty in English Thought 1630–1690* (The Hague: Martinus Nijhoff, 1963), p. ix.

the *necessary connections* between the qualities of bodies? In other words, did the assumption of a structure formed by qualities and powers in the world entail knowledge of it? Both Robert Boyle, as we saw in Chapter 7, and John Locke answered these questions by reference to the premise of weakness of knowledge and the deficient state of contemporary science.[9] In true corpuscularian spirit, Locke wrote in *An Essay Concerning Human Understanding* that 'our *Idea*, the word *Man* stands for, is only an imperfect Collection of some sensible Qualities and Powers in him'.[10] Moreover, the acceptance of precariousness was the precondition for fostering the type of ambitious inquiry and greater knowledge that characterized the new science. Both philosophers assumed that there ought to be (some) necessary connections among atoms, and thus the necessary causality. However, unlike Hobbes, they did not presume to know when and how these operated.[11] Hence, the principle of necessary causality was dropped from natural and moral sciences in the extreme form defended by Hobbes.[12]

The second scientific assumption that Locke shared with Boyle was that an omnipotent God stood behind the design of that structure. After all, in Boyle's view, God was the donor of each of the powers of nature. In this and other instances the stimulus of the Scientific Revolution was theological, which meant not merely religious beliefs, but doing science with the help of the notion of God as the omnipotent maker and infinite container.[13] As

[9] 'I have here instanced in the corpuscularian Hypothesis, as that which is thought to go farthest in an intelligible Explication of the Qualities of Bodies; and I fear the Weakness of humane Understanding is scarce able to substitute another, which will afford us a fuller and clearer discovery of the necessary Connexion, and *Co-existence*, of the Powers, which are to be observed united in several sorts of them. This at least is certain, that which ever Hypothesis be clearest and truest, (for that it is not my business to determine,) our Knowledge concerning corporeal Substances, will be very little advanced by any of them, till we are made see, what Qualities and Powers of Bodies have a *necessary Connexion or Repugnancy* one with another; which in the present State of Philosophy, I think, we know but to a very small degree.' Locke, *An Essay Concerning Human Understanding*, IV.3.16, p. 547. See the helpful explanation by Kochiras, 'Locke's Philosophy of Science'.

[10] Locke, *An Essay Concerning Human Understanding*, IV, 6. §15, p. 590.

[11] Which is not the same than to affirm that they held a radical scepticism, but that their theories are richly complex, and arising from scepticism, try to overcome it. Some scholars argue about their extreme scepticism, for example, Stephen Buckle has described Locke as the most skeptic about natural knowledge of all seventeenth-century philosophers, denying the possibility of any insight into the constitution of the world, but opposed, in principle, to moral and religious skepticism. Stephen Buckle, 'British Sceptical Realism: A Fresh Look at the British Tradition' in Udo Thiel (ed.), *Locke: Epistemology and Metaphysics* (Darmouth: Ashgate, 2002), p. 17.

[12] See Chapter 2.

[13] See for instance with regard to the argument of design, Wragge-Morley, *Aesthetic Science*.

Aquinas had put it in *On the Power of God* (*De potentia Dei*), as 'founder and designer of nature' (*conditor et ordinator naturae*), what God did *was* nature.[14] God was moreover superior to nature and therefore not limited by nature – a superior power does not depend on an inferior one.[15] According to Cornelio Fabro, Aquinas's understanding of power was novel, implying Aristotelian concepts of form, essence and action contained in the same notion of 'powers' participating of God's order. A new and more complex metaphysical conception of the world than Aristotelian nature would then transpire from Aquinas's 'On the Power of God'.[16] Locke's lengthy chapter XXI, 'Of Power', in the second book of *An Essay Concerning Human Understanding*, starts similarly with the premise ('I confess') that power is 'a relation to Action or Change'. Later in the chapter, he notes that 'God, is only active [power]'.[17] Aquinas's ambition to explain everything through the notion of God's power had been breathtaking. For example, the issues discussed in *On the Power of God*, in a very rich question five include the following: movement in order, the preservation of God's free will, the uniqueness of each individual, the maintenance of creatures in existence through participation, the fact that human beings naturally do not only care for themselves individually but for the whole city and even for the entire world. The theologian's underlying argument in that text was that by *being power*, God is action and goodness.[18]

Boyle endorsed Aquinas's cosmology of *power* and *powers*, but as we also saw in Chapter 7, he wanted to distil the theologian's notion of nature and purify it of Aristotelian forms, or as he put it, of 'the lazy Aristotelian

14 'Ad primum ergo dicendum, quod verbum Augustini in Glossa illa non est intelligendum quod Deus non possit facere aliter quam natura faciat, cum ipse frequenter faciat contra consuetum cursum naturae; sed quia quidquid in rebus facit, non est contra naturam, sed est eis natura, eo quod ipse est conditor et ordinator naturae'. *De potentia Dei*, q.1.arg.3.ad.1; 'Hoc autem agens incorporeum, a quo omnia creantur, et corporalia et incorporalia, Deus est, sicut in alia quaestione ostensum est, a quo non solum sunt formae rerum, sed etiam materiae. Et quantum ad propositum non differt utrum immediate, vel quodam ordine, ut quidam philosophi posuerunt. Unde sequitur quod divina operatione cessante, omnes res eodem momento in nihilum deciderent, sicut auctoritatibus est probatum in argumentis sed contra'. Aquinas, *De potentia Dei*, q. 5 a1.co.

15 *De potentia Dei*. q.6 a1. s.c.2.

16 Fabro, *La nozione metafisica di partecipazione secondo San Tommaso d'Aquino*, p. 329.

17 Locke, *An Essay Concerning Human Understanding*, II. 21. §3, p. 234; 23. §28, p. 312.

18 See for instance in *De potentia Dei*, question 5 of q.5.a1.co; q. 5. a1.ad1; q. 5a3.ad.8; q. 5. arg. 6 ad.3. 'Ad tertium dicendum, quod homo naturaliter non solum de se ipso sollicitatur, sed etiam de statu communitatis cuius est pars, sicut vel domus vel civitatis, aut etiam totius orbis; et ideo utrumque fuit necessarium ad hominis cautelam occultari, et finem propriae vitae, et finem totius mundi'.

way of Philosophizing'.[19] Arguably, Boyle also rejected the Neoplatonist giver of forms as incompatible with the species of atomism that he favoured, and possibly with Christianity. Corpuscular philosophers seemingly sought to overcome the earlier Neoplatonist dualism. Similarly to Aquinas, they employed the idea of God as a Necessary Existence, as described in Chapter 2, but they did not reduce the conception of God solely to this.[20] I contend that Boyle's new philosophy of nature, and that of the group of philosophers he was in conversation with, undertook such a radical and imaginative break with Aristotelianism and Neoplatonism that beyond single areas of study it engendered a new cosmology that influenced future conceptions of natural law.

John Locke encountered this constellation of ideas in Oxford as a young protégé of Robert Boyle. Without denying his own intellectual originality, Locke's evolution as a natural lawyer must be placed in this context.[21] In combination with his profound interest and knowledge of scholastic theology and his expertise in medical works, corpuscularianism provided Locke with a change of perspective on both old and new moral, economic, political and epistemological themes. While there existed a physical system to which human beings related as bodies and thinking beings, they could

[19] Boyle, *The Origin of Forms and Qualities*, p. 270. That Locke also follows Aquinas in the adoption of a cosmology of powers appears both in the *Two Treatises* and *An Essay*. In the response to Mr. Norris's critique to *An Essay*, Locke exposed his understanding of it for natural sciences: 'For I hope they will not deny God the privilege to give such a power to motion, if he pleases. Yes, say they, they be the occasional, but not the efficient cause; for that they cannot be because that is in effect to say, he has given this motion in the optic nerve a power to operate on himself, but cannot give it a power to operate in the mind of man; it may by this appointment operate on himself, the impassible infinite spirit, and put him in mind when he is to operate on the mind of man, and exhibit to it the idea which is in himself of any colour. The infinite eternal God is certainly the cause of all things, the fountain of all being and power. But, because all being was from him, can there be nothing but God himself? or, because all power was originally in him, can there be nothing of it communicated to his creatures? This is to set very narrow bounds to the power of God, and, by pretending to extend it, takes it away. For which (I beseech you, as we can comprehend) is the perfectest power; to make a machine, a watch, for example, that when the watchmaker has withdrawn his hands, shall go and strike by the fit contrivance of the parts; or else requires that whenever the hand, by pointing to the hours, minds him of it, he should strike twelve upon the bell?' John Locke, 'Remarks upon Some of Mr. Norris's Books. Wherein he asserts P. Malebranche's Opinion of our seeing all Things in God' (1693) in *The Works of John Locke in Ten Volumes*, X (London: Thomas Tegg and Co., 1823), p. 254.

[20] Locke, 'Deus- Descartes's Proof of a God from the Idea of a Necessary Existence, examined', pp. 133–139; using the idea, see for instance, in Locke, *An Essay*, II. 17.§5. p. 212; §20. p. 221.

[21] On Locke and corpuscularianism see also, Locke, *An Essay on Human Understanding*, II.2. §2, p. 120; II.8. §8, 134; II.8. §21, p. 139.

also perceive the actual material world with which they interacted daily. In a sense, the corpuscular theory established the ambitious framework and goal for the future of science, including knowledge about God the Designer of nature. On the other hand, Locke's realism – which described a capacity for perception through the senses of a kind not radically unlike that which proceeded from Aristotelian-Thomism – considered human beings to be equipped with the capacities to interact with that world.[22]

10.1.2 Necessities

Locke's economic thinking benefits from the new perspective of the physical world as an interdependent system, a 'self-moving Engine' that works through motion. Chapter 7 described how the concept of 'Nature' was rendered superfluous in Boyle's philosophy. Instead, he regarded the physical world as an *oeconomy*. In the work of Locke – possibly Boyle's most brilliant student – signs of a rapprochement between the *oeconomy* of nature and the *oeconomy* of the nation started to appear early on.[23] Locke regarded investment of money in the form of capital as being the natural way for the system or economy of a nation to function.[24] Crucially, he described the cycle of trade as a quasi-natural phenomenon, similarly to Boyle's description of the natural system as quasi-artificial.

> For money, as necessary to trade, may be doubly considered – 1° As in his hands that payes the labourer and Landholder, (for here its motion terminats, and through whose hands soever it passes between these he is but a Broker) and if this man want money (as for Example the Clothier) the

[22] On Locke's perception realism see John W. Yolton, *Locke and the Compass of Human Understanding: A Selective Commentary on the 'Essay'* (Cambridge: Cambridge University Press, 1970), pp. 118–138.

[23] With reference to what he read of Boyle, there are sixty-two of Boyle's works listed in Locke's library. Harrison and Laslett, *The Library of John Locke.*

[24] The economist William Petty (1623–1685), another illustrious member of the Hartlib circle, Reformer in Ireland, scientist, friend of Hobbes and Hobbesian, promoted the adoption of statistics to regulate taxes in order to improve trade in his groundbreaking and witty *A Treatise of Taxes*. Between him and Locke exists certainly a family resemblance in the intelligent use of the notion of the necessaries of nature and the stress on labour. For instance, when composing the price of commodities Petty includes the labour required to obtain the 'necessaries': 'That Natural dearness and cheapness depends upon the few or more hands requisite to the Necessaries of nature'; or he defines taxes on consumption with it: 'the very perfect Idea of making a Leavy upon Comsumptions, is to rate every particular Necessary, just when it is ripe for Consumption', William Petty, *A Treatise of Taxes*, in C. H. Hull (ed.), *The Economic Writings of Sir William Petty*, vol 1. (Cambridge: Cambridge University Press, 1899 [1662] Online Library of Liberty), p. 109; p. 111.

> Manifactury is not made, and so the Trade stops and is lost – 2 ° as in the Merchants hands who buys the Commodity when made and if he want money the value of the Commodity when made is lessened and soe the Kingdome looses in the price.[25]

Money thus *moved* within a system of trade in which it was necessary. Moreover, without money the system would stop. Locke's originality in his unpublished writings on money (1668–1674) lay in showing that lending money at interest was not a question of moral theology, but about 'necessity' and 'necessaries' for the individual and for the nation, or for trade (the economy). Locke's *Essays of the Law of Nature*, we might recall, left open the question of how to flesh out the seemingly impossible equation as between the primacy of individuals and the primacy of the public. I will argue that the means of aligning private and public interests appear for the first time in his remarkable studies on money. These show that the commonality of citizens has a common economic project as a nation, which he could demonstrate scientifically. The texts were one important intervention in engineering 'people's zeal for the public, by a prospect of private advantage'.[26] There was a pressing need to adapt values to the process of commercialization that was radically transforming the country.[27] These new values had at their core the aim of encouraging citizens of every status – men and women alike – to become active participants in the financial life of the nation, particularly to help finance the public debt. The activity of lending money at interest as Locke theorized provided the common roots for citizens' participation in the economy. This was achieved through citizens acting as agents in oiling the wheels of trade with money and thus directly contributing to raising credit for the government and for trade, and in a word, contributing to building the public space, while at the same time guaranteeing their own preservation.

Writing in the 1690s against the devaluation of money as being harmful to investors and to private banks, Locke lumped together a variety of techniques, that had all been helpful at a moment of pressing need and impending 'necessities'– including stock market speculation and lottery loans

[25] John Locke, 'Some of the Consequence that Are Like to Follow Upon Lessening of Interest to 4 per Cent' (1668) in Patrick Hyde Kelly (ed.), *Locke on Money*, v. I (Oxford: Clarendon Press, 1991), p. 169.

[26] This was written in praise of the state lotteries, anonymous author quoted in Lee Krim Davison, *Public Policy in an Age of Economic Expansion: The Search for Commercial Accountability in England, 1690–1750* (PhD Harvard University, 1990), p. 97.

[27] Wrighson, *Earthly Necessities, Economic Lives in Early Modern Britain, 1470–1750*, p. 455; Muldrew, *The Economy of Obligation*.

in which investors have the chance to win a prize the size of which was determined by a draw.[28] Locke wrote that reducing the content of precious metal in a coin without changing its denomination,

> will weaken, if not totally destroy the publick Faith, when all that have trusted the Publick, and assisted our present necessities, upon Acts of Parliament, in the *Million Lottery*, *Bank Act*, and other *Loans*, shall be defrauded of 20 *per Cent.* of what those Acts of Parliament were security for.[29]

The necessities that these new financial schemes remedied were public necessities – public debt that constituted revenue for the country by raising credit through public or parliamentary legislation, and all those pitching in were supposed to receive benefit as well. National legislation guaranteed their contribution. Crucially, these contributors had *trusted* that there was some common project in England which they were supporting. Locke sought to stress on a continuous basis that the new financial system belonged to a structure of national necessity with regard to a fundamental triad of publicness, nature and truth. His diatribes against greed and luxury show less interest in stressing scarcity (as that was a fact of life) than in pointing out what he considered, in the tradition of the Reformers studied in chapter 4, the true normativity of moral natural law: human beings' necessities.[30] He took the view that meeting the necessities of the public clearly belonged to the moral sphere of acts and deeds that demanded performance. As this chapter will show, for all intents and purposes Locke employed the notion of 'necessities' politically. This is visible in a sort of conflict of homonyms across all his writings that revolve around the notion of the 'necessary'.[31] In Locke's *œuvre* 'necessity' and the 'necessary' often denote an epistemological claim about truth, standing between chance and interest or, if you will, between *fortuna* and *virtue.*[32]

'Necessity' may also indicate the entirety of a metaphysical structure or constitution of the world or of a certain domain within it, as we saw in the case of Hobbes and the ensuing Cudworth's critique in relation to freedom. However, 'necessity' also refers to a mere contingent economic human need, or indeed a need of the state. Locke played with all these

[28] The Million Lottery of 1694 was the first very successful lottery loan in England.

[29] John Locke 'Further Considerations Concerning Raising the Value of Money', in Patrick Hyde Kelly (ed.), *Locke on Money* (1696), vol. II, p. 417.

[30] Cfr. John O'Brien, 'John Locke, Desire, and the Epistemology of Money' in 15 *British Journal for the History of Philosophy* (2007).

[31] 'Homonyms are two or more words of different origin and different meaning that are spelled the same or sound the same.' Cambridge Dictionary.

[32] Pocock, *The Machiavellian Moment.*

meanings in developing his political philosophy, pointing to laws of nature for areas in which he saw that certainty and predictability was needed, or where he aimed, wisely, at reinforced a theme of tradition. His emphasis in *An Essay Concerning Human Understanding* on 'human beings' necessary search for happiness' is a case in point. Nowhere did Locke engage in a discussion or theoretical description of what exactly he meant by his concept of natural necessities.[33] Nevertheless 'natural necessities' are his bottom-line working tool in each text in which he puts forward a theoretical argument about politics, morality, philosophy, economics or epistemology, crucially so in the law of nature and theory of government set out in his masterpiece, the *Two Treatises of Government*. This suggests that he took for granted the notion's capacity to transmit meaning and that it was common currency – in a similar way to the equally powerful notion of self-interest, against which, I argue, Locke was competing.

The language of necessities was indeed ubiquitous in the period in question.[34] Often, as in Locke's work, it appears to be employed to distinguish the right course of action from one characterized by vice or superfluity. Lee Krim Davison's study on public policy at the end of the seventeenth century offers one among many possible examples that show how necessity was equated with the category of moral right. In the course of the rise of speculation for big and small money from the 1690s onwards, derivatives appeared, including the *renting* of national lottery tickets for short periods. The slang for this was 'hiring a horse', while the paradoxically named 'lottery insurance' was another available instrument.[35] In the case of the former, there was the chance that the holder of a rented lottery ticket would win a prize during the rent time. The moralist writing for a weekly publication noted the difficulty of resisting the chance this represented, since 'the Avaritious and Necessitous are alike drawn in, and fixing their Eyes upon the gilded Bait, the Twenty Thousand, it hinders them from

[33] As we saw in Chapter 8, he briefly explains the meaning of 'the necessary' in the English Tract.

[34] But interestingly the very similar language on necessities employed by James Tyrrell in *Patriarcha non Monarcha* is attributed by Richard Tuck to conversations with his friend John Locke, see Tuck, *Natural Rights Theories*, p. 169; also see Peter Laslett comment in Locke, *Two Treatises of Government*, p. 287.

[35] On 'Lottery insurance' and valuable statistics to understand the impact of lottery loans, see François R. Velde, 'Lottery Loans in the Eighteenth century', *Working Paper, No. 2018-07, Federal Reserve Bank of Chicago, Chicago, IL* (2018) http://dx.doi.org/10.21033/wp-2018-07, p. 19. On the historical importance of lottery loans for public finance in England and the Low Countries, in Belgium also in the twentieth century see, the same and Davison, *Public Policy in an Age of Economic Expansion.*

regarding the Immensity of Odds, and the Improbability of Success'.[36] The ethical concern in this case was that despite the obvious risk and very low prospects of achieving a return inherent in these financial instruments, both the greedy and those in need were equally transfixed by what the author considered a ruse.

Viewing the system of public debt and investments as an aspect of patriotism was a relatively new approach in the 1690s. Anne Murphy mentions the moral dilemma and troubles of conscience of an investor – an experienced moneylender – in deciding whether to invest in the Million Lottery in 1694.[37] However, in the 1660s the idea that investing and lending money at interest amounted to an objective *necessity* was at once observed as a fact by everyone knowledgeable about politics and as an impossibility from a traditional moral perspective. This and the next chapter focus on the context and content of Locke's ideas on money to show their novel departure from moral natural law and how they belonged to the sphere of an emerging science of economics.[38] In this perspective economic matters were no longer treated as issues in which the main agents were human beings interacting morally and socially and seeking to be virtuous. Instead, in Locke's early writings on money, the key issue concerns economic phenomena that belong to an interdependent scientific system. This is not to say that previous authors had not observed the economic connections involved in the use of money. However, Locke *only* observed the systemic connections of the economy – primarily the national economy – from the perspective of purely economic phenomena; and 'necessities' is the main instrument through which he described the phenomena of the emerging monetary economy. As William Letwin put it in a chapter on Locke's scientific economic thinking, the English philosopher offered the 'economist's view of the world, which the public cannot yet (!) comfortably stomach'. In a somewhat incoherent manner, Letwin rejected any suggestion of a natural science influence in Locke and attributed his remarkable novelty in economic scientific thinking to his

36 The story and the quote from Davison, *Public Policy in an Age of Economic Expansion*, p. 102.

37 'He consulted two works on the subject, "Gataker's book of the Nature & Use of Lotts" and Dr Ames's "Marrow of Divinity & Cases of Conscience," before declaring himself to be willing to invest in the Million Adventure but remaining "an utter Enemy" to other forms of lottery.' Anne L. Murphy, 'Dealing with Uncertainty: Managing Personal Investment in Early English Debt' 91 *History* (2006), p. 208.

38 Exposing currently a certain stagnation on the historiography of economics and wondering 'who gets to determine what economics *was*?' see Ian Kumekawa, 'Reconsidering the History of Political Economy. Review Essay' *Modern Intellectual History* (2022) 1–11. doi:10.1017/S147924432200049X

studies of natural law.[39] However, Letwin's description of Locke's natural law as a 'fusion of scientific principle and moral standard' and his noting of the similarities between Locke's laws of nature and those of Boyle and Newton and their assumption of physical necessities makes it clear that it was the notion of natural laws that had undergone substantial change. Interestingly, Letwin added that 'Locke implicitly assumed that economic relations are akin to the facts of nature'.[40]

Whether Locke in fact made that assumption or not, it is not crucial in observing that the issue of necessities is a novel thread in his thinking – which is partly theological and moral, partly medical and philosophical and above all drawn from the natural sciences – and concerns the strict sense of belonging to the physical body. I argue in chapter 12 that far beyond Locke's capacity to synthesize earlier natural rights theories with great clarity, as scholars have previously argued – notwithstanding the exceptional nature of that ability – the focus in *Two Treatises of Government* and *An Essay Concerning Human Understanding* on 'necessities' rather than on 'rights' shows Locke's originality with respect to previous thinkers.[41] His theory concerning 'the necessaries' and 'necessities' rather than 'rights' gives systematic coherence not only to his economic writings, but to his entire philosophical theory. This novel approach is what made it possible for him to develop the theory of the public good with which he attempted to turn the foundation of capitalism on self-interest.

10.1.3 The (Sometimes Dark) Politics of Necessities

Locke, we are told, wrote the *Two Treatises of Government* during the *Restoration* period, to provide a theoretical foundation for resistance against

[39] As we will see below, Locke only adopted a strong moral attitude in his economic writings in the polemic against coin debasement in the mid-1690s.

[40] 'His interest in science left no discernible trace in Locke's economic writings'. Arguably Letwin's argument arises from the outlook of his own epistemic community that did not perceive themselves to be borrowing from natural sciences. Letwin's discussion of laissez-faire and nature introduces very aptly the political aspect of the naturalist methodology. Letwin, *Origins of Scientific Economics*, p. 148; p. 155; p. 176; p. 178. Also, on the influence of natural sciences, in what is probably the sole monograph on Locke as an economist, Vaughn, *John Locke: Economist and Social Scientist*, p. 29.

[41] Locke's 'clearsightedness' as the mark of his work on natural rights in Tuck, *Natural Rights Theories*, p. 171. On Locke's theory of natural rights, see A. John Simmons, *The Lockean Theory of Rights* (Princeton: Princeton University Press, 1992); Gordon Schochet review notes that 'the closer he [Simmons] comes to a "theory," I would argue, the further he is from Locke', Schochet, '"Guards and Fences": Property and Obligation in Locke's Political Thought', p. 380.

the absolutist encroachments of an undesired dynasty.[42] However, it was published, without substantial change, in radically different circumstances, after the triumphant moment of the 1688 Glorious Revolution. This shows that Locke's project in the book went beyond Jacobite opposition. John Dunn, James Tully, Mark Goldie, Ian Harris, Timothy Stanton and Paul Bou-Habib[43], among others, have proposed a theological and specifically a New Testament interpretation of Locke's natural law that is hard to deny when one looks at his entire *œuvre*.[44] What is less obvious is the manner in which Locke's ambiguity may be explained.[45] Locke's natural law theory in the *Two Treatises of Government* supports capital and labour, public and private interest, natural rights for everyone and the accumulation of money, confirms his dread of covetousness and hoarding, and yet sanctions it.[46] In short, Locke simultaneously works with a theology of equality and natural law,[47] *and* with a history of political theory and a political economy that are designed to undermine that theology. Together with a reconsideration of the place of natural rights in Locke's natural law theory, the second aim of the three chapters on Locke in this book is to *disambiguate* this aspect of Locke. It does so by pinpointing the centrality of the concept of 'human necessities', and the relevant role of the 'nation' in *Two Treatises of Government*.

The paradox seems clear from the outset. The nation needs the wealth that comes through the accumulation of money and lands by the very rich, and natural law commands the provision of necessities and the preservation of every human being, something which the very rich seem to prevent with their egoistic tendencies. This, however, Locke corrects through the role of the nation. The authority of the nation is the invisible but fundamental element in the design of Locke's natural law theory and in his lifelong political project. He regards the nation as probably the outcome of

[42] Laslett, 'Introduction' in Locke, *Two Treatises of Government*; James Farr and Clayton Robert, 'John Locke on the Glorious Revolution: A Rediscovered Document' 28 *The Historical Journal* (1985); Mark Goldie, 'John Locke on the Glorius Revolution: A New Document' 42 *History of Political Thought* (2021).

[43] Dunn, *The Political Thought of John Locke*; Tully, *A Discourse on Property*; Harris, *The Mind of John Locke*; Stanton, 'John Locke and the Fable of Liberalism'; Bou-Habib, 'Locke, Natural Law and Civil Peace'; Mark Goldie, in 2021 *The Carlyle Lectures: John Locke and Empire*.

[44] Lisa T. Sarasohn, who by reading Locke through Gassendi, gives him a too hedonistic tone, seems less persuasive, Sarasohn, *Gassendi's Ethics*, p. 168–197.

[45] An ambiguity that has gained him enemies, such as Strauss Leo, *Natural Right and History*.

[46] Also exposing how to educate in liberality in John Locke, 'Some Thoughts concerning Education' in *The Works of John Locke* (London: Rivington, 1824, 12th ed.; Indianapolis: Liberty Fund).

[47] 'What he is attacking is the exploitation of a huge majority by a small minority.' Dunn, *The Political Thought of John Locke*, p. 171.

original sin, or at any rate of 'the corruption, and vitiousness of degenerate Men'. In the beginning it was not like that. By 'the Law of Nature' a human being 'and the rest of Mankind are on Community' and were it not for the existence of evil individuals 'there would be no need of any other; no necessity that Men should separate from this great and natural Community'.[48] Now, however, the nation was necessary.

M. J. Silverthorne has noted that in the late seventeenth century the term 'the nation' acquired a political and ideological connotation that it did not have before.[49] The idea of a 'nation' was pressed at the time even in terms of urging a change in parliamentary vocabulary. For instance, on the occasion of a parliamentary motion on 27 November 1697 to resolve the 'Grievances of the Kingdom', an amendment to omit that expression and replace it with a motion that the entire House of Commons would form itself into a Committee to consider 'the State of the Nation' was passed.[50] Leo Strauss and, more recently, Ian Hunter have tended to describe Locke's theory of natural law as if designed to craft a minimal government. Locke would have understood government negatively, meaning that governance in relation to the individual should be as liberal as possible. Hence, the single motive for individuals in Locke's state of nature to establish a common authority would be that of continuing their rational self-governance and protecting the rights that flowed from it – particularly in relation to property – with the 'unparalleled capacity' for that purpose offered by political authority.[51] From the outset the theme of minimal government is at odds with Gordon Schochet's statistical analysis of the frequency of use of the expressions 'common good', 'publick good' and 'good of the society' in *Two Treatises of Government*, which appear more than 60 times in the text. Schochet concluded that the significance of the public good was, though indeterminate, 'self-evident'.[52] A government must offer a remedy for the inconveniences of the state of nature, albeit that

48 Locke, *Two Treatises of Government*, II §128.

49 In England 'commonwealth' and 'political' and 'civil society' seemed to be the most usual terms for *civitas* and in extremely rare cases, 'state' see M. J. Silverthorne, 'Civil Society and State, Law and Rights: Some Latin Terms and Their Translation in the Natural Jurisprudence Tradition' in *Acta Conventus Neo-Latini Toronotonensis* (Medieval and Renaissance Texts and Studies) (Binghamton, 1991).

50 'House of Commons Journal Volume 11: 10 March 1697', in *Journal of the House of Commons: Volume 11, 1693–1697* (London, 1803), pp. 734–735.

51 This is, for example in Hunter, 'Natural Law as Political Philosophy', p. 485.

52 Schochet, '"Guards and Fences": Property and Obligation in Locke's Political Thought', p. 386. A good example of this is: 'For hereby he (any Man) authorizes the Society, or which is all one, the Legislative thereof to make Laws for him as the publick good of the Society shall require; to the Execution whereof, his own assistance (as to his own Decree) is due.' Locke, *Two Treatises of Government*, Book II, §89. 8.

not just *any* government is equipped to do this.[53] Although it makes sense in relation to the dettament of government from theological questions, against the theory of the minimal government, my argument is that Locke's studies of philosophy, money and medicine produced a novel form of natural law that focuses on the necessities of humanity and of the nation's and promotes vigorous governments and richly complex civil societies.

Furthermore, the universality of natural rights appears to be achieved through the nation. Locke's politics assume that legal and political measures taken by the government should act as a restraint upon monied men and curb their excesses. The common good, comprising both the nation and the individual, incorporates the new economic thinking through necessities. Working selfishly against the provision of necessities of other human beings, provision of which are sanctioned by God and reason, also means acting against the nation. The *Two Treatises of Government* repeatedly elaborate on the preservation of the individual and of mankind, usually together, thus underlining the importance of a common social project of subsistence. Therefore, in Locke's work natural rights are not imbued with a sense of individualist rights. As John Dunn and James Tully have written, Locke always considers people in terms of their relations with God and other human beings, not as atomized individuals.[54] In the absence of an abstract, political humankind in reality it is in the nation where all these relationships occur. The origins of commonwealths were virtuous but poor, while the future seems to promise richness and insincerity.[55] Therefore, the government of the nation ought to keep in check the excesses and immorality of materialism. Further, the nation – any nation – needs wealth, virtuous individuals and labourers.[56]

My argument that Locke was putting forward the idea of a nation whose governance in respect of natural necessities stemmed from universalist obligations is partly biographically and partly textually based. Locke was from the beginning of his career a professional philosopher and a natural lawyer.[57] However, in his early thirties, he became a public servant, a fact that tempered the troubled universalism of his early natural law. As became

[53] Locke, *Two Treatises of Government*, Book II, §13.

[54] Tully, *A Discourse on Property*, p. 11. Dunn, *The Political Thought of John Locke*, pp. 229–241.

[55] 'That poor but vertuous Age' when commonwealths originated. Locke, *Two Treatises of Government*, II. §110.

[56] Compare Vaughn, *John Locke: Economist and Social Scientist*, p. 76.

[57] However, perhaps to highlight his work as a political theorist, Laslett stated that 'at Oxford he was never a philosopher at all' and that Locke 'was never to get much further as a Natural Law theorist', a view that is indefensible. Peter Laslett, 'Introduction', p. 19; p. 22.

clear to him in the 1660s, the English nation required capital and labour for the unemployed and the poor. It was also the nation that would make real the will of God on earth for every human being. The nation would ensure that private interests thrived but did not take precedence over everything else. In this sense, Locke followed, in terms of fundamentals, the principles of the Protestant Reformers of the Long Parliament, and in particular of the Hartlib circle. He shared their cult of science and empiricism, their piety, their interest in the public good and in achieving general economic prosperity, and their expertise in and obsession with money and trade. He was personally acquainted with many of the main political, economic and scientific figures of this movement, often worked with them and learned from them. However, in all his writings the English philosopher eschewed the naïveté of their theoretical approach and of some of their beliefs and idealism, and was more brilliant, cautious and pragmatic in pursue of the same goals – his experience of real politicians, starting with Lord Ashley, Anthony Ashley Cooper, later 1st Earl of Shaftesbury (1621–1683) – may have had a significant impact on his philosophical style.[58] It is also true that, put simply, Locke took a commonsense approach to many of their wild financial, philosophical and other schemes (some of which were discussed in Chapter 4), curbing their excesses and enthusiasms in his own way. It also appears that the question of money rather than trade held more attraction for Locke in terms of service to the English nation and its necessities. This is clear not only from the centrality of money in his writings but also evidenced by his wish to be appointed to the position of 'Comptroller of the Mint' in 1695. This post went instead to the scientist Isaac Newton who had already been recommended for it. I. K. Steele writes that Locke's participation in the activities of the Board of Trade was initially desired by the government, rather than being something either Locke or Sir John Somers (Lord Keeper and Locke's patron) (1651–1716) had sought.[59]

'Necessities' seemed to have taken its most evil turn in the political context of the empire generally, and in a manner that at least tarnish Locke's fame when they referred to human beings under slavery.[60] Barbara Arneil and David Armitage have read Locke's legal and political theory as either a

[58] Peter H. Nidditch, 'Introduction' in John Locke, *An Essay Concerning Human Understanding*, p. xii.

[59] I. K. Steele, *Politics of Colonial Policy: The Board of Trade in Colonial Administration* (Oxford: Clarendon Press, 1968), pp. 178.

[60] Jennifer Welchmann, 'Locke on Slavery and Inalienable Rights' 25 *Canadian Journal of Philosophy* (1995); the review on the question of Locke and slavery by Jeremy Waldron is helpful, Waldron, *God, Locke and Equality*, p. 197. John Dunn notes that Locke sheepishly

defence or at least in 'complicity' with English colonialism.[61] Hence, it was argued that in late seventeenth-century England the natural appropriation of land through labour defended by Locke in the *Two Treatises* justified the appropriation of America's soil. It is useful therefore to look at Locke's activities before the publication of the *Two Treatises of Government*. Locke started his collaboration with Lord Ashley as doctor and advisor in 1667. He later became Lord Ashley's principal secretary, between 1672 and 1675, helping him in his official responsibilities as a colonial and business administrator.[62] It was thanks to Ashley that the obscure Oxford academic became known to the world. The beginnings of their relationship were very propitious. Locke was 34 years old when he played a key role in a complicated surgery suffered by Lord Ashley Cooper and in his convalescence, both very hazardous at the time.[63] In return, Lord Ashley aided Locke's transformation from a scholar into a civil servant working in the public administration of the English nation and empire. Peter H. Nidditch opines that Lord Ashley probably added an 'economic dimension' to Locke's developing liberal ideas.[64] And, as I will argue, Robert Boyle also contributed on this issue. Ashley had been already active in colonial policy. He invested in and was a public administrator of some of the biggest companies in existence at the time, including the Royal African Company and the Hudson Bay Company, and was one of the eight Lords Proprietor of Carolina. In 1670, he became Commissioner of the Treasury and member of the inner Cabinet, and in 1672 Lord Chancellor and President of the Council for Trade and Foreign Plantations.[65]

glossed over his own involvement with investments in the Royal African Company or Barbados, in order to construct a coherent scientific work, Dunn, *The Political Thought of John Locke*, p. 255.

61 Barbara Arneil, *John Locke and America: The Defence of English Colonialism* (Oxford: Clarendon Press, 1996); Armitage, *Foundations of Modern International Thought*, pp. 90–113; p. 112.

62 Laslett, 'Introduction' in John Locke, *Two Treatises of Government*; Kelly 'General Introduction: Locke on Money' in the same ed. *Locke on Money*; Leng, 'Shaftesbury's Aristocratic Empire'.

63 The extraordinary narration of Lord Ashley's case and his recovery and Locke's intervention in it, with Locke's own report on the case, in Peter R. Anstey and Lawrence M. Principe, 'John Locke and the Case of Anthony Ashley Cooper' 16 *Early Science and Medicine* (2011). Locke writes there about the 'animal oeconomy'.

64 Peter H. Nidditch, 'Introduction' John Locke, *An Essay Concerning Human Understanding*, p. xii.

65 Kelly 'General Introduction: Locke on Money'; Leng, 'Shaftesbury's Aristocratic Empire'; J. R. Milton, 'The Unscholastic Statesman: Locke and the Earl of Shaftesbury', in John Spurr (ed.), *Anthony Ashley Cooper, First Earl of Shaftesbury 1621–1683* (Surrey, Burlington: Ashgate, 2011).

Lord Ashley oversaw improving the disastrous management of the colonies and promoting trade with them and introduced the inexpert but very sharp Locke to contemporary thinking on trade and money for political and imperial purposes. During this period Ashley had a great deal of power, as can be seen from records of his dealings, in relation to seeking to make the 'Southern Plantations' (e.g. in Barbados and Carolina) flourish.[66] His *protegé* learned at first hand the aristocrat's early attempts to create a situation of mutual benefit as between landed proprietors and investors and the empire at large. Through his collaboration with Lord Ashley, Locke the civil servant was in a key position, able to witness important events and learn from them, while also initiating development of the constitutional framework for the common prosperity of the colonies and the nation. Famously, Locke was involved in the drafting of the Constitution of Carolina, which, despite the contemporary disregard of the settlers, are now assessed as amounting to ingenious legal drafting that greatly contributed to the stability of the life of the colony.[67] Lord Ashley invested hope above all in well-managed plantations with abundant crops that could be traded successfully. As Thomas Leng writes, the implementation of this vision lay in his 'aristocratic' understanding of empire as amounting to the burden and privilege of landed proprietors.[68] Locke's substantial involvement in the amendment of the provisions of the *Fundamental Constitutions of Carolina*, which reinforced the settlers' power of life and death over African slaves over the years, is a historical fact.[69] Nevertheless, that pragmatic support of slavery is irreconcilable with Locke's philosophical and theological thinking. He fundamentally opposed the notion that God had given one human being dominion over another.[70] The perspective that the greater dream of production and riches for the economy of the empire took priority above almost every other political consideration is one way in which to rationalize his involvement in drafting the consent to these powers. Other ideas about the 'necessaries' for the colony seem to be derived from that clear set of goals. Thus, in a letter to a merchant who transported settlers to Carolina, Ashley instructed him as follows:

66 Leng, 'Shaftesbury's Aristocratic Empire'.
67 Leng, 'Shaftesbury's Aristocratic Empire'.
68 Leng, 'Shaftesbury's Aristocratic Empire'.
69 Armitage, *Foundations of Modern International Thought*, ch. 6.
70 So his most famous political work starts: 'Slavery is so vile and miserable an Estate of Man, and so directly opposite to the generous Temper and Courage of our Nation; that 'tis hardly to be conceived, that an *Englishman*, much less a *Gentleman*, should plead for't.' Locke, *Two Treatises of Government*, I. §1; §26; §27; §28;

> forbeare to invite the poorer sort yet a while ... it being substantiall men and theire Familyes, that must make the Plantation which will stock the country with Negroes, Cattle and other Necessarys, whereas others relye and eate upon us.[71]

The meaning of 'necessaries', referring to enslaved human beings, was here an aspect of the management of a wider colonial economic policy that probably derived more from Ashley than Locke, who was at all times a subordinate of a very shrewd statesman.[72] Since also Lord Ashley appears to have personally abhorred slavery, his view on this matter reflects the concept of economy as a reason of state, which was becoming sadly general during the period in question.[73] This approach has similarities to Boyle's imperial dreams in relation to the utility of science as discussed in Chapter 6. Lord Ashley's economic thinking was undoubtedly influenced by the Reformers' scientific views and specifically by another of his protegés, Benjamin Worsley, whom we have met already. The self-described author of the Navigation Acts, Worsley depicted the colonies as a happy and rare instance in which the nation could gain territory and trade at the same time. To those one may add, capital, since Ashley was determined to further enrich himself in the process, seemingly without embarrassment. On the contrary, he viewed capital increase as the mark of the success of the imperial enterprise – while the Reformers and probably also Locke cared more for the 'happy levellinge' of rich and poor.[74]

It is also remarkable that Locke's rise in influence and power coincides with Lord Ashley's fall from grace: he was dismissed from his post of Lord Chancellor in 1674, was removed from his position in the Privy Council the following year and later became dangerously unstable. He was the prime mover in the conspiracy against the King in 1682 and perhaps in the plan to assassinate Charles II and the Duke of York in March 1683, in what came to be known as 'the Rye House Plot'; he died in exile in Holland in January

[71] Leng, 'Shaftesbury's Aristocratic Empire', p. 109. The schemes to inhabit Jamaica with 'Vagabond and condemned Persons and such as are here useless' and 'enslaved African men and women' in Kate Luce Mulry, *An Empire Transformed: Remolding Bodies and Landscapes in the Restoration Atlantic* (New York: New York University Press, 2021), pp. 293–294.

[72] Milton, 'The Unscholastic Statesman: Locke and the Earl of Shaftesbury'.

[73] In the words of Damaris Masham's account of what Locke thought about Shaftesbury: 'Everything in him (Shaftesbury) was natural, and had a noble air of freedom, expressive of the character of a mind that abhorred slavery, not because he could not be the master, but because he could not suffer such an indignity to human nature.' Cranston, *A Biography*, p. 225.

[74] Leng, 'A Potent Plantation Well Armed and Policeed', p. 190; Leng, 'Shaftesbury's Aristocratic Empire'.

1683, before the events in question took place.[75] The prudent Locke had already established some distance from Ashley, in view of these matters, spending the period from 1675 to 1678 in France. However, he was tainted by his proximity to the late lord and had to fight to prove his innocence.[76] He travelled to Holland in August 1683 and did not return until 1689, during which period he wrote *An Essay Concerning Human Understanding*. According to his biographers, and despite his strenuous denial of the fact at the time, it appears that he was also involved in revolutionary politics during his time in Holland.[77] When William and Mary acceded to the throne after the Glorious Revolution, Locke was appointed Commissioner of Excise Appeals in 1689. From 1696 to 1700 he was a member of the newly established Board of Trade and Plantations, which seems to have been the first 'really weighty body of expert opinion on political and economic matters' in England. He sat on the Board as an expert in a matter that he had certainly mastered thanks to the training received with his early patron.[78]

Locke's writings show varying perspectives on the same theme – that is, how to preserve human nature and the nation – and the necessities of human nature were of key importance in the development of his theories in each of his main philosophical works. The unity of his thought is thus facilitated by the notion of necessities as (a) being instruments of sense and reason by

[75] Milton, 'John Locke and the Rye House Plot', p. 653.

[76] 'Some of my friends, when they considered how small an advancement of my fortune I had made in so long an attendance (of Shaftesbury) have thought I had no great reason to brag of the effects of that kindness. I say not this to complain of my dead master, it would be in no way decent in me. But in this extremity I cannot but complain of it as a hard case: that having reaped so little advantage from my service to him whilst living I should suffer so much on that account now he is dead.' Locke's letter to Lord Pembroke, dated 8 December 1684, quoted in Craston, *A Biography*, p. 247.

[77] Richard Ashcraft, 'Revolutionary Politics and Locke's *Two Treatises of Government*: Radicalism and Lockean Political Theory' 8 *Political Theory* (1980); Craston, *A Biography*; Milton shows the mental instability of Shaftesbury in the later period, which undermines, in a sense, Locke's radicalism. Milton, 'John Locke and the Rye House Plot'. Arguably, the only mystery in Locke's life is why he did not marry Damaris Cudworth when both were still single. With a proverbial control of his passions, Locke guarded his heart well. Although he had several female correspondents that displayed their affection in their letters, he never married. The one woman with him in his correspondence he appeared to be most intimate with, in fact, in romantic terms, Damaris Cudworth got married with Sir Francis Masham, a widower father of nine children, while Locke was in Holland. Nevertheless, they remained close. An arrangement was accepted in which Locke, for whose health London air was very detrimental, literally he could not breath, went to live with the Mashams. About his life in Oates with the Mashams, see Harrison and Laslett, *The Library of John Locke*, p. 7; and Knights, 'Sir Francis Masham, 3rd Bt.'

[78] Laslett, 'John Locke, the Great Recoinage, and the Origins of the Board of trade: 1695–1698', p. 372.

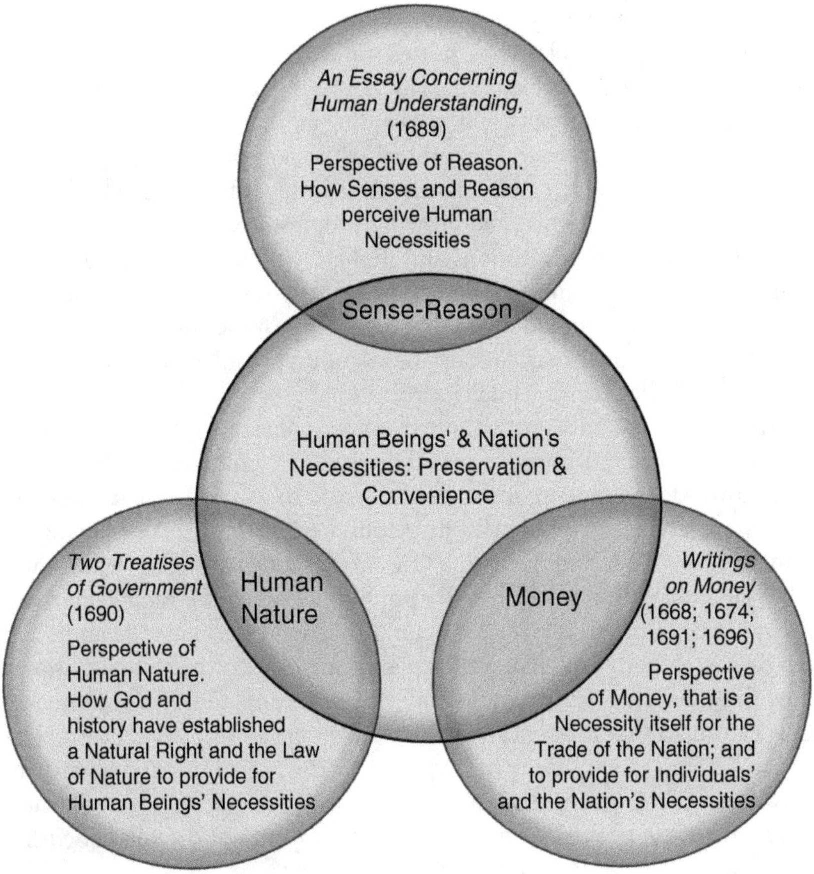

Figure 10.1 Locke's Doctrine of Necessities

which to perceive the world around us, (b) constituting the content of the natural law that seeks to preserve human nature, and (c) being a core economic notion that also explains the circle of trade through money. Through the doctrine of necessities it is explained how Locke modified moral natural law and established human necessities at its heart. Figure 10.1 shows that 'necessities' is a shared foundational concept in Locke's main works.

10.2 Usury, Interest and Science

In mid-seventeenth century, England monetary interest remained an acutely religious and moral issue. This fact highlights the originality and boldness of Locke's 1668 proposal to allow interest on money to fluctuate freely with the market. The traditional trouble did not of course lie with money lending per se: all laws permitted it and divine and natural law, in particular, encouraged it. What divine law, the laws of charity and Aristotelian philosophical tradition censured was lending at interest, especially onerous rates of interest.[79] However, in a country 'without mines' as contemporaries put it, whose goal was to participate in burgeoning international trade, and which experienced a remarkable growth in domestic consumption of goods, the lack of monetary institutions and monetary policy had become a burden.[80] Voicing the opinion of some, in the early seventeenth century, the learned Francis Bacon had noted that the disappearance of usury belonged in Utopia. Bacon did not encourage the relentless pursuit of lending but, as a necessary evil, he recommended its toleration.[81]

Apart from Bacon's short, though influential essay 'On Usury' (1612), several canonical authors are usually regarded as having led the movement towards opening up the reformed world to usury. These include the Protestant civil lawyer Charles du Moulin (1500–1566), the theologian Calvin (1509–1564) and the Dutch Calvinist Claude Saumaise (Salmasius) (1588–1653). Furthermore, the very popular *Consuetudo, vel lex mercatoria* by Gerard Malynes (1586–1641), published in London in 1622 and written by a merchant who had a thorough knowledge of his subject, shows how this issue was being handled in practice in England. Du Moulin and Calvin argued that usury was in causing damage and fraud to our neighbours, and not in extracting utility of them. The French jurist's essentially anti-Aristotelian position wrote that 'conscience does not bind when nature does not oblige' (*Conscientia non ligat quos natura non obligat*).[82]

[79] Some historical laws *tolerating* usury appear in Gerard Malynes, *Consuetudo, vel lex mercatoria, or The ancient law-merchant Diuided into three parts: according to the essentiall parts of trafficke* (London: Adam Islip, 1622) Early English Books Online Text Creation Partnership, 2011, http://name.umdl.umich.edu/A06786.0001.001, pp. 331–332. About Malynes see Perry Gauci, (4.10.2008) 'Malynes [Malines, de Malines], Gerard [Garrett, Gerald] (fl. 1585–1641), Merchant and Writer on Economics.' *Oxford Dictionary of National Biography;* about his economic doctrine, E. A. J. Johnson, 'Gerard de Malynes and the Theory of the Foreign Exchanges' 23 *The American Economic Review* (1933).

[80] William Robert Scott, *The Constitution and Finance of English, Scottish and Irish Joint-Stock Companies to 1720* (Cambridge: Cambridge University Press, 1912) vol. I. *The General Development of the Joint-Stock System Up to 1720*; Muldrew, *The Economy of Obligation.*

[81] Francis Bacon, 'On Usury' in *Bacon's Essays and Wisdom of the Ancients*, with a biography by A. Spiers and preface by B. Montagu, with notes by different writers, (Boston: Little Brown and Co., 1884), pp. 231–236.

[82] Carolus Molinaeus, *Tractatus commerciorum, et usurarum, redituum*, (Pariisis, apud Ioannem Lodoicum Tiletanum, 1546), p. 5. On Calvin see, Matthias Schmoeckel, *Das Recht der Reformation. Die epistemologische Revolution der Wissenschaft und die Spaltung der*

Salmasius was more aggressive, approving of moneylenders that derived their profits from the poor. In his magisterial history of the practice, Eugen von Böhm-Bawerk, would, as a neoclassical economist, censure the condemnation of usury, and not the practice itself.[83]

10.2.1 Fraternal Love versus Love of Money

The evils arising from generalised usury were grave and were felt immediately. Its social consequences included increased covetousness, extorsion and damage to fraternal love. In the context of Christian theology, its worse effect was a threat to each individual's relationship with God. In Aquinas's phrase, the correct use of material goods depends on a good will, meaning a will that naturally loves God more than oneself.[84] Love of money posed a great impediment to the attitude that the Christian God demanded. Usury first devoured the souls of those practising it and then destroyed the community. As is well known, that was not an exclusively Christian standpoint. The communitarian Aristotelian position stated that in a society of friends, of virtuous, liberal individuals, money would flow freely and cash transfers for those in need would be the outcome of virtue. Albert the Great's

Rechtsordnung in der Frühen Neuzeit (Tübingen: Mohr Siebeck), pp. 250–252. About the canonical figures and the situation in England see Jones, *God and the Moneylenders: Usury and Law in Early Modern England*; R. H. Tawney, 'Introduction' to Thomas Wilson, *A Discourse Upon Usury* (London: G. Bell and Sons, Ltd., 1925). An overview of the evolution of the Catholic doctrine on usury in John T. Noonan Jr., *The Scholastic Analysis of Usury* (Cambridge: Harvard University Press, 1957) and the comprehensive study of scholastic economic thought touching also upon the doctrine of usury in the classic, Odd Langholm, *Economics in the Medieval Schools. Wealth, Exchange, Value, Money and Usury according to the Paris Theological Tradition, 1200–1350* (Leiden, New York, Köln: Brill, 1992). See also defending that neither Calvinism, nor Protestantism for that matter, was particularly important in approving usury, which if the connection is taken to be straightforward makes some sense, Charles H. George, 'English Calvinist Opinion on Usury, 1600–1640' 18 *Journal of the History of Ideas* (1957). Arguing for Luther's rejection of practices that entailed hoarding of money, Philipp Rössner, 'Burying Money? Monetary Origins and Afterlives of Luther's Reformation' 48 *History of Political Economy* (2016). Also a helpful study of the anti-usury campaigns of the Church and its economic impact by John H. Munro, 'The Usury Doctrine and Urban Public Finances in Late-Medieval Flanders: Annuities, Excise Taxes, and Income Transfer from the Poor to the Rich' *University of Toronto Working Paper*, (11 June 2007)

83 Eugen von Böhm-Bawerk, *Capital and Interest. A Critical History of Economical Theory*, trans. with and Introduction by William Smart (London: MacMillan and Co. 1890).

84 *Summa theologiae*, I pars, q. 48, a. 6. co; q. 60. a 5. co. Aquinas deals with usury in passim in several places, and specifically in *Summa theologiae* II-II, q. 78, where he considered it to be against natural law and a sin, but also sometimes, a necessary evil in the commonwealth.

description of usurers and merchants (in the thirteenth century) was that they were 'illiberal', whereas 'the liberal uses moneys well'.[85]

In a nutshell, the classic theory against usury, though not strictly monolithic, possessed an important core.[86] It was not in the nature of money to yield fruits. Money was consumed through transference (*per translationem*). The theologian and finance expert Henry of Ghent wrote that in relation to money it was impossible to allocate separate prices in respect of 'substance' and 'use' and that therefore no profit could be derived from its use.[87] The argument concerned respecting the nature of the thing – in this case, money. Odd Langholm points to Aquinas's very similar negative argument against usury:

> The principal use of silver plate is not in its consumption; and therefore one can licitly sell its use retaining the dominion of the thing. The primary use of silver coin, however, is its disbursement in commercial transactions. It is, therefore, not legitimate both to make a charge for its use and to expect the money lent to be restored.[88]

Consequently, Aquinas and, later, Henry regarded the divided dominion of money (between principal dominion and its use) as sinful. In view of the nature of money, changes in time and place did not entitle a person to obtain more than an amount reflecting its substance or quantity.[89] As is

[85] Among the illiberal Albert names the gamblers, always in need of money, and all who for love of money enrich themselves in shameful though licit ways, like beggars or illicit, like the seducers of prostitutes and the usurers. They have in common the dishonorable enrichment. Other illiberal, are those who enrich themselves from friends but spare no one, and also are illiberal the 'merchants', who travel across the seas in misery and endure great dangers for the charm of gain ('et hi, idest alii illiberales sicut mercatores, sustinent magna pericula gratia lucri; unde dicit Horatius: "Per mare pauperiem fugiens, per saxa, per ignes"'). Money signifies everything which is given or exchanged (*communicantur*) by money. *Super Ethica commentum et quaestiones*, I-V, ed. W. Kübel, *Alberti Magni opera omnia, XIV/1* (Münster 1968–1972), p. 221, 43; 87; p. 236, l. 78; p. 241, 30. For commerce as a 'necessary evil' in Aquinas see, Langholm, *Economics in the Medieval Schools*, pp. 221–222.

[86] The argument of Odd Langholm is partly that there was not one single approach of theology to trade, and, similarly to matters purely theological, theologians followed different theoretical avenues, Langholm, *Economics in the Medieval Schools*, pp. 221–248.

[87] Henry of Ghent, Quodlibet I, q. 39, 1. *Henrici de Gandavo, Opera Omnia*, R. Macken (ed.), vol. V.

[88] *Summa theologia*, II-II, q. 78, 1, ad 6. The Dominican Fathers translate 'sell the right to use'. Aquinas did not employ that expression of 'right to use' but simply 'use': 'usus eorum potest vendi licite servato dominio rei', 238–239; Langholm, *Economics in the Medieval Schools*, p. 243.

[89] 'pro nummi locatione nihil potest iuste ultra substantiam eius recipi'; 'si autem uti ea vis, necesse est ut eam transferas, nec plus quam pretium et valorem eius pro ea recipias.' Quodlibet I, q. 39. 1. For Henry, the theologian is the main authority to judge on the

well known, Aristotle had deeply influenced theologians on this issue. The famous passage of the first book of *Politics* stating that profiting from something naturally sterile like money went against nature is worth quoting:[90]

> The most hated sort (of money-making), and with the greatest reason, is usury, which makes a gain out of money itself, and not from the natural use of it. For money was intended to be used in exchange, but not to increase at interest. And this term usury, which means the birth of money from money, is applied to the breeding of money because the offspring resembles the parent. Whereof of all modes of making money this is the most unnatural.[91]

These efforts to establish a bulwark against the practice of usury in the Western philosophical and theological traditions alike had exploded by the mid-sixteenth century, giving rise to a shift from the condemnation of usury per se towards more or less general censure and regulation of fraudulent practices in the context of usury, similar to the positive regulation that exists today.[92] However, it took some time before there was general acceptance of the rightness of this approach, in respect of which von Böhm-Bawerk stated that the 'Church, the law and the learned world had condemned [usury] with one voice and opposed [it] with arguments drawn from all sources'.[93] So much so, that the historian Richard Henry Tawney, writing in the twentieth century, viewed the question of usury and money as one of the main economic controversies of sixteenth-century England.[94] The intermittent social, religious and theological chaos characteristic of the period surely did not help. Robert Ingram's argument that in the eighteenth century the English long Reformation was still underway is a plausible estimate of its duration.[95] With that in mind, we may only imagine

economic matters of secular society, see on this question Marialucrezia Leone, 'The Theologian and the Contracts: Henry of Ghent and the *Emptio-Venditio Reddituum*' in 75 *Recherches de théologie et philosophie médiévales* (2008), p. 151.

90 See a comment in Odd Langholm, *The Aristotelian Analysis of Usury* (Bergen: Universitetsforlaget, 1984); Noonan, *Scholastic Analysis of Usury*.

91 Aristotle, *Politics*, I.10, 1258b.

92 A short analysis of the extreme liberal position of Jeremy Bentham challenging Adam Smith's state-imposed caps on the rate of interest, slightly above the lowest price of money in the market is Joseph Persky's study, which suggests that the latter's standpoint is the general position today, Joseph Persky, 'From Usury to Interest' 21 *The Journal of Economic Perspectives* (2007).

93 v. Böhm-Bawerk, *Capital and Interest*, p. 32.

94 Tawney, 'Introduction' to Thomas Wilson, *A Discourse Upon Usury*.

95 Ingram's argument is, with John Neville Figgis, that the Reformation has not yet ended. Robert G. Ingram, *Reformation Without End: Religions, Politics and the Past in Post-Revolutionary England* (Manchester: Manchester University Press, 2018).

what the situation was like in the late sixteenth and seventeenth centuries. In summary, the situation was confusing, and doctrinal positions as to theology and the law were extremely uncertain and sharply divided.

10.2.2 *The Acts against Usury*

An overview of the discussions in Parliament from 1614 to 1660 for and against the abatement of usury shows not only economic reasons – such as fluctuations in the price of land, the problem of the hoarding of money and the fact that usurers would send their money abroad if interest rates were lower at home – but also an element of religious scandal. The legislative evolution that took place in the 1640s was culturally very relevant. What Vera Keller has referred to more broadly as 'the Interregnum Christianizing of Interest' occurred literally in the House of Commons.[96] It started in 1648 with the consultation of 'the Divines' on the notion of 'Usury':

> *Ordered*, That as to the Word 'Usury', in the Paragraph of the Large Catechism, be re-committed to the Assembly of Divines: And it is referred to the Assembly of Divines, to explain what they mean by the Word 'Usury', in that Place; and to return their Opinions to the House.[97]

This was followed in 1651 by new neutral language about 'Interest of money' and legislation ordering at once a reduction of the interest rate to 6 per cent and the removal of the word 'usury':

> The Question being put, That the House doth agree with the Committee, that this Proviso, 'Provided That no Words in this Law contained shall be construed or expounded to allow the Practice of Usury, in point of Religion or Conscience', be left out.[98]

With the Restoration, this concept was stoutly revived, and thus we read in the records that in the summer of 1660, in discussing the reduction of the interest rate to 6 per cent, the House '*Resolved*, That the Title of the said Bill be, An Act for Restraining the Taking of excessive Usury'.[99]

96 Keller, *Knowledge and the Public Interest, 1575–1725*, p. 377.

97 'House of Commons Journal Volume 5: 24 July 1648', in *Journal of the House of Commons: Volume 5, 1646–1648* (London, 1802), pp. 644–646. *British History Online* www.british-history.ac.uk/commons-jrnl/vol5/pp644-646 (accessed 21 January 2021).

98 'House of Commons Journal Volume 6: 20 May 1651', in *Journal of the House of Commons: Volume 6, 1648–1651* (London, 1802), pp. 575–576. *British History Online* www.british-history.ac.uk/commons-jrnl/vol6/pp575-576 (accessed 21 January 2021).

99 'House of Commons Journal Volume 8: 22 August 1660', in *Journal of the House of Commons: Volume 8, 1660–1667* (London, 1802), pp. 130–131. *British History Online* www.british-history.ac.uk/commons-jrnl/vol8/pp130-131 (accessed 21 January 2021).

In *God and the Money Lenders*, Norman Jones relates the history of the Acts against usury and the indignities that the spread of usury caused in late sixteenth-century English society.[100] These included the imposition of interest rates of up to 25 per cent or more, the appearance of professional middlemen, and so-called 'brokers' squeezing the borrower to the extreme, especially the poor. In 1570 preachers decried the universality of the vice of usury in England, in which everyone 'was involved'.[101] After a more lenient prohibition by Henry VIII in 1545, and a drastic one by Edward VI in 1552, the 1571 Act Against Usury was enacted. In his phenomenal though occasionally Whiggish, early history of joint-stock companies in England, Ireland and Scotland, William Scott points to two positions in the parliamentary discussions of April 1571, prior to passing the act.[102] There was one group of moderates as well as another, which 'relying on Scripture, Aristotle, Canon Law and other authorities' was wary of the danger to young gentry of falling into the traps set by usurers and to the Queen's Custom if people put their money into usury attracted by high interest, rather than into trade.[103] A study of the parliamentary discussions of that day, however, reveals that those against usury did not merely employ the scriptural and 'Praeter Naturam' argument against lending money at interest, but also quoted the 'most ancient laws of this realm'.[104] The antiquarian Sir William Fleetwood (1525–1594) noted that many laws and inquiries against 'Christian usury' appeared in the records.[105] Soon to be Recorder of

100 Jones, *God and the Moneylenders*; see for the seventeenth-century Acts 'House of Commons Journal' Volumes 1–8 (1621–1661), *British History Online* www.british-history.ac.uk; another overview of the general practice also in Tawney, 'Introduction' to Thomas Wilson, *A Discourse Upon Usury*; an example is the generalized practice of usury in the city of Leicester, not as a trade, but as 'the sideline of the business, and the stand-by of retired traders and moneyed widows'. It produced 'very high interest rates' and 'a large amount of desperate debts', in R. A. McKinley 'The City of Leicester: Social and Economic History, 1506–1660', in R. A. McKinley (ed.), *A History of the County of Leicester: Volume 4, the City of Leicester* (Victoria County History, London, 1958), pp. 76–109.

101 Jones, *God and the Moneylenders*, p. 67.

102 William Robert Scott, *The Constitution and Finance of English, Scottish and Irish Joint-Stock Companies to 1720* (Cambridge: Cambridge University Press, 1912) vol. I. *The General Development of the Joint-Stock System Up to 1720.*

103 Scott, *The Constitution and Finance of English, Scottish and Irish Joint-Stock Companies to 1720*, p. 54.

104 Simonds d'Ewes, 'Journal of the House of Commons: April 1571', in *The Journals of All the Parliaments During the Reign of Queen Elizabeth* (Shannon, Ire, 1682), pp. 155–180. *British History Online* www.british-history.ac.uk/no-series/jrnl-parliament-eliz1/pp155-180 (accessed 19 January 2021).

105 'So do the Laws made in *Lucious* his time, and those of *Athelred*; whereby it was ordained, that Witches and Usurers should be banished. King *Edward* the Saint

London, a legal office of conservator of the peace and supreme judge in the city, and valued by the Queen in that position, Fleetwood knew the ancient laws and manuscripts well.[106] Hence, he declared

> that Usury was *malum in se*, for that of some other transgressions, her Majesty may dispence afore with; but for Usury, or to grant that Usury may be used, she possibly cannot.[107]

A notorious anti-papist and priest hunter, who ended up in jail after breaking into the Portuguese Ambassador's residence in search of English Catholics participating in the Mass, Fleetwood was, probably due to that zeal, dubbed the Earl of Leicester's 'mad Recorder' in *Leicester's Commonwealth*, a libellous text written against Robert Dudley, Elizabeth's favourite and a leading political figure at the time.[108] Fleetwood has been rescued from obscurity on account of his having been a very knowledgeable antiquarian both of the history of England and of more contemporary authors such as Macchiavelli and Bodin.[109] That in opposition of those advising to concentrate the prohibition on the degree of usury, that is, the modern position, Fleetwood had such an uncompromising standpoint against the entire practice, is remarkable as a proof of the strong prohibition against usury in traditional English law and the conflicting feelings that this fact provoked at the time.

referreth and appointeth the Offenders herein to suffer *ordalium*. Then was there a great kind of Usury known, which was called *Torus*, and a lesser known by the name of .... *Glanvile*, in the Book *de legibus antiquis*, maketh mention of an inquiry of Christian Usurers.' Fleetwood's speech is summarised in d'Ewes, 'Journal of the House of Commons: April 1571'.

106 P. R. Harris, 'William Fleetwood, Recorder of the City, and Catholicism in Elisabethan England' 7 *Recusant History* (1963), pp. 109–118; J. D. Alsop, 'William Fleetwood and Elisabethan Historical Scholarship' 25 *The Sixteenth Century Journal* (1994), pp. 155–176; Christopher W. Books, 'Fleetwood, William' (c. 1525–1594) *Oxford National Biography*, 23.9.2004, https://doi.org/10.1093/ref:odnb/9690

107 Fleetwood in d'Ewes, 'Journal of the House of Commons: April 1571'. This was the position of Aquinas: 'Respondeo. Dicendum quod dare pecuniam mutuo ad usuram est peccatum mortale. Nec ideo est peccatum quia est prohibitum; sed potius ideo est prohibitum, quia est secundum se peccatum; est enim contra iustitiam naturalem'. *De malo*, q. 13 a. 4 co. www.corpusthomisticum.org/qdm08.html#63279; for a discussion, Langholm, *Economics in the Medieval Schools*, p. 238.

108 Anonymous, *Leicester's Commonwealth: The Copy of a Letter Written by a Master of Art of Cambridge (1584) and Related Documents*, D. C. Peck (ed.) (Athens: Ohio University Press, 1985). On the authorship of the libel *Leicester's Commonwealth* see, Peter Holmes 'The Authorship of 'Leicester's Commonwealth' 33 *The Journal of Ecclesiastical History* (1982), pp. 424–430.

109 Also, 'William Fleetwood and Elisabethan Historical Scholarship'.

The new Act of 1571 tolerated usury and prohibited interest rates above 10 per cent. It also recognized some charitable forms of lending money at interest, as in the case of orphans' and widows' states. Despite the command to limit the rate, lending at interest on a large scale generalized at any rate of interest that could be got. Hence, the issue of public policy became the manner in which to secure enforcement of the law through informants. Jones links the transformation of attitudes towards usury at the end of the sixteenth century to broader theological issues concerning grace and good works. The dangers of covetousness and idolatry in relation to money were glossed over and the divines now began to refer to lending with purity of heart and good intentions. Since only God knows what is in one's heart, so this argument went, the important thing was to keep a pure conscience. Jones takes the view that this perspective lay at the heart of the 1624 Act against usury that allowed lending at 8 per cent and reminded lenders of the need to maintain a pure conscience.[110] The merchant scholar Gerard Malynes stated that position clearly in 1622. Usury was more subjective, than objective. A loan in which the interest compensated for loss (*ex damno habito*) or loss of profit (*lucro cessante*) was not usury. The circumstances justifying the application of interest to a loan included the profits that the borrower may acquire through use of the loan, whether he or she is in real need, the rate of interest and so on. A person granting loans would of course react to economic events but should do so with mercy for those in need and with each particular borrower in mind.[111] As studies of English economy up to the end of the seventeenth century make clear, in a deeply experimental and disorganized economy the issue of the rate of interest to be applied to money was interlocked with other measures designed to stimulate economic growth. These measures remained underexplored and not fully understood. In particular the scarcity of money in specie (bullion coins) remained an unexplained curse at the time.[112] In the early 1620s, Sir Thomas Culpeper (1578–1662) declared that high interest rates on money discouraged trade in favour of the business of lending and chilled communal attitudes in society by a 'care upon one another with usury'.[113]

110 Jones, *God and the Moneylenders*.

111 'So that your conscience is stil the surest guide to direct you with prudence, as the load-stone doth the variation of the Pole.' Malynes, *Consuetudo, vel lex mercatoria*, p. 331.

112 Kelly, 'General Introduction: Locke on Money'; on the disorganisation of the state see Muldrew, *The Economy of Obligation*, p. 182; on money experiments in the end of the seventeenth century, Richard A. Kleer, *Money, Politics and Power. Banking and Public Finance in Wartime England 1694–96* (Abingdon, New York: Routledge, 2017).

113 Sir Thomas Culpeper, *A Tract Against Usurie Presented to the High Court of Parliament* (London: William Iaggard, 1621), Early English Books Online Text Creation Partnership, http://name.umdl.umich.edu/A19689.0001.001 (accessed 8 June 2022).

10.2.3 The Concerns of Gerard Malynes

Malynes's voluminous *Consuetudo, vel lex mercatoria* of 1622 offers probably the most thorough and informed contemporary account about interest on money from a merchant's perspective and was rightly praised by Hartlib.[114] According to his biographer, Malynes had a long career of disasters and mischiefs as a merchant, but managed to stay consistently close to the upper echelons of government. He seems to have redeemed himself by this learned work, six chapters of which are devoted to usury.[115] In Baconian spirit Malynes expressed the need for usury for 'traffick', while he rather opted for not allowing very high rates of interest, apparently agreeing with Sir Thomas Culpeper. Still a Renaissance man, Malynes was all for order and harmony, and thus for contemplating different interest rates for different groups of people, merchants, humble householders and the poor. But where Malynes appears more original was in his call to address the 'Usurie politike', in relation to which, in a country without banks or similar institutions, he urged the government to intervene by means of economic policies to promote the common good on a large scale.[116] Craig Muldrew's study on the expansion of credit makes it clear that Malynes was right to point to the problems that resulted from lack of governmental intervention. Societal interpersonal relations were carrying the burden of the rapid development of the market, and legislation allowing usury for everyone only increased that pressure. Malynes realistically depicted the widespread practice of usury and its main effects on the humblest workers, 'the mechanick' men and women, who were often tricked into receiving loans for very short time periods, resulting in having to pay interest of up to '400 percent in the hundred' per year – while the law allowed 10 per cent. Malynes critically applied the ubiquitous seventeenth-century metaphor of the clock in *Consuetudo,*

114 Hartlib called it a 'great book', Samuel Hartlib, *The Reformed Common-Wealth of Bees* (Londong, Printed for Giles Calbert, 1655), Early English Books Online Text Creation Partnership, http://name.umdl.umich.edu/A45759.0001.001 (accessed 8 June 2022), p. 159.

115 Gauci, (4.10.2008) 'Malynes [Malines, de Malines], Gerard [Garrett, Gerald] (fl. 1585–1641), Merchant and Writer on economics.'

116 Other important economic questions that had been debated in recent times were the elimination of monopolies in the beginning of the seventeenth century, for instance, by Sir Edwin Sandys, who would ironically promote himself in the 1620s the monopoly of tobacco of the Virginia Company. See Sandys's "Instructions touching the Bill for free Trade", in 'House of Commons Journal Volume 1: 19 May 1604', in *Journal of the House of Commons: Volume 1, 1547–1629* (London, 1802), pp. 214–215. *British History Online* www.british-history.ac.uk/commons-jrnl/vol1/pp214-215 (accessed 21 January 2021). On Edwin Sandys see T. Rabb (23 September 2004). Sandys, Sir Edwin (1561–1629), politician and colonial entrepreneur. *Oxford Dictionary of National Biography*.

vel lex mercatoria. He wanted to show how the wheels of crime were all connected, like in a clock, since the 'brokers' who extort money from the people 'have their money masters, to whom they pay twentieth in the hundrethe'. He took the view that the lack of governmental policy in this area was the chief cause of the abuses and accordingly recommended 'a godly work' that would be equivalent to 'the Bridges' in the Low Countries or 'the *Montes pietatis*' ('Banks of Charity') in Italy where people in need could pawn things or receive loans without interest. Malynes mentioned a list of 1500 charitable persons he had prepared that would be willing to donate money to that enterprise. However, he added, nothing had come of it due to the intrigues of a person in whom he had placed trust.[117]

In effect, the merchant scholar was all for the money business. However, he also reflected on the need for some sort of institutional effort for the common good of the people – for a policy that would go beyond the current legislation that merely allowed usury. That collective effort would afford every decent person that wished to do so an opportunity to participate in the economic life of the nation, without danger of falling into the hands of usurers. This would have the added advantage of getting rid of criminals, since 'according to the Prouerbe, *If there were no receiuers, there would be few theeues*'.[118] Hence the significance of Malyne's pioneering 'Usurie politike' lay in its advising political control over the new financial life of the nation in a manner that would stimulate and multiply citizens' economic transactions while also preventing organized crime and observing the rules of charity.

For all the widespread practice of usury and the legislation encouraging the application of up to 10 per cent of interest for money, the moral issue relating to this practice continued to be a subject of hot debate for decades. In *The English Usurer or Usury Condemned*, John Blaxton showed that doubts over the morality of usury were not put to rest with the new legislation. There was a difference, he suggested, between the legislation and what a pious Anglican would do. The legality of usury, Blaxton wrote, could not 'excuse the usurer in the court of conscience'.[119]

10.2.4 *The Scholars' Discussion*

Responding to a collective of divines and despite a more scientific bent in some of its parts, Robert Filmer's tract *A Discourse Whether it May be*

117 Malynes, *Consuetudo, vel lex mercatoria*, ch. 13.

118 Malynes, *Consuetudo, vel lex mercatoria*, p. 337.

119 John Blaxton, *The English Usurer, or Usury Condemned: By the Most Learned and Famous Divines of the Church of England* (London: John Norton, 1634), p. 60.

Lawful to Take Use for Money argued in favour of the morality of usury, largely as a response to Roger Fenton's *A Treatise of Usury Divided into Three Books* of 1611.[120] Filmer's text on usury is altogether Biblical, advising, nevertheless in the style of the new science to use 'the light of Nature' and 'reason or sense'. Following revision of the various laws, Filmer concluded that 'the law of God no where in plain terms forbids the increase of Mony'.[121] Overall Filmer proved again, as he did in *Patriarcha*, that he was a tough man of innovative but obscure theological credentials. He was influential though, and it is remarkable and indicative of his impact that, though probably written in the 1630s, *A Discourse* was first published in 1653, the year of Filmer's death.[122] Peter Laslett's appraisal that *Patriarcha* reflects 'conventional theology' is nowadays discredited.[123] Johann P. Sommerville has shown that it is untenable to pin Filmer as the orthodox Anglican against Locke, the secular libertarian. In fact, the two authors' ideas share the same roots, with Filmer being, interestingly, the more radical in theological terms.[124] For example, *Patriarcha* contains a number of departures from the Bible. In noting that Jewish Law prohibits practising usury on the poor, Filmer stated as follows: 'But with us it is otherwise; if by any other meanes we do sufficiently relieve the poor, then even the taking of Usury of them is no sin, nor oppression.'[125] Filmer did not fail to mention the question of usury again in his well-known 'Observations

[120] See on Fenton's critique to the idea that usury was a necessity of trade, and generally her chapter on the retreat of moral economy during the period examined here, Appleby, *Economic Thought and Ideology in Seventeenth-Century England*, pp. 52–71; p. 66.

[121] Robert Filmer, *A Discourse Whether it may be Lawful to take Use for Money*, (London: Printed for Will Crook, 1678), Early English Books Online Text Creation Partnership, 2011, http://name.umdl.umich.edu/A41301.0001.001 (accessed 8 June 2022), p. 97.

[122] The date of 1653 in Peter Laslett, 'Concise Bibliography of the Works of Sir Robert Filmer' in Sir Robert Filmer, *Patriarcha and Other Writings*, pp. liv–lv; the later date of 1678 in Johann P. Sommerville 'Sir Robert Filmer, Usury and the Ideology of Order', in Daniel Carey (ed.), *Money and the Political Economy of Enlightenment*, Oxford University Studies in the Enlightenment (Oxford: Oxford Voltaire Foundation, 2014), pp. 31–56.

[123] Laslett, 'Introduction' of Robert Filmer, *Patriarcha and Other Political Works*, p. xxxv.

[124] Sommerville 'Sir Robert Filmer, Usury and the Ideology of Order'.

[125] Filmer, *A Discourse*, p. 50. He was writing at the same time that Salmasius, perhaps influenced by him whose views were in turn praised by v. Böhm-Bawerk as the high-water mark of interest theory, determining 'the direction and substance of the theory of interest for more than a hundred years'. von Böhm-Bawerk, *Capital and Interest*, p. 36. On the Monte di Pietà and its function of lending money to the poor, with a tax or an interest that could for example oscillate between 0.5 and 7 per cent see, Paola Avallone 'Il credito su pegno nel Regno di Napoli (XVI–XIX secolo) in *Prestare ai poveri. Il credito su pegno e I Monti di Pietà in area Mediterranea* (secoli XV–XIX) (Torino, Napoli: Consiglio Nazionale delle Ricerche, Instituto di Studi sulle Società del Mediterraneo, 2007), pp. 69–100; p. 86.

Upon Aristotles Politiques Touching Forms of Government', this time placing the political relevance of usurious practices in its historical context.[126] The 'Commons' in Rome found themselves terribly in debt after the wars that endangered their estates, and 'as they thought, oppressed by usury', complained 'of usury and of the power of the Consuls' and managed by sedition to obtain the election of magistrates that represented them as the tribunes of the people.[127] He also noted the 'incredible gains' achieved in terms of public revenue from 'the usury of the Jews' in Venice,

> for in every city they keep open shops of interest, taking pawns after fifteen in the hundred, and if at the year's end, it be not redeemed, it is forfeited, or at the least, sold at great lost. The revenues which the very courtesans pay for toleration, maintain no less than a dozen galleys.[128]

Through this kind of public policy, Filmer seemed to suggest, the practice of usury spread in society and the Jews were exploited at the same time.

In *A Treatise of Taxes*, William Petty devoted a chapter to 'Usury' and commented on the reasonableness of paying interest on loans on the grounds of the inconvenience caused to the lender through making the loan, which amounts to an elaboration of the classic argument also put forward by Aquinas in terms of the 'loss of the lender' (*damnun emergens*).[129] Petty astutely changed the perspective: instead of criticising the morality of usury on the basis of the borrower's need, he defended its licit nature by looking at 'the necessities' of the lenders:

> Wherefore when a man giveth out his money upon condition that he may not demand it back until a certain time to come, whatsoever his own necessities shall be in the mean time, he certainly may take a compensation for this inconvenience which he admits against himself: And this allowance is that we commonly call Usury[130]

More to the point and, and seemingly with similar ideas to Locke's, he employed the conception of 'simple natural interest' as 'the Rent of so much Land as the money lent will buy'. Where security was uncertain, and troublesome, as in England, Petty thought that interest must be employed;

126 Filmer, 'Observations Upon Aristotles Politiques Touching Forms of Government', p. 165.

127 Robert Filmer, 'Observations on Mr. Hobbes's Leviathan: Or his Artifical Man-A Commonwealth' in Filmer, *Patriarcha and Other Political Works*; Robert Filmer, 'Observations on Mr. Milton Against Salmasius', in Filmer, *Patriarcha and Other Political Works*.

128 Filmer, 'Observations Upon Aristotles Politiques Touching Forms of Government', p. 170.

129 *Summa theologiae*, II-II, 78.2, ad 1; Langholm, *Economics in the Medieval Schools*, p. 245.

130 Petty, *A Treatise of Taxes*, p. 80.

that was in itself unpredictable, amounting to 'any height below the Principal'. It was fruitless, in Petty's view, to seek to limit usury at any given time and in any given place, and was akin to making 'Civil Positive Laws against the Laws of Nature' – an activity that involved 'a vanity and fruitlessness', and Petty could only think 'that those who make such Laws were rather Borrowers then Lenders'.[131]

Among the books in Locke's library was *A Letter to a Friend Concerning Usury*, published in London 1690.[132] The Catalogue produced by John Harrison and Peter Laslett indicates that it was the only work on the issue of usury that he possessed. It argues against high interest rates and is concerned with summarizing the ideas for and against the reduction of interest in works penned by Sir Thomas Culpeper in 1621, Sir Thomas Culpeper junior (1668), Sir Josiah Child (1668) and Thomas Manley (1669). These works are in the main economic tracts, although all also touch upon the moral uncertainty of usury. This is particularly true in the writings of Sir Thomas Culpeper junior, who made a point of demonstrating that it was unlawful. Josiah Child's *Brief Observation Concerning Trade, and Interest of Money*, published in 1668, adopted an international perspective through which he sought to show the negative aspects of a high interest rate. While Child – who was soon to be Governor of the East India Company – acknowledged that a high rate of interest might attract Dutch money, he stated that was a 'meer Chymera' which would not increase the circulation of money in the country on a consistent basis. At any moment the Dutch could withdraw their money. Quoting the Bible, once again with reference to interest, Child recalled the lesson of 'that wise legislator', Moses, forbidding the use of money at interest among Jews and permitting it to foreigners. The Nation would become richer without high interest at home and no public good could ensue from consenting to it. Moreover, in terms of moral behaviour, the accrual of high interest on money also led to all sorts of vices, such as idleness.[133] The staunch defence of a higher rate of interest in Thomas Manley's controversial *Usury at six per cent examined* takes much less of a moral tone. Its main point was that abatement of usury was only possible in a rich country, while forcing 'Usury as low amongst us, a needy and declining people' was as reasonable as expecting fruitfulness

[131] Petty, *A Treatise of Taxes*, p. 80.

[132] R. C., *A Letter to a Friend Concerning Usury* (London: 1690), Early English Books Online Text Creation Partnership, 2011, http://name.umdl.umich.edu/A31146.0001.001.

[133] Sir Josiah, Child, *Brief observations concerning trade and interest of money* (London: Printed for Elizabeth Calvert and Henry Mortlock, 1668), p. 16.

from a barren land, thus repeating the strategy of painting a dark picture of the economy employed by those who called for higher interest rates. One of a cohort of pamphleteers, Manley blamed the bad economic situation (as he saw it) upon the idleness of the poor and was probably among the first to openly praise usurers for their service to the commonwealth.[134] Sir Thomas Culpeper senior was the most original of the writers under consideration, and his approach probably set the tone for many subsequent tracts, including Locke's. His insistence that 'Land and money are euer in ballance one against the other' may have given Locke impetus to think the issue through.[135]

It was, of course, a moral approach that Robert Sanderson took when discussing usury, but the winds of change are already visible in the respected moralist's work. Almost writing from the trenches of morality, attacked from all flanks, he wrote that one *ought not be forced* to lend at interest. He discussed usury in the context of necessary evil, as well as in other contexts. As 'an evil thing', similarly to other evils – divorce is the other example he gave –usury may be permitted by the law, since there were some evils that could be made to disappear only at great inconvenience to the public. Therefore it 'pertaineth to the political prudence of Government' to moderate how it was used, and in order to make it 'subservient to the Publick profit', delimit the bounds within which it was lawful. Permitting an evil, however, did not force anyone to commit it. Sanderson underlined that 'nevertheless this is certain, that were it never so lawful, no man by that permission is obliged to the exercising of it'.[136]

The letter from the physician and religious controversialist Lewis du Moulin (1605–1680) to 'the very noble' Robert Boyle on the question of usury testifies to the anxieties Boyle suffered on account of this issue, perhaps due to his own activities, or in the light of the proposal to readmit the

134 Thomas Manley, *Usury at six per cent. examined, and found unjustly charged by Sir Tho. Culpepper and J.C. with many crimes and oppressions, whereof 'tis altogether innocent* (…) (London: Pr. by Thomas Ratcliffe, and Thomas Daniel, 1669), Early English Books Online Text Creation Partnership, 2011, http://name.umdl.umich.edu/A51784.0001.001, p. 59. In a letter to a patron of his Manley was again supplying arguments against Culpeper in 1673, among them also of theology: 'The Lawfulness of ye encreas of monie both from Nature & reason, & yt ye prohibition of it among ye Jewes related to them as Jewes only, & so not binding to Christians.' See the letter and generally on Manley in the debate, Tim Keirn and Frank T. Melton, 'Thomas Manley and the Rate-Of-Interest Debate, 1668–1673', 29 *Journal of British Studies* (1990), p. 172.

135 Culpeper, *A Tract Against the High Rate of Usurie*, p. 18.

136 Sanderson, *Several Cases of Conscience Discussed*, p. 221.

Jews to England.[137] Du Moulin wrote that moral law and natural equity prohibited usury, but that one also must distinguish between loans that helped and loans that bit (*juvantis* or *laedentis*), the former being allowed and the latter prohibited.[138] However du Moulin's larger conclusion was that 'all the usury that benefits the debtor is licit'.[139] As a means of allowing a debtor to use someone else's money, it was permissible for creditors to demand interest on their money. It was true that God had prohibited the Jews from practising usury among themselves. Nevertheless, it was permissible if practised in accordance with moral law and natural equity. And, like Filmer, du Moulin noted that that prohibition of usury that applied to the Israelites did not affect Christian countries.[140] In addition, he considered that the arts of banking and commerce though more prone to vice than other liberal arts gave no cause to suspect dishonesty or deception if practised 'within the bounds of the rigor of the law'.[141] Here du Moulin contributed two interesting ideas. First, he focused on the promotion of the borrower's commercial activities. Second, in describing banking as being like any other profession and endorsing a legalist conception of the state, he indirectly pointed to the urgency of having *good laws* to regulate moneylenders' activities.

[137] Hunter, *Boyle: Between God and Science*, p. 85; p. 101. On Lewis du Moulin, see Vivienne Larminie (23 September 2010). Du Moulin, Lewis (1605?–1680), physician and religious controversialist. *Oxford Dictionary of National Biography*. Retrieved 30 October 2020, from www-oxforddnb-com.libproxy.helsinki.fi/view/10.1093/ref:odnb/9780198614128.001.0001/odnb-9780198614128-e-19428. The letter is inserted in a work that du Moulin dedicated to William Sydenham, the military man, older brother of Thomas, the physician. Ludovici Molinaei, 'Ad Nobilissimum & Praestantissimum Virum Robertum Boyle' in *Corollarium ad Paraenesim suam* (London, 1657), pp. 247–270. See also Michael Hunter, 'The Disquieted Mind in Casuistry and Natural Philosophy: Boyle and Thomas Barlow' in Michael Hunter (ed.), *Aspects of the Life and Thought of Robert Boyle (1627–91)* (Farnham: Ashgate, 2015).

[138] Molinaei, 'Ad Nobilissimum & Praestantissimum Virum Robertum Boyle', p. 261.

[139] 'sed in omnibus constitutionibus quibus societas & commercium inter homines constant eo spectet ut commodis utriusque partis consulat, quod fit per contractum usurarium aequum & moderatum. Unde colligere est eiusmodi usuram à legislatore prohibitam quae in damnum debitoris cedit, eam verò usuram concessam per quam ipse rem facit sine cujusquam fraude. sed ne praesidium petam ab illa distinctione, assero quantumvis apud omnes in confesso esset eam usuram quae debitori fructuosa est licitam esse, eamque probe concordare cum lege morali & aequitate naturali.' Molinaei, 'Ad Nobilissimum & Praestantissimum Virum Robertum Boyle', p. 262.

[140] Molinaei, 'Ad Nobilissimum & Praestantissimum Virum Robertum Boyle', p. 265

[141] 'etiam cum ex aequo omnes tum trapezitae, tum alii mercenarii seu mercatores seu opifices intra legum rigorem professione sua defunguntur: trapezitae enim nec cause nec occasion pejerandi aut dejerandi datur.' Molinaei, 'Ad Nobilissimum & Praestantissimum Virum Robertum Boyle', p. 269.

10.2.5 Economists and Scientists

Appeals to the divines in relation to usury began during the last years of the reign of Charles I, prior to the breakthrough on usury made during the Interregnum. This is evidenced by Henry Robinson's *England's Safety in Trades Encrease*, presented to the High Court of Parliament in 1641. Robinson (1605–1673) is regarded as one of the most brilliant and versatile English economic thinkers of the seventeenth century and one of the leading non-ecclesiastical theorists of Independency.[142] Lord Ashley Cooper was not only one of Robinson's protectors, but apparently also one of his pupils in economic matters during the busy years before the Restoration.[143] *England's Safety in Trades Encrease* contains a long list of reforms Robinson deemed necessary to resuscitate trade and the national economy.[144] The text also shows that he was the main inspiration behind later economic schemes, that figures such as Worlsey and Locke put forward as their own. As a member of a family that had been successfully involved in the practice of trade for more than a century, his expertise went beyond the theoretical and chiefly lay in his capacity to think about economy and trade with the breadth that the contemporary English context demanded. Robinson knew how to take into account the West Plantations, the East India Trade, and all the English territories in reordering the economic life of the country, with the ambitious goal of making 'of England the Emporium' of the world.[145] In the context of recommending the introduction of 'Faires or Money marts' such as that of Lyon in France or Placentia in Italy, Robinson – who faced issues in an upfront manner – produced an instructive and detailed discussion of usury. His purpose was to encourage the employment of bills of exchange, by which merchants could be given the money they needed immediately, to be paid back at an agreed time at a level slightly higher than the prevailing rate of interest. Catholic merchants, Robinson argued, had invented the 'unnaturall use of Exchange' as a means to obtain absolution in their confessions, a pardon that was denied if they presented their dealings openly as usury. Robinson's remark also shows how much of an influence Aristotle

[142] W. K. Jordan, *Men of Substance: A Study of the Thought of Two English Revolutionaries, Henry Parker and Henry Robinson* (Chicago: University of Chicago Press, 1967); Aylmer, *The State's Servants*, p. 225.

[143] Jordan, *Men of Substance*, p. 60; p. 216; p. 222.

[144] Henry Robinson, *Englands Safety in Trades Encrease* (London, 1641) Early English Books Online Text Creation Partnership, http://name.umdl.umich.edu/A57437.0001.001

[145] An 'emporium' is the Latin word for a trading station, a market town or market. See Robinson, *Englands Safety in Trades Encrease*, p. 22.

remained on mid-seventeenth-century English consciousness. The usurers of Venice avoided the charge of being in that business by sending their money abroad, for example to London, with no other purpose than to put the money to use and obtain interest on it, while also helping merchants that endorsed the bills of exchange by relieving them of the need to carry coins.[146]

Robinson's discussion of the contemporary theory of usury in a tract on how to increase trade is representative of an approach in which the 'safety of trade' included both economic and moral aspects of 'safety'. Nevertheless, the fact that the matter was now being addressed by a professional merchant was equally characteristic of the change of atmosphere. Robinson's aim was to shine a light on the muddle reigning in relation to the question of usury. 'Protestants and Papists Doctors, Divines and Lawyers' all disagreed in what exactly the definition was, but Robinson considered the following to be the most useful general definition: 'Usury is received profit from a debtor for the use of a thing given in loan' (*Usura est lucrum receptum à Creditore pro usu rei mutuó datae*). However, in his view that definition was incomplete, since it did not include the 'mutuall' and 'intentionall' usury, which was also condemned in *foro conscientiae.* It also disregarded the complex nature of 'giving in loan' (*dare in mutuum*): a house may be rented, wages may be paid, a horse may be lent, and these did not constitute usury. For Robinson, demanding either 2 or 10 per cent was usury – the exact rate was immaterial. That did not mean, he suggested, that one ought to oppose absolutely the practice of usury. Those who read Luke 6:35, *Date mutuum, nihil inde sperantes* ('lend without expecting anything back') as an absolute prohibition, were undertaking a radical interpretation that was not altogether justified since it disregarded the fact that in Deuteronomy 23:20 the Lord allowed the Jews to practice usury in relation to foreigners. Thus, Robinson's argument was that the discussion about making the use of money legitimate ought to move beyond 'need'. Robinson went to the heart of the matter when he pointed to the distinction between 'need' and 'profit' and made an argument in favor of virtuous facilitation of one's neighbour's profit.[147]

[146] Almost thirty years later Child was still urging to start the practice of Bills of Exchange, this time from the Netherlands. However, Child was already unconcerned about its possible usurious uses. Child, *Brief observations concerning trade and interest of money.*

[147] 'In regard there may be an occasion of borrowing, as in a rich man that cannot be said to doe it for need: for which cause I am not bound to lend him, but because he sees certaintie of profit, and rather than I will bee his hindrance of such profit, me thinks I find my selfe in a manner oblig'd to lend him what I could, and intended otherwise to imploy my selfe not without good hopes of benefit: and may not I in this care of certaine profit to my neighbor

In *England's Safety in Trades Encrease* Robinson launched a momentous challenge aimed at addressing the gulf between moral theory and commercial practice. He proposed that the divines should take the matter into serious consideration and declare what percentage of interest amounted to usury. All authors agreed currently, he noted, that taking 8 or 10 per cent of interest on the use of money was usury and unlawful, while nonetheless being practised by entire nations, 'so sweetly and powerfully doth gaine and lucre benumbe the conscience'. England, and the entire world, accordingly needed an 'adequate' definition that would not 'vitiate most contracts, bargaines, and sales, so commonly practised by all nations to the multiplying of trade, and reliefe of whole Kingdomes'. Reformation of trade ought not to signify 'the ruine of ⅔ of all commerce throughout the Universe' – a reformed commonwealth must therefore make usury legal and legitimate.[148] In line with the ideals of the new science of the advancement of laypersons he urged: 'at this studie and consultation of our Divines I crave leave to be bold, and entreat them not to disdaine that light which experts Merchants might give them in this poynt'.[149]

However, fears as to the irreligiosity of usury persisted throughout the Interregnum among the pious Reformers. William Potter's 1650 tract, *The Key of Wealth, or a new Way for Improving of Trade*, is probably the most remarkable text on this topic to have appeared in the period in question. It evidences again that in the England of the new science the question of the 'lawfulness' of putting money out at interest was both a delicate moral matter and a pressing economic quandary.[150] After half a century of reflection upon Bacon's call to consider usury in practical terms, the greater part of the problem that remained was as to what those *practical* terms comprised. Which were the correct means by which to obtain credit and thus resuscitate trade in the defunct post-Civil War economy? Furthermore, how could more bullion, and thus money, be obtained in a country without mines?

Published on 15 September 1650, *The Key of Wealth* appears pitched somewhere between fantasy and reality but contains an array of brilliant

in borrowing, and certain dammage, (for the imploying it is alwayes valued at somewhat) to my selfe by lending, take interest for my money, and so he get more by borrowing, and I by lending?' Robinson, *Englands Safety in Trades Encrease*, p. 41.

148 Robinson, *Englands Safety in Trades Encrease*, p. 41.

149 Robinson, *Englands Safety in Trades Encrease*, p. 42.

150 William Potter, *The Key of Wealth Or, a New Way, for Improving of Trade: Lawfull, Easie, Safe and Effectuall* (Printed by R.A., 1650). Early English Books Online Text Creation Partnership, 2011 http://name.umdl.umich.edu/A90881.0001.001

ideas. It is a futurist tract, which proposes the establishment of a company as 'A Certain Myne of Gold' built upon security provided by land and by insurance mechanisms that would create a new form of paper money.[151] For 'the use and possession of the said Myne', Potter asked for a number of investors to lay out the money to purchase the land and guarantee the insurance system. Then, in order to increase their trade, rich and poor traders alike would be able to borrow from the money generated by the land rents, in whatever sum as they could offer security for, on the basis of a bond that required repayment of the money in six months.[152] Wennerlind regards Potter's *Key of Wealth*, along with several of Robinson's and Hartlib's writings of the 1650s that were inspired by it, as a turning point in the endeavours of Hartlib's scientific circle. He takes the view that this was the moment at which alchemy and experiments aimed at transforming base metals into gold were abandoned in favour of the far more realistic idea of monetizing land as security and the promotion of land-banking as the means to supply much-needed credit. In ideological terms, this represented a movement from the 'transmutation of nature' to the 'passive security of nature'.[153]

The religious and moral question of usury also arises in the context of the connection between alchemy and credit-money. The undesirable social consequences of usury – enriching the few and entailing money being sent out of the country – plainly conflicted with the Reformers' religious ideals. They were democratic and suspicious of greed, but at the same time the entire political project of the Commonwealth depended on England's economic success. In the pursuit of wealth, recourse to alchemy, the land-banks and other means of producing credit were indicative of the efforts undertaken by the intelligentsia in their search for alternatives to usury.

In his correspondence with Hartlib, William Potter emerges as an unhonoured man, unsuccessful in his business career as an inventor and, perhaps for this reason, something of a fatalist in outlook. At the same time, Potter stands out among his peers as being not only incredibly knowledgeable about money but as a visionary who was half a century ahead in his creative approach to it.[154] In 1690 the Government of Massachusetts produced paper money for the first time, as proposed in *The Key of*

151 Schumpeter praise of Potter's analytical work in Joseph A. Schumpeter, *History of Economic Analysis*, Elizabeth Boody Schumpeter (ed.), with and Introduction by Mark Perlman (New York: Routledge, 1987), p. 280

152 Potter, *The Key of Wealth*.

153 Wennerlind, 'Credit-Money as the Philosopher's Stone', p. 250; p. 256.

154 *Hartlib Papers*.

Wealth, to pay for the invasion of Canada, and the link between that event and Potter has been only recently established.[155] Potter weighed the communal aspects of adopting a security in relation to land and creating a common fund of credit against interest-driven usury and its intolerable elitist aspects. The book's introduction explains that this entailed going beyond 'nature alone, (without improvement by the use of mans Reason)' and unlike 'the brutish people of America' who lived 'upon Roots and Acornes' to benefit from the 'Accomodations' furnishing 'Art'; it was also about providing 'help, for the crying and the dying poor', and that 'the Rich may wealth increase' and fundamentally that 'none shall neede (who now will Work) to want their dayly-bread'.[156]

Potter took the view that the way to revive the 'decayed trade' in any place was to 'encrease money', which, in his opinion, would not cause the prices of commodities to increase.[157] On the contrary, extraordinary quick trade, in which the market takes as much as it can, would make commodities and produce cheaper, and thus land-rents would fall. At the same time, landlords would benefit, and traders would see a quick return and a level of profit that would enable them to increase their stock year on year, thus further increasing profits. Finally, cheap commodities in England would attract bullion to the country from overseas. At the foundation of the whole enterprise, 'the Myne', was land, with the advantage that if it were a real mine it would give rise to much more jealousy than a mine crafted through human ingenuity.[158]

In *The Key of Wealth* Potter envisaged the circulation of paper money which, crucially, unlike gold coins, could not be hoarded.[159] He was aware of imitating the Dutch in this regard.[160] Furthermore, the paper money or bills would be *private* to those committed by a bond and this commitment would be made visible by means of flags or signs in one's businesses, and of course, since Hartlib was somehow involved, its complex management would be done through 'an Office'.[161] When everyone, or many, was willing to borrow 'gratis' on such a firm security as 'the Myne' the use of the

155 Katie A. Moore, 'The Blood that Nourishes the Body Politic: The Origins of Paper Money in Early America' in 17 *Early American Studies: An Interdisciplinary Journal* (2019), pp. 1–36.

156 David Brown 'Introduction' in William Potter, *The Key of Wealth*.

157 Potter, *The Key of Wealth*, p. 15.

158 Potter, *The Key of Wealth*, p. 23.

159 Dunn, 'Milton among the Monopolists'.

160 'The way of trading upon Bills is, (I confess) used in Flanders'. Potter, *The Key of Wealth*, p. 57.

161 Potter, *The Key of Wealth*, p. 45.

new money that the company would provide could become general, and hence function as real credit and real money.

> as the case now stands with us, *the only feasible means, whereby both to receive and multiply the decayed Trade of this Land, is by increasing amongst Tradesmen some firm and known Credit or Security, equal to that of the Chamber of* London, *Banke of* Amsterdam, *or any Bills of* Exchange, *which being given in written or printed Evidences, may be fit to transfer from hand to (hand).*[162]

Significantly, one of the novelties of the entire enterprise was that borrowing money would be possible 'without paying any *Interest*', which poor merchants could not afford and that would keep the price of the commodities low.[163] Instead of serving usurers' sectorial private interest, the Company would have a communitarian aspect. The rationale behind this was to help poor merchants. In fact, one of the effects of the whole enterprise would be 'to diminish the Interest for monies'. For who would

> put in *security* to borrow *money* upon *Interest*, when he may upon like *security*, have such Bills as will passe in the place of *money* lent him *gratis*, & that in such a way, as whereby to be brought into a capacity of *multiplying his trading to the utmost degree possible?*[164]

Therefore, borrowing conditions would be most favourable for the poor merchants:

> the procuring of sufficient security, for the borrowing of any considerable sums of money, may be too hard a task for the poorer sort of Tradesmen to perform; yet there will be nothing required of them, in order to the putting themselves into a capacity of multiplying their trading, and that with ready pay.[165]

Potter did not consider this Company more risky than usury itself: 'there is (as I have already proved) greater hazard in letting out moneys to Interest, then in this undertaking,' and yet people, 'in hopes of a small profit of Interest, and by that small profit, do one time with another gain more then (sic) they loose by such hazard, as is evident, by mens continuing this practice'.[166] Moreover, he envisaged the possibility of multiplication

[162] Potter, *The Key of Wealth*, p. 38.
[163] Potter, *The Key of Wealth*, p. 22; pp. 29–30.
[164] Potter, *The Key of Wealth*, p. 72.
[165] Potter, *The Key of Wealth*, p. 26.
[166] Potter, *The Key of Wealth*, p. 25.

'ad infinitum' of returns.[167] And if business was unsuccessful for traders, all borrowers had to do was to return the bills, while the insurance system and land rents would make good their losses.

> Yet considering that *those who borrow of it pay no Interest*, it follows, that if they cannot make it to be taken for *Commodity, all they are Ingaged unto, is but to return it again at the time appointed;* although indeed if it be remembred, that *this money is such as will yield the Value without any considerable losse, though sold to the Gold-smith*; it cannot be doubted, but that *all wise Tradesmen, will take it much rather then turne away a Chapman.*[168]

In sum, despite the almost general benefit Potter prophesied, the only ones who would not benefit from 'the Myne' in the Commonwealth would be 'Usurers, Brokers and Lawyers' who would 'lose all their customers' and the 'money mongers' that 'hoard money to raise the interest'.[169]

This review of positions on usury concludes with Locke. His analysis followed the same path of promoting commerce. Money was put to work in the context of trade through the industry of the borrower in the same way as land that would otherwise be left fallow was put to use through the tenant's work. The premise, however, was inequality.

> For as the unequall distribution of Land, You having more then you can or will manure, and another Lesse brings you a Tenant for your Land, and the same unequall distribution of mony I having more then I can or will Imploy and another Lesse brings me a Tenant for my mony.[170]

Locke did not deny that the 'usurer' and the landlord were reaping the results of other peoples' work.

> his 6 li per Cent may seeme to be the fruit of another mans Labour as he that Letts Land to a Tenant for without the Tenant Industry (supposeing as before the owner would not manage it himself) his Land would yield him Little or noe profit.[171]

But the reason for paying interest on it lay in the fact that the borrower and tenant received more from the use of money than they paid. A merchant borrowing 1000 pounds at 6 per cent, would, if he knew the business, obtain profit exceeding the 60 pounds paid in interest. Those with

167 Potter, *The Key of Wealth*, p. 6.

168 Potter, *The Key of Wealth*, p. 33.

169 Potter, *The Key of Wealth*, p. 60; p. 68; p. 72.

170 John Locke, 'Supplement' of 'Some of the Consequences that are Like to Follow Upon Lessening of Interest to 4 per Cent', p. 182.

171 Locke, 'Supplement' of 'Some of the Consequences that are Like to Follow Upon Lessening of Interest to 4 per Cent', p. 182.

skills in trade and husbandry but neither money nor land were able to obtain their livelihood through the usurer and the landlord. In this way Locke explained why borrowing money was unavoidable on the grounds of 'the necessity of affaires and the Constitution of Humane society', and the unequal distribution of land and money; and why receiving profit from lending money was equitable and lawful as it was for the landlord to receive rent from the tenant.[172] Locke's point was that the individual was entitled to obtain a livelihood and eventually enrichment thanks to the loan. Locke's suggestion sounded commonsensical as more money needed to be in circulation in order to resuscitate the national economy. As discussed in his economic writings of the 1690s, the funds needed to meet the costs of government as well as both the necessities required and the luxuries desired by people would certainly not come from conquest and plunder, especially in England. As he realistically put it:

> In our present circumstances, no Body is vain enough to entertain a Thought of our reaping the Profits of the World with our Swords, and making the Spoil and Tribute of Vanquished Nations, the Fund for the supply of the Charges of the Government, with an overplus for the wants and equally craving Luxury, and fashionable Vanity of the People. Commerce, therefore is the only way left to us.[173]

Locke was original in that he developed a scientific discussion outside the narrative of moral theology. His philosophical methodology, which treats money as a necessity, deserves closer study.

[172] Locke, 'Supplement' of 'Some of the Consequences that are Like to Follow Upon Lessening of Interest to 4 per Cent', pp. 182–183.
[173] Locke, 'Some Considerations of the Consequences of the Lowering of Interest, and Raising the Value of Money', pp. 222–223.

11

The Scientification of Money

11.1 The Science of Interest

The common understanding of money underwent change during the seventeenth century in tandem with changes in the conception of nature within corpuscularianism. Chapter 10 discussed key theoretical experiments made in order to separate money from its metallic constitution, such as William Potter's *The Key of Wealth*. This chapter analyses the theoretical transformation of money into a necessary element, inter alia, of the economic process. Specifically, when money became a necessity, it disappeared from the radar of moral natural law and theology though not from that of philosophy and studies of trade. Money underwent a process of 'scientification', for the systematic knowledge that Locke produced 'in the spirit of "truth-seeking" science' about how money works in the economy, became the new and primary source of legitimisation.[1] Not only was money placed outside theology and moral philosophy, but as a necessity, money operated now outside the sphere of deliberation of practical reason devoted to contingents. Considered as an indispensable element of the system of trade (the economic system), it became the object of study of the emergent branch of political economy, whose avowed aim was a type of imitation of nature. Significantly, William Petty's advice with regard to macroeconomic measures looked to adopt the 'more natural way', rather than the 'resisting of Nature'. For instance, if food could be produced much cheaper in England than in Holland, the natural way forward would be 'to take away burthensome, frivolous, and antiquated Impositions and Offices' (taxes). In the case of trade, if the Dutch had outdone the English

[1] Weingart who studied some years ago the process in the context of the politics of new knowledge production writes that '"scientification" is a process whereby the use of and claim to systematic and certified knowledge produced in the spirit of "truth-seeking" science becomes the chief legitimating source for activity in virtually all other functional subsystems', Weingart, 'From Finalization to Mode 2': Old Wine in New Bottles?', p. 610.

in the manufacture of cloth 'by more art', a good course would be for example to send people to Holland to learn from Dutch methods.

> We must consider in general, that as wiser Physicians tamper not excessively with their Patients, rather observing and complying with the motions of nature, then (*sic*) contradicting it with vehement Administrations of their own; so in Politicks and Oconomicks the same must be used.[2]

Locke may be set apart from the scholars and merchants writing on usury mentioned in the previous chapter. No reference was made in his remarkable piece, *Some of the Consequence that are Like to Follow Upon Lessening of Interest to 4 per Cent* (1668) to Josiah Child's statement about the 'multiplying Nature' of interest which 'make the Lenders monstrous rich' and the rest extremely poor.[3] His discussion did not deal with usury, richness, wealth, prosperity or desire, but with scarcity, necessity and needs. With razor-sharp thinking and armed with the rhetorical tools to rebuff critique concerning unlawful usury, the depravity of greed and the scandalous iniquity of wealth, he eliminated all elements from the phenomenon of 'money' that would be unsuitable in a discourse of natural philosophy. Carl Wennerlind has recently described the renewed enthusiasm about the 'achievement' of money among Enlightenment philosophers.[4] My argument is that Locke's purification of money of its theological and philosophical past, which he carried out by means of scientific analysis, was instrumental in that enlightened appraisal of money.

This chapter introduces William Potter's proposals to ensure the quality of Irish money and compares it with Locke's position. It contains detailed analysis of Locke's understanding of money as a necessity. This reveals the goal of constructing publicness, for the achievement of which Locke's natural sciences method was put to work. Joyce Oldham Appleby famously considered that Locke's position on the 'intrinsick value' of silver in the Recoinage controversy of the 1690s amounted to a naturalization of money. Locke, Appleby argued, went on to '[turn] a mint standard into an immutable fact of nature', while rejecting 'the ideological implications of assigning

[2] Petty, *A Treatise of Taxes*, p. 88.

[3] Locke, 'Some of the Consequence that are Like to Follow Upon Lessening of Interest to 4 per Cent' (1668). Josiah Child, who was a merchant, thought that high rate of interests damaged trade, Child, *Brief Observations Concerning Trade and Interest of Money*.

[4] Carl Wennerlind, 'Money and Its Ideas: Enlightenment Debates about the Morality of Money', in Christine Desan (ed.), *A Cultural History of Money in the Age of Enlightenment* (London: Bloomsbury Academic, 2021), p. 131.

to money an extrinsic value manipulatable by the sovereign'.[5] Appleby's essentialist critique is difficult to support in the face of the evidence provided by the answer Locke made to his opponent William Lowndes, on the issue of devaluing money, in *Further Considerations Concerning Raising the Value of Money* (1696). In this work, the words 'nature' or 'natural' are not employed, except once in the Preface.[6] Moreover, Daniel Carey has argued convincingly that Locke's 'intrinsick value' is in reality 'an external value', founded on reason and on public authority, and not on nature.[7] It is impossible to do justice to Carey's treatment of the notion of 'species' in this brief comment, but ultimately, it shows that Locke knew that money would be always the result of a convention, and in the late seventeenth century, an *international convention* at that.[8] On the other hand, Courtney Weiss Smith shows that the most articulate authors participating in the debate on coinage on both sides were involved in a naturalized discourse on money.[9] My study of money as necessity makes sense of Appleby's intuition about the naturalization of money and its consequences. In the words of Stefan Eich, Locke's 'politics of depoliticizing money' can be denied only with great difficulty.[10]

However, my argument, perhaps a nuance of that idea, is that Locke's goal was the scientification of money along the lines of the New Science. In this endeavour, his doctrine of necessities was crucial. I would suggest first that Locke's method of naturalization was less straightforward than adhering to a natural value of silver, second that it was implemented much earlier in his life, and third that it represented a piece in the puzzle of his

[5] Joyce Oldham Appleby 'Locke, Liberalism and the Natural Law of Money', 71 *Past and Present* (1976), p. 61; p. 64; Appleby, *Economic Thought and Ideology in Seventeenth-Century England*, pp. 199–241.

[6] Locke, 'Further Considerations Concerning Raising the Value of Money' in *Locke on Money*, vol. II.

[7] 'The use of Coin'd Silver or Money is, that every Man in the Country where it is current by publick Authority, may, without the trouble of refining, essaying or weighing, be assured what quantity of Silver he gives, receives, or contracts for, under such and such denominations.' Locke, 'Further Considerations Concerning Raising the Value of Money', p. 414.

[8] Carey, 'Locke's Species: Money and Philosophy in the 1690s'; and Daniel Carey, 'John Locke, Money and Credit', in Daniel Carey and Christopher J. Finlay (eds.), *The Financial Revolution in the British Atlantic World, 1688–1815* (Dublin Portland: Irish Academic Press, 2011).

[9] Courtney Weiss Smith, 'A "Foundation in Nature": New Economic Criticism and the Problem of Money in 1690s England', 53 *The Eighteenth Century* (2012).

[10] Eich, 'John Locke and the Politics of Monetary Depolitization' 17 *Modern Intellectual History* (2020), pp. 1–28. And more recently within a larger argument of money being always political, Eich, *The Currency of Politics*.

broader methodological aim to develop a new natural law and government thinking that could operate within the system of the new science.

After official investigations, consensus had already been reached in the 1620s that scarcity of money was the key reason for the commercial depression.[11] Up until the creation of the Bank of England in the late 1690s, many solutions were proposed, some of them colourful: alchemy, lotteries – which William Petty had defined as early as 1662 as 'a Tax upon unfortunate self-conceited fools'[12] – job stocking and, starting with those put forward by Robinson, Potter and many others, innumerable schemes for institutions of credit.[13] Oliver Cromwell successfully developed a plan to readmit the Jewish communities, who had been banished from England since 1290, particularly to benefit from their economic knowledge.[14] On the other hand, William Petty had written about the main implication of the publicness of money, that is, that citizens ought to pay their taxes. In order to achieve that end, he had devised a better tax system.[15] The question of the scarcity of money was further complicated by a generalized clipping of coins to extract silver from them, and hoarding the good coins, and it is in this context that Potter devised his project for Ireland.

[11] Analysing the different philosophies underlying the techniques to solve the scarcity of money see, Wennerlind, *Casualties of Credit: The English Financial Revolution, 1620–1720*, p. 31.

[12] He considered that not everyone in the world that could be cheated ought to be cheated, but since there were in the world rather plenty of this kind enthralled with lottery, it was 'rather ordained that the Sovereign should have the Guardianship of these fools'; 'in the way of Lottery men do also tax themselves in the general, though out of hopes of Advantage in particular', Petty, *Treatise of Taxes*, p. 91.

[13] Christine Desan, *Making Money* (Oxford: Oxford University Press, 2014) Ch. 8; Daniel Carey, 'Money and the Issues of the Age. Thinking about Money in the Eighteenth Century', in Christine Desan (ed.), *A Cultural History of Money in the Age of Enlightenment* (London: Bloomsbury Academic 2021).

[14] Benjamin Dew, 'Jewish Exclusions: Eighteenth-century Historians and the Expulsion of England's Jews, 6 *Intellectual History Archive* (2018); Webster, *The Great Instauration. Science*, p. 8; p. 454; on the economic and millenarian aspects of the readmission; Hunter, *Boyle: Between God and Science* (Yale University Press, 2009), pp. 85–86; p. 101.

[15] William Petty was the expert of the times on taxation starting with *Treatise of Taxes* (1662) mentioned before, until the famous *Political Arithmetic* (1676) in which he devised a method to establish a correct base for taxation by making an estimation of the stock of national wealth and the national exchanges of money, goods and services. See *The Economic Writings of Sir William Petty*, Charles Henry Hull (ed.) (Cambridge University Press, 1899), vol. I. For an assessment of the impact of Petty see, Mark Blaug, *Pre-classical Economists: Charles Davenant (1656–1714) and William Petty (1623–1687)* (Aldershot: Elgar Publishing, 1991).

11.1.1 *From Potter to Ireland: Money Is Running Debt*

A series of letters (1658–1659) between Samuel Hartlib, Benjamin Worsley, William Potter and Robert Wood, an Oxford scholar writing from Dublin Castle, are among Hartlib's papers. It appears that either Worsley or Wood consulted Potter on how to solve, immediately, in Ireland the dramatic scarcity of money and its poor and clipped physical condition with a view to applying the solution offered later in England.[16] In his study of the Reformers, Charles Webster took a close look at the content of Wood and Potter's discussion on 'the intrinsick value' of money. Webster noted that to some extent William Petty took these questions up later in order to translate the intrinsic value of land into its 'monetary or "extrinsick value"', and thus to ascertain a relationship between the intrinsic value of bullion and other commodities.[17] In turn, Locke started his discussion where Petty left off. Potter's original scheme (now lost) was, again, based on creating new money. It was prepared directly to Hartlib with the hope of its being made available to the Lord Deputy of Ireland, Henry Cromwell and the Council through 'the Gentleman in Ireland' (perhaps Wood). The latter wrote later in the spring from Dublin Castle asking for clarifications, which again Potter sent. These last two letters make Potter's project clear.[18] His proposal was to regulate the creation of farthings with base metals in a manner that could not be 'counterfaited'. In between, Potter was very ill, to the point that he required the services of one Thomas Babington to put his response in writing. He was also very secretive about the practical means by which clipping could be avoided. Potter's poor health and other calamities – the Lord Protector died in 1659 and Charles II returned to England the following year, leading to the fall of many of the Reformers – ensured that the resulting scheme came to nothing.[19] However, in the process, although Potter was

[16] Benjamin Worsley to William Potter, 7.4.1658 39/2/62A-63B (copy); Hartlib to Robert Boyle, 27.4.1658, in 'The Works of the Honourable Robert Boyle', T. Birch. (ed.) 2nd edition, 6 vols. (*London*, 1772). vol. VI, pp. 102–106; Benjamin Worsley to Hartlib, 20.1.1658/1659 33/2/11A-12B; Copy in Scribal Hand Thomas Babington (for Potter) to Hartlib 13.12.1658 53/30/1A-8B; Robert Wood, 'Objections to Potter's Further Work on Coinage, 15.1.1659, 33/1/41A-42B; William Potter to Robert Wood[?] 15.3.1659 30/3/11A-12B; Robert Wood to Hartlib, 21.3.1659, 33/1/48A-49B, in M. Greengrass, M. Leslie and M. Hannon (2013). in *The Hartlib Papers.*

[17] Webster, *The Great Instauration*, pp. 450–454; p. 453.

[18] Webster apparently had no access to Potter's reply to Wood's objection, Webster, *The Great Instauration*, p. 450.

[19] 'Sir, I perceive yow was informed by Mr Hartlib, that I had promised to impart unto you my way to prevent the counterfeiting of the designed Coyne which though I thinke a mistake for I remember noe such promise.' William Potter to Robert Wood[?] 15.3.1659 30/3/11A-12B in *The Hartlib Papers.*

not appointed to any public post, he again demonstrated his knowledge of money.[20] As Locke's work contains certain ideas that are similar to those expressed in the correspondence discussed here, it is possible that he knew its contents.

Quantities of money were needed for foreign trade, in order to provide shipping and all the necessaries for the transportation of commodities, to furnish the plantations and for the people there, and, obviously for domestic trade. Thus Potter proposed 'Lead & Iron, as Tin, Brass & Copper to be coyned in great peeces of 5^{li} or 10^{li} value a peece, according to their true intrinsick value as it is called'.[21] The way to make that new baser money valid currency was by means of a new law to return, or rather force into the people the money by means of the money that was owed them in taxes and public charges. The County would back that new money and, when it would be current, 'make it good' by accepting it back in the form of payment of taxes.[22] Instead of security in the form of land, Potter now argued for security to be provided through public institutions. A law would establish that 'the whole County' would be liable during six months or one year, a period in which anyone could exchange the new money for bullion if they wished. There was no danger, in Potter's view, that this would happen. No one would seek to exchange money that was valid currency. That he had England also in mind was evident when he noted as follows:

> This I thinke cannot possibly give distaste, especially if it bee begun in Ireland only, the rather, for that the silver coyned there is most exceedingly liable to counterfeiting as I heare.[23]

According to Joseph Johnson, debasing their money was among the recurrent punitive measures taken against the rebel Irish. The fact that there was no continuously open mint in Ireland for a period of three centuries following the reign of Queen Elizabeth I seems to have been the main cause of the disastrous state of Irish currency, since old, worn and debased silver coins were never replaced. Hence, when new coins were introduced, they immediately disappeared. In the middle of the seventeenth century, loan interest reached the previously unheard-of rate of 40 per cent. Johnson wrote that in 1660 currency was 'outlandish', mostly

[20] Also on the expertise of Potter, Wennerlind, 'Money and Its Ideas', pp. 107–113.
[21] Babington/Potter, 1658, 53/30/1B, in *The Hartlib Papers*.
[22] Babington/Potter, 1658, 53/30/1A, in *The Hartlib Papers*.
[23] Babington/Potter, 1658, 53/30/2A, in *The Hartlib Papers*.

clipped and counterfeited and that everyday exchanges were made 'through tradesmen's tokens' valid only locally. On the other hand, the Cromwellian settlers started to expand the foreign trade and thus good-quality foreign coins appeared in large quantities.[24] Potter also suggested that widows and orphans, who were unable to engage in trade, 'should have the priviledge to turne their estates into Bullion & deliver the same to the county office'. Since, as a consequence of the scheme, 'interest will fall to little or nothing', their stock would be managed discreetly and they would obtain a certain level of payment for it, not necessarily the interest 'that money commands', if it was too low. To become popular then, the charitable aspects ought to be emphasized, 'for cleering of all scruples, shewing the benefit thereof both towards the employment of the poore & many other wayes'.[25]

Wood was sceptical, and objected to Hartlib: 'I cannot but admire how that Chimæra should enter into his braine'.[26] Potter was sure, however, that once the new money became valid currency and one could buy things with it, no one would want to 'make it good' (i.e. demand bullion in return for it). The whole point of money was 'to procure something else therewith'. Money was after all, merely a 'medium'. The main benefits of the new currency would lie in achieving increase in the volume of money in circulation in order to enable trade and therefore acquire bullion for the County without the need to levy taxes and in 'the preventing of the plague & intolerable mischiefs that follow upon trading on private trust'. A nation needed trade or credit, and making it independent from private borrowing could only be done by having enough bullion or credit 'that will passe currant through a Nation'.

Robert Wood was especially concerned that the new money was made out of a base metal, in defiance of the universal view that coins should be made of gold or silver. In his response, Potter emphasized how little persons understood about money if they took the view that 'money of bullion [was] anything else but the running currant of the Debts of the World'. Gold and silver were not in themselves *universal* to any extent except that they passed for 'money'. And although gold and silver were accounted the best metals on which to base money, this could be changed and would mean only that a new form of money would be established in

[24] Joseph Johnston, 'Irish Currency in the Eighteenth Century' 27 *Hermathena* (1938), p. 9.

[25] Babington/Potter, 1658, 53/30/1B, in *The Hartlib Papers*.

[26] Robert Wood, 'Objections to Potter's Further Work on Coinage, 15.1.1659, 33/1/41A-42B, in *The Hartlib Papers*.

their place. In fact, 'the best money is nothing else but a token or a bill of a publique faith debt secured by its currantness'. In laying out his ideas Potter explained:

> money is nothing else, but that ticket bill, or token which all men among whom it runns currant & doth procure thereby Commodities upon it, are either by Law bound, or at least willing to make good in the behalf of any man that payes the same, for hee that payes money is discharged of the debt, which hee that receives it, would not consent to, but that he hopes all men will acknowledge and satisfy the money, bill or toke upon sight thereof.[27]

In this theoretical sense, of 'money as a public token of debt' that is accepted as currency, money did not belong to any 'particular persons' but to a 'whole body of those men amongst whom such money runns currant', a commonwealth, which was in Potter's view 'the Commonwealth of mankind'.[28] Against the objection that the scheme would provoke the exportation of bullion due to falls in interest, he employed an argument that Locke would also use later. People imagined that when the Dutch lend money to England, they sent over the physical bullion, but they did not. Only bills of exchange would come over to England. If Dutch loans were no longer needed, in effect, no bullion would be lost. In Potter's view the real drain of bullion, occurred through the East India trade, and that would not be stopped since it achieved abundant profit that came in from overseas.

Potter arrived also at the language of 'necessities' in his response to the complaint voiced by some that coining brass money was not an honourable measure. There was 'noe reasoning against necessity', since everyone knew that debased coinage was allowed to pass for authentic and no one was allowed to denounce it 'unlesse it plainly appeare to bee counterfeit'. This, Potter noted, was tantamount to encouraging all 'the Nations and Merchants' to employ individuals skilled in clipping money or cheating in other ways. Moreover,

> Our want of bullion, & the necessityes growing thereby cannot be hid from the world, & to seeme unwilling to have those necessityes knowne which cannot be hid, doth not diminish, but not att all preserve reputation.[29]

Potter thus exposed, again, what everybody knew: that in both England and Ireland lack of money was a source of economic distress. In order to

[27] Babington/Potter, 1658, 53/30/5A, in *The Hartlib Papers*.
[28] Babington/Potter, 1658, 53/30/5A, in *The Hartlib Papers*.
[29] Babington/Potter, 1658, 53/30/6B, in *The Hartlib Papers*.

avoid further lending from private trust, his proposal, which had futuristic or perhaps prophetic overtones, was to produce a different type of money with base metals and to have it backed by the Commonwealth. Money was a medium and tantamount to debt agreed by people to take a certain physical form. Therefore, he made no bones as to detaching it from the traditional precious metal used for it, silver and gold.

11.1.2 Theorizing on Interest and Money

Influential economists of the past two centuries grasped that Locke's ideas on money were momentous. Karl Marx, although quoting Nicholas Barbon, was paraphrasing Locke on the key question of 'need' in the first chapter of *The Capital*.[30] John Maynard Keynes borrowed certain ideas for his monetary theory and enriched them with psychological insights lacking in Locke. Keynes considered that despite his great ideas Locke remained within a dimension of a natural sense of necessities that does not cover all that happens when human beings deal with money.[31] However, Locke's outlook was appropriate in relation to topics of natural philosophy, as evidenced in his writings on money. Less fulsome in his praise, Schumpeter nevertheless filled his *History of Economic Analysis* with Locke's novel insights.[32] The fact that money was scarce and yet a necessity seemed to have prompted Locke's economic reasoning to revolve around explaining the natural economic mechanism that made money a necessity, how to make money more abundant within that quasi-natural constitution, and the relationship of money with the other main source of wealth in England, land. Again, Boyle's mentorship is visible in this question. As early as 1665 Locke wrote to Boyle from Düsseldorf in the following terms:

[30] It is remarkable then that Nicholas Barbon, translated 'desire' as 'want of the mind', presumably to be able to establish a dialogue with Locke in his response to the latter's text in the recoinage controversy. Marx also mimicked the tendency and wrote about 'human wants' that 'spring from the stomach or from fancy, makes no difference'. Marx, *Capital: A Critique of Political Economy*, p. 27.

[31] The rate of interest Keynes wrote is 'the reward for parting with liquidity'; 'the "price" which equilibrates the desire to hold wealth in the form of cash with the available quantity of cash.' 'Locke' did not consider 'fluctuations of liquidity preference' that may occur for example for psychological motives of a wish to speculate with money. John Maynard Keynes, *General Theory of Employment, Interest and Money* (London: Macmillan, 1936), p. 107.

[32] Schumpeter, *History of Economic Analysis*.

> As I once heard you say, I find it true here, as well as in other places, that the great cry is ends of gold and silver.[33]

Remarkably, and unlike Potter, Locke no longer considered money only as a token of debt, but also as a function of interest. In particular, Locke produced a naturalistic account of usury. In one memorandum written in 1668 and enlarged in 1674, which had an innovative scientific style uncharacteristic of the period (in which texts dealing with similar issues usually displayed a polemic tendency), he noted that lending money at interest that fluctuated with the market – i.e. 'natural interest' – was a key element of the nation's economy.[34] For money was a necessity and lending it at interest at the natural level of the market was also necessary. Here, as in the other sections, the question of 'necessity' marks the ethical absence of freedom or of a voluntary element. In his *Nichomachean Ethics* Aristotle had excluded things that must necessarily happen from the sphere of deliberation as to the best and most virtuous course to take in any given situation.[35] Since virtue does not deal with necessity, as Aristotle had hinted, it was by implication meaningless to question the morality of a necessity. In the case of Locke, the language of necessity was

[33] 'Locke to Robert Boyle, 22 December 1665' in *The Correspondence of John Locke in 8 volumes*, v. I. And two years later, he reported to him, with what seemed to be a sort of common joke at the expense of the philosopher's stone, how with another colleague he was in charge of levying a tax on scholars: 'He and I are now upon a new sort of chemistry, i.e. extracting money out of the scholars pockets; and if we can do that, you need not fear but in time we shall have the lapis [the philosophers' stone]; for he that can get gold and silver out of scholars, cannot doubt to extract it any where else.' 'Locke to Robert Boyle, 6 March 1667' in *The Correspondence of John Locke in 8 volumes*, v. I.

[34] Kelly 'General Introduction: Locke on Money' in *Locke on Money*, p. 9.

[35] 'Now about eternal things no one deliberates, e.g. about the material universe or the incommensurability of the diagonal and the side of a square. But no more do we deliberate about the things that involve movement but always happen in the same way, whether of necessity or by nature or from any other cause. (…) We deliberate about things that are in our power and can be done; and these are in fact what is left. For nature, necessity, and chance are thought to be causes, and also reason and everything that depends on man. Now every class of men deliberates about the things that can be done by their own efforts. And in the case of exact and self-contained sciences there is no deliberation, e.g. about the letters of the alphabet (for we have no doubt how they should be written); but the things that are brought about by our own efforts, but not always in the same way, are the things about which we deliberate, e.g. questions of medical treatment or of money-making (….) Deliberation is concerned with things that happen in a certain way for the most part, but in which the outcome is obscure, and with things in which it is indeterminate. We call in others to aid us in deliberation on important questions, distrusting ourselves as not being equal to deciding. We deliberate not about ends but about means.' Aristotle, *The Nichomachean Ethics*, Book III, 1112a15–1112b15; Adamson, 'Making a Virtue of Necessity', p. 13.

also the idiom of a young and responsible civil servant. Locke wrote this report during his first years as a secretary of Lord Ashley, and though it remained unpublished, the memorandum soon found its way to Ashley, who apparently distributed it widely among those occupying the highest level of officialdom.[36] John Spurr notes that the Chancellor of the Exchequer (Ashley) had been distrusted from 1661 onwards on account of his changing alliances, but nonetheless valued on the strength of his knowledge of finance and administration.[37] The fact that Locke wrote the piece on money during that early period also provides a wider political context to his recommendation on economic legislation about the rate of interest.

From May 1667 onwards, Lord Ashley was one of the six members of a board of commissioners that had been given control of the Treasury, then in a critical state after the Dutch war. C. D. Chandaman has explained the crucial role played by these men in overcoming the economic crisis, noting that despite appearances their work was successful. Their muscular handling of the situation and the novelty of their ideas allowed them to postpone until 1672 the repudiation of state debt known as the 'Stop of the Exchequer'. Chandaman takes the view that the gist of the new financial experiment they came up with entailed employing a credit-raising technique, during the extraordinary war finance situation of 1665, within the system by which ordinary revenue was produced.[38] Crucially, in the context of the study of Locke's ideas on money, the core of 'the Order system' was an attempt to attract, beyond professional moneylenders and financiers, a great multitude of small English investors to lend money to the government.[39] That this was, indeed, revolutionary may be also ascertained by comparing it with the credit-raising methods used in

[36] That the memorandum was widely distributed and is to be found among the papers of high officials in Letwin, *The Origins of Scientific Economics*, p. 156; that probably it was written for Ashley in Kelly, 'General Introduction: Locke on Money'; his work for Ashley during these years acquainted Locke with the major administrators and politicians of Restoration England, see Milton, 'The Unscholastic Statesman: Locke and the Earl of Shaftesbury'.

[37] 'Although Charles II allegedly had little faith in Ashley's integrity', presumably due to his swapping allegiance during the Civil Wars, 'he made good use of his administrative and financial acumen and his parliamentary eloquence.' Ashely had changed allegiance from Royal to Parliamentarian during the Civil Wars in 1644, and then again in support for the returning King in February 1660, John Spurr, 'Shaftesbury and the Seventeenth Century' in *Anthony Ashley Cooper*, pp. 11–14; quote in p. 15.

[38] They were the Duke of Albemarle, Lord Ashley, Sir Thomas Clifford, Sir William Coventry and Sir John Duncombe, Chandaman, *The English Public Revenue 1660–1688*, p. 213.

[39] I follow C. D. Chandaman on the system devised by the Commissioners and its successes and failures, Chandaman, *The English Public Revenue 1660–1688*, generally ch. 6; p. 212.

previous years.[40] The Commissioners thought in terms of an attractive offer involving simple and guaranteed means of repayment from funds reserved for that purpose, specifically from the farm and collection of certain taxes, that was clearly more appealing than the previous complex repayment system involving tallies.[41] Registered orders could be used as security and as payment for goods and services.[42] Chandaman notes that during 1667/68 this new financial system performed a vital service for the government. However, it was impossible for the system to keep pace with alarming rises in state debt by raising more credit, not even by 'increasing the rate of interest to 10 per cent'.[43] Furthermore, an overly optimistic estimate of tax revenues on which the Treasury counted appears to have led to the system's ultimate failure. Although the financial scheme was ingenious, without sufficient funds to pay the interest, the system led into a trap. Chandman notes that credit had not only been encouraged, but artificially created. Katharina Pistor also recalls that people paid the tax collectors with notes issued by goldsmiths backed by sovereign debt. When the debt was due, the tax collector could exchange it for coined money. With the meagre quantities of coined money in England, that was another recipe for disaster. When Crown or goldsmiths defaulted, tax collectors 'would impose a "coins only" rule' for collecting taxes, due to the fear that the notes would be worthless.[44] The colossal burden placed on Ashley and the other Treasury Commissioners as public servants is clear and explains the feeling at the time that money was desperately

[40] Examples of how the government had risen credit abroad in times of crisis, basically going abroad to find professional lenders, in John Guy, *Gresham's Law, The Life and World of Queen Elizabeth I's Banker* (London: Profile Books, 2019); Ian Blanchard, 'English Royal Borrowing at Antwerp 1544–1564', in M. Boone and W. Prevenier (eds.), *Finances publiques et finances privées au bas moyen âge* (Leuven-Apledoorn : Garant, 1996). Moshe Arie Milevsky casts a less heroic frame, suggesting that powerful moneylenders might have been influencing new thinking on rate of interest at the time; he relates the connections between the wealthy moneylender John Banks, who survived contemporary upheavals and was richer after them, and Locke. Moshe Arie Milevsky, *The Day the King Defaulted. Financial Lessons from the Stop of the Exchequer in 1672* (Cham: Springer, Palgrave, Macmillan, 2017).

[41] A version of which we find again in the 1690s, Richard A. Kleer, *Money, Politics and Power. Banking and Public Finance in Wartime England, 1694–1696*, (Routledge, 2017). On the seventeenth-century systems of issuing public bonds and minting money see Desan, *Making Money*, ch. 6.

[42] Chandaman, *The English Public Revenue 1660–1688*, p. 212

[43] Chandaman, *The English Public Revenue 1660–1688*, p. 220.

[44] Katharina Pistor, 'From Territorial to Monetary Sovereignty' 18 *Theoretical Inquiries in Law* (2017), p. 509.

needed. Looking at this specific crisis as a moment in which Locke started to focus on 'necessities' as a method confirms Daniel Carey's recent thesis that economic and financial crisis generated the most striking theoretical thinking.[45]

Locke wrote and published on the question of money on several other occasions, significantly in the *Two Treatises of Government* and in various writings on the 'Recoinage Controversy' of the 1690s. In tune with his ideas on natural law, his proposals over the 30 years during which he wrote on money were in favour of promoting freedom of trade and against protectionism, regulation and monopolies. As long as a quasi-natural system, as the bottom line of a healthy and honest economy was respected, non-constraint was Locke's preferred strategy for the national economy. A sense of encouragement to all citizens to participate in monetary transactions, which in his view would have distributive effects across the nation emerges from the recommendation in his writings that the 'legal Use' or interest on money be kept very near to the 'Natural Use', which he defined as 'that Rate of Money which the present Scarcity of it makes it naturally at'. On the contrary, with a lower legal use of money or interest rate, Lombard Street, or in other words the professional lenders would drive all the business on money there, due to the fact that people would not lend at so low a price or not risk breaking the law.[46] Over time, Locke developed the fundamental axiom of natural philosophy that in order to avoid epistemological and moral chaos rational individuals ought to take hints from nature as guidance. In the economic arena, the balance between freedom and nature is also mirrored in the manner in which Locke viewed the relationship between natural law and natural philosophy.

In his early writings, Locke stated the scientific fact that money and general moneylending were necessities for the national economy and argued in favour of paying the natural interest or the interest of the market for the use of money, without regulatory constraints, in a local and general environment of scarcity. From this followed the effect, subtly articulated, though clearly unpacked in the texts, that moneylending, traditionally known as usury, was unrelated to personal moral conscience. Locke was the first theoretician to exhibit an absolute detachment from tradition with regard to usury, more so even than those who only knew 'the

[45] Carey starts to consider Locke's spectacular intervention in the Recoinage crisis in the 1690s, Carey, 'Money and the Issues of the Age. Thinking about Money in the Eighteenth Century', p. 279.

[46] Locke, 'Some Considerations of the Consequences of the Lowering of Interest', p. 216.

practick'.[47] Moreover, in defining money as a necessity, Locke also justified that a price – interest – must be paid for it.

He also articulated analytically his conviction that the use of money and land behave similarly when producing economic value. At every stage when thinking about money and trade he framed his reasoning in terms of natural law and natural philosophy through his idea of 'the international' – of what lies outside England – and of the foreigner, who will return when he or she pleases to the reality and truth that exists beyond the borders. His opposition to devaluing money sprang from this outlook.[48] The international is a space which checks almost with the force of nature all value and reasoning about trade and money. In that sense, money was for Locke intrinsically universal. In Locke's main text on political theory, *Two Treatises*, money was regarded as being the result of an agreement among human beings and thus part of the public reason. Its accumulation was not only allowed but convenient for the economy as a means of putting money to use and fostering industriousness – i.e. transforming money into capital and thus multiplying production. On the other hand, he was also defending the economic independence of the sovereign nation when he described money as a necessity of the nation.[49] That the public money was integrated in an international global system, was clear for every one, as the system of public debt had worked like that for centuries. But to think of money as a necessity assumes that also private money is integrated in the national economic system.

Locke's view in the 1660s and again in 1691 was that the most prosperous course for government was to let the rate of interest gravitate to its natural level according to market forces. As scholars now acknowledge, during the disputes on the recoinage of the clipped money of the 1690s that made him famous, Locke displayed a mastery of theory, and his

[47] Towards the end of the century the merchant Nicholas Barbon reproached Locke (wrongly, as visible in his correspondence) that he did not know the practice, but was 'only acquainted with the Speculation and Theory of Foreign Coins.' Nicholas Barbon, *A Discourse Concerning Coining the new Money Lighter in Answer to Mr. Lock's Considerations about Raising the Value of Money* (London: Printed for Richard Chiswell) Early English Books Online Text Creation Partnership 2011, http://name.umdl.umich.edu/A30882.0001.001, p. 19.

[48] Carey notes that this was one of the strongest points in the 1690s recoinage controversy: 'foreign traders would expose arbitrary manipulations of value and raise their prices accordingly, calculating according to international not domestic valuations of silver'. Carey, 'Money and the Issues of the Age', p. 285.

[49] See on this question, Pistor, 'From Territorial to Monetary Sovereignty'.

argument evidently founded on experience, was accordingly the most far-reaching, logical, prudent, sophisticated and modern, and therefore the most convincing, of those being urged at the time.[50]

11.1.3 Locke's Theory of Interest

Locke's early texts, akin to memoranda, were written, as mentioned before, during his tenure as Lord Ashley's secretary from 1666 onwards at which time public debates concerning lowering interest on money were taking place.[51] The most impressive aspect of his study was his ability to see all the systemic dependencies of a series of elements: the use of money and its price, the intensity of trade, land rents, land prices, commodity prices, labourers' wages, food prices, the balance of trade and the role of public authority. Interest falls and rises, Locke explained, did not in themselves help produce more commodities or more profit from land, contrary to the view taken by other commentators who looked to Holland for this purpose. Since in England only private banks existed, whose aim was to make a profit, they had the advantage of always having the possibility to place their money on the international market in search of a better price. An uncontrolled flow of money to foreign countries, Locke argued, would stop trade. Thus, money being a 'necessity' to trade, the safest course by which to face the contemporary scarcity of specie was to leave interest at the natural level of the market.[52] That would not tempt moneylenders and borrowers to go abroad, which would be detrimental for the nation.

At the outset, Locke, the natural philosopher, described money as having a double nature: it was a commodity that was employed as a means by which to achieve exchange for other commodities;[53] and it was also equivalent to land, that is, fruitful in itself. As noted, Potter did not identify this latter attribute, regarding money as having rather the quality of running

[50] Locke, 'Some Considerations of the Consequences of the Lowering of Interest, and Raising the Value of Money'; Locke 'Further Considerations Concerning Raising the Value of Money'; Appleby 'Locke, Liberalism and the Natural Law of Money'; Kelly, 'General Introduction: Locke on Money'; Carey, 'John Locke, Money and Credit'; Ormazabal, 'Lowndes and Locke on the Value of Money'; Carey, 'Locke's Species: Money and Philosophy in the 1690s'; Felix Waldmann, 'Additions to De Beer's Correspondence of John Locke' 15 *Locke Studies* (2015); Eich, 'John Locke and the Politics of Monetary Depolitization'.

[51] See Kelly, 'General Introduction: Locke on Money', pp. 6–12.

[52] Locke, 'Supplement' of 'Some of the Consequences that are Like to Follow Upon Lessening of Interest to 4 per Cent', p. 171.

[53] An explanation of this Aristotelian doctrine, in Kaye, *Economy and Nature in the Fourteenth Century*, pp. 46–51.

debt. For Locke the receipt of interest in relation to the use of money was therefore analogous to the receipt of rents for the use of land. Locke recalled the classic theory about the nature of money as something unfruitful, without including its damnatory critique.

> for Land produces naturally something new profitable and of value to man kinde, But mony is a Barren thing and produces nothing, but by compact transfers that mony was the reward of one mans Labour into an other mans pocket.[54]

This explanation also described money as the result of the agreements between human beings, and not as a natural thing. However, the interesting difference between money and land, in Locke's view, was that, unlike land, money never lay fallow or barren. Money was constant and held its value across the country, making it possible for the public magistrate to establish a fixed rate of interest – money was in this sense a sound instrument of government.[55] In its capacity of being equivalent to land, interest was a legitimate reality – 'profit for the Loane of mony, is as equitable and Lawfull as receiving rent for Land and more Tolerable to the borrower'.[56]

As noted, it was the fact that money was unequally distributed – that it was both a means of exchange and a source of wealth – that allowed for lending.[57] Locke defined interest in the exchange of money as *commodity*, 'addeing to mony by agreement or publique authority a quality which naturally it hat not, vizt. a faculty of increasing every yeare 6 li per Cent'.[58] At the outset, this definition made clear that Locke neither held

54 Locke, 'Supplement' of 'Some of the Consequences that are Like to Follow Upon Lessening of Interest to 4 per Cent', p. 181; Aristotle's *Politics* considered unnatural that money, an artificial thing would generate more money. The scholastics pick up this idea, e.g. Duns Scotus: 'Money has not of its *nature* have any fruit' or Jean Gerson 'it is against nature that money should breed money'. See about this and the quotes in Langholm, *The Aristotelian Analysis of Usury*, ch. 3; p. 59. See also section 10.2.1.

55 Locke, 'Supplement' of 'Some of the Consequences that are Like to Follow Upon Lessening of Interest to 4 per Cent', p. 180.

56 Locke, 'Supplement' of 'Some of the Consequences that are Like to Follow Upon Lessening of Interest to 4 per Cent', pp. 182–183.

57 See on the function of money as a store of wealth, explaining John Maynard Keynes's theory of the monetary framework of economic life in Gordon A. Fletcher, *The Keynesian Revolution and Its Critics: Issues of Theory and Policy for the Monetary Production of Economy* (New York: Palgrave Macmillan, 1987), pp. 98–100. That Keynes was another keen reader of 'the great Locke' is visible in Keynes, *General Theory of Employment, Interest and Money*. Keynes's analysis of these ideas of Locke that he attributed to a controversy with William Petty, p. 213.

58 Locke, 'Supplement' of 'Some of the Consequences that are Like to Follow Upon Lessening of Interest to 4 per Cent', 189.

a naturalistic conception of money nor of any immutable natural laws governing it.[59] His position in the recoining controversy described below may be partly interpreted as an effort to educate the ruling class in how to develop international credit and trust. The point is important because it confirms his consistent anti-essentialist position as a natural philosopher. Instead, Locke borrowed the centrality of the idea of 'system' and 'needs' from natural sciences to develop his theory of the economic process.

It follows from Locke's thinking outlined earlier that it would therefore be prejudicial for the nation to have a low interest rate on money. A nation became wealthy as a man became wealthy. A positive balance of trade and avoidance of expenditure on foreign luxury goods were necessary conditions for that. Furthermore, in order to maintain strong production of commodities and be able to trade with them, landlord, labourer and merchant needed money. These three together constitute 'trade', whereas it is startling that he did not include the 'moneylender' in the group. By 'money' Locke primarily meant bullion, silver and gold. He took the view, at least initially, that other kinds of payment founded on trust were in principle suspect. Silver and gold, on the other hand, were universal means of payment, and thus had almost an 'intrinsicke naturall worth'.[60] Locke employed the language of necessities of nature in a sophisticated, philosophical way, removed from simplistic analogies still in use even in the 1690s. For instance, James Hodges referred to the needs of human beings, but he was adamant about the absurdity of comparing the natural substance of silver with that of a 'nourishing' bread. That 'he who is hungry cannot eat Silver, nor he who is thirsty drink it; nor he who is naked clothe himself with it; nor he, who is cold, warm himself with it; nor he who is faint, make a Cordial of it, to revive him; nor he who is wounded or sick, make a Plaster or Medicin of it, etc.' Silver had, in a word, no possibility of supplying for 'any useful necessity or convenience' farther than 'in its capacity into certain Vessels or Instruments'.[61]

Unlike Josiah Child's psychological insights about the English economy, which were relevant, but disconnected, Locke provided all his facts and economic analysis within the framework of a unifying

[59] See on the point against Locke's naturalism on money in particular, Carey, 'John Locke, Money and Credit'.

[60] Locke, 'Supplement' of 'Some of the Consequences that are Like to Follow Upon Lessening of Interest to 4 per Cent', p. 189.

[61] James Hodges, *The Present State of England, as to Coin and Publick Charges: Treating of the Necessity of More Money before Taxes can be effectual & other questions* (London: A. Bell, 1697), p. 267; p. 78; see on this question Weiss Smith, 'A "Foundation in Nature", p. 280

psychology.[62] Locke employed a natural psychology according to which *needs rule people's behaviour* – and not, as later would be usual, desire.[63] The necessities of life and trade that only money can provide force all individuals, as individuals and as merchants, to crave money. And that necessity for money that made all equal could not be controlled through legislation.

> If you doe want money that want will still force you to borrow of your Neighbours and at the rate your Necessity not your Lawes shall set, Or else if there be scarcity of money it must hinder the Merchants buying and the Labourers manufactury.[64]

Since 'necessity' ruled demand for money, lowering the legal interest rate to 4 per cent would increase the size of the market for those with the skill and capacity to circumvent the law, that is, usurers. It would also increase the hoarding of money by those hoping for better opportunities to come along in the future. The upshot of both these things would be to make money scarcer. Locke's solution was therefore to allow money to remain at its natural rate of interest. When this rate was very high, his solution – restating some of Robinsons' tropes – lay in 'Generall frugallity and Industrey' and 'being Masters of the trade of some commodity' on which the English would be able to set the price.[65] The most common way in which the 'naturall Interest' was raised occurred when money was 'little in proportion to the trade of a Country for in trade every body calls for money according as he wants it'.[66] Any attempt to lay down a legal interest rate in times when money was scarce was a lost enterprise, 'the want of Money being that alone which regulates its price'. And to show how money was really a necessity, Locke made the comparison between setting a price 'upon wine or silks', which was hard enough, and to set a price on 'Victualls in a time of famin' that was 'impossible'. For money was to trade what food was to life: 'necessary'.[67]

62 Child, *Brief Observations Concerning Trade and Interest of Money*.
63 As John O'Brien has noted, Locke deliberately refrained from employing the term 'desire' in the context of money. O'Brien, 'John Locke, Desire, and the Epistemology of Money'.
64 Locke, 'Some of the Consequence that are Like to Follow Upon Lessening of Interest to 4 per Cent' (1668), p. 168.
65 Locke, 'Some of the Consequence that are Like to Follow Upon Lessening of Interest to 4 per Cent' (1668), p. 171.
66 Locke, 'Some of the Consequence that are Like to Follow Upon Lessening of Interest to 4 per Cent' (1668), p. 172.
67 'For money being a Universall commodity, and as necessary to trade as food is to life, every body must have it at what rate they can get it, and unavoidably pair deare when it is Scarce'. Locke, 'Some of the Consequence that are Like to Follow Upon Lessening of Interest to 4 per Cent' (1668), p. 170; p. 172.

The scarcity therefore made money more expensive. Remarkably, however, scarcity was not the primary cause for money being more in demand: it was always necessary that the individual, labourer, merchant and landlord constantly exchanged money for goods and labour.

> Every man therefore ... must have at least soe much money, or soe timely recruites as may in hand or in a short distance of time satisfie him who supplies him with the necessaries of his life or of his trade, for nobody hath any longer those supplies then he has money or Credit, which is noething else but an assurance of money in some short time, so that it is requisite to trade. There should be soe much money as will keepe up the Landholders Labourer's and Brokers Credit, and therefore ready money must be constantly Exchainged for wares and Labour or follow within a short time after.[68]

In the 'Supplement' to the 1668 text, Locke went on to show how lowering the interest rate would increase the value of land and annuities but not immediately the price of commodities. The reason for this was that the price of the latter depended on the scarcity of the commodity and on its nature – exactly as it happened with money. Locke drew a distinction here between money as a form of commodity and money as a substitute for land. As he explained it, money as a commodity provides *directly* for the necessaries of human life: 'mony has a value as it is capable by exchange to procure us the necessaries or conveniencies of life, and in this it has the nature of a commoditie'.[69] The corollary was that 'things absolutely necessary for Life, must be had at any rate' but 'things convenient', would be obtained only as they stand in relation to other conveniences.[70] Locke's argument was then that the relative scarcity of a commodity affected its price, especially if no other thing could be used as a substitute for it, and also the proportion of their quantity and 'their vent, which vent is nothing Else but the passing of Commodities from one owner to another in Exchange'. Again, 'the vent' of a commodity, to use Locke's own expression, was explained by necessity. The 'vent' of a commodity

> depends upon its necessity or usefulness for whatever is necessary men give any proportion of mony for it, rather than goe without it, and in such things the scarcity of them alone makes their prices.[71]

68 Locke, 'Some of the Consequence that are Like to Follow Upon Lessening of Interest to 4 per Cent' (1668), pp. 173–174.
69 Locke, 'Supplement' of 'Some of the Consequences that are Like to Follow Upon Lessening of Interest to 4 per Cent', p. 180.
70 Locke, 'Supplement' of 'Some of the Consequences that are Like to Follow Upon Lessening of Interest to 4 per Cent', p. 179.
71 Locke, 'Supplement' of 'Some of the Consequences that are Like to Follow Upon Lessening of Interest to 4 per Cent', p. 178.

In turn, the function of money as a substitute for land, yielding interest on its use, was to serve *directly* the necessities of trade. In sum, as an instrument of exchange money offered a means of meeting individuals' needs, while as equivalent to land, yielding interest, it served the needs of society and trade more generally and in particular of the economy of the country. Similarly, that it was fair that the tenant paid rent to the landlord: 'he that has skill in trafficke but has no money too, enough to exercise it, has not only reason to exercise it and drive his trade and get a Livelihood', but evidently 'to pay use for that mony'. Since money was a necessity for country and trade, to pay interest for it was legitimate, notwithstanding opinions of the immorality of the practice:

> From whence it is Cleere that borrowing mony upon use is not onely by the necessity of affaires and the Constitution of Humane society unavoidable to some men, but that also to receive profit for the Loane of mony is as equitable and Lawfull as receiving rent for Land and more Tolerable to the borrower, notwithstanding the opinion of some overscrupulous men.[72]

The gist of Locke's reasoning was, in conclusion, that lowering the interest, although it would make 'money as land' cheaper, it would make money as a commodity scarce, and thus 'dearer' – in turn this would make the value of land in relation to money more expensive.[73]

In 1691 he finally published a tract entitled *Some Considerations of the Consequences of the Lowering of Interest and Raising the Value of Money*, where Locke repeated many of the ideas outlined earlier, often in the same words, adding perspectives on debt and credit to his insights on trade.[74] The 'unusual' agreement he signed in 1691, stating that 'the sole right' in relation to that tract belonged to him, indicates that he considered the need to establish his original authorship pressing enough to take that uncharacteristic trouble.[75] If anything, the emphasis on the 'necessities of nature' is intensified in that text. Locke described again money as a necessity in a civilized society, as it was the only way by which human beings' natural needs could be met. Indeed, it was only out of necessity that anyone would ever request a loan:

[72] Locke, 'Supplement' of 'Some of the Consequences that are Like to Follow Upon Lessening of Interest to 4 per Cent', pp. 182–183.

[73] Locke, 'Supplement' of 'Some of the Consequences that are Like to Follow Upon Lessening of Interest to 4 per Cent', pp. 183–184; pp. 188–189.

[74] 'Upon this new survey of them, I find not my thoughts now to differ from those I had near twenty years since: they have to me still the appearance of truth' Locke, 'Some Considerations of the Consequences of the Lowering of Interest, and Raising the Value of Money', p. 210.

[75] Kelly 'General Introduction: Locke on Money' in *Locke on Money*, p. 132.

> no Man's borrows money, or pays Use, out of mere Pleasure: 'Tis the want of money drives Man to that Trouble and charge of Borrowing: And proportionally to this Want, so will everyone have it, whatever Price it cost him.[76]

As was the case in his early writings, the level of necessity – 'the want' – is the only instrument by which to determine the rate of interest on money. 'Law cannot keep him from taking more *Use* than you set (the Want of Money being that alone which regulates its Price)'.[77]

The philosophers discussed in the previous chapter worked also on the principle that money was necessary. Potter argued that money was a public matter and therefore must be secured on the basis of public and not private trust. Utilizing a different and more sophisticated philosophical approach to the monetary economy, Locke described money as a *necessity*. This scientific way of dealing with money contributed to stabilizing its meaning and its function, which was universal. The direction in which the philosophical anti-essentialism of corpuscularianism might lead, radical nominalism, with money only having nominal value, posed a risk to morality and politics.[78] With his natural sciences approach based on necessities, Locke built a middle way in terms of method between corpuscularianism and Aristotelian metaphysics that suited social sciences and institutions such as money.

11.1.4 Money as Necessity

First in an article for the *British Journal of Philosophy* and then recently on a book on the unconscious culture of companies in modernity, John O'Brien has addressed the connections between Locke's logic of desire in *An Essay Concerning Human Understanding* and the epistemology of money in his economic writings.[79] The central question that O'Brien poses, which is also relevant here, concerns Locke's strenuous efforts, noted before, to avoid incorporating desire in his published writings on money. In fact, O'Brien argues, 'Locke goes to the trouble of inventing a new economic term [vent] in order to keep desire out of representation'.That is what, as tradition has it, most distinguishes him from the era of the classical economists identified with Adam Smith's economy of

[76] Locke, 'Some Considerations of the Consequences of the Lowering of Interest, and Raising the Value of Money', p. 211.

[77] Locke, 'Some Considerations of the Consequences of the Lowering of Interest, and Raising the Value of Money', p. 214.

[78] This point in Carey, 'Locke's Species: Money and Philosophy in the 1690s'.

[79] O'Brien, 'John Locke, Desire, and the Epistemology of Money'.

desire.[80] O'Brien goes on to interpret Locke's epistemology and morality in *An Essay* as an idealized version of the symbolic economy of the period. Locke successfully resisted a new devaluation of money in the 1690s, when clipped coins had lost much of their original weight, and stubbornly advocated new minting as to regain the lost weight of the coinage on the ground of the intrinsic value of silver.[81] In O'Brien's view, the connection that Locke unconsciously drew between his economy and his philosophy was to contain desire for money by keeping it scarce.[82] The interpretation is suggestive. However, O'Brien's depiction of Locke associating 'negativity' and 'desire' goes against the thesis in Book II of *An Essay*.[83] There Locke explains that human beings are exclusively motivated by forms of desire – up to the desire for God – which is ultimately another way of stating that are only motivated by love.

> I am forced to conclude, that *good*, the *greater good*, though apprehended and acknowledged to be so, does not determine the *will*, until our desire, raised proportionably to it, makes us *uneasy* in the want of it.[84]

In *An Essay*, desire is not defined through negativity but through consciousness of 'want' or 'lack' of something, of a necessity. O'Brien accurately notes Locke's ambivalence about money and how he avoided integrating the idea of desire into his monetary texts, while others, made profligate use of it.[85] Here is worth noting Daniel Carey's view that Locke's position in the recoining controversy, in terms of his insistence that 'the meaning of money must remain the existing definition of its value at the Mint, i.e. 5s. 2d. per ounce' was in fact a moral argument about rigour and curbing the tendency to tamper endlessly with the value

80 'Desire, for so long condemned as mere avarice, was now widely heralded as the force that drove the trade upon which the social order depended, and, naturalized into an irreducible constant that motivated all participants in the marketplace, it lent economic thought a degree of coherence that guaranteed its systematicity.' John O'Brien, *Literature Incorporated. The Cultural Unconscious of the Business Corporation, 1650–1850* (Chicago: University of Chicago Press, 2016), p. 40; and O'Brien, 'John Locke, Desire, and the Epistemology of Money', p. 696.

81 This standpoint would be proudly maintained until the twentieth century.

82 O'Brien, *Literature Incorporated: The Cultural Unconscious of the Business Corporation, 1650–1850*, p. 51.

83 O'Brien, *Literature Incorporated: The Cultural Unconscious of the Business Corporation, 1650–1850*, p. 58.

84 Locke, *An Essay*, II. 21 §35.

85 O'Brien also describes Nicholas Barbon's *A Discourse of Trade* (1690) as 'a virtual hymn to desire'. O'Brien, 'John Locke, Desire, and the Epistemology of Money', p. 705.

of money.[86] Nevertheless, as O'Brien recalls the charge that James Hodges levelled against Locke was that he avoided to describe desires in an area that was ruled by them:

> And seeing it is equally known to every one that neither the Government nor any Trader do call for Money, to give one Piece for another, or one bag or Sum for another in the same Quantity and Fineness of Silver; what can be expected to the Purpose from a Discourse of Coin, which standeth wholly upon such a fundamental Point, as considereth Silver only in respect of it self, and not in respect of any of those Ends for which it is desired, and for which it is only needful or useful?[87]

In comparison with Locke's own theory of money, Hodges described money here merely as a commodity of exchange, not as equivalent to land, thus yielding the equivalent to rent. But, what if the desire for money was not for something that one may buy with money, but for money *itself*? Money could be desired in that double nature, as a commodity or for itself. Locke, I want to suggest, was well aware of the psychological appeal of the promising future of profit, and also of its extreme selfish expressions, in a word, of the greed for money itself or the love for money. Despite the fact that he lived in a society threatened by materialism, money is conspicuously absent from moral discussions of good and bad desire in *An Essay Concerning Human Understanding*. However, his anthropology exposes the role of desires in morality and stresses the distinction between good and bad desires. Unlike apparently James Hodges in the quote mentioned earlier, Locke recognised the possibility of desiring money only for the sake of having more money.[88] But remarkably, in his theory of money, he opted to gloss over the ungodly desires, plausibly as a moral pedagogical exercise: money ought not to be viewed as an object of selfish desire. Hence he explained it only as a necessity, that is as a means to serve the public sphere of the commonwealth.

I have argued in this section that in his economic writings Locke treated money as a 'necessity' of the basic economic system he described.

[86] Carey, 'Locke's Species: Money and Philosophy in the 1690s', p. 379; see also Felix Waldmann, 'Additions to De Beer's Correspondence of John Locke' 15 *Locke Studies* (2015), pp. 31–42.

[87] Hodges, *The Present State of England, as to Coin and Publick Charges*, pp. 149–150; also O'Brien, 'John Locke, Desire, and the Epistemology of Money'.

[88] With regard to James Hodges's hedonistic naivité, it is telling that one of the measures he proposed to King William was to confiscate all the plate of the people and turned it into money and that he marvelled about 'the unreasonable Fondness, wherewith many are affected towards their Plate' Hodges, *The Present State of England, as to Coin and Publick Charges*, p. xiv.

This was a theory he developed early on, in the late 1660s. In the particular context of the scarcity of money to the point where the national economy stagnates, money embodies in literal terms the necessities of the nation. Hence his proposal to stimulate the use of money by means of allowing a natural price to interest, rather than lowering it legally. Moreover, his scientific theory of promoting an unchecked interest for the use of money glossed over the traditional caution against money made by moralists and theologians alike. Instead, Locke continued to develop the insights that his philosophical theory of necessities offered for monetary theory. On the one hand, this is consistent with his continuous concern over the scarcity of money and the promotion of means to make good money abundant. On the other hand, his means of making an intervention as a moral philosopher appeared to have been in the spirit of Jan Comenius's 'Professor of Necessities': by exposing the right knowledge about which things were necessary, in this case, money. As we will see in the last chapter, instead of disapproving of money in particular, what Locke did as a moralist was to map out a new philosophical means of determining what was necessary for salvation, and human necessities and the necessities of the nation – and so money – were important in it by signalling a right moral decision.

11.2 The Morality of Capital

11.2.1 Money as Reason of State

The 1690s were a period of intense capitalization when the London stock market took off.[89] From the beginning of the reign of William and Mary, moneyed men embodied the reason of state.[90] At the very least the eternal truth that land, rather than stocks, constituted the wealth of the country started to be questioned. Locke was both traditional, following James Harrington, in holding the view of the importance of land; but also modern with a view to the global economy of natural resources that Boyle had

[89] A fact attributed partially to the war finances, see Giles Parkinson, 'War, Peace and the Rise of the London Stock Market', in Sophus A. Reinert and Pernille Røge (eds.), *The Political Economy of Empire in the Early Modern World* (Hampshire: Palgrave Macmillan, 2013), pp. 131–146.

[90] Kleer, *Money, Politics and Power, Banking and Public Finance in Wartime England, 1694–98*; Marjolein T. Hart, 'The Devil or the Dutch: Holland's Impact on the Financial Revolution in England, 1643–1694' 11 *Parliaments, Estates and Representation* (1991), pp. 39–52.

envisaged.[91] The nation was, of course, becoming the centre of an empire during that period. From his return to England from Holland in 1689 up until his death in 1704, Locke immersed himself in developing a new view of economic policymaking for the country. Through his work with the Board of Trade, his political and economic pieces, his contribution to shaping legislation before parliament and working in close collaboration with the leading statesmen of the day such as Sir John Somers John Locke made history as a practical philosopher.[92] His correspondence shows that Locke invested money in trade and capital in the London Stock Market – rather a steady investor than a greedy one. His commitment to the government, to 'the publick good' and to the English nation shone through in the intensive work he carried out for the Board of Trade and in the promotion of English trade and capital, despite seriously failing health, but also in the way he personally invested in the public debt caused by war.

'Commerce' was the only way to finance the needs of the state, but as he had explained scientifically, commerce needs money.[93] Moreover, commerce was not enough in itself. Istvant Host has described the point at which free trade became a reason of state. Influential English economists and analysts of trade such as Charles Davenant (1656–1714) advocated the advantages of free trade as being equal to ensuring that resources gained on the international markets would suffice to service public debt, even for a war economy.[94] In his response to Davenant, John Pollexfen one of the seven members, alongside Locke, of the first Board of Trade made clear the position of key political actors. He entertained major doubts as to the prudency of leaving public finances to the hazards of the (international) market.[95] Credit was key to addressing many problems of the state and

[91] 'But the *chief matter of Property* being now not the Fruits of the Earth, and the Beasts that subsists on it, but the *Earth it self*; as that which takes in carries with it all the rest: I think it is plain, that Property in that too is acquired as the former [through labour].' Locke *Two Treatises of Government*, II §32; Harrington, *The Oceana*; on this question of Boyle, see ch. 6.

[92] 'What are we to think then of the relationship between the two men in 1695, when we find Somers the leading figure in the government, in the Cabinet Council when William III was in England, and amongst the Lords Justices who governed in the King's name when he was out of the country?' Laslett, 'John Locke, the Great Recoinage, and the Origins of the Board of trade: 1695–1698', p. 379. On this period may be watched, the *2021 Carlyle lectures: John Locke and Empire* by Mark Goldie.

[93] Locke, 'Some Considerations of the Consequences of the Lowering of Interest, and Raising the Value of Money', p. 222.

[94] Hont, 'Free Trade and the Economic Limits to National Politics: neo-Machiavellian Political Economy Reconsidered', p. 45; p. 57 and generally.

[95] Hont, 'Free Trade and the Economic Limits to National Politics: neo-Machiavellian Political Economy Reconsidered', pp. 96–100;

money would not come merely from fluctuating trade. Moreover, bringing about mass participation in financing the national debt also called for general moral approval of the financial system that emerged after the Whig Revolution.[96] The operation termed 'the financial revolution' occupied the English nation for almost a century and it is certain that the first shot was fired with the arrival of William and Mary from Holland, and also John Locke, who had been in that country in an exile of sorts for five years.[97] Debates are still ongoing as to how he occupied himself during his stay in Holland. He completed his *Essay*, which must have been enough work for the period. But what we know of Locke would tend to indicate with some degree of certainty that he spent much of his time in Holland *learning* from the Dutch also in the field of finances.

John Munro has argued that in effect the financial revolution had occurred in Flemish cities by the late medieval period and that it was general in Europe by the sixteenth century. Its most important aspect was, according to Munro, that public debt changed the means of finance from interest-bearing loans to the sale of life annuities or rents. He argues that that occurred due to the Church's anti-usury campaigns in the late Middle Ages. In this respect, Locke's personal preference for annuities is intriguing. Peter King, his cousin, once suggested to Locke that he invest £1000 in malt tickets since he envisaged that a new and beneficial bill would be passed. Locke was doubtful whether the bill would ever pass with the new government, and although he trusted King completely, he answered:

> I who aime not at growing mightily rich could be content with less profit upon surer funds and therefore I am inclind to have it laid out either in Bank or East India stock or some such other funds where it might pay interest and yet be ready at any time to be had, when I could get a good land security for it. For there is my desire to place it.[98]

[96] P. G. M. Dickson, *The Financial Revolution in England: A Study in the Development of Public Credit 1688–1756* (London: Macmillan, 1967); Parkinson 'War, Peace and the Rise of the London Stock Market'; Murphy 'Dealing with Uncertainty: Managing Personal Investment in the Early English National Debt'. On Locke's expressions for unity after the Revolution, James Farr and Robert Clayton, 'John Locke on the Glorious Revolution: A Rediscovered Document' 28 *The Historical Journal* (1985); Mark Goldie, 'John Locke on the Glorius Revolution: A New Document' 42 *History of Political Thought* (2021).

[97] Dickson, *The Financial Revolution in England*; on how the King was made dependent on Parliament, see Clayton Roberts, 'The Constitutional Significance of the Financial Settlement of 1690, 20 *The Historical Journal* (1977).

[98] The bill was meant for supplying deficiencies ('deficiencies in the return of the taxes on which the Exchequer Bills were issued') promising a discount of '18 or 19 l. per cent' 'Peter King, later First baron King to Locke, London April 25 1702'; 'Locke to Peter King, later

It seems safe to think that the aim of addressing money matters by means of the new scientific temper and scientific methods of the day was characteristic of the English financial revolution, and that Locke's monetary thinking was instrumental in this regard. The financial innovations involved a complex combination of historical and political factors. In relation to public debt, commerce and speculation with capital, the architects of the new state sought to imbue economic thinking with notions drawn from the new science. Their success was mixed. Peter Dickson describes the circumstances that culminated in the South Sea Bubble collapse in the early 1720s, and he attributed the general involvement in fraud and bribery to the encouragement of speculation and the belief that wealth was a measure of worth – a lack of principles that after the event and for a long time checked the activities of the capital enthusiasts.[99] Despite the fact that in theory money was no longer considered such a serious moral danger as the old theologians and natural lawyers had feared, in practice after the 1688 Revolution the sources show that it could easily get out of control.

11.2.2 *The Right Stock-Jobbing*

After 1688, all the fear in relation to interest on money displayed by some of the most pious and brilliant Reformers had vanished. But when usury was finally erased from official records none of the moral concerns with dishonesty disappeared with it. Science had taken over the money matters and the moment of explosion of the stock market had arrived and with it the possibilities of vice.[100] That wealth on a large scale for the nation ought not to come at the price of virtue was a mantra among the Whig politicians of the 1690s. 'God' was 'a God of reason', and so ought to be his creature when dealing with money and property, but virtuously.[101] Between

first Baron King Oates, 27 April 1702' in E. S. de Beer (ed.), *John Locke: Correspondence* (Oxford at the Clarendon Press, 1980), vol. VI, p. 611.

99 Dickson, *The Financial Revolution in England*, Chs. 5 and 6.

100 Dickson, *The Financial Revolution: A Study in the Development of Public Credit, 1688–1756*; Kleer, *Money, Politics and Power, Banking and Public Finance in Wartime England, 1694–96*; a helpful and detail view is provided in Giles Parkinson, *The London Stock Market in the 1690s* (MPhil, Cambridge University 2006).

101 John Houghton, for instance, was arguing that God would also agree with land enclosure due to its economic benefits, John Houghton, *England's great happiness, or a dialogue between Content and Complaint wherein is demonstrated that a great part or our complaints are causeless, and we have more wealth now, than ever we had at any time before the restauration of His Sacred Majestie* (London, 1677) Early English Books Online Text Creation Partnership 2011, http://name.umdl.umich.edu/A70268.0001.001; Wood, *John Locke and Agrarian Capitalism*, pp. 64–65.

good realism and naïveté, the new architects of the nation envisaged an unproblematic capacity of human reason to be both immersed in money business and above it. That was expressed at its best in their promotion of capital investments.

On 8 June 1694, John Houghton, publisher of a popular periodical, a weekly collection of letters for *Improvement of Husbandry and Trade*, considered that 'a little diversion from natural history' was proper and 'thought fit to treat of *joint-stocks*, and of the various dealings therein, commonly called *stock-jobbing*'.[102] Houghton's letters on stock-jobbing are a marvellous specimen of the style of the new science, combining both teaching of the truth, subtle moral instruction and warning to the well intended. Education, encouragement, exposition of what a worthy gentleman careful of the public interest would do, and the lengths to which a corrupt individual would go – all this was embodied in the letters designed to boost active economic participation and curb vicious economic practices through economic knowledge passed on by the printed press.[103] Houghton was a nationalist and an early convert to the happiness that luxury, consumption and market were able to impart, as trumpeted in his *England's Great Happiness* (1677).[104] His boldness was rewarded by prominence. However, other fellows of the Royal Society complained to Robert Boyle on account of Houghton's lack of moral substance in defending prodigality and luxury.[105] His letters on stock-jobbing show an altogether different style.

In his weekly letters, Houghton addressed a public composed of gentlemen, the middle class and traders, generally those interested in the new advances of science. On the strength of his periodicals, he has been considered important to the history of journalism and book-reviewing.[106]

[102] F.R.S., that is, Fellow of the Royal Society, accompanied the signature of Houghton's weekly letters, see John Houghton, *Husbandry and Trade Improved: Being a Collection of Many Valuable Materials relating to Corn, Cattle, Coals, Hops, Wool, etc.*, Revised with a Preface by Richard Bradley, F.R.S. (Lyon, London: Printed for Wooman, 1777).

[103] See the many attempts in the same period to check economic vices through public measures in Davison, *Public Policy in an Age of Economic Expansion.*

[104] Houghton, *England's great happiness*; see specially, Paul Slack, 'The Politics of Consumption and England's Happiness in the Later Seventeenth Century' 122 *The English Historical Review* (2007); Joyce Appleby, 'Ideology and Theory: The Tension Between Political and Economic Liberalism in Seventeenth-Century England' *The American Historical Review* (1976).

[105] Slack writes that perhaps *England's Great Happines* earned him the Fellowship in the Royal Society; also the complaint of John Beale to Robert Boyle against Houghton's irreligious defence of luxury, in Slack, 'The Politics of Consumption', p. 613.

[106] See Roger Philip McCutcheon, 'John Houghton, a Seventeenth-Century Editor and Book-Reviewer', 20 *Modern Philology* (1923), pp. 255–260.

What he published amounted to efficient interventions in the education of the public on, among other matters, husbandry, general history, code-breaking, trade, banking, and as we will see next, stock-jobbing. Evidently, increasing knowledge for the good of the nation was his key concern.[107] Houghton was also extremely well connected, as shown by his numerous notes on discussions about books with specialists, for example on mathematics and theology. His relevance is also made clear by the fact that he had sponsored the admission to the Royal Society of none other than the Quaker William Penn (1644-1718), then a close friend of William Petty, Robert Boyle and John Locke. Penn was elected as a member *in absentia* on 2 November 1681. On that day Houghton presented the Society with a map of Pennsylvania in Penn's name.[108]

Houghton himself introduced his several letters on stock-jobbing as a defence of trade. The issue in question concerned explaining the mysteries of stocks and dispelling prejudices and false notions as being the only hindrances 'to a man's coming to the true knowledge of any thing'. He wrote that he personally did not trade in stock, but noted that Descartes had already suggested that without certainty no one ought to consider that they had achieved truth. It was proper therefore to examine and scrutinize the reason behind opinions with objectivity.[109] There had been 'some abuses', Houghton admitted, 'by traders', but that did not make the thing unlawful in itself. Was wine bad because some people did not know how to consume it? The 'Gentlemen' he knew, 'worthy persons of great honour and probity, who deal in stocks' had to suffer 'the censures of mankind, who inveigh against all traders and trading in stock', while those critics were generally ignorant about the matter. Therefore Houghton promised that starting in the next Friday's paper he would give an account of 'the original and *necessity* of joint-stocks', of 'the lawfulness and usefulness of trading therein', and also of its 'abuses'.[110] Notwithstanding this style of

107 In a paper given at the Royal Society five years later, Houghton described 'the Political uses of Coffee' through a calculation of tons of consumption in each of the kingdoms. If the 70 tons of coffee consumed in England annually, at a cost of £14 a ton, were to be sold in coffee houses, this would result in employment for 6174 persons – since coffee houses made people 'sociable', facilitated trade and arts, and 'improved useful knowledge very much', meaning that that business represented a good source of employment. John Houghton F. R. S., 'A Discourse of Coffee, read at a Meeting of the Royal Society', 21 *Philosophical Transactions* (1699), pp. 311–317.

108 On Houghton, Penn and his friends see Marion Balderston, 'The Mystery of William Penn, the Royal Society, and the First Map of Pennsylvania' 55 *Quaker History* (1966), pp. 79–87.

109 Houghton, *Husbandry and Trade Improved*, p. 258.

110 Houghton, *Husbandry and Trade Improved*, p. 260 (emphasis mine).

presentation, Houghton's subsequent letters contained not only a guide to stock-jobbing but a portrait of it, placing the investor in the wider context of the needs of the nation.[111] Stock-jobbing was necessary and lawful, but not *any* stock-jobbing – Houghton had no doubt that a distinction could be made between virtuous and vicious stock-jobbing, despite many and well-entrenched blunders in the system.

Houghton's nativist account of the history of stocks held that the trade was as old as the East India Company (i.e. it had been going on for almost a century), but the impetus recently observed was due to the war with France, which had obstructed maritime commerce. The business itself was explained by the fact that transferring stocks from one person to another was easier than investing money in land, houses or commodities, and because many took the view that money should not lay idle, despite its owner's lack of employment. 'This put them upon contrivances, whereby some were encouraged to buy, others to sell, and this is that is called *stock-jobbing*.'[112] Everything started with an invention, a discovery of a mine, a new trade that promised gain, but due to the amount of money needed or the hazard implied, it could not be done 'by a private purse'. The individual would then find 'some friends', who draft an agreement divide the shares. Everyone then would bring 'in his friends' and continue 'till all the shares be bought at such a price as stated'.[113] Houghton recommended paying down all the money immediately in view of the trouble caused when someone lagged in paying his quota. The organs of this new enterprise were a general court, composed of all the owners of the shares, a committee that would manage the whole, 'except ordering the raising or dividing of money' and usually a chairman, a treasurer and a clerk. They would meet either in houses established for the purpose, if they were big, or in particular coffee houses, 'where they may have some refreshment without great charge'.[114] The business to be done started when 'the monied man goes among the brokers', usually dwelling on the 'Exchange' or at 'Jonathan's coffee-house'. He would ask 'how stocks go'. With this 'information, (he) bids the broker to buy or sell so many shares of such and such

111 I am borrowing here John Brewer's expression. Brewer referred to *The General Shop Book or Tradesman Universal Director* of mid eighteenth century that helped placing the small shopkeeper in the larger context of the British Empire, John Brewer, *The Sinews of Power: War, Money and the English State, 1688–1783* (Cambridge: Harvard University Press, 1988), p. 228.

112 Houghton, *Husbandry and Trade Improved*, p. 261.

113 Houghton, *Husbandry and Trade Improved*, p. 262.

114 Houghton, *Husbandry and Trade Improved*, p. 263.

stocks' at certain prices, then he would mingle with the share owners or brokers to strike a bargain.[115]

On other occasions, he would ask what they will have for refuse of so many shares: that is, how many guineas a share he shall give for liberty to accept or refuse such shares, at such price, at any time within six months, or other time they shall agree for.[116]

Houghton also published an example of the type of contract used for that type of commitment to sell on demand and explained in detail what it meant in substance. It concerned the right to require the owner of a £75 share, for instance, that on receipt of a payment of three guineas, he or she would not sell it in the next three months. Price fluctuations would determine whether that owner lost or gained. If the share price rose substantially, whoever paid the three guineas would demand its acquisition and would have to pay only the original £75 for the share. Hence 'in plain English, one gives three guineas for all the profits if they should rise, the other for three guineas runs the hazard of all the loss if they should fall'.[117] Dealers might also make a profit by buying and selling shares in the same stock for different prices.

Another variation of the same idea of contracting on future handlings was 'putting', in which those who needed money would sell their shares in exchange for some form of security. For a certain price (e.g. a guinea and a half), they would agree to take the shares again at the same price for a certain period of time. The security of *putting upon* someone was the demand to buy again the shares he or she sold before. For the buyer, this type of transaction represented a means of obtaining profit, while for the seller it was a means of obtaining money immediately that he or she might need for other businesses. One ventured the guinea and a half and interest (dividend) on the share, hoping for profit; and the other, for the same sum, bore the risk that the shares would fall during the period that the security lasted, while being able to use the other's money in the meantime. 'Putting' functioned well in encouraging many people to buy in transactions whose success, as Houghton noted, was 'very uncertain'.[118] It was also employed in order to manipulate the prices of shares on the market, holding up shares for some time, and thus tempting others to buy, but without security. It was possible 'by the contrivances of a few men in confederacy' to have prices 'rise or fall', but, Houghton clarified,

[115] Houghton, *Husbandry and Trade Improved*, p. 264.
[116] Houghton, *Husbandry and Trade Improved*, p. 264.
[117] Houghton, *Husbandry and Trade Improved*, p. 265.
[118] Houghton, *Husbandry and Trade Improved*, p. 269.

this could happen easily where small stocks were concerned, but not in relation to the bigger ones.[119]

Houghton also described 'the great mystery of all', or 'the mystery of buying more than all', which involved an intrigue to secure all the shares in a stock, and also to pay people who had no shares a sum in return for refusing offers to purchase them. 'Putting' and 'refusing' operated similarly with lottery tickets. Those who were to refuse offers would not imagine that the price would rise above the amount they had received, or they would think that they could buy from others before it did so. However, they could not, as under this scheme the closure of the sale period was arranged in advance. Once the price has risen,

> such takers of guineas for refuse as have no stock, must buy of the other that have, so many shares as they have taken guineas for the *refuse of*, at such rates as they or their friends will sell for tho' ten or twenty times the former price.[120]

Houghton's letters evidence that in the 1690s the rising stock market was causing the wider English public some apprehension. The whole point of his letters was to show the truth of stock-jobbing, and he did so. While it is clear that some of its mathematical secrets escaped him, the gist of stock-jobbing did not. His description vividly showed that it was about 'risk dealings' and the all too obvious uncertainty of the entire business, which was created not least by the uncertainty of human beings themselves – scoundrels, ruffians and villains were involved in stock-jobbing, Houghton explained, alongside numerous honest folk.

Houghton's letters are also indicative of an effort to teach the public that in the making of money one ought to remain virtuous and vigilant. Moreover, the system of stock-jobbing itself, with its aura of mystery, seemed to lend itself to vicious machinations and abuses. The dissemination of knowledge was the strategy followed by Houghton and his friends, with a view to disarming the evildoers by uncovering their mischievous methods. However, he concluded firmly that it was worth continuing with stock-jobbing and expanding it for the sake of the nation.

In his seventh and last letter on the question, Houghton highlighted particular companies that provided advantages to 'the nation' and in which it was worth investing.[121] He highlighted the profitability of companies

[119] Houghton, *Husbandry and Trade Improved*, pp. 269–270.
[120] Houghton, *Husbandry and Trade Improved*, p. 272.
[121] Houghton, *Husbandry and Trade Improved*, p. 274.

involved in the following: glass bottles, japan (lacquers), sword blades (in Newcastle, but formerly imported from Holland and Germany), tapestries, copper and coal mines, 'night engines' (streetlights), firefighters, Greenland fishing, the trade of the Guinea company, leather from Turkey and Russia, 'lutestring' (silk clothes in the French style), all trade from India, (with the increasing of the city population), drinking water, paper, 'salt petre' and colonies such as New Jersey and Pennsylvania. In summary, companies were useful for the country, and Houghton concluded that 'if an hundred stocks more arise, we have no reason to be offended.'[122] His advice was that it was safer to confine one's investment activity to the big companies. But the truth is that the 'good' stock market of the great companies became highly exclusive by dint of the exorbitant price of a single share, which only the richest could afford.[123] Despite Houghton's instruction on stock-jobbing only a few, roughly 1 per cent of London's population at the time (above half a million inhabitants), would be capable of benefiting from the business honourably and with certainty, without involvement in the stock-jobbers' dubious schemes.[124] Thus access to virtue was open to the very rich, but not for everyone.

Houghton's seven letters on stock-jobbing did not stem merely from his private inspiration. They aligned with prevalent assumptions as to the ties between knowledge, profit and public good. Hence the course of action adopted by the government and parliament in the following decades entailed a series of bold measures by which to put greater quantities of private capital in motion with a view to facilitating rational public policies.[125] Interestingly, they also belong to a philosophical view on political economy that was definitively separated from theological discourse and based on notions of necessity developed by John Locke from the 1670s on, the techniques of which he had learned from his predecessors and placed in a new philosophical context. As argued in this chapter, what happened between the Reformers and Houghton, was Locke.

122 Houghton, *Husbandry and Trade Improved*, p. 276.

123 These companies with value £100.000 or more were the Bank of England, the White Paper, the East India and the Royal African Companies and the Orphan's Fund, Parkinson, *The London Stock Market in the 1690s*, p. 74; p. 158.

124 Giles Parkinson's study shows that only around five thousand investors at a time owned the capital of the biggest corporations that by 1697 composed 98% of the market index, from where I calculate the number of 1 per cent. Parkinson, *The London Stock Market in the 1690s*.

125 Brewer, *The Sinews of Power*, pp. 221–249.

12

The Doctrine of Necessities and the (Public) Good

12.1 Necessity and Necessities in Knowledge and Morality: *An Essay Concerning Human Understanding*

It is in the absence of thinking, not merely of power as Hobbes had it, that necessity occurs. This is how Locke put it: 'Where-ever Thought is wholly wanting, or the power to act or forbear according to the direction of Thought, there *Necessity* takes place.'[1] Thinking is therefore the opposite of necessity. We are ignorant of 'the Nature' of 'that thinking thing that is in us, and which we look on as ourselves', save for the fact that it is free to design her own destiny, misery or happiness.[2] It is possible to ascertain the centrality of human necessities in Locke's wider theory of knowledge and human morality as set out in *An Essay Concerning Human Understanding*. First, human beings navigate this world securely through the knowledge provided by necessities.

> If any one pretends to be so sceptical, as to deny his own Existence, (for really to doubt of it, is manifestly impossible,) let him for me enjoy his beloved Happiness of being nothing, until Hunger, or some other Pain convince him of the contrary.[3]

Second, the particular knowledge constituted by necessities provides a helpful guide to the correct moral action to be taken towards happiness, as it is necessary to assess whether human desires, which are numerous and constant, are fixed on their proper objects. As a rule of thumb of proper conduct, necessities lead to the preservation of life; while following desires threatens its loss if these desires are not examined with the goal of eternal life in mind. As any reader of *An Essay Concerning Human Understanding* will see, there is much more to Locke's epistemology and

[1] See also in Locke, *An Essay Concerning Human Understanding*, II. 21. §13, p. 240.
[2] Locke, *An Essay Concerning Human Understanding*, II.27. §27, p. 347.
[3] Locke, *An Essay Concerning Human Understanding*, IV, 10 §1.

moral philosophy than human necessities. However, human necessities are the hinge that unites knowledge and morality.

12.1.1 Epistemology and Necessities

In *An Essay Concerning Human Understanding* Locke traced how ideas originate, in order to distinguish between knowledge and opinion. Matthew Priselac has called the epistemology of that book a 'genetic structure' of knowledge.[4] Naturally, ideas start when the human body experiences the external world and the senses inform the mind of this. Together with awareness of the existence of an infinite and omnipresent God, human necessities unproblematically relate human beings to the reality surrounding them. Thus 'necessities' have a fundamental role in avoiding general scepticism. Despite Locke's adherence to corpuscularianism and his conception that everything is composed of atoms in constant flux, it is clear in his epistemology that human beings are equipped to know what will help them to survive in the world, and more than survive.

> That *the certainty of* Things existing *in rerum Naturâ*, when we have *the testimony of our senses* for it, is not only *as great* as our frame can attain to, but *as our Condition needs*. For our Faculties being suited not to the full extent of Being, nor to a perfect, clear, comprehensive Knowledge of things free from all doubt and scruple; but to the Preservation of us, in whom they are; and accommodated to the use of Life: they serve to our purpose well enough, if they will but give us certain notice of those Things, which are convenient or inconvenient to us.[5]

Significantly, knowledge depends on 'the right use' of the powers that nature had bestowed on us, human beings.[6] Thus both the *burden* and the advantage of knowledge lie in the reasoning subject.[7] This demand for

[4] Priselac, *Locke's Science of Knowledge*, p. 15. On Locke as an 'indirect realist' to whom ideas are 'the immediate objects of perception' through which our mind reaches out to the real world. Walter Ott, 'Locke on Sense Perception', in Jessica Gordon-Roth and Shelley Weinberg (eds.), *The Lockean Mind* (Abingdon, New York: Routledge, 2022), Ch. 15.

[5] Locke, *An Essay Concerning Human Understanding*, IV. 9. §8, p. 634.

[6] 'But this only by the bye, to shew how much our *knowledge depends upon the right use of those Powers Nature hats bestowed upon us*, and how little upon such innate Principles, as are in vain supposed to be in all Mankind for their direction,' Locke, Locke, *An Essay Concerning Human Understanding*, I. 4, §22, p. 100.

[7] 'Since it is the Understanding that sets Man above the rest of sensible beings, and gives him all the Advantage and Dominion, which he has over them; it is certainly a Subject, even for its Nobleness, worth our labour to inquire into.' Locke, *An Essay Concerning Human Understanding*, I, p. 43.

the correct use of reason constitutes, in an important sense, Locke's theory of the burden of freedom. He shares with Boyle the awareness of the immensity of unknown things – created, after all, by an omnipotent God. There are many phenomena that our senses cannot perceive, of which we consequently know nothing.[8] However, Locke writes, in this 'Globe of Earth allotted for our Mansion' we know what we need to know.[9]

> The infinite wise Contriver of us, and all things about us, has fitted our Senses, Faculties and Organs, to the conveniences of Life and the Businesses we have to do here.[10]

Senses allow us to distinguish things and examine them in a manner that allows us to 'apply them to our Uses' and diversely 'accommodate the Exigencies of this Life'.[11] Hobbes had declared that the fool is wrong. In turn Locke would defend that 'the skeptic is wrong.'[12] In this endeavour human necessities appear to be instrumental. Furthermore, the rejection of innate principles in the theory of knowledge that Locke presented in *An Essay* may be paralleled with Boyle's rejection of a metaphysical concept of nature as mentioned in Chapter 7. Both concepts were (in their view) of doubtful authority and provenance and prevented the advancement of science. Locke regarded innate principles as putting difficulties in the way of acquiring better understanding of how the faculty of reasoning works.

> On this faculty of Distinguishing one thing from another, depends the evidence and certainty of several, even very general Propositions, which have passed for innate Truths; because Men over-looking the true cause, why those Propositions find universal assent, impute it wholly to native uniform Impressions; whereas it in truth depends upon this clear discerning Faculty of the Mind, whereby it perceives two Ideas to be the same or different.[13]

[8] Anstey, *John Locke and Natural Philosophy*, Chs. 2 and 3.

[9] Thousands of changes happen in the bodies we may handle that we may 'never suspect, because they never appear in sensible effects.' Locke, *An Essay Concerning Human Understanding*, II. 23. §9, p. 301; §12, p. 302. By contrast others like Robert Hooke (1635–1703) or Benjamin Worsley highlighted the relevance of invisible nature for science and faith, see Chapter 7 and Wragge-Morley, *Aesthetic Science.* On the humorous critique arising against this latter view that Jonathan Swift and his *Gulliver's Travels* exemplify see Denys van Renen, *Nature and the New Science in England, 1665–1726* (University of Oxford, Voltaire Foundation: Liverpool University Press, 2018).

[10] Locke, *An Essay Concerning Human Understanding*, II. 23. §12, p. 302; Kochiras, 'Locke's Philosophy of Science'.

[11] Locke, *An Essay Concerning Human Understanding*, II. 23. §12, 302.

[12] See, Priselac, *Locke's Science of Knowledge*, p. 15.

[13] Locke, *An Essay Concerning Human Understanding*, II. 11. §1, pp. 155–156; II. 11. §15, p. 162.

Further, in his important discussion of liberty and necessity in the context of power (Book II, chapter IX), Locke concedes that human beings necessarily want happiness and considers that perfection lies in the determination of human will by choosing what is good.[14] One could argue that these two claims resemble in practice a description of innate principles, but Locke consistently adheres to the terminology of an elusive principle of *necessity*. My intention, however, is not to contest Locke's extraordinary analysis of human morality but to highlight the instrumental role played by human necessities in his epistemological and moral method. *An Essay* may well be read as an extremely accomplished effort to appease the anxiety of the era struggling to grapple with disparate elements left over from a past theological period by means of a rational moral philosophy. Timothy Stanton has emphasized that Locke took the view that God was the foundation of all morality and that an atheist could accordingly have no morality.[15] A 'company of poor insects' is the comparison Locke used to describe what would become of humanity without God.[16] At the same time his moral theory is superbly empirical and thus rational, and that is of course its strength. In that empirical perspective the importance of human necessities cannot be doubted because human beings' sole motivation for action lies in 'uneasiness' of mind or body.[17] 'Uneasiness' represented by desire might be natural, such as thirst, hunger, or indeed love, or 'fantastical', such as honours.[18]

That the desire for self-preservation moves everyone to act and that the assumption that human needs bring people together, we might recall, appear in the *Essays on the Law of Nature* and they embody the elements for beginning a political society specified in the *Two Treatises of Government* – these are necessity, convenience and inclination, as we will see in this chapter.[19] Desires are numerous, either through natural wants or custom and habit.[20] At any rate, the most pressing uneasiness,

14 Locke, *An Essay Concerning Human Understanding*, II. 21. §48, p. 264.

15 Stanton is quoting from Locke's, *An Essay Concerning Toleration*, in his exchange with John William Tate, Stanton, 'On (Mis) Interpreting Locke: A Reply to Tate', p. 232.

16 'Supposing them only like a Company of poor insects; whereof some are Bees, delighted with Flowers and their sweetness; others Beetles, delighted with other kinds of Viands, which having enjoyed for a season, they would cease to be, and exist no more for ever.' Locke, *An Essay Concerning Human Understanding*, II. 21. §55, p. 270.

17 Pleasure and pain indicate to the human being the divine design for human beings according to Rossitter see for this, Elliot Rossiter, 'Hedonism and Natural Law in Locke's Moral Philosophy' 54 *Journal of the History of Philosophy* (2016).

18 Locke, *An Essay Concerning Human Understanding*, II. 9. §7, p. 145.

19 Locke, *Essays on the Law of Nature*; Harris, *The Mind of John Locke*, p. 99.

20 Locke, *An Essay Concerning Human Understanding*, II. 21. §45.

for instance a terrible pain, an addiction to alcohol or a passionate love or hunger determines action in the absence of conflicting desires.[21]

Moreover, everything starts with necessities as he noted in the argument on the origin of ideas set out in Book II.

> Therefore I doubt not but *Children*, by the exercise of their Senses and Objects, that affect them *in the Womb, receive some few Ideas,* before they are born, as the unavoidable effects, either of the Bodies that environ them, or else of those Wants or Diseases they suffer, amongst which, (if one may conjencture concerning things not very capable of examination) I think the *Ideas* of Hunger and Warmth are two: which probably are some of the first that Children have, and which they scarce ever part with again.[22]

He took the view that the order and variety of ideas that a child receives after their birth is very uncertain.[23] However, he asserted that a certain process occurs when the child is still in the mother's womb. Intellectual perception accordingly starts through surrounding bodies, necessities and diseases, and specifically with necessities.

12.1.2 Between Aquinas and Henry of Ghent

The aim of freedom, whose existence Locke strongly defends, is that we attain the good we choose. The only determinations in human beings' moral action that he admits are first that when faced with a decision, the will necessitates (a) to will this or (b) not to will it – *tertium non datur*;[24] and second, that individuals will always choose what they think best for themselves in order to achieve happiness. Experience and observation show that people choose the good that they regard as constituting a necessary part of their happiness, which might or might not be 'the greatest good'.[25] However, the true perfection of an intellectual nature is to achieve true and solid happiness, and such a person accordingly chooses 'the proper Object of desire', that is to say, one that identifies affection and truth.[26] Locke follows Aquinas in this description of how the objects

21 Locke, *An Essay Concerning Human Understanding*, II. 21. §40.

22 Locke, *An Essay Concerning Human Understanding*, II. 9. §5, p. 144.

23 Locke, *An Essay Concerning Human Understanding*, II. 9. §7, p. 145.

24 He meant to want this or not to want this. Locke, *An Essay Concerning Human Understanding*, II. 21. §24.

25 Locke, *An Essay Concerning Human Understanding*, II. 21. §54

26 Locke, *An Essay Concerning Human Understanding*, II. 21. §51. On the question of the harmonization of desire, see recently Juan Andrés Mercado y Pía Valenzuela, 'L'armonizzazione del desiderio per la fioritura umana', in S. Langela, M. S. Vaccarezza, M. Croce (eds.), *Virtù, legge e fioritura umana. Saggi in onore di Angelo Campodonico* (Milano: Mimesis, 2022).

of desire move to action.[27] In fact, what Locke accomplished in *An Essay Concerning Human Understanding* may be understood as recovering a Christian moral language and as transmuting self-interest into terms of necessity, and hence as a vocation to perfection.

> Every Man is put under a necessity by his constitution, as an intelligent Being, to be determined in willing by his own thought and judgment, what is best for him to do.[28]

Anything else, Locke concluded, would be determination by some else and thus lack of freedom. In his understanding, the 'necessity of being happy' contains a preference for eternal happiness, rather than a present but transient happiness.[29] However, misjudgements of reason about happiness abound. Moreover, according to Locke, freedom was also honoured when an individual willingly opted for the lowest good, a present pleasure that however causes that individual to lose the chance of eternal bliss – it was a madman's freedom, but freedom nonetheless.[30] Locke commented in this context on the classical case of the prisoner who suddenly realized that he had no chains.

Famously, in one of his three solutions to this case contained in *Questio* 26 of his *Quodlibet* IX produced in Lent of 1286, the Parisian theologian Henry of Ghent had attributed to the man sentenced to death a licit power (*licit potestas*) to flee.[31] On the strength of this solution, Henry is often mentioned as an introductory author in the histories of natural rights, since he utilized a remarkably novel language in this

27 'So it is clear that there is ultimately one mover, the object desired. For this both moves appetition and affords a starting point for the practical intellect – the two motive principles which have been assumed. And it is reasonable that these two principles should be reduced to unity in the object of desire; for if both intellect and appetition are principles with respect to one and the same movement they must, as such, share the same specific nature; since a single effect implies always a single cause of precisely one effect. Now it cannot be said that appetite is a moving principle through sharing the specific nature of intellect, but rather e converso, for intellect only moves anything in virtue of appetition. It moves by means of the will, which is a sort of appetition. The explanation of this is that the practical reason is essentially balanced between alternatives; nor can it initiate movement unless appetition fixes it exclusively upon one alternative' *Aristotle's De Anima with the Commentary of St. Thomas Aquinas*, trans. By Kenelm Foster, and Silvester Humphries, with an Introduction by Ivot Thomas, (New Haven and London: Yale University Press, 1951) §823–825, p. 472

28 Locke, *An Essay Concerning Human Understanding*, II. 21. §48, p. 264.

29 Locke, *An Essay Concerning Human Understanding*, II. 21. §49, p. 265.

30 Locke, *An Essay Concerning Human Understanding*, II. 21. §70, p. 283

31 Henrici de Gandavo, *Opera Omnia*, Macken ed. *v. XIII, Quodlibet IX*: 'Utrum condemnatus morti licite possit abire, si tempus et locum habeat', pp. 306–310.

regard.[32] In answering the question of whether 'one man sentenced to death can licitly flee if he has the time and place', Henry declared that if the circumstances of place and time were favourable – for instance 'he would be without chains and the door would be open' – the criminal was a 'homicide' if he 'did not provide for himself as he should' and fled, as necessity compelled him to do. Unlike the necessity of the judge to punish him, the prisoner's necessity was of a higher calibre and compelled him to search for his freedom.[33] The condemned man 'had like a power of using the same body' in order to guard his life as had the judge in order to punish him.[34] However, as custodian of the life dwelling in the body, the soul's power over the body was greater than the judge's. Henry posed the problem as the criminal's licit *power* of using his body, which was also his right (*ius suum*) according to the law of nature, and if necessary of exercising that right (*exsequendi ius suum*). 'Over a certain thing' Henry had stated 'there can be a power or right' (*potestas sive ius*) in two ways. One, like the ownership in the substance of the thing. In the case of the body, 'only the soul under God has property in the substance of the body', and 'the other like a use in determined actions that can be exercised over the thing,' hence the judge's right to enchain etc. (*ius in vinculando etc.*).[35]

[32] Marialucrezia Leone, 'Henry of Ghent on Divine Law, Natural Law and Divine Law', pp. 383–398, pp. 390–391; and Virpi Mäkinen, 'Duty to Self-Preservation or Right to Life? The Relation between Natural Law and Natural Rights' (1200–1600)', pp. 457–470, p. 466, both in Andreas Speer and Guy Guldentops (eds.) *Das Gesetz – The Law – La Loi* (Berlin: De Gruyter, 2014); Tierney, *The Idea of Natural Rights*, pp. 78–89; Porro, 'Individual Rights and Common Good: Henry of Ghent and the Scholastic Origins of Human Rights'.

[33] 'quia iudex non tanta necessitate compellitur eum detinere aut occidere, quanta necessitate propter iustum metum mortis compellitur damnatus quod sibi provideat, ne vitam et perfectionem suam in corpore amittat, quia, si in hoc non provideret si posset invenire locum et tempus, ut si forte esset sine vinculis et ostia essent aperta, nec adesset impedimentum abeundi et per hoc vitam salvandi, sui ipsius homicida esset, non providendo sibi sicut deberet.' Henrici de Gandavo, *Quodlibet IX*, p. 309.

[34] 'quoad animam potestatem super idem corpus utendi eo ad vitae suae in corpore custodiam, in qua consistit eius perfectio sine iniuria alterius. Et hoc non solum aequitate naturae quae fas est circa rem alienam, sed quae licitum est. Et non solum licitum tamquam a lege naturae indultum in aliquale alterius praeiudicium, sed quae ius est secundum legem naturae. Et non solum ius, sed in casu necessitas exsequendi ius suum.' Henrici de Gandavo, *Quodlibet IX*, p. 309.

[35] 'Ad cuius intellectum sciendum est quod supra rem aliquam dupliciter haberi potest potestas sive ius: una quoad proprietatem in substantia rei, alia quoad usum in actione aliqua exercenda circa rem. Primam potestatem aut ius nullatenus habet iudex saecularis super corpus damnati plus quam super animam illius, sed secundam tantum, quae consistit in tribus, scilicet in corpus capiendo, in vinculando sive incarcerando, et in occidendo. Potestatem autem quoad proprietatem in substantia corporis sola anima habet sub Deo, et tenetur ius suum in hoc custodire absque iniuria alterius.' *Quodlibet IX*, p. 309.

In his discussion of the text, Brian Tierney situates Henry's novel language in the context of the dawn of the idea of natural rights in the late Middle Ages, tracing how this solution was taken up by another Parisian theologian, Jacques Almain, in around 1500.[36] Furthermore, Aquinas had discussed the case, explaining that someone sentenced to death ought to act according to reason and not only be guided by the natural instinct of survival. A just individual would escape if he or she was innocent and stay in prison if guilty.[37]

> Reason has been given to human beings in order to carry on what nature inclines them to, not randomly, but according to the order of reason. Hence not all defense of themselves is licit, but only that which is done with due guidance.[38]

Instead, preservation of life and the natural rights of *the soul* over the body took precedence in Henry's discussion. His goal was to determine the criminal's rights and duties. What is plain, however, is that while Aquinas transferred the moral decision to the individual sentenced to death in the particular situation, and to his or her capacity of reasoning, Henry's solution is that of the casuistic theologian who determines who had always

[36] See the series of articles and chapters by Brian Tierney, in particular, Brian Tierney, 'Natural Rights in the Thirteenth Century: A *Quaestio* of Henry of Ghent' 67 *Speculum* (1992), pp. 58–68; 'Historical Roots of Modern Rights Before Locke and After' 3 *Ave Maria Law Review* (2005); 'Dominion of Self and Natural Rights Before Locke and After', in Virpi Mäkinen and Petter Korkman (eds.), *Transformations in Medieval and Early-Modern Rights Discourse* (Springer, 2006). In his study on natural rights, also dealing with Henry's 26 *Quaestio* on the 'ownership of self', Tierney considers Hobbes an 'aberration' in the tradition of natural rights and Grotius, Locke and Pufendorf followers of that tradition, Tierney, *The Idea of Natural Rights*, pp. 83–89; ch. 13; p. 340.

[37] 'Respondeo dicendum quod aliquis damnatur ad mortem dupliciter. Uno modo, iuste. Et sic non licet condemnato se defendere, licitum enim est iudici eum resistentem impugnare; unde relinquitur quod ex parte eius sit bellum iniustum. Unde indubitanter peccat. Alio modo condemnatur aliquis iniuste. Et tale iudicium simile est violentiae latronum, secundum illud Ezech. XXII, *principes eius in medio eius quasi lupi rapientes praedam ad effundendum sanguinem*. Et ideo sicut licet resistere latronibus, ita licet resistere in tali casu malis principibus, nisi forte propter scandalum vitandum, cum ex hoc aliqua gravis turbatio timeretur.' Aquinas, *Summa theologiae*, IIª-IIae q. 69 a. 4 co.

[38] 'Ad primum ergo dicendum quod ideo homini data est ratio, ut ea ad quae natura inclinat non passim, sed secundum rationis ordinem exequatur. Et ideo non quaelibet defensio sui est licita, sed quae fit cum debito moderamine.' Aquinas, *Summa theologiae*, IIª-IIae q. 69 a. 4 ad 1. Comparing Aquinas and Henry on this issue see Porro, 'Individual Rights and Common Good: Henry of Ghent and the Scholastic Origins of Human Rights'.

the better right and even the obligation to exercise the natural right of preservation.[39]

No matter how general the view may be, Tierney has rightly noted the impossibility of regarding Locke's famous position in the *Two Treatises* on the right of property over one's person as a radical departure of scholasticism.[40] In this context, critiques emphasizing links between the slavery system and Locke's natural right of property over one's person (rather than with slavery as the classic institution of *ius gentium*) need to be complicated with studies on Scholasticism and with perceptions as to how Neoplatonism made it conceptually possible in the first place for this type of appropriation by the soul of everything material, even one's body.[41] It is also clear that at the outset people like Henry pursued the autonomy of individuals by means of a robust dualism connecting the soul and God, with no authority in between – certainly the opposite project to slavery. Locke asserted that 'every Man has a *Property* in his own *Person*. This no Body has any Right to but himself. The *Labour* of his Body, and the *Work* of his hands, we may say, are properly his'. If taken literally, these statements amount more to an anti-slavery manifesto than a justification for it.[42] In an era in which commercial exploitation of natural resources and enslavement of human beings became of paramount economic importance, the development of a natural law mingled with civil law notions of property rights seems to have played an ambiguous role. But with a view to what key theologians like Henry wrote on the natural rights of individuals, Locke appears less an original thinker on the question and more a continuator of a tradition favouring autonomy, especially of classic Parisian theologians.[43]

Brian Tierney mainly analysed Locke's position on natural rights in the *Two Treatises*. However, in *An Essay* the philosopher's use of the prisoner

[39] Compare with Mäkinen who argues that natural law and natural right 'are both derived as correlative doctrines from the same fundamental view of human personality.' Mäkinen, 'Duty to Self-Preservation or Right to Life? The Relation between Natural Law and Natural Rights' (1200–1600), p. 460.

[40] Tierney, 'Natural Rights in the Thirteenth Century'.

[41] This type of connection between Locke's property on one's person and modern slave capitalism in the piece by Jennifer Rae Greeson, 'The Prehistory of Possessive Individualism' 127 *PMLA* (2012); O'Brien, *Literature Incorporated. The Cultural Unconscious of the Business Corporation, 1650–1850*, p. 32; p. 48.

[42] Locke, *Two Treatises of Government*, II §27, pp. 287–288.

[43] This fact should not come as a surprise, since whatever else he did in France during around four years, he certainly passed many hours studying. Milton, 'Locke's Life and Times'. Maurice Cranston gives a lively description of the years in France. Although he wrote that Locke wanted to get 'away from the vague glamour of medieval things, from reverence for tradition, from mysticism, enthusiasm and *gloire*' this is not what transpires from his

example was not about rights. Intriguingly it seemed to be more in line with Aquinas's theory of freedom of moral decision, but with an argument that evidences that naturalist ideas of self-preservation had attained centrality in his line of thinking. Locke's prisoner is all alone, and no one threatens him but the inhospitality of life outside the prison. He is able to decide what to do – but this is the most difficult part, for there is no normative principle that compels him to act beyond his necessary search for happiness. In *An Essay* this example serves to demonstrate the individual's power to suspend judgment and examine the morality of each situation before acting. While due examination of the good and evil involved, was 'all that [he] needs [to do]', the prisoner was no less free if he chose to 'stay in his Prison'. Locke depicts this choice as being prompted by the convenience urged by the prisoner's physical body, but crucially, not its necessities: 'the darkness of the Night', 'the illness of the Weather' or 'the want of other Lodgings' made him prefer to stay.[44] However, Locke remarked that the highest perfection of an intellectual nature demanded that a human being would be increasingly free from 'any necessary determination of our will or from a necessary compliance with our desire'.[45] Locke's employment of the classical case of the prisoner who finds himself without chains suggests that, in extreme cases, excessive care for the body beyond necessities may prevent people from attaining the superior freedom that awaits them.

12.1.3 Necessary Happiness

This *thing* that human beings have of searching for true happiness, Locke depicted as the 'necessity' of pursuing a higher happiness and 'the necessity' of suspending judgment in favour of deliberation in order to achieve that goal.[46] That he was more inclined to theological optimism is apparent in that in *The Reasonableness of Christianity* he rejected a parallel 'necessity of sinning', thus marking a distance between his ideas and those

recorded sightseeing. Rather Locke seemed to have been opened to everything French. Cranston, *John Locke: A Biography*, Ch. 13; 163; Locke, *Locke's Travels in France 1675–1679, as Related in his Journals.*

44 Locke, *An Essay Concerning Human Understanding*, II. 21. §50, p. 266.

45 Locke, *An Essay Concerning Human Understanding*, II. 21. §51, p. 266.

46 'Whatever necessity determines to the pursuit of real Bliss, the same necessity, with the same force establishes *suspence, deliberation*, and scrutiny of each successive desire, whether the satisfaction of it, does not interfere with our true happiness, and mislead us from it.' Locke, *An Essay Concerning Human Understanding*, II. 21. §52, p. 267.

of Calvinist influence.[47] Hence, Ian Harris, in his discussion of Locke's assessment of the consequences of original sin, writes that the capability of human beings to live as good Christians in *An Essay* is complementary to his theological convictions.[48] God cares tenderly for human beings. This is not the place to discuss whether John Locke, who was a physician, employs the figure of God the merciful Father – fundamental in any discussion of original sin – with a therapeutic or a theological purpose. However, I would be inclined to consider that both were relevant.[49]

Nevertheless, experience also showed that many people chose the worse before the better, and not always guiltily.[50] Locke tones down Boyle's doctrine of 'scientist as priest' by teaching that at the end of the day everyone is an experimental philosopher in relation to his or her own moral conduct, which Michael Ben-Chaim has termed the doctrine of experience as a divine gift.[51] In Locke's division of sciences, ethics was 'the skill of Right applying our own Powers and Actions, for the Attainment of things good and useful'.[52] Bad choices stemmed from lack of skill and impossible situations. The 'bodily torments' of a person on the rack or suffering want or disease made it difficult to make a right moral decision. Necessity made one act disgracefully (*Necessitas cogit ad turpia*), noted Locke, as Robert Burton had also done in his scorn of poverty, which was the mother of all vices and ridicule.[53] Furthermore, there was the issue of time in the relationship between the distant, but 'greatest absent good' – the 'proper object of our desires' – and the present fulfilment of a desire.[54] Ignorance, rash judgment due to passion that prevented deliberation, and so on, resulted in our mistaking desire for a present pleasure for genuine good.

47 J. Locke, *The Reasonableness of Christianity*, p. 8. 'For Calvin, despair had a necessary and unequivocally positive eschatological function' that if understood adequately was a sign of 'the punishment preceding redemption that manifested itself in the afflicted conscience'. Gowland, 'The Problem of Early Modern Melancholy', p. 105.

48 Harris, *The Mind of John Locke*, Ch. 10.

49 'God, who knows our frailty, pities our weakness and requires of us no more than we are able to do, and sees what was and what was not in our power, will judge as a kind and merciful Father'. Locke, *An Essay Concerning Human Understanding*, II. 21. §53, p. 268.

50 Again, following Boyle's steps, Locke adopted empiricism, observance of others' and one's experiences for understanding *what* is thinking, also in terms of moral action. Ben-Chaim, *Experimental Philosophy and the Birth of Empirical Science*.

51 Michael Ben-Chaim, 'Locke's Ideology of Common Sense', 33 *Studies in History and Philosophy of Science* (2000), pp. 473–501.

52 Locke, *An Essay Concerning Human Understanding*, IV. 21. §3, pp. 720–721.

53 Locke, *An Essay*, II. 21. §57, 272; Robert Burton, *The Anatomie of Melancholy* (Oxford, Printed for Henry Cripps, 1651), p. 159.

54 Locke, *An Essay Concerning Human Understanding*, II. 21. §61, 274.

As his repeated moral guidance in this direction shows in *An Essay*, rather than being glorified, 'desire' is dissected, isolated and scientifically anatomized. Pleasure could be in itself a way to God or a means to lose eternal life. It depended on the situation that proper reasoning must discern. Alexander Wragge-Morley argues that the Fellows of the Royal Society were of the view that the pleasure obtained through the human senses was both a way to nature and God.[55] In this regard defining Locke's discussion of pleasure in *An Essay* as having a purely hedonistic character ignores the depth of his theological and epistemological background.[56]

Locke used the language of necessities in *An Essay* to present his position in relation to the weighty problem of liberty and necessity. His solution is rather classic and uncompromising on freedom and virtue, but methodologically novel. Necessities helped him to describe free individuals acting in the world and, as he was persuaded, freely choosing the gift of walking in the world or not towards their Creator.

12.2 Necessities, Dominion and Money in the *Two Treatises of Government*

12.2.1 Dominion for Necessities

In the *Two Treatises of Government* human necessities connect the arguments as to the divine design of the world, the obligation of natural law and the function of government. The fundamental law of nature in that text is an obligation of self-preservation directing human beings' lives – it is also practically the only one together with 'the *Fundamental Law of Property*'.[57] Human beings perceive that the desire to preserve themselves is implanted in their hearts. That understanding, in fact a law of reason, obliges an individual first to provide for his or her necessities, and then for those of humankind at large.[58] The remainder of natural rights derives from that fundamental law of nature. Human beings grasp this obligation quasi-rationally. Moreover, they understand that the obligation to obey the fundamental law of nature of preservation is the result of how

55 'Pleasure, as they saw it, was a symptom of the sensory encounter with specimens of God's wisdom and power'; and also 'Hooke proposed a form of inquiry in which pleasure accompanied the discovery of the truth.' Wragge-Morley, *Aesthetic Science*, p. 8; p. 13.

56 Cfr. Wolfgang von Leyden, 'Introduction', John Locke, *Essays on the Law of Nature*.

57 Locke, *Two Treatises of Government*, I §86; II §16; II. §140.

58 'For *Law*, in its true Notion, is not so much the Limitation as *the direction of a free and intelligent Agent* to his proper Interest, and prescribes no farther than is for the general Good of those under that Law.' Locke *Two Treatises of Government*, II §57.

the world has been designed by Someone Else.[59] To defy that design, to disobey the inner call to provide with the products of nature for human necessities, amounts to challenging the subjection owed to the Creator. Hence, human necessities became an important means by which Locke integrated faith and reason. Experienced empirically by everyone and thus showing to human beings the rationality of a creation free willed by God, human necessities are at once contingent and universal, prudential and theoretical. Locke constructed his doctrine of human necessities as the philosopher's companion to the theologian's argument of a Maker, hence intended, albeit not always successfully, to be compatible with theological tradition.[60]

In the *First Treatise*, Locke emphasizes the polemical intent of uniting freedom and political obligation with human necessities. This is first done through a brief critique of the absolutist politics of necessity espoused by Filmer. Next, and more importantly, Locke unites the liberty of natural law and his preferred method of government – popular assembly – by placing the origin of property in the context of the natural desire for self-preservation. Robert Filmer had marked his absolutism by means of 'Laws of Necessity'. When Kings were absent in wars, subjects must find

[59] Kari Saastamoinen emphasises this aspect of Locke's understanding of equality rather than taken it to be also a political or moral project. Kari Saastamoinen, 'Natural Equality and Natural Law in Locke's *Two Treatises*', in Ian Hunter and Richard Whatmore (eds.), *Philosophy, Rights and Natural Law. Essays in Honour of Knud Haakonssen* (Edinburgh University Press, 2019), pp. 127–146.

[60] An important case in point of incompatibility of Locke's theory of human necessities with traditional natural law is Locke's proposal to further inquiry about the temporary nature of natural marriage, on the grounds that a natural lasting union would be only required as long as the issue needs to be provided for. In beasts of prey the union last longer than the mere act of copulation: 'The same is to be overserved in all Birds (…) whose Young needing Food in the Nest, the Cock and Hen continue Mates, till the Young are able to use their wing and provide for themselves. And herein I think lies the chief, if not the only reason *why the Male and Female in Mankind are tyed to a longer conjunction* than other Creatures, *viz.* because Female is capable of conceiving, and *de facto* is commonly with Child again, and Brings forth too a new Birth long before the former is out of dependency for support on his Parents help'. Locke notes that the lasting society of man and woman encourages industry, common interest and provision for the future for them and their children, but he continues. 'But though these are Ties upon *Mankind*, which make the *Conjugal Bonds* more firms and lasting in Man than the other Species of Animals; yet it would give one reason to enquire, why this *Compact*, where Procreation and Education are secured, and Inheritance taken care for, may not be determinable, either by consent, or at a certain time, or upon certain Conditions, as well as any other voluntary Compacts, there being not necessity in the nature of the thing, nor to the ends of it, that it should be always for Life; I mean, to such as are under no Restraint of any positive Law, which ordains all such Contracts to be perpetual.' Locke, *Two Treatises of Government*, II §79; §80; §81.

the sovereign's will 'in the Tables of his Laws'. Filmer sought to trace this slavery of 'Absolute Dominion' back to Adam and thus to God. Locke argued, however, that Filmer's purpose had in reality been to leave people with nothing, and thus appease their conscience and convince them by 'Undeniable proofs of its Necessity' that they must submit peacefully to that 'Absolute Dominion'.[61] In this sense, such a reasoning of necessity annulled conscience. Filmer's theory had given a theological foundation to a political dominion with absolutist characteristics, that is, with absolute power and dominion of life and death. Against Filmer's idea that Adam was 'Proprietor of the world' with private dominion over it, Locke famously defended a common dominion of all humankind over animals, 'the dominion of the whole species of Mankind over the inferior Species of Creatures'.[62] In this early part of the *First Treatise*, Filmer's absolutist political dominion soon becomes, in Locke's hands, a common property over inferior animals. This turns remarkably evident when Locke brings Eve into the picture: had she also not received God's grant as to be 'Lady', as Adam was 'Lord of the World?' Thus, Filmer's theory would have the result of hindering 'her *Dominion* over the Creatures or *Property* in them'.[63]

The point is relevant in relation to the core function of human necessities. If there was someone that had private dominion over 'the Food and Rayment, and other Conveniences of Life' – i.e. who had an exclusive right of use – how could the rest of mankind fulfil the commandment of increasing and multiplying? If 'their Subsistence' depended on the will of one, dreary results could be expected, as Locke notes, recalling how the multitude are deprived of the 'conveniences of life' in 'the Absolute Monarchies of the World'.[64] That one had a natural right over another in that respect had been never God's design: 'we know God hath not left one Man so to the Mercy of another, that he may starve him if he please'.[65] The foundation of sovereignty could therefore not be 'anothers necessity'. Instead, only the *consent* that someone in need gave – who ended up in

[61] Locke *Two Treatises of Government*, I §10; Locke quotes from Filmer's Patriarcha: 'When Kings were either busied with Wars, or distracted with public Cares, so that every private Man could not have Access to their Persons, to learn their Wills and Pleasure, then were Laws of Necessity invented, that so every particular Subject might find his prince's Pleasure decypher'd unto him in the Tables of his Laws In a Monarchy, the King must by necessity be above the Laws' Locke, *Two Treatises of Government*, I.§8.

[62] Locke, *Two Treatises of Government*, I, §16; §28–§30. Probably the best analysis so far of Locke's innovative way in Tully, *A Discourse on Property.*

[63] Locke, *Two Treatises of Government*, I §29.

[64] Locke, *Two Treatises of Government*, I §41.

[65] Locke, *Two Treatises of Government*, I §42.

that situation through human injustice, chance or lack of industriousness – was valid. That individual preferred to be a subject than to starve, while the sovereign could access only so much power as he or she consented to renounce.[66] Neither did this principle of sovereignty apply to children, born in need – as Locke wrote in the *Second Treatise*, 'the necessities of his Life, the Health of his Body, and the Information of his Mind would require him to be directed by the Will of others and not his own'.[67] However, a small child's precarious status never amounted to dominion over the person of the child. Rather the main intention of nature was that humanity be preserved and increased through the care of parents, while even animals may sometimes 'neglect their own Private good' in order to care for their baby animals.[68]

Locke did what he was supposed to do in his exposition of natural law, that is, he acknowledged the philosophical tradition and wrote within it.[69] Although he had a novel contribution to make by arguing the centrality of labour as a means to acquire private property to provide for the necessities of human beings, Locke did not deviate remarkably in style from previous writings on natural law.[70] However, since his epistemology was radically new, the author of *An Essay Concerning Human Understanding* imbued his political theory with innovative depth through his scientific method. Reason, for Locke, is like a 'dark room', similar to 'a Closet wholly shut from light', with small openings through which 'Ideas of things' are brought in by means of sensation.[71] Unconventionally, as we have seen already, he conceived neither of a weakened light of nature nor of reason as active sources of light in themselves. Instead, he regarded experience as crucial for human action. In terms of natural law, this leads to a concentration on questions of material self-preservation. Putting aside the tradition of practical moral reasoning, Locke's moral reasoning is more about the individual human

[66] Locke, *Two Treatises of Government*, I §43; II §23; see Quentin Skinner's discussion of this same point in Hobbes, Skinner, *Hobbes and Republican Liberty*, pp. 205–206.

[67] Locke *Two Treatises of Government*, II §61.

[68] And thus the beast forgot, 'that general rule which Nature teaches all things of self Preservation' putting first the Preservation of their Young'. Locke *Two Treatises of Government*, I, §56; §59.

[69] Tuck, *Natural Rights Theories*, Ch. 8.

[70] On the other hand, as Peter Laslett noted, when Locke established the preservation of each human being and the rest of mankind as the *fundamental* law of nature, Locke avoided the usual method of listing laws of nature, and thus turned into a 'very unconventional natural-law writer, much more so than Hobbes' Laslett, 'Introduction' to Locke, *Two Treatises of Government*, p. 98.

[71] Locke, *An Essay Concerning Human Understanding*, II. 11.§ 17, pp. 162–163

being mastering 'the Dominion of Man in his little World of his own Understanding'.[72] Moreover, the truth of things is *outside* the individual who thinks and must be discovered in the Maker's design.

It is important to note, however, that rights of dominion over the earth – and not virtue ethics, or other expressions of practical reason – are also at the core of the law of nature in the tradition of natural rights.[73] A. John Simmons is right in urging a reading of Locke's moral theory that is multifaceted and has a variety of levels, taking seriously duty-based, rights-based and virtues-based theory, but ultimately becoming none of them.[74] What Locke never did, however, was to dwell on matters of practical reasoning in the manner that had been understood at least since Aristotle's *Nichomachean Ethics*. In the *Two Treatises of Government* Locke follows the theological tradition of dominion rights of the type inaugurated early on by Henry of Ghent, as we saw in the previous section, imbuing it with his theory of an experiential discovery of God's will. This theoretical depth transformed his idea of property rights into a complex theme, so rich that it would be a hollow claim to label him a theorist of capitalism.[75] Property founded on self-preservation was central to a theological tradition of care for each individual that Locke evidently mastered and useful to address and oppose the already general commentary on self-interest, which, as we

[72] Locke, *An Essay Concerning Human Understanding*, II. 2, §2, p. 120; Corneanu, *Regimens of the Mind. Boyle, Locke, and the Early Modern Cultura Animi Tradition*.

[73] Villey, 'Les Origines de La Notion Du Droit Subjectif'; Villey, 'La Genèse du droit subjectif chez Guillaume d'Occam'; Strauss, *Natural Rights and History*; Tuck, *Natural Rights Theories*; Simmons, *The Lockean Theory of Rights*; Ernest L. Fortin, 'On the Presumed Medieval Origin of Individual Rights', in J. Brian Benestad (ed.), *Classical Christianity and the Political Order: Reflections on the Theologico-Political Problem* (Lanham, Boulder, New York, London: Rowman & Littlefield Publishers, Inc., 1996); Brett, *Liberty, Right and Nature*; Finnis, *Natural Law and Natural Rights*; Mäkinen, *Property Rights in the Late Medieval Discussion on Franciscan Poverty*; Tierney, *The Idea of Natural Rights*; Peter Landau, 'Reflexionen über Grundrechte der Person in der Geschichte des kanonischen Rechts', in Heinrich J. F. Reinhardt, *Theologia et Jus Canonicum, Festgabe für Heribert Heinemann zur Vollendung Seines 70. Lebenjahres* (Essen: Ludgerus Verlag, 1995), pp. 517–532; Brian Tierney, 'Review Article – Medieval Rights and Powers: On a Recent Interpretation', 21 *History of Political Thought* (2000); Dan Edelstein, *The Terror of Natural Right: Republicanism, the Cult of Nature, and the French Revolution* (Chicago: University of Chicago Press, 2009); Jacob Giltaj and Kaius Tuori, 'Human Rights in Antiquity? Revisiting Anachronism and Roman Law', in Pamela Slotte and Miia Halme-Tuomisaari (eds.), *Revisiting the Origins of Human Rights* (Cambridge: Cambridge University Press, 2015), pp. 39–63; Dan Edelstein, 'Is There a "Modern" Natural Law Theory? Notes on the History of Human Rights', 7 *Humanity* (2016), pp. 345–364.

[74] Simmons, *The Lockean Theory of Rights*, p. 11.

[75] MacPherson, *The Political Theory of Possessive Individualism*.

saw in the Chapter 8, he rejected from the beginning. Given its capacity to connect the past and the future, property was very fitting a focus for a natural philosopher concerned with necessities. All begins by feeling in one's body the pain of need, for food and other necessaries, and this awakens the desire, divinely implanted, for self-preservation.

The core doctrine about God's natural design for human beings, on which the concept of property is founded, appears in the crucial paragraph 86, on which the *First Treatise* hinges. In this way, Filmer's idea of Adam's being granted exclusive private dominion is definitively demolished. Locke devotes the remainder of the text to confute Filmer's argument as to a sacred authority that God granted to Adam. Thus the reader is led to the *Second Treatise* to read Locke's robust explanation of the origins and content of government, or in other words, of the origins of dominion as imperium and authority. Due to his close commentary on Filmer in the previous paragraph on the origin of property and in order to avoid confusion, Locke writes in paragraph 86, he would state plainly his own case.[76]

> God having made Man, and planted in him, as in all other Animals, a strong desire of Self-preservation, and furnished the World with things fit for Food and Rayment and other Necessaries of Life, Subservient to his design, that Man should live and abode for some time upon the Face of the Earth, and not that so curious and wonderful a piece of workmanship by its own Negligence, or want of Necessaries, should perish again, presently after a few moments continuance: God, I say, having made Man and the World thus, spoke to him, (that is) directed him by his Senses and Reason, as he did the inferior Animals by their Sense, and Instinct, which he had place in them to that purpose, to the use of those things, which were serviceable for his Subsistence, and given him as means of his *Preservation*.[77]

The obligation to preserve oneself and mankind was not only the outcome of the design of nature, but the very will of God planted in our heart, a will that human reason could understand and pursue through a natural right to use things, or in other words, through property. Reason thus confirmed Revelation while the reality that reason grasped was antecedent to the letter of the Bible.[78] Moreover, all this revolved around the needs of human beings, the necessaries created to satisfy them and God's plan that it ought to be so.

[76] 'But not to follow our A. too far out of the way, the plain of the Case is this.' Locke *Two Treatises of Government*, I §86.

[77] Locke, *Two Treatises of Government*, I §86.1–14.

[78] Locke, *Two Treatises of Government*, I §86.15.

> And thus Man's *Property* in the Creatures, was founded upon the right he had, to make use of those things that were necessary or useful to his Being.[79]

In the wonderful paragraph 86, Locke made much of the innate principle of self-preservation through necessities, the only innate principle he admitted on the grounds that it was not planted in reason. In the *Second Treatise* it exceptionally appeared 'writ in the Hearts of all Mankind' and gave certainty to the law of nature.[80] Human beings were therefore connected to their material surroundings through necessities. Here Locke dwelt as what in fact he was, a medical doctor, a philosopher of needs and a theologian too, in the original care of a God that was merciful to his creatures in providing them with necessaries for their subsistence. Crucially that was the manner in which God had originally designed the world, governed by a fundamental law of nature that bound a man 'to preserve himself' and, as stated in the *Second Treatise*, 'when his own Preservation' came not in competition he ought 'as much as he can, *to preserve the rest of Mankind*'.[81]

The desire for (self)-preservation substantiated the law of nature that, as Locke repeatedly affirms, in turn generated the radical equality of human beings, endowed with similar faculties, a community of nature and, hence, without subordination among them. Since this was the reason and foundation of Adam's property, '[e]very Man had a right to the Creatures, by the Same Title Adam had'.[82] Every creature 'of the same species' was 'born to all the same advantages of Nature'.[83] The question of subsistence and preservation, despite its naturalistic and Hobbesian overtones, was squarely placed within theological tradition, and more so in its connection with the right over natural things or necessaries.

> Whether we consider natural *Reason*, which tells us, that Men, being once born, have a right to their Preservation, and consequently to Meat and Drink, and such other things, as Nature affords to their Subsistence: or *Revelation*, which gives us an account of those Grants God made of the World to *Adam*, and to *Noah*, and his Sons, 'tis very clear, that God, as King *David* says, *Psal. CXV. xvj. Has given the Earth to the Children of men*, given it to Mankind in common.[84]

79 Locke, *Two Treatises of Government*, I §86. Compare Aquinas who states that these things they 'could use for their utility' Aquinas, *Summa theologiae*, II-II, q. 66, a.1. co; ad 1.

80 Locke, *Two Treatises of Government*, II, §11.31; §12.10. See Peter Laslett's note, p. 274.

81 Locke, *Two Treatises of Government*, II, §7.1–22; Simmons, *The Lockean Theory of Rights*, pp. 38–66.

82 Locke, *Two Treatises of Government*, I.§87; II, §7.14–15.

83 Locke, *Two Treatises of Government*, II, §4.10.

84 Locke, *Two Treatises of Government*, II §25.

The same idea appears, among others, in the famous *De vita spirituale animae* by the French theologian Jean Gerson (1363–1429).

> There is the natural dominion, a gift of God, by which the creature has a right directly from God to draw other inferior things for her use and conservation, available to all equally and inalienably, according to the original justice or natural integrity.[85]

M. J. Silverthorne writes that Hobbes held that self-preservation was a right, 'Iuris naturalis fundamentum primum' and not a law; while Locke, sharing Pufendorf's vocabulary of obligation, transformed it into a desire planted by God, which became both a law of preservation and a right.[86] Blending old Scholasticism with the thinking of Hobbes and Pufendorf in relation to natural law, natural rights and property, but also utilizing an original method based on natural sciences and theology, the process of Locke's thinking generated the useful new idiom of necessities. Not fear, but necessities and convenience – and hence the hazard of protecting property from the uncertainties of the state of nature is Locke's most peculiar principle, which he dovetailed with principles and theories drawn from the theological tradition.

12.2.2 Private Property and Money

Reason, evil passions, freedom under God, the public good and money at once heighten and shatter this divine natural law that the Creator wanted for his workmanship. Human beings entered societies gradually when they understood that the state of nature held difficulties and dangers, and that it would be more convenient for their preservation to unite

[85] 'Erit igitur naturale dominum donum Dei quo creatura jus habet immediate a Deo assumere res alias inferiores in sui usum et conservationem, pluribus competens ex aequo et inabdicabile servata originali justitia seu integritate naturale.' Iohannes Gerson, *Liber de vita spirituali animae*, in *Opera omnia*, L. Ellies du Pin (ed.), (Antwerpiae, 1706; Hildesheim: G. Olm Verlag, 1987) III, 26–27, p. 145. (my translation) On Gerson, see Brian Patrick McGuire, 'Jean Gerson and the Renewal of Scholastic Discourse 1400–1415', in Joseph Canning, Edmund King and Martial Staub (eds.) *Knowledge, Discipline and Power in the Middle Ages, Essays in Honour of David Luscombe* (Leiden Boston, 2011).

[86] M. J. Silverthorne, 'Civil Society and State, Law and Rights: Some Latin Terms and Their Translation in the Natural Jurisprudence Tradition' in Alexander Dalzell, Charles Fantazzi and Richard J. Schoeck (eds.), *Acta Conventus Neo-Latini Torontonensis. Proceedings of the Seventh International Congress of Neo-Latin Studies* (Medieval and Renaissance Texts and Studies, Binghamton, New York, 1991,) p. 686; there are many more instances on self-preservation as 'a duty to God' in the text, than as a right, see Dunn, *The Political Thought of John Locke*, p. 160.

for a common project of public good. They also established governments, whose end was the protection and preservation of their lives, liberties and estates – i.e. their property.[87] The property in their lives and liberty, and the private property in their estates is what individuals wanted to protect by uniting in civil societies. Private property was therefore usual in the state of nature, and so was its accumulation. As a matter of fact, as soon as human beings started *to use* the goods of creation, private property *begun*.

Both in the state of nature and in civil society human beings are free. Submission to an absolute power always entails going against the law of self-preservation.[88] For in order to survive, one must never subject oneself to 'the inconstant, uncertain, unknown Arbitrary Will of another Man', but only to legislative power that has been consented to, and only to the extent of the trust put in it.[89] According to the *Two Treatises*, human beings have been created with all the potential to become prosperous and happy individuals. Hence, the freedom of human beings did not originate in government. Union in a society entrusted with a government became the most pressing and rational course of action due to the existence of 'degenerate Men' – corrupt individuals 'biassed by their Interest' – who were unable to apply the law of nature and that threatened the life and property of others with violence.[90] The state of nature lacked a settled and well-known law, an objective and known judge and a power to back the implementation of legal decisions, and all this was what people chose when they united in commonwealths under government to achieve 'the Preservation of their Property'. In Locke's often repeated triad, life, liberty and estate constitute 'Property'. Correspondingly, a violator of the law of nature or a bad government would endanger property and 'impoverish, harass, or subdue' the members of the commonwealth.[91]

With all this Locke made clear that Filmer's supposition that Adam was attributed private dominion was unnecessary. Perhaps with the aim of endowing private property with positive content that would not resonate with ideas of evil and sin, Filmer had defended its adamite and biblical origin, to explain how the earth and its goods, granted to the children of God, had become private. Instead, God had willed that in the world com-

[87] 'Man being born, as has been proved, with a Title to perfect Freedom, and an uncontrouled enjoyment of all the Rights and Priviledges of the Law of Nature, equally with any other Man, or Number of Men in the World, hath by Nature a Power' … 'to preserve his Property, that is, his Life, Liberty and Estate' Locke, *Two Treatises of Government*, II §87; §124.

[88] Locke, *Two Treatises of Government*, II §23; §59; §104.

[89] Locke, *Two Treatises of Government*, II §22.

[90] Locke, *Two Treatises of Government*, II §124; §128.

[91] Locke, *Two Treatises of Government*, II §124; §125; §126; §201; see also § 123; §173.

mon property becomes private property naturally when human beings *appropriate* for their use the goods necessary for their preservation.[92] The human reason that God also gave to human beings in the moment of creation enables human beings 'to make use of it [the World in Common] to the best advantage of Life, and convenience', their 'support and comfort'.[93]

Therefore, it is proper of the rationality of human beings to thrive in all respects and to make use of the earth in that sense. But is must be underlined that the entirety of creation has never been common. Each individual human being that has been created in history is master of their soul and body. His or her 'Person' is his or her 'Property'. As a consequence, 'Labour' is also 'the unquestionable Property of the Labourer'.[94] Thus 'labour' allows human beings to 'fix' their property in the necessaries of life. 'Acorns', 'apples' and 'turfs' belong to the individual or the master and owner of servants and animals that picks, cuts and eats them.[95] In fact, Locke notes, since the commonality of property comprises necessaries and conveniences that allow the subsistence of human beings, finding the origin of private property 'in the consent of all Mankind' would have meant the death of all, and an absurd death at that.[96] Instead, private property was founded in the individual's right to the necessaries for her preservation, in the state in which 'Nature' has provided them, and by mixing them with her labour, making them her own. Locke's solution underlines the positive aspect of private property and he also emphasizes that it is not mere survival that is at stake under natural law, but people's 'benefit and the greatest Conveniencies of Life they were capable to draw from it'.[97] Human beings had therefore in themselves the 'great Foundation of property'.[98] Private property started with the appropriation of necessities and materialized through the hard work and ingenuity that multiplied the value of things. For 'Nature and the Earth furnished only the almost worthless Materials'.[99] In a word, God 'gave' the world 'to the use of the Industrious and Rational', not to the 'Fancy or Covetousness of the Quarrelsom and Contentious'. 'Labour' therefore constitutes human beings' title to the goods of the world necessary for their preservation. Locke added the caveat that natural law obliged one not to take more than

[92] Locke, *Two Treatises of Government*, II §26; §39.
[93] Locke, *Two Treatises of Government*, II §25; §26; §39.
[94] Locke, *Two Treatises of Government*, II §27.
[95] Locke, *Two Treatises of Government*, II §28.
[96] Locke, *Two Treatises of Government*, II §28; §29.
[97] Locke, *Two Treatises of Government*, II §33.
[98] Locke, *Two Treatises of Government*, II §44.
[99] Locke, *Two Treatises of Government*, II §43.

one may consume and enjoy. Beyond that, a violation of the law of nature occurred if foods and goods spoiled in one's possession. That is, 'the measure of Property, Nature has well set, by the Extent of Mens *Labour and the Conveniency of Life*'.[100] Allowing fruit to rot or meat to putrefy was an offence against the law of nature that was, significantly, liable to be punished by anyone.[101] By this means the concept of property escalates from being common property in the first natural stage to also being private property in a second natural moment, but still with a token of equality for preservation.

The passing from common to private property was meant to happen from the beginning and was not a consequence of the original sin. This is well highlighted by contrasting Locke's theory of the use of goods with an example drawn from English canon law of the Middle Ages. One of the special characteristics of canon law is that it regulates many aspects of the lives of persons called to perfection – i.e. to live in accordance with the law of the Gospel and within monasteries.[102] What canon lawyers stated in these instances was not meant to be generalized because they would hardly make any sense in the absence of a monk's previous vows. The *Summa De iure canonico tractaturus* to Gratian *Decretum* by the canonist Magister Honorius of Kent is one of the main works of the French and Anglo-Norman school of the last decade of the twelfth century. It contains one good example of the transition of common to private property within the bounds of the monastery, constituting a legal space under the imposition of a law of common property.[103] For canon lawyers, common property was a precept of natural law through monks' vows that meant that nothing is one's own, 'neither bread nor hood'. One ought to give only to a monk in need, otherwise one was always required to ask the prior before giving, because through the vow, monks 'did not only renounce property, but also pleasure' (of sharing). The interest in this issue lies in the level of detail with which it is presented. However, can the monk say that this bread is mine, when it is cut for his use (*fractus*), or chewed (*masticates*)? The canonist's radical answer was that the thing stops being common when use by another is no longer possible.[104]

100 Locke, *Two Treatises of Government*, II § 34; §36.

101 Locke, *Two Treatises of Government*, II § 37.

102 Honori Magistri Summa, *De iure canonico tractaturus*, Ediderunt, Rudolf Weigand, Peter landau, Waltraud Kotzur, adlaborantibus Stephan Haering, Karin Miethaner-Vent, Martin Petzolt, (Città del Vaticano: Biblioteca Apostolica Vaticana, 2004), p. 25.

103 Peter Landau, 'Introduction' to Honori Magistri Summa, *De iure canonico tractaturus*.

104 Set quando potest dici panis proprius, vel fractus vel masticates? Resp.: Tunc desinet esse communis cum ad usum alterius est omnino inutilis.' Honori Magistri Summa, *De iure canonico tractaturus*, p. 25

Certainly God had not imposed such a law of common property on human beings. But he obliged commitment to a personal law of self-preservation, fulfilled through private property and, to the extent that this was possible, in the service of the entire humankind. Preservation is at issue also in the case Locke presented concerning a conqueror in a just war who assumes the right to reparations from the vanquished. Despite having the law on its side, the victorious commonwealth could never gain dominion over what was needed to ensure the survival of children. Since the fundamental law of nature was 'that all, as much as may be, should be preserved', if there was not enough money available to compensate in full the losses incurred as well as ensure the survival of the children, the former must give way to the latter to the extent that their survival is secured.[105]

It appears that big families and even cities emerged in the state of nature, and 'possessions enlarged with the need of them'.[106] However, in the beginning 'right and conveniency' worked together:

> This left no room for Controversie about the Title, nor for Incroachment on the Right of others; what Portion a Man carved to himself, was easily seen; and it was useless as well as dishonest to carve himself too much, or take more than he needed.[107]

This manner of living, still in the state of nature, 'out of the bounds of Societie', changed dramatically with the invention of something imperishable, *money*, and the 'tacit Agreement of Men to put a value on it'.[108] Now people started to desire goods beyond necessity, to long for things that were not really useful.[109] Such objects as diamonds or pieces of yellow metal could be exchanged for perishable things that have intrinsic value which 'depends only on their usefulness to the Life of Man'.[110] Individuals could then possess more land that they needed and produce, dig and build more that they could use, with the purpose of exchanging the surplus for money, gold and silver. Hoarding up money could be done without violating the law of nature, and 'without injury to any one, these metalls not spoileing or decaying in the hands of the possessor'.[111] The *Two Treatises*

[105] Locke, *Two Treatises of Government*, II 138; §139.
[106] Locke, *Two Treatises of Government*, II § 38; §39.
[107] Locke, *Two Treatises of Government*, II § 51.
[108] An account of Locke's property, that includes labour but not yet money, Helga Varden, 'Locke on Property', in Jessica Gordon-Roth and Shelley Weinberg (eds.), *The Lockean Mind* (Abindgdon, New York: Routledge, 2022), Ch. 44.
[109] Locke, *Two Treatises of Government*, II § 50; §36; §42.
[110] Locke, *Two Treatises of Government*, II § 37.
[111] Locke, *Two Treatises of Government*, II § 50.

describes this entire process that a monetary economy enables mostly as a positive evolution, the result of the ingenuity and industriousness of human beings as rational creatures. In paragraph 43 of the *Second Treatise* Locke explains that it is 'Labour' that '*puts the greatest part of Value upon Land*'. That appears plainly from his calculation of the productivity of acres of wasteland in America as compared to that of fertile and well-cultivated soil in Devonshire (England) at least to be 10/1000.[112]

However, Locke seemed to be in two minds in his normative appraisal of the contribution of money in relation to human beings. With the employment and foundation of 'Labour', money was clearly the means that facilitated 'the Benefit of Mankind' by producing a greater amount of product from the same land. It was also money that made possible 'the desire of having more than Men needed'. Moreover, securing protection and encouragement 'to the honest industry of Mankind' was how the philosopher envisaged a wise and godlike Prince. Intriguingly, Locke noted that as soon as something that has the function of money appears, an individual 'will begin presently to enlarge his Possessions'.[113] Was that something he considered to be *wrong* in the conduct of an individual? It does not seem to be Locke's opinion, since

> the *exceeding of the bounds of his* just *Property* not lying in the largeness of his Possession, but the perishing of any thing uselessly in it.[114]

The chapter on 'Property' contains a long explanation to the effect that the function of private property is to provide for necessities. When money appears, 'the temptation to enlarge possession' beyond necessities accompanies it. However, this is apparently not merely to satisfy the evil concupiscence, *amor sceleratus habendi.*[115] Despite Locke's proverbial ambiguity, it is possible to argue that the accumulation of property that money enables has ultimately a public function of providing for the necessities of the nation and even of mankind, if regulated by law. But this requirement seems to be only possible within a commonwealth – either on a domestic or a larger scale – that gives rise to an even more pressing need to leave the state of nature after the invention of money.

12.2.3 *Preservation, Government and the Public Good*

Indeed, money is not the last word in *Two Treatises of Government.* Locke's decisive proposal in that text is to put the public good at the centre both of the

[112] Locke, *Two Treatises of Government*, II § 43.
[113] Locke, *Two Treatises of Government*, II § 43; §37; §42; §49.
[114] Locke, *Two Treatises of Government*, II § 46.
[115] Locke, *Two Treatises of Government*, II § 108; §111.

act of constituting a nation and its government. By constituting the end of government, necessities and preservation again serve the purpose of establishing the theoretical foundation in the *Second Treatise*. In this way, the private dominion of necessities of the *First Treatise* becomes the justification of imperium and dominion as authority. In view of the extent of the critique of his individualism, it is surprising to ascertain that a communitarian and political Locke emerges from a textual analysis of the concluding part of the text second treatise. Furthermore, he arrived at that position by underscoring the law of nature of self-preservation of the people. The public good seems, therefore, to be the political articulation of the moral theory of self-preservation analysed so far.

Scholarship of the twentieth century tended to highlight the novelty of the centrality of labour in the *Two Treatises* and its influence on Adam Smith and Karl Marx.[116] It was again Locke's wonderful ambiguity and the liberal use he made of his knowledge of economy and theology that emboldened him to describe labour as the main source of economic value. The background to this lay in the Book of Genesis: God 'put [Adam] in the Garden of Eden to work it and take care of it'.[117] In response to Macpherson's pro-capitalist thesis about Locke, John Dunn noted how inadequate it was to view Locke as the 'convinced lyricist of the moral sufficiency of *any* system of economic production'.[118] Dunn went on to describe Locke as a Calvinist calling to *labour*, and he introduces an incomparable quote from a letter from Locke to his friend William Molyneux dated 19 January 1694:

> I think every one, according to what way Providence has placed him in, is bound to labour for the public good, as far as he is able or else he has no right to eat.[119]

Locke's argument on the theological centrality of labour is strong and consistent and, Dunn argues, he considered the human being with respect to

[116] E. J. Hundert, 'The Making of Homo Faber: John Locke between Ideology and History' 33 *Journal of the History of Ideas* (1972); MacPherson, *The Political Theory of Possessive Individualism*.

[117] 'Tulit ergo Dominus Deus hominem, et posuit eum in paradiso voluptatis, ut operaretur, et custodiret illum'. 'Genesis 2 will shortly develop the understanding of the human vocation in terms of a priestly care for God's garden' … 'The wording of Genesis 2.15 is particularly significant in this context: "The LORD GOD took the man and put him in the Garden of Eden to work it and take care of it' – literally, 'to serve it and keep/guard it' (Hb. 'avad and shamar). This is religious language, which underlines the importance and sacred nature of the task.' Iain Provan, *Discovering Genesis: Content, Interpretation, Reception* (Grand Rapids, Michigan: Eerdmans Publishing Company, 2015), p. 66.

[118] Dunn, *The Political Thought of John Locke*, p. 250.

[119] Locke quoted in Dunn, *The Political Thought of John Locke*, p. 250

society and family as 'a recipient of the commands of God', and not merely as 'economic producer, a proprietor of his labour'. However, it may be the case that Dunn's answer on economic spiritualism was framed to a certain extent by the fact that he was responding to Macpherson's argument concerning economic materialism.[120] To set this out plainly, in this quote, 'labour' and 'public good' are equally important and the latter has the greater textual relevance in the *Two Treatises of Government* overall.[121]

Locke started his discussion of political society with two principal forms of society – marriage and civil society – into which a human being enters 'under strong Obligations of Necessity, Convenience, and Inclination'.[122] It is tempting to suggest an analogy between commonwealth and marriage in the *Two Treatises*: where of the two the former demands more from a person than the latter. Both require express consent – tacit consent is not enough – and by incorporating him to the Commonwealth a man

> by his uniting himself thereunto, annexed also, and submits to the Community those Possessions, which he has or shall acquire that do not already belong to any other Government.[123]

However, it is not necessary to press this point further but only to highlight the level of life commitment that signifies membership of the commonwealth for Locke – far from the notorious 'possessive individualism'.[124] The reason for renouncing the 'Empire' that human beings had in the state of nature and subjecting themselves to the power of another's 'Dominion' was the insecurity involved in maintaining power over one person and possessions. The rights existed, but their enjoyment was always at potential risk of being threatened by others. After entering the commonwealth things change quite radically in the sense that one is no longer alone with one's family, but

> with others who are already united, or have a mind to unite for the mutual Preservation of their Lives, Liberties and Estates, which I call by the general Name, *Property*.[125]

120 Dunn, *The Political Thought of John Locke*, p. 261.
121 See Simmons, that Locke's common good is distributive, unlike the additive common good of later utilitarians, Simmons, *The Lockean Theory of Rights*, p. 57.
122 Locke, *Two Treatises of Government*, II § 77.
123 Locke, *Two Treatises of Government*, II § 119; §120.
124 Armitage approaches the topic from a different angle, an analysis of whether Locke was theorising on the empire; he concludes similarly, that Locke was 'a theorist of the commonwealth, or state, and not a theorist of empire.' Armitage, *Foundations of Modern International Thought*, p. 125; see also Chapter 1 in this book.
125 Locke, *Two Treatises of Government*, II § 123.

The preservation of property is now *mutual*. Self-preservation is easier in a commonwealth because there are laws, rulers and judges – individuals have given up their power to do whatever they thought appropriate in order to maintain self-preservation and to punish the crimes against the law of nature. However, the commonwealth represents a more complex situation because laws must be laid down to provide for the public good.[126] No one, moreover, after having given up equality, liberty and executive power, would be satisfied with mere survival in civil society. Instead, people seek to better their condition with respect to the state of nature: '[f]or not rational creature can be supposed to change his condition with an intention to be worse'. In fact, the ultimate state of a flawed government is exactly that, when things no longer function, and the situation is worse than the state of nature. It amounts to what we would call today a failed state, lacking proper administration of justice, power to direct the military and the capacity to 'provide for the Necessities of the publick'.[127] Legislation that is properly in force, objective judges, and executive power must be in place to achieve the goal of ensuring the '*Peace, Safety* and *publick good* of the People'.[128]

Therefore, governments must carry out their role with care.[129] The more primitive and golden time with almost no covetousness of the first governments was over. In its place, 'Ambition and Luxury' would lead to constant attempts to increase power without attending to the business for which the government was established.[130] A good government ought to meet the obligations placed upon it by the people 'for their good, and the Preservation of their Property'.[131] Human beings had no arbitrary power over their life or liberty, as this power lay with God. Furthermore, they only had power over the life, liberty and property of others to the extent required to meet the obligation of self-preservation. Consequently, they could not confer greater jurisdiction on the government than they had. That was, in a sense, the responsibility of rational creatures. Locke wrote of legislators in the following terms:

126 Locke, *Two Treatises of Government*, II § 128.
127 Locke, *Two Treatises of Government*, II § 219.
128 Locke, *Two Treatises of Government*, II §131.
129 This agrees with Mark Goldie's recent interpretation of Locke as defender of an active government, see Mark Goldie, 'Locke and Executive Power', in Jessica Gordon-Roth and Shelley Weinberg (eds.), *The Lockean Mind* (Abingdon, New York: Routledge, 2022), Ch. 46.
130 Locke, *Two Treatises of Government*, II § 43; §111.
131 Locke, *Two Treatises of Government*, II § 171.

> Their Power in the utmost Bounds of it, is *limited to the publick good* of the Society. It is a Power, that hath no other end but preservation, and therefore can never have a right to destroy, enslave, or designedly to impoverish the Subjects.[132]

Remarkably, legislative power is not only immediately concerned with preservation of the commonwealth, but beyond the domestic limits it is bound to comply with a universal obligation: 'the fundamental law of nature' being 'the preservation of Mankind'.[133] Thinking with Hobbes that the whole community or commonwealth is, as a body, in the state of nature with respect to the other 'States or persons' outside the commonwealth, his conclusion is relatively un-Hobbesian.[134] The *Executive Power* and its prerogative (a 'Power to do good') acts together with the legislator. It intervenes in 'All Accidents and Necessities that may concern the Publick', sometimes acting in the absence of law, or even against the letter of the law, if it is 'for the publick good'.[135] Property must be respected in the commonwealth, in the sense that it cannot be touched without the owner's consent, which Locke justifies on two grounds. First, because individuals entered the political society to protect their property. Hence, they must have a right to their property in accordance with the laws of the community. Second, and more importantly, if supreme power lies with the legislator (in the form of either a lasting assembly or a monarch), situations may arise in which the individuals in the assembly or the monarch develop 'a distinct interest from the rest of the community' and seek to enrich themselves by taking from the people.[136] In fact this potential for abuse of power is the key reason why the people always remain the supreme power. Although he might have looked with personal disdain on the desire to accumulate riches, it does not seem that Locke was troubled by individuals' 'disproportionate and unequal possession', to which the people at large have consented and even facilitated by means of money

[132] Locke, *Two Treatises of Government*, II § 111; §135.

[133] Locke, *Two Treatises of Government*, II §135; Simmons, *The Lockean Theory of Rights*, p. 38.

[134] Locke, *Two Treatises of Government*, II §145; Martti Koskenniemi, 'The Hobbesian Structure of International Legal Discourse, in Timo Airaksinen and Martin A. Bertman (eds.), *Hobbes: War Among Nations* (Avebury : Aldershot, 1989), pp. 168–177.

[135] Locke, *Two Treatises of Government*, II § 160; § 164.

[136] 'For if any one shall claim a Power to lay and levy Taxes on the people, by his own Authority, and without such consent of the People, he thereby invades the Fundamental Law of Property, and subverts the end of government. For what property have I in that which another may by right take, when he pleases to himself?' Locke, *Two Treatises of Government*, II §140; quote in §138.

and other artificial means of representing value.[137] However, Locke's conception of property cannot be merely fixed as 'property of unlimited amount as a natural right of the individual'.[138] What made Locke's case for the protection of property vital was that it offered the means to ensure people's preservation. And for that reason, in his view, the people could get rid of any government, even of the legislative power – whose end is 'the preservation of the Community' – that is perceived by the people, consistently and unequivocally, to go against 'this Fundamental, Sacred and unalterable Law of Self-Preservation'.[139] However, Locke asked, who can say whether the moment has arrived to overthrow a government that has abandoned the goals of safety and public good? *Quis iudicabit*? Since 'God and Nature' never allow the neglect of self-preservation, the response is that it is people who judge whether they must appeal to heaven in relation to their case.[140]

The reasoning of Locke's *Two Treatises* is that *within* government, the purpose of which is the preservation of all, the accumulation of property through labour and money will provide for the necessities of the nation, and even of all mankind

[137] Locke, *Two Treatises of Government*, II § 50.
[138] C. B. Macpherson (ed.), *Property* (Toronto: University of Toronto Press, 1978), p. 14.
[139] Locke, *Two Treatises of Government*, II § 149; §160.
[140] Locke, *Two Treatises of Government*, II § 168.

Conclusions

This book has spelled out the important impact of the principle of necessity and of necessities in structuring modern natural law. Recourse to an imperative though elusive idiom of *necessity* is ubiquitous in seventeenth-century scholarship and political thinking. But how it changed natural law and moral and political philosophy has not been addressed before in scholarship. Chapter 2 traces the specific influence of ideas about necessity in Thomas Hobbes's 'doctrine of necessity' to the necessitarian metaphysics of the type proposed by the Arabic philosopher Avicenna, which were adopted after the thirteenth century by a number of theologians at the prestigious faculty of theology at the University of Paris. Further, also for the first time John Locke's 'doctrine of necessities' has been identified in the book. This term denotes a thread running through Locke's work that comprises a means by which he devised a new political theory and epistemology employing human necessities as an instrument to connect diverse traditions: Hobbes's political philosophy, Neotestamentarian theology and the naturalist philosophy of the philosopher-physicians that he had studied closely. What Hobbes's doctrine of necessity and Locke's doctrine of necessities have in common is the attempt to reconstruct moral philosophy in the face of rampant scepticism and their recourse to epistemology founded on the natural sciences, in which human thinking started with the physical body. Nevertheless, the service provided to natural lawyers and political thinkers by Locke's philosophical effort to combine freedom and publicness in the natural law of an sceptical era is 'widespread', to use Peter H. Nidditch's expression.[1]

The book has demonstrated that the rise of a modern natural law, marked by the sceptical reason and without a robust theological and moral anthropology, characteristic of the seventeenth century is linked with the birth of the nation, the prehistory of classical economics and with

[1] Peter H. Nidditch, 'Foreword' in John Locke, *An Essay Concerning Human Understanding*, p. x.

the ideological origins of the Anthropocene, when human activity started to have a significant impact on the earth's ecosystems, including the ecosystem of humanity. All these novel phenomena occurred within the powerful worldview proposed during the early Scientific Revolution. It is remarkable that among natural scientists during this period the notion of right reason was under the wing of radical voluntarist theology. Hence, the influence of 'right reason' in scientific works was almost non-existent and certainly much weaker than among the most sceptical of natural lawyers. Thus, Robert Boyle, one of the main initiators of the Scientific Revolution, argued in favour of the immense possibilities for reason to acquire knowledge about the physical world and, in practical terms, argued that moral right reason did not exist. I have identified both the cross-fertilization and the tensions that developed between the philosophical projects of natural philosophers and legal philosophers. The second contribution offered by this study is methodological in nature: the appraisal of changes in modern natural law encompassing natural philosophers' perspectives and their novel views on nature, natural laws and voluntarist theology. The book thus seeks to undermine the modern paradigm that separates human nature from nature and the human spirit from the corporeal body.

It is significant that the shift in the theology as to the use of the world – the use of material things – towards utilitarianism occurred both by glossing over the divine commands to human beings to be the guardians of nature *and* the theological and ethical precepts referring to the dangers posed to human beings by money. The book relates this change in moral theology to changes in moral natural law and specific ideas that were in vogue during the Scientific Revolution. Before the seventeenth century, theologians stressed as a matter of course that the use of the world – of material things of the world – ought to be done with a good or virtuous will, and that it was not to be presumed that individuals would do that. Hence the admonitions, prohibitions and counsels about how to deal with riches and money. In contrast to this approach, an ideology of multiplication seized the scientific imagination of seventeenth-century English society – entailing the multiplication of benefits, investments, money, harvests, productions – in such manner that all previous religious and moral strictures that hindered such multiplication started to be vigorously resisted. Suddenly human nature and physical nature appeared immune to hazard and greed.

England – the European country that during that period witnessed more radical constitutional and social changes than any other – also produced the most original transformations in natural law. This book has analysed changes in the classical idea of moral freedom founded on practical reason, in the notion of a sacred nature that only God the giver of order may alter, in the idea of a universal natural law, and in the conception of money that was traditionally thought to be dangerous for the moral integrity and eternal destiny of human beings. These classical principles were partially replaced by new and exciting formulas by which to organize the moral life of individuals in space and rationalize political and economic goals. The scientific and theological heterodoxy of Protestant Reformers described in Chapter 4, whose political influence was felt from the 1630s to the Restoration, prompted them to turn to practical arts and trades and seek there the *unum necessarium*: the path to salvation. Nature was observed as the ultimate source of gold within the idiosyncratic alchemical programmatic endeavours that took place at the time. The new natural law was thus conceived in the context of plans for scientific development and economic expansion. The first participants in the Scientific Revolution – natural lawyers, natural scientists and early political economists – endorsed changing conceptions of nature, which led to the manipulation of nature and to the exploitation of natural resources on a massive industrial scale. Buttressed by the novel philosophical influences, the intelligentsia's new moral philosophy shifted from seeking what is good to searching for what is necessary and useful.

With increasing denial of the existence of the principles of moral practical reason, a tenet which was encapsulated in the disappearance at the time of a cogent notion of the light of reason, the human body became the focus of human beings' source of knowledge. The core of the capacity of reason was thus conceived through a reliance on the body's necessities and by following ever more ambitious patterns of reasoning. These new empirical epistemologies arose as a reaction to the different ways in which Neoplatonist philosophers of the seventeenth century emphasized that human knowledge about the world was a replication of that world within the human mind. In reaction to this, existential and empiricist natural lawyers argued that thinking starts when the human body reacts to its environment. Experimental practice has been at the forefront of science ever since. However, scientists also represented human beings as passive agents of needs and desires and posited that God had created physical nature to satisfy them. Conceptually, nature and economy started to meld together. With the new emphasis on methodological physicalism, money started to be described as a necessity of the nation, in parallel to the needs of the human body. The expectation of profit yields from moneylending was reinterpreted scientifically as a rational, and thus as a morally neutral issue. Greed, derided everywhere, begun its course as a private vice, receding from concerns as to how the public space ought to be constructed.

This book argues that Hobbes's focus on thinking in terms of body and his recourse in manifold ways to a rich causal principle of necessity greatly facilitated his robust natural law and resilient political philosophy. Certainly, it is more congenial vis-à-vis received tradition to describe Hobbes merely as a mechanistic philosopher. However, I have argued that Hobbes endorsed the materialism or physicalism of Avicenna's philosophy and that this was a novelty within the web of ideas of European natural law that has not been recognized to date. In Hobbes's work, these principles culminated in *Leviathan*. The deterministic stance taken by Avicenna and Hobbes thwarted further thinking on, and the development of, a theory of moral freedom, and indeed of a foundational political theory of freedom. This has been a classic critique of the philosophical work of Hobbes, but also of Avicenna, who – aside from thoughts expressed in certain very minor pieces – never, as discussed in Chapter 9, developed a moral theory. Chapter 3 highlights Hobbes's effort to accommodate a Christian understanding of the liberty of human beings within his doctrine of necessity by uniting them under the umbrella principle of the divine will of God. God had designed, for all eternity, an order of necessary events. However, since knowledge of this was inaccessible to humans, they thought themselves to be free due to ignorance or lack of awareness of the necessary events arranged by God.

Robert Boyle boldly aimed at reinventing knowledge while rejecting the (ultimate) atheist implications of the mechanistic principle of necessary causality. Natural laws and matter became the sole object of his study. He adopted corpuscularianism, a species of atomism influenced by Aristotelian principles, and was thus ready to deconstruct nature. Boyle transformed nature into a system, an *oeconomy*, both in conceptual and literal terms. His writings treat nature as an important asset for the country's economic growth that also gives meaning to the British imperial project. The economic benefits of the exploitation of nature became, after the 1660s, the principle that cemented the utility of empirical science. The fantastic increase in the popularity of natural sciences went hand in hand with their becoming an instrument of political and economic engineering of the English nation which was then emerging from the ashes of the Civil Wars (1642–1646; 1648–1651). The revolution carried out by the Puritans, in whose circles Boyle's experimental work was first nurtured, greatly contributed to his radical stance in relation to knowledge and epistemology and to its economic bent. Chapters 4, 6 and 7 demonstrate that Boyle shared with his mentors an anti-metaphysical stand and a messianic view of science, which he toned down in the Restoration period, leaning towards a utopian theology that made prolific use of analogies between the scientist and the priest, the world and the temple. The bulk of Boyle's scientific ideas are supported by a boldly voluntarist theology and an argument in favour of divine design. Despite his piety and faith Boyle did not take a public stand against the burgeoning slave trade. I have argued that this attitude was a consequence of his early abandonment of the study of ethics and his conception of nature as simply matter and movement. The nature of human beings remained, as it were, outside his philosophical study of nature.

John Locke was the heir and admirer of both Boyle and Hobbes. From the outset, his reasoning was founded on their physicalism and atomism and on his own studies of classic natural law and medicine. Locke, who was born into the political and religious chaos of the Civil Wars and the 'economic sociability' of the period, is a theoriser of the public sphere. Chapter 8 shows that his initial and enduring preoccupation is to honour individuals' political and religious identities while constructing a commonwealth at the same time. Very early on Locke took up a position against innate ideas in natural law. It would appear that from the outset he radicalized the separation of knowledge and nature in natural law, but in fact, his position was more complex and original than that. Grounded on his studies of theology and of classic philosopher-physicians, Locke inverted Hobbes's case of a war against all due to human needs. In a sceptical era, Locke identified the needs of the individual as the secure foundation for all knowledge and politics, which constituted his attempt to reunite nature and knowledge under the category of natural law. The result was tenuous, since knowledge of natural law would be only tantamount to the principles of the law that human beings may acquire due to the promptings of physical needs. Knowledge would also, however, be certain since there is no empirical or theoretical way of denying human needs. Locke's epistemology is very sophisticated, and I have not considered it in its entirety in this book. Instead, I have benefited from the latest studies, which emphasize the naturalism of his work on the theory of knowledge and traced the way he employed the notion of the necessities of human nature to underpin his conception of what it means to be human and how a human being understands the world.

As a political theologian, Locke recovered the traditional relevance of human necessities in relation to ideas of charity and the common good and elevated them to constitute the main principles of his theory of government: the foundation of property and of the public good. Moreover, he employed these ideas about human necessities as a methodological tool by which to provide a basis for his groundbreaking monetary theories. Chapter 10 has reviewed biographical aspects of Locke as a civil servant involved not only with the plantations of the empire but, as a secretary of Lord Shaftesbury between 1667 and 1675, responsible for saving England from collapsing in a situation of disastrous public debt. It shows that money was a key element in building the publicness of Restoration England. In a period of sceptical reason, stressed sociability and political fragmentation, with the ensuing crisis about the common good, Locke's method of aligning private and the public interest manifests itself for the first time in his remarkable studies on money. Through these studies, he came to understand that the country's inhabitants shared a common project as a nation. A fundamental part of that common project was a monetary economy, and he was able to demonstrate scientifically how it should work: thus money became a necessity.

After a long period in which the (English) people had wrestled their political power and authority from Emperor, Pope and King the theories of modern English natural law became nation-centred in practice. Consonant with the emphasis on the body in philosophical thinking during the period, the main expressions of the foundation of physical natural law were articulated as (a) being the principle of a basic equality of wealth among individuals and (b) the growth of the economy of the nation. Locke viewed labour, rather than the hereditary principle, as the natural foundation of property – and money as the consensual means for its accumulation. Thus he integrated both natural and artificial consent into the terms of political obligation. His political theory, as described in Chapter 12, suggests that clashes between these two universalist principles (money and labour) could be avoided by means of rational domestic legislation concerned with the public good and that the *oeconomy* could accordingly be adapted to the proportions of the nation. The relevance attributed to government *for the public good* together with his faith in the rational power of Christianity seem to have been Locke's foundational political principles.

English natural law displays a massive originality as a unified body of thought that has not been recognized to date. My conclusion is that for a postmodern natural law, theirs is an unfinished project and that their accurate conviction in terms of philosophy that the human being is 'a body among bodies' ought to be supplemented by a theology of the human body that aims at discovering the spiritual meaning of that peculiar corporeality.[2]

2 On this question see John Paul II, *Theology of the Body*.

Further, in modern political theory, modern international law and contemporary moral philosophy, the space for thinking about issues regarding the morality of money has remained empty. Since around the end of the seventeenth century, moral considerations in respect of money have played no formal role in global governance, jurisprudence or moral philosophy and, even more worryingly, they are also absent from theological thinking. This glossing over of a theory of the morality of money has had a huge impact, not always positive, on theories of growth – to the extent that even John Maynard Keynes of all people wrote in disparaging terms of 'the love of money', which he viewed as both enhancing economic growth while at the same time denuding society of its values. The critique of benefiting from putting money to interest should, according to Keynes, become relevant again.

Perhaps two arguments that Keynes put forward in the 1930s help to substantiate this final idea. The British economist predicted that by now, the decade of 2020–2030, exactly the moment we are living through, global society would reconsider its stance towards money. Although himself an ambivalent figure fascinated by the possible uses of interest for the public economy of a country, Keynes also developed intriguing philosophical positions on the matter. In his successful *General Theory of Employment, Interest and Money*, and, as he put it, even though he had been educated in that belief, the British economist felt it important to underscore that the doctrines of the 'Medieval Church' on the use of money were not absurd. The complicated efforts of theologians, he now understood, rather than being a means of escaping moral law in practice, were 'honest intellectual efforts' to distinguish between the marginal efficiency of money and interest. Rule, custom and the moral law ought to maintain the latter at a low rate.[3] More explicitly, in a futurist essay he wrote in 1930 entitled 'Economic Possibilities for our Grandchildren', Keynes predicted in gripping terms that with sufficient accumulation of wealth, by about a century later – that is, in a decade from now:

> The love of money as a possession – as distinguished from the love of money as a means to the enjoyments and realities of life – will be recognised for what it is, a somewhat disgusting morbidity, one of those semi-criminal, semi-pathological propensities which one hands over with a shudder to the specialists in mental disease. All kinds of social customs and economic practices, affecting the distribution of wealth and of economic rewards and penalties, which we now maintain at all costs, however

[3] Keynes, *General Theory of Employment, Interest and Money*, p. 218.

> distasteful and unjust they may be in themselves, because they are tremendously useful in promoting the accumulation of capital, we shall then be free, at last, to discard.[4]

In his 1930s economic utopia Keynes envisaged that when our economic necessity and that of our neighbours was appeased, people would start to think again about their purpose in life, human beings would again be free to return to principles of 'religion and traditional virtue' and openly recognize that 'the love of money is detestable'.[5] We would no longer think only about enjoying the future, but we would simply learn 'how to pluck the hour and day virtuously and well'. This would be looked at with dread in the beginning, since we have been accustomed to striving for the future. Whereas 'for the first time since his creation' a human being would be faced with the real and perennial problem of how to use one's freedom wisely and well, and what to do with the leisure that 'science and compound interest' will have won for them.[6] However, Keynes warned in the 1930s, the time was not yet ripe for that, and we had to hold on a little longer:

> For at least another hundred years we must pretend to ourselves and to every one that fair is foul and foul is fair; for foul is useful and fair is not.[7]

After almost the century, from the date of Keynes's prediction of a period in which we will be free of 'avarice and usury', and with a completely transformed postcolonial global economic situation, his musings are valuable and worth reconsidering.[8] Keynes's ideas on the pathological love of money are also enlightening in the context of this book. His vision that possessiveness would disappear with scientific and economic development showed Keynes to be the true heir of the authors dealt with in the previous chapters. Notwithstanding the success of the City, the triumph of the Empire and the ideas of some few radical Independents, the English

[4] John Maynard Keynes 'Economic Possibilities for our Grandchildren', in Donald Moggridge (ed.), *Collected Writings of John Maynard Keynes*, vol. IX (London: Macmillan for the Royal Economic Society, 1972), pp. 321–332, p. 329. On his utopianism in this regard and the view that 'love of money' was 'the cancer of economies', in Robert Skidelsky, *John Maynard Keynes. The Economist as Saviour 1920–1937* (London: Macmillan, 1992), pp. 234–238, p. 425.

[5] 'Assuming no important wars and no important increase in population' occurred, Keynes 'Economic Possibilities for our Grandchildren', p. 326.

[6] Keynes 'Economic Possibilities for our Grandchildren', p. 324.

[7] Keynes 'Economic Possibilities for our Grandchildren', p. 331.

[8] 'Avarice and usury and precaution must be our gods for a little longer still.' Keynes 'Economic Possibilities for our Grandchildren'.

natural law tradition shows a recurrent uneasiness about what Keynes termed 'the love of money'.

In Locke's theory economic equality and distribution revolved around the governmental operations of the nation state. In a scenario of universal international law without a political legislative organ of government to regulate the market for the common good, it is imperative to develop anew a moral law of money concerned with the individual human being, the nations and global society. And in that effort human necessities, rather than interests might be a good theme to start with.

INDEX

CAMBRIDGE STUDIES IN INTERNATIONAL AND COMPARATIVE LAW

Books in the Series

179 *The Necessity of Nature: God, Science and Money in 17th Century English Law of Nature*
Mónica García-Salmones Rovira

178 *Making the World Safe for Investment: The Protection of Foreign Property 1922–1959*
Andrea Leiter

177 *National Governance and Investment Treaties*
Josef Ostřanský and Facundo Pérez Aznar

176 *Who Owns Outer Space? International Law, Astrophysics, and the Sustainable Development of Space*
Michael Byers and Aaron Boley

175 *Intervening in International Justice: Third States before Courts and Tribunals*
Brian McGarry

174 *Reciprocity in Public International Law*
Arianna Whelan

173 *When Environmental Protection and Human Rights Collide*
Marie-Catherine Petersmann

172 *The International Law of Sovereign Debt Dispute Settlement*
Kei Nakajima

171 *The Everyday Makers of International Law: From Great Halls to Back Rooms*
Tommaso Soave

170 *Virtue in Global Governance: Judgment and Discretion*
Jan Klabbers

169 *The Effects of Armed Conflict on Investment Treaties*
Tobias Ackermann

168 *Investment Law's Alibis: Colonialism, Imperialism, Debt and Development* David Schneiderman

167 *Negative Comparative Law: A Strong Programme for Weak Thought*
Pierre Legrand

166 *Detention by Non-State Armed Groups under International Law*
Ezequiel Heffes

165 *Rebellions and Civil Wars: State Responsibility for the Conduct of Insurgents*
Patrick Dumberry

164 *The International Law of Energy*
Jorge Viñuales

163 *The Three Ages of International Commercial Arbitration*
Mikaël Schinazi

162 *Repetition and International Law*
Wouter Werner

161 *State Responsibility and Rebels: The History and Legacy of Protecting Investment Against Revolution*
Kathryn Greenman

160 *Rewriting Histories of the Use of Force: The Narrative of 'Indifference'*
Agatha Verdebout

159 *The League of Nations and the Protection of the Environment*
Omer Aloni

158 *International Investment Law and Legal Theory: Expropriation and the Fragmentation of Sources* Jörg Kammerhofer

157 *Legal Barbarians: Identity, Modern Comparative Law and the Global South* Daniel Bonilla Maldonado

156 *International Human Rights Law Beyond State Territorial Control*
Antal Berkes

155 *The Crime of Aggression under the Rome Statute of the International Criminal Court*
Carrie McDougall

154 *Minorities and the Making of Postcolonial States in International Law*
Mohammad Shahabuddin

153 *Preclassical Conflict of Laws*
Nikitas E. Hatzimihail

152 *International Law and History: Modern Interfaces*
Ignacio de la Rasilla

151 *Marketing Global Justice: The Political Economy of International Criminal Law*
Christine Schwöbel-Patel

150 *International Status in the Shadow of Empire*
Cait Storr

149 *Treaties in Motion: The Evolution of Treaties from Formation to Termination*
Edited by Malgosia Fitzmaurice and Panos Merkouris

148 *Humanitarian Disarmament: An Historical Enquiry*
Treasa Dunworth

147 *Complementarity, Catalysts, Compliance: The International Criminal Court in Uganda, Kenya, and the Democratic Republic of Congo*
Christian M. De Vos

146 *Cyber Operations and International Law*
François Delerue

145 *Comparative Reasoning in International Courts and Tribunals*
Daniel Peat

144 *Maritime Delimitation as a Judicial Process*
Massimo Lando

143 *Prosecuting Sexual and Gender-Based Crimes at the International Criminal Court: Practice, Progress and Potential*
Rosemary Grey

142 *Capitalism As Civilisation: A History of International Law*
Ntina Tzouvala

141 *Sovereignty in China: A Genealogy of a Concept Since 1840*
Adele Carrai

140 *Narratives of Hunger in International Law: Feeding the World in Times of Climate Change*
Anne Saab

139 *Victim Reparation under the Ius Post Bellum: An Historical and Normative Perspective*
Shavana Musa

138 *The Analogy between States and International Organizations*
Fernando Lusa Bordin

137 *The Process of International Legal Reproduction: Inequality, Historiography, Resistance*
Rose Parfitt

136 *State Responsibility for Breaches of Investment Contracts*
Jean Ho

135 *Coalitions of the Willing and International Law: The Interplay between Formality and Informality*
Alejandro Rodiles

134 *Self-Determination in Disputed Colonial Territories*
Jamie Trinidad

133 *International Law as a Belief System*
Jean d'Aspremont

132 *Legal Consequences of Peremptory Norms in International Law*
Daniel Costelloe

131 *Third-Party Countermeasures in International Law*
Martin Dawidowicz

130 *Justification and Excuse in International Law: Concept and Theory of General Defences*
Federica Paddeu

129 *Exclusion from Public Space: A Comparative Constitutional Analysis*
Daniel Moeckli

128 *Provisional Measures before International Courts and Tribunals*
Cameron A. Miles

127 *Humanity at Sea: Maritime Migration and the Foundations of International Law*
Itamar Mann

126 *Beyond Human Rights: The Legal Status of the Individual in International Law*
Anne Peters

125 *The Doctrine of Odious Debt in International Law: A Restatement*
Jeff King

124 *Static and Evolutive Treaty Interpretation: A Functional Reconstruction*
Christian Djeffal

123 *Civil Liability in Europe for Terrorism-Related Risk*
Lucas Bergkamp, Michael Faure, Monika Hinteregger and Niels Philipsen

122 *Proportionality and Deference in Investor-State Arbitration: Balancing Investment Protection and Regulatory Autonomy*
Caroline Henckels

121 *International Law and Governance of Natural Resources in Conflict and Post-Conflict Situations*
Daniëlla Dam-de Jong

120 *Proof of Causation in Tort Law*
Sandy Steel

119 *The Formation and Identification of Rules of Customary International Law in International Investment Law*
Patrick Dumberry

118 *Religious Hatred and International Law: The Prohibition of Incitement to Violence or Discrimination*
Jeroen Temperman

117 *Taking Economic, Social and Cultural Rights Seriously in International Criminal Law*
Evelyne Schmid

116 *Climate Change Litigation: Regulatory Pathways to Cleaner Energy*
Jacqueline Peel and Hari M. Osofsky

115 *Mestizo International Law: A Global Intellectual History 1842–1933*
Arnulf Becker Lorca

114 *Sugar and the Making of International Trade Law*
Michael Fakhri

113 *Strategically Created Treaty Conflicts and the Politics of International Law*
Surabhi Ranganathan

112 *Investment Treaty Arbitration As Public International Law: Procedural Aspects and Implications*
Eric De Brabandere

111 *The New Entrants Problem in International Fisheries Law*
Andrew Serdy

110 *Substantive Protection under Investment Treaties: A Legal and Economic Analysis*
Jonathan Bonnitcha

109 *Popular Governance of Post-Conflict Reconstruction: The Role of International Law*
Matthew Saul

108 *Evolution of International Environmental Regimes: The Case of Climate Change*
Simone Schiele

107 *Judges, Law and War: The Judicial Development of International Humanitarian Law*
Shane Darcy

106 *Religious Offence and Human Rights: The Implications of Defamation of Religions*
Lorenz Langer

105 *Forum Shopping in International Adjudication: The Role of Preliminary Objections*
Luiz Eduardo Salles

104 *Domestic Politics and International Human Rights Tribunals: The Problem of Compliance*
Courtney Hillebrecht

103 *International Law and the Arctic*
Michael Byers

102 *Cooperation in the Law of Transboundary Water Resources*
Christina Leb

101 *Underwater Cultural Heritage and International Law*
Sarah Dromgoole

100 *State Responsibility: The General Part*
James Crawford

99 *The Origins of International Investment Law: Empire, Environment and the Safeguarding of Capital*
Kate Miles

98 *The Crime of Aggression under the Rome Statute of the International Criminal Court*
Carrie McDougall

97 *'Crimes against Peace' and International Law*
Kirsten Sellars

96 *Non-Legality in International Law: Unruly Law*
Fleur Johns

95 *Armed Conflict and Displacement: The Protection of Refugees and Displaced Persons under International Humanitarian Law*
Mélanie Jacques

94 *Foreign Investment and the Environment in International Law*
Jorge E. Viñuales

93 *The Human Rights Treaty Obligations of Peacekeepers*
Kjetil Mujezinović Larsen

92 *Cyber Warfare and the Laws of War*
Heather Harrison Dinniss

91 *The Right to Reparation in International Law for Victims of Armed Conflict*
Christine Evans

90 *Global Public Interest in International Investment Law*
Andreas Kulick

89 *State Immunity in International Law*
Xiaodong Yang

88 *Reparations and Victim Support in the International Criminal Court*
Conor McCarthy

87 *Reducing Genocide to Law: Definition, Meaning, and the Ultimate Crime*
Payam Akhavan

86 *Decolonising International Law: Development, Economic Growth and the Politics of Universality*
Sundhya Pahuja

85 *Complicity and the Law of State Responsibility*
Helmut Philipp Aust

84 *State Control over Private Military and Security Companies in Armed Conflict*
Hannah Tonkin

83 *'Fair and Equitable Treatment' in International Investment Law*
Roland Kläger

82 *The UN and Human Rights: Who Guards the Guardians?*
Guglielmo Verdirame

81 *Sovereign Defaults before International Courts and Tribunals*
Michael Waibel

80 *Making the Law of the Sea: A Study in the Development of International Law*
James Harrison

79 *Science and the Precautionary Principle in International Courts and Tribunals: Expert Evidence, Burden of Proof and Finality*
Caroline E. Foster

78 *Transition from Illegal Regimes under International Law*
Yaël Ronen

77 *Access to Asylum: International Refugee Law and the Globalisation of Migration Control*
Thomas Gammeltoft-Hansen

76 *Trading Fish, Saving Fish: The Interaction between Regimes in International Law*
Margaret A. Young

75 *The Individual in the International Legal System: Continuity and Change in International Law*
Kate Parlett

74 *'Armed Attack' and Article 51 of the UN Charter: Evolutions in Customary Law and Practice*
Tom Ruys

73 *Theatre of the Rule of Law: Transnational Legal Intervention in Theory and Practice*
Stephen Humphreys

72 *Science and Risk Regulation in International Law*
Jacqueline Peel

71 *The Participation of States in International Organisations: The Role of Human Rights and Democracy*
Alison Duxbury

70 *Legal Personality in International Law*
Roland Portmann

69 *Vicarious Liability in Tort: A Comparative Perspective*
Paula Giliker

68 *The Public International Law Theory of Hans Kelsen: Believing in Universal Law*
Jochen von Bernstorff

67 *Legitimacy and Legality in International Law: An Interactional Account*
Jutta Brunnée and Stephen J. Toope

66 *The Concept of Non-International Armed Conflict in International Humanitarian Law*
Anthony Cullen

65 *The Principle of Legality in International and Comparative Criminal Law*
Kenneth S. Gallant

64 *The Challenge of Child Labour in International Law*
Franziska Humbert

63 *Shipping Interdiction and the Law of the Sea*
Douglas Guilfoyle

62 *International Courts and Environmental Protection*
Tim Stephens

61 *Legal Principles in WTO Disputes*
Andrew D. Mitchell

60 *War Crimes in Internal Armed Conflicts*
Eve La Haye

59 *Humanitarian Occupation*
Gregory H. Fox

58 *The International Law of Environmental Impact Assessment: Process, Substance and Integration*
Neil Craik

57 *The Law and Practice of International Territorial Administration: Versailles to Iraq and Beyond*
Carsten Stahn

56 *United Nations Sanctions and the Rule of Law*
Jeremy Matam Farrall

55 *National Law in WTO Law: Effectiveness and Good Governance in the World Trading System*
Sharif Bhuiyan

54 *Cultural Products and the World Trade Organization*
Tania Voon

53 *The Threat of Force in International Law*
Nikolas Stürchler

52 *Indigenous Rights and United Nations Standards: Self-Determination, Culture and Land*
Alexandra Xanthaki

51 *International Refugee Law and Socio-Economic Rights: Refuge from Deprivation*
Michelle Foster

50 *The Protection of Cultural Property in Armed Conflict*
Roger O'Keefe

49 *Interpretation and Revision of International Boundary Decisions*
Kaiyan Homi Kaikobad

48 *Multinationals and Corporate Social Responsibility: Limitations and Opportunities in International Law*
Jennifer A. Zerk

47 *Judiciaries within Europe: A Comparative Review*
John Bell

46 *Law in Times of Crisis: Emergency Powers in Theory and Practice*
Oren Gross and Fionnuala Ní Aoláin

45 *Vessel-Source Marine Pollution: The Law and Politics of International Regulation*
Alan Khee-Jin Tan

44 *Enforcing Obligations Erga Omnes in International Law*
Christian J. Tams

43 *Non-Governmental Organisations in International Law*
Anna-Karin Lindblom

42 *Democracy, Minorities and International Law*
Steven Wheatley

41 *Prosecuting International Crimes: Selectivity and the International Criminal Law Regime*
Robert Cryer

40 *Compensation for Personal Injury in English, German and Italian Law: A Comparative Outline*
Basil Markesinis, Michael Coester, Guido Alpa and Augustus Ullstein

39 *Dispute Settlement in the UN Convention on the Law of the Sea*
Natalie Klein

38 *The International Protection of Internally Displaced Persons*
Catherine Phuong

37 *Imperialism, Sovereignty and the Making of International Law*
Antony Anghie

36 *Principles of the Institutional Law of International Organizations*
C. F. Amerasinghe

35 *Necessity, Proportionality and the Use of Force by States*
Judith Gardam

34 *International Legal Argument in the Permanent Court of International Justice: The Rise of the International Judiciary*
Ole Spiermann

33 -

32 *Great Powers and Outlaw States: Unequal Sovereigns in the International Legal Order*
Gerry Simpson

31 *Local Remedies in International Law (second edition)*
Chittharanjan Felix Amerasinghe

30 *Reading Humanitarian Intervention: Human Rights and the Use of Force in International Law*
Anne Orford

29 *Conflict of Norms in Public International Law: How WTO Law Relates to Other Rules of International Law*
Joost Pauwelyn

28 -

27 *Transboundary Damage in International Law*
Hanqin Xue

26 -

25 *European Criminal Procedures*
Edited by Mireille Delmas-Marty and J. R. Spencer

24 *Accountability of Armed Opposition Groups in International Law*
Liesbeth Zegveld

23 *Sharing Transboundary Resources: International Law and Optimal Resource Use*
Eyal Benvenisti

22 *International Human Rights and Humanitarian Law*
René Provost

21 *Remedies against International Organisations*
Karel Wellens

20 *Diversity and Self-Determination in International Law*
Karen Knop

19 *The Law of Internal Armed Conflict*
Lindsay Moir

18 *International Commercial Arbitration and African States: Practice, Participation and Institutional Development*
Amazu A. Asouzu

17 *The Enforceability of Promises in European Contract Law*
James Gordley

16 *International Law in Antiquity*
David J. Bederman

15 *Money Laundering: A New International Law Enforcement Model*
Guy Stessens

14 *Good Faith in European Contract Law*
Reinhard Zimmermann and Simon Whittaker

13 *On Civil Procedure*
J. A. Jolowicz

12 *Trusts: A Comparative Study*
Maurizio Lupoi and Simon Dix

11 *The Right to Property in Commonwealth Constitutions*
Tom Allen

10 *International Organizations before National Courts*
August Reinisch

9 *The Changing International Law of High Seas Fisheries*
Francisco Orrego Vicuña

8 *Trade and the Environment: A Comparative Study of EC and US Law*
Damien Geradin

7 *Unjust Enrichment: A Study of Private Law and Public Values*
Hanoch Dagan

6 *Religious Liberty and International Law in Europe*
Malcolm D. Evans

5 *Ethics and Authority in International Law*
Alfred P. Rubin

4 *Sovereignty over Natural Resources: Balancing Rights and Duties*
Nico Schrijver

3 *The Polar Regions and the Development of International Law*
Donald R. Rothwell